AQA
Law
for A2

Third Edition

Jacqueline Martin
& Chris Turner

Editor: Denis Lanser

HODDER
EDUCATION
AN HACHETTE UK COMPANY

Orders: please contact Bookpoint Ltd, 130 Milton Park, Abingdon, Oxon OX14 4SB.
Telephone: (44) 01235 827720. Fax: (44) 01235 400454. Lines are open from 9.00 – 5.00,
Monday to Saturday, with a 24 hour message answering service. You can also order
through our website www.hoddereducation.co.uk

If you have any comments to make about this, or any of our other titles, please
send them to educationenquiries@hodder.co.uk

British Library Cataloguing in Publication Data
A catalogue record for this title is available from the British Library

ISBN: 978 0 340 97364 6

First Edition Published 2004
Second Edition Published 2007
This Edition Published 2009

Impression number   10 9 8 7 6 5 4 3 2 1
Year   2013 2012 2011 2010 2009

Hachette UK's policy is to use papers that are natural, renewable and
recyclable products and made from wood grown in sustainable forests.
The logging and manufacturing processes are expected to conform to the
environmental regulations of the country of origin.

Artwork by Ian Foulis
Cover photo © Pegaz/Alamy
Typeset by Dorchester Typesetting Group Ltd
Printed in Italy for Hodder Education, an Hachette UK company, 338 Euston Road,
London NW1 3BH

Contents

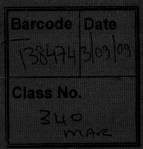

Barcode | Date
138474 | 3/09/09

Class No.
340
MAR

Unit 3
Section B: Law of Contract

Preface

This book is designed to cover both criminal law and law of contract in Unit 3 for AQA Law, and the options of criminal law and the law of tort in Unit 4 for AQA Law. There is complete coverage of the AQA A2 specification for those taking any combination of the options of criminal law, contract law and tort. Although consumer protection and human rights are not covered as separate units there is some consideration of these in the chapters on the synoptic Unit 4 Section C. In addition there is some coverage of consumer law in Unit 3 Section B (contract).

The first part of the book deals with Unit 3, with Chapters 1-5 containing the criminal law option and Chapters 6-10 setting out the law on contract. The sections on Unit 4 follow a similar pattern with Chapters 11-16 on criminal law and Chapters 16-22 on tort. The final section contains five chapters on the synoptic unit, mirroring the specification's requirements.

As well as explaining the relevant law there are sections within most chapters on problems in that particular area of law and comments on possible reforms. These sections should give students material for the final part of the AQA questions set in Units 3 and 4, which are targeted at the satisfactoriness of the law and/or reform.

Instead of having one table of cases at the beginning of the book, a table of cases has been created for each Option and will be found at the start of each Option.

The book is in the same general style as AQA Law for AS by one of the co-authors of this book, Jacqueline Martin. The text is broken up into manageable sections with plenty of headings. The student's understanding of topics is reinforced with diagrams and Key Facts charts and there are also activities to test knowledge and understanding. Important cases are highlighted within the text making it easier for students to refer to them.

The law is stated as we believe it to be on 1 January 2009.

Acknowledgements

The authors and publishers would like to thank the following for permission to reproduce copyright material:

Daily Telegraph for extract from 'Mercy for mother who was driven to kill her Down's syndrome son', page 34. *Kent Messenger* for extract from 'Thug jailed for stamping on policeman's face', page 66. Courier Media Group Ltd for extracts from 'Armed raid at off-licence', page 245; and 'Clingfilm-wrapped yob wrecks lights', page 274. © Crown Copyright material is reproduced with permission of the controller of HMSO.

Every effort has been made to trace and acknowledge ownership of copyright. The publishers will be glad to make suitable arrangements with any copyright holders whom it has not been possible to contact.

List of Figures

Table of statutes and other instruments

EU Legislation

UNIT 3

Section A: Criminal Law (Offences Against the Person)

Table of Cases

Chapter 1

Murder

Homicide is the unlawful killing of a human being. There are different offences depending on the *mens rea* of the defendant and whether there is a special defence available to the defendant. The most serious homicide offence is murder.

Murder is a common law offence. This means that it is not defined by any Act of Parliament. It has been defined by the decisions of judges in cases and the accepted definition is based on one given by a seventeenth century judge, Lord Coke. This is that murder is:

'the unlawful killing of a reasonable person in being and under the King's (or Queen's) Peace with malice aforethought, express or implied'.

The different elements of this definition are considered in detail under the *actus reus* and *mens rea* of murder below at 1.1 and 1.3.

Jurisdiction over murder extends to any murder in any country by a British citizen. This means that if the defendant is a British citizen, he may be tried in an English court for a murder he is alleged to have committed in another country.

1.1 *Actus reus* of murder

The *actus reus* of murder is the unlawful killing of a reasonable creature in being and under the Queen's Peace. The killing must be unlawful. It is not unlawful if what is done is in self-defence, or in the prevention of crime and the defendant used reasonable force in the circumstances (see Chapter 5). The *actus reus* can be an act or omission but it must cause the death of the victim. Murder is a result crime; the defendant cannot be guilty unless his act or omission caused the death. The law on causation is considered at 1.2 below.

1.1.1 Omissions as *actus reus*

In nearly every case the *actus reus* will be an act such as stabbing the victim, shooting them or running over them in a car. The normal rule is that an omission cannot make a person guilty of an offence. This was explained by Stephen J, a nineteenth-century judge, in the following way.

> 'A sees B drowning and is able to save him by holding out his hand. A abstains from doing so in order that B may be drowned. A has committed no offence.'

Exceptions to the rule

There are exceptions to the rule that an omission cannot make a person guilty of an offence. In some cases it is possible for a failure to act (an omission) to be the *actus reus*.

An omission is only sufficient for the *actus reus* where there is a duty to act. There are four main situations in which such a duty can exist.

- A contractual duty.
- A duty because of a relationship.
- A duty which has been taken on voluntarily.
- A duty which arises because the defendant has set in motion a chain of events.

A contractual duty

In *Pittwood* (1902) a railway crossing keeper failed to shut the gates of the crossing when a train was

due. As a result a person crossing the line was struck and killed by the train. The keeper was guilty of manslaughter. A more modern example would be of a lifeguard at a pool who leaves his post unattended. His failure to do his duty under his contract of employment could make him guilty of an offence if a swimmer were injured or drowned.

A duty because of a relationship

This is usually a parent–child relationship since a parent has a duty to care for young children. A duty can also exist the opposite way round, where a grown-up child is caring for their elderly parent. A case example involving a parent–child duty is *Gibbins and Proctor* (1918).

Gibbins and Proctor (1918)

The father of a seven-year-old girl lived with a partner. The father had several children from an earlier marriage. He and his partner kept the girl separate from the father's other children and deliberately starved her to death. They were both convicted of murder.

The father had a duty to feed her because he was her parent and the mistress was held to have undertaken to look after the children, including the girl, so she was also under a duty to feed the child. The omission or failure to feed the child was deliberate with the intention of killing or causing serious harm to her. In these circumstances they were guilty of murder. The failure to feed the girl was enough for the *actus reus* of murder.

A duty which has been undertaken voluntarily

In the above case of *Gibbins v Proctor* (1918) the partner had voluntarily undertaken to look after the girl. She therefore had a duty towards the child. When she failed to feed the child she was guilty of murder because of that omission.

Another example of where a duty had been undertaken voluntarily is *Stone and Dobinson* (1977).

Stone's elderly sister, Fanny, came to live with the defendants. Fanny was eccentric and often stayed in her room for several days. She also failed to eat. She eventually became bedridden and incapable of caring for herself. On at least one occasion *Dobinson* helped to wash Fanny and also occasionally prepared food for her. Fanny died from malnutrition. Both defendants were found guilty of her manslaughter.

As Fanny was Stone's sister, he owed a duty of care to her. Dobinson had undertaken some care of Fanny and so also owed her a duty of care. The duty was either to help her themselves or to summon help from other sources. Their failure to do either of these meant that they were in breach of their duty.

A duty which arises because the defendant set in motion a chain of events

This concept of owing a duty and being liable through omission was created in the case of *Miller* (1983), where a squatter had accidentally started a fire.

Miller (1983)

D was living in a squat. He fell asleep while smoking a cigarette. He awoke to find his mattress on fire. He did not attempt to put out the fire or to summon help but went into another room and went back to sleep. The house caught fire. He was convicted of arson.

In *Miller* (1983) it was not the setting of the mattress on fire which made him guilty. Instead, it was the fact that he had failed to take reasonable steps to deal with the fire when he discovered his mattress was on fire. This failure or omission meant that he had committed the *actus reus* for arson. The House of Lords pointed out that Miller was only expected to take reasonable steps. He

did not have to put himself at risk. So if, when he woke and found the fire, it was very small and could easily be put out then he was expected to do that. However, if it was too dangerous for him to deal with it personally then his duty was summon the fire brigade.

1.1.2 Reasonable creature in being

This phrase means a human being – for murder to be committed a person must be killed. Normally this part of the definition does not cause any difficulties. The only two problem areas are:

- Is a foetus in the womb a 'reasonable creature in being'?
- Is a victim still considered to be alive (and so a 'reasonable creature in being') if they are 'brain-dead' but being kept alive by a life-support machine?

Foetus

A homicide offence cannot be charged in respect of the killing of a foetus. The child has to have an 'existence independent of the mother' for it to be considered a 'creature in being'. This means that it must have been expelled from her body and have an independent circulation. However, the umbilical cord connecting the child and the mother need not have been cut. Also it is probable that the child need not have taken its first breath for it to be considered a 'reasonable creature in being'. In addition in *Attorney-General's Reference (No 3 of 1994)* (1997) it was stated by the House of Lords that where the foetus is injured and the child is born alive but dies afterwards as a result of the injuries, this can be the *actus reus* for murder or manslaughter.

Attorney-General's Reference (No 3 of 1994) (1997)

The defendant stabbed his girlfriend who was about 23 weeks' pregnant. She recovered from the stab wound but it caused her to give birth prematurely some seven weeks after the stabbing. The baby was born alive but died at the age of four months as a result of the premature birth. The defendant was charged with the murder of the child. At the trial the judge directed the jury that a foetus was not a 'reasonable creature in being' and so the defendant could not in law be guilty of either the murder or manslaughter of the child. The defendant was acquitted.

The House of Lords agreed that this was correct where the foetus died before being born but held that:

'violence towards a foetus which results in harm suffered after the baby has been born alive can give rise to criminal responsibility'.

However, they held that in the circumstances the offence was manslaughter, as there was no *mens rea* for murder. (See 1.3 for the discussion on *mens rea*.)

Brain-dead

It is probable that a person who is 'brain dead' would not be considered as 'reasonable creature in being'. Doctors are allowed to switch off life-support machines without being liable for homicide. In *Malcherek* (1981) doctors had carried out many, but not all, of the tests for brain death. The Court of Appeal held that switching off the victim's life support machine did not break the chain of causation (see 1.2.3). This meant that the original attacker was liable for murder.

Year and a day rule

There used to be a rule that death must have occurred within a year and a day of the unlawful act. This rule was sensible in past centuries when medical knowledge was not sufficient to prove that an attack had caused the death after such a long time. However, with improvements in medical skill, the rule became outdated. In particular it meant that where a victim was kept

alive by a life-support machine so that his death did not occur until more than a year after the attack, the attacker could not be charged with his murder. So the year and a day rule was abolished by the Law Reform (Year and a Day Rule) Act 1996. There is now no time limit on when the death may occur after the unlawful act but, where it is more than three years after the attack, the consent of the Attorney-General is needed for the prosecution.

Queen's Peace

Under the Queen's Peace means that the killing of an enemy in the course of war is not murder. However, the killing of a prisoner of war would be sufficient for the *actus reus* of murder.

1.2 Causation

Where a consequence must be proved, then the prosecution has to show that the defendant's conduct was:

- the factual cause of that consequence; and
- the legal cause of that consequence; and
- that there was no intervening act which broke the chain of causation.

1.2.1 Factual cause

The defendant can only be guilty if the consequence would not have happened 'but for' the defendant's conduct. An example of where the death was held to have occurred because of the defendant's conduct is *Pagett* (1983).

Pagett (1983)

The defendant used his pregnant girlfriend as a shield while he shot at armed policemen. The police fired back and the girlfriend was killed. Pagett was convicted of her manslaughter. She would not have died 'but for' him using her as a shield in the shoot-out.

The opposite situation was seen in *White* (1910).

1.2.2 Legal cause

The defendant's conduct must be more than a 'minimal' cause of the consequence but it need not be a substantial cause. In *Cato* (1976) the victim had prepared an injection of heroin and water which the defendant then injected into the victim. The victim died and Cato was convicted of manslaughter. The Court of Appeal said that:

> 'it was not necessary for the prosecution to prove that the heroin was the only cause of death. As a matter of law, it was sufficient if the prosecution could establish that it was a cause, provided it was a cause outside the *de minimis* range, and effectively bearing on the acceleration of the moment of the victim's death.'

In *Kimsey* (1996) the Court of Appeal held that instead of using the Latin phrase *de minimis*, it was acceptable to tell the jury it must be 'more than a slight or trifling link'. There may be more than one person whose act contributed to the death. The defendant can be guilty even though his conduct was not the only cause of the death.

Thin-skull rule

The defendant must also take the victim as he finds him. This is known as the 'thin-skull rule'. It means that if the victim has something unusual about his physical or mental state which makes an injury more serious, then the defendant is liable for the more serious injury. So, if the victim has an unusually thin skull which means that a blow to his head gives him a serious injury, then the defendant is liable for that injury. This is so even though that blow would have only caused bruising in a 'normal' person.

An example is the case of *Blaue* (1975).

1.2.3 Intervening acts

The chain of causation can be broken by:

- an act of a third party
- the victim's own act
- a natural but unpredictable event.

In order to break the chain of causation so that the defendant is not responsible for the consequence, the intervening act must be sufficiently independent of the defendant's conduct and sufficiently serious enough.

Where the defendant's conduct causes foreseeable action by a third party, then the defendant is likely to be held to have caused the consequence; as in *Pagett* (1983), where his girlfriend was shot when he held her as a shield against police bullets.

Medical treatment

Medical treatment is unlikely to break the chain of causation unless it is so independent of the defendant's acts and 'in itself so potent in causing death' that the defendant's acts are insignificant. The following two cases illustrate situations where the chain of causation was not broken.

Smith (1959)

Two soldiers had a fight and one was stabbed in the lung by the other. The victim was carried to a medical centre by other soldiers, but was dropped on the way. At the medical centre the staff gave him artificial respiration by pressing on his chest. This made the injury worse and he died. Had the proper treatment been given, his chances of recovering would have been as high as 75 per cent. However, the original attacker was still guilty of his murder.

Cheshire (1991)

The defendant shot the victim in the thigh and the stomach. The victim had problems breathing and was given a tracheotomy (ie a tube was inserted in his throat to help him breathe). The victim died from rare complications of the tracheotomy, which were not spotted by the doctors. By the time he died the original wounds were no longer life-threatening. The defendant was still held to be liable for his death.

In addition, the switching off of a life-support machine by a doctor when it has been decided that the victim is brain-dead does not break the chain of causation. This was decided in *Malcherek* (1981).

The next case illustrates a situation in which it was held that the chain of casuation was broken.

Jordan (1956)

The victim had been stabbed in the stomach. He was treated in hospital and the wounds were healing well. He was given an antibiotic but suffered an allergic reaction to it. One doctor stopped the use of the antibiotic but the next day another doctor ordered that a large dose of it be given. The victim died from the allergic reaction to the drug. In this case the actions of the doctor were held to be an intervening act which caused the death. The defendant was not guilty of murder.

Victim's own act

If the defendant causes the victim to react in a foreseeable way, then any injury to the victim will have been caused by the defendant. This occurred in *Roberts* (1971).

Roberts (1971)

A girl jumped from a car in order to escape from sexual advances. The car was travelling at between 20–40 mph, and the girl was injured through jumping from the car. The defendant was held to be liable for her injuries.

However, if the victim's reaction is unreasonable, then this may break the chain of causation as in *Williams* (1992).

Williams (1992)

A hitch-hiker jumped from Williams' car and died from head injuries caused by his head hitting the road. The car was travelling at about 30 mph. The prosecution alleged that there had been an attempt to steal the victim's wallet and that this was the reason for his jumping from the car. The Court of Appeal said that to make the defendant guilty the victim's act had to be foreseeable and also had to be in proportion to the threat. The question to be asked was whether the victim's conduct was:

'within the ambit of reasonableness and not so daft as to make his own voluntary act one which amounted to a *novus actus interveniens* (an intervening act) and consequently broke the chain of causation.'

This makes it necessary to consider the surrounding circumstances in deciding whether the victim's conduct has broken the chain of causation. Where the threats to the victim are serious, then it is more likely for it to be reasonable for him to jump out of a moving car (or out of a window, or into a river etc). Where the threat is very minor and the victim takes drastic action, it is more likely that the courts will hold that it broke the chain of causation.

The main rules on causation are shown in a flow chart at Figure 1.1

Figure 1.1 The rules on causation

Activity

Read the following situations and explain whether the *actus reus* for murder is present.

1. Jane is angry because Karina is pregnant by Jane's boyfriend. When Karina is eight months pregnant, Jane stabs her in the stomach, intending to kill the foetus. Karina is rushed to hospital where a caesarian section is carried out. The baby is alive when it is removed from Karina's womb, but dies two hours later.
2. Anya is offered a lift home by Barnaby. After a few minutes she realises he is driving away from her home. He then puts his hand on her thigh as he is driving and says that they can enjoy themselves. Anya is so afraid that she jumps out of the car while it is going at about 40 mph. She is hit by another car and killed.
3. Toyah stabs Steve in the arm. His injury is not serious but he needs stitches, so a neighbour takes Steve to hospital in his car. On the way to the hospital the car crashes and Steve sustains serious head injuries, from which he dies.
4. Lily decides to kill Kevin. She takes his shotgun and loads it. She waits until he has gone to sleep then she goes into his bedroom and shoots him in the head. Unknown to her, Kevin died from a drug overdose twenty minutes before she shot him.
5. Ross stabs Paul in the chest. Paul is taken to hospital where he is given a blood transfusion. Unfortunately, he is given the wrong blood and he dies.

1.3 *Mens rea* of murder

1.3.1 Malice aforethought

The *mens rea* for murder is stated as being 'malice aforethought, express or implied'. This means that there are two different intentions either of which can be used to prove the defendant guilty of murder:

1. express malice aforethought (the intention to kill); or
2. implied malice aforethought (the intention to cause grievous bodily harm).

A defendant has the *mens rea* for murder if he has either of these intentions. This means that a person can be guilty of murder even though they did not intend to kill. This was decided in *Vickers* (1957).

Vickers (1957)

Vickers broke into the cellar of a local sweet shop. He knew that the old lady who ran the shop was deaf. However, the old lady came into the cellar and saw Vickers. He then hit her several times with his fists and kicked her once in the head. She died as a result of her injuries. The Court of Appeal upheld his conviction for murder. They pointed out that if a defendant intends to inflict grievous bodily harm and the victim dies, this has always been sufficient in English law to imply malice aforethought.

In *Cunningham* (1981) the House of Lords confirmed that the Court of Appeal's decision in *Vickers* was correct.

Cunningham (1981)

The defendant hit the victim over the head with a stool. The victim died from head injuries. The defendant claimed that he did not intend any life-threatening injuries to the victim. The House of Lords held that an intention to cause really serious harm was sufficient for the *mens rea* of murder.

DPP v Smith (1961) decided that 'grievous bodily harm' has the natural meaning of 'really serious'. However, a direction to the jury which left out the word 'really' was not considered a misdirection.

In the *Attorney-General's Reference (No 3 of 1994)* (1997) it was held that it was not possible for a defendant to have the *mens rea* to kill or seriously injure a foetus. This was because it did not have a separate existence from the mother.

1.3.2 Foresight of consequences

The main problem with proving intention is in cases where the defendant's main aim was not the death of the victim, but something quite different. However, in achieving the aim, death or serious injury is caused. This is referred to as 'oblique intent'. The defendant does not have the *mens rea* for murder unless he foresaw that he would also cause death or serious injury. This is known as 'foresight of consequences'.

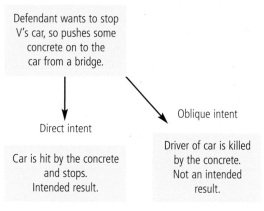

Figure 1.2 Oblique intent

The usual example given to explain these ideas of oblique intent and foresight of consequences is where a man wants to claim insurance money. He decides to put some fake cargo on a plane and then arrange for it to explode when the plane is over the sea. This has the effect of killing the crew of the cargo plane. The man's direct intention is to claim the insurance money on the loss of the cargo. The oblique intent is the killing of the crew. This is not an intended result. If the man foresaw that death or serious injury was a virtual certainty, then he has foresight of the consequences.

The starting point for foresight of consequences is s 8 of the Criminal Justice Act 1967 which states that:

 'A court or jury, in determining whether a person has committed an offence –

(a) shall not be bound in law to infer that he intended or foresaw a result of his actions by reason only of its being a natural and probable consequence of those actions; but

(b) shall decide whether he did intend or foresee that result by reference to all the evidence, drawing such inferences from the evidence as appear proper in the circumstances.'

This wording has been considered in several murder cases. The important point of the section is that the defendant must intend or foresee a result. In murder this means that the defendant must intend or foresee that death or really serious injury will be caused. The leading case on this now is *Woollin* (1998), but to understand the law and the problems it is necessary to look at cases which came before *Woollin*. The first of these was *Moloney* (1985).

Moloney (1985)

D and his stepfather had drunk a considerable amount at a family party. After the party they were heard talking and laughing. Then there was a shot. D phoned the police saying he had just murdered his father. D said that they had been seeing who was the fastest at loading and firing a shotgun. He had loaded his gun the fastest. His stepfather then said he hadn't 'got the guts' to pull the trigger. D said 'I didn't aim the gun. I just pulled the trigger and he was dead.' D was convicted of murder but this conviction was quashed on appeal.

In the case of *Moloney* the House of Lords ruled that foresight of consequences is only evidence of intention. It is not intention in itself. This part of the House of Lords' judgment is still law.

Other parts of this judgment have, however, been overruled by later cases. This was because Lord Bridge stated that jurors should be told to consider two questions. First, was death or really serious injury a natural consequence of the defendant's act, and second, did the defendant foresee that consequence as being a natural result of his act? The problem with these questions (which are often referred to as the *Moloney* guidelines) is that the word 'probable' is not mentioned.

If you look back to s 8 of the Criminal Justice Act 1967, you will see that the section uses the phrase 'natural and probable consequence'. Lord Bridge referred only to a natural result. This omission of the word 'probable' was held in *Hancock and Shankland* (1986) (see below) to make the guidelines defective. So they are no longer law.

Hancock and Shankland (1986)

Ds were miners who were on strike. They tried to prevent another miner from going to work by pushing a concrete block from a bridge onto the road along which he was being driven to work in a taxi. The block struck the windscreen of the taxi and killed the driver. The trial judge used the *Moloney* guidelines to direct the jury and Ds were convicted of murder. On appeal the Court of Appeal quashed their conviction. This was upheld by the House of Lords.

The problem with *Moloney* was explained by Lord Scarman, who stated that the guidelines in *Moloney* were unsafe and misleading. He said:

> 'In my judgment, therefore, the *Moloney* guidelines as they stand are unsafe and misleading. They require a reference to probability. They also require an explanation that the greater the probability of a consequence the more likely it is that the consequence was foreseen and that if that consequence was foreseen the greater the probability is that that consequence was also intended.'

The next case was *Nedrick* (1986) where the Court of Appeal thought that the judgments in the two earlier cases of *Moloney* and *Hancock and Shankland* needed to be made clearer.

Nedrick (1986)

D had a grudge against a woman. He poured paraffin through the letterbox of her house and set it alight. A child died in the fire. D was convicted of murder but the Court of Appeal quashed the conviction and substituted one of manslaughter.

To try to make the law easier for juries to apply, the Court of Appeal said it was helpful for a jury to ask themselves two questions:

1. How probable was the consequence which resulted from D's voluntary act? and
2. Did D foresee that consequence?

So, it was necessary for the consequence to be a virtual certainty and for D to have realised that. If this was so then there was evidence from which the jury could infer that D had the necessary intention. Lord Lane CJ put in this way:

> 'The jury should be directed that they are not entitled to infer the necessary intention unless they feel sure that death or serious bodily harm was a virtual certainty (barring some unforeseen intervention) as a result of the defendant's actions and that the defendant appreciated that such was the case.'

The next case was *Woollin* (1998), in which the House of Lords approved of Lord Lane's direction in *Nedrick*, but disapproved of the use of the two questions above.

Woollin (1998)

The defendant had been feeding his three-month-old baby son. The baby choked on the food and the defendant admitted he 'lost his cool' and threw the baby towards his pram which was some three or four feet away against a wall. The baby suffered head injuries and died. The trial judge had directed the jury that they could infer intention if they were satisfied that when he threw the baby the defendant appreciated that there was 'substantial risk' of causing serious harm. The House of Lords quashed his conviction for murder and substituted a conviction for manslaughter.

The House of Lords did this because they said that 'substantial risk' was not the correct test. Using this phrase blurred the line between intention and recklessness. They approved the direction given in *Nedrick* (1986), provided the word 'find' was used instead of 'infer'. So the jury should be directed that they are not entitled to *find* the necessary intention unless they feel sure that death or serious injury was a virtual certainty as a result of the defendant's actions, and that the defendant appreciated that such was the case.

In his judgment Lord Steyn also said that the effect of the direction is that 'a result foreseen as virtually certain is an intended result'. He also pointed out that in *Moloney* (1985) the House of Lords had said that if a person foresees the probability of a consequence as little short of overwhelming, this 'will suffice to establish the necessary intent'. Lord Steyn emphasised the word 'establish'. This seems to suggest that the House of Lords in *Woollin* regarded foresight of consequences as the same as intention, when *Moloney* had clearly stated that it was not.

Subsequent cases have not helped to clarify this point. In *Re A* (2000), a civil case, doctors asked the courts whether they could operate to separate conjoined twins when they foresaw that this would kill the weaker twin. The Court of Appeal (Civil Division) clearly thought that *Woollin* (1998) laid down the rule that foresight of consequences *is* intention. They therefore had to find a defence to justify the actions of the doctors in order to give permission for the operation to go ahead.

Key facts

	Law	Source/case
Definition	'The unlawful killing of a reasonable person in being and under the King's (or Queen's) Peace, with malice aforethought, express or implied'.	Lord Coke (17th century)
Actus reus	Must unlawfully kill a person under the Queen's Peace.	
	Can be an act or an omission. A foetus is not considered a person for the purposes of murder.	*Gibbins and Proctor* (1918) *Attorney-General's Reference (No. 3 of 1994)* (1997)
	Causation D's conduct has to be: ● factual cause of death ● legal cause of death and ● there must not be a break in the chain of causation	*Pagett* (1983); *White* (1910) More than minimal cause *Blaue* (1975); *Cheshire* (1991)
Mens rea	Intention to kill *or* intention to cause grievous bodily harm.	*Vickers* (1957); *Cunningham* (1981)
	Foresight of consequences is evidence of intention.	*Moloney* (1985)
	Jury can *find* intention death or serious injury was a virtual certainty as a result of D's actions and D appreciated this.	*Woollin* (1998)

Key facts chart for murder

However, in *Matthews and Alleyne* (2003) the Court of Appeal (Criminal Division) thought that Lord Steyn's judgment in *Woollin* meant that foresight of consequences is *not* intention; it is a rule of evidence. If a jury decides that the defendant foresaw the virtual certainty of death or serious injury, then they are entitled to find intention but they do not have to do so.

Matthews and Alleyne (2003)

The defendants had thrown the victim into the middle of a wide river from a bridge. The victim had told them he could not swim. They watched him 'dog paddle' towards the bank but left before seeing if he reached safety. The victim drowned. The trial judge explained that there were two different ways of the prosecution proving intention in murder. One was by proving a direct intent to kill. The other was by proving that the victim's death was a virtual certainty and that at the time the victim was thrown off the bridge, the defendants appreciated that this was the case.

The defendants argued on appeal that this direction was suggesting that foresight of consequences is intention. The Court of Appeal held that *Woollin* (1998) only lays down a rule that evidence of foresight of consequences is not intention. However, even though there may have been a technical misdirection, they upheld the convictions as it would not have made any difference to the jury.

1.4 Transferred malice

Transferred malice is the principle that the defendant can be guilty if he intended to commit a similar crime but against a different victim. An example is aiming a blow at one person with the necessary *mens rea* for an assault causing actual bodily harm, but actually hitting another person. This occurred in the old case of *Latimer* (1886).

Latimer (1886)

D aimed a blow with a belt at a man in a pub because that man had attacked him. The belt bounced off the man and struck a woman in the face. Latimer was guilty of an assault against the woman, although he had not meant to hit her.

The principle of transferred malice was also accepted in the case of *Mitchell* (1983).

Mitchell (1983)

D tried to push his way into a queue at the post office. A 72-year-old man told him off for this. D then punched the man, causing him to stagger backwards into an 89-year-old woman. The woman was knocked over and injured and a few days later died of her injuries. D was convicted of unlawful act manslaughter.

However, where the *mens rea* is for a completely different type of offence, then the defendant may not be guilty. This was the situation in *Pembliton* (1874), where the defendant threw a stone, intending it to hit people with whom he had been fighting. The stone hit and broke a window. The intention to hit people could not be transferred to the window.

The doctrine of transferred malice was confirmed in an *obiter* statement by the House of Lords in the case of *Attorney-General's Reference (No 3 of 1994)* (1997). (See 1.1.2 for details of the case.)

1.5 Coincidence of *actus reus* and *mens rea*

In order for an offence to take place, both the *actus reus* and the *mens rea* must be present at the same time. For example, if you decide to go round to your next-door neighbour intending to assault them, but when you get to their house you change your mind and do not actually assault them, you cannot be guilty of an assault, even though you had the *mens rea*.

If, two hours later, you are driving your car out of your driveway and knock down your neighbour because you did not see them, you have now done what could be the *actus reus* for an assault. However, you are not guilty of any criminal offence since at the moment you hit your neighbour you did not have the necessary *mens rea*. The *mens rea* and the *actus reus* were not present at the same time.

This principle applies to all offences, including murder as is shown by the case of *Thabo Meli v R* (1954). In this case the court had to decide if the *actus reus* and *mens rea* were present together. If they were, then the defendants were guilty of murder, if they were not then the defendants would be not guilty of murder.

Thabo Meli v R (1954)

Ds attacked a man and believed they had killed him. They then pushed his body over a low cliff.

In fact the man had survived the attack and died of exposure when unconscious at the foot of the cliff. The court held that they were guilty of murder.

The defendants argued in their defence that there were two separate acts. The first was the attack and the second was the pushing over the cliff. They accepted that they had the *mens rea* for murder during the attack, but pointed out that this did not actually kill the defendant. They argued that they did not have the *mens rea* for murder when they pushed the victim over the cliff as they thought he was already dead.

The Privy Council held that the two parts of the defendants' plan could not be divided up in this way. Both acts were part of the plan to murder and if they had the *mens rea* for murder at any point during those acts they were guilty of murder.

Activity

In each of the following situations, explain whether the defendant has the required intention for murder.

1. Ainsley dislikes Vince and decides to attack him. Ainsley uses an iron bar to hit Vince on the head. Vince suffers serious head injuries from which he dies.
2. Jamie is annoyed because Harry has being trying to date Jamie's girlfriend. Jamie sees Harry in a local pub and punches him hard in the face saying, 'Perhaps that will make you leave my girlfriend alone'. Harry has a thin skull and the punch causes a brain haemorrhage from which he dies.
3. Selina throws a large stone into a river to see how much of splash it will make. Jake is swimming in the river and is hit on the head by the stone and dies as a result.
4. Diana intends to kill Edward. She fixes an explosive booby trap to the front door of his house, so that when he opens it the explosive will go off. Unknown to Diana Edward has given Felix the keys to his house and told him to collect some papers from there. Felix opens the door and is killed by the explosion.
5. Conway throws a large stone from a bridge onto the motorway below. It is rush-hour and there is a lot of traffic on the motorway. The stone smashes through the windscreen of Ashley's car and causes severe head injuries from which he dies.

This rule also applies to manslaughter, as shown by *Church* (1965). In this case the defendant had a fight with a woman and knocked her out. He tried unsuccessfully for about half an hour to bring her round. He thought she was dead and he put her in the river. She drowned. His conviction for manslaughter was upheld.

1.6 The need for reform of the law

In 2006 the Law Commission published a report, *Murder, Manslaughter and Infanticide* (Report Law Com 304). In this report the Law Commission pointed out that there were many problems with the law on murder.

In its general comments on the law of murder, the report said (at paragraph 1.8):

> 'The law governing homicide in England and Wales is a rickety structure set upon shaky foundations. Some of its rules have remained unaltered since the seventeenth century, even though it has long been acknowledged that they are in dire need of reform. Other rules are of uncertain content, often because they have been constantly changed to the point that they can no longer be stated with any certainty or clarity.'

In the report the Law Commission set out the existing problems with the law on murder. They listed the following:

- The law on murder has developed bit by bit in individual cases and is not a coherent whole.
- A defendant can be convicted of murder even though he only intended to cause serious harm (the serious harm rule).
- There is no defence available if excessive force is used in self defence.
- The defence of duress is not available as a defence to murder.
- The mandatory life sentence and the government's sentencing guidelines do not

allow sufficient differentiation in sentencing to cover the wide variety of levels of blameworthiness in the current law of murder.

Each of these is discussed in the section below.

The Law Commission also pointed out that there are problems with the special defences to murder of diminished responsibility and provocation. These problems are considered in the chapter on these defences at 2.1.5 and 2.2.5.

1.6.1 Bit by bit development of the law

One of the main areas where the bit by bit development by the courts has caused problems is the meaning of 'intention'. Intention is a concept which affects all specific intent offences but most of the cases which have been heard by the House of Lords have involved murder. Section 8 of the Criminal Justice Act 1967 tried to make the law clear on this point. It states:

> 'A court or jury in determining whether a person has committed an offence—
> (a) shall not be bound in law to infer that he intended or foresaw a result of his actions by reason only of its being a natural and probable consequence of those actions; but
> (b) shall decide whether he did intend or foresee that result by reference to all the evidence, drawing such inferences from the evidence as appear proper in the circumstances.'

The main problems in the law are on foresight of consequences. The House of Lords has tried on many occasions to explain what the effect of foresight of consequences has. In *Moloney* (1985) it ruled that foresight of consequences was not intention; it was only evidence from which intention could be inferred in accordance with s 8(b) above.

However, the later decision in *Woollin* (1998), where the House of Lords speaks about intention being *found* from foresight of consequences, has made the law uncertain. It is not clear whether there is a substantive rule of criminal law that foresight of consequences is intention, or if there is only a rule of evidence that intention can be found from foresight of consequences. In *Matthews and Alleyne* (2003) the Court of Appeal even said that there was little to choose between a rule of evidence and one of substantive law, leaving it even more unclear.

1.6.2 The serious harm rule

The Law Commission, in their report, *Murder, Manslaughter and Infanticide,* points out that Parliament, when it passed the Homicide Act 1957, never intended a killing to amount to murder unless the defendant realised that his or her conduct might cause death. They state that in their view the present offence of murder is too wide.

Under the present law on murder, a defendant is guilty of murder if he had the intention to cause grievous bodily harm and actually causes the victim's death. In some of these cases the defendant may not even realise that death could occur. Yet he is just as guilty of murder as the man who deliberately sets out to kill his victim.

The Law Commission give the following example in their report (paragraph 1.17):

> 'D intentionally punches V in the face. The punch breaks V's nose and causes V to fall to the ground. In falling, V hits his or her head on the curb causing a massive and fatal brain haemorrhage.'

They point out that, if the jury decide that the harm D intended the punch to cause can be described as 'serious', then this would be murder. Yet, most people would agree that this should not be the most serious offence of homicide and D should not receive a mandatory life sentence for it.

Not only are the Law Commission very critical of this rule, but the problem had already been

pointed out by judges as far back as 1981 in the case of *Cunningham* (1981). When the law was considered by the House of Lords, Lord Edmund Davies stated that he thought the *mens rea* for murder should be limited to an intention to kill. He said:

> '[It is] strange that a person can be convicted of murder if death results from, say, his intentional breaking of another's arm, an action which, while undoubtedly involving the infliction of "really serious harm" and as such, calling for severe punishment, would in most cases be unlikely to kill.'

Although he was very critical of the law, Lord Edmund Davies felt that any change to the law had to be made by Parliament. This was because the law has been the same for over 200 years and it would therefore be wrong for judges to change such a well-established law.

The Law Commission has made very specific proposals for how the law could be reformed. These proposals are discussed at section 1.6.6.

1.6.3 No defence where excessive force is used

If a defendant can show that he used reasonable force in self-defence or prevention of crime in doing the killing, he is not guilty of murder. However, where force is necessary in self-defence or prevention of crime but the defendant uses excessive force in the circumstances, he is guilty of murder. This 'all or nothing' effect of the defence is very harsh in murder cases, as the defendant is either acquitted or given a life sentence. He was justified in using some force and his only 'fault' was that he used more force than was reasonable. This surely does not justify a life sentence.

Two recent cases have highlighted this problem. The first was *Clegg* (1995).

Clegg (1995)

D was a soldier on duty at a checkpoint in Northern Ireland when a stolen car came towards him at speed. D fired at the car. His final shot hit a passenger in the back and killed her. The evidence showed that the car had gone past D by the time this last shot was fired. It was held that he could not use self-defence or defence of another as there was no danger when he fired that shot. The force was excessive in the circumstances and his conviction for murder was upheld.

Note that in 1999 the case of *Clegg* was referred back to the Court of Appeal by the Criminal Case Review Commission. On this occasion his conviction was quashed because new forensic evidence cast doubt on whether the fatal shot had actually been fired by Clegg.

The second case was *Martin (Anthony)* (2002).

Martin (Anthony) (2002)

Two burglars entered the defendant's house in the night. The house was in an isolated place and had been burgled before. On this occasion the noise of entry woke Martin, who got up, armed himself with a shotgun, and without warning fired three shots in the dark. One of the burglars was killed. Martin was convicted of murder. His appeal on the ground of self-defence was rejected as the force was not reasonable. However, his conviction was reduced to manslaughter because of evidence that he was suffering from diminished responsibility.

Both these decisions have been criticised. Many people believe that a person who kills where he has an honest, but unreasonable, belief as to the degree of force needed is not as blameworthy as a 'true' murderer. It is unjust that such a person is found guilty of the same crime of murder and sentenced to the same punishment.

The Law Commission proposes that use of excessive force in a situation where some force is justified should be a partial defence to murder. If the defence was successful, the offence would be reduced to manslaughter. The judge would then have more discretion over sentencing in such a case. A life sentence could be given but it would not be mandatory.

1.6.4 No defence of duress

Duress is where the defendant is threatened with death or serious injury so that he takes part in an offence. Duress is allowed as a defence to almost all offences, but it is not allowed as a defence to murder (or attempted murder). See 16.1 for full discussion of the defence of duress.

The Law Commission give the following example:

> 'A taxi driver has his vehicle commandeered by a gunman who holds a gun to the driver's head and tells him to drive to a place where the gunman says he may shoot someone. The taxi driver does as the gunman demands and the gunman goes on to shoot and kill someone.'

The report points out that, under the existing law, the taxi driver is an accomplice in the killing and could be convicted of murder. He would then receive a mandatory life sentence just as the gunman would. This is clearly not fair.

The Law Commission proposes that duress should be a complete defence to murder. However, a defendant claiming this defence would have to prove that he or she was threatened with death or life-threatening harm and had had no realistic opportunity to seek police protection. The jury would also have to find that a person of ordinary courage might have responded in the same way as D did by taking part in the commission of the crime.

1.6.5 Mandatory life sentence

If a defendant aged 18 or over is convicted of murder, the judge has to pass a sentence of life imprisonment. For offenders aged 10–17 who are found guilty of murder, the judge has to order that they be detained at Her Majesty's Pleasure. Because the judge has no discretion in what sentence to impose, this is known as a *mandatory* sentence. The judge cannot give a different sentence even if he feels that the defendant is not as blameworthy as a deliberate killer.

For other offences, including attempted murder, the judge can decide what the most appropriate sentence is for the offence and the offender. This makes it possible for a judge to give even a community sentence where the circumstances justify it. This happened in the case of *Gotts* (1992), where the father of a 16-year-old boy threatened to kill the boy unless he stabbed his mother. The boy did stab her and seriously injure her, but the injury did not kill her. He was convicted of attempted murder and because of the circumstances the judge put him on probation for three years. If the stabbing had caused the death of the mother, the judge would have had to order the boy (because of his age) to be detained at Her Majesty's Pleasure.

It is because of the mandatory life sentence for murder that the 1957 Homicide Act sets out special defences: of diminished responsibility and provocation (see Chapter 2), which reduce the charge to manslaughter. This allows the judge flexibility in passing sentence which he does not have when the defendant is convicted of murder.

Minimum sentences

In each case the judge will impose a life sentence but will then state the minimum number of years the offender must serve before any application can be made for release on licence.

The sentencing problems have been aggravated by the Government's guidelines on these minimum sentences as laid down in the Criminal Justice Act 2003. This gives three starting points for adult offenders:

- a whole life term for exceptionally serious cases, such as premeditated killings of two or more people, sexual or sadistic child murders or politically motivated murders;
- 30 years' minimum for serious cases such as murders of police or prison officers, murders involving firearms, sexual or sadistic killings or killings aggravated by racial or sexual orientation; and
- 15 years' minimum for murders not falling within the two higher categories.

Under these rules *Martin (Anthony)* who shot and killed a burglar would have had to be given a minimum sentence of 30 years. This is the same length of sentence that a contract killer who deliberately kills a victim would receive. The guidelines do not allow sufficient differentiation between levels of blameworthiness.

The Law Commission was not asked to consider sentencing. However, in their proposals for making murder into a two tier offence, they state that the mandatory life sentence and the guidelines on minimum sentences should only apply to first degree murder. This would create a fairer sentence structure.

1.6.6 Law Commission's proposals for reform

The Law Commission proposed that murder should be reformed by dividing into two separate offences:

- first degree murder; and
- second degree murder.

First degree murder would cover cases in which the defendant intended to kill. It would also cover situations where the defendant intended to cause serious harm and was aware that his or her conduct posed a serious risk of death.

Cases in which the defendant intended to do serious injury but was not aware that there was a serious risk of death would be second degree murder. By dividing murder into two separate categories the mandatory life sentence would apply only to first degree murder. Second degree murder would carry a maximum of a life sentence but would allow the judge discretion in sentencing.

1.6.7 Government's response to the Law Commission's proposals

In July 2008 the Government issued a consultation paper, *Murder, manslaughter and infanticide: proposals for reform of the law*, CP 19/08. This paper rejected the Law Commission's proposal of completely reforming murder by making it a two-tier offence. The Government's proposals do not, therefore, address the problems of no intent to kill, the difficulty of the meaning of intention, the lack of a defence of duress and the use of the mandatory life sentence. These would continue to be problems in the law of murder.

The only area where the Government accepted that reform is needed is the lack of a defence for those who use excessive force in self-defence. For this the Government proposes that there should be a partial defence of 'killing in response to a fear of serious violence'.

This would form part of a new defence which it is proposed would replace the partial defence of provocation. See 2.2.7 for discussion of how this would affect provocation.

The Government's consultation paper points out that there are two likely scenarios where the partial defence of 'killing in response to a fear of serious violence' would be available. These are where:

- a victim of sustained abuse kills his or her abuser in order to thwart an attack which is anticipated but not immediately imminent; or
- someone overreacts to what they perceive as an imminent threat.

If this proposal is accepted then defendants in cases such as *Clegg* (1995) and *Martin (Anthony)* (2002) would have a partial defence to a charge of murder which could reduce the charge to manslaughter.

1.6.8 Euthanasia

There is also the problem of euthanasia. This is also known as 'mercy killing' and is where D kills V because V is suffering through an incurable illness. Quite often, D is the spouse or partner of V and has seen V suffering for a long period of time.

Under the present law, if D kills V because he or she can no longer bear to see V in such pain then D is guilty of murder. This is so even if V has begged D to do the killing. This means that D will be sentenced to life imprisonment with a minimum term of 15 years before D can be considered for release on licence.

As such a defendant is unlikely to be a dangerous person, surely there should be more discretion in the sentence that the courts impose.

In some countries, especially The Netherlands, doctors are allowed to end the life of terminally ill patients. There are, of course, strict controls on when this can be done.

In this country although euthanasia is not allowed, doctors can withdraw treatment from patients in certain circumstances under the decision in *Airedale NHS Trust v Bland* (1993).

Airedale NHS Trust v Bland (1993)

Bland had been suffocated in the Hillsborough Stadium tragedy. This had so starved his brain of oxygen that he had been in a persistent vegetative state in hospital for over three years. He was being fed through tubes. The hospital applied for permission to stop feeding him.

The House of Lords stated that there was no rule that a patient's life be prolonged regardless of the quality of life. Sanctity of life was an important principle, but quality of life could also be considered. If it was in the best interests of the patient to discontinue life-support, then that was allowed to happen.

So although doctors can withdraw treatment where a patient is in a persistent vegetative state, the doctors are not allowed to do anything positive to kill the patient. It can be argued that it is better to administer a drug which kills such a patient painlessly, rather than deprive them of food and drink, so that they effectively starve to death.

1.7 Exam tips

When considering a murder problem in an examination question, remember that it is likely to involve a number of points. It may be a situation where the *mens rea* for murder is uncertain and it is necessary to consider involuntary manslaughter which is explained in the next chapter.

Alternatively there may be a defence available to the defendant. Different types of defence have different effects on the verdict. For example, in Chapter 2 we look at three special defences to murder; if any of these is successful then the verdict is not guilty of manslaughter but guilty of voluntary manslaughter.

In Chapter 5 some general defences are considered. If the defendant proves he was insane at the time of the killing, he is found not guilty by reason of insanity. If the defendant successfully pleads automatism, mistake or self-defence he is entitled to be acquitted of murder.

The following flow chart takes you through the different points you may have to consider.

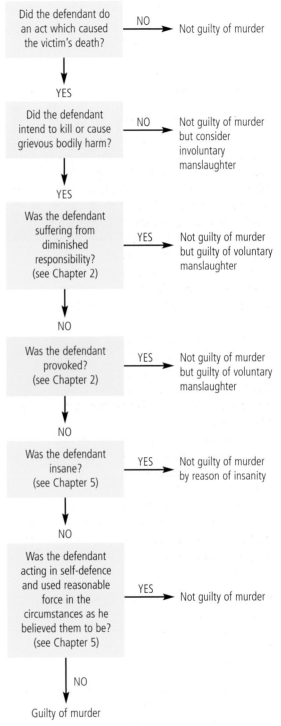

Figure 1.3 Points to consider in a murder question

Chapter 2

Voluntary manslaughter

There are three special defences to a charge of murder. These are where the killing occurs when the defendant is under:

- diminished responsibility;
- provocation; or
- suicide pact.

All of these defences are set out in the Homicide Act 1957. These defences are available only to murder. They are also only partial defences, which means that the defendant is not completely acquitted. Instead, when one of these defences is successful the charge of murder is reduced to manslaughter.

This is important because it means that the judge has discretion in the sentence which he imposes. When a person is found guilty of murder the judge has to pass a sentence of life imprisonment. However, for manslaughter the judge can choose any sentence which is suitable. This means that where the defendant is dangerous and his mental problems cannot be treated then the judge may pass a sentence of life imprisonment as happened in *Byrne* (1960) (see 2.1.1). However, if the defendant is not dangerous then he or she may be given a short term of imprisonment or even a community sentence. If the defendant has mental problems which can be treated, then the most suitable sentence is one which orders the defendant to have treatment, either in a hospital or in the community.

For the AQA specification, you are only required to deal with diminished responsibility and provocation.

2.1 Diminished responsibility

This defence was introduced by the Homicide Act 1957; it did not exist in English law until then. Before 1957 if a person with mental problems killed, then their only defence was insanity. The test for insanity is a very narrow one and defendants who clearly suffered from a mental illness do not always come within it. (See Chapter 5 for further information on the defence of insanity.)

Section 2(1) of the Homicide Act states that:

> 'Where a person kills or is party to a killing of another, he shall not be convicted of murder if he was suffering from such abnormality of mind (whether arising from a condition of arrested or retarded development of mind or any inherent causes or induced by disease or injury) as substantially impaired his mental responsibility for his acts and omission in doing or being a party to the killing'.

The burden of proving the defence is on the defendant, but the defendant need only prove it on the balance of probabilities.

This means that a defendant who pleads diminished responsibility must prove:

- he was suffering from an abnormality of mind;
- this was caused by arrested or retarded development of mind or an inherent cause or disease or injury; and
- that the abnormality of mind substantially impaired his mental responsibility for the killing.

2.1.1 Abnormality of mind

Abnormality of mind covers a wide range of situations. In *Byrne* (1960) the Court of Appeal described it as 'a state of mind so different from that of ordinary human beings that the reasonable man would term it abnormal'.

Byrne (1960)

The defendant was a sexual psychopath who strangled a young woman and then mutilated her body. The medical evidence was that, because of his condition, he was unable to control his perverted desires. He was convicted of murder but the Court of Appeal quashed the conviction and substituted a conviction for manslaughter.

The Court of Appeal held that 'abnormality of mind' is wide enough to cover:

- the perception of physical acts and matters;
- the ability to form a rational judgment as to whether an act is right or wrong; and
- the ability to exercise willpower to control physical acts in accordance with that rational judgment.

This final point covers 'irresistible impulse' as in this case where he could not resist his perverted desires. This meant that the defence of diminished responsibility was available to Byrne. However, although the Court of Appeal substituted a conviction for manslaughter, Byrne was still sentenced to life imprisonment.

In *Byrne*, the medical experts had described his condition as amounting to 'partial insanity' and the Court of Criminal Appeal had approved of this. In *Seers* (1984), where the defendant was suffering from chronic reactive depression, the trial judge had directed the jury that the defence was only available to those who were 'partially insane' or 'on the borderline of insanity'. Seers was convicted of murder but the Court of Appeal quashed this conviction and substituted a conviction for manslaughter, holding that comparisons with insanity should be avoided.

Diminished responsibility covers a wide range of mental conditions including depressive illnesses, paranoia, epilepsy, pre-menstrual tension and battered wives' syndrome.

2.1.2 Causes of the abnormality of mind

The abnormality of mind must be caused by one of the matters set out in the brackets within s 2(1) Homicide Act 1957. These are:

- a condition of arrested or retarded development of mind; or
- any inherent cause; or
- induced by any disease; or
- induced by injury.

Inherent cause means one which comes from within the defendant as opposed to an outside factor. It does not have to be permanent. A totally external factor such as alcohol, drugs, a traumatic event or environmental influences is not an inherent cause. However, if a traumatic event causes the defendant to suffer from post-traumatic stress disorder then this is recognised as a disease.

The important point is that there must be medical evidence given at the trial of an abnormality of mind arising from one of the specified causes.

2.1.3 Substantially impairs

The abnormality of mind must substantially impair the defendant's mental responsibility for his acts or omissions in doing or being a party to the killing.

In *Byrne* (1960) the appeal court said that the question of whether the impairment was substantial was one of degree and that it was for

the jury to decide. In *Lloyd* (1967) it was held that substantial does not mean total, nor does it mean trivial or minimal. It is something in between and it is for the jury to decide if the defendant's mental responsibility is impaired and, if so, whether it is substantially impaired. However, as it is a question of fact, the judge can withdraw the point from the jury if there is no evidence on which a reasonable jury could conclude that the defendant's mental responsibility was substantially impaired.

2.1.4 Diminished responsibility and intoxication

The defence of diminished responsibility becomes more complicated when the defendant was also intoxicated at the time of the killing. There are various combinations of intoxication and diminished responsibility that have to be considered. These are:

- intoxication only
- intoxication and a pre-existing abnormality of mind not connected to the intoxication
- intoxication which has caused brain damage
- intoxication due to addiction/dependency.

Intoxication only

There is a clear rule that intoxication alone is not diminished responsibility. In *Di Duca* (1959) the Court of Appeal held that the immediate effects of taking alcohol or drugs was not an injury, even if it did have an effect on the brain. So a 'transient' state of intoxication was not an abnormality of mind.

So, if the jury decide that the defendant was not suffering from an abnormality of mind, the defence of diminished responsibility is not available. The defendant will be guilty of murder.

Intoxication and a pre-existing abnormality of mind

There are difficulties in cases where the defendant has some abnormality of mind but, in addition, is intoxicated at the time he does the killing. This occurred in *Gittens* (1984).

Gittens (1984)

The defendant suffered from depression and had medication for this. One night he drank heavily and also took several anti-depressant pills. He then clubbed his wife to death and strangled his step-daughter. He was convicted of murder. The conviction was quashed because the trial judge had misdirected the jury on the effect of intoxication in the case. The Court of Appeal held that where there was a combination of factors, one of which was intoxication, the jury had to decide whether the combination of the factors excluding the intoxication amounted to a substantial impairment of the defendant's responsibility for his acts.

This decision was later interpreted as meaning that the defendant could only prove diminished responsibility if he could satisfy the jury that he would have killed because of the abnormality of mind even if he had not been intoxicated. However, in *Dietschmann* (2003) the House of Lords said that this was the wrong approach and was not what had been decided in *Gittens* (1984).

Dietschmann (2003)

The defendant was upset by the fact that, in his view, the victim was behaving in a way which was disrespectful to the memory of the defendant's aunt who had just died. He killed the victim by repeatedly kicking him and stamping on him. The psychiatrists called by both the prosecution and the defence agreed that the defendant was suffering from an adjustment disorder in the form of depressed grief reaction to the death of his aunt. However, they disagreed on whether this had substantially impaired his mental

responsibility for the killing. The defendant had also drunk about a third of a bottle of whisky, and two and a half pints of cider before the killing. He was convicted and appealed. The Court of Appeal dismissed the appeal, but the House of Lords allowed it.

Although the Court of Appeal dismissed the appeal, they certified the following questions for the House of Lords:

> '(1) Does a defendant seeking to prove a defence of diminished responsibility under section 2(1) of the Homicide Act 1957 in a case where he had taken drink prior to the killing of the victim, have to show (a) he would have killed as in fact he did; and (b) he would have been under diminished responsibility when he did so?
>
> (2) If not, what direction ought to be given to a jury as to the approach to be taken to self-induced intoxication which was present at the material time in conjunction with an abnormality of mind which falls within under section 2(1) of the 1957 Act?'

In the House of Lords Lord Hutton said that the meaning of s 2(1) was reasonably clear. It meant that if the defendant satisfied the jury that, notwithstanding the alcohol he had consumed and its effect on him, his abnormality of mind substantially impaired his mental responsibility for his acts in doing the killing, the jury should not find him guilty of murder but, instead guilty of manslaughter under s 2(1).

Lord Hutton also pointed out that s 2(1) does not require the abnormality of mind to be the sole cause of the defendant's acts in doing the killing. Even if the defendant would not have killed if he had not taken the drink, the causative effect of the drink does not necessarily prevent an abnormality of mind from substantially impairing his mental responsibility. Lord Hutton highlighted three points from the decision in *Gittens* (1984):

1. The abnormality of mind and the drink might each play a part in impairing the defendant's mental responsibility for the killing.
2. The jury's task was to decide whether, despite the disinhibiting effect of the drink on the defendant's mind, the abnormality of mind nevertheless substantially impaired his mental responsibility for his fatal acts.
3. It was not correct for the judge to direct the jury that unless they were satisfied that if the defendant had not taken drink he would have killed, the defence must fail. The direction was incorrect because it failed to recognise that drink and the abnormality of mind might each play a part in impairing the defendant's mental responsibility for the killing.

The House of Lords allowed the appeal and sent the case back to the Court of Appeal to decide whether to substitute a verdict of manslaughter or to order a new trial.

Intoxication which has caused brain damage

If the brain has been injured through alcoholism then that injury or disease can support a finding of diminished responsibility. This was stated in *Tandy* (1989) (see below).

Intoxication due to addiction/dependency

In *Tandy* (1989) the Court of Appeal held that where the defendant is unable to resist drinking, so that it is involuntary, this may amount to diminished responsibility.

Tandy (1989)

Mrs Tandy had been an alcoholic for a number of years, usually drinking barley wine or Cinzano. One day, she drank nearly a whole bottle of vodka. That evening she told her mother that her (Tandy's) second husband had sexually interfered with her 11-year-old daughter. She then strangled her daughter. The trial judge told the jury to decide whether Tandy was suffering from an abnormality of mind as a direct result of her alcoholism or whether she was just drunk. She was convicted. The Court of Appeal dismissed her appeal because Tandy had not shown that her brain had been injured or that her drinking was involuntary.

The decision in this case has been criticised as it only looks at whether the defendant was unable to prevent themselves from drinking. It does not consider whether alcoholism is a disease.

The point was considered again in *Wood* (2008) when the Court of Appeal pointed out that the 'sharp effect of the distinction drawn in *Tandy* between cases where brain damage has occurred as a result of alcohol dependency syndrome and those where it has not, is no longer appropriate'.

Wood (2008)

The defendant, after drinking heavily, had gone to the victim's flat. The defendant claimed he had fallen asleep there and been woken by the victim trying to perform oral sex on him. The defendant repeatedly hit the victim with a meat cleaver, killing him. At the trial medical experts agreed that the defendant was suffering from alcohol dependency syndrome, but disagreed as to whether this had damaged his brain.

The judge directed the jury that if they found that the defendant had suffered brain damage from his long-term abuse of alcohol then the defence of diminished responsibility was available to him. But if they found that he had not suffered brain damage, they then had to decide whether the drinking had been voluntary or not. If it was voluntary then the defendant could not use the defence of diminished responsibility.

> The defendant was convicted. He appealed and the Court of Appeal quashed the conviction, holding that the judge was wrong to direct the jury that all of the defendant's drinking had to be involuntary.

When hearing the appeal in the case of *Wood* the Court of Appeal considered the effect of the judgment in *Dietschmann* on the decision in *Tandy*. They held that alcohol dependency syndrome could be considered as a possible source of abnormality of mind. This was for the jury to decide. If the jury found that it was an abnormality of mind, then they had to consider the effect of any alcohol consumed by the defendant as a result of his dependency.

This involved questions such as whether the defendant's craving for alcohol was or was not irresistible and whether his consumption of alcohol in the period leading up to the killing was voluntary – and if so, to what extent.

The view in *Tandy* that all the drinking had to be involuntary for the defence of diminished responsibility to be available was incompatible with the House of Lords' approach in *Dietschmann*.

The jury could take into consideration the effect of any drinking which they decided was involuntary when determining whether the defendant's mental responsibility for his actions at the time of the killing was substantially impaired.

Although the approach recognises that a person suffering from alcohol dependency syndrome cannot always control their drinking, it does make the task for the jury a difficult one. They have to decide which drinks were involuntary and then consider the effect of those while ignoring any consumption of alcohol which they decide was voluntary.

2.1.5 Problems in the law on diminished responsibility

Although diminished responsibility has provided a more satisfactory defence than insanity for defendants who kill but are suffering from a mental abnormality, there are still problems with the defence.

Burden of proof

A main point is that the burden of proof should not be on the defendant; in most other defences the defendant only has to raise the issue and the prosecution has to disprove it. This should also apply to diminished responsibility. At the moment, defendants pleading diminished responsibility are at a disadvantage which is not faced by those raising provocation.

There is also the possibility that putting the burden of proof on the defendant may be a breach of Art 6(2) of the European Convention on Human Rights which states that 'everyone charged with a criminal offence shall be presumed to be innocent until proven guilty according to law'. Making the defendant prove diminished responsibility could be considered a breach of this right to be presumed innocent.

Wording of s 2

There are also problems with the wording in s 2 of the Homicide Act 1957. The definition in s 2 has been constantly criticised. Lord Justice Buxton described the wording as a 'disgrace'.

The Law Commission in their report, *Murder, Manslaughter and Infanticide* (2006), pointed out two principal problems with the current law. These were:

1. The section does not explain what is involved in a 'substantial impairment of mental responsibility'.

   Section 2 implies that the effects of an abnormality of mind must significantly reduce the offender's culpability. But the Act does not make this clear. The Act also fails to say in what way the effects of an abnormality of mind can reduce the culpability for an intentional killing so as to make a manslaughter verdict the right one instead of murder.

2. The definition in s 2 was not drafted with the needs and practices of medical experts in mind.

    In particular the term 'abnormality of mind' is not a psychiatric term. This has had the effect that the meaning of the phrase has had to be developed through case law. It would be better to have a clearer medical definition.

    In addition, medical knowledge of mental illness has developed beyond the simple list given in the words in brackets in the section (whether arising from a condition of arrested or retarded development of mind or any inherent causes or induced by disease or injury).

    The Law Commission quote one psychiatrist as pointing out that:

> [A]ttempting to specify the cause of mental disorders... is irrelevant [and] misleading, and in fact there are almost always multiple causes stemming from the interaction between genetic vulnerability and life events.

An example of medical knowledge improving is the recognition of what is commonly called 'battered wife syndrome'. This is where a woman has been physically and mentally abused over many years to the point where she has lost touch with reality and is no longer fully responsible for her actions.

2.1.6 Proposals for reform

The Law Commission, in their report, *Murder, Manslaughter and Infanticide* (2006), recommended that the definition of diminished responsibility should be modernised so as to take into account changing medical knowledge. The Law Commission also thought that the definition should be flexible enough to allow for future developments in medical knowledge.

The Government, in their consultation paper, *Murder, manslaughter and infanticide: proposals for reform of the law*, CP 19/08, accepted the Law Commission's recommendations and proposed that there should be a new partial defence of diminished responsibility. The definition they suggest in the consultation paper is:

> (1) A person (P) who kills or is a party to the killing of another is not to be convicted of murder if P was suffering from a relevant mental impairment which provides an explanation for P's acts and omissions in doing or being a party to the killing.'

The paper gives the following explanation of 'relevant mental impairment':

> 'Relevant mental impairment' means an abnormality of mental functioning which –
> (a) arises from a recognised medical condition, and
> (b) substantially impairs P's ability to do one or more of the following –
>   (i) to understand the nature of P's conduct; or
>   (ii) form a rational judgment; or
>   (iii) to exercise self-control.'

This would base the defence on a 'recognised medical condition'. This wording allows for the law to develop with changing medical knowledge of mental health conditions. It does not restrict it as the present wording of the defence does.

It also sets out clearly what aspects of the defendant's functioning must be substantially impaired in order for the partial defence of diminished responsibility to succeed.

The Law Commission had also recommended that developmental immaturity in those under 18 should also be included. Their reason for this was because there is evidence to show that frontal lobes of the brain which play an important role in the development of self-control and in controlling impulsive behaviour do not mature until the age of 14.

If there is no such defence children as young as 10 may be convicted of murder when they are developmentally immature. They cannot use the defence of diminished responsibility under the existing law as they are not suffering from an abnormality of mind.

However, the Law Commission recognised that this proposal was controversial, and the Government rejected it and it was not included in their consultation paper published in July 2008.

Key facts

	Law	Act/Case
Definition	• suffering from an abnormality of mind • caused by arrested or retarded development of mind, an inherent cause, disease or injury • the abnormality of mind substantially impaired his mental responsibility for the killing	s 2(1) Homicide Act 1957
Abnormality of mind	A state of mind so different from that of ordinary human beings that the reasonable man would term it abnormal	*Byrne* (1960)
Substantially impaired	A question of degree for the jury to decide Substantial does not mean total nor trivial or minimal but something in between	*Byrne* (1960) *Lloyd* (1967)
Effect of intoxication	• Transient effect of drink or drugs on brain is not an injury	*Di Duca* (1959)
	• Where the defendant has a pre-existing mental disorder, intoxication does not prevent him using the defence; the abnormality of mind does not have to be the sole cause of the defendant doing the killing	*Dietschmann* (2003)
	• Brain damage caused by alcohol/drug abuse can be diminished responsibility	*Tandy* (1989)
	• Alcohol dependency syndrome can be an abnormality of mind – jury must consider effects of involuntary drinking	*Wood* (2008)
Burden of proof	It is for the defence to prove on the balance of probabilities	s 2(2) Homicide Act 1957
Effect of defence	The charge of murder is reduced to manslaughter	s 2(3) Homicide Act 1957
Proposal for reform	Partial defence where P was: • suffering from a relevant mental impairment: and • this substantially impairs P's ability to: (i) understand the nature of P's conduct; or (ii) form a rational judgment; or (iii) exercise self-control	2008 Government consultation paper

Key facts chart on diminished responsibility

Activity

Read the following extract from a newspaper report by Stewart Payne which appeared in the *Daily Telegraph,* 3 November 2005, and answer the questions which follow.

Mercy for mother who was driven to kill her Down's syndrome son

The desperate plight of a loving mother who killed her Down's syndrome son after caring for him for 36 years led a judge to spare her a jail sentence yesterday.

Wendolyn Markcrow, 67, described as having lived a 'saintly' life, finally reached her wits' end, a court heard.

During another sleepless night she 'snapped' and gave her son Patrick 14 tranquillisers and suffocated him with a plastic bag.

She then slashed her neck and arm with a kitchen knife and sat down in the garden shed where she hoped to die.

She was 'overwhelmed with despair' and wanted to end her life. Yet she feared for what would happen to Patrick if she were not there.

Oxford Crown Court heard that she had never thought to put her own needs before those of her son and, in the end, 'spiralled into depression'. Markcrow, a mother of four, who admitted manslaughter on the grounds of diminished responsibility at an earlier hearing, survived her suicide attempt. She told police: 'I feel sad, desperate, defeated and ashamed.'

Mr Justice Gross sentenced her to two years' prison, suspended for 18 months, and told her: 'The pressures you faced were extreme.'

Questions

1. Which section of which Act allows a defence of diminished responsibility?

2. What would Mrs Markcrow's lawyers have had to prove to establish the defence of diminished responsibility?

3. What points in the extract support the defence?

4. The original charge against the defendant would have been murder. What effect does the defence of diminished responsibility have to that charge?

5. What sentence did the judge pass on the defendant?

6. The mandatory sentence for murder is life imprisonment. Why was the judge able to pass such a lenient sentence?

2.2 Provocation

Provocation had been a common law defence prior to the Homicide Act 1957, and the Act recognised and built on that old common law defence. However, the Act only amended some of the elements of provocation. It did not completely replace the common law. Section 3 Homicide Act 1957 states:

> 'Where, on a charge of murder, there is evidence on which the jury can find that the person charged was provoked (whether by things done or by things said or by both together) to lose his self control, the question whether the provocation was enough to make a reasonable man do as he did shall be left to be determined by the jury.'

This section does not explain what can amount to provocation except to state that it can be 'things done or by things said or by both together'. The section also imposes a two-stage test for the jury to apply:

1. A subjective test – did the defendant lose his self-control?
2. An objective test – would a reasonable man have lost his self-control?

2.2.1 What can be provocation?

The Act states that provocation can be things done or said or both. This has been held to include a wide range of behaviour such as:

- physical assaults, both on the defendant or on his relatives; *Pearson* (1992)
- homosexual advances;
- the continual crying of a 19-day-old baby; *Doughty* (1986)
- a denial of stealing the defendant's tools; *Smith (Morgan James)* (2000)
- the actions of the wife's lover in going to meet her, where the husband was provoked into killing his wife; *Davies* (1975)
- threats made to the defendant's son by a drug dealer; *Baillie* (1995).

From these examples it can be seen that the victim does not have to deliberately aim the provocation at the defendant. In *Doughty* (1986) the defendant killed his baby son aged 19 days because the child would not stop crying. He was convicted but the Court of Appeal quashed the conviction because it should have been left to the jury to decide if the baby's crying was provocation by 'things done'. Clearly a 19-day-old child is not deliberately trying to provoke anyone.

The acts which provoke the defendant can also be aimed at another person. This happened in *Pearson* (1992) where the father abused the defendant's younger brother. Although this behaviour was not aimed at the defendant, it was still 'things done' which caused the defendant to lose his self-control.

The provocation can also be by someone other than the victim. An example would be where someone tells a man that his wife has been having an affair, so that the man loses self-control and rushes off and kills his wife. The words which were the provocation were not by the victim.

This has to be provocation.

2.2.2 Loss of self-control

The first test is that the jury must be satisfied that the defendant lost his self control as a result of the provocation. In *Duffy* (1949) (before the Homicide Act 1957) it was said that there must be 'a sudden and temporary loss of self-control, rendering the accused so subject to passion as to make him or her for the moment not master of his mind'. This way of putting it has been approved by the Court of Appeal in later cases since the 1957 Act.

One of the points that may be looked at to decide whether there was a 'sudden and temporary' loss of self-control is the time lapse between the provocation and the killing. The longer the time lapse between the provocation and the killing, the less likely that the defence will succeed. This was shown in the case of *Ibrams and Gregory* (1981).

Ibrams and Gregory (1981)

The ex-boyfriend of Ibrams' current girlfriend had been visiting the flat which Ibrams and the girlfriend shared and terrorising them. On 7 October Ibrams called the police but the police did nothing. On 10 October the two defendants made a plan to attack the ex-boyfriend, and they carried out this plan and killed him on 12 October. They were convicted of murder. The Court of Appeal upheld their convictions because there was no evidence of any provocation after 7 October, and the gap of five days between this and the attack negated their claims that they had lost their self-control.

In *Baillie* (1995) the defendant discovered that a drug dealer had supplied his teenage sons with drugs and was now threatening the sons with violence. The defendant armed himself with a sawn-off shotgun and a cut-throat razor; he drove to the drug dealer's home and shot him. The judge had ruled that the time lapse and the defendant's actions meant that the defence of provocation was not available to the defendant. The Court of Appeal held that the jury should have been given the opportunity to consider the issue, as the defendant's loss of self-control when he discovered what had happened could have continued from this discovery to the time of the killing.

It is argued that this need for a sudden loss of self-control makes the defence more available to men than women. This is because men are more likely than women to respond quickly with violence. In many cases women will take longer before they lose their self-control. This is known as 'slow burn' and was considered in *Thornton (No 2)* (1996).

Thornton (No 2) (1996)

Sara Thornton's husband was jealous and possessive, and physically abused her. He also drank heavily. One night when Sara returned home, her husband was lying on the sofa in the living room. He called her names and told her he would kill her when she was asleep. Sara went into the kitchen and sharpened a bread knife. She returned to the living room and stabbed her husband in the stomach. She was convicted of murder and her first appeal failed, but on the second appeal the Court of Appeal held that there could be a sudden loss of self-control triggered by a minor incident. In other words, it is the last straw which sparks the killing. The Court of Appeal also said that medical evidence that the defendant was suffering from 'battered woman syndrome' could be relevant in explaining the 'slow burn' reaction. They quashed the conviction and ordered a re-trial at which the jury acquitted the defendant.

This 'slow burn' was also seen in *Ahluwalia* (1992).

Ahluwalia (1992)

The defendant had been physically abused over many years by her husband. One night her husband, before he went to bed, threatened her with violence the next day unless she paid a bill. Later, after the husband was asleep, the defendant poured petrol over him and set him alight. He died six days later. She was convicted of murder and appealed. The Court of Appeal did not allow her appeal on the basis of provocation. They pointed out that the defendant's reaction to the provocation had to be 'sudden' rather than 'immediate' and the longer the delay, the more likely that the act had been deliberate, so that the prosecution could negate the defence of provocation. However, the Court of Appeal did allow her appeal on the basis of diminished responsibility.

2.2.3 The reasonable man test

Under s 3 Homicide Act 1957, the jury must take into account the effect which the provocation would have on a reasonable man. This phrase 'reasonable man' has caused many problems. Before the 1957 Act the courts ruled that the reasonable man was an adult who was normal both mentally and physically. This ruling often appeared unfair, as in *Bedder v DPP* (1954) where the defendant was impotent. A prostitute taunted him about this and he stabbed her to death. His conviction for murder was upheld because under the reasonable man test the jury had to ignore the fact of impotence and the effect it would have on the provocation.

This was the leading case until *Camplin* (1978) when the House of Lords held that the 1957 Act had effectively overruled *Bedder* (1954). In *Camplin* it was held that age, sex and other relevant characteristics should be taken into account when considering how the reasonable man would have responded to the provocation.

Camplin (1978)

The defendant, a 15-year-old boy, had been sexually abused by an older man who had then laughed at him. Camplin had reacted to this by hitting the man over the head with a chapatti pan. At the trial the judge directed the jury to ignore the boy's age and consider what effect the provocation would have had on the reasonable adult. He was convicted of murder, but on appeal the House of Lords overruled *Bedder* (1954) and allowed the appeal, substituting a conviction for manslaughter.

In the judgment of the House of Lords Lord Diplock said:

'... the reasonable man is a person having the power of self-control to be expected of an ordinary person of the sex and age of the accused, but in other respects sharing such of the accused's characteristics as they think would affect the gravity of the provocation to him; and that the question is not merely whether such a person would in like circumstances be provoked to lose his self-control but whether he would react to the provocation as the accused did.'

This made it clear that there were two parts to the reasonable man test in s 3 Homicide Act 1957. These were:

1. For the purposes of self-control, the level is the power of self-control to be expected from a person of the age and sex of the defendant; but
2. For the gravity of the provocation, the reasonable man shares such of the defendant's characteristics as the jury think would affect the gravity to the defendant.

Gravity of the provocation

In *Camplin* (1978) the House of Lords gave examples of a number of characteristics which could affect the gravity of the provocation where the provocation was aimed at one of those characteristics. These included age, sex, race, colour, ethnic origin, physical deformity or infirmity, impotence (as in *Bedder* (1954)), a shameful incident in the past or an abcess on the cheek where the provocation relied on was a blow to the face. Also, for female defendants they accepted that pregnancy or menstruation might be a relevant characteristic if the provocation was aimed at this. Subsequent cases tried to set down which 'other characteristics' might be relevant. For example, in *Morhall* (1995) the fact that the defendant was a glue-sniffer was a relevant characteristic to be taken into account. Morhall had been persistently criticised by the victim about this fact immediately before the killling.

Power of self-control

Camplin (1978) clearly stated that age and sex could be taken into account when considering the power of self-control to be expected from the reasonable man. However, the courts were uncertain as to whether any other characteristics could be taken into account on this point. In *Thornton (No 2)* (1996) the Court of Appeal stated that 'battered woman syndrome' might be relevant to the level of self-control. However, in *Luc Thiet Thuan* (1997), where the defendant had suffered a previous head injury which caused him to have outbursts of temper which he could not control, the Privy Council held that mental abnormality could not be taken into account when considering the level of self-control to be expected from the defendant.

The same point on the level of self-control was considered by the House of Lords in *Smith (Morgan James)* (2000) when the House of Lords held that the defendant's characteristics could be taken into account in deciding the level of self-control a defendant should be expected to show.

This was the law for the next five years but in *A-G for Jersey v Holley* (2005) the Privy Council had to consider the same point. A panel of nine judges was used to decide this case.

A-G for Jersey v Holley (2005)

D was an alcoholic who had been drinking heavily. He claimed that his long-standing girlfriend told him she had had sex with another man and taunted him. He struck and killed her with an axe he was using to chop wood. He was convicted of murder and his conviction was upheld by the Privy Council by a majority of six judges to three.

The conclusion of the majority of judges in Privy Council was that only age and sex should be considered when identifying and applying the objective standard of self-control. Other characteristics of D are not relevant. So D is, for the purposes of the defence of provocation, to be judged by the standard of a person having ordinary powers of self-control. This has the merits of being a constant, objective standard in all cases.

This decision obviously differs from the House of Lords' decision in *Smith (Morgan James)*. Indeed, in *Holley,* Lord Nicholls stated that the decision in *Smith (Morgan James)* was 'erroneous'.

The decision in *Holley* was by the Privy Council. Normally, in the system of judicial precedent which operates in the courts in England and Wales, decisions by the Privy Council are only persuasive. But decisions by the House of Lords are binding on all lower courts. So it was not immediately certain what influence the decision in *Holley* would have. However, in *Mohammed* (2005) the Court of Appeal followed *Holley* rather than the decision in *Smith (Morgan James)*. Also more recently, in *James, Karimi* (2006), a five-member Court of Appeal confirmed that the decision in *Holley* had overruled *Smith (Morgan James)*.

Although the defendant's characteristics cannot be taken into account for the purpose of deciding the level of self-control expected from the defendant, the Privy Council did accept that other characteristics can be taken into account in assessing the gravity of the provocation to D. There is still a subjective test for the gravity of the provocation to the defendant. For this purpose the jury must 'take the defendant as they find him, "warts and all"'.

So the law now is that decided in *Holley*. There is a subjective test for the gravity of the provocation in which characteristics of the defendant can be taken into account. There is an objective test for the standard of self-control. It is that of the reasonable person of the same age and sex as the defendant. Any other characteristics of the defendant cannot be taken into account.

2.2.4 Proof of provocation

The judge decides if there is evidence of provocation for the defence to be left to the jury. If there is evidence which raises the possibility of provocation, the prosecution must then prove beyond reasonable doubt that the accused was not provoked.

2.2.5 Problems in the law on provocation

In 2003, when the Law Commission was reviewing

Key facts

	Law	Section/case
Definition	Evidence on which the jury can find that the person charged was provoked (whether by things done or by things said or by both together) to lose his self-control.	Common law as amended by s 3 Homicide Act 1957
Examples of provocation	• physical assaults, both on the defendant or on his relatives • the continual crying of a 19-day-old baby • a denial of stealing the defendant's tools • supplying drugs to the defendant's son	*Pearson* (1992) *Doughty* (1986) *Smith (Morgan James)* (2000) *Baillie* (1995)
Loss of self-control	• There must be a sudden and temporary loss of self-control, so that the defendant is not master of his mind • A time lapse may negate this • It must be sudden but need not be immediate	*Duffy* (1949) *Ibrams and Gregory* (1981) *Thornton (No 2)* (1996)
Reasonable man test	• Was the provocation enough to make a reasonable man do as D did? • For the gravity of the provocation the characteristics of D are taken into account • For the standard of self-control expected of D, the test is objective. D is judged by the standard expected of a reasonable person of the age and sex of D	s 3 Homicide Act 1957 *Morhall* (1995) *Camplin* (1978) *Holley* (2005)
Effect of defence	The charge of murder is reduced to manslaughter.	s 3 Homicide Act 1957

Key facts chart on provocation

the law on special defences to murder, it issued a consultation paper on the subject. In this it pointed out a number of problems with the defence of provocation, including that:

• The defence as stated in s 3 of the Homicide Act 1957 contradicts itself; it raises the question of whether a reasonable man would ever respond to provocation.
• The term 'reasonable man' has proved difficult for the judge to explain. The phrase has been considered by the House of Lords four times in 20 years and on the last occasion in *Smith (Morgan James)* (2000) the judges were split 3:2. (The matter has also now been considered by the Privy Council in *Holley* (2005) when the panel of nine judges were split 6:3.)
• There is no limit to the conduct which is capable

of 'provoking', so that completely innocent conduct may be regarded as provocation. This was seen in *Doughty* when the crying of a very young baby was held to be provocation.
• It allows a defence for anger, when there is no defence if the defendant kills in fear, despair or compassion.
• The effect of the decision in *Smith (Morgan James)* was to reduce the threshold of self-control that people are entitled to demand of all members of society. (Note that if the case of *Holley* continues to be followed by the courts in England and Wales, then this criticism disappears.)

As already pointed out in section 2.2.2, the defence is also seen as a 'male' defence, because men are more likely to suffer a sudden loss of self-control.

2.2.6 Proposals for reform

The Law Commission's report, *Murder, Manslaughter and Infanticide* (Law Com 304) (2006), suggested reforming the defence of provocation in the following way.

1. An unlawful homicide that would otherwise be murder should instead be manslaughter if:

    (a) the defendant acted in response to:
       (i)   gross provocation (meaning words or conduct or a combination of words and conduct which caused the defendant to have a justifiable sense of being seriously wronged); or
       (ii) fear of serious violence towards the defendant or another; or
       (iii) a combination of (i) and (ii);

    (b) a person of the defendant's age and of ordinary temperament, i.e. ordinary tolerance and self-restraint, in the circumstances of the defendant might have acted in the same or a similar way.

2. In deciding whether a person of ordinary temperament in the circumstances of the defendant might have acted in the same or a similar way, the court should take into account the defendant's age and all the circumstances of the defendant other than matters whose only relevance to the defendant's conduct is that they bear simply on his or her general capacity for self-control.

3. The partial defence should not apply where:

    (a) the provocation was incited by the defendant for the purpose of providing an excuse to use violence; or
    (b) the defendant acted in considered desire for revenge.

These proposals would make several changes to the current law on provocation.

The first main difference between the proposals and the current law is that only 'gross provocation' would suffice under the proposals. This would presumably prevent such matters as

the crying of a 17-day-old baby being provocation as in *Doughty* (1986).

A second difference is that a test of whether the words and/or conduct caused the defendant to have a justifiable sense of being seriously wronged would be introduced. Two words appear to be especially important in the phrase 'justifiable sense of being seriously wronged'. These are 'justifiable' and 'seriously'. The combination of the two would be likely to restrict the operation of the defence of provocation compared to its present operation. Again it would prevent the crying of a 17-day-old baby being provocation. This could scarcely give rise to a phrase 'justifiable sense of being seriously wronged'.

It is also notable that there is no mention of sudden or immediate loss of control. This raises the question as to whether these proposals would allow a defence of provocation where there was a considerable delay between the provocation and the killing.

Finally, the proposal would mean that those who act out of fear of violence would be able to rely on the defence of provocation.

Abolition of the defence

The Law Commission also raised the possibility that the mandatory sentence of life imprisonment for murder should be abolished. This would then allow the defence of provocation to be abolished as the judge would have discretion in sentencing.

However, this would leave two problems. First, if the prosecution did not accept the defendant's version of what had happened, then there would still need to be an investigation of the facts before the judge could decide on a suitable sentence. Secondly, surely a jury is better placed than a judge to decide on the level of self-control to be expected by society from a defendant. If the defence of provocation is abolished then the matter will be entirely in the hands of a judge.

2.2.7 The Government's response

In its consultation paper, *Murder, manslaughter and infanticide: proposals for reform of the law*, CP 19/08, the Government proposed a different approach to reform of provocation. They wish to abolish the current defence of provocation. Instead they would like to replace it with a defence of:

 'Killing in response to words and conduct which caused the defendant to have a justifiable sense of being seriously wronged.'

The draft clause for this new partial defence to murder states:

(1) Where a person ("D") kills or is a party to the killing of another ("V"), D is not to be convicted of murder if –
   (a) D's acts and omissions in doing or being a party to the killing resulted from D's loss of self-control,
   (b) the loss of self-control had a qualifying trigger, and
   (c) a person of D's sex and age, with a normal degree of tolerance and self-restraint and in the circumstances of D, might have reacted in the same or in a similar way to D.

The first point to note is that under this there would still be a requirement that the defendant had lost self-control but this loss would not have to be 'sudden'. This would allow for situations where the defendant's reaction has been delayed or builds gradually. This would solve the problem of cases such as *Thornton*.

Reasonable person

The Government propose that this new partial defence should apply only if a person of the defendant's sex and age, with a normal degree of tolerance and self-restraint and in the circumstances of the defendant, might have reacted in the same or a similar way.

Other limitations

The Government also proposes limiting when the defence is available. They propose that words and conduct should be a partial defence to murder only in exceptional circumstances.

Also, under their proposals, they make it clear that a partner having an affair does not of itself constitute such conduct for the purposes of the partial defence.

Activity

Explain whether any of the special defences to murder could apply in the following situations.

1. Roscoe, aged 25, has a mental age of eight. In a fit of temper he attacks Max and kicks him to death.
2. Cameron and Jacob are working together on a building site. Cameron knows that Jacob's wife is having an affair with another man. He taunts Jacob about this. Jacob loses his temper and hits Cameron on the head with a brick, killing him.
3. Ellie's husband, Glen, is an alcoholic and when drunk is often violent to her. Ellie has recently been suffering from depression for which she takes medication. One evening Glen comes home drunk and hits Ellie several times. He then goes to bed. Ellie stays up and after about four hours, in a sudden burst of rage, she gets a knife and stabs Glen, killing him.
4. Brigid, an immature, attention-seeking, 16-year-old, tries to commit suicide by slashing her wrists with a knife, but the cuts she makes are only superficial. Carol teases her about her inability to do anything properly. Brigid rushes at Carol and stabs her with the knife, killing her.

Chapter 3

Involuntary manslaughter

Involuntary manslaughter is an unlawful killing where the defendant does not have the intention to kill or cause grievous bodily harm. The lack of this intention is what distinguishes involuntary manslaughter from murder. It is also important not to confuse involuntary manslaughter with voluntary manslaughter. For voluntary manslaughter the defendant has the intention to kill or cause grievous bodily harm, but the charge is reduced from murder because the defendant can use one of the special defences to murder. Those special defences were explained in Chapter 2.

Involuntary manslaughter covers a wide range of circumstances. At the top end of the range the behaviour of the defendant which caused the death can be highly blameworthy as there was a high risk of causing death or serious injury. At the bottom end of the range the defendant's behaviour may verge on carelessness, and only be just enough to be considered blameworthy. There have been criticisms that the same offence covers such a wide range of behaviour, and there have been proposals for reform which are considered at 3.3.

The maximum sentence for involuntary manslaughter is life imprisonment, thus giving the judge discretion to impose any sentence which is suitable for the particular circumstances of the offence. In some cases the judge may even pass a non-custodial sentence.

There are three ways of committing involuntary manslaughter. These are:

- unlawful act manslaughter
- gross negligence manslaughter
- subjective recklessness manslaughter.

3.1 Unlawful act manslaughter

This is also known as constructive manslaughter because the liability for the death is built up or constructed from the facts that the defendant has done a dangerous unlawful act which caused the death. This makes the defendant liable, even though he did not realise that death or injury might occur.

The elements of unlawful act manslaughter are:

- the defendant must do an unlawful act
- that act must be dangerous on an objective test
- the act must cause the death
- the defendant must have the required *mens rea* for the unlawful act.

3.1.1 Unlawful act

The death must be caused by an unlawful act which must be a criminal offence. A civil wrong (tort) is not enough. In *Franklin* (1883) the defendant threw a large box into the sea from the West Pier at Brighton. The box hit and killed a swimmer. It was held that a civil wrong was not enough to create liability for unlawful act manslaughter. Another case illustrating that there must be a criminal unlawful act is *Lamb* (1967).

Lamb (1967)

Lamb and his friend were fooling around with a revolver. They both knew it was loaded with two bullets in a five chamber cylinder but thought that it would not fire unless one of the bullets was opposite the barrel. They knew that there was no bullet in this position, but did not realise that the cylinder turned so that a bullet from the next chamber along would be fired. Lamb pointed the gun at his friend and pulled the trigger, killing him. It was held that the defendant had not done an unlawful act. The pointing of the gun at the friend was not an assault as the friend did not fear any violence from Lamb.

In many cases the unlawful act will be some kind of assault, but any criminal offence can form the unlawful act, provided it involves an act which is dangerous in the sense that it is likely to cause some injury. Examples of the offences which have led to a finding of unlawful act manslaughter include arson, criminal damage and burglary.

Omission not enough

There must be an act. An omission cannot create liability for unlawful act manslaughter. In *Lowe* (1973) the defendant was convicted of wilfully neglecting his baby son and of his manslaughter. The trial judge had directed the jury that if they found the defendant guilty of wilful neglect, he was also guilty of manslaughter. The Court of Appeal quashed the conviction for manslaughter because finding of wilful neglect, involved a failure to act and this could not support a conviction for unlawful act manslaughter.

In *Khan and Khan* (1998) the Court of Appeal again pointed out that an omission was not sufficient to convict the defendants of unlawful act manslaughter.

Khan and Khan (1998)

The defendants supplied a young prostitute with heroin. They knew she was a new user. She injected herself in their presence but went into a coma. The defendants left the flat and when they returned next day she was dead. The Court of Appeal quashed their conviction for unlawful act manslaughter as they had not done an unlawful act. They had omitted to get help for her when she was in a coma, but that omission was not an act for the purposes of unlawful act manslaughter.

3.1.2 Dangerous act

The unlawful act must be dangerous on an objective test. In *Church* (1966) it was held that it must be:

> 'such as all sober and reasonable people would inevitably recognise must subject the other person to, at least, the risk of some harm resulting therefrom, albeit not serious harm'.

From this it can be seen that the risk need only be of 'some harm'. The harm need not be serious. If a sober and reasonable person realises that the unlawful act might cause some injury, then this part of the tests for unlawful act manslaughter is satisfied. It does not matter that the defendant did not realise there was any risk of harm to another person. The case of *Larkin* (1943) illustrates both the need for an unlawful act and for there to be, on an objective viewpoint, the risk of some harm.

Larkin (1943)

The defendant threatened another man with an open cut-throat razor in order to frighten him. The mistress of the other man tried to intervene and, because she was drunk, accidentally fell onto the open blade which cut her throat and killed her. On appeal his conviction for manslaughter was upheld. The act of threatening the other man with the razor was a technical assault. (See Chapter 4 for explanation of assaults.) It was also an act which was dangerous because it was likely to injure someone.

Humphries J explained this in the judgment when he said:

> 'Where the act which a person is engaged in performing is unlawful, then, if at the same time it is a dangerous act, that is, an act which is likely to injure another person, and quite inadvertently he causes the death of that other person by that act, then he is guilty of manslaughter.'

The act need not be aimed at the victim. In *Mitchell* (1983) the defendant tried to push his way into a queue at the post office. A 72-year-old man told him off for this. The defendant then punched the man, causing him to stagger backwards into an 89-year-old woman. The woman was knocked over and injured and a few days later died of her injuries. The defendant was convicted of unlawful act manslaughter. He had done an unlawful act by punching the man. This act was dangerous as it was an act which was likely to injure another person. Finally the act inadvertently caused the death of the woman. All the elements put by Humphries in the statement in *Larkin* (1943) above are present. The defendant is guilty of unlawful act manslaughter despite the fact that in each case the person threatened (or punched) was not the one who died.

The act need not even be aimed at a person; it can be aimed at property, provided it is 'such that all sober and reasonable people would inevitably recognise must subject another person to, at least, the risk of some harm'. This is illustrated by *Goodfellow* (1986).

I'm only playing dominoes.

Goodfellow (1986)

The defendant decided to set fire to his council flat so that the council would have to rehouse him. The fire burned out of control and his wife, son and another woman died in the fire. He was convicted of manslaughter and appealed. The Court of Appeal upheld the conviction because all the elements of unlawful act manslaughter were present. These were:

● the act was committed intentionally

● it was unlawful

● reasonable people would recognise it might cause some harm to another person

● the act caused the death.

The risk of harm includes causing a person to suffer shock. However, mere 'emotional disturbance' is not sufficient. This was decided in *Dawson* (1985).

Dawson (1985)

Convictions for manslaughter were quashed where three defendants attempted to rob a petrol station. They were masked and armed with pickaxe handles. The petrol station attendant managed to sound the alarm but then dropped dead from a heart attack. The judge directed the jury that 'harm' meant either 'emotional or physical disturbance'. The Court of Appeal held that this was a misdirection as 'emotional disturbance' on its own was not enough to amount to harm.

There was also the problem in *Dawson* of whether a sober and reasonable person would have foreseen the risk of harm (shock) to the petrol station attendant.

However, where a reasonable person would be aware of the victim's frailty and the risk of physical harm to him, then the defendant will be liable. This was stated in *Watson* (1989) where the two defendants threw a brick through the window of a house and broke into it, intending to steal property. The occupier was a frail 87-year-old man who heard the noise and came to investigate what had happened. The two defendants physically abused him and then left. The man died of a heart attack 90 minutes later. Although the Court of Appeal quashed the convictions for manslaughter, the court stated that the act of burglary could be 'dangerous' in that it became dangerous as soon as the old man's condition would have been apparent to the reasonable man.

3.1.3 Causing the death

The unlawful act must cause the death. The rules on causation are the same as for murder, and are set out at 1.2.

An important point is that if there is an intervening act which breaks the chain of causation then the defendant cannot be liable for manslaughter.

This point has caused problems in cases where

the defendant has supplied V with an illegal drug. If the defendant also injects the drug into V, then there is no break in the chain of causation. This was shown in the case of *Cato* (1976).

Cato (1976)

D and V each prepared an injection of a mix of heroin and water. They then injected each other. V died. By injecting V with the heroin, D had committed the unlawful act of administering a noxious substance to V, contrary to s 23 of the Offences Against the Person Act 1861. As D died from the effects of the injection, *Cato* was convicted of unlawful act manslaughter.

The problem has been with situations where the defendant has prepared the injection, handed the syringe to V, and V has then injected himself. There have been several cases on this. There are two points at issue. These are:

- whether the defendant has done an unlawful act; and
- has the defendant caused the victim's death or is the self-injection an intervening act.

The first case on this was *Dalby* (1982).

Dalby (1982)

D supplied a drug called Diconal which the victim then self-injected. The defendant's conviction for manslaughter was quashed because the Court of Appeal held that although supplying the drug was an unlawful act, it was not the act of supplying which had caused the death. The injection was the cause of the death and, as this was a voluntary act by the victim, it had broken the chain of causation.

However, in later cases it was suggested that the defendant could be guilty in similar circumstances as he was considered to have administered a noxious substance to V, contrary

to s 23 of the Offences Against the Person Act 1861. This was an unlawful act and if V died the defendant could be guilty of unlawful act manslaughter. This idea was criticised and was not followed in all cases, thus causing confusion in the law.

The debate was finally settled in *Kennedy* (2007) when the House of Lords ruled that there was no unlawful act by the defendant under s 23. The defendant did not administer the noxious substance by filling a syringe and handing it to V. The act of self injection was a voluntary intervening act by V which broke the chain of causation.

Kennedy (2007)

D had prepared an injection of heroin and water for V to inject himself. He handed the syringe to V who injected himself and then handed the syringe back to D. V died. Initially Kennedy was convicted and the Court of Appeal upheld his conviction. The case was then referred back to the Court of Appeal by the Criminal Cases Review Commission. Again the Court of Appeal upheld the conviction on the basis that filling the syringe and handing it to V was administering a noxious substance and an unlawful act.

The case was then appealed to the House of Lords. They quashed the conviction on the basis that D had not done an unlawful act which caused the death. D had not administered a noxious substance for an offence under s 23 of the Offences Against the Person 1861. V's act in injecting the heroin himself was an intervening act which broke any chain of causation.

In *Kennedy* the Law Lords pointed out that the criminal law generally assumes the existence of free will. The victim had freely and voluntarily administered the injection to himself. The defendant could only be guilty if he was involved in administering the injection. In this case he had not been.

Joint involvement

The Law Lords did accept that there could be situations in which it could be regarded that both defendant and victim were involved in administering the injection. However, they did not give any examples of when this could be considered to have happened. In fact they specifically stated that the case of *Rogers* (2003) had been wrongly decided.

In *Rogers* the defendant had participated in the injection of heroin by holding his belt round the victim's arm as a tourniquet to make it easier for the victim to find the vein to inject. The Court of Appeal had held that the act causing death was the injection of the heroin and it was 'artificial and unreal' to separate the tourniquet from the injection. By applying and holding the tourniquet, the defendant was playing a part in the mechanics of the injection. This made him guilty of an offence under s 23 and, if death occurred as a result, he was also guilty of manslaughter.

The case of *Rogers* was not appealed to the House of Lords. However, the Law Lords stated in *Kennedy* that *Rogers* was wrongly decided. There was no unlawful act of administering a noxious substance by helping V inject by providing a tourniquet. If this is not administering a noxious substance then it is difficult to think of situations in which D and V could be regarded as being jointly involved in the act of injecting.

3.1.4 *Mens rea* for the unlawful act

It must be proved that the defendant had the *mens rea* for the unlawful act. Where the defendant has committed a deliberate assault on the person of another, such as punching someone in the face, then it is obvious that the defendant intended the *mens rea* of that unlawful act. So if, when the defendant punches the person, that person falls down, hits their head on the kerb and dies as a result, then there is no difficulty in establishing all the elements of unlawful act manslaughter.

Key facts

Elements	Comment	Cases
Unlawful act	Must be unlawful A civil wrong is not enough It must be an act; an omission is not sufficient	*Lamb* (1967) *Franklin* (1883) *Lowe* (1973)
Dangerous act	The test for this is objective – would a sober and reasonable person realise the risk of some harm? The risk need only be of some harm – not of serious harm An act aimed at property can still be such that a sober and reasonable person would realise the risk of some harm There must be a risk of physical harm; mere fear is not enough	*Church* (1966) *Larkin* (1943) *Goodfellow* (1986) *Dawson* (1985)
Causes death	Normal rules of causation apply; the act must be the physical and legal cause of death. An intervening act such as the victim self-injecting a drug breaks the chain of causation. But merely preparing the injection is not a cause of death. V's self-injection breaks the chain of causation	*Dalby* (1982) *Kennedy* (2007)
Mens rea	The defendant must have *mens rea* for the unlawful act but it is not necessary to prove that the defendant foresaw any harm from his act	*Newbury and Jones* (1976)

Key facts chart on unlawful act manslaughter

However, it is not necessary for the defendant to realise that the act is unlawful or dangerous. In *Newbury and Jones* (1976) the defendants were two teenage boys who pushed a piece of paving stone from a bridge on to a railway line as a train was approaching. The stone hit the train and killed the guard. They were convicted of manslaughter and the House of Lords was asked to decide the question of whether a defendant could be convicted of unlawful act manslaughter if he did not foresee that his act might cause harm to another. The House of Lords confirmed it was not necessary to prove that the defendant foresaw any harm from his act. The defendant could be convicted provided the unlawful act was dangerous and the defendant had the necessary *mens rea* for that act.

3.2 Gross negligence manslaughter

Gross negligence manslaughter is another way of committing manslaughter. It is completely different from unlawful act manslaughter. It is committed where the defendant owes the victim a duty of care but breaches that duty in a very negligent way, causing the death of the victim. It can be committed by an act or an omission, which does not have to be unlawful. The leading case on gross negligence manslaughter is *Adomako* (1994).

Adomako (1994)

The defendant was the anaesthetist for a man who was having an operation on a detached retina. During the operation one of the tubes supplying oxygen to the patient became disconnected. The defendant failed to notice this until some minutes later, when the patient suffered a heart attack due to the lack of oxygen. The patient suffered brain damage and died six months later as a result. Doctors giving evidence in the trial said that a competent anaesthetist would have noticed the

disconnection of the tube within 15 seconds and that the defendant's failure to react was 'abysmal'. The trial judge directed the jury on gross negligence and they convicted. The conviction was upheld by the House of Lords.

From *Adomako* (1994) it appears that the elements of gross negligence manslaughter are:

- the existence of a duty of care towards the victim
- a breach of that duty of care which causes death
- gross negligence which the jury considers to be criminal.

3.2.1 Duty of care

A duty of care has been held to exist for the purposes of the criminal law in various situations including the duty of a doctor to his patient as in *Adomako* (1994). In this case Lord Mackay said that in his opinion the ordinary principles of negligence in the civil law applied to ascertain whether there was a breach of duty of care, and whether that duty had been breached. These principles come from a statement made in the case of *Donoghue v Stevenson* (1932) where it was stated that:

> ❝ 'You must take reasonable care to avoid acts and omissions which you can reasonably foresee would be likely to injure your neighbour. Who then is my neighbour? The answer seems to be – persons who are so closely and directly affected by my act that I ought reasonably to have them in contemplation as being so affected when I am directing my mind to the acts or omissions which are called into question.' ❞

This civil test is very much wider than the duty situations in which the criminal law recognises can lead to criminal liability for an omission. This suggests that gross negligence manslaughter may cover a wide range of situations.

In *Singh* (1999) the courts recognised a duty to manage and maintain property where a faulty gas fire caused the deaths of tenants. In *Litchfield* (1998) it was held that the owner and master of a sailing ship owed a duty to the crew when he sailed knowing that the engines might fail because of contamination to the fuel. The ship was blown on to rocks and three crew members died. His act of sailing when he knew there was such a risk was gross negligence. In all of these situations there is a contractual duty.

However there does not need to be a contractual duty. In *Adomako* (1994) the House of Lords approved the decision in the case of *Stone and Dobinson* (1977) where the defendants had undertaken to care for Stone's elderly sister who became bedridden and unable to care for herself. The defendants failed to feed her or to summon medical help, and the sister died. They were convicted of manslaughter, as they had voluntarily undertaken a duty to care for the sister, and they had failed in this duty.

Also in *Khan and Khan* (1998) the Court of Appeal stated *obiter* that duty situations could be extended to other areas. In this case the defendants had supplied heroin to a new user who took it in their presence and then collapsed. They left her alone and by the time they returned to the flat she had died. Their conviction for unlawful act manslaughter was quashed, but the Court of Appeal thought that there could be a duty to summon medical assistance in certain circumstances.

A further extension of the type of duty recognised by the courts occurred in *Wacker* (2002).

Wacker (2002)

The defendant agreed to bring 60 illegal immigrants into England. They were put in the back of his lorry for a cross-channel ferry crossing. The only air into the lorry was through a small vent and it was agreed that this vent should be closed at certain times to prevent the immigrants being discovered. The defendant closed the vent before boarding the ferry. The crossing took an hour longer than usual and at Dover the Customs officers found that 58 of the immigrants were dead.

At the trial the judge expressed the duty of care owed to the victims as being under the ordinary principles of the law of negligence, which applied to ascertain whether or not the defendant has been in breach of a duty of care towards the victims who died; but that, unlike in civil law, it was irrelevant that the victims were parties to an illegal act

On this point the Court of Appeal held that the purposes of civil and criminal law were different. So the fact that no action could arise in a civil case did not mean that there was no breach of a duty of care in a criminal case; this was largely based on public policy.

The defendant also argued that it was impossible to determine the extent of his duty, but the Court of Appeal held it was a simple matter on the facts. The defendant knew that the safety of the immigrants depended on his own actions in relation to the vent and he clearly assumed the duty of care. This case indicates that this area of the law may be extended in the future, and it is difficult to predict what duties may be recognised.

In *Willoughby* (2005) the Court of Appeal confirmed that the fact that the defendant and the victim were engaged in a criminal activity did not prevent the defendant owing the victim a duty of care.

Willoughby (2005)

D owned a disused public house. V was killed when this building was set on fire. The prosecution alleged that D had asked V to help him set fire to the building using petrol. An explosion from the petrol catching fire had killed V. D was convicted of gross negligence manslaughter and reckless arson contrary to s 1(2) and 1(3) Criminal Damage Act 1971.

D appealed on the basis that he did not owe V a duty of care.

The Court of Appeal upheld the conviction and ruled that:

- a duty could not arise merely because D was the owner of the premises;

- a duty could arise out of the combination of factors (D was the owner, the pub was to be destroyed for his financial benefit, he enlisted V and V's role was to spread the petrol inside the building);

- whether a duty arises can be determined in part by public policy; as in *Wacker* (2003) the fact that D and V are engaged in a criminal enterprise does not prevent a duty of care arising;

- the role of the judge is to decide that there is evidence capable of establishing a duty of care; the jury then decide if a duty of care exists.

3.2.2 Gross negligence

The fact that a defendant has been negligent is not enough to convict him of gross negligence manslaughter. The negligence has to be 'gross'. In *Bateman* (1925), which involved negligent treatment of a patient by a doctor, it was stated that the negligence is 'gross' when it goes 'beyond a matter of mere compensation between subjects and showed such disregard for the life and safety of others as to amount to a crime against the State and conduct deserving of punishment'.

In *Adomako* (1994) the House of Lords approved this test and stressed that it was a matter for the jury. The jury had to decide whether, having regard to the risk of death involved, the conduct of the defendant was so bad in all the circumstances as to amount, in their judgment, to a criminal act or omission. The jury has to consider the seriousness of the breach of duty in all the circumstances in which the defendant was placed when it occurred. In *Adomako* Lord Mackay said:

> 'The jury will have to consider whether the extent to which the defendant's conduct departed from the proper standard of care incumbent upon him, involving as it must have done a risk of death to the patient, was such that it should be judged as criminal.'

There have been criticisms of these tests because it is left to individual jury panels to decide the appropriate standard for 'gross' negligence. This may lead to inconsistent decisions in similar cases. There is also little guidance on what should be considered as 'gross' negligence.

If you look back at case examples you can see the sort of level of negligence that juries have considered to be 'so bad in all the circumstances' as to amount to gross negligence.

For example, in *Adomako* (1994), part of an anaesthetist's job during an operation is to keep checking the patient's breathing. So when the defendant failed to notice for several minutes that a tube had become disconnected, the jury decided that it amounted to gross negligence.

In *Litchfield* (1998) the owner and master of the sailing ship knew that the engines could fail because of the contaminated fuel. The jury found that his decision to sail without safe engines as a back up in bad weather was gross negligence.

3.2.3 Risk of death

It is also not clear if the test is that there has to be a risk of death through the defendant's conduct or whether the risk need only be to 'health and welfare' of the victim. In *Stone and Dobinson* (1977) the test was expressed as the risk being to the 'health and welfare' of the sister who died. In *Adomako* (1994) Lord Mackay giving judgment approved this way of explaining reckless in *Stone and Dobinson* (1977). However Lord Mackay also approved the test in *Bateman* (1925) where the test is 'disregard for the life and safety of others'. In addition, Lord Mackay specifically mentioned 'a risk of death' on two occasions in his judgment.

This appeared to leave the law uncertain on this point, though given the seriousness of the charge of manslaughter, it would seem fair that the test should be 'a risk of death'.

This apparent uncertainty was the subject of an appeal in *R v Misra; R v Srivastava* (2004). The defendants argued that the offence of gross negligence manslaughter breached Art 7 of the European Convention on Human Rights as it was too uncertain.

R v Misra; R v Srivastava (2004)

The appellants were doctors who had the post-operative care of V. V had had surgery to repair a tendon in the knee. He then developed an infection which the doctors failed to diagnose or treat. The infection caused V's death. Both doctors were charged with gross negligence manslaughter and convicted. The Court of Appeal upheld the convictions. On the issue of whether the risk had to be of death or only of injury, the Court of Appeal held that it was clear from *Adomako* and subsequent cases that the risk must relate to death. It was not enough to show that there was risk of bodily injury or injury to health.

The Court of Appeal held that the elements of the offence of gross negligence manslaughter were made clear in *Adomako* (1994). They were that:

Key facts

Elements	Comment	Cases
Duty of care	The defendant must owe the victim a duty of care The civil concept of negligence applies Covers wide range of situations eg maintaining a gas fire May even cover a duty not to supply drugs The fact that the victim was party to an illegal act is not relevant	*Adomako* (1994) *Adomako* (1994) *Singh* (1999) *Rogers* (2003) *Wacker* (2003)
Breach of duty	This can be by an act or an omission	
Gross negligence	Beyond a matter of mere compensation and showed such disregard for the life and safety of others as to amount to a crime Conduct so bad in all the circumstances as to amount to a criminal act or omission	*Bateman* (1925) *Adomako* (1994)
Risk of death	Not clear if the risk need only be to 'heath and welfare' or disregard for the life and safety or a risk of death	*Stone and Dobinson* (1977) *Bateman* (1925) *Adomako* (1994)

Key facts chart on gross negligence manslaughter

- a duty of care was owed;
- that duty had been broken;
- the breach of the duty of care amounted to gross negligence; and
- the negligence was a substantial cause of the death of the victim.

As the elements of gross negligence manslaughter were clear, there was no breach of Art 7.

3.3 Subjective reckless manslaughter

After the decision in *Adomako* (1994), it was thought that reckless manslaughter no longer existed. However, in *Lidar* (2000) the Court of Appeal upheld the defendant's conviction for manslaughter even though the judge referred to recklessness (rather than gross negligence) in his directions to the jury.

Lidar (2000)

D and others had been asked to leave a public house in Leicester. They went into the pub car park and got into a Range Rover, with D as driver. One of the passengers shouted something at V, who was the doorman of the pub. V approached the vehicle and put his arms through the open front passenger window. D then drove off, with V half in and half out of the window. After about 225 metres, V was dragged under the rear wheel of the Range Rover and suffered injuries from which he died. D was convicted of manslaughter.

Although the trial judge directed the jury on the basis of recklessness, it is obvious from the facts that the defendant could have been convicted on the basis of gross negligence manslaughter. The defendant clearly owed V a duty of care. In fact, all road users owe a duty of care to others on the road (whether as drivers, passengers or pedestrians). By driving off with V half in and half out of the window, the defendant was in breach of that duty of care. It was open to the jury to decide that the breach was gross negligence.

In view of this, it is difficult to see why it is necessary to have a separate category of reckless manslaughter.

Activity

Explain whether the following situations could be unlawful act manslaughter and/or gross negligence manslaughter.

1. Alvin is throwing stones at passing cars. One of the stones goes through the open side window in Dawn's car and hits her on the side of the head. She loses control of the car and hits a pedestrian, Keith, who is killed.

2. Justine and Oliver have spent the evening at Justine's flat drinking heavily. Oliver also knows that Justine has taken an ecstasy tablet, although he has not taken any drugs. Justine passes out and Oliver who is afraid he may get into trouble decides to leave. The next morning Justine is discovered to be dead.

3. Liam, who is very angry with Sam, kicks out at Sam. This causes Sam to trip and fall down some steps, breaking his neck and killing him.

4. Patsy has been caring for her elderly aunt who is very frail and unable to walk without assistance. Patsy goes away on a fortnight's holiday, leaving her aunt on her own. The aunt dies through lack of food and cold.

5. Brett decides to rob a local post office. He puts a mask over his face and takes an imitation gun with him. He enters the post office and tells the two members of the staff who are there, Karina and Sven, to put their hands up. Karina is so shocked that she suffers a heart attack. When her colleague, Sven, tries to go to her assistance, Brett pushes him away. Sven falls, hits his head and dies. Karina dies two hours later.

Chapter 4

Non-fatal offences against the person

The main offences are set out in the Offences Against the Person Act 1861 (OAPA). They are based on whether or not the victim was injured; if there were injuries, their level of seriousness; and the intention of the defendant. The main offences are, in ascending order of seriousness:

- assault – s 39 Criminal Justice Act 1988
- battery – s 39 Criminal Justice Act 1988
- assault occasioning actual bodily harm – s 47 OAPA
- malicious wounding or inflicting grievous bodily harm – s 20 OAPA
- wounding or causing grievous bodily harm with intent – s 18 OAPA

4.1 Common assault

There are two ways of committing this:

- assault
- battery.

Assault and battery are common law offences. There is no statutory definition for either assault or for battery. However statute law recognises their existence, as both of these offences are charged under s 39 Criminal Justice Act 1988 which sets out that the maximum punishment for them is six months' imprisonment or a fine of £5,000, or both.

The act involved is different for assault and battery. For assault there is no touching, only the fear of immediate, unlawful force. For battery there must be actual force. There are often situations in which both occur. For example, where the defendant approaches the victim shouting that he is going to 'get him', then punches the victim in the face. The approaching, shouting and raising his arm prior to the punch constitute an assault, while the punch is the battery. As the act is different for each it is easier to consider assault and battery separately.

4.1.1 *Actus reus* of assault

An assault is also known as a technical assault or a psychic assault. There must be:

- an act
- something in the act which causes the victim to apprehend the infliction of immediate, unlawful, force.

Act

An assault requires some act or words. An omission is not sufficient to constitute an assault. However, words are sufficient for an assault. These can be verbal or written. In *Constanza* (1997) the Court of Appeal held that letters could be an assault. The defendant had written 800 letters and made a number of phone calls to the victim. The victim interpreted the last two letters as clear threats. The Court of Appeal said there was an assault as there was a 'fear of violence at some time, not excluding the immediate future'. In *Ireland* (1997) it was held that even silent telephone calls can be an assault. It depends on the facts of the case.

Apprehend immediate unlawful force

The important point is that the act or words must cause the victim to apprehend that immediate force is going to be used against them. There is no assault if the situation is such that it is obvious that the defendant cannot actually use force. For example, where the defendant shouts threats from a passing train, there is no possibility that he can carry out the threats in the immediate future. It was decided in *Lamb* (1967) that pointing an unloaded gun at someone who knows that it is unloaded cannot be an assault. This is because the other person does not fear immediate force. However, if the other person

thought the gun was loaded then this could be an assault.

Fear of immediate force is necessary; immediate does not mean instantaneous, but 'imminent', so an assault can be through a closed window as in *Smith v Chief Superintendent of Woking Police Station* (1983).

Smith v Chief Superintendent of Woking Police Station (1983)

The defendant broke into a garden and looked through the victim's bedroom window on the ground floor at about 11 pm one evening. The victim was terrified and thought that he was about to enter the room. Although the defendant was outside the house and no attack could be made at that immediate moment, the court held that the victim was frightened by his conduct. The basis of the fear was that she did not know what he was going to do next, but that it was likely to be of a violent nature. Fear of what he might do next was sufficiently immediate for the purposes of the offence.

The point that immediate does not mean instantaneous was also seen in *Ireland* (1997).

Ireland (1997)

The defendant made several silent phone calls to three women. All three women suffered psychiatric illness as a result. He was convicted of offences of causing actual bodily harm under s 47 of the Offences Against the Person Act 1861. It is necessary to prove an assault for this offence. The House of Lords held that silent phone calls could be an assault. They pointed out that a victim of a silent phone call might fear that the caller was about to arrive at her home. The victim could fear the possibility of immediate personal violence.

The use of mobile phones today makes it even more likely that such a caller could be just outside the victim's house. The fear of immediate personal violence is a very real threat in such situations.

Words indicating there will be no violence may prevent an act from being an assault. This is a principle which comes from the old case of *Tuberville v Savage* (1669) where the defendant placed one hand on his sword and said, 'If it were not assize time, I would not take such language from you'. This was held not to be an assault because what he said showed he was not going to do anything.

Fear of any unwanted touching is sufficient: the force or unlawful personal violence which is feared need not be serious.

There are many examples of assault:

- raising a fist as though about to hit the victim
- throwing a stone at the victim which just misses
- pointing a loaded gun at someone within range
- making a threat by saying 'I am going to hit you'.

Unlawfulness of the force

The force which is threatened must be unlawful. If it is lawful, there is no offence of common assault. Whether force is lawful or unlawful is discussed in detail in the next section.

4.1.2 *Actus reus* of battery

The *actus reus* of battery is the application of unlawful force to another person. Force is a slightly misleading word as it can include the slightest touching, as shown by the case of *Collins v Wilcock* (1984).

Collins v Wilcock (1984)

Two police officers saw two women apparently soliciting for the purposes of prostitution. They asked the appellant to get into the police car for questioning but she refused and walked away. As she was not known to the police, one of the officers walked after her to try to find out her identity. She refused to speak to the officer and again walked away. The officer then took hold of her by the arm to prevent her leaving. She became abusive and scratched the officer's arm. She was convicted of assaulting a police officer in the execution of his duty. She appealed against that conviction on the basis that the officer was not acting in the execution of his duty, but was acting unlawfully by holding her arm as the officer was not arresting her. The court held that the officer had committed a battery and the defendant was entitled to free herself.

The court pointed out that touching a person to get his attention was acceptable provided that no greater degree of physical contact was used than was necessary, but that physical restraint was not.

A similar point arose in *Wood (Fraser) v DPP* (2008) where a police officer took hold of Wood's arm to check his identity.

Wood (Fraser) v DPP (2008)

The police had received a report that a man named Fraser had been disruptive in a public house and had thrown an ashtray at another person. This had missed that person but had caused the ashtray to smash. Three police officers went to the scene. They saw a man (the appellant, W) who fitted the description of 'Fraser' come out of the public house. One of the police officers took hold of W by the arm to prevent him leaving and asked if he was Fraser. W denied this and struggled trying to pull away. At that point another officer took hold of W's other arm. W was charged with assaulting two of the police officers while they were acting in the execution of their duty.

The police officer who had first caught hold of W's arm said that he had done this in order to detain W, but was not at that time arresting him. It was held that as the officer had not arrested W before he struggled and assaulted the police, then there was a technical assault (battery) by the police officers. This meant that W was entitled to struggle and was not guilty of any offence of assault against the police.

Even touching the victim's clothing can be sufficient to form a battery. In *Thomas* (1985) the defendant touched the bottom of a woman's skirt and rubbed it. The Court of Appeal said, *obiter*, 'There could be no dispute that if you touch a person's clothes while he is wearing them that is equivalent to touching him'.

Continuing act

A battery may be committed through a continuing act as in *Fagan v Metropolitan Police Commissioner* (1968).

Fagan v Metropolitan Police Commissioner (1968)

The defendant parked his car with one of the tyres on a police officer's foot. When he parked he was unaware that he had done this, but when the police officer asked him to remove it, he refused to do so for about half a minute. The court said that at the start there was an act which could be a battery, but the full offence of battery was not committed at that point because there was no element of intention. However, it became an offence of battery the moment the intention was formed to leave the wheel on the officer's foot.

Indirect act

A battery can also be through an indirect act such as a booby trap. In this situation the defendant causes force to be applied, even though he does

not personally touch the victim. This occurred in *Martin* (1881) where the defendant placed an iron bar across the doorway of a theatre. He then switched off the lights. In the panic which followed several of the audience were injured when they were trapped and unable to open the door. Martin was convicted of an offence under s 20 OAPA 1861.

A more modern example is *DPP v K* (1990).

DPP v K (1990)

The defendant was a 15-year-old schoolboy who took sulphuric acid without permission from his science lesson to try its reaction on some toilet paper. While he was in the toilet he heard footsteps in the corridor, panicked and put the acid into a hot air hand drier to hide it. He returned to his class intending to remove the acid later. Before he could do so another pupil used the drier and was sprayed by the acid. The defendant was charged with assault occasioning actual bodily harm (s 47). The magistrates acquitted him because he said he had not intended to hurt anyone (see 4.2.2 for the *mens rea* of s 47). The prosecution appealed by way of case stated to the Queen's Bench Divisional Court which held that a common assault (remember, this includes both an assault and a battery) could be committed by an indirect act.

Another example of indirect force occurred in *Haystead v Chief Constable of Derbyshire* (2000) where the defendant caused a small child to fall to the floor by punching the woman holding the child. The defendant was found guilty because he was reckless as to whether or not his acts would injure the child. It is worth noting that, in this case, the conviction could also be justified by the principle of transferred malice.

Omissions

Criminal liability can arise by way of an omission, but only if the defendant is under a duty to act. Such a duty can arise out of a contract, a relationship, from the assumption of care for another, or from the creation of a dangerous situation.

One scenario which could make a defendant liable by way of omission is where the defendant has created a dangerous situation which may lead to force being applied to the victim. This is what occurred in *DPP v K* (1990) when he failed to remove the acid from the drier.

Another scenario is by analogy with *Miller* (1983) where the defendant accidentally set fire to his mattress but failed to do anything to prevent damage to the building in which he was sleeping. He was convicted of arson. However, if there had been other people asleep in the room and Miller had not awakened them to warn them of the danger and one of them had been hit by plaster falling from the ceiling as a result of the fire, then there appears no reason why Miller could not have been charged with battery of that person.

Unlawful force

For a battery to be committed, the force must be unlawful. If the victim gives genuine consent to it then the force may lawful (see 5.4 for further information on consent as a defence). Force may also be lawful where it is used in self-defence or prevention of crime. This can only be so if the force used is reasonable in the situation as the defendant believed it to be (see 5.5). If the force is lawful, then the person using the force is not guilty of a battery.

Another situation where force may be lawful is in the correction of a child by a parent. English law recognises that moderate and reasonable physical chastisement of a child is lawful. However, in *A v UK* (1998) where a jury had acquitted a father who had beaten his son with a garden cane, the European Court of Human Rights ruled that a law allowing force to be used on children offends Article 3 of the European Convention on Human Rights. This Article prohibits torture and inhuman or degrading treatment or punishment.

However, the Children Act 2004 now means that a battery committed on a child is not lawful if it results in any injury.

Self-defence/defence of another

Where reasonable force is used to defend oneself (or another) against attack, then this is lawful. For example, in *Wood (Fraser) v DPP* (2008), where the defendant tried to pull away from police who were holding him, the defendant's use of force was lawful. This meant that he was not guilty of any assault against the police. The police had not lawfully detained him, so he was entitled to use reasonable force. (See earlier in this section for full details of this case.)

Battery without an assault

It is possible for there to be a battery even though there is no assault. This can occur where the victim is unaware that unlawful force is about to be used on him such as where the attacker comes up unseen behind the victim's back. The first thing the victim knows is when he is struck; there has been a battery but no assault.

4.1.3 *Mens rea* of assault and battery

The *mens rea* for an assault is either an intention to cause another to fear immediate unlawful personal violence, or recklessness as to whether such fear is caused. The *mens rea* for battery is either an intention to apply unlawful physical force to another or recklessness as to whether unlawful force is applied. So intention or recklessness is sufficient for both assault and battery.

The test for recklessness is subjective. For an assault, the defendant must realise that there is a risk that his acts/words could cause another to fear unlawful personal violence. For a battery the defendant must realise that there is a risk that his act (or omission) could cause unlawful force to be applied to another.

Assault and battery are classed as offences of basic intent. This means that if the defendant is intoxicated when he does the relevant *actus reus*, he is considered as doing it recklessly. This was stated by the House of Lords in *DPP v Majewski* (1976).

DPP v Majewski (1976)

The defendant had consumed large quantities of alcohol and drugs and then attacked people in a public house and also the police officers who tried to arrest him. The Law Lords held that getting himself intoxicated by drink and drugs was a reckless course of conduct and recklessness is enough to constitute the necessary *mens rea* in assault cases.

This ruling in *Majewski* can be criticised, as the point at which the drink or drugs is taken is a quite separate time to the point when the *actus reus* for the offence is committed. It is difficult to see how there is coincidence of the two. It is reasonable to say that the defendant is reckless when he takes drink or other intoxicating substances, but this does not necessarily mean that when he commits an assault or battery three or four hours later he is reckless for the purposes of the offence. The decision can be viewed as a public policy decision.

4.2 Section 47

We now look at assaults where an injury is caused. The lowest level of injury is referred to the 1861 Act as 'actual bodily harm' and the offence under s 47 Offences Against the Person Act 1861, which is triable either way, states:

Activity

Explain whether there is an assault and/or battery in the following situations.

1. At a party Tanya sneaks up behind William, whom she knows well, and slaps him on the back.
2. Vince throws a stone at Lily, but misses. He picks up another stone and this time hits the edge of Lily's coat.
3. Grant turns round quickly without realising that Harry is standing just behind him and bumps into Harry. Harry shouts at him 'If you were not wearing glasses, I would hit you in the face'.
4. Ramsey and Sue are having an argument. During the argument, Ramsey says 'If you don't shut up, I'll thump you'. Sue is so annoyed at this that she gets out a penknife and waves it in front of Ramsey's face. Ramsay pushes her away.

"

'Whosoever shall be convicted of any assault occasioning actual bodily harm shall be liable ... to imprisonment for five years.'

"

As can be seen from this very brief section there is no definition of 'assault' or 'actual bodily harm'. Nor is there any reference to the level of *mens rea* required. For all these points it is necessary to look at case law.

4.2.1 *Actus reus* of section 47

It is necessary to prove that there was an assault or battery and that this caused actual bodily harm. This means that there must the *actus reus* of either an assault or a battery to establish a s 47 offence.

An example of an assault as the *actus reus* of a s 47 charge is *Ireland* (1971), where the defendant made silent phone calls to his victims. He put them in fear of immediate personal violence. His three victims suffered psychiatric illness as a result so he was guilty of a s 47 offence.

It is more usual for there to be a battery when there is a s 47 offence. For example, if the defendant kicks someone causing bruising to that person's leg, then the kick is a battery. It is the application of unlawful force.

The difference between common assault and a s 47 offence is that the victim suffers actual bodily harm as a result of the assault or battery.

Actual bodily harm

In *Chan Fook* (1994) it was held that the words 'actual bodily harm' were ordinary words. The word 'harm' means injury, hurt or damage. The word 'actual' means that there must be more than merely trivial hurt or injury. The harm must not be so trivial as to be effectively without significance.

In *R(T) v DPP* (2003) loss of consciousness, even momentarily, was held to be actual bodily harm.

In *DPP v Smith (Michael)* (2006) D cut off his ex-girlfriend's pony tail with a pair of kitchen scissors without her consent. The magistrates ruled that there was no case to answer on a s 47 charge. The prosecution appealed by way of case stated to the Divisional Court, which held that cutting hair was actual bodily harm and remitted the case to continue in the magistrates' court.

The court said that, even though scientifically the hair above the surface of a person's head is dead tissue, it remains part of the body and is intrinsic to each individual. For this reason the act could amount to an assault occasioning actual bodily harm.

Section 47 can be charged where there is any injury. Bruising, grazes and scratches all come within this. Psychiatric injury is also classed as 'actual bodily harm'. This was decided by the Court of Appeal in *Chan Fook* (1994). However, they pointed out that actual bodily harm does not include 'mere emotions such as fear, distress or panic' nor does it include 'states of mind that are not themselves evidence of some identifiable clinical condition'.

This decision was approved by the House of Lords in *Burstow* (1997) where it was said that 'bodily harm' in ss 18, 20 and 47 Offences Against the Person Act 1861 must be interpreted so as to include recognisable psychiatric illness.

4.2.2 *Mens rea* of section 47

The section in the Act makes no reference to *mens rea* but, as the essential element is a common assault, the courts have held that the *mens rea* for a common assault is sufficient for the *mens rea* of a s 47 offence.

This means that the defendant must intend or be subjectively reckless as to whether the victim fears or is subjected to unlawful force. This is the same *mens rea* as for an assault or a battery. It is important to note that there is no need for the defendant to intend or be reckless as to whether actual bodily harm is caused.

An example of where the defendent was reckless as to whether the victim feared unlawful force is *Roberts* (1971).

Roberts (1971)

The defendant, who was driving a car, made advances to the girl in the passenger seat and tried to take her coat off. She feared that he was going to commit a more serious assault and jumped from the car while it was travelling at about 30 mph. As a result of this she was slightly injured. He was found guilty of assault occasioning actual bodily harm even though he had not intended any injury or realised there was a risk of injury. He had intended to apply unlawful force when he touched her as he tried to take her coat off. This satisfied the *mens rea* for a common assault and so he was guilty of an offence under s 47.

This decision was confirmed by the House of Lords in the combined appeals of *Savage* and *Parmenter* (1991) (see 4.3.4 for details of *Parmenter*).

Savage (1991)

A woman in a pub threw beer over another woman. In doing this the glass slipped from the defendant's hand and the victim's hand was cut by the glass. The defendant said that she had only intended to throw beer over the woman. She had not intended her to be injured, nor had she realised that there was a risk of injury. She was convicted of a s 20 offence but the Court of Appeal quashed that and substituted a

Key facts

Offence	*Actus reus*	Consequence (injury) required	*Mens rea*
Assault	Causing V to fear immediate unlawful violence. Requires an act but can be by silent telephone calls (*Ireland* (1997)) or letters (*Constanza* (1997))	None needed	Intention of, or subjective recklessness as to, causing the victim to fear immediate unlawful violence
Battery	Application of unlawful violence even the slightest touching (*Collins v Wilcock* (1984))	None needed	Intention of, or subjective recklessness as to, applying unlawful force (*DPP v Majewski* (1976))
NB Assault and battery are both charged under s 39 Criminal Justice Act 1988 and are known as common assault.			
Assault occasioning actual bodily harm s 47 (OAPA1861)	Assault ie an assault or battery	Actual bodily harm (eg bruising) This includes: ● nervous shock *Miller* (1954) ● psychiatric harm *Chan Fook* (1994) ● cutting hair *Smith (Michael)* (2006)	Intention or subjective recklessness as to causing fear of unlawful violence or of applying unlawful force; ie the *means rea* for an assault or battery

Key facts chart on assault, battery and s 47

conviction under s 47 for assault occasioning actual bodily harm. She appealed against this to the House of Lords. The Law Lords dismissed her appeal. The fact that she intended to throw the beer over the other woman meant she had the intention to apply unlawful force and this was sufficient for the *mens rea* of the s 47 offence.

4.3 Section 20

This is the next offence in seriousness. It is an offence under s 20 Offences Against the Person Act 1861 which states:

> 'Whosoever shall unlawfully and maliciously wound or inflict any grievous bodily harm upon any other person, either with or without a weapon or instrument, shall be guilty of an offence and shall be liable ... to imprisonment for not more than five years.'

The offence is triable either way and the maximum sentence is five years. This is the same maximum sentence as for a s 47 offence, despite the fact that s 20 is seen as a more serious offence and requires both a higher degree of injury and *mens rea* as to an injury.

For the offence to be proved it must be shown that the defendant:

- wounded; or
- inflicted grievous bodily harm

and that he did this:

- intending some injury to be caused; or
- being reckless as to whether bodily harm was inflicted.

4.3.1 Wound

Wound means a cut or a break in the continuity of the whole skin. A cut of internal skin, such as in the cheek, is sufficient, but internal bleeding where there is no cut of the skin is not sufficient. This is shown by *JCC v Eisenhower* (1983).

JCC v Eisenhower (1983)

The victim was hit in the eye by a shotgun pellet. This did not penetrate the eye but did cause severe bleeding under the surface. As there was no cut, it was held that this was not a wound.

The cut must be of the whole skin, so that a scratch is not considered a wound. This is because only the surface layer of the skin is broken in a scratch. The inner layers are not cut.

Even a broken bone is not considered a wound, unless the skin is broken as well. In the old case of *Wood* (1830), the victim's collar bone was broken but, as skin was intact, it was held there was no wound.

4.3.2 Grievous bodily harm

It was held in *DPP v Smith* (1961) that grievous bodily harm means 'really serious harm'. The harm does not have to be life-threatening and in *Saunders* (1985) it was held that it was permissible to direct a jury that there need be 'serious harm' and not include the word 'really'.

In *Bollom* (2004) it was held that the severity of the injuries should be assessed according to the victim's age and health.

Bollom (2004)

A 17-month-old child had bruising to her abdomen, both arms and left leg. D was convicted of causing grievous bodily harm. The Court of Appeal quashed his conviction and substituted a conviction for assault occasioning actual bodily harm. However, the Court stated that bruising could amount to grievous bodily harm. Bruising of this severity would be less serious on an adult in full health than on a very young child.

In *Burstow* (1997), where the victim of a stalker suffered a severe depressive illness as a result of the stalker's conduct, it was decided that serious psychiatric injury can be grievous bodily harm.

In October 2003 in *Dica* there was the first ever conviction for causing grievous bodily harm through infecting the victims with HIV. The defendant had had unprotected sex with two women without telling them he was HIV positive. Both women became infected as a result.

4.3.3 Inflicting grievous bodily harm

Section 20 uses the word 'inflict'. Originally this was taken as meaning that there had to be a technical assault or battery. Even so it allowed the section to be interpreted quite widely, as shown in *Lewis* (1974) where the defendant shouted threats at his wife through a closed door in a second-floor flat and tried to break his way through the door. The wife was so frightened that she jumped from the window and broke both her legs. Lewis was convicted of a s 20 offence. The threats could be considered as a technical assault.

In *Burstow* (1997) it was decided that 'inflict' does not require a technical assault or a battery. This means that it need only be shown that the defendant's actions have led to the consequence of the victim suffering grievous bodily harm. The decision also means that there now appears to be little, if any, difference in the *actus reus* of the offences under s 20 and s 18 which uses the word 'cause'. In fact, in *Burstow* Lord Hope said that for all practical purposes there was no difference between the two words.

4.3.4 *Mens rea* of section 20

The word used in the section is 'maliciously'. In *Cunningham* (1957) it was held that 'maliciously' did not require any illwill towards the person injured. It simply meant either:

- an intention to do the particular kind of harm that was in fact done; or
- recklessness as to whether such harm should occur or not (ie the accused has foreseen that

the particular kind of harm might be done, and yet gone on to take the risk of it).

Cunningham (1957)

The defendant tore a gas meter from the wall of an empty house in order to steal the money in it. This caused gas to seep into the house next door where a woman was affected by it. Cunningham was not guilty of an offence against s 23 Offences Against the Person Act 1861 of maliciously administering a noxious thing, as he did not realise the risk of gas escaping into the next-door house. He had not intended to cause the harm.

In *Parmenter* (1991) the House of Lords confirmed that the *Cunningham* meaning of recklessness applies to all offences in which the statutory definition uses the word 'maliciously'.

For the *mens rea* of s 20, the prosecution can prove either that the defendant intended to cause another person some harm, or that he was subjectively reckless as to whether another person suffered some harm.

It is not necessary to prove that the defendant had intention to cause serious harm or was reckless about whether serious harm was caused. This means that there is a difference between the level of injury for the *actus reus* of s 20 (grievous bodily harm or wound) and the level for the *mens rea* of s 20 which only requires intention or recklessness as to some harm. It was decided by the House of Lords in *Parmenter* (1991) that, although the *actus reus* of s 20 requires a wound or grievous bodily harm, there is no need for the defendant to foresee this level of serious injury.

Parmenter (1991)

Parmenter had injured his three-month-old baby when he threw the child in the air and caught him. Parmenter said that he had often done this with slightly older children and did not realise

Offence	Mens rea	Injury
s 18	Specific intent to wound or cause GBH or resist arrest etc	Wound or grievous bodily harm
s 20	Intention or recklessness as to some harm	
s 47	Intention or recklessness as to putting the victim in fear of unlawful force or applying unlawful force assault	Actual bodily harm
Common assault		No injury

Figure 4.1 Different levels of *mens rea* and injury for assault cases

that there was risk of any injury. He was convicted of an offence under s 20. The House of Lords quashed this conviction as there was no evidence that he foresaw any injury. They did, however, substitute a conviction for assault occasioning actual bodily harm under s 47.

4.4 Section 18

This offence under s 18 Offences Against the Person Act 1861 is often referred to as 'wounding with intent'. In fact it covers a much wider range of behaviour than this implies. It is considered a much more serious offence than s 20 as can be seen from the difference in the maximum punishments. Section 20 has a maximum of five years' imprisonment whereas the maximum for s 18 is life imprisonment. Also s 20 is triable either way but s 18 must be tried on indictment at the Crown Court. The definition in the Offences Against the Person Act 1861 states:

> 'Whosoever shall unlawfully and maliciously by any means whatsoever wound or cause any grievous bodily harm to any person, with intent to do some grievous bodily harm to any person, or with intent to resist or prevent the lawful apprehension or detainer of any person, shall be guilty of … an offence.'

4.4.1 *Actus reus* of section 18

This can be committed in two ways:

* wounding
* causing grievous bodily harm.

The meanings of 'wound' and 'grievous bodily harm' are the same as for s 20.

The word 'cause' is very wide so that it is only necessary to prove that the defendant's act was a substantial cause of the wound or grievous bodily harm.

4.4.2 *Mens rea* of section 18

This is a specific intent offence. The defendant must be proved to have intended to:

* do some grievous bodily harm; or
* resist or prevent the lawful apprehension or detainer of any person.

Intent to do some grievous bodily harm

Although the word 'maliciously' appears in s 18, it has been held that this adds nothing to the *mens rea* of this section where grievous bodily harm is intended. The important point is that s 18 is a specific intent crime. Intention must be proved; recklessness is not enough for the *mens rea* of s 18.

In the majority of cases there is no problem with proving intention. Where the defendant's aim is to carry out a serious attack on another person it is straightforward to prove the intention to do grievous bodily harm.

However, there are some situations where the defendant's aim or purpose is something quite different, but in the course of carrying out that purpose someone is seriously injured. This is where the concept of foresight of consequences is important. The law on this is stated in a series of cases on murder. The first point is that, as decided in *Moloney* (1985), foresight of consequences is not intention; it is only evidence from which intention can be inferred or found. And following the cases of *Nedrick* (1986) and *Woollin* (1998) intention cannot be found unless the harm caused was a virtual certainty as a result of the defendant's actions and the defendant realised that this was so. (See 1.3.1 for a fuller discussion on these cases and the meaning of intention.)

These principles also apply to s 18 offences. An example would be where a man decides to set fire to his shop in order to claim insurance money. His aim is to damage the shop and get the insurance money. Unfortunately he starts the fire when staff are working there and some of them are seriously injured in the fire. If the man is charged with a s 18 offence, then it is necessary to show that serious injury was a virtual certainty as a result of his actions and that he realised this. Then the jury are entitled to find that he had the intention for a s 18 offence.

Resisting or preventing arrest

Where the defendant is trying to resist or prevent arrest or detention, then the level of intention regarding the injury is lower. The prosecution must prove that he had specific intention to resist or prevent arrest, but so far as the injury they need only prove that he intended to or was reckless as to whether his actions would cause some harm or injury.

This was decided in *Morrison* (1989).

Morrison (1989)

A police officer seized hold of the defendant and told him that she was arresting him. He dived through a window, dragging her with him as far

Key facts

Offence	*Actus reus*	Consequence (injury) required	*Mens rea*
Maliciously wounding or inflicting grievous bodily harm s 20 OAPA 1861	A direct or indirect act or omission – *Martin (1881)* No need to prove an assault – *Burstow* (1998)	Either a wound, a cutting of the whole skin – *JCC v Eisenhower* (1984) or grievous bodily harm (really serious harm) which includes psychiatric harm – *Burstow* (1998)	Intention or subjective recklessness as to causing some injury (though not serious) – *Parmenter* (1991)
Wounding or causing grievous bodily harm with intent s 18 OAPA 1861	A direct or indirect act or omission which causes the victim's injury	A wound or grievous bodily harm (as above)	Specific intention to wound or to cause grievous bodily harm, or specific intention to resist or prevent arrest plus recklessness as to causing injury – *Morrison* (1989)

Key facts chart on s 20 and s 18

as the window so that her face was badly cut by the glass. The Court of Appeal held that as the word 'maliciously' is used in respect of this part of the section, it must have the same meaning as in *Cunningham* (1957). This means that the prosecution must prove that the defendant either intended injury or realised there was a risk of injury and took that risk.

Activity

Read the following newspaper article from the *Kent Messenger* and answer the questions below.

Thug jailed for stamping on policeman's face

A thug has been jailed for two-and-a-half years for a vicious attack on a police officer after New Year's Eve celebrations erupted in violence.

Kevin Vidler assaulted the PC and then stamped on his face, fracturing his cheekbone, and kicked him in the head.

His brother Neil was given 240 hours' community punishment order for assaulting another man. He was ordered to pay his victim £250 compensation.

Maidstone Crown Court heard in October how the party at a working men's club in Southborough was in full swing when the victim, a club member, intervened in a couple's heated argument. There was a 'verbal tirade' and he asked one of the men to leave.

Soon afterwards he was punched in the face by 37-year-old Neil Vidler. The police were called but the trouble continued outside.

When the PC and a fellow officer arrived, a teenager hit out at them. Kevin Vidler, aged 36, tried to help the youth, grabbing the constable by the throat and punching him in the head.

Kevin Vidler was convicted of causing grievous bodily harm with intent. Neil Vidler was convicted of assault causing actual bodily harm.

Kent Messenger, 5 December 2003
© Kent Messenger Group

Questions

1. What offence was Kevin Vidler convicted of?

2. Which section of the Offences Against the Person Act 1861 would this come under?

3. What are the elements which have to be proved for this section?

4. Explain what Kevin had done to make him guilty of this offence.

5. What offence was Neil Vidler convicted of?

6. Which section of the Offences Against the Person Act 1861 would this come under?

7. What are the elements which have to be proved for this section?

8. What had Neil done to make him guilty of this offence?

9. What sentences were the two brothers given?

10. Explain why they received different sentences.

4.5 CPS charging guidelines

When deciding which offence should be charged when a victim is injured, the type of injury is important as it distinguishes between common assault where there is no injury, s 47 offences where there must be actual bodily harm and s 20/18 offences where there must be grievous bodily harm or a wound.

The Crown Prosecution Service has guidelines about what offence should normally be charged for certain types of injury. These are only guidelines. They do not always match the law accurately. This is because they are intended to ensure convictions and make efficient use of resources.

Actual bodily harm

The CPS charging guidelines state that the following injuries should normally be prosecuted under s 47:

- loss or breaking of tooth or teeth
- temporary loss of sensory functions, which may include loss of consciousness
- extensive or multiple bruising
- displaced broken nose
- minor fractures
- minor, but not merely superficial, cuts of a sort probably requiring medical treatment (eg stitches)
- psychiatric injury that is more than mere emotions such as fear, distress or panic.

Some of these are, according to decided cases, more serious than actual bodily harm. For example, a cut which requires stitches comes within the definition of wound. Also, extensive bruising may be considered as grievous bodily harm if the victim is a child, as in the case of *Bollom*.

Grievous bodily harm

The Crown Prosecution charging guidelines stress that grievous bodily harm means serious bodily harm and it is for the jury to decide whether the harm is serious. However, examples of what would usually amount to serious harm include:

- injury resulting in permanent disability or permanent loss of sensory function
- injury which results in more than minor permanent, visible disfigurement
- broken or displaced limbs or bones, including fractured skull
- compound fractures, broken cheekbone, jaw, ribs, etc
- injuries which cause substantial loss of blood, usually necessitating a transfusion
- injuries resulting in lengthy treatment or incapacity
- psychiatric injury.

4.6 Reform

This area of the law is in need of reform, and recommendations have been made by both the Criminal Law Revision Committee and the Law Commission. The Law Commission pointed out that there are three main problems with the Offences Against the Person Act 1861. These are:

- it uses complicated, obscure and old-fashioned language; eg the words 'maliciously' and 'grievous'
- the structure of the Act is complicated
- non-lawyers find the Act completely unintelligible.

In fact some of the difficulties have been resolved by the judges in case decisions. For example, there was considerable debate as to whether the word 'inflict' in s 20 meant that a technical assault had to take place. This was resolved by the case of *Burstow* (1998) (see 4.3.3) in which the House of Lords ruled that it did not. Also the courts have extended the meaning of 'bodily harm' to include injury to mental health so that defendants causing such injury can also be convicted.

4.6.1 Inconsistency between offences

There are inconsistencies in the Act, especially with regard to the *mens rea* required for each offence. In particular, s 47 has the same *mens rea* as for an assault or battery. It does not require the defendant to intend or even realise that there is a risk of any injury. This appears unjust.

It is also unjust that a person who causes a small cut can be charged with the more serious offence of s 20 instead of the offence of 'occasioning actual bodily harm' under s 47. This is because s 20 refers to 'wound or grievous bodily harm'. Yet clearly there are different levels of wound and many of them do not equate with grievous bodily harm.

It is also inconsistent that a defendant who only intends or foresees the risk of minor injury can be convicted of the very serious offence of s 18 if serious injury then occurs when he intends to resist arrest. This is the effect of the decision in *Morrison* (1989) (see 4.4.2). Is it right that the fact that the defendant intends to resist arrest makes him liable for the same offence as someone who has intended to cause very serious injuries?

In fact the situation can be even more unfair as someone who intends to resist arrest can be charged with s 18 even though they only caused a small wound to the victim. This means that such a defendant can be guilty of the same offence as a defendant who intended to cause serious harm and did in fact cause very severe injuries.

4.6.2 Sentencing

The inconsistencies between the offences also apply to the maximum sentences available for each level of offence.

For an assault or battery the maximum sentence is six months' imprisonment. For s 47 the maximum sentence is five years' imprisonment. Yet the *mens rea* for the two offences is the same. To have such a big difference in the maximum sentence where the defendants have the same *mens rea* is unjust.

The other main criticism of the sentences available is that the maximum for s 47 and s 20 is the same. They both have a maximum sentence of five years' imprisonment. Yet both the *mens rea* and level of injury are much more serious for s 20.

For s 47 the *mens rea* is intention or recklessness

as to whether the victim fears physical force or intention or recklessness in applying physical force. The level of injury is actual bodily harm. For s 20 the *mens rea* is intention or recklessness as to whether some harm is inflicted, while the level of injury is grievous bodily harm or a wound. Both of these are much more serious than the required element of s 47. So it is difficult to understand why the maximum sentences should be the same for the two offences.

4.6.3 Modern understanding of 'bodily harm'

The 1861 Act uses the phrase 'bodily harm' in sections 47, 20 and 18. When the Act was passed nearly 150 years ago, medical knowledge was comparatively limited. In particular, psychiatric illness was not understood.

With the improvement in medical knowledge, it is now known that it is possible to cause psychiatric illness through putting someone in fear. This meant that judges have had to develop the law in cases such as *Burstow* and *Ireland* to match modern knowledge and understanding.

It is only because of judicial development that 'bodily harm' is now interpreted as including psychiatric illness. If the judges had not included this, then the law would have failed to protect victims. However, it would be much more satisfactory if the law was re-written and made clearer.

Another area in which judges have had to adapt the law to modern knowledge is in the transmission of disease. Defendants can now be liable for infecting others with diseases such as HIV. However, it would be more satisfactory if the law were re-written to cover such situations expressly.

4.6.4 Law Commission's proposals

In 1993 the Law Commission proposed a new law to take its place, but the Government did nothing about this until 1998 when the Home Office issued a Consultation Document, *'Violence: Reforming the Offences Against the Person Act 1861'*. This included a draft Bill which set out four main offences. These were intended to replace s 18, s 20, s 47 and assault and battery. In order, starting with the most serious (which is in clause 1 of the draft Bill), they are:

1. Intentional serious injury where person would be guilty if he intentionally caused serious injury to another.
2. Reckless serious injury where a person would be guilty if he recklessly caused serious injury to another.
3. Intentional or reckless injury where a person would be guilty if he intentionally or recklessly caused injury to another.
4. Assault where a person would be guilty if he intentionally or recklessly
   (a) applied force to or caused an impact on the body of another, or
   (b) caused the other to believe that any such force or impact is imminent.

In each of these the level of injury and the required *mens rea* is made clear by the wording. In addition the draft Bill also defined the word 'injury', making it clear that both physical and mental injury were included. The word 'wounding' is not used. So this would mean that a serious cut would be considered to be a serious injury, while a small cut would be considered to be merely an injury. This would have cleared up most of the problems in the present law.

The draft Bill also set out a new sentencing framework. This matched the blameworthiness of the offence to the maximum sentence available in a more structured and sensible way than the current system. Unfortunately, although the Bill was sent out for consultation in 1998, the Government has done nothing more, so the law still remains in an unsatisfactory state.

In the draft Bill, the Law Commission defined injury. They said it included both physical and mental illness and they gave a definition for both of these:

- Physical injury was defined as including pain, unconsciousness and any other impairment of a person's physical health.
- Mental injury was defined as any impairment of a person's mental health.

They also included disease as a physical injury for the purposes of the most serious offence. However, this meant that it would be almost impossible to convict a defendant of infecting another person with HIV, since the proposed most serious offence (no.1 in the list above) can only be committed where the defendant has intentionally caused serious injury. This would mean that convictions for recklessly transmitting HIV as in the case of *Dica* (2004) (see 4.3.2) would not be possible.

Activity

Explain in each of the situations below, what type of offence may have been committed.

1. In a football match Billy is kicked by Rio as Rio tries to get control of the ball. This causes bruising to Billy's leg. Billy is annoyed at this and punches Rio in the face, causing a cut to his lip.
2. Anish is walking along a canal bank. Carol, who is in a hurry, pushes past him, knocking him into the canal. Anish hits his head on the side and suffers a fractured skull.
3. A police officer sees Jason damaging a parked car. The officer puts his hand on Jason's shoulder and says 'I am arresting you for criminal damage'. Jason punches the officer hard in the face, breaking his jaw. Jason then runs off.
4. Karl waves a knife at Lily, saying 'I am going to cut that silly smile off.' Lily is very frightened and faints. She falls against Mary, who is knocked to the ground and suffers bruising.

Chapter 5

Defences

When a person is charged with an offence, there are various defences that may be available to them. Some defences can be used for any offence; other defences can only be used for certain offences. If a defence is used successfully, the defendant is usually acquitted of the crime and is free. The exception to this is the defence of insanity where a special verdict of 'not guilty by reason of insanity' is given. This means that the judge then makes an order on what should happen to the defendant. The type of order will depend on the nature of the defendant's mental state. It can range from an order to detain the defendant in hospital, down to an absolute discharge.

Figure 5.1 shows the availability of the defences discussed in this chapter to offences in Unit 3 of the AQA A2 specification. It also shows whether there are limitations on when they can be used.

Defence	Availability	Limitation
Insanity	All offences where *mens rea* is required	Not available for strict liability offences where no mental element is required
Automatism	All offences	
Intoxication	Offences of specific intent murder, s 18 OAPA 1861	Not available for offences of basic intent, manslaughter, ss 20 and 47 OAPA, assault, battery
Self-defence	All offences	
Consent	Assaults where there is no injury or only a minor injury	Never available for murder. Not always available for ss 18, 20 and 47 OAPA

Figure 5.1 Availability of defences

5.1 Insanity

The rules on insanity are based on *M'Naghten* (1843). M'Naghten suffered from extreme paranoia. He thought he was being persecuted by the 'Tories' (the then Government). He tried to kill a member of the Government, Sir Robert Peel, but instead killed his secretary. Because of his mental state M'Naghten was found not guilty of murder. In fact he was committed to a mental hospital because of his mental state, but this was not a result of the verdict. The fact that he could be found not guilty and was not automatically sent to a mental hospital caused a public outcry, and led to the judges in the House of Lords being asked to answer a series of questions in order to clarify the law in respect of insanity. The answers to those questions have created the rules on insanity (M'Naghten Rules) which are used in legal cases today.

The main rule is that 'in all cases every man is presumed to be sane and to possess a sufficient degree of reason to be responsible for his crimes'. For the defence of insanity to be established the defendant must prove that at the time of committing the act:

> 'he was labouring under such a defect of reason, from disease of the mind, as not to know the nature and quality of the act he was doing, or if he did know it, that he did not know he was doing what was wrong.'

From this it can be seen that three elements need to be proved. These are:

1. a defect of reason
2. this must be the result of a disease of the mind
3. this causes the defendant not to know the nature and quality of his act, or not to know he was doing wrong.

The burden of proving insanity is on the defence, who must prove it on the balance of probabilities.

Where a defendant is found to be insane the verdict is 'not guilty by reason of insanity'.

It used to be thought that insanity was a defence to all offences. However, in *DPP v H* (1997), where the defendant was charged with driving with excess alcohol, it was held that insanity is not a defence to offences of strict liability where no mental element is required.

5.1.1 Defect of reason

This means that the defendant's powers of reasoning must be impaired. If the defendant is capable of reasoning but has failed to use those powers, then this is not a defect of reason.

This was decided in *Clarke* (1972) where it was held that the defect of reason must be more than absent-mindedness or confusion.

Clarke (1972)

The defendant went into a supermarket, picked up three items including a jar of mincemeat, put them into her own bag and then left the store without paying. She was charged with theft but claimed in her defence that she lacked the *mens rea* for theft as she had no recollection of putting the items into her bag. Indeed, she did not even want the mincemeat as neither she nor her husband ate it. She said she was suffering from absent-mindedness caused by diabetes and depression. The trial judge ruled that this amounted to a plea of insanity, so she then pleaded guilty to the theft but appealed against it.

The Court of Appeal quashed the conviction. They held that the phrase 'defect of reason' in the M'Naghten Rules applied only to 'persons who by reason of a "disease of the mind" are deprived of the power of reasoning'. The Court of Appeal also said that the rules of insanity do not apply to people who simply have moments of confusion or absent-mindedness.

5.1.2 Disease of the mind

The defect of reason must be due to a disease of the mind. This is a legal term, not a medical one. The disease can be a mental disease or a physical disease which affects the mind. For example, in *Kemp* (1956) the defendant was suffering from hardening of the arteries which caused a problem with supply of the blood to the brain. This caused the defendant to have moments of temporary loss of consciousness. During one of these he attacked his wife with a hammer, causing her serious injury. He was charged with inflicting grievous bodily harm under s 20 Offences Against the Person Act 1861.

At his trial the question arose as to whether this condition came within the rules on insanity. Kemp admitted that he was suffering from a 'defect of reason' but said that this was not due to a 'disease of the mind' as it was a physical illness causing the problem and not a mental illness. He was found 'not guilty by reason of insanity' and appealed against this finding. The Court of Appeal upheld this finding, stating that the law was not concerned with the brain but with the mind. Kemp's ordinary mental faculties of reason, memory and understanding had been affected and so his condition came within the rules on insanity.

In *Sullivan* (1983) the House of Lords was asked to decide whether epilepsy came within the rules of insanity.

Sullivan (1983)

The defendant, aged 51, had suffered from epilepsy since childhood. He was known to have fits and had shown aggression to those trying to help him during a fit. He injured an 80-year-old man during a friendly visit to a neighbour's flat. The trial judge ruled that on the facts, he would be directing the jury to return a verdict of 'not guilty by reason of insanity'. As a result of this the defendant pleaded guilty to assault occasioning actual bodily (s 47 OAPA). The defendant then appealed. Both the Court of Appeal and the House of Lords confirmed the conviction.

The House of Lords ruled that the source of the disease was irrelevant. It could be 'organic, as in epilepsy, or functional', and it did not matter whether the impairment was 'permanent or transient and intermittent', provided that it existed at the time that the defendant did the act.

This ruling in *Sullivan* means that for the purpose of the M'Naghten Rules the disease can be of any part of the body provided it has an effect on the mind.

This decision in *Sullivan* has extended the legal meaning of insanity far beyond the medical meaning. So long as there is a disease which affects the mind, it does not matter what the type of disease is. As the House of Lords stated, it can be 'functional', that is affecting the functioning of the defendant such as in schizophrenia, paranoia or manic depression.

However, it can also be 'organic', that is a disease of the organs of the body. This includes such diseases as epilepsy, arteriosclerosis (as in *Kemp*), brain tumours and diabetes, as shown by *Henessy* (1989).

Hennessy (1989)

Hennessy was a diabetic who had not taken his insulin for three days. He was seen to get into a car which had been reported stolen and drive off. He was charged with taking a motor vehicle without consent and driving while disqualified. He had no recollection of taking or driving the car. The disease of diabetes was affecting his mind, and so comes within the definition of insanity.

In *Burgess* (1991) it was decided that in some instances sleep-walking was also within the legal definition of insanity. The defendant and his girlfriend had been watching videos. They fell asleep and in his sleep Burgess attacked the girl.

There was no evidence of any external cause for the sleep-walking, and a doctor at the trial gave evidence that in this instance it was due to an internal cause: a sleep disorder. The judge ruled that this was evidence of insanity and the defendant was found 'not guilty by reason insanity'. The Court of Appeal upheld the finding.

However, if the sleep-walking is due to an external cause, such as a blow to the head, then it is not insanity but will allow the defendant the defence of automatism (see 5.2).

External factors

Where the cause of the defendant being in a state where he does not know what he is doing is not a disease but an external cause, then this is not insanity. This was shown in *Quick* (1973).

Quick (1973)

The defendant was a diabetic who had taken his insulin but then not eaten enough. This causes low blood-sugar levels which can affect the brain. In this state Quick, who was a nurse at a mental hospital, assaulted a patient. The Court of Appeal ruled that his condition did not come within the definition of insanity. It was caused by an external matter, in this case the drug insulin. This meant that he could rely on the defence of automatism (see 5.2) and was entitled to be acquitted of the charge.

This decision has the odd effect that diabetics may be classed as insane when they have not taken any insulin, as in *Hennessy*, or not insane when they have taken insulin but not eaten, as in the situation in *Quick* (1973).

This is because of the internal/external cause of the automatic state that the defendant was in. If he has not taken any drugs and it is the disease causing the problem, then this is an internal cause and it is a 'disease of the mind'. If the defendant has taken a drug and this is the cause of his automatic state, then it is an external cause and not within the definition of insanity.

5.1.3 Not knowing the nature and quality of the act or not knowing that it is wrong

Nature and quality refers to the physical character of the act. There are two ways in which the defendant may not know the nature and quality of the act. These are:

1. because he is in a state of unconsciousness or impaired consciousness; or
2. where he is conscious but due to his mental condition he does not understand or know what he is doing.

If the defendant can show that either of these states applied to him at the time he did the act, then he satisfies this part of the M'Naghten Rules.

The defendant may not know the nature and quality of the act because he is in an automatic state. He does not know what he is doing. This was the situation in the cases of *Kemp* (1956), *Sullivan* (1983), *Henessy* (1989) and *Burgess* (1991). All those defendants were unaware of what they were doing.

It is also possible for someone not to know the nature and quality of their act because they suffer from delusions. If a person believes that the devil is standing next to them and hits out at 'the devil' with a knife, but in actual fact kills a person, they do not know the nature and quality of their act. The same is true if an insane person believes they are squeezing an orange when in fact they are squeezing someone's throat.

Where the defendant knows the nature and quality of the act, he still can use the defence of insanity if he does not know that what he did was wrong. Wrong in this sense means legally wrong, not morally wrong. If the defendant knows the nature and quality of the act and that it is legally wrong, he cannot use the defence of insanity. This is so even if the defendant is suffering from a mental illness. This was seen in *Windle* (1952).

Windle (1952)

The defendant's wife constantly spoke of committing suicide. One day the defendant killed her by giving her 100 aspirins. He gave himself up to the police and said 'I suppose they will hang me for this'. He was suffering from mental illness, but these words showed he knew what he had done was legally wrong. As a result he could not use the defence of insanity and was found guilty of murder.

Note that this case was in 1952 and the special defence of diminished responsibility to a charge of murder did not exist. That defence was only created in 1957, so Windle could not use it.

The case of *Windle* was followed more recently in *Johnson* (2007).

Johnson (2007)

D forced his way into a neighbour's flat and stabbed him. D was charged with wounding with intent (s 20 Offences Against the Person Act 1861). At his trial two psychiatrists gave evidence that he was suffering from paranoid schizophrenia and suffering from hallucinations. However, they both agreed that, despite this, D knew the nature and quality of his acts and that they were legally wrong. One psychiatrist was of the view that D did not consider that what he had done was wrong in the moral sense. The judge ruled that the defence of insanity was not available to D and D was convicted of wounding with intent.

The Court of Appeal upheld the judge's ruling that insanity was not available as D knew the nature and quality of his acts and that they were legally wrong. They followed the decision in *Windle* where the court had held that the word 'wrong' meant knowing that the act was contrary to law.

In their judgment in *Johnson*, the Court of Appeal pointed out that there had been an Australian case in which the Australian courts had refused to follow *Windle*. The view of the Australian court was that if a defendant believed his act to be right according to the ordinary standard of reasonable men, then he was entitled to be acquitted even if he knew that it was legally wrong.

The Court of Appeal felt they were obliged to follow *Windle,* but they did express the opinion that the Australian case contained 'illuminating passages indicating the difficulties and internal inconsistencies which can arise from the application of the M'Naghten rules if the decision in *Windle* is correct'.

5.1.4 Problems with the law of insanity

The first major problem is that the definition of insanity was set by the M'Naghten Rules in 1843. At that time medical knowledge of mental disorders was very limited. Much more is known today about mental disorders and a more modern definition should be used.

Legal definition of insanity

Another major problem is that the definition has become a legal one rather than a medical one. This causes two problems.

1. People suffering from certain mental disorders do not come within it; for example, those suffering from irresistible impulses and who are psychopaths such as *Byrne* (1960). They do not come within the M'Naghten Rules as they know what they are doing and that it is wrong. However, they cannot prevent themselves from acting and have a recognised mental disorder.
2. On the other hand those suffering from physical illnesses such as diabetes (*Hennessy* (1989)), brain tumours or hardening of the arteries (*Kemp* (1956)) are considered to be legally insane. Even a sleep-walker has come within the definition (*Burgess* (1991)). The

justification for this is that there is an internal cause of their actions: the behaviour may recur and it may be possible to treat it.

The overlap with automatism

Insanity overlaps with automatism. It is necessary to decide whether the defendant's automatic state is due to a mental illness or due to external factors. The courts have decided that those suffering from any illness, mental or physical, which affects their mind or puts them into an automatic state amounts to insanity. This means that the defence of non-insane automatism has been removed from such people as epileptics and diabetics.

This has serious consequences, as those successfully using the defence of automatism are entitled to a complete acquittal. Whereas, on a finding of not guilty by reason of insanity, the judge has to impose some order on the defendant.

The position of diabetics

The way that the legal definition of insanity works means that diabetics are sometimes classed as insane and at other times not. In *Sullivan* it was held that he came within the M'Maghten rules as it was the disease of diabetes which caused him to go into an automatic state and not know what he was doing.

However, in *Quick*, where he had taken insulin for the diabetes but then failed to eat, it was held that the cause of his automatic state was not a disease but the external cause of taking the drug. This meant that he did not come within the definition of insanity. Instead he could use the defence of automatism and was entitled to a full acquittal.

Decision in *Windle*

Following the decision in *Windle* (1952), a defendant who is suffering from a serious recognised mental illness and who does not know that his act is morally wrong cannot have a

defence of insanity when he knows that his act is legally wrong. An Australian case refused to follow this decision. In *Johnson* (2007) the Court of Appeal clearly thought that the Australian case had some merit but they were obliged to follow *Windle.*

Social stigma

Even the use of the word 'insanity' is unfortunate. It carries a social stigma. It is bad enough to apply it to people who are suffering from mental disorders, but it is entirely inappropriate to apply it to those suffering from such diseases as epilepsy or diabetes.

Proof of insanity

The defendant has to prove that he is insane. This places the burden of proof on him. It is possible that this is in breach of Article 6 of the European Convention on Human Rights which states that the defendant is innocent until proven guilty.

There is also the point that the jury are required to decide if the defendant is insane or not. This is not an appropriate function for a jury. It is a matter which should be decided by medical experts. Where there is dispute the jury have to listen to medical evidence and try to understand technical and complex psychiatric issues.

5.1.5 Proposals for reform

There have been several proposals for reform of the law on insanity. In 1953, the Royal Commission on Capital Punishment suggested that the M'Naghten Rules should be extended so that a defendant would be considered insane if he 'was incapable of preventing himself' from committing the offence. If this had been acted upon, then those suffering from 'irresistible impulses' would have come within the definition of insanity.

However, instead of making this reform, the Government introduced the defence of diminished responsibility. This gives a special

Key cases

Case	Facts	Law
M'Naghten (1843)	Suffering from paranoia, shot Sir Robert Peel's secretary. Acquitted but House of Lords asked to clarify the law on insanity.	D must be labouring under a defect of reason, from disease of the mind: AND must either not know the nature and quality of the act he was doing, or not know he was doing wrong.
Clarke (1972)	Absent-mindedly took items from a supermarket.	Mere absent-mindedness or confusion is not insanity
Kemp (1956)	Suffering from hardening of the arteries which causes blackouts.	Was within the rules of insanity as his condition affected his mental reasoning, memory and understanding.
Sullivan (1984)	Injured friend during epileptic fit.	Insanity included any organic or functional disease. It also applied even where it was temporary.
Hennessy (1989)	Diabetic who took a car after failing to take his insulin.	If the disease affects the mind then it is within the definition of insanity.
Burgess (1991)	Injured his girlfriend while he was asleep.	If the cause of sleep-walking is internal, then it is a disease within the definition of insanity.
Quick (1973)	Diabetic who failed to eat after taking his insulin.	This was an external cause (the effect of the drug) and so not insanity.
Windle (1952)	Was suffering from a mental disorder and killed his wife, who had constantly spoken of committing suicide.	Because he knew what he had done was legally wrong, he was not insane by the *M'Naghten* rules.
Johnson (2007)	D, who was suffering from paranoid schizophrenia and suffering from hallucinations, stabbed his neighbour.	Because he knew what he had done was legally wrong, he was not insane by the *M'Naghten* rules.

Figure 5.2 Key cases on insanity

defence to those charged with murder (see section 8.1). It does not give a defence to any other offence, but judges have discretion on sentencing for all other offences.

In 1975 the Butler Committee suggested that the verdict of not guilty by reason of insanity should be replaced by a verdict of not guilty on evidence of mental disorder.

In 1989 the Law Commission's Draft Criminal Code proposed that a defendant should be not guilty on evidence of severe mental disorder or severe mental handicap.

None of these proposals have been made law. However, the change to the ways in which judges can deal with a defendant after they are found not guilty by reason of insanity has improved matters. As explained in section 12.1.4, a judge can now make a supervision and treatment order or even give an absolute discharge where that is suitable.

5.2 Automatism

In *Bratty v Attorney-General for Northern Ireland* (1961) automatism was defined as:

> 'an act done by the muscles without any control by the mind, such as a spasm, a reflex action or a convulsion; or an act done by a person who is not conscious of what he is doing such as an act done whilst suffering from concussion or whilst sleep-walking'.

In fact this definition covers two types of automatism:

1. **insane automatism**: where the cause of the automatism is a disease of the mind within the M'Naghten Rules. In such a case the defence is insanity and the verdict not guilty by reason of insanity;
2. **non-insane automatism**: where the cause is an external one. Where such a defence succeeds, it is a complete defence and the defendant is not guilty.

5.2.1 Non-insane automatism

This is a defence because the *actus reus* done by the defendant is not voluntary. In addition the defendant does not have the required *mens rea* for the offence. The cause of the automatism must be external. Examples of external causes include:

- a blow to the head
- an attack by a swarm of bees
- sneezing
- hypnotism
- the effect of a drug.

In *R v T* (1990) it was accepted that exceptional stress can be an external factor which may cause automatism. In this case the defendant suffered post-traumatic stress disorder after being raped.

Reduced or partial control of one's actions is not sufficient to constitute non-insane automatism. In *A-G's reference (No 2 of 1992)* (1993) the Court of

Appeal held that there must be 'total destruction of voluntary control'. In this case the defendant had driven his lorry into a stationary car, killing two people. He said that he was suffering from the condition 'driving without awareness' which puts a driver into a trance-like state. This may be brought on by driving for long distances on motorways. The jury acquitted him. The Attorney-General referred the point of law to the Court of Appeal who ruled that because this condition only causes partial loss of control, it did not amount to automatism.

5.2.2 Self-induced automatism

This is where the defendant knows that his conduct is likely to bring on an automatic state, for example, a diabetic failing to eat after taking insulin. The law on this comes from the case of *Bailey* (1983).

Bailey (1983)

D was a diabetic who had failed to eat enough after taking his insulin to control the diabetes. He became aggressive and hit someone over the head with an iron bar. The Court of Appeal ruled that if the offence charged is one of specific intent, then self-induced automatism can be a defence. This is because the defendant lacks the required *mens rea*.

However, if the offence charged is one of basic intent then:

1. The prosecution will have to prove the necessary element of recklessness for the particular offence the defendant has been charged with. For example, in cases of assault if the defendant knows that his conduct is likely to make him aggressive, unpredictable or uncontrolled with the result that he may cause some injury to others, then it is open to the jury to find that he was reckless.
2. Where the self-induced automatic state is caused through drink or illegal drugs or other intoxicating substances the defendant cannot

Insanity	Automatism
For defence to prove on the balance of probabilities	For defendant to raise, the prosecution must then disprove
Must have a defect of reason due to disease of the mind M'Naghten Rules	Must be caused by an external factor
Example: Diabetic affected by disease *Hennessey* (1989)	Example: Diabetic affected by (drug) insulin *Quick* (1973)
Verdict: not guilty by reason of insanity	Verdict: not guilty

Figure 5.3 Comparison of insanity and automatism as defences

use the defence of automatism. This is because *DPP v Majewski* (1976) decided that becoming voluntarily intoxicated is a reckless course of conduct (see 5.3.1).

3. Where the defendant does not know that his actions are likely to lead to a self-induced automatic state in which he may commit an offence, he has not been reckless and can use the defence of automatism.

This third situation was seen in *Hardie* (1984).

Hardie (1984)

The defendant was depressed because his girlfriend had told him to move out of their flat. He took some valium tablets which had been prescribed for his girlfriend. He then set fire to a wardrobe in the flat. He said he did not know what he was doing because of the valium. The trial judge directed the jury to ignore the effect of the tablets and he was convicted of arson.

The Court of Appeal quashed his conviction as the defendant had taken the drug because he thought it would calm him down. This is the normal effect of valium. So the defendant had not been reckless and the defence of automatism should have been left to the jury.

5.2.3 Problems with the law on automatism

The main problem is that in each case it has to be decided whether the situation is one of insane

automatism or non-insane automatism. This is very important as the effect of these two types of automatism as a defence is so different.

Situations which would seem to the non-lawyer to be ones of non-insane automatism, such as a diabetic being in a high blood sugar state, or someone sleep-walking, may at law be considered to be insane-automatism.

5.2.4 Proposals for reform

In the Draft Criminal Code (1989) the following definition was suggested:

> 'A person is not guilty of an offence if –
> (a) he acts in a state of automatism, that is his act
>   (i) is a reflex, spasm or convulsion; or
>   (ii) occurs while he is in a condition (whether of sleep, unconsciousness, impaired consciousness or otherwise) depriving him of effective control of his act; and
> (b) the act or condition is the result neither of anything done or omitted with the fault required for the offence nor of voluntary intoxication.

This definition would include those who act during an epileptic convulsion, so that cases such as *Sullivan* (1984) would be able to use the defence of non-insane automatism instead of insanity. This would be a welcome improvement to the law.

Also cases of sleep-walking would come under this defence. This would have given *Burgess* (1991) the defence of non-insane automatism. Under the present law he was found not guilty by reason of insanity.

In both these cases the defendants under the proposals for reform would have had a full defence. On the other hand, the present system allows a judge to order medical treatment for those who are found not guilty by reason of insanity. Should there be some way of making sure that those who commit dangerous offences whilst in an automatic state, and who would benefit from treatment, do in fact receive treatment?

5.3 Intoxication

This covers intoxication by alcohol, drugs or other substances, such as glue-sniffing. Intoxication does not provide a defence as such, but is relevant as to whether or not the defendant has the required *mens rea* for the offence. If he does not have the required *mens rea* because of his intoxicated state, he may be not guilty.

Whether the defendant is guilty or not depends on:

1. whether the intoxication was voluntary or involuntary; and
2. whether the offence charged is one of specific or basic intent.

Specific intent offences are generally those which require specific intention for their *mens rea*. For the purposes of AQA Unit 3 specification, specific intent offences are murder and s 18 OAPA.

Basic intent offences are generally those for which recklessness is sufficient for the *mens rea*. For the purposes of AQA Unit 3 specification, basic intent offences are manslaughter, s 20 and s 47 OAPA and assault and battery.

5.3.1 Voluntary intoxication

Voluntary intoxication is where the defendant has chosen to take an intoxicating substance. This can be by taking alcohol, illegal drugs or other intoxicants such as through sniffing glue. It can also occur where the defendant knows that the effect of a prescribed drug will be to make him intoxicated.

Voluntary intoxication and specific intent offences

Voluntary intoxication can negate the *mens rea* for a specific intent offence. If the defendant is so intoxicated that he has not formed the *mens rea* for the offence, he is not guilty. For example, in *Sheehan and Moore* (1975) the defendants were very drunk when they threw petrol over a tramp and set fire to him. They were too drunk to have formed any intent to kill or cause grievous bodily harm. It was held that because they did not have the *mens rea* for murder their intoxication was a defence to that offence. However, they were found guilty of manslaughter as that is a basic intent offence.

Where the defendant has the necessary *mens rea* despite his intoxicated state, then he is guilty of the offence. The intoxication does not provide a defence. It has been held that a drunken intent is still an intent. This was shown by *AG for Northern Ireland v Gallagher* (1963) where the defendant decided to kill his wife. He bought a knife to do the killing and also a bottle of whisky. He drank a large amount of the whisky before killing his wife. His conviction for murder was upheld.

Voluntary intoxication and basic intent offences

Where the offence charged is one of basic intent then intoxication is not a defence. This is because voluntarily becoming intoxicated is considered a reckless course of conduct, and recklessness is enough to constitute the necessary *mens rea*. This was decided in *DPP v Majewski* (1976).

Majewski (1976)

The defendant had taken both alcohol and drugs. In a very intoxicated state he then attacked people in a public house and also the police officers who tried to arrest him. He was convicted of three offences of assault occasioning actual bodily harm (s 47 OAPA) and three of assaulting a police officer in the execution of his duty. The House of Lords upheld all these convictions; his intoxicated state was not a defence.

This decision has caused problems because it appears to have the effect that voluntary intoxication can never be a defence to a basic intent offence.

Lord Elwyn-Jones in his judgment in the House of Lords said that a defendant who voluntarily gets into an intoxicated state:

> 'supplies the evidence of *mens rea*, of guilty mind certainly sufficient for crimes of basic intent. It is a reckless course of conduct and recklessness is enough to constitute the necessary *mens rea* in assault cases.'

This seems a very harsh line to take and the courts have adopted a different approach in some other cases. They have taken the view that the jury should consider whether the defendant would have realised the risk had he not been intoxicated. This was the line taken in *Richardson and Irwin* (1998).

Richardson and Irwin (1998)

The defendants and the victim were university students. They had each drunk about five pints of lager. They then started 'horseplaying'. During this the victim was lifted over the edge of a balcony and dropped about ten feet, suffering serious injury. The defendants' convictions under s 20 of the Offences Against the Person Act 1861 were quashed. The Court of Appeal held that the jury should have been directed to consider whether the defendants would have realised the risk if they had not been drinking.

So, if the jury in such a case decide that the defendants would not have realised the risk of some injury to the victim even if they had been sober, then the jury should find the defendants not guilty. The mere fact of being intoxicated does not automatically make the defendants guilty.

5.3.2 Involuntary intoxication

Involuntary intoxication covers situations where the defendant did not know he was taking an intoxicating substance. This may be where, for example, a soft drink has been 'laced' with alcohol or drugs. It also covers situations where prescribed drugs have the unexpected effect of making the defendant intoxicated.

The test is, did the defendant have the necessary *mens rea* when he committed the offence? If so, it was decided in *Kingston* (1994) that he will be guilty. The involuntary intoxication will not provide a defence. This is so even though the defendant would not have committed the offence without the intoxication lowering his resistance to committing the offence.

Kingston (1994)

The defendant's coffee was drugged by someone who wanted to blackmail him. He was then shown a 15-year-old boy who was asleep and invited to abuse him. The defendant did so and was photographed by the blackmailer. The House of Lords upheld his conviction for indecent assault. They held that if a defendant had formed the *mens rea* for an offence then the involuntary intoxication was not a defence.

Where, however, the defendant did not have the necessary intent, he will be not guilty. He has no *mens rea* and so cannot be guilty of a specific intent offence. Neither can he be guilty of a basic intent offence. This is because the defendant has not been reckless in getting intoxicated. An example of this is *Hardie* (1984) (see 5.2.2) where the defendant took valium tablets not knowing they could make his behaviour unpredictable. See also 5.4.1 for the effect of a drunken mistake.

5.3.3 Problems in the law on intoxication

Some areas of the law on intoxication appear to be contrary to the normal rules on *mens rea* and *actus reus*. In particular this is seen in the decision in *DPP v Majewski* (1977). The decision in this case, that the defendant is guilty of a basic intent offence because getting drunk is a 'reckless course of conduct', ignores the principle that *mens rea* and *actus reus* must coincide. The decision to drink may be several hours before the defendant commits the actus reus of any offence. For example, in *O'Grady* the defendant had fallen

Shorry, I thought you were a martian.

asleep and only committed the act of hitting his friend some hours afterwards.

In addition, the recklessness in becoming

Key facts

	Specific intent crimes	Basic intent crimes
Voluntary intoxication	If defendant has *mens rea* he is guilty – *Gallagher* (1963) If defendant has no *mens rea* he is not guilty	Becoming intoxicated is a reckless course of conduct – *Majewski* (1977). The defendant is guilty of the offence
Involuntary intoxication	If defendant has *mens rea* he is guilty – *Kingston* (1994) If defendant has no *mens rea* he is not guilty – *Hardie* (1984)	The defendant has not been reckless in becoming intoxicated, so not guilty – *Hardie* (1984)
Drunken mistake	If the mistake negates *mens rea* the defendant is not guilty If the mistake is about the need to defend oneself it is not a defence. The defendant will be guilty – *O'Grady* (1987) *Hatton* (2005)	Getting drunk is a reckless course of conduct, so the defendant is guilty

Key facts chart on intoxication as a defence

intoxicated means that the defendant takes a general risk of doing something 'stupid' when drunk. At the time of getting intoxicated the defendant has no idea that he will actually commit an offence. Normally, for offences where recklessness is sufficient of the *mens rea* of an offence, it has to be proved that D knew there was a risk of the specific offence being committed.

This point was considered by the Law Commission in a consultation paper in 1993. They said in that paper that the *Majewski* rule was arbitrary and unfair. However, the Law Commission's proposals for changing the law were severely criticised and by the time they published firm proposals for reform of the law in 1995 they had changed their opinion. By this time they thought that the present law operated 'fairly, on the whole, and without undue difficulty'.

The alternative approach to the *Majewski* decision as taken in *Richardson and Irwin* does make the law fairer. Under this the magistrates or the jury have to consider whether a defendant would have realised the relevant risk if he had not been drinking. The mere fact of being intoxicated does not automatically make a defendant guilty.

However, there are problems with this approach as it is very difficult to know what a particular defendant would have realised if he had been sober. In *Richardson and Irwin* one of the judges in the Court of Appeal pointed out that 'the defendants were not hypothetical reasonable men, but University students'. So would they have realised the risk of dropping someone over a balcony if they had been sober?

Specific intent/basic intent

Where a defendant is charged with murder or a s 18 assault he can use intoxication as a defence. However, because intoxication is not a defence to a basic intent offence, such a defendant can be found guilty of a lower level offence. These are manslaughter where murder is charged or an offence under s 20 of the Offences Against the Person Act 1861 where a s 18 offence has been charged.

However, for other crimes there is often no 'fall-back' offence. If a defendant is charged with theft and successfully claims that he did not form the *mens rea* for theft because he was too intoxicated, he will be not guilty of any offence.

Involuntary intoxication

A final point where the law could be thought to be in need of reform is where the defendant's inhibitions are broken down by being made intoxicated involuntarily. The decision in *Kingston* (1994) makes such a defendant guilty if he formed the necessary *mens rea*. This ignores the fact that the defendant was not to blame for the intoxication.

Public policy issues

Many of the contradictions in the law on intoxication have arisen because the law in this area is largely policy based. This is because of two main reasons:

1. Intoxication is a major factor in the commission of many crimes; many offences are committed when D is in an intoxicated state;
2. There is a need to balance the rights of the defendant and the victim; if intoxication were always to be a defence, then victims' rights would not be protected.

Public policy can be clearly seen in the law on self-defence, defence of another and prevention of crime. Parliament has enacted (in s 76(5) Criminal Justice and Immigration Act 2008) that D cannot rely on 'any mistaken belief attributable to intoxication that was voluntarily induced' when claiming any of these defences.

5.4 Self-defence/defence of another

This covers not only actions needed to defend oneself from an attack, but also actions taken to defend another. The defences of self-defence and defence of another are common law defences which justify the defendant's actions. In addition there is a statutory defence of prevention of crime under s 3(1) of the Criminal Law Act 1967 which states that:

> 'a person may use such force as is reasonable in the circumstances in the prevention of crime'.

There are two main points to be decided. These are:

- was the use of force necessary? If it was, then
- was the force used reasonable in the circumstances?

5.4.1 Was force necessary?

The first point to be decided if the defence is to succeed is whether force was necessary. This is a question for the jury. In many cases it is straightforward. For example, if the facts are that the victim had a knife in his hand and came towards the defendant saying 'I'm going to slash you to pieces', it is quite clear that force is necessary in self-defence in this situation.

However, if someone taps you on the arm but does nothing else, it is almost certain that force is not necessary. The situation would be different if after tapping you on the arm, the person then said something threatening, indicating that a further assault was about to take place. Force might be now necessary in self-defence. It depends on the circumstances in each case.

5.4.2 Mistaken use of force in self-defence

Where the defendant has made a mistake about what is happening it is more difficult to decide if force was necessary. Where the defendant makes a genuine mistake the jury have to decide whether force was necessary in the circumstances that the defendant honestly believed existed.

For example, what if, while walking home in the dark, the defendant sees a large man who is shaking a club above his head in a threatening

way coming towards him? D thinks it is necessary to defend himself and punches the man hard, knocking him to the ground. However in reality, the 'large man' was an elderly woman, and the 'shaking a club' was the woman trying to open an umbrella above her head.

The jury have to decide if D honestly believed he was being threatened. If they decide that he did, then he has the defence of self-defence. He can use force, even though there was no actual threat to him. In this situation an innocent person (the woman trying to open her umbrella) has been punched but D's behaviour is not a criminal offence.

Genuine mistake

In looking at the circumstances, the defendant must be judged on the facts as he genuinely believed them to be. In *Williams* (1987) it was ruled that the defendant should be judged according to his genuine mistaken view of the facts, regardless of whether this mistake was reasonable or unreasonable. This allowed *Williams* to use the defence of protection of others.

Williams (1987)

D was on a bus when he saw what he thought was a man assaulting a youth. In fact it was a man trying to arrest the youth for mugging an old lady. D got off the bus and asked what was happening. The man said that he was a police officer arresting the youth, but when D asked him to show his police ID card he could not do so. There was then a struggle between D and the man in which the man was injured. D was convicted of assault after the judge directed them that D only had a defence if his mistake was a reasonable one.

The Court of Appeal quashed his conviction because the jury should have been told that if they thought the mistake was genuine they should judge the defendant according to his genuine mistaken view of the facts, regardless of whether this mistake was reasonable or unreasonable.

Section 76 of the Criminal Justice and Immigration Act 2008 puts the decision in *Williams* onto a statutory footing. The section states:

 S.76(4) If D claims to have held a particular belief as regards the existence of any circumstances –
(a) the reasonableness or otherwise of that belief is relevant to the question whether D genuinely held it; but
(b) if it is determined that D did genuinely hold it, D is entitled to rely on it for the purposes of subsection (3), whether or not –
(i) it was mistaken, or
(ii) (if it was mistaken) the mistake was a reasonable one to have made.

So in each situation, the important point is what were the facts as the defendant genuinely believed them to be. If the defendant genuinely made a mistake then he is to be judged on the facts as he believed them to be. This is so even if the mistake was unreasonable.

Drunken mistake

Section 76(5) of the Criminal Justice and Immigration Act 2008 makes it clear that a defendant cannot rely on any mistaken belief if that mistake is made due to the defendant being voluntarily intoxicated.

If the defendant made the mistake because he had voluntarily got drunk or taken drugs, and makes a mistake because of his intoxicated state, then he cannot rely on his mistaken belief. An example would be where a defendant had taken drugs which caused hallucinations causing him or her to believe that they were being attacked by snakes. If the defendant then assaults someone believing that person is a snake then the defendant cannot use the defence of self-defence. He genuinely believes he is being attacked by a snake, but this mistake has been caused by the defendant's voluntary intoxication.

5.4.3 Degree of force

The amount of force which can be used in self-defence, defence of another or in prevention of crime is now explained in the Criminal Justice and Immigration Act 2008. This states that, in deciding whether the force used is reasonable in the circumstances:

 '(a) that a person acting for a legitimate purpose may not be able to weigh to a nicety the exact measure of any necessary action; and
(b) that evidence of a person's having only done what the person honestly and instinctively thought was necessary for a legitimate purpose constitutes strong evidence that only reasonable action was taken by that person for that purpose.'

This allows for the fact that a person who is facing an attack by another is under stress and cannot be expected to calculate the exact amount of force which needs to be used in the circumstances. If there is evidence that the person 'honestly and instinctively' thought the level of force he used to protect himself or another or to prevent crime, then this provides strong evidence that the defensive action taken was reasonable in the circumstances.

However, if the force is used after all danger from the assailant is over (ie as retaliation or revenge), the defence is not available.

The Criminal Justice and Immigration Act 2008 makes it clear that the degree of force has to be measured against the circumstances as the defendant believed them to be. So, if the defendant genuinely believed that his attacker had a gun, the degree of force is what would be reasonable in those circumstances.

However, if the defendant makes a mistake about the degree of force needed because he was voluntarily intoxicated, then he cannot rely on that mistake. This rule is set out in s 76(5) of the Criminal Justice and Immigration Act 2008.

5.4.4 Problems in the law on self-defence etc

Pre-emptive strike

One point is whether a person has to wait until they are attacked before they can use force. The law appears to be clear that they can act to prevent force. It is not necessary for an attack to have started. In the example in 5.4.2 of the defendant believing he was about to be attacked by a large man with a club, no attack had started. D thought he was about to be attacked and reacted to save himself from being attacked. This appears to be a sensible rule, since it would be ridiculous if a person had to wait until they were stabbed or shot before being allowed to defend themselves.

In *Attorney-General's Reference (No 2 of 1983)* (1984) it was held that someone who fears an attack can make preparations to defend himself. This is so even if the preparations involve breaches of the law.

Attorney-General's Reference (No 2 of 1983) (1984)

D's shop had been attacked and damaged by rioters. Fearing further attacks, he made petrol bombs. D was charged with possessing an explosive substance in such circumstances as to give rise to a reasonable suspicion that he did not have it for a lawful object (contrary to s 4(10) of the Explosive Substances Act 1883). D pleaded self-defence and the jury acquitted him. The Attorney-General referred the point of law to the Court of Appeal which decided that it was correct that D could make preparations in self-defence.

Excessive force

A major problem is where a defendant uses excessive force in self-defence. If this is so they cannot use self-defence as a defence. If they are charged with any assault charge then the judge can only take any issues of self-defence into consideration when passing sentence. However, where such a defendant is charged with murder they must be given a life sentence as the judges have no discretion in sentencing.

This was seen in the cases of *Clegg* (1995) and *Martin (Anthony)* (2002). The facts of both cases are set out in Chapter 1 at section 1.5.5.

However, the Government consultation paper *Murder, manslaughter and infanticide: proposals for reform of the law* has a proposal for a partial defence of 'killing in response to a fear of serious violence'. This would be available to someone who overreacts to what they perceive as an imminent threat and would reduce the charge to manslaughter. If this proposal becomes law, then defendants such as *Clegg* and *Martin (Anthony)* would be able to use this partial defence.

Relevance of D's characteristics

Another point is whether D's characteristics can be taken into account in deciding if D thought that he needed to defend himself.

In *Martin (Anthony)* (2002) the Court of Appeal held that psychiatric evidence that D had a condition that meant that he perceived much greater danger than the average person was NOT relevant to the question of whether D had used reasonable force. One of the reasons for this decision was that self-defence is usually raised in cases of minor assault and it would be 'wholly disproportionate to encourage medical disputes in cases of that sort'.

Also, in *Cairns* (2005) the Court of Appeal followed the decision in *Martin* and held that when deciding whether D had used reasonable force in self-defence, it was not appropriate to take into account whether D was suffering from a psychiatric condition (such as paranoid schizophrenia) which may have caused him to have a delusion that he was about to be attacked.

It is difficult to know whether these decisions are still effective following the passing of the Criminal Justice and Immigration Act 2008. Section 76 of that Act makes it clear that the question of whether the degree of force used by D was reasonable in the circumstances is to be decided by reference to the circumstances as D believed them to be. The section goes on to say that if the jury (or magistrates) decide that D did genuinely have a belief in the existence of particular circumstances, then D is entitled to rely on it.

If D's psychiatric condition makes him genuinely believe that force is necessary and the court accepts that he believed this, then surely, under the wording of the Act, D must be able to claim self-defence. However, it is doubtful that this is the interpretation that the courts will use. It would have been helpful if the Act had made it clear whether a psychiatric condition which caused D to believe in the existence of circumstances was to be taken into account or not.

5.5 Consent

Consent is always a defence to a common assault or battery. This is because there is no injury caused. In these circumstances the law will not interfere with people's rights to do what they wish.

However, where an injury is caused, then consent is not a defence unless the situation is one recognised as an exception to this rule on the basis of public policy. These are discussed in 5.5.3.

Consent is strictly speaking not a defence, since where the other person consents this means there is no offence. For example, where the other person consents to being touched then there is no battery as there is no unlawful force.

This was illustrated by *Slingsby* (1995) where the defendant was charged with involuntary manslaughter by an unlawful act.

Slingsby (1995)

The defendant and the victim had taken part in sexual activity which was described as 'vigorous' but which had taken place with the victim's consent. During this a signet ring which the defendant was wearing caused small cuts to the victim, which led to blood poisoning from which she died. The victim's consent meant that there was no battery or other form of assault and so the defendant was held to be not guilty of manslaughter as there was no unlawful act.

There must, however, be true consent. This was illustrated in *Tabassum* (2000).

Tabassum (2000)

The defendant had persuaded women to allow him to measure their breasts for the purpose of preparing a database for sale to doctors. The women were fully aware of the nature of the acts he proposed to do, but they said they consented only because they thought that the defendant had either medical qualifications or medical training. The Court of Appeal approved the trial judge's direction when he said:

'I should prefer myself to say that consent in such cases does not exist at all, because the act consented to is not the act done. Consent to a surgical operation or examination is not consent to sexual connection or indecent behaviour'.

The fact that the victim submits to the defendant's conduct through fear does not mean the consent is real. This was shown by *Olugboja* (1982).

The victim had already been raped by D's companion and seen her friend raped by the same man. When D tried to have sexual intercourse with her, she submitted. D claimed that this meant she had consented. The Court of Appeal held that there was a difference between real consent and mere submission. It was for the jury to decide if the consent was real.

Informed consent

In the old case of *Clarence* (1888) 22 QBD 23 the courts had ruled that if a person consented to sexual intercourse there was no assault. It did not matter that V was unaware that the defendant was suffering from a sexually transmitted disease.

Clarence (1888)

Unknown to the wife, the husband was suffering from a venereal disease and the wife became infected. She had consented to sexual intercourse with him. It was held that her consent meant that there was no assault, even though she did not know that her husband was infected.

This remained the law until *Dica* (2004), when the Court of Appeal confirmed that *Clarence* (1888) was wrongly decided.

Dica (2004)

D, who knew he was HIV positive, had unprotected sex on a number of occasions with two women. They said they did not know that he was HIV positive and, that if they had known, they would not have agreed to unprotected sex. Both women became infected. D was convicted of two counts of inflicting 'biological' GBH contrary to s 20 OAPA 1861. Although his

convictions were quashed by the Court of Appeal because of a judicial misdirection and a re-trial was ordered, the Court took the opportunity to overrule *Clarence*. They did this on the basis that, following the decision in *Burstow* (see 4.3.3), it is no longer necessary to prove an assault for s 20 and that the victim had to consent to the risk of being infected by the disease.

At *Dica's* retrial in March 2005, he was again convicted of inflicting 'biological' GBH and sentenced to $4^1/_2$ years in prison. The *Dica* ruling was relied on shortly afterwards in the similar case of *Konzani* (2005) where the defendant had had unprotected sex with three women. He knew that he was HIV positive, but none of the three women knew this.

The judge in *Konzani* directed the jury as follows: 'If a little bird had whispered in the ear of one of the women as she was about to have unprotected sex with [D], "Would you be doing this if you knew he was HIV infected?", would she reply "No I wouldn't", or would she reply "It doesn't matter, I'll be all right."? If it's the former you have to find him guilty, if it's the latter you must find him not guilty.'

5.5.1 Implied consent

There are situations in which the courts imply consent to minor touchings, which would otherwise be a battery. These are the everyday situations in which there is a crowd of people and it is impossible not to have some contact. In *Wilson v Pringle* (1987) it was held that the ordinary 'jostlings' of everyday life were not battery. Nobody can complain of the jostling which is inevitable from his presence in, for example, a supermarket, an underground station or a busy street; nor can a person who attends a party complain if his hand is seized in friendship, or even if his back is (within reason) slapped.

This also applies to contact sports. When a person takes part in sport such as rugby or judo he is agreeing to the contact which is part of that sport. However, if the contact goes beyond what is allowed within the rules then it is possible for an offence to be committed. For example, a rugby player consents to a tackle within the rules of the game, but he does not consent to an opposition player stamping on his head.

5.5.2 Consent to minor injuries

There have been arguments as to whether consent could be a defence to an offence under s 47 of the Offences Against the Person Act 1861. It used to be thought that consent could always be a defence where the injuries were not serious. However, in *Attorney-General's Reference (No 6 of 1980)* (1981) the Court of Appeal held otherwise.

Attorney-General's Reference (No 6 of 1980) (1981)

Two young men agreed to fight in the street to settle their differences following a quarrel. The Court of Appeal held that consent could not be a defence to such an action as it was not in the public interest. They said:

'It is not in the public interest that people should try to cause, or should cause, each other bodily harm for no good reason. Minor struggles are another matter. So, in our judgment, it is immaterial whether the act occurs in private or public; it is an assault if actual bodily harm is intended and/or caused. This means that most fights will be unlawful regardless of consent.'

In *Brown* (1993) the House of Lords had to consider whether consent could be a defence to offences under s 47 and s 20 of the Offences Against the Person Act 1861.

Brown (1993)

Five men in a group of consenting adult sado-masochists were convicted of offences of assault under s 47 and s 20. They had carried out acts which included applying stinging nettles to the genital area and inserting map pins or fish hooks into the penises of each other. All the victims had consented and none had needed medical attention. Their convictions were upheld by the House of Lords.

The defence argued that the defence of consent should be allowed for s 47 offences, even if it was not allowed for s 20 offences. This was rejected. Lord Templeman said:

> ❝ 'I do not consider this solution is practicable. Sado-masochistic participants have no way of foretelling the degree of bodily harm which will result from their encounters.' ❞

So it is now accepted that consent is not a defence to a s 47 offence, unless the situation is one of the exceptions which have been recognised by the courts.

5.5.3 Public policy exceptions

The courts have recognised the following as public policy exceptions where consent is a defence to an assault charge even if injury is caused:

- properly conducted games or sports
- reasonable surgical interference
- tattooing
- body piercing
- horseplay
- dangerous exhibitions.

It is seen as being in the public interest to allow consent as a defence in these situations. For example, many sports could not be played if consent was not a defence. Also, in surgical operations, it is usually necessary to cut the patient's skin in order to deal with their health problem.

5.5.4 Contact sports

In general, consent is not available as a defence where actual bodily harm is intended or likely to be caused. However, as seen above, public policy exceptions include 'mutual manly contests' and 'rough and undisciplined sport or play where there is no anger and no intention to cause bodily harm'.

This applies to contact sports. When a person takes part in a sport such as rugby or judo, he is agreeing to the contact which is part of that sport. However, if the contact goes beyond what is allowed within the rules then it is possible for an offence to be committed. For example, a rugby player consents to a tackle within the rules of the game, but he does not consent to an opposition player stamping on his head.

However, the breach of the rules of the sport must be a serious one. The Court of Appeal said in *Barnes* (2004) that where an injury is caused during a match, then a criminal prosecution should be reserved for those situations where the conduct was sufficiently grave to be properly categorised as criminal.

Barnes (2004)

D made a late tackle on V during an amateur football match. V suffered a serious leg injury. D's conviction of an offence under s 20 of the Offences Against the Person Act 1861 was quashed.

The Court of Appeal said that the starting point was the fact that most organised sports had their own disciplinary procedures for enforcing their particular rules and standards of conduct. They also pointed out that there was the possibility of an injured player obtaining damages in a civil action. A criminal prosecution should be reserved for situations where the conduct was sufficiently grave to be properly categorised as criminal. In all contact sports, the participants impliedly consent to the risk of certain levels of harm.

The Court of Appeal set out the following points:

- consent is not normally available as a defence where there is bodily harm, but sporting activities are one of the exceptions to this rule;
- the exceptions are based on public policy;
- in contact sports, conduct which goes beyond

what a player can reasonably be regarded as having accepted by taking part, is not covered by the defence of consent;
- however, in a sport in which bodily contact is a commonplace part of the game, the players consent to such contact, even if through an unfortunate accident serious injury may result.

In deciding whether conduct in the course of a sport is criminal or not the following factors should be considered:

- intentional infliction of injury will always be criminal;
- for reckless infliction of injury – did the injury occur during actual play, or in a moment of temper or over-excitement when play has ceased;
- 'off the ball' injuries are more likely to be criminal;
- the fact that the play is within the rules and practice of the game and does not go beyond it will be a firm indication that what has happened is not criminal.

The type of sport, the level at which it was played, the nature of the act, the degree of force used, the extent of the risk of injury and D's state of mind are all likely to be relevant in determining whether D's actions went beyond a breach of the rules and became a criminal offence.

5.5.5 Body adornment

Tattooing is accepted as body adornment. It is accepted that people can consent to it.

Wilson (1996)

A defendant branded his initials on his wife's buttocks with a hot knife at her request. However, she had to seek medical attention for the burns which were caused and her husband was charged with an offence under s 47 of the Offences Against the Person Act 1861. The Court of Appeal held the branding was not an unlawful act, even though it had caused injury. It was not in the public interest that such consensual behaviour should be criminalised. This was a situation of 'personal adornment', like having a tattoo.

The important point was that the act was for body adornment. The court compared it to piercing of nostrils or tongues for the purposes of inserting decorative jewellery. They also pointed out that the husband did not have any aggressive intent. It was for these reasons that consent was allowed as a defence.

5.5.6 Horseplay

In *Jones* (1986) the Court of Appeal held that consent could be a defence to an assault charge where the activity the defendants and victim had engaged in was 'rough and undisciplined horseplay'.

Jones (1986)

Two schoolboys aged 14 and 15 were tossed into the air by older youths. One victim suffered a broken arm and the other a ruptured spleen. The defendants claimed they believed that the two victims consented to the activity. The Court of Appeal quashed their convictions for offences under s 20 of the Offences Against the Person Act 1861 because the judge had not allowed the issue of mistaken belief in consent to go to the jury. The court held that a genuine mistaken belief in consent to 'rough and undisciplined horseplay' could be a defence, even if that belief was unreasonable.

This exception is more difficult to reconcile with the idea that it is in the public interest. It does not seem to be so very different from the youths agreeing to fight in case of the *Attorney-General's Reference (No 6 of 1980)*. However, a distinguishing feature is that those engaging in

such behaviour do not usually intend to cause injury, whereas when two people agree to fight they intend to cause each other injury.

5.5.7 Mistaken belief in consent

Where the defendant genuinely, but mistakenly, believes that the victim is consenting, then there is a defence to an assault. In this area the decisions of the courts are even more difficult to reconcile with the general principle that 'it is not in the public interest that people should try to cause, or should cause, each other bodily harm for no good reason'. This was seen in the case of *Jones* (1986) above.

A similar decision was reached in *Aitken* (1992).

Aitken (1992)

RAF officers poured white spirit over a colleague who was wearing a fire-resistant flying suit, but who was asleep and drunk at the time this was done. They then set the suit on fire, and he suffered 35 per cent burns. Their convictions under s 20 were quashed as the mistaken belief in the victim's consent should have been left to the jury.

In *Richardson and Irwin* (1999) it was even held that a drunken mistake that the victim was consenting to horseplay could be a defence to a charge under s 20.

Richardson and Irwin (1999)

The Ds, who were students, had often indulged in horseplay. On this occasion they had drunk about five pints of lager when they started 'playing about'. They dropped V from a balcony causing him to be seriously injured. The Court of Appeal allowed their appeals as their belief in V's consent should have been considered.

5.5.8 Need for a defence of consent

It is important to allow a defence of consent in some situations. For example, if there was no defence of consent then contact sports would all be illegal. This is why the Court of Appeal in *Attorney-General's Reference (No 6 of 1980)* (1981) stated that, although consent was not a defence to street fights, there were exceptions where consent was a defence.

The list of exceptions that the Court of Appeal gave in that case included 'properly conducted games and sports, reasonable surgical interference, dangerous exhibitions, etc'. These exceptions are based on public policy.

If there was no defence of consent in 'properly conducted games and sports' then team games such as football, rugby and hockey could never be played. There would also be a large number of individual sports which would be prevented, for example, judo, karate and boxing.

The important phrase in the judgment is 'properly conducted games and sports'. There has to be a distinction between playing according to the rules and behaviour which is outside the rules. A deliberate 'off the ball' tackle aiming at another player's legs with the intention of causing serious injury must surely be considered as criminal behaviour. A player who is injured in this way has not consented to such behaviour.

The case of *Barnes* (2004) set out matters which were to be considered in deciding whether an assault had taken place in the course of a match. The court said that in deciding whether conduct in the course of a sport is criminal or not the following factors should be considered:

- intentional infliction of injury will always be criminal
- for reckless infliction of injury – did the injury occur during actual play, or in a moment of temper or over-excitement when play has ceased
- 'off the ball' injuries are more likely to be criminal
- the fact that the play is within the rules and practice of the game and does not go beyond it

will be a firm indication that what has happened is not criminal.

Medical procedures

Another exception where consent is allowed as a defence is 'reasonable surgical interference'. Clearly where the surgery is needed to save the patient's life or to improve a patient's health in some way, then consent to the operation is a defence to any charge of assault.

Mentally capable adults can consent to reasonable medical treatment or they can refuse it. If they refuse consent, if surgery or other treatment was then performed it would be a criminal act. For example, if a person refuses a blood transfusion because of their religious beliefs then such treatment cannot be given.

If a patient is unconscious and their consent cannot be asked, medical staff will try to obtain consent from relatives. If this is not possible then, where treatment is necessary and must be performed quickly, then such an operation can be performed without actual consent.

5.5.9 Problems in the law on consent

It is difficult to reconcile the decisions by the courts in cases on consent. For example, compare the case of *Brown* (1994) with the case of *Wilson* (1997).

In *Brown* the House of Lords ruled that consent could not be a defence to sado-masochistic behaviour between consenting adult homosexuals. In *Wilson* the Court of Appeal ruled that consent could be a defence where a husband had branded his wife's buttocks with his initials. These decisions were made despite the fact that none of the 'victims' in *Brown* had needed medical attention whereas the wife in *Wilson* had had to receive medical attention. These cases can be distinguished by the fact that causing pain for sexual gratification is not allowed, but causing pain for body adornment is allowed.

However, these cases can suggest that the courts are prepared to condone acts where the parties are consenting adult heterosexuals, but not where the parties are consenting adult homosexuals. Are the courts trying to impose their own moral values on the law?

There are also contradictory decisions within cases involving heterosexuals. In *Emmett* (1999), where 'high-risk' sexual activity between a man and a woman had resulted in the woman suffering haemorrhages to her eyes on one occasion and burns to her breast on another occasion, the Court of Appeal held that consent could not be a defence. The basis for this decision was that consent cannot be a defence where the harm caused is more than 'transient or trivial' injury. Yet in *Wilson* the Court of Appeal had accepted consent as a defence even though the wife had needed medical attention. However, a distinction can again be made on the basis that causing pain for sexual gratification is not allowed, but causing pain for body adornment is allowed.

Horseplay

Another area of law where the courts are prepared to accept consent as a defence is in what is called 'horseplay'. That is where those of a similar age use 'friendly' violence to each other. This is seen in the playground of schools where boys, in particular, often push each other or trip each other up in play.

Even where such behaviour results in serious injury the courts have ruled that consent can be a defence. This is the legal basis that the aggressor does not have the *mens rea* for assault. Even more surprisingly, the courts have held that honest belief in consent provides a defence although the victim in fact has not consented.

This is shown in the cases of *Jones and another* (1986) and *Aitken* (1992). In *Jones* two schoolboys aged 14 and 15 were tossed into the air by older youths. One victim suffered a broken arm and the other a ruptured spleen. In *Aitken* the victim suffered 35 per cent burns when RAF officers poured white spirit over him when he was asleep

and drunk. At the time he was wearing a fire-resistant flying suit. In both cases the courts accepted that the defence of consent was available, even though there was a mistaken belief in the existence of consent.

When these cases are contrasted with *Brown* (1994) and *Emmett* (1999) above there appear to be further inconsistencies in the law. Why should consent be refused as a defence for disapproved types of sexual behaviour and yet allowed for horseplay which results in serious injury, even where the victim was not actually consenting?

5.5.10 Consent and sexual offences

There are specific problems for offences under the Sexual Offences Act 2003 as the defence of consent is not always available. One such offence is section 5 of the Act which covers the offence of rape of a child under 13. For the purposes of this offence a girl under 13 is presumed never to be able to consent to sexual intercourse. The offence is also a strict liability one.

These two facts mean that if a 15-year-old boy has consensual sex with a girl whom he genuinely believes is the same age as himself, but is in fact only 12, he will be guilty of rape of a child under 13.

This situation occurred in *G* (2008). At the appeal to the Court of Appeal, the court had stated that consent was relevant only to sentence. G appealed against his conviction on the basis that his human rights had been breached. The House of Lords rejected his appeal by a majority of three judges to two. But the fact that two House of Lords judges would have decided the case in favour of the defendant shows how difficult this area of law is.

5.5.11 Consent and euthanasia

There is also a problem that no-one can consent to their own death. This means that if a terminally ill patient wishes to die, they must take their own life. If anyone kills them, it is murder. Even if anyone assists them to take their own life that person is guilty of the offence of assisting suicide. This was decided in *R (on the application of Pretty) v DPP* (2001).

R (on the application of Pretty) v DPP (2001)

Mrs Pretty was suffering from motor neurone disease. As a result she was becoming more and more incapable of movement. She knew that eventually she would suffocate to death. She wanted her husband to be able to assist her to take her own life when she felt that her life had become intolerable.

She applied to the courts for a judicial declaration that, if her husband assisted her to commit suicide, he would not be prosecuted. The House of Lords refused the declaration on the basis that any assistance of the husband would be a criminal act.

This decision leads to the situation where the law recognises that people are entitled to take their own life and do not commit any crime by trying to do so. But in cases where the person who wishes to commit suicide is physically incapable of doing it, they are denied their wishes as anyone who helps them will be guilty of an offence.

Note that prior to 1961 it was a criminal offence to commit suicide, so that if the person was not successful then they would be prosecuted for attempting to commit suicide.

Key facts

Offence	Can consent be a defence?	Comment/case
Murder	Never a defence.	Not in the public interest.
s 18 OAPA 1861 s 20 OAPA 1861 s 47 OAPA 1861	Generally not a defence.	Not in the public interest, eg fighting (*Attorney-General's Reference (No 6 of 1980)* (1981)) or sado-masochistic acts (*Brown* (1993)).
	BUT there are exceptions where consent is a defence.	Properly conducted sports, surgery, dangerous exhibitions (*Jones* (1986)) or personal adornment such as tattoos (*Wilson* (1996)).
Battery	Always allowed as a defence.	Consent can also be implied to the 'jostlings' of everyday life (*Wilson v Pringle* (1986)).

Key facts chart on consent as a defence

Activity

Explain whether there would a defence available in the following situations.

1. Alice took some illegal drugs. She is told that while she was under the influence of the drugs, witnesses saw her hit Peter in the face with a saucepan, breaking his jaw. Alice cannot remember doing this. What defence(s) might be available to her if she is charged with offences under s 18 and s 20 of the Offences Against the Person Act 1861?

2. Courtney is a diabetic. One morning he gets up late and in his rush to get to work he forgets to take his insulin. As a result he becomes violent later in the day and punches Jemima in the face. What defence(s) might be available to him if he is charged with an offence under s 47 of the Offences Against the Person Act 1861?

3. Gary is hit on the head by a slate which accidentally falls off a building. He loses consciousness briefly but is then able to walk home. Later that day he attacks his partner, Lynne, causing serious injuries to her. He has no recollection of doing this. What defence(s) might be available to him if he is charged with offences under s 18 and s 20 of the Offences Against the Person Act 1861?

4. Martha has an argument with her husband, Desmond. Desmond then goes into the kitchen and a few minutes later comes out shouting abuse at her. Martha sees what she thinks is a knife in his hand, although it is actually a child's toy. Believing that he is about to stab her, Martha throws an ash-tray at Desmond's head. This hits him on the temple and kills him. What defence(s) might be available to her if she is charged with murder?

5. Joe plays rugby for his college team. During one match Joe is tackled very hard by Dave. Joe is angry about this and makes sure that every time Dave has the ball, he (Joe) tackles Dave hard. When they are leaving the pitch at the end of the match Joe pushes Dave. What defence(s) might be available to him if he is charged with battery in respect of the tackles and the push?

Examination-style questions

Question 1

Angela, who is married to Barry, has just had a baby and is suffering from postnatal depression. Clive, a friend of Barry's, comes to their home to see Barry, who has not returned from work. Clive sees Angela crying. He tries to cheer her up by saying how good-looking the baby is, but goes on to say that the baby is far too good-looking to be Barry's son.

Angela becomes angry as Barry has already accused her of having an affair and she thinks that Barry must have been talking to his friends about this. At that moment Barry comes home. Angela leaves the room and goes into the kitchen. She keeps hearing them laughing, and after about an hour this makes her angrier. She rushes out of the kitchen and stabs Clive with a knife. Barry grabs hold of Angela and in a very rough manner he pulls the knife out of her hand. In doing this he breaks Angela's wrist.

Clive dies from his injuries.

1. Discuss Angela's criminal liability for the murder of Clive. (In discussing any defences consider only those which are defences to murder alone.) (25 marks)
2. Discuss Barry's criminal liability for the injury suffered by Angela. (25 marks)
3. Consider how satisfactory the special defences to murder are. (25 marks)

Question 2

Deborah is with her boyfriend, Ewan, in a local pub when they see Deborah's ex-boyfriend, Fraser. Fraser has already drunk several pints of beer. He goes up to Deborah and puts his arm around her. She tells him to let go, but he refuses to do so unless she lets him kiss her. Ewan objects to this and an argument starts between the two men.

They eventually agree to go outside and fight to see who is the better man. During the fight Fraser hits Ewan in the face, causing a split lip. Ewan then punches Fraser hard on the chin, briefly knocking him out. Fraser gets up after a few seconds. Disorientated, he goes back into the pub and pushes Gail, a customer in the pub. She falls over and Fraser, thinking that she is a dog on the floor about to bite him, kicks out at her. This breaks one of her ribs and causes internal injuries.

1. Discuss Fraser's criminal liability for both the incident with Deborah and the incident with Gail. (25 marks)
2. Discuss both Ewan and Fraser's criminal liability for the incidents in the fight. (25 marks)
3. Explain what reforms are need to the law on assault. (25 marks)

Question 3

Harry and Ivan are both drug users. One day they
are in Harry's flat when Jayne, Ivan's girlfriend
who is not used to taking drugs, asks them to
help her 'take a trip'. Harry prepares a syringe of
heroin but then hands it to Jayne saying she
needs to learn to do it herself. Jayne has
difficulties and cannot get the needle in so Ivan
presses on the vein in her arm to make it easier
for her. Jayne injects herself with heroin.

   She later starts to lose consciousness. Ivan says
to Harry that he thinks Jayne's breathing is 'odd'.
Harry says it's nothing to do with him but 'not to
worry'. Harry then leaves the flat. Ivan tries to
rouse Jayne, but is unable to do so. He decides to
take some drugs himself. When Harry returns to
the flat some hours later he finds that Jayne has
died and Ivan is asleep. Harry pours water over
Ivan to wake him up. Ivan is suffering from the
effects of the drugs and in his drugged state he
thinks that Harry is going to kill him. He picks up
a chair and hits Harry with it, causing Harry to
suffer cuts and severe bruising to his face and
concussion.

1. Discuss Harry and Ivan's criminal liability for
   the death of Jayne.   (25 marks)
2. Discuss Ivan's liability for the injuries to
   Harry.   (25 marks)
3. Discuss what criticisms can be made of the
   law of unlawful manslaughter.
                                    (25 marks)

UNIT 3

Section B:
Law of Contract

Table of Cases

Chapter 6

Formation

6.1 The basic character of agreement

The Law of Contract concerns 'bargains' which are made between parties. The major significance of the word 'bargain' is that it involves an agreement that is binding on both parties. In Contract Law, then, it is insufficient merely that an agreement exists between two parties, but rather that it involves that specific type of agreement which is *enforceable* by both parties.

A contract is completed when both sides honour an agreement by carrying out their particular side of the bargain. It is a breach of contract when a party fails to do so.

However, because of the special nature of contractual agreements, we cannot identify a breach of contract where we may feel that we have not received what we paid for or 'bargained' for, without first showing that the agreement was indeed a contract.

So our first objective in a contract case may be to prove that there is actually a contract in existence. We can tell if it is a contract because to be so it must have been formed according to certain standard rules.

It will only be a contract where there is:

1. an **agreement** – which is based on mutuality;
2. **consideration** – which means that both sides are bound to give something to each other; and
3. **intention** – to be legally bound by the terms of the agreement.

These elements are considered in these next three sections.

A contractual agreement is said to exist when a valid **offer** is followed by a valid **acceptance**. This appears straightforward, and if one person offers to sell something to another party who accepts the price and agrees to buy, then there is no difficulty.

In practice, negotiations can be much more complex than this, and agreements can be identified which appear to have no formal negotiating steps; for example, purchasing goods from a vending machine.

In *Butler Machine Tool Co v Ex-Cell-O Corporation* (1979) Lord Denning MR suggested that judges should decide whether a contract existed by examining the evidence in its totality rather than trying to apply a strict test of offer and acceptance.

Even if other judges sympathised with the logic of this they would not publicly admit it, so we still have to return to the traditional test of offer and acceptance.

6.2 Offer

6.2.1 Offers and invitation to treat

A person making an offer is called an **offeror**. The person to whom the offer is made, and who thus can accept it, is called the **offeree**.

The offer is a statement of intent by the offeror to be legally bound by the terms of the offer if it is accepted, and the contract exists once acceptance has taken place.

If the offer is plainly stated, eg 'Would you like to buy my car for £8,000?' there is no problem.

The question is easily identified as an offer, and you only have to say 'Yes I will buy your car for £8,000' for there to be an easily identifiable acceptance too.

It is not always the case, however, that the first stage in negotiations is an offer. Often the first step is an entirely passive state and is not therefore open to acceptance; eg a tin of beans sitting on a supermarket shelf. This is not an offer and is called an **invitation to treat**; in other words an invitation to the other party to make an offer, usually an offer to buy. The contract is then formed by the agreement to sell which is the acceptance in this case. See Figure 6.1 for an illustration of this.

Figure 6.1 The point at which a contract is made in a standard offer and acceptance, and where there is firstly an invitation to treat

6.2.2 Examples of invitation to treat

Goods displayed on shelves in a self-service shop

This is not an offer which is then accepted when the customer picks the goods from the shelves. The goods are an invitation to treat – an invitation to

the buyer to make an offer to buy. This is done by the customer taking them to the cash desk where the contract is formed when the sale is agreed.

Pharmaceutical Society of GB v Boots Cash Chemists Ltd (1953)

Boots altered one of their shops to self-service. Under s 18 Pharmacy and Poisons Act 1933 a registered pharmacist was required to be present at the sale of certain drugs and poisons. It was important to know where the contract was formed. The Court of Appeal held that the contract was formed when goods were presented at the cash desk where a pharmacist was present, not when taken from the shelf.

The rule preserves the freedom of contract of the shopkeeper and sensibly allows the shopkeeper to accept or refuse a sale. This might be particularly important where a child selects alcohol from shelves in an off-licence and tries to buy it.

Goods on display in a shop window

Again there is no offer, only a display of the goods that the customer might go into the shop and offer to buy.

Fisher v Bell (1961)

A prosecution under the Offensive Weapons Act 1959 failed due to bad drafting of the Act. The offence was to offer for sale prohibited weapons. The shopkeeper displaying a flick knife in the window was not offering it for sale. It was a mere invitation to treat.

Goods or services advertised in a newspaper or magazine

Here a contract will not be formed until the person seeing the advertisement has made an offer to buy, which is then accepted.

A prosecution for 'offering for sale' a wild bird under the Protection of Birds Act 1954 failed. The advertisement 'Bramblefinch cocks, bramblefinch hens, 25s each' was not an offer but an invitation to treat.

An invitation to council tenants to buy their property

Gibson v Manchester City Council (1979)

Gibson returned his completed application form when receiving an invitation to buy his house from the council. When there was a change of policy by the council, Gibson's action for breach of contract failed. His completed application was an offer to buy, not an acceptance of any offer by the council.

A mere statement of price

The mere fact that a party has indicated a price which he would find acceptable does not make it an offer.

Harvey v Facey (1893)

Harvey wanted to buy Facey's farm and sent a telegram 'Will you sell me Bumper Hall Penn? Telegraph lowest price.' Facey's telegram replied 'Lowest price acceptable £900.' Harvey tried to accept this but could not. It was merely a statement of price, not an offer

Lots at an auction

The rule in fact derives from auctions. The lot is the invitation to make a bid. Bidding is an offer to buy, and the acceptance is the fall of the auctioneer's hammer at which point the contract is formed. The contract is formed between the highest bidder and the owner of the goods. The auctioneer is merely acting on behalf of the owner of the goods.

British Car Auctions v Wright (1972)

A prosecution for offering to sell an unroadworthy vehicle failed. At the auction there was no offer to sell, only an invitation to bid.

The consequence of this is that there is an absolute entitlement to withdraw any lot prior to the fall of the auctioneer's hammer. This is no more than an example of the rule that an offer can be withdrawn any time prior to acceptance (see 6.4).

Harris v Nickerson (1873)

Here Harris had attended the auction, hoping to buy certain furniture which was advertised as being in the sale in the catalogue of the auction. The auctioneer had withdrawn these items from the sale and Harris sued arguing a breach of contract. The court held that the advertising of the goods in the catalogue was no more than an invitation to treat. Moreover any contract could only be formed on fall of the auctioneer's hammer when a bid was accepted.

The result may be different in an auction that is advertised as being 'without reserve'. This means that there is no minimum sale price that must be reached by the bidders before a sale can be concluded, so that the goods are sold to the highest bidder.

6.2.3 More complex situations

Sometimes in situations that we would normally associate with invitation to treat, the circumstances involved or the nature of the words used mean that there has in fact been an offer rather than an invitation to treat. These include:

Advertisements including a unilateral offer

If the advertisement indicates a course of action in return for which the advertiser makes a promise to pay, then he is bound by this promise.

Carlill v The Carbolic Smoke Ball Co Ltd (1893)

The company advertised a patent medicine, the smoke ball, with the promise that if a purchaser used it correctly and still got flu, then the company would pay them £100. Mrs Carlill did contract flu after using the smoke ball in the correct fashion. The court enforced her claim for the £100. The promise was an offer that could be accepted by anyone who used the smoke ball correctly and still contracted the flu.

A statement of price where an offer is also intended

A mere statement of price is not binding, but if other factors indicate that an offer is included in the statement, then it will be binding if it is accepted.

Biggs v Boyd Gibbins (1971)

In response to the offer of a lower price the claimant wrote 'For a quick sale I will accept £26,000.' The defendant replied 'I accept your offer.' The claimant then wrote 'I thank you for accepting my price of £26,000. My wife and I are both pleased that you are purchasing the property.' His first letter was an offer that the defendant had accepted.

Competitive tendering

Normally an invitation to tender for the supply of goods or services is an invitation to treat. For instance, a company want to have their office painted. They invite tenders, and various decorators respond with different prices for the work. The company is free to choose any of the decorators, not necessarily the cheapest. If, however, the company has agreed in the advertisement that the work will go to the tender with the lowest price, then it is bound to give the work to the bidder with the lowest price.

Harvela Investments Ltd v Royal Trust Co of Canada Ltd (1986)

The Trust company had invited tenders from two interested parties for the purchase of some land. The sale would go to the party making the highest bid. The party making the lowest bid had tendered a price of $2,100,000 or $101,000 in excess of any other offer. When it was accepted and Harvela, the party making the higher bid, found out they sued successfully. The wording of the invitation to tender made it an offer that could only be accepted by the highest bidder.

There may also be an obligation on the party inviting tenders, to consider all tenders regardless of whether a tender is accepted.

Blackpool and Fylde Aero Club Ltd v Blackpool Borough Council (1990)

The club had held the concession to run pleasure flights from the council's airport for many years. When the concession was due for renewal the council put it out to competitive tender, and invited tenders from other parties. All tenders were to be submitted in unmarked envelopes in a particular box by twelve noon on a specific date. The council stated that it would not be bound to accept any bid. The club placed its bid in the box at 11.00 am but by accident the box was not emptied after this time and its bid was not therefore considered. The concession was given to another group, R.R. Helicopters. When the council later discovered its mistake they at first decided to repeat the exercise but were threatened with legal action by R.R. Helicopters. The club claimed breach of a contract to consider all tenders delivered by the due time. Their claim was upheld. The court felt that there was an implied undertaking to operate by the rules that they had set, even though the invitation to tender for the concession was only an invitation to treat.

Auctions advertised as 'without reserve'

Traditionally an auction might take two forms. The first includes a 'reserve price' (a minimum price acceptable to the seller). In this case no sale can take place, and thus no contract is formed, unless the bidders reach this reserve price. See *McManus v Fortescue* (1907).

In the case of an auction held by reserve then there is only one possible outcome – the goods will become the property of the highest *bona fide* bidder. It had, however, been held in *obiter* that no contract of sale can materialise between the owner of the goods and the highest bidder where the auctioneer refuses the sale or for any reason fails to accept the bid of the highest *bona fide* bidder. In this instance it was said that a collateral contract is created between the highest *bona fide* bidder and the auctioneer himself, so that the auctioneer may then be sued for breach of contract. See *Warlow v Harrison* (1859). This point has been examined more recently.

Barry v Heathcote Ball & Co (Commercial Auctions) Ltd (2000)

Here in an auction advertised as 'without reserve' the auctioneer withdrew two lots, machinery worth £14,251, from the auction. In doing so he refused bids of £200 for each machine made by the claimant and which were the highest bids. The auctioneer then sold them on privately at £750 each. The claimant bidder sued arguing that the highest bid rule should apply. The court, approving *Warlow v Harrison* (1859), accepted the existence of a collateral contract between the bidder and the auctioneer and awarded the claimant £27,600 damages.

Activity

Explain whether the following situations involve offers or mere invitations to treat

1. A sign in a shop window reading:

2. My friend has an old sports car that I particularly like. When I ask him how much he would sell it for he replies: 'You could not buy a car like that for less than £20,000 these days.'

3. An advertisement in a local newspaper which reads:

Activity

Now do the same in a simpler form and suggest whether or not an offer exists in the following examples

1. I tell you that I have a thousand copies of my new Contract Law text book, the price of which is only £14.99.

2. My new Contract Law text book is advertised in the College Handbook at only £14.99.

3. I write you a letter in which I say 'Would you like a copy of my new Contract Law text book? It is only £14.99.'

6.2.4 The rules of offer

Once we know whether a party is making an offer, and is then intending to contract, we must be satisfied that the offer conforms to the rules to show whether it is a valid offer or not.

The offer must be communicated to the offeree

It is impossible to accept something of which you have no knowledge.

Taylor v Laird (1856)

Taylor gave up the captaincy of a ship and then worked his passage back to Britain as an ordinary crewmember. His claim for wages failed. The ship owner had received no communication of Taylor's offer to work in that capacity.

An offer can be made to one person but it can also be made to the whole world

Anyone can then accept the offer who has had notice of it.

Carlill v The Carbolic Smoke Ball Co Ltd (1893)

The company's claim that they had no contract with Mrs Carlill failed. They had made their offer generally and she had accepted by buying the smoke ball, using it and still contracting flu.

The offeree must have knowledge of the offer for it to be valid and enforceable

Inland Revenue Commissioners v Fry (2001)

The IRC claimed that Fry owed them £113,000. Her husband sent a cheque for £10,000 to the IRC with a letter stating that the cheque was 'in full settlement' and that if presented for payment this would be acceptance of her offer. IRC procedure was for cashiers to bank cheques received before accompanying correspondence was then sent on to a caseworker. The caseworker here immediately phoned the defendant to say that the £10,000 could be treated as part payment or she could have the money back. Fry insisted that the Revenue were bound to accept the offer, having cashed the cheque. The court held that while an offeree could accept a unilateral offer which prescribed its manner of acceptance by acting in accordance with that manner, there had to be knowledge of the offer when the act was done. IRC were actually ignorant of the offer here so there was no acceptance.

The terms of the offer must be certain

If the words of the offer are too vague then the parties might not really know what they are contracting for and should not then be bound.

Guthing v Lynn (1831)

When a horse was purchased a promise to pay £5 more '… if the horse is lucky…' could not be an offer. It was too vague.

It is possible to withdraw an offer, at any time before the offer is accepted

Routledge v Grant (1828)

Grant had offered his house for sale on the understanding that the offer would remain open for six weeks. When he took it off the market within the six weeks that was legitimate because there had been no acceptance.

If, however, the offeree paid money to the offeror to keep the offer open, then he would be bound to do so.

Activity

In the following examples, consider whether the terms of the offer are certain enough for a contract to be formed if they are accepted.

Sukky agrees to sell an important book on contract law for:

1. A fair price.
2. A price which will be fixed by Sukky's friend Dalvinder when he next sees him.
3. A price that is half of the normal retail price.
4. A price to be agreed between Sukky and myself at a later date.

The offeror must communicate the withdrawal of the offer to the offeree

Byrne v Van Tienhoven (1880)

On 1 October Van Tienhoven wrote to Byrne offering to sell certain goods.

On 8 October he changed his mind and sent a letter withdrawing the offer.

On 11 October Byrne accepted the offer in a telegram.

On 15 October he confirmed this in writing.

On 20 October Byrne received Van Tienhoven's letter withdrawing the offer. It was invalid because it had not been received until after Byrne's acceptance.

This shows how important it is to keep a track of dates as well as other information during contractual negotiations.

Communication of withdrawal of the offer can be by a reliable third party

It need not be done personally but the third party must be a reliable source of information.

Dickinson v Dodds (1876)

Dodds had offered to sell houses to Dickinson. When Berry notified Dickinson that Dodds had withdrawn the offer this was acceptable. Berry was shown to be a mutual acquaintance on whom both could rely.

A unilateral offer cannot be withdrawn while the offeree is performing

In a unilateral contract the offeree actually accepts by performing his side of the bargain (as in *Carlill* (1893)). It would clearly be unfair to prevent this once the other party had begun.

> ### *Errington v Errington & Woods* (1952)
>
> A father bought a house and mortgaged it in his own name. He promised his son and daughter-in-law that it would become theirs when they had paid off the mortgage. When the father died and other members of the family wanted possession of the house their action failed. The father's promise could not be withdrawn so long as the couple kept up the mortgage repayments, after which the house would be theirs.

6.2.5 Termination of offer

An offer can be terminated in a number of ways:

- It can be accepted, in which case there is a contract (or indeed it could be refused or met with a counter-offer, in which case there is no contract).
- It can be properly withdrawn, as we have seen above.
- The time for acceptance can lapse.
- A reasonable time can have lapsed (it would be rare that an offer could stay open indefinitely).

> ### *Ramsgate Victoria Hotel Co Ltd v Montefiore* (1866)
>
> Montefiore had offered to buy shares in June but the company only issued the shares in November. It was held that his offer to buy had lapsed.

- When one of the parties dies. Generally this may operate in different ways depending on which party dies.

(a) If the offeree dies then this will cause the offer to lapse and his representatives will be unable to accept on his behalf.

(b) If an offeror dies, however, he may still be bound by an acceptance that is made in ignorance of the offeror's death.

(c) Although if the offeror dies and the offeree knows of this then it is unlikely that he could still claim to accept the offer.

Activity

1. What is an offer?
2. What is the major difference between an offer and an invitation to treat?
3. What would happen if a customer in a supermarket took tins of beans from a shelf but changed her mind and discarded them before reaching the cash desk?
4. What would happen if I ordered goods advertised in a magazine and the seller wrote back to say that supplies were exhausted?
5. What makes a unilateral offer different to an invitation to treat?
6. Is it possible for an offer to be made to more than one person?
7. Why is it important to notify an offeree before withdrawing the offer?
8. Is it true to say that it is better for an offeree that negotiations prior to a contract are all carried out by letter, and if so, why is that so?
9. What factors would you take into account in determining whether a reasonable time for an offer to stay open had lapsed?
10. If you find my lost dog and return it to me and later see an advertisement in the newspaper offering a reward for return of the dog, can you claim it?

6.3 Acceptance

6.3.1 The basic rules of acceptance

The acceptance must be communicated to the offeror

Just the same as for the offer, communication is required, otherwise the unscrupulous might hold people to offers of which they were unaware. It goes without saying then that the acceptance must be a positive act, and that acceptance cannot be taken from silence.

Felthouse v Bindley (1863)

An uncle and nephew had negotiated over the sale of the nephew's horse. The uncle had said 'If I hear no more from you I shall consider the horse mine at £30: 15s.' On sale of the nephew's stock, the auctioneer failed to withdraw the horse from the sale as instructed by the nephew. The uncle tried to sue the auctioneer in tort but failed. He could not prove the horse was his. The nephew had not actually accepted his offer to buy.

The acceptance can be in any form

It can be in writing, by words, or conduct. Of course if the offeror requires it to be in a specific form then it must be in that form, or it will be invalid.

Yates v Pulleyn (1975)

An option to purchase land was required to be exercised by notice in writing '...sent by registered or recorded delivery post.' When the option was sent by ordinary post only, it was invalid.

Acceptance can be construed from the conduct of the parties: *Brogden v Metropolitan Railway Co* (1877), but only if this can be objectively demonstrated to have been the intention of the offeree: *Day Morris Associates v Voyce* (2003).

The acceptance must be unconditional

This is the so-called 'mirror image rule'. The acceptance must conform exactly with the terms of the offer or it is invalid and no contract will have been formed. It follows that any attempt to vary the terms of the offer is a counter-offer, terminating the original offer, which cannot then be accepted.

Hyde v Wrench (1840)

Wrench offered to sell his farm to Hyde for £1,000. Hyde rejected this and offered to pay £950, which Wrench rejected. When Hyde then tried to accept the original price and Wrench would not sell, Hyde's action failed. The original offer was no longer open for him to accept.

Mere enquiries do not count as rejection

A mere enquiry about the contract is not a counter-offer, as it does not reject the terms of the offer. This means that the offer is still open to acceptance by the offeree.

Stevenson v McLean (1880)

In a response to an offer to sell iron, the price and quantity were accepted but the offeree wished to know whether delivery could be staggered. Hearing nothing further the claimant sent a letter of acceptance. He sued on discovering that the iron had been sold to a third party. The defendant's claim that there had been a counter-offer failed. It was not a rejection of the offer, merely an enquiry about it, and the offer was still open to acceptance.

Technical counter-offers may not count as a rejection

Where counter offers concern merely ancillary terms of no importance to the parties the court may ignore the counter offer.

Brogden v Metropolitan Railway Co (1877)

The parties had a long-standing informal arrangement for the supply of coal. They then formalised the arrangement and the railway company sent a draft contract to Brogden. Brogden inserted the name of an arbitrator in a section left blank for that purpose, signed the agreement and returned it. The railway company secretary signed and returned it without looking at it. Brogden continued supplying coal and was paid for deliveries. Brogden then tried to avoid his obligations and argued that there was no contract because of a counter offer by the railway company. The House of Lords held that the insertion of the arbitrator's name was technically a counter offer but it had no effect on the parties so Brogden had accepted it.

6.3.2 Problems with different forms of communication

The 'postal rule'

Where use of the ordinary postal system is the normal, anticipated or agreed means of accepting, then the contract is formed at the time the letter of acceptance is posted, not when it is received (the postal rule).

Adams v Lindsell (1818)

The rule began with this case where wool was offered for sale, an acceptance by post was requested and sent, but not received until long after the wool had been sold. The rule developed then from the possible injustices caused by delays in the postal system in its early days.

The rule applies even where the letter is never received, rather than merely delayed.

Household Fire Insurance v Grant (1879)

Grant made a written offer to purchase shares. Notification of acceptance was posted but never received. When the company went into liquidation, Grant's claim that he was not a shareholder and should not be liable for the value of the shares failed. He had become a shareholder even though unaware of it.

It is possible to avoid the effects of the postal rule by stating in the offer that there will be no contract until the acceptance is actually received, in which case the contract is only complete on communication of the acceptance.

Holwell Securities v Hughes (1974)

An attempt to use the postal rule failed where the acceptance was required to be 'by notice in writing'. The fact that actual notice was required meant that the postal rule did not apply.

Modern methods of communication

In the case of more modern methods of communication the picture is not so clear. The important factor seems to be how instantaneous the method is.

Brinkibon Ltd v Stahag Stahl (1983)

Previous case law had stated that an acceptance by telex, like telephone, was immediate enough communication to be effective straightaway. This case, however, concerned a telex received out of office hours. The House of Lords held that this could only be effective once the office was reopened.

Activity

Activity

1. Why is it necessary for acceptance to 'mirror' the offer?
2. What are the different consequences of a counter-offer and a mere enquiry?
3. How does the judge decide whether something is a counter-offer or a mere enquiry?
4. In what way can a counter-offer operate to influence the formation of a contract?
5. Is there a satisfactory method of resolving a 'battle of forms'?
6. In what possible situations might a silent response nevertheless lead on to a contractual relationship?
7. Is there any justification for the postal rule in the modern day?
8. What problems result from modern day rapid or instantaneous forms of communication and how have they been resolved?

Faxes and e-mail are more modern forms of communication and the same problems and the same principles very often apply.

More recently as a result of having to implement EU Directive 97/7, the Distance Selling Directive, the Consumer Protection (Distance Selling) Regulations 2000 have been introduced.

- These apply to contracts for the sale of goods and provisions of services made by a variety of modern methods; eg telephone, fax, internet shopping, mail order, e-mail and television shopping.
- The Regulations do not apply to transfers of land, building contracts, financial services, purchases from vending machines and auctions.
- Under reg 7 the seller/supplier is bound to provide the purchaser with certain minimum information, including the right to cancel the contract within seven days, description, price, arrangements for payment and delivery (and how long all of these remain open for), the identity of the supplier. Written confirmation must also be given according to reg 8.
- Inevitably if these rules are not complied with then the contract is not formed.

The Electronic Commerce Directive 2000/31 (implemented in the Electronic Commerce (EC Directive) Regulations 2002) has an impact also on offer and acceptance by electronic means. Article 11 says that:

> 'where [a purchaser] in accepting [a seller's] offer is required to give his consent through technological means, such as clicking on an icon, the contract is concluded when the recipient of the service has received from the service provider, electronically, an acknowledgement of receipt of the recipient's acceptance.'

So this would appear to clear up some of the problems formerly encountered in determining when such agreements are actually complete and a contract formed.

6.4 Basic problems with offer and acceptance

Many contracts in a modern commercial context are not formed as the result of one party straightforwardly accepting the simple offer of the other. This would be too restrictive and rigid. Businesses contract in a variety of ways and may be subject to disagreements, rejections, compromises and even threats before ever an agreement is reached. Sometimes people will negotiate to try to gain something different from what is first offered. We have already seen the effect that a counter-offer can have on the parties. When does a mere enquiry end and a counter-offer begin? That is a question that judges will often be called on to answer.

A further complication is the common use of 'standard forms' by businesses. These are used so that the business can be sure of always dealing on terms advantageous to it. This may not cause any problems in a consumer sale. When two businesses are contracting, however, it can prove a nightmare. This is the so-called 'battle of the forms'. One business makes an offer on its standard forms. The customer accepts on its own forms. The two forms may be entirely contradictory. The question is, which terms are taken as being the contractual ones in the case of a conflict between the two businesses?

Key facts

Offer	Case
A contract is made where there is an agreement between two parties An agreement is a valid offer followed by a valid acceptance Offer must be distinguished from: (a) an 'invitation to treat'	*Pharmaceutical Society of GB v Boots Cash Chemists* (1953)
(b) a mere statement of price Competitive tendering is different	*Harvey v Facey* (1893)
An offer must be communicated ● The offeree must be aware of the existence of the offer ● An offer can be made to the whole world	*Harvela Investments v Royal Trust Co of Canada* (1986) *Taylor v Laird* (1856) *IRC v Fry* (2001)
The terms of the offer must be certain ● An offer can be withdrawn any time up to acceptance ● The withdrawal must be communicated to the offeree ● This can be by a reliable third party ● Unilateral offers do not require acceptance, only performance An offer ends: (a) on acceptance (b) on proper withdrawal (c) on lapse of time (d) on death of one of the parties.	*Carlill v The Carbolic Smoke Ball Co Ltd* (1893) *Guthing v Lynn* (1831) *Routledge v Grant* (1828) *Byrne v van Tienhoven* (1880) *Dickinson v Dodds* (1876) *Errington v Errington and Woods* (1952)
Acceptance	**Case**
Acceptance must be communicated If use of the post is the normal, anticipated method of acceptance the contract is formed on posting (the postal rule) This applies even if the acceptance is never received	*Felthouse v Bindley* (1863) *Adams v Lindsell* (1818) *Household Fire Insurance v Grant* (1879)
Acceptance must be unconditional But mere enquiries are not rejections of the offer Modern methods of communicating such as fax, e-mail and internet cause problems in determining when a contract is formed Some problems have now been resolved by the e-commerce directive and the Consumer Protection (Distance Selling) Regulations.	*Hyde v Wrench* (1840) *Stevenson v McLean* (1880)

Key facts chart on offer and acceptance

The general rule in the modern day is to take the last counter-offer as having been accepted, and give effect to its terms in the contract.

Davies & Co Ltd v William Old (1969)

Shop fitters, following their successful tender, contracted with the architects in a building contract to sub-contract to the builders. The builders under instruction from the architects issued an order for work to the shop-fitters. They did this on their own standard form that included a clause that they would not pay for work until they themselves had been paid. When the shopfitters later sued for some work that had not been paid for, their action failed. The builders' standard form was a counter-offer that the shopfitters had accepted by carrying on with the work.

The problem is further compounded because often the services or goods are provided before any settled agreement is reached. In a later conflict the courts may find a contract does exist provided there has been no major disagreement between the parties. Sometimes, however, this is impossible.

British Steel Corporation v Cleveland Bridge and Engineering Co (1984)

Cleveland Bridge were sub-contracted to build the steel framework of a bank in Saudi Arabia. The work required four steel nodes which they asked BSC to manufacture. BSC wanted a disclaimer of liability for any loss caused by late delivery. The parties were never able to agree on this and so no written agreement was ever made. BSC, however, did make and deliver three of the nodes, but the last was delayed because of a strike. Cleveland Bridge refused to pay for the three nodes and claimed that BSC was in breach of contract for late delivery of the fourth. Because there was a total disagreement over a major term, the judge in the case found it impossible to recognise that a contract existed. He did order that BSC be paid for what they had supplied.

6.5 Consideration

6.5.1 The nature and purpose of consideration

As we have already seen, the law of contract deals with bargains. The rules of contract seek to differentiate between agreements where there is something to be gained by both parties (as is the case in a contract), and agreements which are purely gratuitous (as are gifts).

Originally contracts were only recognised if in a deed. This was logical in the case of land transfers but otherwise inconvenient. The giving of 'consideration' by both sides became the traditional method of ensuring that other types of agreement were contractual. It was the *quid pro quo*, the proof that a bargain in fact existed, and if no consideration could be found then the agreement could not be enforced. The exception is an agreement made by deed.

6.5.2 Defining consideration

Originally it proved impossible to give a simple, single definition of consideration, and the pragmatic view was often taken that it was no more than the reason why the promise should be binding in law. Often in any case it was taken as being no more than a rule of evidence.

Many nineteenth century cases looked for definitions based on benefit gained and detriment suffered. So for instance it was variously defined as:

- 'loss or inconvenience suffered by one party at the request of the other' – *Bunn v Guy* (1803)
- 'some detriment to the plaintiff or some benefit to the defendant' – *Thomas v Thomas* (1842).

A simple, early way of defining consideration came in *Currie v Misa* (1875) where it was described in terms of benefit and detriment:

> 'some right, interest, profit or benefit accruing to one party, or some forbearance, detriment, loss or responsibility given, suffered or undertaken by the other'.

So if I contract with you over my contract law textbook for £15, I am gaining the benefit of the £15 but have the detriment of giving up the book. For you it is the other way round.

A more sophisticated definition was later provided in *Dunlop v Selfridge* (1915), a case involving issues of both absence of consideration and lack of privity of contract by the party seeking to enforce contractual provisions. Here the House of Lords approved Sir Frederick Pollock's definition contained in his 'Principles of Contract' that:

> '… an act of forbearance or the promise thereof is the price for which the promise of the other is bought, and the promise thus given for value is enforceable …'

In fact, although the judges are saying that they will not in contract law enforce a promise which has not been paid for in some way, in modern cases they have been shown to be willing to see almost any promise made in a commercial context as contractual. Therefore consideration can be surprisingly little, and it can seem difficult to fit the theory to real situations.

6.5.3 Executory and executed consideration

Contract law would have no meaning unless it enforced promises as well as actual acts. **Executory** consideration is simply the exchange of promises to carry out acts or pass property at a later stage. If one party breaks their promise and fails to do what they are supposed to do under it,

then they are in breach of contract and may be sued.

In unilateral contracts, however, the party making the unilateral offer is under no obligation until the other party performs (executes) their side of the bargain. This is called **executed** consideration, and a common example is a reward. We have already seen this principle in operation in Mrs Carlill's case (see 6.2.3).

6.5.4 The rules of consideration

Consideration need not be adequate but it must be sufficient

This sounds like complete nonsense because adequacy and sufficiency appear to be the same thing.

Adequacy

In fact lawyers are using adequacy in its everyday form, ie whether the parties are promising things of fairly equal value. What is adequate is a decision of the parties themselves. Freedom of contract would be badly affected if we could not decide ourselves if we are satisfied with the bargain we have made. In certain circumstances, in any case, it may actually work to our ultimate advantage to make a bargain that on the face of it appears to be a bad one.

The courts then are not interested in whether there has been a good or a bad bargain made, only that a bargain exists, and they will seek to enforce the bargain that is actually agreed upon by the parties.

Thomas v Thomas (1842)

A man before his death expressed the wish that his wife should be allowed to remain in the house although this was not in his will. The executors carried out this wish and charged the widow a nominal ground rent of £1 per year. When they later tried to dispossess her they failed. The moral obligation to carry out the man's wishes was not consideration but the payment of ground rent, however small and apparently inadequate, was.

Sufficiency

On the other hand, sufficiency is used here as a legal term, and it means that what is promised must:

- be real
- be tangible
- have some actual value.

White v Bluett (1853)

A son owed his father money on a promissory note. When the father died and his executors were trying to recover the money, the son tried to claim that he was not bound to pay. He claimed an agreement with his father that the debt would be forgotten in return for the son's promise not to complain about the distribution of the father's assets in his will. The son failed. The promise was too intangible to be consideration for the father's promise to forego the debt.

What is real, tangible and of value is not always easily distinguishable.

Ward v Byham (1956)

A father of an illegitimate child promised the mother money towards its upkeep if she would keep the child '… well looked after and happy …'. The mother would be doing nothing more than she was already bound by law to do in looking after the child. The court were prepared to enforce the agreement, however, since there is no obligation in law to keep a child happy, and the promise to do so was seen as good consideration.

In fact even things of no apparent worth have been classed as amounting to valuable consideration.

Chappell v Nestle Co (1960)

Nestle offered a record, normally retailing at 6/8d (not quite 34p), for 1/6d (7.5p) plus three chocolate bar wrappers to promote their chocolate. On receipt the wrappers were thrown away. They were still held to be good consideration when the holders of the copyright of the record sued to prevent the promotion because they would receive substantially fewer royalties from it.

The accusation that if a court wishes to enforce a promise in a commercial context it will always find something to act as consideration seems to be proved when set against the reasoning in certain cases (see later for instance: *Williams v Roffey Bros & Nicholls Contractors Ltd* (1990)).

Past consideration is no consideration

This rule simply means that any consideration given cannot come before the agreement but must follow it.

It is a sensible rule in that it can prevent the unscrupulous from forcing people into contracts on the basis of providing goods or services, which they have not ordered. Quite simply, in any case it is a promise that has not been agreed to by both parties in their contract.

The basic rule

It will usually occur where one party has done a voluntary act and is trying to enforce the other party's later promise to pay.

Re McArdle (1951)

A son and his wife lived in his mother's house that on her death would be inherited by her son and three other children. The son's wife paid for substantial repairs and improvements to the property. The mother then made her children sign an agreement to reimburse the daughter-in-law out of her estate. When she died the children refused to keep this promise and the daughter-in-law sued unsuccessfully. Her consideration for their promise was past. It came before they signed the agreement to repay her.

The exception to the rule

The rule will not always work justly, as the above case shows. In certain circumstances the rule will not apply. Where one of the parties has requested a service, the law sensibly concludes that he is prepared to pay for it. Even though that service is then carried out without any mention of payment, or any apparent contractual agreement, a promise to pay coming after the service is performed will be enforced by the courts. This is known as 'the rule in *Lampleigh v Braithwaite*' from the case of that name.

Lampleigh v Braithwaite (1615)

Braithwaite was accused of killing a man and asked Lampleigh to obtain a King's pardon for him. Lampleigh did so at considerable expense to himself, and Braithwaite, in gratitude

promised to pay him £100, which he in fact never did. Lampleigh's claim that there was a contract succeeded. Because the service was requested, even though no price was mentioned at the time, it was clear that both parties would have contemplated a payment. The later promise to pay was clear evidence of this.

There are more modern examples of the operation of the exception in *Lampleigh v Braithwaite* in a commercial context.

Re Casey's Patent (1892)

Joint-owners of a patent wrote to the claimant agreeing to give him a third share of the patent in return for his services as manager of their patents. When the claimant wished to enforce this agreement they then claimed that the agreement was in respect of his past services and unenforceable for past consideration. He had in fact given no consideration following the agreement. Bowen LJ held that there was inevitably an implied promise that in managing the patents, the claimant would be paid for his work. The later agreement to pay was therefore enforceable. It was an example of the exception in *Lampleigh v Braithwaite*.

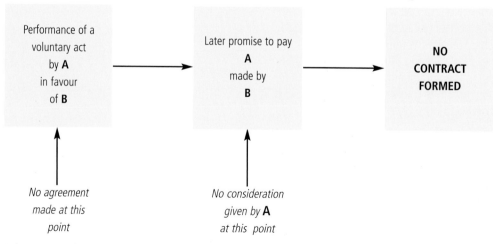

Figure 6.2 The operation of the past consideration rule

The agreement

| **A** requests a service from **B** with no mention of payment | **B** carries out what he is asked to do | A grateful **A** now promises **B** a payment for the service | **CONTRACT FORMED** |

This is not yet an agreement, but the request shows a willingness to pay

This is not yet consideration

This promise supports the idea of willingness to form an agreement

Figure 6.3 The exception in *Lampleigh v Braithwaite* (1615) in operation

The consideration must move from the promisee (the person to whom the promise is made)

Again the rule sounds somewhat complex but in fact it simply means that a person cannot sue or indeed be sued under a contract unless he has provided consideration. (This rule is interchangeable with the rule requiring privity of contract.)

Tweddle v Atkinson (1861)

Fathers of a young couple who intended to marry agreed in writing to each settle a sum of money on the couple. The young woman's father died before giving over the money and the young man then sued the executors to the estate when they refused to hand over the money. Even though he was named in the agreement he failed because he had given no consideration for the agreement himself.

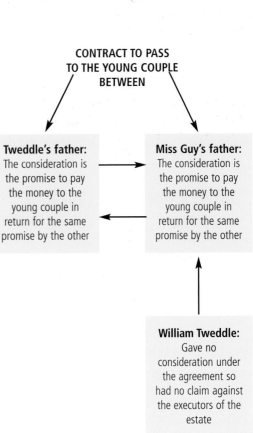

CONTRACT TO PASS TO THE YOUNG COUPLE BETWEEN

Tweddle's father: The consideration is the promise to pay the money to the young couple in return for the same promise by the other

Miss Guy's father: The consideration is the promise to pay the money to the young couple in return for the same promise by the other

William Tweddle: Gave no consideration under the agreement so had no claim against the executors of the estate

Figure 6.4 *Tweddle v Atkinson* (1861) illustrates the rule that consideration must move from the promissee

Activity

Consider the following events and decide whether an enforceable contract has been formed or whether consideration is only past.

1. While I was away on holiday in Goa it was very hot at home too. My neighbour Alison noticed that some of my flowers were dying and so she watered them every day, saving them. I was very pleased when I returned and I told her that I would give her £20 for all her trouble. In fact I have not given Alison the money and she wonders if she is actually entitled to it.

2. Last month I had to go to an Exam Board meeting in Birmingham. My car would not start so I asked one of my students, Neera, who has a car if she would take me there. She happily agreed and gave me a lift there, and even waited for the meeting to finish so that she could also give me a lift back. After returning I gave Neera the appropriate amount of money for the petrol that she had used but I also promised her that I would buy her a new copy of a law textbook costing £58.50p that she had been saving hard for. However, last week when Neera asked when she could have the money for the book I told her that I no longer intend to buy the book for her.

Performing an existing duty cannot be the consideration for a new promise

The basic rule

Merely doing something that you are already bound to do can never be sufficient to amount to consideration. This applies firstly where the duty is a public one.

Collins v Godefroy (1831)

A police officer was under a court order to attend and give evidence at a trial. It was important to the defendant that the officer attended so he promised to pay him a sum of money to ensure that he did so. The promise to pay was not enforceable. There was no consideration for it.

It also applies where the duty has arisen under an existing contract.

Stilk v Myrick (1809)

Two members of a ship's crew deserted. The captain promised the remaining crew that they could share these two men's wages if they got the ship safely home. The promise was held not to be binding on the ship's owner. Sailors were bound by their contract to cope with the normal contingencies of the voyage, which could include these desertions, so there was no consideration for the captain's promise.

The exceptions to the rule

It will be consideration where what is given is more than could be expected from the duty. The extra element is the consideration for the new promise. Again this will apply where a public duty is exceeded.

Glassbrook Bros v Glamorgan County Council (1925)

During a strike a pit-owner asked for extra protection from the police and promised a payment in return. When the strike was over the pit-owner refused to pay, claiming that the police were in any case bound to protect his pit. His argument failed. The police had provided more men than they would normally have done so there was consideration for the promise.

The exception to the basic rule has also been seen even in apparently social arrangements, where it is arguable whether it can in reality be considered that there is also an intention to create legal relations.

Shadwell v Shadwell (1860)

At a time when an action for breach of promise to marry was still available in law, a young man became engaged to marry. His uncle wrote to him congratulating him and promising to pay him £150 per year until he reached an income of £600 per year as a chancery barrister. The young man did in fact marry and claimed the money from his uncle when it remained unpaid. The court held that even though the claimant was legally bound to marry, doing so was good consideration for the uncle's promise and the promise was enforceable.

Again it also applies where the existing duty is contractual and a party has given more than was necessary under the contract.

Hartley v Ponsonby (1857)

This case involved similar facts to *Stilk v Myrick* (1809) but only 19 members of a crew of 36 remained. A similar promise to pay more money to the remaining crew was enforceable because the reduction in numbers made the voyage much more dangerous. In agreeing to continue in these circumstances they had provided good consideration for the promise to pay them extra money.

The exception has been upheld even in situations where the consideration is not straightforwardly identifiable.

Scotson v Pegg (1861)

Claimants contracted with a party to deliver coal to him or to his order. The contracting party then sold the coal to the defendant and instructed the claimant to deliver the coal to a third party, the defendant. The defendant then agreed with the claimant that in consideration of the claimant delivering the coal to him, the defendants would unload the coal at a fixed rate per day. The defendant failed to keep this arrangement and the claimant sued. The defendant argued that there was no consideration for the agreement with the claimant. The court rejected this argument and held that the performance of a duty owed to a third party could in fact provide consideration for a promise made by a third party.

It has also been accepted, albeit by the Privy Council, that a promise to perform an existing obligation made to a third party can be valid consideration for a fresh agreement.

Pao On v Lau Yiu Long (1980)

Both parties owned companies. The major asset in Pao's company was a building that Lau wished to purchase. An agreement was made whereby Lau's company would buy Pao's company in return for a large number of shares in Lau's company. To avoid the damage that sudden trading in this number of shares might cause, Lau inserted a clause in the contract that Pao should retain 60 per cent of the shares for at least one year (we could call this agreement 1). Pao wanted a guarantee that the shares would not fall in value, and a subsidiary agreement was made at the same time by which Lau would buy back 60 per cent of the shares at $2.50 each. Pao later realised that this might benefit Lau more if the shares rose in value, and therefore refused to carry out the contract unless the subsidiary arrangement was scrapped and replaced with a straightforward indemnity by Lau against a fall in the value of the shares. Lau could have sued at this point for breach of contract but, fearing a loss of public confidence in his company as a result, agreed to the new terms (we could call this agreement 2). When the value of the shares did then fall, Lau refused to honour the agreement and Pao then sought to enforce the indemnity. Lao offered two defences. Firstly that the second agreement, the agreement to indemnify Pao, was past consideration. Secondly that Pao had given no consideration for the second agreement since it only involved doing what he was bound to do under the first agreement – pass the company in return for the shares. In response to Lau's first defence, the Privy Council applied the rule in *Lampleigh v Braithwaite*. Lau's demand that Pao should not sell 60 per cent of the shares for one year was a request for a service that carried with it an implied promise to pay. This implied promise was later supported by the actual promise to indemnify Pao. Lau's second defence also failed. There was consideration. Pao, by continuing with the contract, was protecting the credibility and financial standing of Lau's company and the price payable in return for this was the indemnity.

The same reasoning can be used to find consideration by third parties to a contract where an agency relationship can be identified and where the agreement protects the commercial credibility of the contract.

New Zealand Shipping Co Ltd v AM Satterthwaite & Co Ltd (The Eurymedon) (1975)

This is a complex case demonstrating how far the courts are prepared to strain the simple meaning of consideration in order to enforce an agreement that they believe must be enforced. Carriers contracted with the consignors of goods to ship drilling equipment. The carriers hired stevedores to unload the equipment, and these stevedores by their negligence caused substantial damage to it. A clause in the carriers' contract with the consignors contained a clause limiting their liability in the event of breach. The clause also identified that the protection offered by the limitation would extend to any servant or agent of the carriers.

There were two questions for the court. Firstly the court had to decide whether there was a contractual relationship between the stevedores and the consignors. If so, the court was then required to determine whether the stevedores had provided any consideration for the promise by the consignors to be bound by the limitation clause. This was clearly questionable because the stevedores were doing nothing more than they were contractually bound to do, unload the ship. The Privy Council accepted that there was a contractual relationship based on agency, and that the promise made by the stevedores could provide consideration in return for the promise made by the consignors to be bound by the limitation clause.

A very recent exception to the basic rule occurs where the party making the promise to pay extra receives an extra benefit from the other party's agreement to complete what he was already bound to do under an existing arrangement.

Williams v Roffey Bros & Nicholls Contractors Ltd (1990)

Roffey Bros builders sub-contracted the carpentry on a number of flats they were building to Williams for £20,000. Williams had underquoted for the work and ran into financial difficulties. Because there was a delay clause in Roffey's building meaning they would have to pay money to the client if the flats were not built on time, they promised to pay Williams another £10,300 if he would complete the carpentry on time. When Williams completed the work and Roffey's failed to pay extra, his claim to the money succeeded. Even though Williams was only doing what he was already contractually bound to do, Roffey's were gaining the extra benefit of not having to pay the money for delay to the client. Williams was providing consideration for their promise to pay him more for the work merely by completing his existing obligations on time.

One point to remember is that there was no attempt on Williams' part to extract the extra money by threats or coercion. The rules of economic duress would in any case have prevented him from succeeding.

What is clear from the case is that the courts do not want promises made in a business context to be broken. To prevent this, they will find consideration even though it is hard to find anything real or tangible about it.

A simpler approach has been adopted by the New Zealand Court of Appeal. In *Antons Trawling Co Ltd v Smith* (2003) the court held where the parties merely vary the terms of an existing agreement they should be bound by the variation.

A promise to accept part payment of an existing debt in place of the whole debt cannot be enforced, as there is no consideration for the promise

The basic rule

This was first stated in *Pinnel's Case* (1602) which held that payment of a smaller sum than the debt itself on the due date can never relieve the liability of the debtor to pay the whole debt, so the creditor can always sue for the unpaid balance of the debt.

The rule can operate fairly where the creditor is giving in to pressure by the debtor to accept less.

Activity

In the following situations, select the appropriate statement from the choices which follow:

1. Mary, a student, asks Donald, her teacher, if he will give her good tuition for which she will pay him £100.
   (a) There is a contract. Mary will have to pay £100 to Donald.
   (b) Mary will be able to sue Donald if his tuition is not good.
   (c) Donald cannot demand the £100 from Mary. He is only doing his duty.
   (d) Donald can sue for the £100 if Mary does not pay it.

2. Sid, the manager of a firm promises Danny, a packer, £100 on top of his wages if he will work late one evening to complete a rush order.
   (a) There is no contract. Danny is only doing his job.
   (b) Danny is entitled to the £100. He is doing extra to his normal job.
   (c) Danny can only be paid the £100 if he does £100 worth of extra work.
   (d) Sid can sue Danny if he refuses to stay late.

DC Builders v Rees (1965)

Builders were owed £482 for the balance of work they had completed. After several months waiting for payment, and at a point where they were in danger of going out of business, they reluctantly accepted an offer by the Rees's to pay £300 in full satisfaction of the debt. When the builders then sued for the balance they were successful. They were not prevented by the agreement to accept less, which in any case was extracted from them under pressure.

It can also sometimes seem to operate unfairly where the debtor genuinely relies on the promise of the creditor.

Foakes v Beer (1884)

Dr Foakes owed Mrs Beer £2,090 after a court judged against him. The two reached an agreement for Foakes to pay in installments, with Mrs Beer agreeing that no further action would be taken if the debt was paid off by the agreed date. Later Mrs Beer demanded interest, which is always payable on a judgement debt, and sued when Foakes refused to pay. She was successful as a result of *Pinnel's* rule.

Exceptions to the rule

There are two basic exceptions where the agreement to pay less than the full debt can be enforced.

1. **Accord and satisfaction.** There is an agreement to accept something other than the money from the existing debt. This might take a number of forms:

*   An agreement to accept an earlier payment of a smaller sum than the whole debt. (This was in fact what actually happened in *Pinnel's* case.) As an example, say I owe you £100 that I am due to pay on March 1st. You then agree to accept a payment of £80 made on February 1st.

You will be unable to sue for the remaining £20. In effect the earlier payment reflects consideration for the changed agreement.

*   An agreement to accept something other than money instead of the debt. Say I owe you £1,000 and you accept instead my stereo hi-fi, worth about £800. You have the opportunity to place whatever value you wish on the goods. If you accept them in place of the money, the full debt is satisfied.

*   An agreement to accept a part payment together with something else, not to the value of the balance of the debt. Say I owe you £100 and you agree to accept £50 and a law book worth £21.99p. In cash value you have only received £71.99p but the debt has been paid.

2. **The doctrine of promissory estoppel.** The doctrine acts as a defence to a claim by a creditor for the remainder of the debt where part payment has been accepted.

    The effect of the doctrine is to prevent (estop) the claimant from going back on the promise because it would be unfair and inequitable to do so.

Lord Denning developed the doctrine in *obiter* from the older doctrine of waiver.

Central London Property Trust Ltd v High Trees House Ltd (1947)

From 1937 the defendants leased a block of flats in Wimbledon from the claimants to sublet to tenants. When the Second World War started, it was impossible to find tenants and so the defendants were unable to pay the rent. The claimants agreed to accept half rent, which the defendants continued to pay. By 1945 the flats were all let and the claimants wanted the rent returned to its former level and sued for the higher rent for the last two quarters. They succeeded but Lord Denning stated in *obiter* that had they tried to sue for the extra rent for the whole period of the war, they would have failed.

Estoppel would prevent them from going back on the promise on which the defendants had relied so long as the circumstances persisted. As Lord Denning stated:

'A promise was made which was intended to create legal relations and which to the knowledge of the person making the promise was going to be acted upon by the person to whom it was made, and which in fact was so acted upon. In such cases the courts have said that the promise must be honoured … the logical consequence, no doubt, is that a promise to accept a smaller sum in discharge of a larger debt if acted upon, is binding notwithstanding the absence of consideration.'

Unfortunately Lord Denning's final statement here led some judges to the conclusion that the need for consideration to be proved in contracts had somehow been removed. Lord Denning was then called on to develop a more reliable explanation of the application of estoppel in a later case.

Combe v Combe (1951)

A wife separated from her husband and sued him for a promise that he had quite gratuitously made to her that he would pay her £2 per week (ie it was not under a legal maintenance order). The judge at first instance noted the lack of consideration but held that following the *High Trees* case this was irrelevant and found in the wife's favour. In the Court of Appeal Lord Denning apologised for any confusion he had caused in *High Trees* and explained the doctrine further:

'Where one party has by his words or conduct made to the other party a promise or assurance which was intended to affect the legal conditions between them and be

acted on accordingly, then once the other party has taken him at his word and acted on it the one who gave the promise cannot afterwards be allowed to revert to the previous legal relations as if no such promise had been made.'

Lord Birkett in the case made one further very significant comment in describing estoppel as 'a shield and not a sword'; in other words, it could only operate as a defence to a claim, not a means of bringing one.

The essential elements of the doctrine then as described in the case require the following to be used successfully:

- There must be an existing contractual relationship between the claimant and the defendant.
- The claimant must have agreed to waive (give up) some of his rights under that contract (the amount of the debt that has been unpaid).
- The claimant has waived these rights knowing that the defendant would rely on the promise in determining his future conduct.
- The defendant has in fact acted in reliance on the promise to forego some of the debt.

The possible subsequent development of the doctrine is uncertain, particularly now that Lord Denning has died. In *Brikom Investments Ltd v Carr* (1979), for instance, Lord Justice Roskill stressed that:

> 'it would be wrong to extend the doctrine of promissory estoppel, whatever its precise limits at the present day, to the extent of abolishing in this back-handed way the doctrine of consideration.'

Certainly application of estoppel to the area of part payment of debt as an enforceable replacement for the whole debt is likely to be rejected; see *Re Selectmove* (1995) below.

Re Selectmove (1995)

A company which owed tax to the Inland Revenue offered to pay its debt by installments. The Collector of taxes stated that he would contact the company if the arrangement was unsatisfactory, and the company began to pay off its debt by installments. The IRC then insisted that all arrears of tax should be paid immediately or it would begin winding-up procedures against the company. The company tried to argue on the basis of *Williams v Roffey* (1990) that their promise to carry out an existing obligation was good consideration for the agreement to pay by installments. The Court of Appeal distinguished *Williams v Roffey* as that case involved the provision of goods and services rather than payment of an existing debt. The court as a result felt itself bound rather by the basic precedent in *Foakes v Beer* (1884) and held that IRC was not bound by any agreement to accept payment by installments. There appears still to be a glaring inconsistency here with the reasoning in *Williams v Roffey*.

Attempts to apply the principle in *Williams v Roffey* (1990) to situations involving promises to accept part payment of debts in full satisfaction of the whole debt have been specifically rejected.

Key facts

Consideration	Case
Consideration is 'the price for which the promise of the other is bought'. Executory consideration is where the consideration is yet to change hands. Executed consideration is consideration that has already passed.	*Dunlop v Selfridge* (1915)
Consideration need not be adequate	*Thomas v Thomas* (1842)
But it must be sufficient, that is it must be real, tangible and have value	*Chappel v Nestle Co* (1960)
Consideration must not be past	*Re McArdle* (1951)
Except where the service has been requested	*Lampleigh v Braithwaite* (1615)
A person seeking to sue on a contract must have given consideration under it	*Tweddle v Atkinson* (1861)
Carrying out an existing contractual obligation cannot be consideration for a new promise	*Stilk v Myrick* (1809)
Unless something extra is added to the contract	*Hartley v Ponsonby* (1857)
Or a third party's interests are involved	*Pao On v Lau Yiu Long* (1980)
Or if an extra benefit is to be gained	*Williams v Roffey Bros & Nicholls* (1990)
Part payment of a debt can never satisfy the debt as a whole There are exceptions to the rule including:	*Pinnel's Case* (1602)
accord and satisfaction (where the debt is paid in a different form), and estoppel (where a party waiving rights is prevented from going back on the promise because of reliance by the other party)	*Central London Properties Trust v High Trees House Ltd* (1947)
Williams v Roffey (1990) applies only to existing duties as consideration for fresh agreements and cannot be applied to agreements to accept part payment of a debt in full satisfaction	*Re Selectmove* (1995)

Key facts chart on consideration

Activity

In the following situation select the appropriate statement from the choices which follow:

Dave, a builder, owes his supplier £50,000 for materials. Dave has been unable to sell the house he has recently built at a profit, due to a slump in the property market, and has only £45,000. The supplier agrees to accept the £45,000 to prevent Dave from going out of business. Six months later the supplier has learnt that Dave has just gained a building contract worth £5 million.

(a) Dave will have to pay the remaining £5,000 to the supplier immediately.
(b) Dave can use the supplier's promise as a defence to a claim for the money.
(c) The supplier can recover the materials used by Dave.
(d) Dave can sue the supplier.

Activity

1. Why did the law first develop the doctrine of consideration?
2. What in simple terms is consideration?
3. Why is it unimportant whether the consideration is adequate or not?
4. What is the basic difference between something that is sufficient and something that is adequate?
5. How easy is it to accept cases such as *Chappell v Nestle* (1960) in the light of the accepted legal meaning of sufficiency?
6. Why is it impossible to form a contract with consideration that is past?
7. Exactly how does the exception in *Lampleigh v Braithwaite* (1615) operate?
8. In which ways could the rule that consideration must move from the promisee be said to be unfair?
9. What is the distinguishing feature, if any, between *Stilk v Myrick* (1809) and *Hartley v Ponsonby* (1857)?
10. Why is it difficult to see the distinction between the principles in *Stilk v Myrick* (1809) and *Williams v Roffey Bros & Nicholls* (1990)?
11. Why exactly did Pau On succeed in the case of *Pao On v Lau Yiu Long* (1980)?
12. Is there any relevance to promissory estoppel in the modern day?
13. Do the exceptions to *Pinnel*'s rule always cover every possible problem?
14. What is the effect of the judgment in *Re Selectmove* (1995)?

6.6 Privity of contract

6.6.1 The basic rule

The simple rule is that a person who is not a party to a contract can neither sue nor be sued under it. It is similar to the rule of consideration that a person who has not given consideration cannot sue or be sued. We have seen this in operation in *Tweddle v Atkinson* (1861). Even though the claimant was named in a written agreement, he had no enforceable third party right.

The modern statement of the rule is found in Lord Haldane's judgment in the following case:

Dunlop Pneumatic Tyre Co Ltd v Selfridge & Co Ltd (1915)

In the contract, Dew & Co wholesalers agreed to buy tyres from Dunlop. They did so on the express undertaking that they would not sell below certain fixed prices. They also undertook to obtain the same price fixing agreements from their clients. Dew sold tyres on to Selfridge on these terms but Selfridge broke the agreement and sold tyres at discount prices. Dunlop sought an injunction. They failed for lack of privity. In the House of Lords Lord Haldane said:

'... only a person who is a party to a contract can sue on it. Our law knows nothing of a *jus quaesitum tertio* arising by way of contract. Such a right may be conferred by way of property, as, for example, under a trust, but it cannot be conferred on a stranger to a contract as a right to enforce the contract *in personam* ...'

The rule has a number of consequences:

- A person receiving goods as a gift may be unable to sue personally where the goods are defective.
- It may then prove embarrassing to try to enlist the help of the actual purchaser.
- Even if the purchaser does sue, he may be able to recover only for their own loss, not necessarily the loss suffered by the donee of the gift.
- The rule may well prevent enforcement of services that have already been paid for, as in *Price v Easton* (1833).
- The rule may also mean that a benefactor's express wishes are denied, as in *Tweddle v Atkinson* (1861).
- In commercial contracts, as Lord Dunedin said in *Dunlop v Selfridge* (1915):

" '... the effect ... is to make it possible for a person to snap his fingers at a bargain definitely made, a bargain not unfair in itself, and which the person seeking to enforce it has a legitimate interest to enforce ...' **"**

6.6.2 Exceptions to the rule

Many attempts have been made to avoid the harsh effects of the rule on enforcing third party rights in a contract. This is done using a variety of means, none of which have affected the basic rule. This remains intact.

Statutory exceptions

Parliament is not bound by the strict rules of contract in enacting new provisions, and so there are statutory exceptions to the rule.

Section 148(7) of the Road Traffic Act 1988 obliges a motorist to take out third party liability insurance. Another motorist who is involved in an accident with this motorist can then rely on it. The insurance is enforceable despite the fact that the other motorist lacks any privity in the insurance contract.

However, the courts will not allow an Act to be used for an incorrect purpose.

Beswick v Beswick (1968)

A widow was trying to enforce an agreement between her husband and her nephew for the latter to provide her with a weekly annuity on the death of the former. The agreement was a condition in the sale of her husband's business to the nephew. The widow lacked privity to the agreement and had provided no consideration for it. Her attempt to use a provision in s 56 Law of Property Act 1925 that referred to '... other property ...' failed. The reasoning was that the Act referred only to real property (land or interests in land) and could not be applied to purely personal property.

Trust law

Despite lacking privity, a party identifying third party rights under a contract may show that a trust is created in his or her favour.

Gregory & Parker v Williams (1817)

Parker owed money to both Gregory and Williams. Since he could see no way of organising settlement himself, he assigned all of his property to Williams on the understanding that Williams would then pay off the debt to Gregory. Williams failed to pay over the money to Gregory who, not being a party to the agreement, was unable to sue on it. The court was nevertheless prepared to accept that a trust of the money had been created in Gregory's favour, which was then enforceable against Williams.

But a trust is not created unless a claimant can show an express intention that he should gain a benefit.

Les Affreteurs Reunis SA v Walford (1919) (Walford's Case)

Walford was a broker who negotiated an agreement between a charter party and the owner of the vessel, but was obviously not a party to the agreement. The agreement contained a stipulation that Walford should receive a 3 per cent commission from the shipowners. They failed to pay. The court was prepared to accept that a trust was created only because he was named.

Restrictive covenants

This is another device created by equity by which a party selling land retains certain rights over the use of the land which must be negative restrictions. The covenant is said to run with the land. So, if properly created, it binds subsequent purchasers of the land even though there is no privity between them and the original seller. This applies even if the land retained by the original seller has also been sold on.

Tulk v Moxhay (1848)

Tulk owned land in London that he sold with an express undertaking that it would never be used to build property on. It was then resold on numerous occasions, each time subject to the same undertaking. Moxhay bought it knowing of the limitation but still intended to build on it. Tulk successfully sought an injunction. The court accepted that it would be against conscience for Moxhay to buy, knowing of the restriction.

Procedural rules

In rare instances, procedural rules have been used to get round the effects of privity. This only succeeds if it corresponds to the actual promise made, and because all of the parties are present in the court.

Snelling v John G Snelling Ltd (1973)

Three brothers were all directors of their own company, John G Snelling Ltd, which was financed by loans from the three brothers. When the company borrowed money from a finance company, the three brothers entered an agreement with one another that until such time as the finance company loan was repaid, if any of them resigned their directorship in the company they would forfeit the amount of their own loan to the company. The company was not a party to this agreement. One brother did leave the company and sued the company for his loan. The remaining brothers applied to join the company as defendants and counterclaimed on the agreement reached between the three brothers. The court upheld their argument. Even though the company was not a party to the agreement, the brothers and the company were in many ways the same. A stay of execution of the brother's claim was the appropriate order.

The so-called 'holiday cases'

We will discuss the issue of recovery for mental distress and the 'holiday cases' at a later stage under damages. However, significant development was made in these cases in respect of third party rights.

Jackson v Horizon Holidays (1975)

Mr Jackson had booked a 'family holiday' which fell far short of the contract description. He sued the holiday company not only on his own behalf but for his family also. The company, while accepting liability, disputed that they should pay damages in respect of the family. The House of Lords held that the loss of enjoyment suffered by the family was in effect a loss to the contracting party himself. He had paid for a 'family holiday' but not received it. Damages were awarded on this basis. This appears to strain the law a long way, albeit in order to achieve a just result.

The courts have indicated that this method of getting round the privity rule is confined to 'holiday contracts'. In *Woodar Investment Development Ltd v Wimpey Construction (UK) Ltd* (1980) the House of Lords, while not expressly overruling *Jackson* (1975), held that there was no general principle allowing a party to a contract to sue on behalf of third parties injured by a breach. Lord Wilberforce held that *Jackson* fell into a special group of contracts involving families where it was intended that the benefit should be shared between the family members.

Protecting third parties in exclusion clauses

A party to a contract can include an exclusion or limitation clause in a contract. Traditionally, however, a sub-contractor would be unable to claim the benefit of the exclusion clause, even if named under it.

Scruttons Ltd v Midland Silicones Ltd (1962)

A shipping company carried chemicals for the claimants under a contract containing a clause limiting damages in the event of breach to $500. Stevedores sub-contracted to the shipping company did $583 worth of damage, tried to rely on the clause and failed for lack of privity. However, Lord Reid felt that there could be:

'… success in agency if the bill of lading makes it clear that the stevedore is intended to be protected by the provisions …'

Despite this, in some situations third parties have been able to claim cover under an exclusion clause despite lacking privity.

New Zealand Shipping Co Ltd v A M Satterthwaite & Co Ltd (The Eurymedon) (1974)

In this Privy Council case the stevedores were able to rely on an exclusion clause in a similar action. The reasoning given by Lord Wilberforce was that the stevedores were identified as agents in the contract.

Collateral contracts

This mechanism may succeed if a claimant complains that a contract has been formed through reliance on a collateral promise made by a third party to the contract.

Shanklin Pier v Detel Products Ltd (1951)

Shanklin Pier v Detel Products Ltd (1951)

Owners of a pier were assured by Detel's representatives that their paint was suitable to paint the pier and would last a minimum of seven years. Relying on the assurance, the pier owners instructed their painting contractors to paint the pier with Detel's paint. The paint was in fact unsuitable and peeled. The court held that Detel was liable on the promise despite an apparent lack of privity in the painting contract.

Agency, assignment and negotiable instruments

All of the exceptions so far considered are enforceable because of principles contained in individual cases or because they rely on areas of law other than contract.

There are three major exceptions which are outside of the A Level specifications: agency, assignment and negotiable instruments.

- Where one party acts as an agent for another (known as the principal), the agent can make and carry out contracts with a third party on the principal's behalf. The significance of this is that the agent can make agreements by which the principal is bound, despite the apparent lack of privity. Where all of the appropriate rules are complied with, the principal and the third party are able to sue and be sued by each other under the contract made by the agent.
- Assignment is a system devised for the transfer of property rights. This may be appropriate for instance with debts. If the assignment of the debt conforms to the proper rules, then the party to whom the debt is assigned can sue the debtor despite the apparent lack of privity.
- Negotiable instruments were originally a device of merchant traders. The rules used by

the merchants were eventually given statutory force in the Bills of Exchange Act 1882. One common form of negotiable instrument with which we are familiar in modern times is the cheque. By various processes it is then possible to transfer ownership of the property identified in the instrument; in the case of a cheque, a sum of money.

6.6.3 The Contracts (Rights of Third Parties) Act 1999

The fact that judges have been prepared to allow so many exceptions to the basic rule is a fair indication of a general dissatisfaction with the operation of the doctrine. In many cases indeed judges have themselves called for legislative reform, particularly because of the complexities that are caused by there being so many different exceptions.

The Act followed a Law Commission draft bill. Its major provision is contained in s 1(1) by which:

> '... a person who is not a party to a contract (in this Act referred to as a third party) may in his own right enforce the contract if: (a) the contract contains an express term to that effect; or (b) subject to subsection (2) the contract purports to confer a benefit on the third party.'

The first ground under subsection (a) is self-explanatory. The second ground, subject to subsection (2) states that ground (b) will be unavailable to a third party if:

> '... on the proper construction of the contract it appears that the parties did not intend the contract to be enforceable by a third party ...'

In consequence it seems only those rights given in the contract can be enforced.

Nisshin Shipping Co v Cleaves & Co Ltd (2004)

A contract between ship owners and charterers of the vessel included a clause for payment of commission to the broker who had negotiated the agreement between the parties, but who was not a party to the contract. The commission was not paid so the broker sued. The court held that he was identifiable from the contract so s 1(3) applied and the contract clearly conferred a benefit on him so that s 1(1)(b) was also satisfied and he was able to recover under the Act.

Certain types of contract are excluded, eg those where other legislation applies; a third party cannot sue an employee who is in breach of his contract of employment to protect workers where they take legitimate industrial action; the 'statutory contract' under s 14 Companies Act 1985 gives shareholders the right to sue officers of the company on issues arising from the memorandum and articles of association.

The Act has some important consequences:

- A wide range of third party rights will be enforceable under the Act.
- Certain exceptions to the basic rule become unnecessary, eg the claimant in *Tweddle v Atkinson* (1861) would have an enforceable right as would the family members in *Jackson v Horizon Holidays* (1975).
- Where a third party comes within the scope of an exclusion clause, it will be much easier to enforce in their favour.
- Many exceptions will still apply, eg collateral warranties.
- The Act can still prove ineffective as its provisions can be expressly excluded.

Key facts

Privity and third party rights	Case
The basic doctrine is that nobody can sue or be sued under a contract who is not a party to it	*Dunlop v Selfridge* (1915)
In other words nobody can enforce a contract without giving consideration under it	*Tweddle v Atkinson* (1861)
Since the rule unfairly prevents third parties identified as gaining rights under a contract from enforcing those rights a number of exceptions exist:	
● Statutory exceptions as with Third Party Insurance under the Road Traffic Acts	
● Where a trust is created in favour of the third party	*Gregory & Parker v Williams* (1817)
● Restrictive covenants	*Tulk v Moxhay* (1848)
● Procedural rules	*Snelling v John G Snelling Ltd* (1973)
● The 'holiday cases'	*Jackson v Horizon Holidays* (1975)
● Protection given to third parties in exclusion clauses	*New Zealand Shipping Co v Satterthwaite* (1974)
● Collateral contracts	*Shanklin Pier v Detel Products Ltd* (1951)
● Agency, assignment and negotiable instruments.	
Now parliament has passed the Contracts (Rights of Third Parties) Act 1999 to enable third parties to enforce rights that they are given under a contract – so a third party can enforce provisions in a contract if:	
(a) the contract expressly states so	
(b) the contract purports to confer a benefit on the third party.	

Key facts chart on privity and third party rights

1. What are the major justifications for the rule on privity of contract?
2. What is the connection between the doctrine of privity and the requirement of consideration in a contract?
3. How is the doctrine of privity unfair?
4. What are the most effective exceptions to the basic rule on privity?
5. To what extent does the Contract (Rights of Third Parties) Act 1999 address the problems of all third parties affected by the doctrine of privity?

6.7 Intention to create legal relations

6.7.1 The two presumptions

We all regularly make arrangements with each other, and we may even be doing things in return for something; this seems as though there is consideration too.

However, we do not always intend that if we fail to keep to an agreement the other party should be able to sue us. Nor would it be sensible for the courts to be filled with actions on all of the broken promises that are ever made. My children may expect their pocket money regularly, but would you want them to be able to sue if I forget to give it to them one week?

The law makes a sensible compromise by assuming that in certain situations we would usually not intend the agreement to be legally binding, while in others we usually would. The first covers social or domestic arrangements where it is presumed there is no intention to be legally bound. The second concerns commercial or business agreements where an intention to be legally bound is presumed. In either case the facts can show that the presumption should not apply. So intention is very much decided on the facts in individual cases.

6.7.2 Social and domestic agreements

Arrangements between family members are usually left to them to sort out themselves and are not legally binding.

Balfour v Balfour (1919)

A husband worked abroad without his wife who had to stay in England due to illness, and promised an income of £30 per month. When the wife later petitioned for divorce her claim to this income failed. It had been made at an amicable point in their relationship, not in contemplation of divorce. It was a purely domestic arrangement beyond the scope of the court.

Where husband and wife are estranged, an agreement between them may be taken as intended to be legally binding.

Merritt v Merritt (1970)

Here the husband had deserted his wife for another woman. An agreement to pay the wife an income if she paid the outstanding mortgage was held to be intended to create legally binding obligations.

Sometimes of course families make arrangements that appear to be business arrangements because of their character. In such cases, the court must examine what the real purpose of the arrangement was.

Jones v Padavatton (1969)

A mother gave an allowance to her daughter under an agreement for the daughter to give up her highly paid job in New York, study for the bar in England and then return to practise in Trinidad where the mother lived. When the daughter found it difficult to manage on the allowance, the mother then bought a house for her to live in, part of which the daughter could let to supplement her income. They later quarrelled and the mother sought repossession of the house. The daughter's argument that the second agreement was contractual failed. The court could find no intent.

If money has passed hands, then it will not matter that the arrangement is made socially. It will be held as intended to be legally binding.

Simpkins v Pays (1955)

A lodger and two members of the household entered competitions in the lodger's name but paid equal shares of the entry money on the understanding that they would share any winnings. Their action succeeded.

If parties put their financial security at risk for an agreement, then it must have been intended that the agreement should be legally binding.

Parker v Clarke (1960)

A young couple were persuaded by an older couple to sell their house to move in with them, with the promise that they would inherit property on the death of the old couple. When the couples eventually fell out, the young couple was asked to leave. Their action for damages succeeded. Giving up their security indicated that the arrangement was intended to be legally binding.

6.7.3 Commercial and business agreements

An arrangement made in a business context is presumed to be intended to be legally binding unless evidence can show a different intent.

Edwards v Skyways Ltd (1969)

An attempt to avoid making an agreed *ex gratia* payment in a redundancy failed. Although *ex gratia* indicates no pre-existing liability to make the payment, the agreement to pay it once made was binding.

In identifying that intention exists, the courts also make a distinction between situations where the parties reach a basic agreement where detail is to be added at a later stage, where there is a clear intention to be bound, and situations where a final decision is deferred until some matter is resolved between the parties (*Bear Sterns Bank plc v Forum Global Equity Ltd* (2007)).

The offer of free gifts where this is to promote the business can still be held to be legally binding.

Esso Petroleum Co Ltd v Commissioners of Customs and Excise (1976)

Esso gave free World Cup coins with every four gallons of petrol purchased. Customs and Excise wanted to claim purchase tax from the transaction. As Esso were clearly trying to gain more business from the promotion, there was held to be intention to be bound by the arrangement.

The principle has also been developed to cover situations where prizes are offered in competitions. The purpose of such events is generally to promote the body offering the prize, so there is intention to create a legal relationship which is binding and can be relied on by members of the public who enter the competition.

McGowan v Radio Buxton (2001)

The claimant entered a radio competition for which the prize had been stated to be a Renault Clio car. She was told that she had won the competition but was given a four-inch scale model of a Clio. The defendants argued that there was no legally binding contract. The judge held that was intention to create legal relations. The claimant entered the competition as a member of the public and that 'looking at the transcript of the broadcast, there was not even a hint that the car would be a toy.'

However, it is possible for the agreement to contain no intention to be legally binding where that is specifically stated in the agreement itself.

Jones v Vernons' Pools Ltd (1938)

The Pools company inserted a clause on all coupons stating that '… the transaction should not give rise to any legal relationship … but be binding in honour only …' When a punter claimed that the company had lost his winning coupon and sought payment, he failed. The clause prevented any legal claim.

The same type of principle applies with so-called comfort letters. Although such letters are worded so that they appear almost to amount to a guarantee, they do not and will not give rise to legal obligations.

Kleinwort Benson Ltd v Malaysian Mining Corporation (1989)

Kleinwort lent £10 million to Metals Ltd, a subsidiary of MMC. The parent company would not guarantee this loan but issued a comfort letter stating their intention to ensure Metals had sufficient funds for repayment. When Metals went out of business without repaying Kleinwort, the latter's action based on the comfort letter failed. If they wanted a guarantee they should have insisted on one.

Activity

1. How do courts decide if an agreement is intended to be legally binding?
2. Why should an agreement within a family not be legally binding?
3. Why are the cases of *Balfour v Balfour* (1919) and *Merritt v Merritt* (1970) decided differently?
4. Why should commercial agreements generally lead to a legal relationship?
5. What is an 'honour pledge clause'?
6. What is the reasoning behind making free gifts, prizes in competitions etc part of a legally enforceable agreement?

Activity

Consider whether the courts would identify an intention to be legally bound in the following situations:

1. Alan agrees that he will buy his son a book in return for mowing the lawns.
2. James agrees to take his secretary Dawn out for a meal for finishing an urgent job quickly and at very short notice.
3. I ask my daughter to give up her part-time job for a week to proofread a draft of a textbook, and promise to pay her the same as she would have earned in her job.
4. Skinny Co usually gives their employees a £50 Christmas box but this year they have decided against it.
5. I agree to take my wife to the cinema but I fail to turn up because I have had to stay longer at work.

Key facts

Intention to create legal relations	Case
There are two rebuttable presumptions – that in social and domestic arrangements there is no intention to be legally bound, and in commercial and business dealings there is.	
Domestic:	
● An arrangement between husband and wife will not normally be legally binding	*Balfour v Balfour* (1919)
● Unless the couple is estranged	*Merritt v Merritt* (1970)
● An agreement will be binding where the parties have spent money on it	*Simpkins v Pays* (1955)
● And also where they have acted to their detriment	*Parker v Clarke* (1960)
Business:	
● An agreement made in a business context is usually binding	*Edwards v Skyways* (1969)
● Even where free gifts are promised to promote sales	
● The same can apply to prizes offered in competitions	*Esso v Commissioners of Customs & Excise* (1976)
● Some agreements are binding in honour only	*McGowan v Radio Buxton* (2001)
● Comfort letters create no legal obligations	*Jones v Vernons Pools* (1938)
	Kleinwort Benson v Malaysian Mining Corporation (1989)

Key facts chart on intention to create legal relations

Chapter 7

Contract terms

7.1 Express and implied terms

7.1.1 Distinguishing terms from mere representations

The terms of a contract are its contents and represent what the parties agree to do or to give under it, the obligations that they owe. Both sides have obligations as we have already seen from the *consensus ad idem* in offer and acceptance, and from the doctrine of consideration.

Under a contract, both sides must carry out their side of the agreement for the contract to be completed. It is often failing to meet a contractual obligation, and therefore a breach of a term, that leads to a dispute.

The terms of a contract can be what the parties have expressly agreed upon, but they can also be what the law has said should be included in the contract and therefore is implied into the contract.

Terms that have been expressly agreed by the parties will inevitably arise from the negotiations that have taken place prior to formation and the statements that each party makes to the other at that time. Such pre-contractual statements are generally known as 'representations'.

A pre-contractual statement may be made orally or in writing, or indeed may be implied by conduct, as when a contract is formed on the fall of an auctioneer's hammer. The impact that a pre-contractual statement has on a contract depends very much on the character of the statement and the context in which it is made.

In this way certain statements made by the parties will have no significance at all in law, while some will actually form the obligations of the contract as terms, and are therefore enforceable or their breach will lead to remedies. The significance of certain other pre-contractual statements may depend on whether they have been falsely stated or not, in which case they may be actionable.

Assessing the significance of pre-contractual statements

Basically, any statement made at the time of the contract or in the period leading up to the contract is a representation. The effect of the statement is to represent that the information contained in the statement is true. A further possibility is that the statement represents the stated intention of the party making it.

The law distinguishes between different statements according to the relative significance they will have on a contract. If a contract is in writing, the terms are easily identified in the contract itself. Otherwise the following distinctions can be drawn:

- A statement made by a contracting party which may be intended to induce the other party to enter the contract, but was not intended to form part of the contract, is a **representation**. It may have legal consequences if certain criteria are met. It is **not a term** since it is not incorporated into the contract.

- A statement made by a contracting party by which he intends to be bound will be incorporated and form part of the contract and is therefore a **term**. It will have legal consequences, though these may differ according to what type of term it is.

In all cases the court will determine what the intention of the parties was by use of an objective test – what would a reasonable person consider to be the significance of the statement?

There are also some statements made at the time the contract was formed or in the negotiations leading up to it that will attach no liability and have no legal significance. They will be treated as such because the courts can find no reliance placed upon them, or indeed because no sensible person would believe that they would induce a party to enter a contract.

They are of three different types:

1. trade puffs
2. opinions
3. mere representations.

Trade puffs

Puffs are the boasts or unsubstantiated claims made by, amongst others, advertisers of products or services to highlight the product they are selling. '*Carlsberg, probably the best lager in the world*' is an obvious example of such a boast. It is an exaggerated claim made to boost the saleability of the product. The law will allow the producers some licence to make such statements since it is felt that nobody would be taken in by them, *simplex commendatio non obligat*.

A different view may be taken when the statement, is not a mere boast, but includes a specific promise stated as fact.

Carlill v The Carbolic Smoke Ball Co Ltd (1893)

Here the Smoke Ball company argued that the claim in the advertisement that the product would do as they suggested was a mere advertising gimmick designed to sell more of the product. Their argument failed because of the promise they made to give £100 to anybody contracting one of the prescribed illnesses after using the Smoke Ball correctly. The fact that they had stated in their advertisement that a sum of money was deposited in a bank to cover such claims was even greater proof of their intention to be bound by their promise.

Opinions

Some statements made by a party to a contract attach little legal significance because they lack any weight. An example of this is a mere opinion. An opinion does not carry any liability for the party making it because it is not based on fact.

Bisset v Wilkinson (1927)

Here a vendor was selling two blocks of land in New Zealand. The purchaser was intending to use the land for sheep farming, though it had not previously been used for that purpose, although sheep had formerly been kept on a small part of the land. The vendor told the purchaser that in his judgement the land could carry 2,000 sheep. In fact it could support nowhere near that number. The purchaser argued that the statement was an actionable misrepresentation. The Privy Council held that, owing to the inexperience on which it was based, it was no more than an honest opinion, and not actionable therefore.

Obviously if a statement of opinion is known to be untrue by the party making it, then it is actionable as misrepresentation.

Similarly a party will be able to sue on the basis of a false opinion which has been stated by a party with specialist expertise in that field, and therefore who is in a better bargaining position than the party to whom it is addressed.

Mere representations

Where a party to a contract has made a representation as to fact, which is intended to induce the other party to enter the contract, but which is not intended to form part of the contract, and it is in fact true, there is no further contractual significance. The representation has achieved what it was supposed to do but it is accurate so it has also been complied with.

Esso Petroleum Co Ltd v Marden (1976)

Esso acquired a site on which to build a petrol station. On the basis of professional estimates they represented to Marden, a prospective purchaser, that the filling station would have a throughput of 200,000 gallons per year. In fact the Local Authority refused planning permission for the proposed layout so that pumps would be at the back of the site, and access only from side roads at the rear rather than from the main road at the front of the site. Marden queried the throughput figure but Esso assured him it would be possible. Despite Marden's best efforts sales only ever reached 78,000 gallons; he lost money and was unable to pay back a loan from Esso. Esso sued for repossession and Marden counterclaimed. Esso argued that the statement as to the likely throughput of petrol was a mere opinion. This argument failed because of their extensive expertise in the area.

Activity

1. In what ways does a term differ from a mere representation?
2. Why do some statements made before the contract attach no liability at all?

Activity

Which of the following situations do you think is likely to contain a term?

1. Jasvinder is a greengrocer. He puts a poster in his window which reads 'The tastiest apples around'.
2. Andrew is selling his caravan. He describes it as a 'family caravan'. It has one double bed and two couches on which it would be possible for other people to sleep.
3. Annie has been given a computer for a present that she cannot use so she is selling it to Raj. Raj asks if it has a large memory and Annie says that she thinks it has.
4. Sid is selling his motorbike to Colin. He tells Colin that the bike is 'mechanically perfect'. In fact the bike breaks down as Colin is leaving Sid's house.

Key facts

- The express terms of a contract represent what the parties have agreed upon – these are often identified in the pre-contractual statements.
- Pre-contractual statements are known as 'representations'.
- The law distinguishes between:
  (a) statements which are sufficiently significant to be incorporated into the contract as terms
  (b) statements which, while not incorporated into the contract nevertheless were intended to induce the other party to enter the contract – these are mere representations, but if they are false statements they will be misrepresentations

  (c) statements intended to have no contractual significance at all – these can include: trade puffs and mere opinions.
- A trade puff has no effect on the contract because it is a mere boast which is not taken seriously – unless some other promise is attached; *Carlill v The Carbolic Smoke Ball Co Ltd* (1893).
- An opinion carries no weight unless made by an expert – *Bisset v Wilkinson* (1927).

Key facts

Type of statement	Contractual significance	Reasoning
Terms	These will attach liability (and also a range of remedies when they are breached)	Because they are actually incorporated into the contract, and so they become the obligations under the contract
Mere representations	These attach NO liability	Because, while they may induce a party to enter into the contract, they are not incorporated into the contract and are not intended to create binding obligations
Misrepresentations	These attach liability (and also a range of remedies depending on how deliberately the falsehood was made) *Esso v Marden* (1976)	Because even though they are not part of the contract, being false they may have wrongly induced the other party to enter the contract thus vitiating his or her free will
Mere opinions	These attach NO liability in themselves *Bisset v Wilkinson* (1927)	Because the other party's opinion is no more valid than our own, and we cannot be said to rely on it
Expert opinions	These attach liability (possibly as terms if they are important enough to have been incorporated in the contract. If not they may still amount to innocent misrepresentations) *Esso v Marden* (1976)	Because we do rely, and should be entitled to rely, on the opinion of experts
Trade puffs	These attach NO liability eg 'Carlsberg probably the best lager in the world'	Because the law credits us with more intelligence than to take advertisers' boasts too seriously
Puffs with a specific promise attached	These attach liability *Carlill v Carbolic Smoke Ball Co Ltd* (1892)	Because the promise is quite specific and so we can rely on it rather than the puff, since it creates a separate contractual relationship

Figure 7.1 The relationship between different types of representation and the legal consequences attaching to them

7.1.2 The process of incorporating express terms

Factors relevant to incorporation

Clearly the dividing lines between some of the above categories of statements are not always obvious. Where a contract is in writing, then generally the terms are as stated in the written contract. Where negotiations leading up to the contract are oral, the courts have developed guidelines to determine whether a particular statement is a term of the contract or not.

In order to be a term of the contract, the statement must be incorporated and form part of the contract. Whether or not a statement is incorporated as a term can depend on a number of different factors:

The importance attached to the representation

The more importance that is attached to the statement by either party, then the more likely it is that it is a term. The logic of this is clear. If a party relied on a statement so that without it being incorporated into the contract as a term, it is unlikely that the party would have entered the contract without its inclusion, then the provision identified in the statement is a term.

Birch v Paramount Estates (Liverpool) Ltd (1956)

A couple bought a new house from developers because of a promise that the house would be '… as good as the show house.' In fact the house was not as good and the Court of Appeal held that the statement was so central to the agreement that it had been incorporated into the contract as a term.

In this way, the effect of the statement being so important may make it a warranty rather than a misrepresentation that it might otherwise have been.

Couchman v Hill (1947)

In a written agreement for the sale of a heifer (a young female cow, usually one that has not yet had a calf) the conditions of sale included a clause that lots were sold '… with all faults, imperfections and errors of description.' The sale catalogue actually described the heifer as 'unserved' (meaning not yet having been used for breeding). Prior to the making of the contract the buyer asked both the auctioneer and the seller to confirm that the heifer was unserved, and they both assured him that it was. As a result he bought the heifer. However, not long afterwards he discovered that the heifer was having a calf, and it in fact died as a result of having a calf at too young an age. The Court of Appeal held that, despite the written terms in the contract, the representation was so crucial to the buyer in making the contract that it was incorporated as a term.

Special knowledge or skill affecting the equality of bargaining strength

If the statement is made without the expertise or specialist knowledge to back it up, it is less likely to be seen as a term.

Oscar Chess Ltd v Williams (1957)

The defendant sold a car to motor dealers for £290, describing it as a 1948 Morris 10. He honestly believed that was the correct age of the car since it was the age given in the registration documents. When the car was later found to be a 1939 model, the motor dealers sued for breach of warranty. Their action failed. The defendant had no expertise or specialist skill, was reliant on the registration documents and his statement was no more than an innocent misrepresentation.

However, a statement may well be a term if the person making it has specialist knowledge or expertise and the person to whom it is made is relying on that expertise in deciding to contract.

Dick Bentley Productions Ltd v Harold Smith (Motors) Ltd (1965)

The claimant asked the defendants, who were car dealers, to find him a 'well vetted' Bentley car. In other words, one in good condition. The defendants found a car they falsely stated had only done 20,000 miles since being fitted with a new engine and gearbox. In fact it had done 100,000 miles. The claimant later found the car to be unsuitable as well as discovering that the statement about the mileage was untrue and sued for a breach of warranty. The Court of Appeal upheld the claim since the claimant relied on the specialist expertise of the car dealers in stating the mileage.

The time between making the statement and formation of the contract

Sometimes the court may assess that the time lapse between the statement made in the negotiations and the creation of the contract itself is too great to support a claim that the statement is incorporated in the contract as a term.

Routledge v McKay (1954)

A motorcycle had actually first been registered in 1939 but in a registration book later issued it was wrongly stated as 1941. In 1949 the current owner, who was unaware of this inaccuracy, was selling the motorcycle, and in response to an enquiry about the age by a prospective buyer, gave the age in the registration documents. The prospective buyer then bought the motorcycle a week later in a written contract that did not mention the age. On discovering the true age he tried to sue for a breach of a term but failed. The lapse of time was held to be too wide to create a binding relationship based on the statement.

Whether the agreement, including the statement, is in writing

Where a contract is in writing and a statement made orally between the parties is not included in the written document, then the court will generally infer that it was not intended to form part of the contract but is a mere representation.

Routledge v McKay (1954)

Here, since the written agreement made no mention of the age of the motorcycle, the court held that it had not been considered important enough to be a term.

Furthermore, where a written agreement is signed this generally makes the contents of the agreement binding, irrespective of whether they have been read by the party signing (a clear warning that we should never sign anything without reading it first).

L'Estrange v Graucob (1934)

The claimant bought a vending machine from the defendants on a written contract which in small print contained the clause '… any express or implied condition, statement or warranty, statutory or otherwise not stated herein is hereby excluded'. The machine turned out to be unsatisfactory and the claimant claimed for breach of an implied term as to fitness for purpose under the Sale of Goods Act 1893. (Exclusions of liability for the implied terms were possible under the 1893 Act.) She also argued that she had not read the clause and had no knowledge of what it contained. Judgment was initially given to the claimant but on appeal she failed. As Scrutton LJ put it,

'When a document containing contractual terms is signed, then, in the absence of fraud, or, I will add, misrepresentation, the party signing it is bound, and it is wholly immaterial whether he has read the document or not.'

(Of course judgments like the above would now be subject to the Unfair Contract Terms Act 1977 and Unfair Terms in Consumer Contracts Regulations 1999.)

The extent to which the term is effectively drawn to the notice of the party subject to it

In general a term will not be accepted as incorporated into the contract unless it is brought sufficiently to the attention of the party subject to it prior to or at the time the contract is made. This is one of the basic ways in which judges have developed protections for consumers in the case of exclusion clauses. Rules on incorporation of terms are interchangeable with the rules on incorporation of exclusion clauses, and cases such as *Olley v Marlborough Court Hotel* (1949), *Chapelton v Barry UDC* (1940) (see 7.1.3) and *Thornton v Shoe Lane Parking Ltd* (1971) could all also be used to illustrate the basic point. So the party subject to an alleged term must have real knowledge of it before entering the contract or it may not be incorporated.

O'Brien v MGN Ltd (2001)

The claimant bought a copy of the *Daily Mirror* containing a scratch card. On the card was printed 'For full rules and how to claim see *Daily Mirror*'. The claimant bought another Daily Mirror containing a scratch card on a later day. The card and paper contained the words 'normal Mirror rules apply'. This second card showed a £50,000 prize, but because of a mistake 1,472 other people were also told that they had won. The competition rules provided for a draw to take place in the event that there were more winners than prize money available. The paper organised a draw with one prize of £50,000 and another £50,000 to be divided between all the others (£34 each). The contract included the phrase 'normal Mirror rules apply' and it was held that this was sufficient to incorporate the terms. The newspaper had done just enough to bring the terms to the attention of the claimant since the rules were referred to on the back of each card and were available at the offices of the paper and in back issues of the paper.

The significance of standard forms

It is common in a modern commercial context for parties to contract on their own standard terms and conditions. Very often this can lead to problems when the terms conflict. If the contract has been formed orally, such terms can only be relied on if they have in fact been incorporated into the contract at the time of its formation.

Lidl UK GmbH v Hertford Foods Ltd (2001)

In a contract for supply of corned beef, the seller was able to deliver only part of the order. He was unable to obtain further supplies due to circumstances beyond his control. The buyer then had to obtain supplies elsewhere at extra cost which the buyer then sued for. Both parties then tried to rely on their own standard terms and conditions. The seller's terms included a 'force majeure' clause which would make them not liable. They had done business with each other before so had seen each other's terms, but the terms were inconsistent and had not been incorporated into earlier contracts. As the contract was made on the telephone and neither party had mentioned their standard terms, even though they had later sent them to the other, the Court of Appeal decided that neither set of terms was incorporated. The seller was in breach of contract and liable.

Whether the term is reasonable

Where terms give discretion the discretion should not be used for an improper purpose.

Paragon Finance v Nash (2001)

Mortgage lenders loaned money on variable interest rates with discretion to raise or lower the rates. The claimants fell into arrears and challenged the agreements on the ground that the interest rates were far higher than those of other lenders. The Court of Appeal held that a term should be implied into such contracts that the rates should not be set arbitrarily or dishonestly or for any improper purpose or in a way that no other mortgage lender, acting in a reasonable way, would do. However, the loan agreement was held not to be excessive.

It is important to remember that since the passing of the Misrepresentation Act 1967, many of the above claimants would not necessarily have to try to prove that the statement made to them amounted to a term of the contract. The Act allows a claimant an action even for an innocent misrepresentation, such as that relating to the age of a vehicle found in the registration documents of the vehicle. Prior to this Act there were very limited circumstances in which a claim for misrepresentation could be made. So it was vital for a claimant to prove a statement was a term otherwise he may have had no remedy at all.

The 'parol evidence' rule

Traditionally where a party to a written agreement was trying to show that the written document did not fully reflect the actual agreement, he would come up against the 'parol evidence' rule. By this rule, oral or other evidence that the party tried to introduce would not be admissible if it was to be used to add to, vary or contradict the terms in the written contract.

The rule can easily be justified. Firstly, if the contract was in writing, it was only logical to suppose that things omitted from the written document actually formed no part of the agreement. Secondly, the danger is that adding terms in after the written agreement leads to uncertainty.

However, many contracts are partly written and partly oral, and over time a number of exceptions to the strict rule have emerged rendering the rule unworkable:

Custom or trade usage

Terms can invariably be implied into a contract by trade custom (see later in implied terms).

Rectification

Where it can be shown that a written contract inaccurately represents the actual agreement reached by the two parties, equity will allow rectification of the written document. Parol evidence can be introduced to show what the real agreement was. The inaccuracies are removed and replaced if necessary with the substance of the real agreement.

Webster v Cecil (1861)

Webster was trying to enforce his purchase of land where the written document identified the price as £1,250. Cecil was able to show that he had already refused an offer of £2,000, so that the accurate price was £2,250. The price was amended accordingly.

Invalidation by misrepresentation, mistake etc

Where a claimant is seeking to avoid the consequences of a contract, having discovered that the contract has been made as the result of a mistake or a misrepresentation or other invalidating factor, he is clearly entitled to introduce evidence to that effect. (See Chapter 8.)

Where the written agreement only represents part of a larger agreement

Clearly in some circumstances, as we have already seen, the court is prepared to accept that oral representations because of their significance are intended to be as much a part of the agreement as those included in the written document.

J Evans & Son (Portsmouth) Ltd v Andrea Merzario Ltd (1976)

The claimant regularly used the defendant as carriers to ship machinery from Italy, and did so on the defendants' standard forms. Originally the machines, which were liable to rust if left on deck, were always carried below decks. When the defendants started using containers that are generally kept on deck, the claimants expressed concern about rusting and were given an oral assurance that their machinery would still be stored below decks. One machine being carried for the claimants was put in a container and by error stored on deck. The container was improperly fastened and fell overboard. The

Court of Appeal allowed the claimant to introduce evidence of the oral assurance, the standard forms did not represent the actual agreement, and the defendants were liable.

Where the contract depends on fulfilment of a specified event

Obviously where the parties have a written agreement but have also agreed that the contract will only come into effect on fulfilment of some other condition, then evidence can be introduced to that effect. There is no attempt to vary the terms of the contract. The evidence of the oral agreement is introduced only to show that operation of the contract has been suspended until fulfilment of the condition.

Pym v Campbell (1856)

Here there was a written agreement to buy a share of the patent of an invention. The claimant sued for a breach of this agreement. In fact there was an oral agreement between the parties that the contract would not come into effect until the patent had been examined and verified by a third party. The defendant was allowed to introduce parol evidence of this.

Collateral contracts

We have already seen how the collateral contract is an exception to the basic rules on privity of contract, allowing a party to sue the maker of a promise on which they have relied even though that party is not a party to the actual contract.

Collateral agreements are also relevant as an exception to the parol evidence rule in certain circumstances. For instance, where a promise is made which depends on the making of another contract, the promise is collateral, the making of the other contract is the consideration. Though the promise may only be a representation in the major contract, it can be raised as evidence of the second or collateral contract.

City and Westminster Properties (1934) Ltd v Mudd (1958)

The defendant rented a shop for six years, together with a small room in which he slept, and which was known by the claimant landlords. When the lease was up for renewal the landlords inserted a clause restricting use of the premises to the 'showrooms, workrooms and offices only', the effect of which would be to prevent the defendant from sleeping on the premises. He then gained an oral assurance that he could still

Key facts

- To form part of the contract, express terms must be incorporated.
- If the contract is written then this presents no problem, since the terms are in written form.
- Where the contract is oral, a number of factors can be taken into account to determine whether representations have been incorporated:
  - (a) the importance to the parties – *Birch v Paramount Estates* (1956)
  - (b) the relative bargaining strength of the parties – *Oscar Chess v Williams* (1957)
  - (c) the extent to which one party relied on the expertise of the other – *Dick Bentley Productions v Harold Smith (Motors) Ltd* (1965)
  - (d) whether the term was sufficiently drawn to the other party's attention before the contract was formed – *O'Brien v Mirror Group Newspapers Ltd* (2001)
  - (e) whether the representation was put in writing – *Routledge v McKay* (1954).
- A party is generally bound by anything that he has signed, whether or not he has read it – *L'Estrange v Graucob* (1934).
- Originally the 'parol evidence' rule prevented a party from introducing evidence of oral agreements not actually in the written agreement – but the rule now has many exceptions.

sleep in the room, on which basis he signed the new lease. The landlords then brought an action for forfeiture of the lease for the defendant's breach of the new clause. It was held that he had broken the terms of the lease, but the landlords were unable to enforce its terms against him because of the collateral contract.

Activity

1. In what ways can expertise or specialist knowledge be important in determining what the terms of a contract are?
2. What are the benefits of putting a contract in writing?
3. What is the effect of signing an agreement that you have not read?

7.1.3 Implied terms

Generally the parties to a contract will be deemed to have included all of the various obligations by which they intend to be bound as express terms of the contract.

Sometimes, however, terms will be implied into a contract, even though they do not appear in a written agreement or in the oral negotiations that have taken place leading up to the contract.

Terms will be implied into a contract for one of two reasons:

- because a court in a later dispute is trying to give effect to a presumed intention of the parties, even though the intentions were not expressed (these are terms implied by fact)
- because the law requires that certain obligations are included in a contract irrespective of whether the parties have agreed on them or would naturally include them (these are terms implied by law – usually this results from a statutory provision aimed at redressing an imbalance in bargaining strength or seeking to protect a particular group – but it can be by operation of the common law).

7.1.4 Terms implied by fact

Where terms are implied by fact this is usually from decisions in individual court cases. The courts have implied terms by fact in a variety of different circumstances:

Terms implied by custom or habit

There is an old maxim that 'custom hardens into right'. For instance, customary rights gained by long use, known as prescription, are common features in relation to the use of land. Bridle paths and public rights of way are examples.

Hutton v Warren (1836)

Local custom meant that on termination of an agricultural lease, a tenant was entitled to an allowance for seed and labour on the land. The court held that the lease must be viewed in the light of the custom. As Baron Parke in the Court of Exchequer said:

'It has long been settled that in commercial transactions extrinsic evidence of custom and usage is admissible to annex incidents to written contracts, in matters with respect to which they are silent.'

Terms implied by trade or professional custom

Parties to a contract might be bound by an implied trade custom when it is accepted as their deemed intention even though there are no express terms on the matter. In marine insurance, for instance, it has long been a custom that there is an implied undertaking on the part of the broker that he will pay the premium to the insurer even where the party insured defaults on the payment.

The custom, however, should operate to give effect to the contract by supporting the general purpose, not to contradict the express terms, and therefore defeat the general purpose.

Les Affreteurs Reunis SA v Walford (1919) (Walford's Case)

In privity of contract, Walford was suing for a commission of 3 per cent that he felt he was owed for negotiating a charter party between Lubricating and Fuel Oils Co. Ltd and the owners of the SS 'Flore'. One of the defendant's arguments was that there was a custom that commission was payable only when the ship had actually been hired. In this instance the French government had requisitioned the ship before the charter party had actually occurred. If the custom was accepted then it would conflict with the clause in the contract requiring payment as soon as the hire agreement was signed, so it was held not to have been implied into the contract.

Terms implied to give sense and meaning to the agreement

Sometimes a contract would be rendered meaningless or inoperable without the inclusion of a particular term, which is implied to give sense to the agreement.

Schawel v Reade (1913)

The claimant wanted to buy a stallion for stud purposes. At the defendant's stables he was examining a horse advertised for sale when the defendant remarked 'You need not look for anything: the horse is perfectly sound. If there was anything the matter with the horse I would tell you.' On this recommendation the claimant halted his inspection and later bought the horse. In fact it turned out that the horse was unfit for stud purposes. Lord Moulton held that, even though the defendant's assurances were not an express warranty as to fitness for stud, they were an implied warranty.

Terms implied to give business efficacy to a commercial contract

This also applies in business contracts. Parties would not enter a contract freely that had no benefit for them or indeed that might harm them or cause loss. So courts will imply terms into a contract that lacks them in express form to sustain the agreement as a businesslike arrangement.

The Moorcock (1889)

The defendants owned a wharf with a jetty on the Thames. They agreed with the claimant for him to dock his ship and unload cargoes at the wharf. Both parties were aware at the time of contracting that this could involve the vessel being at the jetty at low tide. The ship then grounded at the jetty and broke up on a ridge of rock. The defendants argued that they had given no undertaking as to the safety of the ship. The court held that there was an implied undertaking that the ship would not be damaged. Bowen LJ held:

'In business transactions such as this, what the law desires to effect by the implication is to give such business efficacy … as must have been intended at all events by both parties who are businessmen …'

Terms implied because of prior conduct of contracting parties

Quite simply, where the parties to a contract have a prior history of dealing on particular terms, if those terms are not included in a later contract, they may be implied into it if the parties are dealing in otherwise essentially similar terms.

Hillas v Arcos (1932)

In a 1931 contract between the two parties for the supply of standard sized lengths of timber, there was included an option clause allowing the claimants to buy a further 100,000 during 1932. The agreement was otherwise quite vague as to the type of timber, the terms of shipment and other features. Despite this the contract was completed and the timber supplied. In 1932 the claimants then wanted the further 100,000 lengths of timber but the defendants refused to deliver them. Their argument was that since the 1931 agreement was vague in many major aspects, it was therefore no more than a basis for further negotiations. The House of Lords held that, while the option clause lacked specific detail, nevertheless it was in the same terms as the contract of sale that had been completed. It was therefore implicit in the original contract that the option be carried out in the same terms if the claimant wished to exercise it.

The classic test to identify if a term will be implied into a contract by fact is that of MacKinnon LJ in *Shirlaw v Southern Foundries Ltd* (1939).

> ❝ *Prima facie* that which in any contract is left to be implied and need not be expressed is something so obvious that it goes without saying; so that if, while the parties were making their bargain, an officious bystander were to suggest some express provision for it in their agreement, they would testily suppress him with a common "Oh, of course!"❞

This is known as the 'officious bystander test'. It is still used, and on the face of it is an adequate way of showing that the court is giving effect to the presumed intention of the parties. However, it imposes a very strict standard and possibly an unrealistic one. While one party will usually be all too willing to accept that the implied term at issue was what he actually intended to be part of the contract, the other party almost inevitably will be arguing the exact reverse, or there would be no dispute.

As a result there are circumstances when the 'officious bystander rule' cannot apply.

One example is where one party is totally unaware of the term it is being suggested should be implied into the agreement. In this case it could never have been his intention to include it, so the test fails.

Spring v National Amalgamated Stevedores and Dockers Society (1956)

An agreement between various trade unions, including the defendant's union, was known as the 'Bridlington Agreement', from the meeting of the TUC at which it was reached. The agreement concerned transfer between unions. The claimant joined the defendant union in breach of this rule on transfer but totally unaware of the existence of the agreement. This breach was reported to the TUC Disputes Committee. It then demanded of the defendant that they expel him. When they tried to do so the claimant sued for breach of contract. The defendant asked that a term should be implied into the agreement with Spring that they should follow the Bridlington Agreement. MacKinnon's 'officious bystander test' was referred to and rejected. If told about the Bridlington Agreement by an officious bystander, Spring would have no idea what it was.

If it is uncertain that both parties would have agreed to the term even if it had been included in the agreement, then it is difficult to demonstrate that it was their presumed intention and include it by implication, so the test fails yet again.

Shell (UK) Ltd v Lostock Garage Ltd (1977)

By an agreement between the two parties, Shell supplied petrol and oil to Lostock who in return agreed to buy these products only from Shell. In a later 'price war', Shell supplied petrol to other garages at lower prices, forcing Lostock to sell at a loss. Lostock wanted to imply a term in the contract that Shell would not 'abnormally discriminate' against them. The Court of Appeal refused since Shell would never have agreed to it.

Lord Denning took a more relaxed view of the process of implying terms by fact. He suggested that the process need be no more than including terms that are reasonable as between the parties in the circumstances. The House of Lords rejected his approach.

Liverpool City Council v Irwin (1976)

Here the council let flats in a 15-floor tower block. There was no proper tenancy agreement though there was a list of tenants' obligations signed by tenants. There were no express undertakings in the agreement on the part of the landlord. The council failed to maintain the common areas such as the stairs, lifts, corridors and rubbish chutes. These became badly vandalised over time, with no lighting and the lifts and rubbish chutes not working. The claimants were tenants in the tower block who withheld the rent in protest. The council sued for repossession. The claimants counterclaimed and argued a breach of an implied term that the council should maintain the common areas. In the Court of Appeal Lord Denning felt that such a term could be implied because it was reasonable in the circumstances. The House of Lords though rejected this approach. Lord Wilberforce said that to do this is to '... extend a long, and undesirable, way beyond sound authority.' Lord Cross stated that:

' ... it is not enough for the court to say that the suggested term is a reasonable one the presence of which would make the contract a better or fairer one ...'

and identifies that the 'officious bystander test' is the appropriate method for a term to be implied into a contract. In the event, the House of Lords was not prepared to accept that the council had an absolute obligation to maintain the common areas. It did accept that there was an implied term to take reasonable care to maintain the common areas, which they did not feel had been breached here by the council.

Courts have recently suggested that they should take into account reasonableness, fairness and the balancing of competing policy considerations when implying terms into contracts.

Crossley v Faithful & Gould Holdings Ltd (2004)

The court was asked to imply a term into an employment contract that the employer had an obligation to take care of the economic well being of his employee. The court held that such an implied term would be too broad, place unreasonable burdens on employers and there were no policy reasons for implying such a general obligation.

Implied terms are what a reasonable person would have understood to be the intention of both parties so the court must look at the context.

Egan v Static Control Components (Europe) Ltd (2004)

SCC supplied Egan's company with components. Before 1999 Egan had signed three guarantees making him personally liable for the company's debts up to £75,000. In 1999 with the debt rising Egan was asked to repay in six weekly instalments and to sign a new agreement guaranteeing the company's debts up to £150,000 in the same form as the previous guarantees. When the company went into liquidation Egan tried to argue that the 1999 guarantee only applied to goods supplied after it was signed. The Court of Appeal held that a reasonable person would assume that the guarantee applied to both existing and future debts.

7.1.5 Terms implied by the common law

Terms implied into a contract are justified because they represent the presumed but unexpressed intentions of the parties. Had the parties thought of the particular term, they would have naturally included it.

Where a term is implied into a contract by process of law, it is being inserted into the contract irrespective of the wishes of the parties. The justification here is that the law, whether the courts or Parliament itself, wishes to regulate such agreements.

The courts might imply a term by law because it is felt that it is the type of term that should naturally be incorporated in a contract of that type. Once the term has been implied, the case will then stand as a precedent for future cases involving the same type of agreement.

Liverpool City Council v Irwin (1976)

Here the House of Lords could not imply a term as a matter of fact that the landlord was responsible for common areas because it failed the 'officious bystander' test. However, it accepted that there should be a general obligation on landlords in tenancy agreements to take reasonable care to maintain common areas.

7.1.6 Terms implied by law – by statute

In the nineteenth century contract law was mostly governed by the maxim *caveat emptor* (let the buyer beware). The law was mostly concerned with the process of contracting and little attention was paid to the fact that often one party to the contract was in a significantly inferior bargaining position to the other. Early statutes such as the Sale of Goods Act 1893 attempted to redress this imbalance. In the latter half of the twentieth century there was much more awareness of the needs of consumers, employees and others in contractual relationships. The old maxim has been found wanting and unacceptable and Parliament, through Acts, has often given greater protection to the party with the weaker bargaining strength in certain types of contracts by the process of inserting or implying terms into the contracts irrespective of the express intentions of the parties.

Such a process is common in Acts governing consumer contracts such as the Sale of Goods Act 1979 (as amended). It is also prominent in employment contracts with not only the Employment Rights Act 1996 but Acts outlawing discrimination such as the Sex Discrimination Act 1975, Race Relations Act 1976 and Disability Discrimination Act 1995, and many other Acts giving a wide variety of protection to employees by the process of implying terms into the contract of employment.

The importance of such terms is that they give statutory protection that can be constantly relied upon as they are applied regardless of what is said in the contract.

The Sale of Goods Act 1979

The Act contains a number of these terms which provide a very clear example of the process and its benefits.

Section 13 – the implied condition as to description

In a sale of goods contract, the goods must correspond to any description applied to them, even possibly the packaging.

Re Moore & Co and Landauer & Co's Arbitration (1921)

A contract for a consignment of tinned fruit was described as being in cartons of 30 tins. When on delivery, half of the cartons were of 24 tins. There was a breach of s 13 even though the actual quantity of tins delivered was correct.

Section 13(2) adds that if the sale is by sample as well as by description, even if the bulk of the goods correspond with the sample this is not enough; they must also correspond with the description. Further, under s 13(3), it can still be a sale 'by description' even if a buyer actually sees and selects the goods.

Beale v Taylor (1967)

A buyer looking over a car was influenced by the description of it as a '1961 Triumph Herald'. It turned out to be a mix of two cars welded together, one of which was an earlier model. The buyer successfully argued breach of s 13.

Much may depend on the relative expertise of the parties and how much the description influenced the purchase.

Harlingdon & Leinster Enterprises Ltd v Christopher Hull Fine Art (1990)

A seller had described a painting as by the artist Munter, but this was not the case. The statement was held not to be a 'description' of the painting, partly because the seller had less expertise than the buyer so the description had not influenced the buyer.

Section 14(2) – the implied condition that the goods are of satisfactory quality

Unlike s 12 and s 13 this implied term, as with s 14(3), applies only when the goods are sold in the course of a business.

Traditionally the requirement was that goods should be of 'merchantable' quality. Merchantability was a legal term with a narrow meaning and in consequence many parties were left without a remedy.

Bartlett v Sidney Marcus Ltd (1965)

In this case a car was bought with a defective clutch. The sellers offered to either repair the clutch or to reduce the price by £25. The buyer accepted the price reduction but very soon had to replace the clutch, costing an extra £45 besides. Lord Denning nevertheless rejected the buyer's claim that the defect was more costly meant that it was not merchantable.

The Sale and Supply of Goods Act 1994 amended s 14(2), replacing merchantable with satisfactory, a concept that should be easily understood by consumers generally. It also inserted a new s 14(2)(b) explaining what is satisfactory including:

> '(a) fitness for all purposes for which goods of the kind in question are commonly supplied
> (b) appearance and finish
> (c) freedom from minor defects
> (d) safety and durability'

Section 14(2)(c) adds that the section does not apply if the defects were brought to the buyer's attention or the goods were examined and the defect should have been noticed. Many sale goods are reduced due to a small defect, like a missing button. If the buyer is told of this, or it is obvious, then s 14 cannot be relied on.

There is little case law on the new provisions but they should make it much easier for consumers to bring claims in respect of defective goods.

Section 14(3) – the implied condition that the goods are fit for their purpose

This applies if the buyer:

> 'either expressly or impliedly makes known to the seller any particular purpose for which goods are being bought regardless of whether or not that is a purpose for which goods of that kind are commonly supplied'.

So the provision mainly applies where the buyer is relying on the skill and judgement of the seller in buying the goods and has expressed a particular purpose for which the goods are required.

Baldry v Marshall (1925)

Here the buyer claimed that a Bugatti car was not fit for the purpose. He had asked the seller to supply him with a fast, flexible and easily-managed car that would be comfortable and suitable for ordinary touring purposes. The Bugatti that he was sold was not such a car.

It may also apply, however, in respect of purposes that are implicit in the contract rather than actually stated.

Grant v Australian Knitting Mills Ltd (1936)

Here the buyer contracted a painful skin disease from chemicals in underpants that he had bought. The court accepted that the buyer would have impliedly made known the purpose for which he was buying the underpants even if he had not actually stated it to the seller.

The Supply of Goods and Services Act 1982

This Act also implies terms into contracts. Sections 3 and 4 apply to the supply of goods, this time where goods are transferred or supplied rather than sold. Examples would be where goods are exchanged (which would not be a sale as no money changes hands) or where goods are supplied along with a service, such as a plumber supplying pipes or a decorator supplying paint. These are conditions, equivalent to ss 13 and 14 of the Sale of Goods Act (SGA), and amended by the Sale and Supply of Goods Act 1994 in the same way.

Sections 13 and 14 of the 1982 Act apply to the supply of services, such as those of the plumber or decorator mentioned above. These implied terms are not stated to be conditions so will be treated as innominate terms.

Section 3(2) – the implied condition as to description

As with SGA, the goods must correspond with any description that is applied to them.

Section 3(3) further provides that if the goods are transferred by sample as well as by description they must still correspond with the description. Under s 3(4) these terms apply even if the goods are selected by the person supplied.

Section 4(2) – the implied condition as to satisfactory quality

As with s 14 SGA, this applies only if the goods are transferred in the course of business. They must be of satisfactory quality and s 4(2)(a) says they are of satisfactory quality if they meet the standard that a reasonable person would regard as satisfactory, taking account of any description of the goods, the price (if relevant) and all the other relevant circumstances.

Under s 4(3) this does not apply to any defects which were brought to the attention of the person, or where the goods were examined and any defects should have been noticed, or where, if supplied by reference to a sample, which would have been apparent on a reasonable examination of the sample.

Section 4(5) – the implied condition that the goods are fit for their purpose

If the goods are being acquired for a particular stated purpose there is a requirement that they are fit for that purpose, whether or not it is one for which they are commonly supplied. For example, interior paint would commonly be suitable for use indoors, but if you state that it is for use outdoors and it is sold on that basis, you can sue for breach of contract if the paint is not suitable for outdoor use. Under s 4(6) this does not apply where the circumstances show that the person supplied does not rely on the skill or judgment of the transferor, or that it is unreasonable to rely on such skill. In the above example, if you were not influenced in any way by the supplier when you bought the paint you cannot rely on s 4(5).

The implied terms as regards the supply of services apply only where the supplier is acting in the course of a business. As these apply to services rather than goods they do not have an equivalent in SGA, but they are fairly straightforward.

Section 13 – the implied term that the service will be carried out with reasonable care and skill

In a contract for the supply of a service, there is an implied term that the supplier will carry out the service with reasonable care and skill.

Wilson v Best Travel (1993)

While on holiday in Greece the claimant fell through a glass door and suffered injuries. Although the glass conformed to Greek safety requirements it was not up to British standards at the time. A claim was brought under s 13 on the basis that the tour operator had supplied a service which had not been carried out with reasonable care and skill. The court held that in the circumstances s 13 meant the tour operator should take reasonable care not to offer holiday accommodation which was of such a nature that clients could not stay in safety. As they had checked the premises, the local safety regulations had been complied with and the danger posed by the glass would not cause 'reasonable holidaymakers' to decline to stay there, they had not breached the implied term.

Section 14(I) – the implied term that the service will be carried out within a reasonable time

In a contract for the supply of a service there is an implied term that the supplier will carry out the service within a reasonable time. This doesn't apply if the time is fixed by the contract, or it is left to be arranged in a manner which has been agreed on (either in the contract or a previous course of dealing between the parties). Under s 14(2) what is a reasonable time is a question of fact, so much will depend on the circumstances.

Remedies for breach of terms implied by these statutes

Breach of a condition allows for rescission of the contract and rejection of the goods. If the term is deemed a warranty then the only remedy is damages.

Conditions and warranties are discussed in chapter 8.

Rescission and rejection

Rescission and rejection usually go together. Rescission means a wronged party can treat the contract as at an end. Both parties are returned to the position they would be in if the contract had *never existed*, unlike damages where they are put in a position as if it existed but was *not breached*. Any goods received can be rejected and returned to the supplier and any payment already made is returned to the person supplied.

Rescission is only possible where there is breach of a *condition*, not a *warranty*. Also, as it is an equitable remedy, it will not be awarded if e.g., it would be unfair.

Repair, replacement or a reduction in price

It is up to the 'wronged party' to accept or reject the goods. This is the buyer under SGA or the person supplied under SOGSA. If preferred, they can require a repair or replacement instead or, if the problem is small, a reduction in the cost.

J H Ritchie Ltd v Lloyd Ltd (2007)

A farmer had bought a combination seed drill and power harrow but when using it noticed a serious vibration. The sellers were in breach of the implied condition under SGA as to satisfactory quality. This gave the farmer a right to reject the goods or choose to accept a repair. The sellers had taken the harrow to inspect it and they repaired and returned it. When asked what had been wrong with it they had refused to say. The farmer found out it had been a major defect and was concerned that other parts might have been affected. He rejected the equipment but the sellers refused to refund his money. The law was not clear on whether the right to reject remained *after* a repair had been carried out.

The House of Lords held that in the circumstances the sellers were under an implied condition to tell the farmer what the fault was so that he could make an informed choice whether to accept or reject the equipment. They were in breach of this condition, so he could reject the repaired equipment.

Activity

1. How are terms implied into a contract?
2. What is the difference between an express term and an implied term?
3. What is the difference between a term implied by fact and a term implied by law?
4. In what ways is the 'officious bystander test' ineffective?
5. For what reasons has Parliament chosen to imply terms into contracts through Acts of Parliament?
6. What are the remedies for breach of the statutory terms?

Key facts

- Terms can be implied in one of three ways:
  (a) by fact – because of the presumed intention of the parties
  (b) by law – because courts feel that such terms should be present – *Liverpool City Council v Irwin* (1976)
  (c) by law – because statutory provisions insert terms into contracts.

- Terms are implied by fact because of:
  (a) custom or common usage – *Hutton v Warren* (1836)
  (b) professional custom – *Walford's Case* (1919)
  (c) business efficacy – *The Moorcock* (1889)
  (d) past conduct – *Hillas v Arcos* (1932).

- Terms are implied by fact according to the 'officious bystander' test – if an officious bystander had asked the parties about a term that was missing from the contract they would have replied that it was obviously included.

- Terms are implied by statute for, eg consumer protection – Sale of Goods Act 1979.

- Sale of Goods Act terms include eg s 13 – goods should correspond with description; s 14(2) – be of satisfactory quality; s 14(3) – and fit for their purpose.

7.2 Conditions and warranties

7.2.1 Classifying terms

We have already seen how with representations made prior to formation of the contract, some are more important than others. As a result, some are incorporated in the contract and others are not.

In the same way not all terms are equally important to the contract. Some are of critical importance, and without them the contract could not be completed. On the other hand some terms are of lesser importance. They may for instance be purely descriptive and even if they are breached this will not mean that the contract cannot be carried out.

If terms are of different significance then the effects of a breach of those terms will also vary in significance; there are of necessity different remedies available to the parties in the event of a breach. The courts have traditionally dealt with the issue by classifying terms into different categories. Broadly speaking then the courts always distinguished in two ways. Firstly, the term can be categorised according to its importance to the completion of the contract. Secondly, it can be categorised according to the remedies available to a party who is a victim of a breach of the term.

7.2.2 Conditions

Until fairly recently judges recognised only two classes of term. The most important of these was the condition, which can be considered in two ways.

Firstly, a condition is a term of a contract which is so important that a failure to perform would render the contract meaningless and destroy the purpose of the contract. As a result a condition is said to 'go to the root of a contract'.

Secondly, as a result of the significance of the term to the contract, the court allows the claimant who has suffered a breach of the term the fullest range of remedies. When a condition is

unfulfilled, the claimant will not only be able to sue for damages but may repudiate his obligations, or indeed do both. Repudiation as a remedy is the right to consider the contract ended as a result of the other party's breach. This may be particularly appropriate as it may mean that the claimant can contract with an alternative party and treat himself as relieved of his obligations under the contract, without fear of the defendant alleging a breach by the claimant instead.

Poussard v Spiers and Pond (1876)

An actress was contracted to appear in the lead role in an operetta for a season. The actress was unable to attend for the early performances, by which time the producers had given her role up to the understudy. The actress sued for breach of contract but lost. She had in fact breached the contract by turning up after the first night. As the lead, her presence was crucial to the production and so was a condition entitling the producers to repudiate and terminate her contract for her non-attendance at the early performances.

7.2.3 Warranties

Warranties are seen as minor terms of the contract or those where in general the contract might continue despite their breach. Almost by default, a warranty is any other term in a contract, one that does not go to the root of the contract. It is a residual category of terms dealing with obligations that are secondary to the major purpose of the contract.

As a result, the remedy for a breach of warranty is merely an action for damages. There is no right to repudiate.

Thus it can be seen that the way in which the terms are classified is critical in determining the outcome of the contract and the remedies available for breach.

Bettini v Gye (1876)

In a case with similar circumstances to the last, a singer was contracted to appear at a variety of theatres for a season of concerts. His contract included a term that he should attend rehearsals for six days prior to the beginning of the actual performances. In the event he turned up only three days before but had been replaced. When the singer sued, the producers' claim that the obligation to attend rehearsals was a condition failed. The court held that it was only ancillary to the main purpose and only entitled the producers to sue for damages, not to end the contract and replace the singer.

7.2.4 Innominate terms

The problem of determining which category a term fits usually happens when the parties have been silent on the subject or where the contract is oral. The effect of the classification is to identify what the term was at the time of the formation of the contract, so all later consequences depend on that classification.

A more recent approach of the courts has been to describe terms as 'innominate', or without specific classification, and in determining the outcome of a breach of the term, to consider the consequence of the breach rather than how it is classified in deciding on the available remedy.

The purpose of distinguishing between different classes of term is ultimately to decide what remedies are available to the victim of the breach. The modern concept of the innominate term has developed out of a desire that the right to repudiate should only be available in the event of a breach when it is fair to both sides.

The rather simplistic process of classifying all terms as either conditions or warranties had problems, and the innominate term was first considered as an alternative means of deciding the appropriate remedy in the event of a breach of a term in the following case.

Hong Kong Fir Shipping Co Ltd v Kawasaki Kisen Kaisha Ltd (The Hong Kong Fir Case) (1962)

The defendants chartered a ship from the claimants under a two-year charter party. A term in the contract required that the ship should be '… in every way fitted for ordinary cargo service.' In fact the ship broke down as a result of incompetence by the engine room staff, and in any case was in a poor state of repair and not seaworthy, which the claimants admitted. As a result, 18 weeks' use of the ship was lost by the defendants and they claimed to treat the contract as repudiated and at an end. The claimants sued, arguing that the term was only a warranty, only entitling the defendants to sue for damages. The Court of Appeal agreed. There were, however, some interesting points made in the judgments. Lord Diplock felt that not all contracts could be simply divided into terms that are conditions and terms that are warranties, and that many contracts are of a more complex character. He considered that:

'… all that can be predicted is that some breaches will, and others will not, give rise to an event which will deprive the party not in default of substantially the whole benefit which it was intended that he should obtain from contract; and the legal consequences … unless expressly provided for expressly in the contract, depend on the nature of the event to which the breach gives rise and do not follow automatically from a prior classification … as a "condition" or a "warranty".'

The process is simple. The proper remedy is only discovered after the consequences of the breach have been identified. The innominate term then could be particularly useful in contracts such as charters where the results of breach vary from rendering the contract impossible to trivial effects.

Nevertheless, there is an uncertainty to the innominate term. Nobody can be really sure what the outcome of a particular situation will be until the term has been breached and the judge in the case has construed the term and declared what remedy is appropriate. The doctrine has however been accepted.

Cehave NV v Bremer Handelsgesselschaft mbH (The Hansa Nord) (1976)

A cargo of citrus pulp pellets to be used as cattle feed was rejected by the buyers because part had suffered overheating and did not conform to the term 'Shipment to be made in good condition.' As the sellers would not refund the price already paid, the buyers applied to the Rotterdam court which ordered its sale. Another party then bought the cargo and sold it on to the original buyers at a much lower price than they had paid the original sellers. The cargo was then used for its original purpose, cattle feed. The buyers argued that the goods were not merchantable within the meaning of the Sale of Goods Act 1979, the term was a condition and so justified their repudiation. This succeeded at first. The Court of Appeal, however, using the *Hong Kong Fir* approach, accepted that, since the goods had been used for their original purpose, there was not a breach of the contract serious enough to justify repudiation. Only an action for damages was appropriate in the circumstances.

Use of the innominate term is particularly appropriate where bargaining strength is unequal or where breaches of the contract are technical rather than material and the traditional methods of classification would lead to an injustice.

Reardon Smith Line Ltd v Hansen-Tangen (1976)

In a contract for the charter of a tanker, the ship was described as 'Osaka 354', a reference to the shipyard at which the tanker would be built. In fact because the shipyard had too many orders the work was sub-contracted to another yard and the tanker became known as 'Oshima 004'. When the need for tankers lessened, the buyers tried to get out of the contract by claiming a breach of a condition that the tanker should correspond with its description. The court held that since the breach was entirely technical and had no bearing on the outcome of the contract, it could not justify repudiation.

However, the court may still classify a term as a condition, regardless of what the possible consequences of a breach might be, if the circumstances demand it.

Bunge Corporation v Tradax Export SA (1981)

In a contract for the sale of soya bean meal, the buyers were required to give at least 15 days' notice of readiness to load the vessel. In the event they gave only 13 days' notice. This would not necessarily prevent the sellers from completing their obligations. As a result, the first instance court held that since the consequences of the breach were minor it would not justify repudiation. The House of Lords, however, held that, since the sellers' obligation to ship was certainly a condition, the obligation to give notice to load in proper time should be a condition regardless of the effects of the breach. Lord Wilberforce felt that stipulations as to time in mercantile contracts should usually be viewed as conditions.

7.2.5 The construction of terms

The remedies available to a party who has suffered a contractual breach depend on the classification given to the term that is not complied with. Parties to a contract do not always think to outline, prior to the contract, the nature of the terms they are incorporating in the contract, or the precise remedies they are contemplating will be available in the event of a breach. Where the parties are silent on the classification of terms or the classifications are vague, the judges must construe what the terms are and their contractual significance.

Judges use certain guiding principles:

- Where terms are implied by law then judges apply the classification given to them in the statute; ie the implied terms in the Sale of Goods Act 1979 are stated as conditions.
- Where terms are implied by fact, the judges will construe them according to the presumed intention of the parties.
- Where terms have been expressed by the parties who have identified how the terms are to be classified or what remedies attach to them, then the judges will usually try to give effect to the express wishes of the parties.
- Where the terms are express but the parties have not identified what type they are or what is the appropriate remedy in a breach, then judges will construe those terms according to what they believe is the true intention of the parties.

It is advantageous if a term is classed as a condition, since a wider range of remedies is available. This has the potential for unscrupulous parties to a contract to classify all of the terms of the contract as conditions. In view of the complexities of modern contracting, and particularly the use of the standard form contract, there may well be occasions when the judges feel that it is impossible to follow the express classification of the terms. In this way, a term stated as being a condition may be construed in fact as a warranty.

Schuler (L) AG v Wickman Machine Tool Sales Ltd (1974)

In an agency contract, Wickman was appointed sole distributors of Schuler's presses. It was stated as a condition of the contract that Wickman's representatives would make weekly visits to six large UK motor manufacturers to solicit orders for presses. A further term stated that the contract could be terminated for a breach of any condition that was not remedied within 60 days. The contract was to last more than four years, amounting to more than 1400 visits. When some way into the contract Wickman's representatives failed to make a visit, Schuler sought to terminate the contract. In the House of Lords Lord Reid felt that it was inevitable that during the contract there would be occasions when maintaining weekly visits would be impossible. He also felt that the effect of accepting the term as a condition would be to entitle Schuler to terminate even if there was only one failure to visit out of the 1400. This would be unreasonable so the term could not be a condition.

Judges may of course be aided in their construction of terms by guidance given in statutory definitions and referring to the market in which the particular contract operates may also assist them.

Maredelanto Cia Naviera SA v Bergbau-Handel GmbH (1970) (The Mihalis Angelos)

A charter party repudiated their contract with ship-owners when the contract contained an 'expected readiness to load' clause and it was clear that the vessel would not be ready to load on time. There was a clear breach of a term but the court had to decide of which type. The House of Lords, using guidance from statutory terms as well as from the commercial character of the contract, decided that the term was a condition justifying repudiation. The judges held that in commercial contracts, predictability and certainty of relations must be the ultimate test.

So while in general a contract drafted by a lawyer should usually conform to the classification of terms given, nevertheless the courts may seek to preserve certainty in commercial contracts whatever the apparent intent of the parties.

Harlingdon & Leinster Enterprises Ltd v Christopher Hull Fine Art Ltd (1990)

Here defendant dealers sold a painting as a Munter (a German expressionist painter). The sellers declared at the time of the contract that they had no expertise on such paintings, whereas the buyers did have. When it was discovered that the painting was a forgery, the buyers tried to claim a breach of description by the sellers. The Court of Appeal held that the sale was not one by description entitling the buyers to repudiate. There was no reliance by the buyers, who had relied on their own superior judgment.

Activity

1. What are the key differences between 'conditions' and 'warranties'?
2. In what circumstances will the court ignore the classification given to a term by the parties themselves?
3. In which ways does a term classed as innominate differ from terms classified normally as conditions or warranties?
4. What are the advantages and disadvantages of defining terms as innominate?

Key facts

- There are different types of term – which category a term falls into is determined by how important it is to the contract.
- In this way terms also vary according to the remedy available on breach.
- A condition is a term which 'goes to the root of the contract' – breach of a condition would render the contract meaningless, so the party who is the victim of the breach can repudiate his obligations under the contract as well as or instead of suing for damages – *Poussard v Spiers and Pond* (1876).
- A warranty is any other term – only damages are available for a breach of a warranty – *Bettini v Gye* (1876).

- Where the parties are silent on what type the term is, judges must construe it from the surrounding circumstances. While judges try to give effect to express intentions of the parties, remedies for breach will only be awarded if the condition operates like a condition – *Schuler v Wickman Machine Tool Sales Ltd* (1974).
- Judges sometimes also view terms as innominate; ie the appropriate remedy is judged from the seriousness of the breach – *The Hong Kong Fir Shipping case* (1962).
- This can prevent the wrong remedy being given for breaches which are purely technical – *Reardon Smith Line v Hansen-Tangen* (1976).

7.3 Exclusion clauses

7.3.1 Common law controls

A clause in a contract that seeks either to limit or exclude liability for breaches of the contract is itself a term of the contract. It is therefore subject to all of the normal rules regarding terms, particularly those concerning incorporation of the term.

Such terms can be harsh on those subject to them and often highlight the inequality of bargaining between providers of goods and services and consumers. Historically *caveat emptor* gave much leeway to a seller and little protection to a consumer.

As a result, judges gradually developed rules to prevent sellers having an unfettered discretion to avoid liability for their contractual breaches. More recently, a trend towards consumer protection has seen the introduction of more effective statutory controls, and the UK has also had to implement controls from EC law.

Incorporating exclusion clauses

Judges insist on exclusion clauses having been properly incorporated. The rules are generally interchangeable with rules regarding incorporation of other terms.

Signed agreements

As with terms in general, the initial proposition is that where a party has signed a written agreement then he is *prima facie* bound by that agreement.

L'Estrange v Graucob (1934)

Here, as we know, the purchaser of the vending machine was bound by the exclusion clause in the contract, regardless of the fact that she had not read it.

Express knowledge of the clause

The first principle used by courts is that exclusion clauses are only incorporated into a contract where the party subject to the clause has actual knowledge of the clause at the time the contract was made.

Olley v Marlborough Court Hotel (1949)

Mr and Mrs Olley booked into the hotel, at which point a contract was formed. When they later went out they left the key at reception as required. In their absence a third party took the key, entered their room and stole Mrs Olley's fur coat. The hotel claimed that they were not liable because of an exclusion clause in the contract that 'the proprietors will not hold themselves liable for articles lost or stolen unless handed to the manageress for safe custody'. The Court of Appeal rejected their claim. The clause was not incorporated in the contract since it was on a notice on a wall inside the Olley's room.

On the other hand, if the parties have dealt on the same terms in the past, it is possible to imply knowledge of the clause from the past dealings provided that there has been a consistent course of dealing. Then it may be incorporated in the contract.

McCutcheon v David MacBrayne Ltd (1964)

The claimant had used the defendants' ferries to ship his car from Islay to the Scottish mainland on many occasions. Sometimes he was asked to sign a risk note including an exclusion clause and sometimes he was not. On the occasion in question the claimant's relative, McSporran, took the car to the ferry. He received a receipt on which was printed the exclusion clause, but did not read it, and was not asked to sign a risk note. Through the defendants' negligence the ferry sank and the car was a write-off. The claimant sought compensation and the defendants tried to rely on the exclusion clause in the risk note and on the receipt. They failed since there was no consistent course of action that allowed them to assume that the claimant knew of the clause so it was not incorporated in the contract. As Lord Devlin put it:

'... previous dealings are only relevant if they prove knowledge of the terms actual and not constructive and assent to them.'

Sufficiency of notice of the exclusion clause

Generally courts do not accept that an exclusion clause has been incorporated into a contract unless the party who is subject to it has been made sufficiently aware of its existence in the contract.

On this basis, an exclusion clause will not be incorporated into a contract when on an objective analysis it is not contained in a document that would usually not be seen as having contractual significance.

Chapelton v Barry Urban District Council (1940)

Here the claimant hired deckchairs on the beach at Barry, and received two tickets from the council's beach attendant on paying for hire of the chairs. On the back of these small tickets were the words 'The council will not be liable for any accident or damage arising from the hire of the chair' though the claimant did not read it, believing it only to be a receipt. The canvas on one chair was defective and it collapsed, injuring the claimant. He claimed compensation and the council tried to rely on their exclusion clause. Their defence failed since the existence of the clause was not effectively bought to the attention of the claimant. It was unreasonable to assume that he would automatically understand that the ticket was a contractual document, and the council was liable for the claimant's injuries.

One further question concerns the extent to which parties inserting exclusion clauses in contracts must go in order to claim that they are brought sufficiently to the attention of the other party, and therefore incorporated in the contract.

Thornton v Shoe Lane Parking Ltd (1971)

The claimant was injured in a car park owned by the defendants. At the entrance to the car park there was a notice that, as well as giving the charges, stated that parking was at the owner's risk. On entering a motorist was required to stop at a barrier and take a ticket from a machine at which point a barrier would lift allowing entry to the car park. On the ticket was printed the words 'This ticket is issued subject to the conditions of issue as displayed on the premises.' Notices inside the car park then listed the conditions of the contract including an exclusion clause covering both damage and personal injury. When the claimant claimed, the defendants argued that the exclusion clause applied but their argument was rejected. Lord Denning identified that the customer in such situations has no chance of negotiating. He:

'… pays his money and gets a ticket. He cannot refuse it. He cannot get his money back. He may protest to the machine, even swear at it. But it will remain unmoved. He is committed beyond recall … The contract was concluded at that time.'

In consequence, Lord Denning says the customer is bound by the terms of the contract '… as long as they are sufficiently bought to his notice before-hand, but not otherwise.'

In other words, for the party including the clause in the contract, a very high degree of notice is required for it to be effective. As he had previously stated in *Spurling v Bradshaw* (1956) when looking at what needs to be done to draw a clause to the attention of the party subject to it, 'Some clauses which I have seen would need to be printed in red ink with a red hand pointing to it before the notice could be held to be sufficient.'

A party is generally bound by a contract that he has signed. Sometimes, however, the party subject to the clause may have enquired about the clause or queried its consequences. If oral misrepresentations have then caused that party to enter the contract with confidence, the exclusion clause may be ineffective as it is the misrepresentation that has induced the other party to enter the contract.

Curtis v Chemical Cleaning and Dyeing Co Ltd (1951)

The claimant took a wedding dress to be cleaned and was asked to sign a document that exempted the defendants from liability for any damage '… howsoever arising.' She sensibly questioned the nature of the document that she was being asked to sign. She was then informed that it only referred to the fact that the defendants would not accept liability for beads or sequins attached to the dress. When the dress was returned, it had a chemical stain for which Mrs Curtis tried to claim. The defendants could not rely on the exclusion clause because of the oral assurances made to the claimant.

The effect of exclusion clauses on third parties to the contract

The privity rule means that the terms of a contract are only binding on the parties to the contract themselves. We have already seen that in general a party trying to enforce third party rights under a contract will fail for lack of privity. In the same way, an exclusion clause in a contract may not offer protection to parties other than the parties to the contract.

Scruttons Ltd v Midland Silicones Ltd (1962)

Carriers had a contract to ship a drum of chemicals for a company, the claimants in the case. The bill of lading contained a clause limiting the liability of the carriers in the event of a breach to $500. The defendants were stevedores who were contracted by the carriers to unload goods. Their contract with the carriers contained terms that they should have the benefit of the limitation clause in the bill of lading. When the stevedores through their negligence did $583 worth of damage to the drum of chemicals, they were sued and tried to rely on the limitation clause in the contract between the claimants and the carriers. Their defence failed because they were not parties to the bill of lading so could not claim any rights under it.

The fact that privity prevents a third party to a contract from relying on exclusions contained in it, may mean that a claimant still has a party to sue despite the existence of the clause, where the third party is responsible for the damage, and is financially worth bringing an action against.

Cosgrove v Horsefell (1945)

A passenger on a bus was injured through the negligence of the driver. The contract with the bus company contained a valid exclusion clause which protected them from liability. However, it did not protect the bus driver from a negligence action.

There have of course been occasions where a party has successfully claimed the protection of an exclusion clause even though not a party to the contract in which the clause was contained. The approach, which is not without its critics, is to argue an agency relationship, and thus to claim that a contractual relationship is created also with the third party.

New Zealand Shipping Co Ltd v A M Satterthwaite & Co Ltd (The Eurymedon) (1975)

Here there was a contract between a consignor and a carrier to ship drilling equipment to New

Zealand. The bill of lading contained an exclusion clause stating that:

'… it is hereby expressly agreed that no servant or Agent of the carrier (including every independent contractor from time to time employed by the carrier) shall in any circumstances whatsoever be under any liability whatsoever to the shipper, consignee or owner of the goods or to any holder of the bill of lading for any loss or damage or delay of whatsoever kind arising or resulting directly or indirectly from any neglect or default on his part …'

and also stating that:

'… every right, exemption, limitation, condition and liberty herein contained … shall extend to protect every such servant or agent of the carrier …'.

In the event stevedores hired by the carriers negligently damaged the equipment and were sued by the consignors. Their attempt to claim protection under the carriers' exclusion clause succeeded. The Privy Council felt that the issue centred on whether the stevedores had given consideration under the contract. The stevedores had accepted a unilateral offer by the consignors that in return for their promise to carry out duties, the consignors would in turn exempt them from any liability. The stevedores had accepted this offer by unloading the ship and could therefore rely on the exclusion clause.

Construction of the contract as a whole

Even though an exclusion clause satisfies the above tests, this does not mean that it will necessarily operate successfully in all cases. The clause might still fail on a construction of the contract as a whole for a number of reasons.

Activity

Consider whether exclusion clauses notified in the following ways will be successfully incorporated into contracts, and say why:

(a) A notice placed on the counter in a shop.
(b) A notice contained in a delivery note where the parties have regularly dealt on the same terms.
(c) A notice on the back of a cloakroom ticket.
(d) A notice posted on the machine at the entrance to a car park.

The *contra preferentum* rule

The *contra preferentum* rule is a device that is basically hostile to ambiguities in a contract. If a party wishes to secure an exemption from liability for contractual breaches by means of incorporation of an exclusion clause in the contract, then the clause must be specific as to the circumstances in which the exemption is claimed otherwise the clause will fail.

The effect of the *contra preferentum* rule as applied to exclusion clauses is that, if there is any ambiguity in the contract, this works against the party seeking to rely on the exclusion clause. That party cannot rely upon it unless it is clear.

Hollier v Rambler Motors (AMC) Ltd (1972)

Hollier left his car with the garage as he had done on previous occasions. The normal conditions of the contract were contained in a form that Hollier had signed on previous occasions but not on the one in question. This form contained a term that 'The company is not responsible for damage caused by fire to customers' cars on the premises.' The car was damaged in a fire caused by the defendants' negligence. The Court of Appeal firstly held that the form was not incorporated into the contract merely by the previous course of dealings in this case. They also concluded that for the garage to rely on the clause, they must have stated in it without ambiguity that they would not be liable in the event of their own negligence. Otherwise the customer might rightly conclude when making the contract that the company would be liable except where the fire damage was caused by other than the defendants' negligence.

Traditionally, after *Canada Steamship Lines Ltd v R* (1952), courts only accepted exclusion of liability for negligence if negligence was expressly excluded by the agreement. Recently a less rigid approach has been introduced with the real test being what the intention of the parties was at the time of contracting.

HIH Casualty and General Insurance v Chase Manhattan Bank (2003)

The bank loaned money for the making of films against the security of the future receipts from the films. To minimise its risk the bank contracted with the insurance company to underwrite the risk. The agreement was negotiated by an intermediary party who was better informed than either of the parties. When a loss occurred the bank successfully relied on an exclusion clause covering its agents.

Fundamental breach

Traditionally the courts were reluctant to allow a party to escape liability for a serious breach by the device of the exclusion clause. One way in which they could control this was by strict construction of the clause and of the contract as a whole, as we have just seen.

Another method that the courts devised and at one time employed to combat the effectiveness of exclusion clauses, was the doctrine of

fundamental breach. By this doctrine a party who had committed a serious breach by breaching a central term of the contract, a 'fundamental breach', would find their clause rendered ineffective by the court. The fundamental breach would be treated as a breach of the whole contract, and therefore the other party would be able to treat the contract as repudiated. The party inserting the exclusion clause would be unable to rely on it since, by the doctrine, he would be treated as being in breach of every term.

Karsales (Harrow) Ltd v Wallis (1956)

The purchaser arranged to buy a second-hand car on a hire-purchase agreement. In this agreement was a clause stating that 'No condition or warranty that the vehicle is roadworthy, or as to its age, condition or fitness for any purpose is given by the owner or implied herein.' Though the purchaser had previously examined the car and found it satisfactory, when it was delivered the cylinder head had been removed, valves in the engine had burnt out, two pistons were damaged, the tyres were damaged and the radio was missing. The purchaser not surprisingly rejected the car. When he was sued the claimants tried to rely on the exclusion clause in the hire-purchase agreement. The Court of Appeal rejected the argument. There had been a fundamental breach of the contract. There was such a substantial difference between the contract as formed and the contract as performed that the breach went to the root of the contract and the claimant could not rely on the exclusion clause.

This approach of the court did not gain universal popularity with judges who found it to be destructive to the general philosophy of freedom of contract. There was also uncertainty as to what actually amounted to a fundamental breach. In consumer contracts judges might be more disposed to accepting the doctrine than they were in commercial contracts where bargaining strength was more equal. As a result, the courts gradually moved to a position of deciding that the doctrine was unsustainable in the form expressed above, and was merely a method of construction rather than a rule of law negating what the parties had freely decided between themselves.

Suisse Atlantique Societe d'Armement Maritime SA v NV Rotterdamsche Kolen Centrale (1967) (The Suisse Atlantique Case)

The owners of a ship sued the party that had chartered the vessel and were to pay them on the basis of the number of journeys made. The owners claimed, and the court accepted, that breaches of the term concerning loading and unloading meant that the party chartering the vessel had made only eight voyages instead of the 14 that they might have been expected to complete. The charter party argued that their liability was limited to a fixed amount of $1,000 per day by virtue of a limitation clause in the contract, rather than the actual loss. The ship owners countered this, arguing that there was a fundamental breach, as a result of which the limitation clause could not apply. The case was decided on the basis that the clause was not a limitation clause but a genuine liquidated damages clause, and in any case it was felt that there was no fundamental breach. Nevertheless, the House of Lords felt that the doctrine of fundamental breach was a restriction on freedom of contract. Lord Wilberforce was a little more guarded since he recognised that where a breach is so serious that it is almost the same as no performance, it is hard to limit liability and still have a contract left.

limitation clauses in commercial contracts where the parties contract on the basis of a more equal bargaining strength. In this way, a clause may be upheld where the parties have freely and genuinely agreed it at the time the contract was formed.

Photo Productions Ltd v Securicor Transport Ltd (1980)

Securicor was under contract on its own standard terms to provide a night patrol service at Photo Productions factory. A clause in Securicor's standard terms stated that:

'Under no circumstances shall the Company be responsible for any injurious act or default by any employee of the company unless such act or default could have been foreseen and avoided by the exercise of due diligence on the part of the Company as his employer.'

The duty security officer on the night in question started a fire that burned out of control, and as a result a large part of the factory was destroyed. It was not disputed that he was suitable for the work, nor was it considered that Securicor was negligent in employing him. While the trial judge held with Securicor, the Court of Appeal applied the doctrine of fundamental breach and found in Photo Productions' favour. The House of Lords, however, disagreed. They affirmed that parties dealing in free negotiations were entitled to include in their contracts any exclusions or limitations or modifications to their obligations that they chose. Since the clause was clear and unambiguous, there was nothing to prevent its use and it therefore protected Securicor from their employee's actions. It was also fairly critical of the continued use of the doctrine of fundamental breach.

The Unfair Contract Terms Act 1977 has given consumers protection against exclusion clauses. Courts have subsequently been prepared to take a more relaxed view towards exclusion and

The approach has since been followed. It seems that in common law it is now immaterial how serious the breach is. If the clause seeking to exclude or limit liability occurs in a contract made out of equal bargaining strength, then the party inserting it can rely on it, provided it is clearly and unambiguously stated.

Ailsa Craig Fishing Co Ltd v Malvern Fishing Co Ltd (1983)

Securicor were under contract to the Aberdeen Fishing Vessels Owners Association Ltd, who acted on behalf of various fishing-boat owners, to provide a security service in the harbour where boats moored. Following negligence by the security guard one vessel fouled another vessel; both sank and became trapped under the quay. The contract was on Securicor's standard terms, and in the ensuing action they sought to rely on a clause in the contract limiting liability:

'… for any loss or damage of whatever nature arising out of or connected with the provision of or failure in provision of, the services covered by this contract … to a sum … not exceeding £1,000 in respect of one claim … and … not exceeding a maximum £10,000 for the consequences of any incident involving fire, theft or any other cause of liability.'

The sums are clearly very small when compared to the likely cost of the damage done to two ships. The court, however, rejected the argument that since Securicor had clearly failed to carry out the terms of their contract at all, they should be unable to rely on the limitation clause. The House of Lords stated that limitation clauses are not to be regarded with the same hostility as exclusion clauses because they relate to the risks to which the defending party is exposed, the remuneration he may receive and the opportunity of the other party to insure against loss. As a result they held that the clause was sufficiently clear and unambiguous to protect Securicor in the case. (The contract was itself made before the enactment of the Unfair Contract Terms Act 1977 otherwise there may well have been a different result.)

These two cases, often referred to as the 'Securicor cases', seem to suggest that the doctrine of fundamental breach can no longer apply. They also suggest that, subject now to statutory controls, where there is equality of bargaining strength and free negotiation, the parties can include terms however onerous, provided that the other side accepts them. These terms will then bind the party agreeing to them even if remedies are lost as a result.

On that level it is probably the case that the Unfair Contract Terms Act 1977 may be more effective in controlling exclusion clauses than the common law is.

George Mitchell Ltd v Finney Lock Seeds Ltd (1983)

Seed merchants agreed to supply farmers with 30lb of Dutch winter cabbage seed for £192. A limitation clause in the contract limited liability on breach to the cost of the seed only or to replacement seed. The farmers planned to sow 63 acres with the seed and calculated that their return would be £61,000. The seed was the wrong sort and was not merchantable and there was no crop. The farmers sued for £63,000 in compensation for lost production. Using the terminology of the Unfair Contract Terms Act 1977, the House of Lords held that the clause was unreasonable and could not be relied on.

In any case there are situations where the courts are reluctant to intervene because the parties have equal bargaining strength and the clause is a common one. An obvious example is in standard form contracts where the offending clause is based on long-standing trade custom.

Overland Shoes Ltd v Shenkers Ltd (1998)

Overland Shoes were importing shoes from China and Schenkers, who were worldwide freight carriers, were contracted to transport the shoes.

The contract was based on the standard forms of the British International Freight Association and included a no set-off clause. When Shenkers sought their freight charges, Overland Shoes tried to set off against these charges sums that Shenkers owed for VAT. Shenkers refused, pointing to the no set-off clause. Overland argued that this was in effect an exclusion clause and was unreasonable under the test in the Unfair Contract Terms Act 1977. The court held that the clause actually satisfied the test of reasonableness since it was based on long-standing established custom.

Activity

1. In which ways does a limitation clause differ from an exclusion clause?
2. In what ways can the rule in *L'Estrange v Graucob* (1934) be described as unfair?
3. What complications are created when a person uses a vending machine or a ticket machine, and how do the courts deal with these problems?
4. Why are the courts reluctant to accept that tickets or receipts can contain contractual terms which then bind the parties?
5. Why were the courts prepared to accept exclusions or limitations in the case of such extreme breaches as those in the '*Securicor* cases'?
6. To what extent did the common law control of exclusion clauses make statutory intervention inevitable?
7. How does the *contra preferentum* rule help to control the use of exclusion clauses?

Key facts

- An exclusion clause is a term of a contract that aims to avoid liability for breaches of the contract; a limitation clause is one which has the effect of reducing damages if there is a breach of contract.
- Again a party is bound by terms where he has signed an agreement – *L'Estrange v Graucob* (1934).
- Judges gradually developed controls on the use of exclusion clauses because of their potential unfairness to consumers.
- An exclusion clause will not be recognised unless it is incorporated into the contract:
  (a) the party subject to it must be aware of it at the time of contracting – *Olley v Marlborough Court Hotels* (1949)
  (b) though it is possible for past dealings to be taken into account if relevant – *McCutcheon v MacBrayne* (1964)
  (c) the party wishing to rely on the clause must bring it to the other party's attention effectively – *Thornton v Shoe Lane Parking Ltd* (1971).
- Misrepresentations about the clause may mean that the party inserting it in the contract cannot rely on it – *Curtis v Chemical Cleaning Co Ltd* (1951).
- In general third parties to the contract cannot rely on the clause (*Scruttons v Midland Silicones* (1962)) – but see *New Zealand Shipping v Satterthwaite* (1975).
- If the clause is ambiguous it cannot be relied upon – *Hollier v Rambler Motors* (1972).
- Courts accept very stringent exclusions where the parties contract on equal terms – *Photo Productions v Securicor Transport Ltd* (1980).
- Providing the clause is clear and unambiguous – *Ailsa Craig Fishing v Malvern Fishing Co Ltd* (1983).

7.3.2 Statutory controls

Provisions created by statute or in regulations are clearly the most effective in controlling the operation of both exclusion and limitation clauses in contracts. However, common law is still relevant. If an exclusion clause has not been successfully incorporated into a contract according to the normal rules, it will be inoperable anyway.

There are two principal provisions provided by Parliament, the Unfair Contract Terms Act 1977, and the Unfair Terms in Consumer Contract Regulations 1999 which were devised in order to comply with EC Directive 93/13.

The Unfair Contract Terms Act 1977 is an effective break on the operation of exclusion clauses, and as such a serious inroad into the principle of freedom of contract when compared, for instance, with the *'Securicor'* cases. The Act applies to exclusions for tort damage as well as contractual breaches.

The 1999 Regulations are based on the Directive which is obviously aimed at harmonising rules on consumer protection throughout the European Union, in order to make the single market more effective. The Regulations are in some senses narrower than the Act. This is because existing UK law already provided many of the features of the directive. Nevertheless, in some ways the Regulations are broader than the Act because the directive was intended to apply in a much broader range of circumstances than the Act, and often imposes stricter duties.

The consequence is that when construing a given exclusion clause it may be appropriate to have regard to the Act, the Regulations, and the common law.

The Unfair Contract Terms Act 1977

When passed, the Act was one of the most significant areas of consumer protection. However, it should be remembered that the Act does not cover all exclusions or indeed every unfair term.

What the Act does try to achieve is to protect the consumer by removing some of the inequalities in bargaining strength. It does this by making certain exclusion clauses automatically invalid; by drawing a distinction between consumer dealings and inter-business dealings; and by introducing a test of reasonableness to apply in inter-business dealings and in certain other circumstances. As a result of this, some of the problems caused by unequal bargaining strength are mitigated.

Exclusions and limitations rendered void by the Act

Certain types of exclusion clauses are invalidated by the Act and will therefore be unenforceable even where they have been successfully incorporated in the contract.

- By UCTA s 2(1) a person cannot exclude liability for death or personal injury caused by his/her negligence.
- By s 5(1) in any consumer contract, clauses seeking to exclude liability by reference to the terms of a guarantee will fail in respect of defects caused by negligence in the manufacture or distribution of the goods.
- By s 6(1) there can be no valid exclusion of breaches of the implied condition as to title in s 12 Sale of Goods Act 1979.
- This same provision applies in respect of Schedule 4 of the Consumer Credit Act 1974 which concerns the same type of condition.
- Section 6(2) invalidates any exclusion clause inserted in a consumer contract to cover breaches of the implied conditions of description (s 13), satisfactory quality (s 14(2)), fitness for the purpose (s 14(3)), and sale by sample (s 15)) in the Sale of Goods Act 1979.
- The provision invalidates breaches of the same conditions in Schedule 4 of the Consumer Credit Act 1974.
- Under s 7(2) similar principles to those in s 6 apply in respect of goods which are transferred under the Supply of Goods and Services Act 1982.

Definitions of consumer contract and inter-business dealing

The Act inevitably is designed to operate mainly for the protection of consumers. As a result, the term 'consumer' has to be defined in the Act. The definition is found in s 12(1) which identifies that a party acts in a contract as a consumer when:

> '(a) he neither makes the contract in the course of a business nor holds himself out as doing so; and
> (b) the other party does make the contract in the course of a business; and
> (c) … the goods passing under or in pursuance of the contract are of a type ordinarily supplied for private use or consumption.'

Activity

Consider which of the following may be consumer dealings:

1. A solicitor buys 200 square yards of carpet to carpet her offices.
2. A carpet salesman sells at cost price to his brother enough carpet to carpet the whole house.
3. A private individual who owns seven large chest freezers buys enough lambs and pigs cut into joints to fill the freezers.
4. A young man buys a second-hand ambulance to use as a normal vehicle.

If the party inserting the exclusion clause in the contract wants to argue that the party subject to it is not a consumer, then by s 12(3) he must prove it.

Whether a contract involves a consumer dealing or not is clearly a matter of construction for the courts. There are many situations where a party might buy goods that are ordinarily for business use, or a businessman buys goods but not for business use. Difficulties can clearly arise. Besides which, a consumer can fall outside the definition in s 12 and thus lose its protection if he holds himself out as acting in the course of a business in order to acquire a trade discount.

Business on the other hand is defined in s 14 as including:

> '... a profession and the activities of any government department or local or public authority.'

Exclusions depending for their validity on a test of reasonableness

The Act identifies a number of contractual situations in which an exclusion clause will be valid, provided that it satisfies a test of reasonableness. If it fails to satisfy these criteria then it will be invalid.

- By s 2(2) a clause seeking to exclude liability for loss, other than death or personal injury, caused by the negligence of the party inserting the clause, can only stand if it satisfies the test of reasonableness in the Act.
- By s 3 in those contracts where the party deals as a consumer, or deals on the other party's standard business forms, the party inserting an exclusion clause cannot rely on a clause excluding liability for his own breach, or for a substantially different performance, or for no performance at all except where to do so would satisfy the test of reasonableness in the Act.
- By s 6(3) a party can only exclude liability for breaches of the implied conditions in ss 13, 14(2), 14(3) and 15 Sale of Goods Act 1979 in inter-business dealings where the test of reasonableness is satisfied.
- This same principle operates in the case of private sellers (those not selling in the course of a business) in respect of exclusions for breaches of ss 13 and 15 Sale of Goods Act 1979.
- By s 7(3) exactly the same requirement of reasonableness operates in respect of exclusions for breaches of the implied conditions in ss 3, 4 and 5 of the Supply of Goods and Services Act 1982.
- Under s 8 a clause seeking to exclude liability for misrepresentations will be subject to the same requirement of reasonableness.
- By s 4 in consumer contracts clauses requiring a party to indemnify the other against loss are only valid where they satisfy the reasonableness test. Such clauses may require the consumer to indemnify the party, inserting the indemnity clause for injury loss or damage caused to third parties.

Thompson v T Lohan (Plant Hire) Ltd & J W Hurdiss Ltd (1987)

A plant hire company hired out a JCB and driver. The contract required that the driver supplied should be competent, but the party hiring them would be liable for all claims arising from the use of the equipment or the work of the driver. Besides this, the contract required them to indemnify the plant hire company for any claims against them. When the claimant's husband was killed as a result of the driver's negligence, the defendants claimed that the clause was a void exclusion clause under s 2(1) of the Act. The court held that it was an indemnity clause covered by s 4 and thus subject to a test of reasonableness in determining its validity.

The test of reasonableness

Guidelines on what is reasonable are contained in both s 11 and Schedule 2 of the Act. These are not absolutely definitive so that the test is one really for judicial interpretation, although there is not a great amount of case law on the area.

Section 11(5) identifies that it is for the party who inserts the clause in the contract and thus seeks to rely on it, to show that it is reasonable in all the circumstances.

Warren v Trueprint Ltd (1986)

A contract contained a limitation clause where the defendants were responsible only for a replacement film and would only undertake further liability if a supplementary charge were paid. They were obliged to but were unable to show that this clause was reasonable when they lost a couple's silver wedding photos.

There are three tests of reasonableness.

1. Under s 11(1) which concerns exclusion clauses in general, the test is whether the insertion of the term in the contract is reasonable in the light of what was known to the parties at the time when they contracted.

Smith v Eric S Bush (1990)

Here surveyors negligently carried out a building society valuation, and a defect was missed which later resulted in loss to the purchaser. The purchaser was obliged to pay for the valuation report. This and the mortgage application contained clauses excluding liability for the accuracy of the valuation report. The attempt to rely on the exclusion clause failed since the court were unwilling to accept that its inclusion was reasonable.

2. Section 11(2) concerns those exclusion clauses referred to in ss 6(3) and 7(3), those involving breaches of the implied conditions in the Sale of Goods Act 1979 and Supply of Goods and Service Act 1982 in inter-business dealings. In the case of these the court should consider the criteria that are set out in Schedule 2:

    (a) Was the bargaining strength of the two parties comparable – for instance, if the buyer could easily be supplied from another source, then it would be.
    (b) Did the buyer receive an inducement or advantage from the supplier that might make insertion of the exclusion clause reasonable, particularly if such an advantage could not be gained from any other source of supply?
    (c) Were the goods manufactured, processed or adapted to the buyer's specifications?
    (d) Were the exclusions or limitations customary practice?

Watford Electronics Ltd v Sanderson CFL (2001)

The defendants provided and integrated software into Watford's existing computer system. When Watford terminated the agreement because the system did not work satisfactorily, the cost stood at £105,000. Watford claimed damages for breach of contract for £5.5 million, or for misrepresentation and negligence of about £1.1 million. In the defendant's standard terms there was a clause excluding liability for any claims for indirect or consequential losses whether arising from negligence or otherwise, and limiting any liability to the price of the goods as supplied. UCTA was held to apply so the question was whether or not the clause satisfied the test of reasonableness. The Court of Appeal held that it did since the parties were of equal bargaining power and the limitation clause was subject to negotiation when the contract was made.

3. Section 11(4) specifically concerns limitation clauses. Here the party inserting the clause must show a capability to meet liability if it arose. Insurance will also be considered.

George Mitchell Ltd v Finney Lock Seeds Ltd (1983)

Here the House of Lords considered that the clause limiting damages to the price of the seeds was unreasonable since the suppliers had often settled out of court in the past and could have insured against such loss without altering their profits substantially.

Contracts not falling within the Act

A number of contracts of specific types will not be covered by the provisions of the Act. These are to be found in Schedule 1:

- Contracts of insurance.
- Contracts for the creation, transfer or termination of interests in land.
- Contracts for patents, copyright and other intellectual property.
- Contracts for the creation or dissolution of companies.

- Contracts for marine salvage, charter parties, or carriage of goods by sea or air (except for incidents falling within the scope of s 2(1)).

The Unfair Terms in Consumer Contracts Regulations 1999

The scope of the regulations

The Regulations are significantly different in operation to the Act because they cover contractual terms in general, not just exclusion clauses. Nevertheless, they will, as their name suggests, operate only in relation to consumer contracts.

Consumer dealing is defined in different terms from in the Act.

- A seller or supplier is defined as:

> '… any person who sells or supplies goods or services and who in making a contract is acting for purposes related to his business.'

This is wider than in the Act.
- A consumer is defined as:

> 'any natural person who is acting for purposes which are outside his trade, business or profession.'

So this is narrower.

By regulation 39(1), the regulations only apply if the parties have not individually negotiated the term in question. So the regulations operate particularly in relation to standard form contracts. In order to avoid the operation of the regulations therefore the seller or supplier will need to show that the contract has been negotiated and is not standard form.

As with the Act, the regulations will not operate in the case of certain types of contract. These are identified in Schedule 1 and include contracts relating to employment, succession, family law rights and partnerships and companies. The regulations will not cover insurance contracts where the risk and the insured are clearly defined. Other than this, the scope of the regulations seems to be much broader than the Act, though their exact scope is uncertain.

Terms falling within the scope of the regulations

The regulations operate in respect of 'unfair terms'. According to regulation 4(1) an unfair term is:

> '… any term which contrary to good faith causes a significant imbalance in the parties' rights and obligations under the contract to the detriment of the consumer.'

So the regulations introduce a general concept of unfairness into the making of contracts, which is then subject to controls.

Schedule 2 identifies a number of factors that must be looked at in order to establish good faith:

- the relative bargaining strength of the parties to the contract
- whether the seller or supplier gave the consumer any inducement in order that he would agree to the term of the contract in question
- whether the goods sold or services supplied under the contract were to the special order of the consumer
- the extent to which the seller or supplier has dealt fairly and equitably with the consumer.

As well as these general guidelines, the regulations in Schedule 3 list a great number of terms that may generally be regarded as unfair, though the list is not intended to be exhaustive.

(a) Terms which limit or exclude liability for the death or personal injury of the consumer arising from an act or omission of the seller or supplier.

(b) Terms which inappropriately limit or exclude liability for a partial performance, a non-performance, or an inadequate performance.

(c) Terms that include provisions binding the consumer but which are only at the discretion of the seller or supplier.

(d) Terms allowing the seller or supplier to retain sums already paid over by the consumer who cancels the contract where there is no such term on cancellation by the seller or supplier.

(e) Terms requiring a consumer who is in breach of the contract to pay excessive sums in compensation to the seller or supplier.

(f) Terms allowing the seller or supplier to dissolve the contract where the same facility is not made available to the consumer by the contract.

(g) Terms that enable a seller or supplier to dissolve a contract that has only indeterminate duration without giving reasonable notice of the dissolution, except where there are serious grounds for doing so.

(h) Terms which automatically allow a seller or supplier to extend a contract of fixed duration where the consumer does not indicate otherwise, when the deadline set for the consumer to indicate a desire not to extend the contract is set unreasonably early.

(i) Terms which irrevocably bind the consumer to terms which he had no real opportunity to become acquainted with, prior to formation of the contract.

(j) Terms that allow the seller or supplier to alter terms unilaterally without any valid reason specified in the contract.

(k) Terms allowing the seller or supplier to unilaterally alter without any valid reason the character of the goods or services supplied.

(l) Terms enabling the price of goods to be determined at the time of delivery or which allow a seller or supplier to alter prices without the consumer having the opportunity to cancel.

(m) Terms giving the seller or supplier the right to interpret terms of the contract or otherwise to determine whether the goods or services supplied correspond to the requirements of the contract.

(n) Terms which limit obligations or commitments made by the agents of the sellers or suppliers.

(o) Terms requiring the consumer to comply with all obligations under the contract but not imposing a similar obligation on the sellers or suppliers.

(p) Terms which grant sellers or suppliers the right to transfer obligations under the contract which might then have the effect of reducing the consumer's rights under any guarantees.

(q) Terms which would have the effect of hindering the right of the consumer to take legal action or which would restrict the availability of evidence.

A further requirement in regulation 6 is that the terms should be expressed in plain and intelligible language. If any term is then found to be unfair under the regulations, it will not bind the consumer.

The regulations still have certain limitations. They do not apply to any term that has been individually negotiated. This sensibly preserves freedom of contract, but also has the effect in some cases of presuming an equality of bargaining strength that does not exist. In introducing the regulations, the government construed the provisions indicated in the directive narrowly. As a result, while the Trading Standards department has the power to challenge the standard form contracts of companies and large corporations, the same facility has not been extended to the consumer groups who may have wished to police contracts. In consequence the directive may not be given full effect.

The Law Commission has proposed reforms for the area of statutory control of terms in Law Commission Report No 292 on unfair contract terms. The suggestion is to combine the 1977 Act and the 1999 Regulations and to simplify the language involved.

Activity

1. To what extent will the Unfair Contract Terms Act 1977 prevent the exclusion or limitation of liability for negligence?
2. In what ways are consumer dealings and inter-business dealings different?
3. Why does the Unfair Contract Terms Act make certain exclusion clauses automatically invalid?
4. Under the Unfair Contract Terms Act, what exactly does reasonable mean?
5. Is there any difference between who is protected by the Unfair Contract Terms Act and the Unfair Terms in Consumer Contracts Regulations 1999?

Key facts

- Common law controls have been supplemented by statutory controls through the Unfair Contract Terms Act 1977 and through the Unfair Terms in Consumer Contracts Regulations 1999 (the latter to comply with European Directive 93/13).
- The Act draws a distinction between consumer and inter-business dealings.
- Clauses in certain types of contract are made void by the Act; eg exclusion of liability for death or injury caused by negligence – s 2(1); exclusions of liability for breaches of the implied terms in the Sale of Goods Act 1979 – ss 6(1), 6(2).
- Clauses in certain other circumstances depend for their validity on a test of reasonableness; eg damage caused by negligence – s 2(2); standard term contracts – s 3; breaches of Sale of Goods Act 1979 implied terms – s 6(3).
- Under s 11, what is reasonable depends on the knowledge of the parties at the time of contracting and a number of factors can be taken into account; eg whether the goods were freely available elsewhere, whether the goods were made to the buyer's specification etc.
- The Regulations are much wider and refer to unfair terms generally, not just exclusion clauses, but apply in consumer contracts only.
- In general they seek to remedy inequality in bargaining strength and remove unequal conditions.

Chapter 8

Vitiating factors

8.1 Effect of void and voidable contracts

If the parties have not complied with all of the necessary requirements that we looked at in Chapter 6, then there will not be a contract in existence. However, even if the rules of formation have been complied with a contract may not be perfect. For instance, if a party contracted on the basis of false information, there is no freedom of contract. That party may not have entered the contract if he had known the true facts.

Thus, even though the various requirements of formation have been fully met, a party may still have legal rights and remedies because of other defects that are later discovered concerning other 'imperfections' at the time the contract was formed. Indeed contracts affected in such a way are often referred to as 'imperfect contracts'.

These defects are generally called **vitiating** factors. A vitiating factor is one that may operate to invalidate an otherwise validly-formed contract, ie one that conforms to all the rules of formation already identified.

To vitiate basically means to impair the quality of, to corrupt or to debase. In a contract this means that factors present at formation of the contract, possibly unknown to one or either party, mean that the contract lacks the essential characteristic of voluntariness, is based on misinformation or is of a type frowned on by the law.

As a result, the role of the law is to provide a remedy to the party who may not have wished to enter the contract given full knowledge of the vitiating factor at the time of formation.

Where a contract is vitiated, it may be void or voidable. Whether the contract is void or voidable in a given case depends on the type of vitiating factor that is complained of.

Void contracts

With certain vitiating factors, the effect of demonstrating the vitiating factor to the court's satisfaction is to render the contract **void**. It is as though it has never been.

Stating that a contract is void is in many ways the same as stating that the contract does not exist. This is because identifying a contract as void is identifying it as having no validity and thus no enforceability in law.

Voidable contracts

If a contract is voidable, there are different possibilities. The vitiating factor is identified and acknowledged but it does not mean that the contract is automatically at an end.

Activity

1. What does vitiating factor mean?
2. What are the basic consequences of a contract being declared void?
3. What are the basic consequences of a contract being declared voidable?
4. Will a contract made on the basis of a misrepresentation generally be void or voidable?

A party who has entered a contract that is voidable for a vitiating factor can continue with the contract if that is to his benefit. Alternatively, that party can avoid their responsibilities under the contract and in effect set the contract aside.

8.2 Misrepresentation

8.2.1 The character of a misrepresentation

We have already considered in Chapter 7 that statements made before or at the time of contracting are known as **representations**. Representations can, if incorporated into the contract, be terms of the contract and as such are actionable if they are breached.

Representations which are not incorporated into the contract will have no contractual significance if they are truly stated. They will have acted to induce the other party into the contract but that is where they end. Alternatively they may be 'puffs', having no contractual significance.

A falsely made representation, however, is a **misrepresentation**. It may be significant even though not forming part of the contract. To be actionable therefore, the statement must not only be false but have acted to induce the other party to enter the contract.

Misrepresentation may refer to the false statement itself or may be the action of making the false statement. The statement may be false or merely incorrect since innocent misrepresentation is now possible.

A misrepresentation can also arise from the conduct of a party.

Spice Girls Ltd v Aprilia World Service BV (2000)

A famous girl group was offered a contract with a scooter manufacturer to promote its products. Before the contract was signed the group filmed a commercial, knowing that one member of the group was about to leave. In a later dispute between the manufacturer and the group the court held that by attending the group represented that none of them intended to leave the group and none of them was aware that one member intended to. Their conduct in attending was a misrepresentation.

The consequences of a contract being formed on the basis of a misrepresentation are for the contract to be voidable at the request of the party who is the victim of the misrepresentation. It is not void because this denies that party the right to continue with the contract if that is in their interest.

Traditionally, misrepresentation was not actionable at common law. Some relief was available in equity, subject to certain qualifications, and later a remedy was available where fraud could be proved. In general though a party had little possibility of claiming against a misrepresentation until the passing of the Misrepresentation Act 1967. For this reason it was critical in the past for a party to prove that a statement made before the contract was a term.

It may still be advantageous to a party to identify that a representation has been incorporated as a term, though this is obviously more difficult where the contract is written. Misrepresentation should still be viewed in the general context of pre-contractual statements and representations.

A final point about misrepresentation is that it also shares some features with common mistake. As a consequence it is not impossible to see both pleaded in a case.

Definition

A misrepresentation occurs when a representation made at or before the time of the contract is falsely stated. A misrepresentation can therefore be defined as a statement of material fact, made by one party to a contract to the other party to the contract, during the negotiations leading up to the formation of the contract; which was intended to operate and did operate as an inducement to the other party to enter the contract, but which was not intended to be a binding obligation under the contract; and which was untrue or incorrectly stated.

This is a very precise definition, and the components of this definition should be considered individually.

The statement complained of is required to be one of material fact

* It cannot therefore have been a mere opinion, unless of course the opinion was not actually held at the time of the making of the statement.

Bisset v Wilkinson (1927)

A representation as to the number of sheep land could hold was not based on any expert knowledge, so could neither be relied upon or be actionable as a misrepresentation.

* Neither can it be a statement expressing future intention which is speculation rather than fact. Though it could be if the statement was falsely representing a state of mind which did not exist.

Edgington v Fitzmaurice (1885)

The directors of a company borrowed money, representing that they would use the loan for the improvement of the company's buildings. In fact they had intended from the start to use the loan to pay off serious, existing debts. They had misrepresented what their actual intentions were.

* Nor could it be a mere 'puff' which attaches no weight and is not intended to be relied upon at all.

Carlill v The Carbolic Smoke Ball Co Ltd (1892)

The company's argument, that their promise to pay £100 to whoever contracted flu was only a puff, failed. The maxim *simplex commendatio non obligat* (loosely, 'a single recommendation carries with it no legal obligation') could not apply as it had supported the promise by lodging £1,000 in a bank to cover possible claims.

The statement that is claimed to be a misrepresentation must have been made by one party to the contract to the other party

As a result, it is not misrepresentation where the false statement that it is argued induced the other party to contract was made by a third party, unless that third party is an agent.

Peyman v Lanjani (1985)

The defendant took the lease of premises under an agreement requiring the landlord's permission. The defendant did not attend the meeting at which the agreement was struck but sent an agent whom he thought would create a better impression with the landlord. He later decided to sell the lease on to the claimant and again this would require the landlord's permission. Once more he sent his agent. The claimant discovered the deception after he had paid over £10,000 under the agreement with the defendant. He then successfully applied to rescind the contract. Using the agent was a misrepresentation of the legitimacy of the lease which had never been agreed between the defendant and the landlord.

The statement complained of must have been made before or at the time of the contract

If the statement was made after the agreement was reached, then it cannot be actionable as a misrepresentation because it had no effect on the formation of the contract.

Roscorla v Thomas (1842)

After a deal had been struck for the sale and purchase of a horse, the seller represented that it was '… sound and free from vice.' In fact the horse was unruly but the purchaser could not claim since the promise was made after the agreement.

The statement has to be an inducement to enter the contract

- It must be materially important to the making of the contract.

JEB Fasteners Ltd v Marks Bloom & Co Ltd (1983)

The claimant engaged in a takeover of another company in order to obtain the services of two directors of the other company. In investigating the company, it relied on accounts which had been negligently prepared. There could be no claim of misrepresentation since the purpose of taking over the company was to secure the services of the directors and the accounts were no inducement. They were not material to the real purpose.

- Though it will not matter that the representation would not generally be an inducement as long as it induced the claimant.

Museprime Properties Ltd v Adhill Properties Ltd (1990)

Three properties were sold by auction. There was a misrepresentation as to the existence of an outstanding rent review which could result in increased rents and therefore increased revenue. The defendants unsuccessfully challenged the claimants' claim for rescission, arguing that the statement could realistically induce nobody to enter the contract.

- It cannot be an inducement where the other party is unaware of the misrepresentation.
- It will not be a misrepresentation where the party to whom it is made already knows the statement to be false.
- It will not be a misrepresentation where the party to whom it was made never actually relied upon the statement in entering the contract.

Attwood v Small (1838)

A mine was purchased and certain information given as to its remaining capacity. This was in fact false. The claimant could not argue a misrepresentation, however, since in buying the mine he had actually relied on his own mineral survey which was also inaccurate.

The statement was not intended to form part of the contract

If it were intended to be contractually binding, then it would be a warranty rather than a misrepresentation.

Couchman v Hill (1947)

Here the statement that the heifer was 'unserved' could not be a misrepresentation because of the significance attached to it. It was a term incorporated into the contract.

The representation was falsely made

Clearly if a representation is true, it has no further contractual significance once the contract is formed.

Activity

1. What is a misrepresentation?
2. How can a misrepresentation be distinguished from an opinion?
3. Why does it matter whether or not the misrepresentation actually induces the other party to enter into the contract?
4. Why is it important to think of misrepresentation in the context of all pre-contractual statements?

8.2.2 The classes of misrepresentation and their remedies

The character of a misrepresentation

A misrepresentation can obviously arise in a number of different ways. It could merely be an inaccurate statement made in all innocence, the inaccuracy being unknown to the maker. It could happen where the maker of the statement is relying on information supplied in manufacturer's specifications, or oral statements made about goods by a previous owner. A misrepresentation can also be a deliberate lie, intended to deceive and stated in full knowledge that it is untrue. In between these, a misrepresentation can be carelessly made by assuming knowledge and failing to check on the actual details.

As a result, misrepresentations can be classified according to type. Since the passing of the Misrepresentation Act 1967, the significance is less marked than it was, but it can still be important in determining what remedy is available to a party who is the victim of the misrepresentation. Traditionally the character of the misrepresentation was vital since only fraudulent misrepresentation was actionable, and in the tort of deceit rather than in the law of contract.

Originally everything that was not a fraud was classed as innocent misrepresentation, and the only remedy was in equity for rescission of the contract. Now it is possible to identify fraudulent,

negligent and innocent misrepresentations, and there are remedies available in common law and under statute.

Fraudulent misrepresentation

At common law, traditionally the only action available for a misrepresentation was where fraud could also be proved. This action itself is fairly recent, coming only at the end of the nineteenth century. This demonstrates clearly how vital it was to many litigants in the past to show that a statement on which they had relied had been incorporated into the contract as a term, otherwise they might be left without any remedy at all.

Derry v Peek (1889)

A tram company was licensed to operate horse-drawn trams by Act of Parliament. Under the Act they would also be able to use mechanical power by gaining the certification of the Board of Trade. They made an application and also issued a prospectus to raise further share capital. In this, honestly believing that permission would be granted, they falsely represented that they were able to use mechanical power. In the event their application was denied and the company fell into liquidation. Peek, who had invested on the strength of the representation in the prospectus and lost money, sued. His action failed since there was insufficient proof of fraud. Lord Herschell in the House of Lords defined the action as requiring actual proof that the false representation was made:

'… knowingly or without belief in its truth or recklessly careless whether it be true or false.'

So those are the three possibilities if an action in deceit is to be successful. 'Knowingly' is straightforward, the representor knew the inaccuracy of his statement. In other words, there is a deliberate falsehood. If the representor acted without belief in the statement, then this is also a statement falsely made. A recklessly made statement must be something more than mere carelessness. In all cases, the essence of liability is the dishonesty of the defendant in making a statement which he did not honestly know to be true. The motive for making the statement is largely irrelevant. If the claimant has suffered loss as a result, then there is a claim.

The simplest defence available then is to show an honest belief in the truth of the statement. It would not have to be a reasonable belief provided it was honestly held. Fraud is therefore extremely difficult to prove.

Remedies for fraudulent misrepresentation

A party suffering loss as the result of a fraudulent misrepresentation can sue for damages in the tort of deceit. The method of assessing any damages awarded then will be according to the tort measure; ie to put the claimant in the position he would have been in if the tort had not occurred, rather than the contract measure which is to put the claimant in the position he would have been in if the contract had been properly performed.

This may result in more being recovered by way of any claim for consequential loss. As Lord Denning put it in *Doyle v Olby (Ironmongers) Ltd* (1969):

> ❝ '... the defendant is bound to make reparation for all the damage flowing from the fraudulent inducement.' ❞

This point has been confirmed so that the defendant is responsible for all losses including any consequential loss, providing a causal link can be shown between the fraudulent inducement and the loss.

Smith New Court Securities v Scrimgeour Vickers (1996)

The claimants had been induced to buy shares in Ferranti at 82.25p per share as a result of a fraudulent misrepresentation that they were a good marketing risk. The shares were actually trading at 78p per share at the time of the transaction. Unbeknown to either party, the shares were worth considerably less since Ferranti itself had been the victim of a major fraud. When the claimants discovered the fraud, they chose not to rescind but to sell the shares on at prices ranging from 49p to 30p per share. The House of Lords held that the losses incurred were a direct result of the fraud that induced the claimants to contract. As a result any losses awarded should be based on the figure paid of 82.25p rather than the 78p.

The clear consequence of the judgment is that heavier claims can be pursued if fraud is alleged, and there is therefore an encouragement to do so if proof is available.

The claimant who suffers loss as the result of a fraudulent misrepresentation then has two choices on discovering the fraud. He may affirm the contract and go on to sue for damages as indicated above. But the claimant might also disaffirm the contract and refuse further performance.

If this is the claimant's choice, then there are two further possible courses of action. Firstly, if there is nothing at this point to be gained by bringing action against the other party, the claimant can discontinue performance of his or her obligations and do nothing. Then if he is sued by the maker of the fraud, he can then use the misrepresentation as a defence to that claim. Alternatively the claimant might seek rescission of the contract in equity on discovering the fraud.

Negligent misrepresentation

Traditionally any misrepresentation that was not identifiable as a fraud would be classed as an innocent misrepresentation, for which the only possible action was for rescission of the contract in equity.

The reason there was no available action for a negligently made misrepresentation was that negligence falls short of the criteria identified by Lord Herschell in *Derry v Peek* (1889).

There have, however, been developments in both common law and statute meaning that an action is now possible for a negligent misrepresentation. The former is again only possible in tort rather than contract and is a much more limited action than that available under the Act.

Common law

An action for a negligent misstatement causing pecuniary (financial) loss to be suffered by the other party is now possible.

Hedley Byrne & Co Ltd v Heller & Partners Ltd (1964)

The claimants were asked to provide advertising work worth £100,000 for another company, Easipower, on credit. Sensibly they sought a reference as to creditworthiness from Easipower's bankers, the defendants. They wrote back confirming that Easipower were a '... respectably constituted company good for its ordinary business engagements.' The bankers also claimed to reply without any responsibility for the reference they had given. When Easipower went into liquidation with the claimants still unpaid, they brought an action in the tort of negligence against the bankers. Their action failed because the bank had validly disclaimed any liability for their reference. Nevertheless, the House of Lords, in *obiter*, considered that such an action would be possible in certain 'special relationships' where the person making the negligent statement owed a duty of care to the other party to ensure that the statement was accurately made. In reaching this conclusion, the House of Lords approved Lord Denning's dissenting judgment in *Candler v Crane Christmas & Co* (1951), where he felt that negligently prepared company accounts should be actionable.

Subsequent case law has both accepted and refined the *Hedley Byrne* principle. The requirements of the tort are threefold. The party making the negligent statement must be in possession of the particular type of knowledge for which the advice is required. There must be sufficient proximity between the two parties that it is reasonable to rely on the statement. The party to whom the statement is made does rely on the statement and the party making the statement is aware of that reliance.

It is also possible for the principle to apply to representations as to a future rather than a present state of affairs.

Esso Petroleum Co Ltd v Marden (1976)

Esso developed a filling station on a new site near to a busy road, and let it to Marden. During negotiations for the lease, their representative indicated that the throughput would amount to 200,000 gallons per year. Marden queried this figure but contracted on the basis of the reassurance of the more experienced representative. In fact the local authority then required pumps and entrance to be at the rear of the site, accessible only from side streets. As a result, throughput was never more than 86,502 gallons per year, and the petrol station uneconomical. Marden lost all his capital in the venture and gave up the tenancy. Esso sued for back rent and Marden counterclaimed with two arguments, both of which were successful. Firstly he claimed that the estimate of throughput was a warranty on which he was entitled to rely. Secondly he claimed that the relationship with Esso was a special one, creating a duty of care. Esso's failure to warn him properly of the changed circumstances and the very different throughput resulting was negligence under *Hedley Byrne*.

Statute

The above case started before the Misrepresentation Act 1967 was in force, or a simpler action may have been available.

The benefit of the Misrepresentation Act 1967 is that it is much broader than any of the actions previously available. It is particularly appropriate where the claimant is unable to prove fraud. It followed the recommendation of the Law Reform Committee that damages should be available for losses arising from a negligent misrepresentation. However, the Act in that sense was based on the law as it existed before *Hedley Byrne,* and so takes no account of that principle but rather operates as an alternative to fraud.

Section 2(1) identifies the means of taking action.

> 'Where a person has entered into a contract after a misrepresentation has been made to him by another party thereto and as a result thereof he has suffered loss, then if the person making the misrepresentation would be liable to damages in respect thereof had the misrepresentation been made fraudulently, that person shall be so liable notwithstanding that the misrepresentation was not made fraudulently unless he proves that he had reasonable grounds to believe and did believe up to the time the contract was made that the facts represented were true.'

All that this basically means is that a party who is the victim of a misrepresentation has an action available without having to prove either fraud or the special relationship for *Hedley Byrne* criteria.

There are then some important differences with the past law.

- Firstly the burden of proof is partly reversed. Where formerly the claimant would have been required to prove fraud, under the Act it will be for the defendant to show that he in fact held a reasonable belief in the truth of the statement, once it is shown to be a misrepresentation.
- If the misrepresentation is negligently made, then the claimant has the choice of whether to

sue under the Act or under the *Hedley Byrne* principle.
- If the Act is chosen, then there is no need to show the relationship required for *Hedley Byrne* type liability.

Howard Marine Dredging Co Ltd v A Ogden & Sons (Excavating) Ltd (1978)

Contractors estimating a price for depositing excavated earth at sea sought advice from the company from whom they intended to hire barges as to their capacity. The Marine Manager negligently based his answer of 1600 tonnes on dead weight figures from Lloyds register, rather than checking the actual shipping register which would have shown a figure of 1055 tonnes. The work was delayed and the contractors refused to pay the hire for the barges. When sued for payment, they successfully counterclaimed using s 2(1) Misrepresentation Act 1967.

Remedies for negligent misrepresentation

Damages are available as a remedy both under the Act and at common law. If the *Hedley Byrne* principle is applied, then damages are calculated according to the standard tort measure. This means that damages will only be awarded for a loss that is a foreseeable consequence of the negligent misrepresentation being made.

Under the Act, damages are again calculated according to a tort measure since the Act is stated as being appropriate where fraud cannot be proved. It is more arguable whether damages follow the normal tort measure or whether the test applied in the tort of deceit is appropriate. The latter is more beneficial and has been accepted in *Royscot Trust Ltd v Rogerson* (1991).

One consequence of damages under the Act being calculated by the tort measures of course is that they can be reduced if contributory negligence can be shown.

The only remedy traditionally available if the

misrepresentation was negligently made was for rescission in equity, which is still possible.

Innocent misrepresentation

Any misrepresentation not made fraudulently was formerly classed as an innocent misrepresentation, regardless of how it was made. There would be no action possible under the common law, only an action for rescission of the contract in equity.

The emergence of the *Hedley Byrne* principle and of s 2(1) Misrepresentation Act 1967 means that possibly the only misrepresentations that can be claimed to be made innocently are where a party makes a statement with an honest belief in its truth. The obvious example of this is where the party merely repeats inaccurate information, the truth of which he is unaware.

In this case, an action under s 2(1) of the Act would not be possible since this can be successfully defended by showing the existence of a reasonable belief in the truth of the statement. Nevertheless, the traditional action for rescission in equity is still a possibility. There is also a possibility of claiming under s 2(2) of the Act.

Remedies for innocent misrepresentation

As we have seen, since damages were not formerly available under common law, they will not be available either under s 2(1).

However, the court has a discretion under s 2(2) to award damages as an alternative to rescission where it is convinced that to do so is the appropriate remedy. The court must consider that:

> '... it would be equitable to do so, having regard to the nature of the misrepresentation and the loss that would be caused by it if the contract were upheld, as well as the loss that rescission would cause to the other party.'

Zanzibar v British Aerospace (Lancaster House) Ltd (2000)

The Zanzibar government purchased a corporate jet aeroplane from British Aerospace in 1992. The Zanzibar government subsequently alleged that they had been induced to enter the contract on the basis of a false representation by British Aerospace as to both the type of jet and its general airworthiness. Zanzibar claimed rescission of the contract and damages as an alternative. The court denied them both, on the ground that the delay in bringing the action meant that the right to rescission had been lost, and so no damages could be paid in lieu of rescission either.

It is important to consider three significant points regarding s 2(2):

1. There is no actual right to damages as there may be in a common law action. The award of damages is at the discretion of the court as an equitable remedy would be.
2. Since damages are to be awarded as an alternative to rescission, then only one remedy can be granted not both.
3. The measure of damages to be awarded is uncertain, but since it is in lieu of rescission then it is unlikely that consequential loss could be claimed.

Prior to the passing of the Act, the only available remedy was rescission. This remedy may be appropriate because, in the words of Sir George Jessell, '... no man ought to seek to take advantage of his own false statements.'

Redgrave v Hurd (1881)

Rescission was ordered in a contract between two solicitors for the sale and purchase of the one's practice. He had misstated the income from the practice, and when the other backed out, tried to claim specific performance of the contract. The other solicitor successfully counterclaimed for rescission.

Activity

1. Why was it traditionally so important to prove that a falsely made representation was actually incorporated into the contract?
2. How would a party traditionally prove a fraudulent misrepresentation?
3. How easy or difficult is it to prove fraud?
4. What did negligently and innocently made representations have in common?
5. Which is the more advantageous action, that under *Hedley Byrne* principles, or tort, or that under s 2(1) of the Misrepresentation Act 1967?
6. What are the major advantages of the Misrepresentation Act 1967 over other actions?
7. Are the remedies better for any particular class of misrepresentation?

Activity

Suggest what type of misrepresentation is involved in the following examples

1. James is selling his car to Frank. Frank asks what is the capacity of the engine. James, after looking at the registration documents, tells him that it is 1299 cc. Unbeknown to James, the documents are incorrect.
2. Sally, a saleswoman, tells Rajesh that a three-piece suite is flame-resistant in order to gain the sale, without checking the manufacturer's specifications that would have revealed that it was not.
3. Howard, who has no qualifications at all, tells prospective employers at an interview that he has a degree in marketing.

8.2.3 Misrepresentation and the role of equity

The availability of damages for a misrepresentation varies, as we have seen, according to the nature of the misrepresentation and the nature of the action bought by the injured party. Rescission, on the other hand, may be available whatever the character of the misrepresentation.

Rescission is of course an equitable remedy and its award is subject to the discretion of the court. It must be remembered that an actionable misrepresentation makes a contract voidable rather than void, so the contract remains valid until such time as it is 'set aside' by the court for the injured party.

The right to rescind is not absolute and it may be lost in a number of circumstances.

- *Restitutio in integrum* is vital to rescission. In essence this means that, since the party claiming is asking to be returned to the pre-contract position, known as the *status quo ante*, this in fact must be possible to achieve. If it is not then rescission of the contract will not be granted.

Lagunas Nitrate Co v Lagunas Syndicate (1899)

A nitrate field was bought by the claimants on an innocent misrepresentation of the defendant as to the strength of the market for nitrates. They made profits for a period but were affected adversely by a general depression in prices, at which point they sought rescission. They failed because they had extracted the nitrates for some time and the field could not be restored to its pre-contract order.

- An affirmation of the contract after its formation by the party seeking rescission will defeat the claim.

Long v Lloyd (1958)

A lorry was bought on the basis of a representation as to its 'exceptional condition'. Several faults were discovered on the first journey that the purchaser then allowed the seller to repair. When the lorry again broke down through its faulty condition, the buyer's claim to rescission was unsuccessful. He had accepted the goods in a less than satisfactory condition and was unable to return them.

- Delay is said to 'defeat equity'. So a failure to claim rescission promptly may mean it is unavailable as a remedy.

Leaf v International Galleries (1950)

A contract for the sale of a painting of Salisbury Cathedral described it as a Constable. When the description later proved false the purchaser's claim to rescission failed because a five-year period had then elapsed.

- If a third party has subsequently gained rights in the goods, then it would be unfair to interfere with those rights by granting rescission.

White v Garden (1851)

A rogue bought 50 tons of iron from the claimant using a bill of exchange in a false name, and resold it on to a third party who acted in good faith. When the claimant discovered that the Bill of Exchange was useless, he seized the iron from the innocent third party. This was illicit since the third party had gained good title to the iron.

- Under s 2(2) Misrepresentation Act 1967 the judge has a discretion on which remedy to apply. Rescission will not therefore be available if the judge has decided that damages are a more appropriate remedy.

It is possible to be granted rescission and an indemnity for other expenses incurred as a result of the misrepresentation.

Whittington v Seale-Hayne (1900)

Poultry breeders took a lease of premises on the basis of an oral representation that the premises were in a sanitary condition. This was untrue. The water was contaminated, the buyer became ill and some poultry died. At the time the claimants were not entitled to consequential loss because they could not prove fraud. However, as well as their claim to rescission, they were awarded an indemnity representing what they had spent out in terms of rent and rates and other costs.

In granting rescission, the court must always take into account the seriousness of the breach and the likely consequences of rescission for both parties.

Activity

1. Why was equity traditionally so important to a party who had entered a contract as a result of a misrepresentation?
2. How fair are the 'bars' to rescission?
3. What types of misrepresentation would be classed as innocent following the Misrepresentation Act 1967?
4. What are the advantages and disadvantages of s 2(2) of the Act?

8.2.4 Non-disclosure and misrepresentation

There is no basic obligation at common law to volunteer information that has not been asked for.

Fletcher v Krell (1873)

A woman who had applied for a position as a governess had not revealed that she had formerly been married. Despite the fact that single women were generally preferred, her failure to reveal her marriage was not a misrepresentation.

In fact silence of itself cannot generally be classed as misrepresentation.

Hands v Simpson, Fawcett & Co (1928)

A commercial traveller acquired employment without advising his new employers that he was disqualified from driving, even though this was an essential part of the work. Even so, he was not obliged to volunteer the information without being asked.

In fact, it has recently been held that the mere fact that if during contractual negotiations one party fails to mention something which the other party then claims was of importance, this will not normally give rise to a cause of action.

Hamilton and Others v Allied Domecq plc (2007)

Allied Domecq purchased a major shareholding in a mineral water business owned by Hamilton and others in order to increase sales distribution. This would be in hotels, restaurants, public houses and also in supermarkets and groceries. Initial discussions focused on marketing in the on licence trade first with a view to later gaining ground in the off licence trade which Hamilton supported. In fact Allied Domecq intended to market initially only in the off licence trade. When the business went into liquidation Hamilton claimed to be a victim of misrepresentation in that he would not have entered the agreement if he had known Domecq's intention. The claim failed on the basis that the actual agreement of the parties was silent on distribution strategy.

However, there are a number of situations where the act of withholding or not offering information is not misrepresentation.

- Contracts which are *uberimmae fides* or where the 'utmost good faith' is required. This principle is commonly applicable to contracts of insurance, on the basis that with full information the insurer may not have been prepared to accept the risk.

Locker and Woolf Ltd v Western Australian Insurance Co Ltd (1936)

The insured party had not revealed to the insurer when entering the contract that another company had refused him insurance. This was clearly material to the contract.

- Fiduciary relationships, where again good faith is required. These may include the relationship between trustees and beneficiaries. A failure to reveal certain information material to the contract may result in its being set aside under the doctrine of constructive fraud.

Tate v Williamson (1866)

A young man heavily in debt was persuaded by an adviser to sell his land to raise money to settle the debts. This adviser then bought the land, having not revealed full details as to its value and thus obtaining it at half value. The contract was set aside.

- Where a part truth amounts to a falsehood.

Dimmock v Hallett (1866)

A person selling land revealed that the land was let to tenants, but not that the tenants were terminating the lease and thus that the income from the land was reducing. This amounted to a misrepresentation.

- Where a statement made originally in truth becomes false during the negotiations. This will then be a misrepresentation.

With v O'Flanagan (1936)

A doctor selling his practice stated the true income at the beginning of negotiations but by the time of the sale, this had dwindled to a negligible figure. Since he failed to reveal this, it was a misrepresentation.

Key facts

- A misrepresentation is a false statement of fact made by one party to the contract to the other at or before the time of contracting, not intended to be part of the contract but intended to induce the other party to enter the contract.
- It will have the effect of making the contract voidable.
- A misrepresentation can be made:
  (a) fraudulently
  (b) negligently
  (c) innocently.

- If fraudulent there is an action in the tort of deceit – *Derry v Peek* (1889) – in which case it must have been made:
  (a) knowingly or deliberately; or
  (b) without any belief in its truth; or
  (c) recklessly as to whether it is true or not – an honest belief is a defence.

- If negligent then there is a possible action:
  (a) in tort under *Hedley Byrne* – provided it is made in a special relationship, where the party making it has expert knowledge relied upon by the other party; or
  (b) under s 2(1) Misrepresentation Act 1967 – *Howard Marine Insurance v Ogden* (1978).

- If innocent, then traditionally the only remedy was for rescission in equity. Now there is also an action for damages under s 2(2) Misrepresentation Act 1967.
- Rescission is only available if:
  (a) *restitutio in integrum* applies – *Clarke v Dickson* (1858)
  (b) the contract is not affirmed – *Long v Lloyd* (1958)
  (c) there is no undue delay – *Leaf v International Galleries* (1950)
  (d) and no third party has gained rights.

- Non-disclosure of information will also amount to misrepresentation:
  (a) in contracts *uberimmae fides* (of utmost good faith) such as insurance – *Locker and Woolf v Western Australian Insurance* (1936);
  (b) where a part truth amounts to a falsehood – *Dimmock v Hallett* (1866); and
  (c) where a true statement later becomes false – *With v O'Flanagan* (1936).

Activity

1. What exactly is non-disclosure?
2. In what circumstances will non-disclosure amount to an actionable misrepresentation?

Chapter 9

Discharge of contract

Discharge of the contract refers to the ending of the obligations under the contract, so that where we have thought of formation being the beginning of the contract, discharge is concerned with its end.

In its simplest form, discharge will be the point at which all of the primary obligations created by the contract have been met. However, the situation is not always so simple or straightforward, and there are times when we refer to the contract being discharged even though the obligations under the contract remain uncompleted.

The obvious example of this latter point is where the contract is breached. Secondary obligations in this case may be substituted for the primary obligations, and a party not carrying out his obligations under the contract may be required to pay damages.

Where all obligations under the contract have been carried out, this is referred to as performance of the contract. The contract is discharged, but even then the area can be complicated by one party completing some but not all of the obligations.

9.1 Discharge by performance

9.1.1 The strict rule on performance

The rule in *Cutter v Powell* (1795)

The starting point for performance of the contract, sometimes known as the 'perfect tender' rule, is that there should be complete performance of all obligations under the contract. If this is the case, then the contract is in effect complete and discharged.

On the other hand, it also means that where a party fails to meet all of his obligations, the contract is not discharged and this may require that the other party be given a remedy.

The potentially unjust simplicity of the rule is seen in the case from which it emerges.

Cutter v Powell (1795)

Cutter was the second mate on a ship, *The Governor Parry*, sailing from Jamaica to Liverpool. The boat set sail on 2 August and reached Liverpool on 9 October. Cutter died during the voyage on 20 September. When his wages were not paid, his wife sued on a *quantum meruit* (meaning 'for the amount owed'). She failed because her husband had signed on for the complete voyage. By dying, he had failed to complete his contract and since it was an entire contract there was no obligation to pay.

An entire contract is one where all of the obligations are seen as a single transaction that cannot be broken down in any way. The case illustrates the effect of failing to perform such a contract. It also shows how it can create an injustice since Cutter could hardly be said to have defaulted by dying, an event that was beyond his control.

Application of the rule

Application of the strict rule can be commonly seen in Sale of Goods contracts, where the description applied to the contract may mean that all rather than part is essential to completion of the contract.

Arcos Ltd v E A Ronaasen & Son (1933)

A buyer of wooden staves, described in the contract as half an inch thick, was allowed to reject the consignment sent to him. Those delivered were a sixteenth of an inch narrower and so did not correspond to the contract description. The strictness of the rule is shown since the staves could still be used for the purpose the buyer wanted them for. Lord Atkin said:

'... a ton does not mean about a ton, or a yard about a yard. If a seller wants a margin he must, and in my experience does, stipulate for it ...'

The strict rule has been applied even in the case of ancillary obligations.

Re Moore & Co v Landauer & Co (1921)

Tinned fruit was sold described as being in cases of 30 tins. When delivered, some of the cartons contained 24 tins, although the overall total number of tins ordered was correct. The buyer intended to resell the goods so the difference would have no impact on him. Nevertheless, the Court of Appeal, applying the strict rule, held that packaging could be included in description and that the buyer was correct in rejecting the goods and repudiating the contract.

Despite that, it is of course always possible that a judge may apply the maxim *de minimis non curat lex* (the law will not grant a remedy for something that is too trivial).

Reardon Smith Line Ltd v Hansen-Tangen (1976)

We have already seen in this case, using innominate terms, how the judges would not accept a repudiation of obligations where the term was a mere technicality describing the shipyard and job number.

This principle that a buyer should not be allowed to reject goods delivered when there is a slight shortfall or excess has now been incorporated in the Sale of Goods Act 1979 as s 30(2A).

9.1.2 Ways of avoiding the strict rule

The potential injustice of the rule in *Cutter v Powell* (1795) has led to judges accepting exceptions when the rule does not operate.

Divisible contracts

Here, contracts can be seen as being made up of various parts. If each part can be discharged separately, then it might also be enforced separately and the strict rule need not apply. This is particularly appropriate for instances where there is delivery by separate instalments, except where the seller has stipulated for a single payment.

Taylor v Webb (1937)

Premises were leased to a tenant for rent. A term in the lease required the landlord to keep the premises in good repair. In the event, the landlord failed to maintain the premises and the tenant then refused to pay the rent. In the landlord's action the court held that the contract had divisible obligations, to lease the premises, and to repair and maintain. The contract was thus not entire and the tenant could not legitimately refuse payment.

Acceptance of part performance

If one party has performed the contract but not completely and the other side is willing to accept the part performed, then the strict rule will usually not apply. Part performance may occur where there is a shortfall on delivery of goods or where a service is not fully carried out. This exception to the rule will only apply though when the party who is the victim of the part performance has a genuine choice of whether or not to accept.

Sumpter v Hedges (1898)

A builder was hired to build two houses and stables. Certain of the work was done when the builder ran out of money and was unable to complete it. The landowner then had the work completed using materials left on the land. The builder was awarded the value of the materials that had been used. His argument that part performance had been accepted was rejected. The landowner had no choice but to complete the work. The alternative was to leave the partly completed buildings as an eyesore on his land.

Substantial performance

If a party has done substantially what was required under the contract, then the doctrine of substantial performance can apply. The party can recover the amount appropriate to what has been done under the contract, providing that the contract is not entire.

Dakin & Co v Lee (1916)

A builder was bound by contract to complete major repair work to a building. He did complete all of the work, but some of it was carried out so carelessly that the owner of the building refused to pay on the grounds that performance was in effect incomplete. The builder was able to sue for the price of the work less an amount representing the value of the defective work.

- The price is thus often payable in such circumstances and the sum deducted represents the cost of repairing the defective workmanship.

Hoenig v Isaacs (1952)

A decorator was hired to decorate and furnish a flat for £750. He finished the work. The owner moved into the flat and paid £400 by instalments. Then because of defects to a bookcase and a wardrobe that would cost about £55 to put right, he refused to pay the remaining £350. The Court of Appeal held that the contract was substantially performed and the balance was payable less the amount representing the defects.

- What is accepted as substantial performance is a question of fact to be decided in each case. It depends on what remains undone and its value in comparison to the contract as a whole.

Bolton v Mahadeva (1972)

An electrical contractor was hired to install central heating. When completed, it gave off fumes and did not work properly. When payment was then refused, the contractor sued for the price. The Court of Appeal rejected his claim on the ground that there was not substantial performance. Part of the reasoning lay in the fact that there were £174 worth of defects in a system costing £560.

Prevention of performance

If one party prevents the other from carrying out his obligations because of some act or omission, then the strict rule cannot apply. In these circumstances the party trying to perform may have an action for damages.

Planche v Colburn (1831)

A publisher hired an author to write one of a series of books. When the publisher decided to abandon the whole series, the author was prevented from completing the work through no fault of his own. He was entitled to recover a fee for his wasted work.

Tender of performance

A similar situation with slightly different consequences occurs where a party has offered to complete his obligations but the other side has unreasonably refused performance. Here the party 'tendering' performance can sue and recover under the contract. He may also consider his own obligations discharged even though there has been no performance.

Startup v Macdonald (1843)

The contract was for ten tons of linseed oil to be delivered by the end of March. The seller delivered at 8.30 pm on 31 March which was a Saturday, and the buyer refused to accept delivery. The seller was able to recover damages. (This might be different now under the Sale of Goods Act 1979 since delivery should be at a 'reasonable hour'.)

In the case of money owed which is tendered and refused, though the debtor is freed from making further offers to pay, the debt will still exist.

9.1.3 Time of performance

Traditionally, a failure to perform on time would give only an action for damages but not to repudiate the contract.

While at common law it was accepted that time could be 'of the essence', this principle was not generally accepted in equity, and this is now the general assumption.

There are three principal occasions when time will be considered to be 'of the essence', and a

Key facts

- The strict rule on performance is that in an 'entire contract', all obligations must be performed – so there can be no payment for part performance – *Cutter v Powell* (1795).
- There are exceptions to this strict rule:
  (a) If obligations are 'divisible' then payment should be made for the part performed – *Taylor v Webb* (1937).
  (b) Where a party has accepted part performance, this should be paid for – *Sumpter v Hedges* (1898).
  (c) Where there has been substantial performance, the full price will be paid, less the sum appropriate to what has not been done – *Hoenig v Isaacs* (1952).
  (d) Unless too much remains to be done under the contract – *Bolton v Mahadeva* (1972).
- A party can sue for damages where his performance has been prevented by the other party – *Planche v Colborn* (1831).
- And also where he has offered to perform but this has been refused – *Startup v Macdonald* (1843).
- Time of performance is 'of the essence' when
  (a) it says so in the contract;
  (b) the circumstances make it so;
  (c) one party has already failed to perform.

repudiation of the contract is therefore available as a remedy:

1. Where the parties have made an express stipulation in the contract that time is of the essence
2. Where the surrounding circumstances show that time of performance is critical, as would be the case with delivery of perishable goods
3. Where one party has already failed to perform his obligations under the contract. In this case the other party is able to confirm that unless performance is completed within a stated period, repudiation will occur.

Activity

1. In what circumstances is a contract considered to be 'entire'?
2. How can the strict rule cause injustice?
3. What is a 'divisible contract'?
4. In what way can the *de minimis* rule be applied to performance?
5. What is the effect of a contract being only partly performed?
6. How is it possible to measure 'substantial performance'?
7. What effect does failing to perform on time have on a contract?

9.2 Agreement

If a contract is formed following an agreement, then it seems almost pure logic to suggest that the contract can also be ended by agreement without necessarily having been performed. Inevitably what is required is mutuality.

There are in fact two ways in which the contract could be discharged by agreement:

1. A **bilateral** discharge – here the assumption is that both parties are to gain a fresh but different benefit from the new agreement;
2. A **unilateral** discharge – the benefit is only to be gained by one party, who is thus trying to convince the other party to let him off the obligations arising under the original agreement. Lack of consideration is an inevitable problem if one party is merely promising to release the other from existing obligations.

So two problems are immediately apparent if a contract is discharged by agreement:

- absence of consideration for the fresh agreement
- possible lack of proper form for the new agreement in speciality contracts.

9.2.1 Bilateral discharge

Wholly executory arrangements

If neither side has yet performed any obligations under the contract, it is possible that there is no problem at all. Each side can release the other from performance and there is consideration for the new promise in each case – not having to perform the obligations under the original agreement.

A further possibility occurs when parties wish to continue a contractual arrangement, but to substitute new terms for the old ones. In this case, it is possible for the parties to 'waive' their rights under the old agreement and to substitute the new agreement.

Arrangements which are partly executory and partly executed

In this situation, one of the parties wishes to give less than full performance and it is possible for the other to waive rights. However, the obvious problem with this is the absence of consideration.

Where form is an issue

Traditionally this would have been subject to the rule in s 40 Law Property Act 1925 and the doctrine of part performance. Now an agreement to vary the terms in a contract requiring specific form may be invalid unless it is evidenced in writing. If a new agreement is substituted for an existing agreement then again this change will be unenforceable unless evidenced in writing.

9.2.2 Unilateral discharge

Where the contract is left unperformed by one party despite the willingness to contract of the other party, there are a number of possible consequences.

Firstly the party not in default might release the other party from performing, but this requires a deed for validity, otherwise it would fail for lack of consideration. However, as we have already seen, in consideration the principle in *Williams v Roffey Bros & Nicholls Contractors* (1990) may be sufficient to discharge obligations in circumstances where there is an extra benefit gained.

It is also possible to discharge the party in default from full performance where there is 'accord and satisfaction'. This could be as indicated in *Pinnel* (1602) either by adding a new

Activity

1. Why should parties to a contract be able to discharge their obligations by agreement without actually performing?
2. What is the difference between a bilateral discharge and a unilateral discharge?
3. In what way is form a problem in discharge by agreement?
4. When is it easiest to discharge a contract by agreement?
5. What is the easiest way of discharging a contract in a unilateral discharge?
6. What exactly is 'accord and satisfaction'?

Key facts

- Since a contract can be formed by agreement, then it can also be discharged without performance by agreement of both parties.
- There are two types of discharge by agreement – a bilateral arrangement and a unilateral agreement. The first is where both parties wish to back out of the arrangement, the second is where in effect only one does.

- Bilateral discharge is simple where the contract is executory – the waiving of rights is given by the one party in return for the waiving of rights by the other.
- Where form is an issue, the discharge will need evidence in writing.
- Where only one party wants to back out of the contract, that party will need to give some consideration, as in accord and satisfaction, unless estoppel applies.

element which counts as consideration, or by making a smaller payment at an earlier time than when the full payment is due.

Finally by promissory estoppel, where the party waiting for performance has agreed to waive rights under the contract, knowing that the other party is relying on this promise to forego performance. The party making the promise may be prevented from going back on the promise.

9.3 Discharge by frustration

9.3.1 The basic doctrine and types of frustrating event

In the strictest sense, discharge of a contract as we have seen requires performance of the obligations under the contract. Inevitably there will be times when the requirement for strict performance will lead to injustice.

This is particularly the case where there is a factor preventing performance that is beyond the control of either party to the contract. It is because of this potential injustice that the doctrine of frustration developed in the nineteenth century.

The original common law rule

The original common law rule was that a party was bound to perform his obligations under the contract, regardless of the effect of intervening events making it more difficult or even impossible to perform.

Paradine v Jane (1647)

Paradine sued Jane for rent due under a lease. Jane's defence was that he had been forced off the land by an invading army. The court held that he had a contractual duty to pay the rent due under the lease, which was not discharged by any intervening event. If he had wished to reduce his liability to take account of intervening events preventing his performance, then he should have made express provision for that in the lease.

This was the strict rule and it would override any circumstances.

The development of a doctrine of frustration

The injustice of the strict rule led inevitably to exceptions. In the nineteenth century, a doctrine developed whereby a party bound by a contractual promise, in circumstances where he was prevented from keeping the promise because of an unforeseeable, intervening event, would be relieved of the strict obligation. As a result, that party would not be liable for a breach of contract.

This is the origin of frustration. The judges achieved the desired result by the fiction of implying into the contract a term.

Taylor v Caldwell (1863)

Caldwell had agreed to rent a music hall to Taylor for four days for a series of concerts. Before the concerts were due to start, the music hall burnt to the ground, making performance impossible. There were no stipulations as to what should happen in the event of fire. Since Taylor had spent money on advertising and other preparations, he sued for damages under the principle in *Paradine v Jane* (1647). The court held that the commercial purpose of the contract had ceased to exist, performance was impossible, and so both sides were excused further performance. Blackburn J stated:

'... in contracts in which performance depends on the continued existence of a given person or thing, a condition is implied that the impossibility of performance arising from the perishing of the person or thing shall excuse the performance ... that excuse is by law implied, because from the nature of the contract it is apparent that the parties contracted on the basis of the continued existence of the particular person or chattel ...'

The doctrine then developed to cover those situations where the frustrating event meant that performance as envisaged in the contract was impossible.

Davis Contractors Ltd v Fareham UDC (1956)

A building firm contracted to build houses for a local council for £92,450 over a period of eight months. In fact, due to a shortage of skilled labour, the work took some 22 months to complete and the builders wanted an extra £17,651. The council paid the contract price. The builders claimed that the contract was frustrated in order to claim the extra on a *quantum meruit*. The House of Lords held that the contract was not in fact frustrated, but Lord Radcliffe did explain those factors that would justify the doctrine when used.

'… without default of either party, a contractual obligation has become incapable of being performed because the circumstances in which performance is called for would render it a thing radically different from that which was undertaken by the contract.'

The immediate consequence of application of the doctrine is that both parties are relieved of the burden of further performance, and of liability for not performing. This will inevitably not remove all apparent injustice, since the one party to the contract is still being denied the performance of the other party through no fault of his, and may have incurred costs in anticipation of the contract being performed.

As a result the doctrine is subject to many limitations, and parties may provide in their contracts for what happens if there are intervening frustrating events, the so-called *force majeure* clauses.

Types of frustrating event

The doctrine has developed largely out of the case law, and will operate in three main types of circumstance:

1. where the intervening event makes performance impossible
2. where performance becomes illegal
3. where the contract becomes commercially sterilised.

Impossibility

The contract may be frustrated because of the destruction of the subject matter.

Taylor v Caldwell (1863)

Destruction of the music hall was the cause of the impossibility and the frustration.

It may alternatively be the case that the subject matter becomes unavailable when the contract is to be performed.

Jackson v Union Marine Insurance Co. Ltd (1874)

A ship was chartered to sail from Liverpool to Newport and from there with a cargo of iron rails to San Francisco. It ran aground and could not be loaded for some time. The court accepted that there was an implied term that the ship should be available for loading in a reasonable time, and the long delay was a frustration of the contract.

In a contract for services, the frustrating event may be the unavailability of the party who is to render the service due to illness.

Robinson v Davidson (1871)

A husband, acting as agent for his wife, a celebrated pianist, contracted for her to perform. Some hours before the performance was due she became ill and the husband contacted the claimant to inform that she would be unable to attend. When the claimant sued, it was held that the contract was conditional on the woman being well enough to perform and her illness excused her. The contract was frustrated.

This principle of impossibility because of unavailability may apply even where there is only a risk that the party will be unavailable.

Condor v The Baron Knights (1966)

A contract entered into by a pop music group allowed that the group should be available to perform for seven evenings a week if necessary. One group member became ill and was advised to rest and work fewer hours. Though he actually ignored this advice, the court still held that the contract was frustrated since it was necessary to have a stand-in musician in case he fell ill.

In fact, any good reason that means that a party cannot perform his obligations may lead to a frustration of the contract.

Morgan v Manser (1948)

A music hall artiste was contracted to his manager for a ten-year period commencing in 1938. Between 1940 and 1946 he was in fact conscripted into the forces during the war years. His absence rendered the purpose of the contract undermined and both parties were excused performance.

An excessive but unavoidable delay in performing may be classed as impossibility, and mean that the contract is frustrated.

Pioneer Shipping Ltd v BTP Tioxide Ltd (1981) (The Nema)

A time charter of nine months was agreed which anticipated a possible seven voyages. In fact, due to strikes at the port where the vessel was loaded, this was reduced to two and the contract was held to be frustrated.

Outbreak of war is also a common frustrating event.

Metropolitan Water Board v Dick Kerr & Co Ltd (1918)

In July 1914 a contract was formed for the construction of a reservoir and a water works. The contract allowed that the work should be completed within a six-year period. In 1916 a government order stopped the work and requisitioned much of the plant. It was held that the contract was frustrated at the time of the government order.

Subsequent illegality

A contract may be frustrated as the result of a change in the law that makes the contract illegal to perform in the manner anticipated.

Denny, Mott & Dickson Ltd v James B Fraser & Co Ltd (1944)

Lord Macmillan said that a contract to import certain goods to an English port would be frustrated if the law was changed so that importing goods of that kind became illegal.

Outbreak of war is an obvious time when laws may change rapidly and cause a contract to be frustrated.

Re Shipton Anderson & Co and Harrison Bros & Co (1915)

A cargo of grain was sold, but before it could be delivered, war broke out. The government requisitioned the cargo and the contract was frustrated.

Commercial sterility

Even where the contract is not impossible to perform, but the commercial purpose has disappeared as a result of the intervening event, the contract might still be held to be frustrated. This is sometimes also known as frustration of the common venture, and it is commonly claimed when an event that is fundamental to the contract does not occur.

Krell v Henry (1903)

A contract was reached for the hire of a room overlooking the procession route for the coronation of King Edward VII. There was no specific mention of the purpose of the hire in the contract. However, when the coronation did not take place because of the King's illness and the defendant refused to pay for the room the court, applying the principle from *Taylor v Caldwell* (1863), accepted that the contract was frustrated. Watching the coronation procession was the 'foundation of the contract'; the defendant was relieved further performance.

All commercial purpose must be destroyed. If any is left, the contract is not frustrated and obligations under it continue.

Herne Bay Steamboat Co v Hutton (1903)

This was another case arising from the delayed coronation. The defendant hired a boat from which to see the review of the fleet by the King. His claim that the contract was frustrated failed. One purpose had disappeared, but it was still possible to use the boat and to see the fleet.

9.3.2 Limitations on application of the doctrine

Because one party to the contract is still left harmed, there are a number of situations where the courts have stated that the doctrine cannot apply.

Self-induced frustration

Frustration demands that the event is beyond the control of either party, so the doctrine is unavailable when the event is within the control of one party.

Maritime National Fish Ltd v Ocean Trawlers Ltd (1935)

A fishing company owned two trawlers but wished to run three and so hired one. They required a licence for each vessel but were granted licences only for two. They used their own and, in failing to pay for the hire of the other, claimed frustration. The court rejected their claim. They chose not to use the hired vessel rather than were prevented from doing so.

Contract more onerous to perform

There is no release from obligations merely because the contract has become less beneficial because of the intervening event.

Davis Contractors Ltd v Fareham UDC (1956)

Here, the builders being unable to make the same profit was not accepted as justifying a claim of frustration.

Foreseeable risk

If the event claimed as frustrating the contract was in the contemplation of the parties at the time of contracting, then the plea will be rejected.

Amalgamated Investment & Property Co Ltd v John Walker & Sons Ltd (1977)

The defendants contracted to sell a building to the investment company who wanted it for redevelopment. Unbeknown to either party, the Department of the Environment then listed the building, meaning that it could not be used for development. This resulted in a drop of £1.5 million from the contract price of £1.71 million. The court rejected a claim of frustration, holding that listing was a risk associated with all old buildings, of which the developers should have been aware.

Provisions made in the contract for the frustrating event

If the parties have contemplated the possibility of a frustrating event and catered for that in the contract, then there can be no release from obligations.

If a *force majeure* clause does not specifically cover the event in question, frustration may still be claimed.

Fibrosa Spolka Akcyjna v Fairbairn Lawson Combe Barbour Ltd (1943) (The Fibrosa case)

A contract for the sale of machinery to a Polish company could not be completed because of the German invasion. The contract contained a 'war clause'. The contract was still frustrated in the event because the clause only anticipated delays in delivery, not the effects of invasion.

Absolute undertaking to perform

Where the contract contains an undertaking that performance should occur in any circumstances, then a frustrating event will not affect the obligations. This was the case with the lease in *Paradine v Jane* (1647).

Activity

Which of the following involve frustrating events and which do not:

1. A famous comedian dies just before he is due to appear on stage.
2. A plumber is contracted to fit central heating in a house. He underestimates the days needed to complete the work and as a result he will lose profit on the price agreed.
3. A car which I had contracted to buy is destroyed when an explosion sets fire to it.
4. As a lecturer I have contracted to take 15 students on my own on a trip to court. An Act is passed requiring teaching and lecturing staff to take no more than 10 students per one member of staff on educational visits.
5. In a contract to supply a Far Eastern state with machinery, one clause in the contract stipulates what happens in the event of war. In fact, war is declared after the making of the contract.

9.3.3 Common law and statutory effects of frustration

Common law

The contract terminates at the point of the frustration. This means that the parties are released from their obligation to perform from that point on. Nevertheless, they would still be bound by obligations arising before the frustrating event occurred.

> ### *Chandler v Webster* (1904)
>
> This was another case arising from the delayed coronation of Edward VII. Again a room was hired. However, unlike in *Krell v Henry* (1903), where the room was to be paid for on the day of the procession, in this case it was paid for in advance. Despite the frustration there could be no recovery of the money.

This is clearly an unsatisfactory situation because it means that the effect on the parties depends entirely on what point in the contract they have reached.

The House of Lords overruled this principle in *Fibrosa* (1943) and modified the harshness of the rule. It held that a party could recover payments made prior to a frustrating event, provided that there was a total failure of consideration. This is an improvement, but still means that one party will lose out and will receive no payment for work done in advance of a contract.

The Law Reform (Frustrated Contracts) Act 1943

Frustration is a common law doctrine originally developed to avoid the harshness of existing rules. Nevertheless, as has been shown, it can produce injustice itself. As a result, the Act was passed specifically to deal with the consequences of frustrating events.

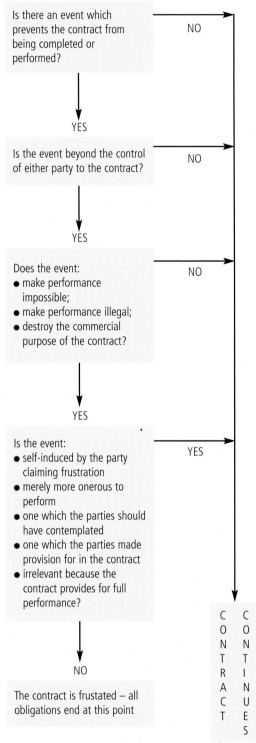

Figure 9.1 When a contract will be considered frustrated

Activity

1. What exactly is 'a frustrating event'?
2. How did *Taylor v Caldwell* (1863) help to modify the harshness in the law?
3. What are the differences between 'impossibility' and 'commercial sterility'?
4. In which ways is the doctrine still unfair on at least one party?
5. Is there really a frustrating event where the frustration is self-induced?
6. How does the *Fibrosa* (1943) case modify the principle?
7. How does the Law Reform (Frustrated Contracts) Act 1943 modify the principle?

The Act covers three main areas:

1. Recovery of money paid in advance of a contract
2. Recovery for work already completed under the contract
3. Financial reward where a valuable benefit has been conferred.

In this way s 1(2) confirms the principle in *Fibrosa* (1943) that money already paid over is recoverable despite the apparent lack of consideration. Money due under the contract also ceases to be payable.

Under s 1(2) the court also has discretion to provide some form of reward for a party who has carried out work under the contract, thus mitigating the harshness of the rule in *Fibrosa* (1943). The sum awarded is discretionary and is what the court believes to be fair, not what was actually incurred in expenses.

Finally, under s 1(3) a party is able to recover for a partial performance which has conferred a valuable benefit on the other party. Again, application of this principle is at the court's discretion.

BP Exploration Co (Libya) Ltd v Hunt (No 2) (1979)

Hunt had a concession to explore for oil in Libya. BP financed him in return for a half share of the concession. Their expenses would be three-eighths of the oil found until they had recovered 120 per cent of their outlay. Oil was discovered but Libya confiscated it. While BP had already spent $87 million, they were awarded $35 million by the court.

Key facts

- A frustrating event is one that prevents performance of the contract but is beyond the control of either party.
- The original rule was that a party was still bound by all obligations under the contract – *Paradine v Jane* (1647).
- A doctrine was developed in the nineteenth century so that in such cases obligations finished at the point of the frustrating event – *Taylor v Caldwell* (1863).
- Frustrating events include:
  (a) Impossibility – eg through the destruction of the subject matter *Taylor v Caldwell* (1863); or unavailability of the other party – *Robinson v Davidson* (1871); or outbreak of war – *Metropolitan Water Board v Dick Kerr & Co* (1918).
  (b) Subsequent illegality – *Re Shipton Anderson & Co* (1915).
  (c) Commercial sterilisation – the commercial purpose in the contract is lost – *Krell v Henry* (1903).
- The courts will not recognise frustration where it is self-induced – *Maritime National Fish Ltd v Ocean Trawlers Ltd* (1935),
  (a) or the contract is merely more burdensome to perform – *Davis Ltd Contractors v Fareham UDC* (1956)
  (b) or risk is foreseeable – *Amalgamated Investment & Property Co Ltd v John Walker & Sons Ltd* (1977).
  (c) or has been provided for – *Fibrosa* (1943).
- The common law was changed so that payments made before the frustrating event could be recovered – *Fibrosa* (1943).
- The Law Reform (Frustrated Contracts) Act 1943 makes more complex provision.

The Act's effectiveness is limited as it does not apply in some circumstances including:

- contracts for the carriage of goods by sea, except time charter parties
- insurance contracts (which in any case are all about risk)
- perishing of goods under the Sale of Goods Act 1979.

9.4 Breach

Whenever a party fails to perform an obligation arising under a contract, then that party can be said to be in breach of contract.

Breach actually occurs in one of two ways:

1. By failing to perform obligations. This situation itself can occur in one of two ways – either the contract is not performed at all, or the contract is not performed to the standard required under the contract, eg providing goods that are not of satisfactory quality.
2. By repudiating without justification.

Breach is described as discharge, although this seems slightly illogical since by definition a breach means that obligations have not been discharged.

Lord Diplock explained this position in *Photo Productions Ltd v Securicor Transport Ltd* (1980). He suggested that the terms of a contract, whether express or implied, are primary obligations. If a party fails to perform what he has promised to do, then this is a breach of a primary obligation which in consequence is then replaced by a secondary obligation; for instance, to pay damages. So breach is not so much a discharge of the contract but a replacing of one set of obligations with a different set.

Lord Diplock also saw there being two basic exceptions to his proposition:

1. The doctrine of fundamental breach – where if breach of a term deprives the other party of the substantial benefit which they would receive under the contract then the whole contract is said to be breached. (This doctrine has probably not survived the *Securicor* cases.)

2. Breach of a condition – where the term is so central to the contract that breach renders the contract meaningless and thus entitles the other party to repudiate their obligations under the contract.

The significant difference between the two traditionally would have been that, while exclusion clauses would be rendered ineffective by the first, it would still be possible to successfully rely on an exclusion clause despite a breach of a condition. This is demonstrated in the *Securicor* cases.

9.4.1 The different forms of breach

There are three identifiable forms of breach.

Breach of an ordinary term

The character of a term is unimportant. Regardless of whether it is a condition or a warranty, if a term is breached there is always an action for damages available.

Breach of a condition

A condition can either be expressed by the parties or indeed implied by law, as in the case of the implied conditions in the Sale of Goods Act 1979. However it must of course conform to the nature of a condition to attract the range of remedies associated with a condition.

Schuler (L) AG v Wickman Machine Tools Sales Ltd (1973)

The claimants could not rely on the term regarding the required frequency of visits by the defendants to the motor manufacturer's to repudiate their obligations. They had already accepted numerous similar breaches. The term obviously did not go to the root of the contract.

A breach of a condition could also in effect include a breach of an innominate term where the effect of the breach was so serious as to justify repudiation by the other party. If the doctrine has survived then it might also include a fundamental breach.

Anticipatory breach

An anticipatory breach occurs whenever one party to a contract gives notice, whether expressly or implied by conduct, that he will not complete obligations under the contract.

Again this does not necessarily mean that all obligations will remain unperformed. It may of course be that the obligations will be performed but not in the manner described in the contract. An obvious example of the latter would be late performance, as in delivery of goods after the contract date.

The doctrine is probably more correctly described as breach by anticipatory repudiation, in effect what is taking place.

Hochster v De la Tour (1853)

The claimant was hired to begin work as a courier two months after the contract date. One month later, the defendants wrote to him cancelling the contract. In answer to his claim they argued that he could not sue unless he could show that on the due date he was ready to perform. The court disagreed. There was no requirement that the victim of a breach of contract should wait until the actual breach to sue.

9.4.2 The effects of breach

The consequences for the party who is the victim of a breach and the remedies available vary according to the categories of breach that we have already considered.

Breach of an ordinary term

An action for damages is always available for breach of any kind of term. If the term is only a warranty or an innominate term where the breach is not serious one, then only an action for

damages is available. Any attempt to repudiate in such circumstances will itself amount to a breach of contract.

Breach of a condition

If, on the other hand, a condition is breached or the breach is sufficiently serious, the party who is the victim of the breach has more choice. He may continue with the contract and sue for damages, or repudiate his own obligations under the contract, or indeed both repudiate and sue for damages.

Before repudiating, of course, a party should be certain that the term is in fact a condition entitling repudiation, or that the breach by the other party is so serious as to justify repudiation, or repudiation may be a breach.

Cehave NV V Bremer Handelsgesselschaft mbH (1975) *(The Hansa Nord)*

Here the buyer's refusal to accept the animal feed was an unlawful repudiation. Using innominate terms it could be shown that, since they went on to buy the goods and use them for the same purpose, the effects of the breach could not have been sufficiently serious to justify repudiation.

The intention of the parties when contracting is clearly significant in determining the outcome of a breach. However, the way the parties describe the term may be less important than whether or not the term was in fact a significant and central term, and thus whether the breach was significant.

Rice v Great Yarmouth Borough Council (2000)

The claimant contracted with the council to provide leisure management and grounds maintenance services for four years. Clause 23 .

identified that if any obligation under the contract was breached, the council could consider the contract ended. The council tried to use the clause to terminate. The Court of Appeal held that repudiation was only possible if the breach was sufficiently serious, and that a common sense approach must be taken. The clause, literally interpreted, gave an unacceptable right to repudiate for breach of any term, even if of no significance.

Anticipatory breach

The party who is victim of the breach has a choice on discovering that the contract will be breached.

He might immediately consider the contract at an end and sue for damages.

Frost v Knight (1872)

At one time a broken promise to marry was actionable. Here the defendant had promised to marry his fiancée when his father died. Before his father did die, he broke off the engagement. The claimant sued successfully for the breach of promise even though the date of the actual breach had not occurred as the father was still alive.

Alternatively it is possible to continue with the contract, wait for the due date of performance and then sue at that point.

Avery v Bowden (1855)

Bowden was contracted to load cargo onto a ship for Avery. When it was clear that Bowden would be unable to meet his obligations, Avery could have sued. He waited, however, in the hope that the contract would be completed, and intending to sue if it was not completed. This actually turned out to be a mistaken strategy since the Crimean War then broke out, frustrating the contract, and Avery thus lost out.

It is always a danger for a party to take this latter course. The contract remains live and as a result it is always possible for the party not only to lose their remedy but also to become liable for a breach themselves.

Fercometal SARL v Mediterranean Shipping Co SA (1989) (The Simona)

A charter party contained an 'expected readiness to load' clause, entitling the charterers to repudiate if the ship was not loaded by 9 June. The shipowners asked for an extension on 2 June and the charterers then chartered another ship. The shipowners, instead of repudiating here for the breach by the charterers, gave notice of readiness to load instead. In fact this was not the case and the charterers continued to use the other vessel. The shipowners' action eventually failed in the House of Lords. Since they had elected to affirm the contract they were bound by their own original terms, of which they were in breach for not being ready to load on 9 June.

It is also possible that the fact of the innocent party having the right to affirm the contract can itself cause apparent injustice to the other party.

White and Carter Ltd v McGregor (1962)

Under a contract one party was to supply litterbins for a local council. The bins were to be paid for from advertising revenue from businesses that would have advertisements placed on the bins for a three-year period. One business backed out before the bins were prepared. The supplier nevertheless prepared the advertising and continued to use it for the whole period of the contract, and then sued successfully for the full price.

If the innocent party decides to accept the repudiatory breach of the other party then he may recover for loss of any benefits that would have resulted from performance of the contract. The party in breach cannot then try to reduce damages because of a subsequent act of the innocent party that has the effect of reducing the overall loss.

Chiemgauer Membrand Und Zeltbau (formerly Koch Hightex GmbH) v New Millennium Experience Co Ltd (formerly Millennium Central Ltd) (No 2) (2002)

The claimant was given the contract to build the roof of the Millennium Dome. Under the contract the defendants could terminate if they paid compensation identified in the contract as 'direct loss and damage'. The claimants then became insolvent. In their claim they argued that 'direct loss' should include their loss of profits and the court, applying the first limb of *Hadley v Baxendale* (1854), agreed. The defendants argued that the claimants could not have completed the contract even without the termination, and that the subsequent insolvency meant that they should not be fixed with the

claimant's loss of profits. The Court of Appeal disagreed, and considered that the facts could be compared with those cases where an innocent party accepts the other party's repudiatory breach and is still entitled to all benefits arising naturally under the contract.

Activity

1. In what way does a breach of contract discharge the obligations under it?
2. What are Lord Diplock's 'primary obligations' and 'secondary obligations'?
3. How limited are the remedies available to a party who has suffered a breach of warranty?
4. Why is there a difference between the remedies available for breach of a condition and those for breach of warranty?
5. What effect does breach of an innominate term have?
6. Exactly what is an anticipatory breach?
7. What possible problems are there in waiting till the actual breach when there is an anticipatory breach?

Key facts

- A breach occurs when one party fails to perform at all, or does less than is required under the contract, or does not perform satisfactorily.
- It will also be a breach where one party wrongly repudiates.
- Breach of a warranty allows only an action for damages.
- Breach of a condition allows for action for damages and/or repudiation, but only if the term is really a condition going to the root of the contract – *Schuler v Wickman Machine Tool Sales Ltd* (1974).
- The same choice applies where the effect of breach of an innominate term is sufficiently serious – *The Hansa Nord* (1975).

- An anticipatory breach occurs where a party makes known before performance is due that the contract will not be performed – *Hochster v De la Tour* (1853).
- The victim of an anticipatory breach has the right to treat the contract at an end and sue immediately – *Frost v Knight* (1872).
- Or to wait until performance is due and then sue – *Avery v Bowden* (1855).
- This can be unfair to the party in breach – *White & Carter Ltd v McGregor* (1962).
- Waiting for the actual breach can also mean losing the remedy – *Fercometal v Mediterranean Shipping Co* (1989).

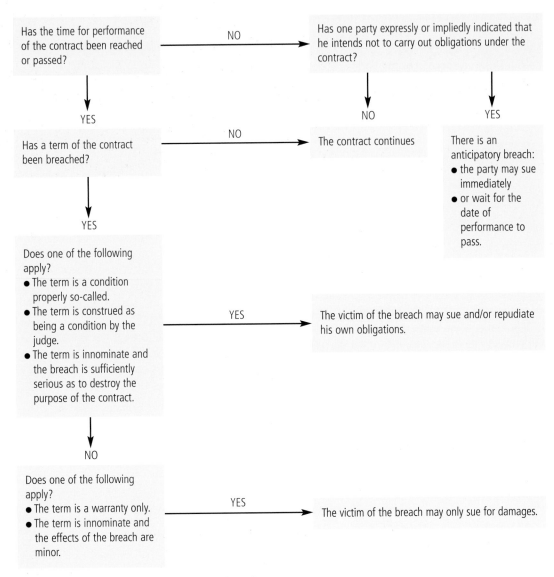

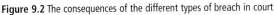

Figure 9.2 The consequences of the different types of breach in court

Chapter 10

Remedies

10.1 Damages

10.1.1 The purpose of damages in contract law

Damages is a sum of money paid by the defendant to the claimant once liability is established in compensation for the harm suffered by the claimant.

The purpose of damages in contract law is to compensate the claimant for the losses suffered as a result of the breach. As Baron Parke put it in *Robinson v Harman* (1848):

> 'the purpose is to put the victim of the breach, so far as is possible and so far as the law allows, into the same position he would have been in if the contract had not been broken but had been performed in the manner and at the time intended by the parties'.

Damages in contract law puts the victim in the position he would have enjoyed if the contract had been properly completed and performed by the defendant.

10.1.2 Remoteness of damage

There are in effect two tests used in assessing an award for an unliquidated sum of damages in contract. The first test concerns the loss in respect of which the claimant can recover. The second concerns the quantity of damages available.

The first of these two questions actually concerns causation. There must be a causal link between the defendant's breach of the contract and the damage suffered by the claimant. There is also a general principle that damages will not be awarded in respect of a loss that it is too remote a consequence of the defendant's breach.

Causation in fact

Causation is a question of fact in each case. The court will decide whether or not the breach is the predominant reason for the loss suffered by the claimant.

London Joint Stock Bank v MacMillan (1918)

A customer of a bank owes a contractual obligation not to draw cheques so that they are easily alterable. Here the client who did so was liable when a third party fraudulently altered the cheque causing loss to the bank.

If the loss arises partly from the breach and partly as the result of intervening events, the party in breach may still be liable provided that the chain of causation is not broken.

Stansbie v Troman (1948)

A decorator was entrusted with keys to the premises where he was contracted to work. When he left the premises unlocked a thief entered and stole property. The decorator was liable for the loss which resulted from his failure to comply with his contractual duty to secure the premises properly on leaving.

Testing remoteness of damage

The test of remoteness was originally derived by Alderson B in the case of *Hadley v Baxendale* (1854):

> 'Where the parties have made a contract which one of them has broken, the damages which the other party ought to receive in respect of such breach of contract should be such as may fairly and reasonably be considered arising either naturally, ie according to the usual course of things, from such breach of contract itself, or such as may be supposed reasonably to have been in the contemplation of both parties at the time they made the contract as the probable result of the breach.'

Hadley v Baxendale (1854)

A mill owner contracted with a carrier to deliver a crankshaft for his mill. The mill was actually not operating at the time because the existing crankshaft was broken. The carrier did not know this when the contract was formed. The carrier was then late with delivery. The mill owner sued unsuccessfully because the carrier was unaware of the importance of prompt delivery.

So in essence the test is in two parts: one is measured objectively according to what loss is a natural consequence of the breach; the second is subjective, based on specific knowledge of potential losses in the minds of both parties when the contract is formed.

The test remains to this day, although it has been modified on occasions.

Victoria Laundry Ltd v Newman Industries Ltd (1949)

The defendants contracted to deliver a boiler to the laundry company and failed to deliver until five months after the contract date. The laundry sued for loss of their usual profits of £16 per week from the date of the breach. They succeeded since this was a natural consequence loss. They also sued in respect of lost profits of £262 per week from a government contract that they had been unable to take up without the boiler. They failed in this action since the government contract was unknown to the defendants at the time the contract was formed. Asquith LJ made some vital points on the issue of remoteness:

- to give the claimant complete indemnity for any loss suffered by the claimant, no matter how remote, is too harsh a test

- as a result, recoverable loss should be measured against a test of reasonable foreseeability

- foreseeability of loss is itself dependent on knowledge at the time of formation

- knowledge is of two types: common knowledge and actual knowledge enjoyed by the defendant – the two types identified in *Hadley v Baxendale* (1854)

- but knowledge can also be implied on the basis of what a reasonable man may have (rather than must have) contemplated in the circumstances.

Nevertheless the test can cause confusion and be made unnecessarily complex.

Koufos v C Czarnikow Ltd (1969) (*The Heron II*)

A vessel was chartered to carry sugar to Basrah, a known sugar market. Owing to the carrier's breach the vessel arrived nine days late, during which time the price of sugar had fallen considerably. The claimant had intended to resell the sugar on its arrival in port, a fact unknown to the defendant carrier. The claimant sued for lost profits following the fall in price of sugar. This was held to be too remote by the Court of Appeal. The House of Lords, however, held that the claimant could recover under the first head of *Hadley v Baxendale* (1854), and held that in some circumstances the reasonable man ought to contemplate that a particular loss was a natural consequence of a breach (although this actually seems more like implied knowledge). It was also suggested that foreseeability differed between contract and tort, although different judges gave different definitions: Lord Reid described it as 'not unlikely … considerably less than an even chance but nevertheless not very unusual and easily foreseeable'; Lord Morris as 'not unlikely to occur … liable to result'; Lord Hodson as 'liable to result'; and Lords Pearce and Upjohn as 'a real danger … a serious possibility'.

However Lord Scarman has subsequently held that the test of remoteness depends not on contemplation of the level of injury, but merely proof that loss could be anticipated.

H Parsons (Livestock) Ltd v Uttley Ingham (1978)

The contract was for the sale and installation of an animal feed hopper. The ventilation hatch was sealed during transit and the installers then forgot to open it. As a result the feed became mouldy, the pigs contracted an intestinal disease

and 254 died. The judge at first instance considered the loss was too remote and not within the contemplation of the defendants, but this was reversed by the Court of Appeal.

What is crucial in any case is what was in the contemplation of the parties at the time that the contract was made.

Jackson v Royal Bank of Scotland plc (2005)

Jackson imported dog chews from Thailand and sold them to a firm, Easy Bag, packaged to its instructions. Both parties banked with the Royal Bank of Scotland. The bank in breach of confidentiality mistakenly revealed to Easy Bag that Jackson was making a 19% mark-up, and Easy Bag stopped dealing with him. The House of Lords held that the termination of the relationship was a clear consequence of the bank's breach of contract. It should have contemplated that this would be the result of breaching Jackson's confidentiality.

10.1.3 Quantifying damages and the bases of assessment

Once the tests of causation and remoteness have established that there is liability for the loss claimed, the court then has to determine how much the claimant can recover.

Nominal damages

If no loss is actually suffered but the breach has been established then the court may award 'nominal damages'. Proof of damage has never been an essential of contract law. The likely motive of the claimant in suing is to ensure that there is a declaration by the court that the contract is at an end.

Staniforth v Lyall (1830)

Lyall was under a duty to load his cargo onto the claimant's boat by a certain date. He failed and the boat owner sued for breach. He had actually hired his boat out to another party immediately following the breach and for a greater profit than he would have made. He succeeded in having the contract declared terminated and, having suffered no loss, was awarded a nominal sum.

In some cases substantial damages have been awarded where, traditionally, nominal damages might have been considered more appropriate.

Experience Hendrix LLC v PPX Enterprises Inc (2003)

After the death of the famous 1960s rock guitarist, Jimi Hendrix, an agreement was reached by which his publisher was entitled to certain recordings from master tapes in return for paying royalties to Hendrix's estate. The publisher breached the agreement by granting licences for recordings that were not in the agreement. The Court of Appeal held that the publisher should pay a reasonable sum to Hendrix's estate, even though Hendrix's estate had suffered no actual loss.

The bases of assessment

There are three bases for assessing awards of damages in contract claims.

Loss of a bargain

The idea here is to place the claimant in the same financial position as if the contract had been properly performed. This may represent a number of positions:

1. The difference in value between the goods or services of the quality indicated in the contract and those actually delivered where they are of inferior value. This sum can be assessed according to the diminution in value or the cost of bringing them up to the contract quality.

Bence Graphics International Ltd v Fasson UK Ltd (1996)

The defendant supplied vinyl film on which the claimant printed decals to put on bulk containers. In the claimant's contract with the container company, there was an implied term that the decals would survive in a readable form for five years. In fact they lasted only two. The claimant sued for the whole purchase price or an indemnity against its customer's claim. This was rejected at first instance, but the Court of Appeal held that the claimants could recover the actual loss.

2. The difference between the contract price and the price obtained in an 'available market' where there is either a failure to deliver the goods or services and an alternative supply has to be found, or where there is a failure to accept delivery and an alternative market has to be found.

If the claimant's ability to make a profit remains, there is no entitlement to damages.

Charter v Sullivan (1957)

The defendant contracted to buy a car then refused to take delivery. Because demand for the particular model at the time easily outstripped supply, there was no interference in the seller's ability to sell the car. As a result he recovered only nominal damages.

However, if there is no available market then the claimant can recover the full loss.

W L Thompson Ltd v Robinson Gunmakers Ltd (1955)

Similar facts to the last case, but here there was an excess in supply of the type of car ordered. Thus when the buyer breached, the seller could recover full damages.

3. Loss of profit – a claimant may recover for the profit that he would have been able to complete but for the breach of contract.
4. Loss of a chance – in rare circumstances the courts have allowed claimants to recover a loss that is entirely speculative, although generally in contract law a speculative loss is not recoverable.

Chaplin v Hicks (1911)

An actress had a contractual right to attend an audition. At this audition 12 actresses would be chosen out of the 50 invited to attend. When she was wrongly prevented from attending, the court awarded her £100 in compensation even though she only had a 50:12 chance of gaining work from the audition. The court stated that the mere fact that damages were difficult to calculate should not prevent her recovering.

Reliance loss

A claimant may also recover for expenses he has had to spend in advance of a contract that has been breached.

Such a claim will normally be made where any loss of profit is too speculative to be able to calculate effectively.

Anglia Television Ltd v Reed (1972)

Anglia paid out a large sum of money in preparing to make a film, including paying scriptwriters, hiring production and technical staff and other necessary expenses. The actor contracted to make the film then backed out in breach of his contract and the company had to abandon the project, since there was no appropriate substitute. Their reliance loss was much easier to account for in the circumstances than any loss of profit.

Generally it is not possible to claim for both loss of profit and reliance loss since it is said to be compensating twice for the same loss. It is possible where the claim for lost profit concerns only net rather than gross profit, which would include the reliance loss.

Western Web Offset Printers Ltd v Independent Media Ltd (1995)

The defendant wrongly repudiated a contract under which the claimant was to print 48 issues of a weekly newspaper. The claimant sued for £176,903, having deducted the costs of printing such as ink and paper from the contract price. The defendant argued that labour costs and other overheads amounting to £38,245 should also be deducted from the claim. The Court of Appeal held that since the claimant had no alternative work for the workforce, the whole claim could be recovered.

It is also possible sometimes to recover damages for the loss of a valuable amenity.

Farley v Skinner (2001)

The claimant hired a surveyor before buying a house and asked the surveyor to specifically report on whether the property was affected by aircraft noise. The report stated that it would not be substantially affected by aircraft noise, but this was wrong and negligent as the house was near a beacon for stacking aircraft at busy times. The claimant paid £490,000 for the house and spent £125,000 on it before moving in. When he discovered the noise, he decided not to move but sued the surveyor for damages for loss of amenity. The House of Lords held that for loss of amenity to succeed, it was not essential for the contract to be one the object of which was to provide pleasure, relaxation etc. The claimant did not forfeit his right to non-pecuniary damages by not moving and was awarded £10,000.

Restitution

This is simply a repayment of any money or other benefits passed to the defendant in advance of the contract that is breached.

Restitution is a huge area of law in its own right and full explanations are only found in books dealing specifically with the subject.

Inevitably restitution in contract law has to do with consideration, and the presence or absence of consideration may determine the appropriateness of the remedy.

Stocznia Gdanska SA v Latvian Shipping Co (1998)

A shipyard entered into a contract under which it was bound to both design and build a ship for the buyers. The shipyard later rescinded the contract before any ownership in the goods had passed to the buyers. The buyers claimed for return of an installment of the contract price on the basis that there was a failure of consideration. The shipyard successfully resisted this claim. The House of Lords held that the true test of whether there was a failure of consideration was not based on whether the buyer had received nothing under the contract, but on whether the seller had done nothing under the contract.

10.1.4 Speculative damages

As has already been said, the purpose of awarding damages in contract is to financially recreate the situation that would have been but for the breach of contract.

We have also seen that courts have been careful to avoid granting damages of a speculative nature since contract damages are awarded for specific loss. Of course there are rare exceptions such as *Chaplin v Hicks* (1911) where damages were awarded for the loss of a chance in an audition.

The courts have always been careful to separate contract and tort. Judges in tort have shown reluctance to allow a remedy for a pure economic loss in negligence, which they see as being more appropriate to principles of contract law. They have been careful in traditionally avoiding allowing recovery in contract law for a claim seen as being more appropriate to principles in tort.

Addis v The Gramophone Company (1909)

The claimant was wrongly dismissed from his post as manager and replaced even before he left. The House of Lords refused his claim for damages for injury to his reputation and the mental distress caused by the humiliating manner of his dismissal, the proper place for this according to Lord Atkin being the tort of defamation. He recovered only for the loss of salary and commission owed.

However, an exceptional group of cases has developed a principle in contract law in recent times allowing damages of a highly speculative nature for mental distress. The cases are known as the 'holiday cases'.

Jarvis v Swan Tours Ltd (1973)

The claimant contracted for a Tyrolean holiday, advertised as a 'house party'. In fact he was on his own for the second week, and the holiday was inferior to most aspects advertised in the brochure. The judge at first instance awarded him £31.72 for the difference between the quality of the holiday as described and the actual holiday. However, the Court of Appeal upheld his claim for disappointment and mental distress and awarded him damages of £125.

The courts had actually previously created an exception to the rule in *Addis* (1909).

Cook v Spanish Holidays (1960)

Travel agents failed in their contractual duty when a honeymoon couple were left without a room on their wedding night. They were awarded damages for loss of enjoyment.

The principle has been extended, effectively as an exception to privity where the claimant recovered not only for his own mental distress but for that of his family also, in *Jackson v Horizon Holidays* (1975). The justification is that in holiday contracts, 'the provision of comfort, pleasure and "peace of mind" was a central feature of the contract.'

The principle may have been extended to certain problems caused by solicitors.

Heywood v Wellers (1976)

The claimant was awarded damages for mental distress where her solicitors, in breach of their contractual obligations, failed to obtain an injunction to prevent her former boyfriend from molesting her.

More recently, damages for 'loss of amenity' have been allowed where the sole purpose of the contract was for 'the provision of a pleasurable amenity'.

Ruxley Electronics and Construction Ltd v Forsyth; Laddingford Enclosures Ltd v Forsyth (1995)

A swimming pool was built six inches shallower than stated in the contract. Since this might prevent the purchaser from safely enjoying the pleasure of diving into the pool, damages were awarded.

Nevertheless, the courts are still reluctant to allow the principle to develop too far or to extend into purely commercial territory. In *Hayes v James and Charles Dodd* (1990) Staughten LJ stated that recovery for mental distress should not include:

> 'any case where the object of the contract was not pleasure or comfort or the relief of discomfort, but simply carrying on a commercial contract with a view to profit'.

Similarly *Woodar Investment Development Ltd v Wimpey Construction UK Ltd* (1980) suggested that the principle is restricted to holiday cases.

10.1.5 The duty to mitigate

There is a clear principle of English law that the party injured by a breach of contract must take reasonable steps to minimise the effects of the breach, known as the duty to mitigate. Any failure to mitigate may be taken into account in awarding damages.

British Westinghouse Electric and Manufacturing Co Ltd v Underground Electric Railways Co of London Ltd (1912)

In a contract for the supply of turbines, the goods delivered did not match the specifications in the contract. As a result, the buyers had to replace them with turbines bought from another supplier. In the event these turbines were so efficient that they soon paid for the difference in price. This could not be claimed for, but losses sustained before the originals were replaced were recoverable. Lord Haldane LC said that a claimant has:

'the duty of taking all reasonable steps to mitigate the loss consequent on the breach [which] debars him from claiming in respect of any part of the damage which is due to his neglect to take such steps.'

However, a claimant is not bound to go to extraordinary lengths to mitigate the loss, only to do what is reasonable in the circumstances.

Pilkington v Wood (1953)

As the result of a solicitor's negligence, the claimant bought a house with defective title, and was unable to take up residence for some time, incurring the extra costs of hotel bills and travelling to and from his old house. The solicitor's argument that the claimant could have brought his action against the vendor instead and thus mitigated the loss in his action against the solicitor was rejected.

Similarly, in an anticipatory breach, the claimant is not bound to sue immediately he knows of the possibility of the breach.

White and Carter v McGregor (1962)

A firm contracted to buy advertising space on litter bins to be fitted by the claimants to lamp posts. When they backed out in breach of their agreement, the claimants continued to produce the bins. The argument that the claimants might have mitigated the loss by not continuing to fit the bins failed.

10.1.6 Liquidated damages

A sum of liquidated damages may be available where the parties have fixed the amount in the contract that will be available in the event of a breach. However, the courts will only accept this sum and deny the victim of the breach a claim for an unliquidated sum, if the sum identified in the contract represents an accurate and proper assessment of loss. If it is not, it is seen as a 'penalty' and will be unenforceable.

Any clause providing for a greater sum than the actual loss is *prima facie* void.

Bridge v Campbell Discount Co (1962)

A depreciation clause in a hire-purchase agreement for a car bore no relation to actual depreciation in value. The clause was declared void as a penalty.

The courts have developed rules for determining the difference between genuine liquidated damages and a penalty.

Dunlop Pneumatic Tyre Co v New Garage and Motor Co (1914)

Under their contract with Dunlop, the garage was bound to pay £5 in respect of breaches such as selling under the recommended price. In this case the House of Lords accepted that the sum represented a genuine assessment so was not a penalty. Lord Dunedin's test included a number of points:

- An extravagant sum will always be a penalty.

- Payment of a large sum for failure to settle a small debt is probably a penalty.

- A single sum operating in respect of a variety of different breaches is likely to be a penalty.

- The wording used by the parties is not necessarily conclusive.

- It is no bar to recovering a liquidated sum that actual assessment of the loss was impossible before the contract.

10.1.7 *Quantum meruit*

This means recovery of an unqualified sum for services already rendered. We have seen its operation in relation to part performance.

There are three common circumstances in which such an award is made:

1. In a contract for services that is silent on the issue of remuneration.

Upton RDC v Powell (1942)

Where a retained fireman provided services with no fixed agreement as to wages, the court awarded a reasonable sum in the circumstances.

2. Where the circumstances of the case show that a fresh agreement can be implied in place of the original one.

Steven v Bromley (1919)

Steven had agreed to carry steel at a specified rate. When the steel was delivered it contained extra goods and thus Steven was able to claim extra for carrying them.

3. Where a party has elected to consider the contract discharged by the other's breach or where a party has been prevented from performing by the other party; in either case they might claim for work they have already done.

Activity

1. What is a court trying to achieve when it makes an award of damages in contract law?
2. When will it be possible to recover damages even though the injured party has suffered no loss?
3. How does a court decide whether the defendant's breach of contract caused the actual damage suffered?
4. What are the basic differences between the judgments in *Hadley v Baxendale* (1854) and *Victoria Laundry v Newman Industries* (1949)?
5. In what ways is the judgment in *The Heron II* (1969) not a sensible one?
6. Why was the case rejected in *Parsons v Utley Ingham* (1978)?
7. How does the 'available market' rule affect an award of damages?
8. When is reliance loss awarded rather than loss of a bargain?
9. Is it possible to recover both?
10. What effect does an anticipatory breach have on an award of damages?
11. What restrictions exist in recovering damages for mental distress?
12. In what ways is a penalty different to liquidated damages?

De Barnady v Harding (1853)

A principal wrongly revoked his agent's authority to act on his behalf. The agent was then entitled to claim for the work he had already done and for expenses incurred.

10.2 Equitable remedies

Equitable remedies are available in both contract and tort, although equity is much more closely associated with contract law. The whole purpose of equitable remedies is that they should operate where an award of damages is an inadequate remedy and justice is not served.

On that basis there are a number of different remedies available to the court, particularly in contract law, which more adequately reflect the needs of the claimant. Equitable remedies are at the discretion of the court, unlike an award of damages, which is an automatic consequence of liability being established. Because the remedies are discretionary, they are awarded subject to compliance with the various 'maxims of equity' such as 'he who comes to equity must come with clean hands'.

10.2.1 Rescission

This is particularly common in both misrepresentation and mistake, and is an order of the court returning the parties to their original pre-contract position. As a result it is only available where to do that is actually possible.

Restitutio in integrum must apply for a successful claim for rescission of a contract. It must be possible to return to the actual pre-contract position without the subject matter of the contract having been substantially altered in any way.

Clarke v Dickson (1858)

Clarke was persuaded to buy shares in a partnership as a result of misrepresentations made to him. Later the partnership became a limited company. When it failed, Clarke then discovered the misrepresentation. He was unable to rescind because the nature of the shares had changed from partnership shares to company shares. The judge gave the example of a butcher who buys live cattle, slaughters them and then wishes to rescind. It would be impossible.

Other important requirements for rescission include that the party seeking rescission must not have already affirmed the contract.

Long v Lloyd (1958)

A lorry was bought which proved defective. The purchaser lost the right to rescind after allowing the seller twice to make repairs to the lorry. He had thus affirmed the contract.

Also that he has not delayed too long in seeking the remedy, as was the case in *Leaf v International Galleries* (1950) where the remedy was lost because the claimant waited five years.

Finally, no third parties have subsequently gained rights over the subject matter, as occurred in *Oakes v Turquand* (1867).

10.2.2 Injunctions

In contract law, injunctions are rarely mandatory and are usually then negative restrictions on the defendant. Injunctions may be either final or interlocutory.

There are three common instances where an injunction is claimed in respect of contracts:

1. To enforce contracts in restraint of trade. Such contractual clauses are *prima facie* void, and so an injunction is only granted if the restraint is reasonable as between the parties and in the public interest, and only if they protect a legitimate interest.

Fitch v Dewes (1921)

A lifelong restraint on a solicitor's clerk from taking up the same employment in a seven-mile radius of Tamworth Town Hall was held to be reasonable.

Fellowes v Fisher (1976)

A five-year restraint on a conveyancing clerk from taking similar employment in Walthamstow was held to be unreasonable by Lord Denning as the clerk was relatively unknown in a densely populated area.

2. To enforce a provision protecting legitimate trade secrets or specialist information.

Faccenda Chicken v Fowler (1986)

The injunction was sought to prevent competition by a former employee who had devised a sales system of fresh chickens from refrigerated vans. The action was unsuccessful because the termination was reasonable and there was no express provision in the contract.

3. To encourage compliance with a contract of personal service.

Since this appears similar to a mandatory injunction, it will only be awarded where there is an express negative restriction in the contract, and will not be awarded where it amounts in effect to a mandatory award.

Page One Records v Britton (1968)

'The Troggs', a 60s pop group, were tied by contract indefinitely to their manager under extremely unfavourable conditions. When they became disillusioned and found a new manager, the old manager tried to enforce the contract but failed.

Similarly it will be unavailable where the clause is unreasonably wide and would prevent the other party from earning a living.

Lumley v Wagner (1852)

An opera singer had a contract with an express stipulation that during its three months' currency she would not take up work with any other theatre. When she did so, she was successfully restrained. In view of the duration of the contract, it did not interfere with her general ability to earn a living.

10.2.3 Specific performance

This is an order of the court for the party in default to carry out his obligations under the contract. It is rarely granted because of the difficulty of overseeing it.

Ryan v Mutual Tontine Westminster Chambers Association (1893)

Under a tenancy agreement the landlord was obliged to provide a hall porter to take care of the common areas. The person employed failed to do the work properly. An order for specific performance was refused since the court could not supervise the work.

This contrasts with *Posner v Scott-Lewis* (1987) which again involves an obligation to provide a hall porter. The court could award the remedy here where the landlord had merely failed to employ one.

Such an order is only usually granted in the case of transfers of land or where the subject matter of the contract is unique in some way, so that it could not be replaced in an 'available market' and an award of damages is thus inadequate. An example would be a valuable work of art as in *Falcke v Gray* (1859). So it will never be able for instance in a contract of service

– *De Francesco v Barnum* (1890) – where it was denied in the case of a breach of a contract of apprenticeship.

Since the remedy is discretionary under equity, it will not be awarded where the claimant's actions in seeking the order are unconscionable, as would be the case with all equitable remedies.

Webster v Cecil (1861)

The claimant was trying to enforce a written document for the sale and purchase of land that he knew contained an inaccurate statement of price. Since there was evidence to show what the actual price should be, his action failed and the document of sale was rectified to accurately reflect the price actually agreed.

10.2.4 Rectification of documents

This is an order of the court to rectify a mistake in a written contract. Since the remedy is discretionary under equity, it will not be awarded where the claimant's actions in seeking the order are unconscionable, as would be the case with all equitable remedies.

Craddock Bros Ltd v Hunt (1923)

Craddock agreed to sell his house to Hunt, not intending an adjoining yard to be included in the sale. By mistake the yard was included in the conveyance so Craddock immediately sought rectification of the document and succeeded.

Activity

1. What are the common features of property that can be the subject of an order for specific performance?
2. In what circumstances will an order for specific performance be denied?
3. Why are the courts reluctant to award mandatory injunctions?
4. When, if ever, is an injunction possible in a contract of employment?
5. In rescission why is the rule relating to *restitutio in integrum* necessary?
6. What other bars to rescission are there?
7. What has gone wrong when rectification of a document is ordered?

Key facts

Damages:

Causation and remoteness of damage	Cases
The breach must be the actual reason for the claimant's loss Two types of loss can be recovered:	*London Joint Stock Bank v MacMillan* (1918)
(i) a natural consequence of breach;	*Hadley v Baxendale* (1854)
(ii) that in contemplation of parties when contract formed; and the latter is based on what is foreseeable	*Victoria Laundry v Newman Industries* (1949)
Bases of assessment	Cases
• Loss of a bargain (difference from bargain made) • Reliance loss (money spent in order to complete the contract) • Restitution (money paid over in advance)	*Charter v Sullivan* (1957) *Anglia TV v Reed* (1972) *Stocznia Gdanska SA v Latvian Shipping Co* (1998)

Speculative damages	Cases
Can sometimes recover for mental distress But not where the loss is not commercial	*Jarvis v Swan Tours* (1973) *Woodar Investment Development Ltd v Wimpey* (1980)

Quantum meruit	Cases
Possible where the contract is silent on payment, or where a fresh agreement should be implied, or where further performance is prevented.	*Upton RDC v Powell* (1942) *Steven v Bromley* (1919) *De Barnady v Harding* (1853)

Equitable remedies:

Rescission	Cases
Puts parties back to pre-contractual position so only available if: ● *restitutio in integrum* is possible ● contract is not affirmed ● there is no excessive delay ● no third party has gained rights ● damages are a better remedy – s 2(2) Misrepresentation Act.	*Clarke v Dickson* (1858) *Long v Lloyd* (1958) *Leaf v International Galleries* (1950) *Oakes v Turquand* (1867)

Injunctions	Cases
Order restraining a party from breaching contract to: ● enforce restraint of trade clauses ● protect confidentiality ● enforce compliance with a contract of personal service.	*Fitch v Dewes* (1921) *Faccenda Chicken v Fowler* (1987) *Warner Bros v Nelson* (1937)

Specific performance	Cases
Order to carry out contractual obligations – only granted if: ● damages would be inadequate ● subject matter is unique ● claimant acts with conscience ● not a contract of personal service ● it is possible for court to oversee.	*Fothergill v Rowlands* (1873) *Adderly v Dixon* (1824) *Webster v Cecil* (1861) *De Francesco v Barnum* (1890) *Posner v Scott-Lewis* (1987)

Key facts chart on damages

Examination-style questions

Question 1

On 16 January, Chris wrote from Wolverhampton to his friend Matt from Manchester, offering to sell Matt a ticket for £60 for the Wolves/Manchester United game to be played on 24 January. Matt posted a letter to Chris on 17 January which said:

> 'Dear Chris,
> £60 seems a bit dear. I don't mind paying a bit over the odds but I'd be happier paying £30. Or could I pay you £30 now and the other £30 when I'm paid again at the end of the month?
> Yours Matt'

Later in the day Matt wrote again to Chris:

> 'Dear Chris,
> I've thought again about that ticket. I really want to go and they've sold out up here so I'll pay you the £60.
> Yours Matt'

He posted the letter the same night.

Chris received Matt's first letter on the morning of 18 January and sold the ticket to another friend Sukhy at work that day.

On 17 January, Matt, believing that the ticket was his, reserved a room at the Britannia Hotel in Wolverhampton for the night of the game so that he could stay over, see a show at the Grand Theatre and return to Manchester the next morning. He paid a deposit of £50 by credit card. He tells the booking clerk over the phone that he is only coming to Wolverhampton to see the football game but will make the most of the day by going to the theatre which is next door to the hotel. When he telephoned Chris on the evening before the match and found out that the ticket was already sold, he then cancelled his booking with the hotel, saying that the purpose of his contract with them no longer existed.

1. Consider what rights if any Matt may have against Chris over the sale of the ticket.

   (25 marks)

2. Consider what rights Matt may have to a return of his deposit from the Britannia Hotel.

   (25 marks)

3. Outline and critically evaluate the rules on either incorporation of terms or the common law rules on incorporation of exclusion clauses.

   (25 marks)

Question 2

Connor needed to post the manuscript of his latest contract law book to his publishers. His printer was broken, and he asked his friend Jane if she would print it off for him. Jane did this and Connor was able to get the manuscript in by the deadline. When he next met Jane he said that he was so grateful that he would pay her £100. He has never done so.

Recently, Connor needed to attend an important business meeting but his car had broken down and he was too late to catch a train. Jane said that she would take him. He was very relieved and, on getting out of the car, Connor said 'I owe you one Jane. I'll pay you £50 when I next see you'.

Connor only bought his printer last year from Dodgy Computers. Connor had explained to the salesman, Sid, that he wrote books and needed a model that would cope. Sid replied that the printer would work forever. In fact when Connor takes it to a computer repair specialist he is told that the model is not suitable for the amount of printing he does and is already worn out and they also think that it is a reconditioned model.

1. Consider what rights if any Jane may have against Connor over the printing of the manuscript.   (25 marks)

2. Consider what rights Jane may have against Connor for driving him to his business appointment.   (25 marks)

3. Outline and critically evaluate the rules in any one of three vitiating factors (mistake, misrepresentation, duress/undue influence).
                                             (25 marks)

Question 3

Rupinder recently went to the SuperRides theme park with her children Dalvinder and Sanjay. On paying for entry Rupinder received a ticket which she had to display to get on each ride. When the family got off the DareDevil, Rupinder discovered that the seat had only recently been painted and the paint had ruined all their clothes. The family's chair on the Devil's Train came off its mountings when they were going round a bend and little Sanjay was badly injured. Rupinder has complained to SuperRides but they have pointed to the back of the ticket on which is printed:

> Customers enter the theme park at their own risk. The proprietors will not be liable for any damage sustained whilst using the rides no matter how caused.

Rupinder is a secretary. Just before Christmas her employer Brian wanted a number of reports typed urgently. He asked Rupinder if she would mind staying late after work for two weeks to complete them. He also promised that, while he could not pay her directly, he would give her a £100 Christmas bonus. He has not done so. Brian and Rupinder also bought raffle tickets from a charity. Brian put his name on the stubs although they both shared the cost of entry. Theirs was the winning ticket and they have won £1,000 but Brian is now refusing to pay Rupinder her share.

1. Consider what rights if any Rupinder may have against SuperRides for the damage to the clothes and for Sanjay's injuries   (25 marks)

2. Consider what rights Rupinder may have against Brian for payment of the Christmas bonus or her share of the raffle winnings.
                                             (25 marks)

3. Outline and critically evaluate the rules in any one of the three elements which must be proved to establish a valid contract (offer and acceptance, consideration, intention to create legal relations).   (25 marks)

UNIT 4

Section A: Criminal Law (Offences Against Property)

Table of Cases

Chapter 11

Theft

Theft is defined in s 1 Theft Act 1968 which states that:
'A person is guilty of theft if he dishonestly appropriates property belonging to another with the intention of permanently depriving the other of it.'

In the next five sections the Act gives some help with the meaning of the words or phrases in the definition. This is done in the order that the words or phrases appear in the definition, making it easy to remember the section numbers. They are:

- section 2 – dishonestly
- section 3 – appropriates
- section 4 – property
- section 5 – belonging to another
- section 6 – with the intention of permanently depriving the other of it.

Remember that the offence is in s 1. A person charged with theft is always charged with stealing 'contrary to section 1 of the Theft Act 1968'. Sections 2 to 6 are definition sections explaining s 1. They do not themselves create any offence.

The *actus reus* of theft is made up of the three elements in the phrase 'appropriates property belonging to another'. So to prove the *actus reus*, it has to be shown that there was appropriation by the defendant of something which is property within the definition of the Act and which, at the time of the appropriation, belonged to another.

There are two elements which must be proved for the *mens rea* of theft. These are that the appropriation of the property must be done 'dishonestly' and there must be the intention of permanently depriving the other person of it.

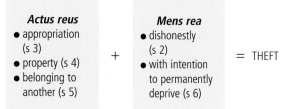

Figure 11.1 The elements of theft

11.1 Appropriation

The more obvious situations of theft involve a physical taking, for example a pickpocket taking a wallet from someone's pocket. But appropriation is much wider than this.

Section 3(1) states that:

> 'Any assumption by a person of the rights of an owner amounts to an appropriation, and this includes, where he has come by the property (innocently or not) without stealing it, any later assumption of a right to it by keeping or dealing with it as owner.'

The important words are 'any assumption by a person of the rights of an owner amounts to appropriation'. The rights of the owner include selling the property or destroying it as well as such things as possessing it, consuming it, using it, lending it or hiring it out. So for there to be appropriation, the thief must do something which assumes (takes over) one of the owner's rights.

The rights of an owner also include the right to sell property. An appropriation by assuming the right to sell is demonstrated by the case of *Pitham and Hehl* (1977).

Pitham and Hehl (1977)

The defendant had sold furniture belonging to another person. This was held to be an appropriation. The offer to sell was an assumption of the rights of an owner and the appropriation took place at that point. It did not matter whether the furniture was removed from the house or not. Even if the owner was never deprived of the property, the defendant had still appropriated it by assuming the rights of the owner to offer the furniture for sale.

The wording in s 3(1) is 'any assumption by a person of *the* rights of an owner'. One question which the courts have to deal with is whether the assumption has to be of *all* of the rights, or whether it can just be of *any* of the rights. This was considered in *Morris* (1983).

Morris (1983)

The defendant had switched the price labels of two items on the shelf in a supermarket. He had then put one of the items, which now had a lower price on it, into a basket provided by the store for shoppers and taken the item to the checkout, but had not gone through the checkout when he was arrested. Lord Roskill in the House of Lords stated that:

> 'It is enough for the prosecution if they have proved … the assumption of any of the rights of the owner of the goods in question.'

So there does not have to be an assumption of all the rights. This is a sensible decision since in many cases the defendant will not have assumed all of the rights. Quite often only one right will have been assumed, usually the right of possession. In fact it seems that 'anyone doing anything whatever to property belonging to another … appropriates it'.

We have seen in *Morris* that switching a label on an item is an appropriation, but the concept means that picking an item off a shelf in a supermarket is also appropriation. Even touching any goods on a shelf without taking them from the shelf is appropriation.

You can't have it – the House of Lords says I've appropriated it.

In *Corcoran v Anderton* (1980) the Court of Appeal expressed the view that the forcible tugging of a handbag, even though the owner of the bag did not let go of it, could amount to an assumption of the rights of the owner. Therefore it was an appropriation of the property. This case concerned a charge of robbery (see 11.2).

11.1.1 Consent to the appropriation

Can a defendant appropriate an item when it has been given to them by the owner? This is an area which has caused major problems. The Theft Act 1968 does not state that the appropriation has to be without the consent of the owner. So, what is the position where the owner has allowed the defendant to take something because the owner thought that the defendant was paying for it with a genuine cheque? This point was considered in *Lawrence* (1971).

Lawrence (1971)

An Italian student, who spoke very little English, arrived at Victoria Station and showed an address to Lawrence who was a taxi driver. The journey should have cost 50p, but Lawrence told him it was expensive. The student offered a £1 note to the driver. Lawrence said it was not enough and so the student opened his wallet and allowed Lawrence to help himself to another £6. Lawrence put forward the argument that he had not appropriated the money as the student had consented to him taking it. Both the Court of Appeal and the House of Lords rejected this argument and held that there was appropriation in this situation.

The point as to whether the appropriation had to be without the consent of the owner was considered again by the House of Lords in *Gomez* (1993).

Gomez (1993)

Gomez was the assistant manager of a shop. He persuaded the manager to sell electrical goods worth over £17,000 to an accomplice and to accept payment by two cheques, telling the manager that they were as good as cash. The cheques had been stolen and had no value. Gomez was charged and convicted of theft of the goods.

The Court of Appeal quashed the conviction, relying on the judgment in *Morris* (1983) that there had to be 'adverse interference' for there to be appropriation. They decided that the manager's consent to and authorisation of the transaction meant that there was no appropriation at the moment of taking the goods. The case was appealed to the House of Lords with the Court of Appeal certifying, as a point of law of general public importance, the following question:

'When theft is alleged and that which is alleged to be stolen passes to the defendant with the consent of the owner, but that has been obtained by a false representation, has:

(a) an appropriation within the meaning of s 1(1) of the Theft Act 1968 taken place, or
(b) must such a passing of property necessarily involve an element of adverse interference with or usurpation of some right of the owner?'

The House of Lords, by a majority of four to one, answered (a) 'yes'. An appropriation has taken place. They answered (b) 'no'. There was no need for adverse interference with or usurpation of some right of the owner. They pointed out that the decision in the case of *Lawrence* (1971) ruled that an act may be an appropriation even if it is done with the consent of the owner.

11.1.2 Consent without deception

So does the decision in *Gomez* (1993) extend to situations where a person has given property to another without any deception being made? This was the problem raised in the case of *Hinks* (2000).

Hinks (2000)

Hinks was a 38-year-old woman who had befriended a very naïve man with a low IQ. He was, however, mentally capable of understanding the concept of ownership and of making a valid gift. Over a period of about eight months, Hinks accompanied the man on numerous occasions to his building society where he withdrew money. The total was about £60,000 and this money was deposited in Hinks' account. The man also gave Hinks a television set. The judge directed the jury to consider whether the man was so mentally incapable that the defendant herself realised that ordinary and decent people would regard it as dishonest to accept a gift from him. The defendant was convicted of theft of the money and the television set.

On appeal it was argued that if the gift was valid, the acceptance of it could not be theft. The House of Lords dismissed the appeal on a majority of three judges to two. Four of the judges decided that, even though the property was a valid gift, there was an appropriation. Lord Hobhouse dissented, ruling that there could not

Activity

Discuss whether there has been an appropriation in each of the following situations.

1. Jake has an argument with his neighbour. When his neighbour is out, Jake holds an auction of the neighbour's garden tools. The neighbour returns before any of the tools are taken away.
2. Saskia goes shopping at the local supermarket and takes her 5-year-old son, Tom, with her. While at the checkout Tom takes some bars of chocolate and puts them in his pocket. Saskia does not realise Tom has done this until she finds the chocolate when they get home. Saskia decides that she will not take the chocolate back to the supermarket.
3. The owner of a shop asks Arnold, a lorry driver, to pick up a load of computer equipment and take it to a warehouse. Arnold agrees to do this, but after collecting the equipment decides that she will not take it to the warehouse but will instead sell it.
4. Otto, aged 18, is infatuated with Harriet, a married woman aged 32. Otto uses his student loan to buy expensive presents for Harriet. She knows he is a student and has very little money but she accepts the gifts from him.

be an appropriation in these circumstances. Lord Hutton, although agreeing with the majority on the point of law, dissented on whether the conduct showed dishonesty.

A major argument against the ruling in *Hinks* is that in civil law the gift was valid and the £60,000 and the television set belonged to the defendant. Lord Steyn in the leading judgment accepted that this was the situation, but he considered it was irrelevant to the decision.

11.1.3 A later assumption of a right

Section 3(1) makes it clear that there can also be an appropriation where the defendant acquires property without stealing it, but then later decides to keep or deal with the property as owner. The appropriation in this type of situation takes place at the point of 'keeping' or 'dealing'.

This could occur where the defendant hires a video from a shop, but instead of returning it decides to keep it. He is acting as though he is the owner with the right to keep the video.

Dealing in the property could occur where the defendant borrows a bicycle (or other property) but then sells it or gives it away. This can also happen where he hires a car. If he sells it instead of returning it, then he has dealt with it as an owner.

11.2 Property

For there to be theft, the defendant must have appropriated 'property'. Section 4 gives a very comprehensive definition of property which means that almost anything can be stolen. The definition is in s 4(1) Theft Act 1968:

> '4(1) "Property" includes money and all other property real or personal, including things in action and other intangible property.'

This section lists five types of items which are included in the definition of 'property'. These are:

- money
- real property (land and buildings)
- personal property
- things in action
- other intangible property.

In this list, money is self-explanatory; it means coins and banknotes of any currency. Personal property is also straightforward as it covers all moveable items. Books, CDs, jewellery, clothes, cars are obvious examples, but the term also includes very large items such as aeroplanes or tanks, and very small trivial items such as a sheet of paper. It has even been held in *Kelly and Lindsay* (1998) that dead bodies and body parts can be personal property for the purposes of theft.

Kelly and Lindsay (1998)

Kelly was a sculptor who asked Lindsay to take body parts from the Royal College of Surgeons where he worked as a laboratory assistant. Kelly made casts of the parts. They were convicted of theft and appealed on the point of law that body parts were not property. The Court of Appeal held that, though a dead body was not normally property within the definition of the Theft Act 1968, the body parts were property as they had acquired 'different attributes by virtue of the application of skill, such as dissection or preservation techniques, for exhibition or teaching purposes.'

11.2.1 Real property

Real property is the legal term for land and buildings. Under s 4(1) land can be stolen, but s 4(2) states that this can only be done in three circumstances. These are where:

- a trustee or personal representative takes land in breach of his duties as a trustee or personal representative
- someone not in possession of the land severs anything forming part of the land from the land
- a tenant takes a fixture or structure from the land let to him.

Under the second point, where someone is not in possession of the land, it is theft to dig up turves from someone's lawn or to dismantle a wall and take the bricks. In 1972 a man was prosecuted for stealing Cleckheaton railway station by dismantling it and removing it. He was in fact acquitted by the jury as he said he acting under a claim of right, but there was no doubt that the station could be property under the Theft Act 1968 definition.

Where someone who is not in possession of the land severs something from land, it is the severing of the item that forms the appropriation.

11.2.2 Things in action

A thing in action is a right which can be enforced against another person by an action in law. The right itself is property under the definition in s 4. An example is a bank account in credit. The bank does not keep coins or banknotes for each customer's account into a separate box! Instead the customer has a right to the payment of the amount in his account. So if the defendant causes the bank to debit another person's account, he has appropriated a thing in action. If he does this dishonestly and with the intention to permanently deprive the other of it, then the defendant is guilty of theft.

A cheque itself is a thing in action, but in being a piece of paper, it is also property which can be stolen; it is a 'valuable security' which can also be stolen under the definition of property.

Other things in action include:

- copyright
- registered trade marks (such as the logos of well-known sports companies)
- a ticket giving the right to attend a theatre performance or concert.

If someone purports to sell any of these rights, then there may be a theft of a thing in action.

11.2.3 Other intangible property

This refers to other rights which have no physical presence but can be stolen under the Theft Act 1968. In *A-G of Hong Kong v Chan Nai-Keung* (1987) an export quota for textiles was intangible property which could be stolen. A patent is also intangible property which can be stolen.

However, there are some types of intangible property which have been held not to be property within the Theft Act 1968 definition. In *Oxford v Moss* (1979) knowledge of the questions on an examination paper was held not to be property.

11.2.4 Things which cannot be stolen

There are some things which cannot be stolen. These are set out in ss 4(3) and 4(4) Theft Act 1968. The first of these concerns plants and fungi growing wild.

> '4(3) A person who picks mushrooms growing wild on any land, or who picks flowers, fruit or foliage from a plant growing wild on any land, does not (although not in possession of the land) steal what he picks, unless he does it for reward or sale or other commercial purpose.'

For the purposes of this subsection, 'mushroom' includes any fungus, and 'plant' includes any shrub or tree.

This only applies to plants etc growing wild, so it is possible to steal cultivated plants. Taking apples from trees in a farmer's orchard would be theft, but picking blackberries growing wild in the hedgerow around the field would not be theft unless it was done for sale or reward or other commercial purpose. Similarly, picking roses from someone's garden would be theft, but picking wild flowers in a field would not (unless for sale or reward). It should be noted that it is an offence to pick, uproot or destroy certain wild plants under the Wildlife and Countryside Act 1981.

Where picking fungi, flowers, fruit or foliage is done with the intention of selling them or for reward or any commercial purpose, then they are considered property which can be stolen. An example of this is picking holly to sell at Christmas time.

Another exception which is not 'property' for the purpose of theft concerns wild creatures.

> '4(4) Wild creatures, tamed or untamed, shall be regarded as property; but a person cannot steal a wild creature not tamed nor ordinarily kept in captivity, or the carcase of any such creature, unless it has been reduced into possession by or on behalf of another person and possession of it has not since been lost or abandoned, or another person is in course of reducing it into possession.'

The effect of this subsection is that it is not theft if a wild creature such as a deer is taken from the grounds of a large estate (though there is an offence of poaching), but it is theft if a deer is taken from a zoo, as in this case it is ordinarily kept in captivity.

Electricity

Electricity is another sort of intangible property which cannot be stolen, but there is a separate offence under s 11 Theft Act 1968 of dishonestly using electricity without due authority, or dishonestly causing it to be wasted or diverted.

11.3 Belonging to another

In order for there to be a theft of the property, that property must 'belong to another'. However, s 5(1) Theft Act 1968 gives a very wide definition of what is meant by 'belonging to another':

> 'Property shall be regarded as belonging to any person having possession or control of it, or having in it any proprietary right or interest (not being an equitable interest arising only from an agreement to transfer or grant an interest).'

From this it can be seen that possession or control of the property or any proprietary interest in it is sufficient. One reason for making it wide is so that the prosecution does not have to prove who is the legal owner.

11.3.1 Possession or control

Obviously the owner of property normally has possession and control of it, but there are many other situations in which a person can have either possession or control of property. Someone who hires a car has both possession and control during the period of hire. If the car is stolen during this time then the thief can be charged

Activity

Explain whether the items in each of the following situations would be property for the purposes of theft.

1. Arnie runs a market stall selling flowers. Just before Christmas, he picks holly from a wood, intending to sell it on his stall. He then digs up a small fir tree for his own use. On his way home he sees some late flowering roses in a garden and picks them to give to his girlfriend.

2. Della finds the examination papers she is to sit next week in the nextdoor office. She writes out the questions from the first paper on to a notepad of her own. The second paper is very long, so she uses the office photocopier to take a copy, using paper already in the machine.

with stealing it from the hirer. Equally, as the car hire firm still own the car (a proprietary right), the thief could be charged with stealing it from them.

The possession or control of the item does not have to be lawful. Where B has stolen jewellery from A and later C steals it from B, B is in possession or control of that jewellery and C can be charged with stealing it from B. This is useful where it is not known who the original owner is, as C can still be guilty of theft. This wide definition of 'belonging to' has led to the situation in which an owner was convicted of stealing his own car.

Turner (No 2) (1971)

Turner left his car at a garage for repairs. It was agreed that he would pay for the repairs when he collected the car after the repairs had been completed. When the repairs were almost finished, the garage left the car parked on the roadway outside their premises. Turner used a spare key to take the car during the night without paying for the repairs. The Court of Appeal held that the garage was in possession or control of the car and so Turner could be guilty of stealing his own car.

It is possible for someone to be in possession or control of property even though they do not know it is there. This occurred in *Woodman* (1974).

Woodman (1974)

A company, English China Clays, had sold all the scrap metal on its site to another company which arranged for it to be removed. Unknown to English China Clays a small amount had been left on the site. There was no doubt that they were in control of the site itself as they had put a barbed wire fence round it and had notices warning trespassers to keep out. The defendant took the remaining scrap metal. He was convicted of theft and the Court of Appeal upheld the conviction as the company was in control of the site.

Section 5 makes it clear that in certain situations a defendant can be guilty of theft even though the property may not 'belong to another'. These are situations in which the defendant is acting dishonestly and has caused a loss to another or has made a gain. These are:

- trust property, where a trustee can steal it
- property received under an obligation
- property received by another's mistake.

11.3.2 Property received under an obligation

There are many situations in which property (usually money) is handed over to the defendant on the basis that he will keep it for the owner or will deal with it in a particular way. As the property has been handed over to the defendant, he has become the owner, so subsection 5(3) tries to make sure that such property is still considered as 'belonging to the other' for the purposes of the law of theft. It states:

> '5(3) Where a person receives property from or on account of another, and is under an obligation to the other to retain and deal with that property or its proceeds in a particular way, the property shall be regarded (as against him) as belonging to the other.'

Under this subsection there must be an obligation to retain and deal with the property in a particular way. So, where money is paid as a deposit to a business, the prosecution must prove that there was an obligation to retain and deal with those deposits in a particular way. If the person paying the deposit only expects it to be paid into a bank account of the business, then if that is what happens there cannot be theft, even if all the money from the account is later used for other business expenses and the client does not receive the goods or service for which he paid the deposit. This is what happened in *Hall* (1972).

Hall (1972)

Hall was a travel agent who received deposits from clients for air trips to America. He paid these deposits into the firm's general account but never organised any tickets and was unable to return the money. He was convicted of theft but on appeal his conviction was quashed because when Hall received the deposits he was not under an obligation to deal with it in a particular way. The Court of Appeal stressed that each case depended on its facts.

In *Klineberg and Marsden* (1999) there was a clear obligation to deal with deposits in a particular way.

Klineberg and Marsden (1999)

The two defendants operated a company which sold timeshare apartments in Lanzarote to customers in England. Each purchaser paid the purchase price on the understanding that the money would be held by an independent trust company until the apartment was ready for the purchaser to occupy. Over £500,000 was paid to the defendants' company but only £233 was actually paid into the trust company's account. The defendants were guilty of theft as it was clear that they were under an obligation to the purchasers 'to retain and deal with that property or its proceeds in a particular way', and that they had not done this.

A problem arises where a person who gives cash towards a charity does not expect the defendant to pay over the exact same notes and coins to the charity. This was considered in *Wain* (1995).

Wain (1995)

D had organised various events to raise money for the Telethon Trust, a charity created by Yorkshire Television Company. D paid the money,

£2,833.25, into a special bank account, but then, with the permission of a representative of the TV company, transferred the money into his own personal bank account. He then spent the money and was unable to pay any money to the charity. He was convicted of theft and the conviction was upheld.

The Court of Appeal considered the point of whether the defendant was obliged to hand over the actual coins and notes or whether there was a more general principle that he was under an obligation to hand over an amount equal to the money he raised. The Court decided that under s 5(3) the defendant was clearly under an obligation to retain the same amount as the money given in sponsorship. It did not matter whether he kept the actual notes and coins or their proceeds, but he was still under an obligation.

There can be an obligation in less formal situations, as shown by *Davidge v Bunnett* (1984).

Davidge v Bunnett (1984)

It was held that the defendant was guilty of theft when she was given money by her flatmates to pay the gas bill but instead used it to buy Christmas presents. There was a legal obligation in this situation as there was an intention to create legal relations under contract law.

It is not clear whether there would be a legal obligation (and so theft) if the situation happened between members of the same family, or whether this would be a domestic arrangement without the intention to create legal relations.

11.3.3 Property obtained by a mistake

Section 5 also provides for situations where property has been handed over to the defendant by another's mistake and so has become his property. If there were no special provision in the

Act then this could not be 'property belonging to another' for the purposes of the law of theft. Subsection 5(4) states:

> 'Where a person gets property by another's mistake, and is under an obligation to make restoration (in whole or in part) of the property or its proceeds or of the value thereof, then to the extent of that obligation the property or proceeds shall be regarded (as against him) as belonging to the person entitled to restoration, and an intention not to make restoration shall be regarded accordingly as an intention to deprive that person of the property or proceeds.'

A-G's Reference (No 1 of 1983) (1985)

The facts were that the defendant's salary was paid into her bank account by credit transfer. On one occasion her employers mistakenly overpaid her by £74.74. She was acquitted of theft but the prosecution asked the Court of Appeal to rule on whether a person in this situation who dishonestly decided not to repay the £74.74 would be guilty of theft. The Court of Appeal held that s 5(4) clearly provided for exactly this type of situation. The defendant was under an 'obligation to make restoration' and if there was a dishonest intention not to make restoration, then all the elements of theft were present.

11.4 Dishonestly

The first point which needs to be proved for the *mens rea* of theft is that when the defendant appropriated the property, he did it dishonestly.

There is no definition of what is meant by dishonesty in the Act but s 1(2) states that it is immaterial whether the appropriation is made with a view to gain, or is made for the thief's own benefit. In other words, if all the elements of theft are present, the motive of the defendant is not relevant. So a modern-day Robin Hood stealing from the rich to give to the poor could be guilty of theft.

The defendant does not have to gain anything from the theft, so destroying property belonging to another can be theft, although it is also, of course, criminal damage. Theft can also be charged where the defendant does not destroy the other's property but throws it away. For example, if the defendant threw a waterproof watch belonging to another into the sea, this could be theft.

The Theft Act 1968 gives three situations which are not dishonest (see 11.4.1). For any other situation the jury or the magistrates have to decide whether the defendant has been dishonest by using the *Ghosh* test which was developed by the Court of Appeal in the case of *Ghosh* in 1982 (see 11.4.3).

11.4.1 Behaviour which is not dishonest

The 1968 Theft Act does not define dishonesty, but it does give three situations in which the defendant's behaviour is not considered dishonest. These are in s 2 which provides that a person's appropriation of property belonging to another is not to be regarded as dishonest if he appropriates the property in the belief that:

(a) he has in law the right to deprive the other of it, on behalf of himself or of a third person; or
(b) he would have the other's consent if the other knew of the appropriation and the circumstances of it; or
(c) the person to whom the property belongs cannot be discovered by taking reasonable steps.

All these three situations depend on the defendant's belief. It does not matter whether it is a correct belief or even whether it is a reasonable belief. If he has a genuine belief in one of these three then he is not guilty of theft.

An example of a defendant believing that he had a right in law to take the property is *Robinson* (1977).

An example of where a person believed he would have the other's consent to the appropriation could be where a student takes a can of lager from his housemate's room, but leaves the money covering the cost of it. If the student believed that his housemate would consent to the taking of the lager, then he is not dishonest under s 2(1)(b).

An example of where a person believes that the owner of the property cannot be discovered by taking reasonable steps is where a £5 note is found at the side of a deserted road. There is no-one else around. So, if the finder decides to keep the note as he believes there is no reasonable way of discovering the owner, then he would not be dishonest under s 2(1)(c).

11.4.2 Willing to pay

In some situations the defendant may say that he is willing to pay for the property or may, on taking property, leave money to pay for it. This does not prevent his conduct from being dishonest as s 2(2) states that 'a person's appropriation of property belonging to another may be dishonest notwithstanding that he is willing to pay for the property'.

At first this may seem severe, but it prevents the defendant taking what he likes, regardless of the owner's wishes. For example, the defendant likes a painting which is hanging in a friend's home. He asks the friend how much it is worth and is told that it is only a copy, worth less than £100, but it was painted by the friend's grandmother and is of sentimental value. A few days later he takes the painting without the friend's consent but leaves £200 in cash to pay for it. His taking of the painting may be considered dishonest even though he left more than the cash value of it.

11.4.3 The *Ghosh* test (1982)

Although the Act does not give a definition of honesty, the Court of Appeal, in *Feely* (1973), did at least give a standard of dishonesty to be applied by the jury.

This test caused a problem in that it was not clear whether the test should be purely objective (the standards of ordinary decent people) or whether it should be subjective (did the defendant realise that what he was doing was dishonest). This was finally solved in *Ghosh* (1982), which is the leading case on what is meant by 'dishonestly'. In this case the Court of Appeal set out the tests to be used.

that they must apply their own standards to decide if what he did was dishonest. He was convicted and appealed against the conviction.

The Court of Appeal decided that the test for dishonesty has both an objective and a subjective element to it. These are:

- Was the action dishonest according to the ordinary standards of reasonable and honest people?
- Did the defendant realise that what he was doing was dishonest by those standards?

So this means that the jury has to start with an objective test. Was the action dishonest by the ordinary standards of reasonable and honest people? If it was not dishonest by those standards, that is the end of the matter and the prosecution fails; the defendant is not guilty. However, if the jury decide that it was dishonest by those standards then they must consider the more subjective test – did the defendant know it was dishonest by those standards?

This second test is not totally subjective as the defendant is judged by what he realised ordinary standards were. This prevents a defendant from saying that, although he knew that ordinary people would regard his actions as dishonest, he did not think that those standards applied to him.

11.5 With intention of permanently depriving

The final element which has to be proved for theft is that the defendant had the intention permanently to deprive the other of the property. In many situations there is no doubt that the defendant had such an intention; for example, where an item is taken and sold to another person or where cash is taken and spent by the defendant. This last example is true even if the defendant intends to replace the money later, as was shown in *Velumyl* (1989).

Velumyl (1989)

The defendant, a company manager, took £1,050 from the office safe. He said that he was owed money by a friend and he was going to replace the money when that friend repaid him. The Court of Appeal upheld his conviction for theft as he had the intention of permanently depriving the company of the banknotes which he had taken from the safe, even if he intended replacing them with other banknotes to the same value later.

Another situation where there is a clear intention to deprive permanently is where the defendant destroys property belonging to another. This can be charged as theft, although it is also criminal damage.

There are, however, situations where it is not so clear and, to help in these, s 6 Theft Act 1968 explains and expands the meaning of the phrase. It provides that, even though a person appropriating property belonging to another does not mean the other permanently to lose the thing itself, he can be regarded as having the intention to deprive the other of it permanently if his intention is to treat the thing as his own to dispose of, regardless of the other's rights.

The Court of Appeal has stated that the meaning of 'dispose of' should be that given by the *Shorter Oxford Dictionary*:

> 'To deal with definitely: to get rid of; to get done with, finish. To make over by way of sale or bargain or sell.'

However, in *DPP v Lavender* (1994) the Divisional Court ruled that the dictionary definition of 'dispose of' was too narrow as a disposal could include 'dealing with' property.

DPP v Lavender (1994)

The defendant took doors from a council property which was being repaired and used them to replace damaged doors in his girlfriend's council flat. The doors were still in the possession of the council but had been transferred without permission from one council property to another. The Divisional Court held that the question was whether he intended to treat the doors as his own, regardless of the rights of the council. The answer to this was yes, so the defendant was guilty of theft.

11.5.1 Borrowing or lending

Another difficulty with s 6 is the point at which 'borrowing or lending' comes within the definition. Normally borrowing would not be an intention to deprive permanently. Take the situation of a student taking a textbook from a fellow student's bag in order to read one small section and then replace the book. This is clearly outside the scope of s 6 and cannot be considered as an intention to deprive permanently.

But what if that student also took another book which he keeps for the whole of the term. He then returns the book to its owner. When the book is returned, the student who owned the book has finished the module for which he needed that book. The book is no longer as valuable to him. Is there an intention to deprive permanently in this situation? The owner gets the complete book back, but it is no longer useful to him. This fact might mean there is an intention to deprive permanently. To decide this, it is necessary to consider what s 6 says about 'borrowing' items.

Section 6 states that borrowing is not theft unless it is for a period and in circumstances making it equivalent to an outright taking or disposal. In *Lloyd* (1985) it was held that this

meant borrowing the property and keeping it until 'the goodness, the virtue, the practical value . . . has gone out of the article'. In this case a film had been taken for a short time and copied, then the original film replaced undamaged. This was not theft.

Another difficulty is where the defendant picks up property to see if there is anything worth stealing. What is the position if he decides it is not worth stealing and returns it? This is what happened in *Easom* (1971).

Easom (1971)

The defendant picked up a handbag in a cinema, rummaged through the contents and then replaced the handbag without having taken anything. He was convicted of theft of the handbag and its contents, but the Court of Appeal quashed this conviction. They held that even though he may have had a conditional intention to deprive, this was not enough.

In *Attorney-General's Reference (Nos 1 and 2 of 1979)* (1979) the Court of Appeal decided that if D had a conditional intent (ie D intended stealing if there was anything worth stealing), D could be charged with an attempt to steal some or all of the contents.

So *Easom* would now be charged with attempting to steal all or some of the contents of the bag, rather than the bag itself and specific items in it.

11.5.2 Intention to treat the thing as his own

If the defendant treats the thing as his own to dispose of, regardless of the other's rights, then the defendant has the intention to permanently deprive. This includes the rather unusual situation seen in *Raphael and another* (2008) where the defendant offered to sell back to the victim his own property.

Key facts

Section of Theft Act 1968	Definition	Comment/Cases
s 1	A person is guilty of theft if he dishonestly appropriates property belonging to another with the intention of permanently depriving the other of it	Full definition of theft Defendant is charged under this section

s 2	**Dishonesty**
	(1) Not dishonest if believes:
	    ● has right in law
	    ● would have the other's consent
	    ● owner cannot be discovered
	(2) Can be dishonest even if intends paying for property
		No definition of dishonesty in the Act
		Ghosh (1982) two-part test:
		    ● is it dishonest by ordinary standards?
		    ● if so, did the defendant know it was dishonest by those standards?

s 3	**Appropriation** (1) 'any assumption of the rights of an owner' Includes a later assumption of rights	Held to be assumption of *any* of the rights of an owner – *Gomez* (1993) Given 'neutral' meaning, so consent irrelevant – *Lawrence* (1971), *Hinks* (2000)
s 4	**Property** Includes money and all other property, real or personal, including things in action and other intangible property Land cannot be stolen except by trustee or tenant or by severing property from land Wild mushrooms, fruit, flowers and foliage cannot be stolen unless done for commercial purpose Wild animals cannot be stolen unless tamed or in captivity	
s 5	**Belonging to another** Property is regarded as belonging to any person having possession or control or any proprietary right Property belongs to the other where it is received under an obligation to retain and deal with it in a particular way Property received by a mistake where there is a legal obligation to make restoration belongs to the other	Not limited to owner – *Turner (No 2)* (1972) stole own car Must be a particular way – *Hall* (1972), *Klineberg and Marsden* (1999) *A-G's reference (No 1 of 1983)* (1985) Must be a legal obligation – *Gilks* (1972)
s 6	**Intention to deprive permanently** Intention Treat the thing as his own to dispose of regardless of the other's rights	The 'goodness' or practical value must have gone from the property – *Lloyd* (1985) *Raphael and another* (2008) – offering to sell V's property back to him was treating it as D's own to dispose of

Key facts chart on theft

Activity

In each of the following situations explain whether all the elements of theft are present.

1. Roland works in a small factory where there are only 20 employees. One day he finds a small purse in the washroom. He opens it. It contains a £10 note and some coins. There is no name or other identification in it. Roland decides to keep the money as he does not think he can find the owner.

2. Venus comes from a country where property placed outside a shop is meant for people to take free of charge. She sees a rack of clothes on the pavement outside a shop and takes a pair of jeans from it.

3. Natalie is given a Christmas cash bonus in a sealed envelope. She has been told by her boss that the bonus would be £50. When she arrives home and opens the envelope she finds there is £60 in it. She thinks her employer decided to be more generous and so keeps the money. Would your answer be different if (a) Natalie realised there had been a mistake but did not return the money or (b) the amount in the envelope was £200?

4. Errol is given permission by his employer to borrow some decorative lights for use at a party. Errol also takes some candles without asking permission. When putting up the lights Errol smashes one of them. He lights two of the candles so that by the end of the evening they are partly burnt down. One of the guests admires the remaining lights and asks if he can have them to use at a disco at the weekend. Errol agrees to let him take the lights.

5. Hari is late for work one day so he takes his neighbour's bicycle to get to work on time. His neighbour is away, but Hari has used the bicycle on previous occasions. He intends returning it that evening when he comes home from work. Hari parks the bicycle at the back of the shop where he works. When he leaves work in the evening he finds that the lamp and the pump have been taken from the bicycle and it has been damaged. He is frightened to return the bicycle in this state so he throws it into the local canal.

Raphael and another (2008)

The two defendants took V's car by force and then demanded payment for its return. It was held that the wording of s 6(1), 'an intention to treat the thing as his own to dispose of, regardless of the other's rights', included the situation when D makes an offer to return to V his own property but subject to a condition which is inconsistent with V's right to possession of his own property. The defendants were guilty of theft.

11.6 Robbery

Robbery is an offence under s 8 Theft Act 1968. In effect it is a theft which is aggravated by the use or threat of force. Section 8 states:

> 'A person is guilty of robbery if he steals, and immediately before or at the time of doing so, and in order to do so, he uses force on any person or puts or seeks to put any person in fear of being then and there subjected to force.'

So the elements which must be proved for robbery are for the *actus reus*:

- theft
- force or putting or seeking to put any person in fear of force.

In addition there are two conditions on the force – it must be immediately before or at the time of the theft, and it must be in order to steal.

For the *mens rea* of robbery it must be proved that the defendant had:

- the *mens rea* for theft and
- intended to use force to steal.

11.6.1 Completed theft

There must be a completed theft for a robbery to have been committed. This means that all the elements of theft have to be present. If a single one is missing then, just as there would no theft, there is no robbery. For example, there is no theft in the situation where the defendant takes a car, drives it a mile and abandons it because he has no intention permanently to deprive. Equally there is no robbery where he uses force to take that car. There is no offence of theft so using force cannot make it into robbery.

The case of *Robinson* (1977) demonstrates that if the elements of theft are not complete then there cannot be robbery.

Robinson (1977)

D ran a clothing club and was owed £7 by V's wife. D approached V and threatened him. During a struggle the man dropped a £5 note and D took it, claiming he was still owed £2. D's conviction for robbery was quashed because the trial judge had wrongly directed the jury that D had honestly to believe he was entitled to get the money in that way. In fact if D had a genuine belief that he had a right in law to the money, then his actions were not dishonest under s 2(1)(a) of the Theft Act 1968.

Where force is used to steal, then the moment the theft is complete there is a robbery. This is demonstrated by the case of *Corcoran v Anderton* (1980).

Corcoran v Anderton (1980)

One of the defendants hit a woman in the back and tugged at her bag. She let go of the bag and it fell to the ground. The defendants ran off without it (because the woman was screaming and attracting attention). It was held that the theft was complete so the defendants were guilty of robbery.

In fact in *Corcoran v Anderton* (1980) the Court of Appeal expressed the view that the forcible tugging of a handbag could amount to an assumption of the rights of the owner (and a completed theft), even if the owner of the bag did not let go of it.

11.6.2 Force or threat of force

As well as theft, the prosecution must prove force or the threat of force. The amount of force can be small. This is clearly shown by the case of *Dawson and James* (1976).

Dawson and James (1976)

One of the defendants pushed the victim, causing him to lose his balance which enabled the other defendant to take his wallet. They were convicted of robbery. The Court of Appeal held that 'force' was an ordinary word and it was for the jury to decide if there had been force.

Another case which shows that only a small amount of force is necessary is *Clouden* (1987).

Clouden (1987)

The Court of Appeal held that Clouden was guilty of robbery when he had wrenched a shopping basket from the victim's hand. The Court of Appeal held that the trial judge was right to leave the question of whether the defendant had used force on a person to the jury.

It can be argued that using force on the bag was effectively using force on the victim as the bag was wrenched from her hand. However, if a thief pulls a shoulder bag so that it slides off the victim's shoulder, would this be considered force? Probably not. And it would certainly not be force if a thief snatched a bag which was resting (not being held) on the lap of someone sitting on a park bench.

The definition of robbery makes clear that robbery is committed if the defendant puts or seeks to put a person in fear of force. It is not necessary that the force be applied. Putting the victim 'in fear of being there and then subjected to force' is sufficient for robbery. This covers threatening words, such as 'I have a knife and I'll use it unless you give me your wallet', and threatening gestures, such as holding a knife in front of the victim.

Robbery is also committed even if the victim is not actually frightened by the defendant's actions or words. If the defendant seeks to put the victim in fear of being then and there subjected to force, this element of robbery is present. So if the victim is a plain-clothes policeman put there to trap the defendant and is not frightened, the fact that the defendant sought to put the victim in fear is enough.

A case illustrating the fact that the victim does not have to be frightened and also that the amount of force does not have to be great is *B and R v DPP* (2007).

B and R v DPP (2007)

The victim, a schoolboy aged 16, was stopped by five other schoolboys. They asked for his mobile phone and money. As this was happening, another five or six boys joined the first five and surrounded the victim. No serious violence was used against the victim, but he was pushed and his arms were held while he was searched. The defendants took his mobile phone, £5 from his wallet, his watch and a travel card. The victim said that he did not feel particularly threatened or scared but that he was bit shocked.

The defendants appealed against their convictions for robbery on the basis that no force had been used and the victim had not felt threatened. The Divisional Court upheld the convictions for robbery on the grounds that:

- there was no need to show that the victim felt threatened; s 8 of the Theft Act 1968 states that robbery can be committed if the defendant 'seeks to put any person in fear of being then and there subjected to force';
- there could be an implied threat of force; in this case the surrounding the victim by so many created an implied threat;
- in any event, there was some limited force used by holding the victim's arms and pushing him.

CPS charging standards

On this part of use of force or threat of force the Crown Prosecution charging standards give examples of when it would be appropriate to charge robbery. These include:

- when a handbag or mobile phone is forcibly snatched from a person's grasp;
- when an 11-year-old hands over a small amount of money following threats of significant violence made by an older and physically larger youth;
- when no force is used or threatened but a weapon is produced or made visible to the victim (on the basis of an implied threat).

They also give examples of when it would NOT be appropriate to charge robbery. These are:

- when a bag has been taken from off the shoulder of a victim without any force being used or threatened;
- when a shoulder strap is cut and the victim is unaware of this until after the handbag has been stolen.

On any person

This means that the person threatened does not have to be the person from whom the theft occurs. An obvious example is an armed robber who enters a bank, seizes a customer and threatens to shoot that customer unless a bank official gets money out of the safe. This is putting a person in fear of being then and there subjected to force. The fact that it is not the customer's property which is being stolen does not matter.

11.6.3 Force immediately before or at the time of the theft

The force must be immediately before or at the time of stealing. This raises two problems. First, how immediate does 'immediately before' have to be? Suppose a person is threatened with violence so that they hand over their credit card and PIN. Obviously there is force at the time of the taking of the credit card so that the defendant could be charged with robbery of the card. But what if the card is used 24 hours later to get money from the victim's account? This is theft of that money, but is the force sufficiently immediate for the offence of taking the money to be robbery? Does this still come within 'immediately before'? There have been no decided cases on this point.

The second problem has come in deciding the point at which a theft is completed, so that the force is not 'at the time of stealing'; see *Hale* (1979).

Hale (1979)

Two defendants knocked on the door of a house. When a woman opened the door they forced their way into the house and one defendant put his hand over her mouth to stop her screaming while the other defendant went upstairs to see what he could find to take. He took a jewellery box. Before they left the house they tied up the householder.

They argued on appeal that the theft was complete as soon as the second defendant picked up the jewellery box, so the use of force in tying up the householder was not at the time of stealing. However, the Court of Appeal upheld their convictions. The Court of Appeal thought that the jury could have come to the decision that there was force immediately before the theft when one of the defendants put his hand over the householder's mouth. In addition, the Court of Appeal thought that the tying up of the householder could also be force for the purpose of robbery as they held that the theft was still ongoing.

In *Lockley* (1995), the defendant was caught shoplifting cans of beer from an off-licence and used force on the shopkeeper who was trying to stop him from escaping. He appealed on the basis that the theft was complete when he used the force, but the Court of Appeal followed the decision in *Hale* (1979) and held that he was guilty.

But there must be a point when the theft is complete and so any force used after this point does not make it robbery. What if in *Lockley* the defendant had left the shop and was running down the road when a passer-by (alerted by the shouts of the shopkeeper) tried to stop him. The defendant then uses force on the passer-by to escape? Surely the theft is completed before this use of force? The force used is a separate act to the theft and does not make the theft a robbery. The force will, of course, be a separate offence of assault.

11.6.4 Force in order to steal

The force must be used in order to steal. So if the force was not used for this purpose, then any later theft will not make it into robbery. Take the situation where the defendant has an argument with the victim and punches him, knocking him out. The defendant then sees that some money has fallen out of the victim's pocket and decides to take it. The force was not used for the purpose of that theft and the defendant is not guilty of robbery, but guilty of two separate offences: an assault and theft.

11.6.5 *Mens rea* for robbery

The defendant must have the *mens rea* for theft; ie he must be dishonest and he must intend to deprive the other of the property permanently. He must also intend to use force to steal.

Activity

Read the following extract from an article from *Sevenoaks Chronicle* on 15 January 2004 and answer the questions below.

Armed raid at off-licence

An armed raider burst into a village off-licence and demanded cash.

The man entered Unwins in The Square, Riverhead at about 6.30 pm on Sunday, and produced what appeared to be a pistol.

He threatened staff with the weapon and demanded money, which the employees handed over from the till.

The raider then fled on foot along London Road, towards Dunton Green.

None of the staff, who have not been identified, were hurt in the attack.

The incident comes less than six months after two men used knives to intimidate employees into giving them cash and cigarettes at the store.'

Questions

1. Identify the offence which was committed at the off-licence.

2. Explain what is required for the *actus reus* of that offence, and identify the acts which form the *actus reus* in this particular raid.

3. Explain what has to be proved for the *mens rea* of the offence.

Key facts

Element	Law	Case
Theft	There must be a completed theft. If any element is missing, there is no theft and therefore no robbery	*Robinson* (1977)
	The moment the theft is completed (with the relevant force) there is robbery	*Corcoran v Anderton* (1980)
Force or threat of force	The jury decide whether the acts were force, using the ordinary meaning of the word	*Dawson and James* (1976)
	It includes wrenching a bag from the victim's hand	*Clouden* (1987)
On any person	The force can be against *any* person. It does not have to be against the victim of the theft	
Immediately before or at the time of the theft	For robbery, theft has been held to be a continuing act	*Hale* (1979)
	Using force to escape can still be at the time of the theft	*Lockley* (1995)
In order to steal	The force must be in order to steal. Force used for another purpose does not become robbery if the defendant later decides to steal	
Mens rea	*Mens rea* for theft plus an intention to use force to steal	

Key facts chart for robbery

Activity

Explain whether or not a robbery has occurred in each of the following situations.

1. Albert holds a knife to the throat of a three-year-old girl and orders the child's mother to hand over her purse or he will 'slit the child's throat'. The mother hands over her purse.

2. Brendan threatens staff in a post office with an imitation gun. He demands that they hand over the money in the till. One of the staff presses a security button and a grill comes down in front of the counter so that the staff are safe and Brendan cannot reach the till. He leaves without taking anything.

3. Carla snatches a handbag from Delia. Delia is so surprised that she leaves go of the bag and Carla runs off with it.

4. Egbert breaks into a car in a car park and takes a briefcase out of it. As he is walking away from the car, the owner arrives, realises what has happened and starts to chase after Egbert. The owner catches hold of Egbert, but Egbert pushes him over and makes his escape.

5. Fenella tells Gerry to hand over her Rolex watch and, that if she does not, Fenella will send her boyfriend to beat Gerry up. Gerry hands over the watch.

Chapter 12

Burglary

12.1 Burglary

This is an offence under s 9 Theft Act 1968. Section 9 provides two different ways in which burglary can be committed. Under s 9(1)(a) a person is guilty of burglary if he enters any building or part of a building as a trespasser with intent to steal, inflict grievous bodily harm or do unlawful damage to the building or anything in it.

Under s 9(1)(b) a person is guilty of burglary if, having entered a building or part of a building as a trespasser, he steals or attempts to steal anything in the building or inflicts or attempts to inflict grievous bodily harm on any person in the building.

Figure 12.1 shows these different ways of committing burglary.

Although ss 9(1)(a) and 9(1)(b) create different ways of committing burglary they do have common elements. These are that there must be:

- entry
- of a building or part of a building
- as a trespasser.

The difference between the subsections is the intention at the time of entry. For s 9(1)(a), the defendant must intend to do one of the three listed offences (known as ulterior offences) at the time of entering. However, there is no need for the ulterior offence to take place or even be attempted. For s 9(1)(b), what the defendant intends on entry is irrelevant, but the prosecution must prove that he actually committed or attempted to commit theft or grievous bodily harm.

12.1.1 Entry

Entry is not defined in the Theft Act 1968, but there have been several cases on the meaning of the word. The first main case on this point was *Collins* (1972) (see 12.1.3), in which the Court of Appeal said that the jury had to be satisfied that the defendant had made 'an effective and substantial entry'.

However, in *Brown* (1985) this concept of 'an effective and substantial entry' was modified to

Burglary	
Section 9(1)(a)	**Section 9(1)(b)**
Enters a building or part of a building as a trespasser	Having entered a building or part of a building as a trespasser
With intent to: • steal • inflict grievous bodily harm • do unlawful damage	• steals or attempts to steal; or • inflicts or attempts to inflict grievous bodily harm

Figure 12.1 Different ways of committing burglary

'effective entry'. The defendant was standing on the ground outside but leaning in through a shop window, rummaging through goods. The Court of Appeal said that the word 'substantial' did not materially assist the definition of entry and his conviction for burglary was upheld as clearly in this situation his entry was effective.

In *Ryan* (1996) the concept of 'effective' entry does not appear to have been followed.

Ryan (1996)

The defendant was trapped when trying to get through a window into a house at 2.30 am. His head and right arm were inside the house but the rest of his body was outside. The fire brigade had to be called to release him. This could scarcely be said to be an 'effective' entry. However, the Court of Appeal upheld his conviction for burglary, saying that there was evidence on which the jury could find that the defendant had entered. This clearly was not an effective entry as the defendant was unable to do anything.

12.1.2 Building or part of a building

The Theft Act 1968 gives an extended meaning to the word 'building' so that it includes inhabited places such as houseboats or caravans, which would otherwise not be included in the offence. However, it does not give any basic definition for 'building'. Usually there is no problem. Clearly houses, blocks of flats, offices, factories and so on are buildings. The word also includes outbuildings and sheds.

The main problems for the courts have come where a structure such as a portacabin has been used for storage or office work. There are two cases on whether a large storage container is a building. In these cases the court came to different decisions after looking at the facts.

- In *B and S v Leathley* (1979) a 25-foot-long freezer container had been in a farmyard for over two years, and was used as a storage facility. It rested on sleepers, had doors with locks and was connected to the electricity supply. This was held to be a building.
- In *Norfolk Constabulary v Seekings and Gould* (1986) a lorry trailer with wheels which had been used for storage for over a year, had steps providing access and was connected to the electricity supply, was held not to be a building. The fact that it had wheels meant that it remained a vehicle.

Part of a building

The phrase 'part of a building' is used to cover situations in which the defendant may have permission to be in one part of the building (and therefore is not a trespasser in that part) but does not have permission to be in another part.

A case example to demonstrate this is *Walkington* (1979).

Walkington (1979)

The defendant went into the counter area in a shop and opened a till. He was guilty of burglary under s 9(1)(a) because he had entered part of a building (the counter area) as a trespasser with the intention of stealing. The counter area was not an area where customers were permitted to go. It was for the use of staff.

Other examples include storerooms in shops where shoppers would not have permission to enter, or a hall of residence where one student would be a trespasser if he entered another student's room without permission.

Going into any other part of a building is entering that new part of the building. There is no need to go through a doorway or other physical barrier. For example, in department stores there are usually different departments, so that entering another department is entering another part of the building.

12.1.3 As a trespasser

In order for the defendant to commit burglary, he must enter as a trespasser. If a person has permission to enter they are not a trespasser. This was illustrated by the unusual case of *Collins* (1972).

Collins (1972)

The defendant, having had quite a lot to drink, decided he wanted to have sexual intercourse. He saw an open window and climbed a ladder to look in. He saw there was a naked girl asleep in bed. He then went down the ladder, took off all his clothes except for his socks and climbed back up the ladder to the girl's bedroom. As he was on the window sill outside the room, she woke up, thought he was her boyfriend and helped him into the room where they had sex.

Collins was convicted of burglary under s 9(1)(a), that he had entered as a trespasser with intent to rape. At that time the intent to rape came within the definition of burglary. (He could not be charged with rape as the girl accepted that she had consented to sex.) He appealed on the basis that that he was not a trespasser as he had been invited in. The Court of Appeal quashed his conviction because there was no evidence that he was a trespasser; the girl had invited him into the room.

The court said that there could not be a conviction for entering premises 'as a trespasser' unless the person entering did so either knowing he was a trespasser or was reckless as to whether or not he was entering the premises of another without the other person's consent.

So to succeed on a charge of burglary, the prosecution must prove that the defendant knew he was trespassing or that the defendant was subjectively reckless as to whether he was trespassing.

Going beyond permission

Where the defendant is given permission to enter but then goes beyond that permission, he may be considered a trespasser. This is shown by the case of *Smith and Jones* (1976).

Smith and Jones (1976)

Smith and his friend went to Smith's father's house in the middle of the night and took two television sets without the father's knowledge or permission. The father stated that his son would not be a trespasser in the house; he had a general permission to enter. The Court of Appeal ruled that:

'a person is a trespasser for the purpose of s 9(1)(b) of the Theft Act 1968 if he enters premises of another knowing that he is entering in excess of the permission that has been given to him to enter, or being reckless whether he is entering in excess of that permission'.

This meant that Smith was guilty of burglary.

The decision in *Smith and Jones* is in line with the Australian case of *Barker v R* (1983) where one person who was going away asked the defendant, who was a neighbour, to keep a eye on the house and told the defendant where a key was hidden should he need to enter. The defendant used the key to enter and steal property. He was found guilty of burglary.

There are many situations where a person has permission to enter for a limited purpose. For example, someone buys a ticket to attend a concert in a concert hall, or to visit an historic building or an art collection. The ticket is a licence (or permission) to be in the building for a very specific reason and/or time. If the defendant buys a ticket intending to steal one of the paintings from the art collection, these cases mean he is probably guilty of burglary.

Shoppers have permission to enter a shop. So,

if a person has been banned from entering a shop they will be entering as a trespasser if they go into that shop. This means that a known shoplifter who is banned from entering a local supermarket would be guilty of burglary if he entered with the intent to steal goods (s 9(1)(a)) or if, having entered, he then stole goods (s 9(1)(b)).

The law is also clear where the defendant gains entry through fraud, such as where he claims to be a gas meter reader. There is no genuine permission to enter and he is a trespasser.

Where a person has permission to enter one part of a building but goes into another part where they have no permission to be, then they are entering that part of the building as a trespasser.

If they intend to steal, inflict grievous bodily harm or do unlawful damage when they enter that

Key facts

Elements	Comment	Case/section
Entry	This has changed from ● 'effective and substantial' entry: to ● 'effective' entry: to ● evidence for the jury to find the defendant had entered	*Collins* (1972) *Brown* (1985) *Ryan* (1996)
Building or part of a building	Must have some permanence Includes inhabited vehicle or vessel Can be entry of part of a building	*B and S v Leathley* (1979) *Norfolk Constabulary v Seekings and Gould* (1986) s 9(4) Theft Act 1968 *Walkington* (1979)
As a trespasser	If has permission, is not a trespasser If goes beyond permission then can be a trespasser	*Collins* (1972) *Smith and Jones* (1976)
Mens rea	Must know or be subjectively reckless as to whether he is a trespasser PLUS EITHER Intention a point of entry to commit: ● theft or ● grievous bodily harm or ● criminal damage OR *Mens rea* for theft or grievous bodily harm at point of committing or attempting to commit these offences in a building	 s 9(1)(a) Theft Act 1968 s 9(1)(b) Theft Act 1968

Key facts chart on burglary

other part of the building, then they are guilty of burglary under s 9(1)(a) at the time they enter.

If they have no intention of doing one of the three ulterior offences, but actually steal or attempt to steal or inflict grievous bodily harm or attempt to inflict grievous bodily harm, they are guilty of burglary under s 9(1)(b).

12.1.4 Mental element of burglary

There are two parts to the mental element in burglary. These are in respect of:

- entering as a trespasser
- the ulterior offence.

First, for both s 9(1)(a) and s 9(1)(b) the defendant must know, or be subjectively reckless, as to whether he is trespassing. In addition, for s 9(1)(a) the defendant must have the intention to commit one of the three offences at the time of entering the building. Where the defendant is entering intending to steal anything he can find which is worth taking, then this is called a conditional intent. This is sufficient for the defendant to be guilty under s 9(1)(a) even if there is nothing worth taking and he does not actually steal anything.

For s 9(1)(b) the defendant must also have the *mens rea* for theft or grievous bodily harm when committing (or attempting to commit) the *actus reus* of one of these offences.

Intention to commit criminal damage

If a defendant intends to commit criminal damage at the time they enter a building or part of a building as a trespasser, then they are guilty of burglary under s 9(1)(a). However, if they do not intend to commit criminal damage when they enter, but in fact do cause unlawful damage, there is normally no offence of burglary as they are not guilty under s 9(1)(a) as they had no intention at the time of entry. Nor are they guilty under s 9(1)(b) as criminal damage is not one of the qualifying offences in that subsection.

The exception is when the damage completely destroys the property. In this case the damage is also considered theft. As theft is a qualifying offence under s 9(1)(b), then they are guilty of burglary under that subsection.

Activity

In each of the following explain whether or not a burglary has occurred, and if so whether it would be an offence under s 9(1)(a) or s 9(1)(b).

1. Jonny has been banned from a local pub. One evening he goes there for a drink with a friend. While he is waiting for the friend to get the drinks at the bar, Jonny sees a handbag under one of the chairs. He picks it up and takes a £10 note from it. He then puts the handbag back under the chair.

2. Ken and his partner, Lola, have split up and Ken has moved out of the flat they shared, taking most of his belongings with him. One evening he goes back there to collect the rest of his belongings. Lola is out and he asks the neighbour to let him have the spare key which the neighbour keeps for emergencies. While Ken is packing his clothes, Lola returns. They have an argument and Ken beats up Lola, causing her serious injuries.

3. Mike works as a shelf-filler in a DIY store. One day when putting packs of batteries onto a shelf, he slips one in his pocket. He does not intend to pay for it. Later in the day he sees the manager leave her office. Mike goes in and takes money from the desk. The door to the office has a notice saying 'Private'.

4. Nigella, who is a pupil at the local comprehensive, goes to the school buildings late in the evening after school. She intends to damage the science lab as she hates the teacher. She climbs in through a window but is caught by the caretaker before she does any damage.

Chapter 13

Blackmail

The common idea of blackmail is the situation where D threatens to reveal some information about V unless V pays him money. This, of course, is blackmail but blackmail also covers many more situations.

The definition of blackmail is set out in s 21 Theft Act 1968 which states that:

'(1) A person is guilty of blackmail if, with a view to gain for himself or another or with intent to cause loss to another, he makes any unwarranted demand with menaces; and for this purpose a demand with menaces is unwarranted unless the person making it does so in the belief—
   (a) that he has reasonable grounds for making the demand; and
   (b) that the use of the menaces is a proper means of reinforcing the demand.'

So, from this it can be seen that there are four points to be proved:

- a demand
- which is unwarranted; and
- made with menaces
- and with a view to gain or intent to cause loss.

The *actus reus* of blackmail is the making of an unwarranted demand with menaces. The *mens rea* of blackmail is an intention to make an unwarranted demand with menaces and with a view to gain or intent to cause loss.

So let's look at the different points to be proved and see how many situations could be blackmail.

13.1 Demand

There must be a demand, but that demand may take any form. So it may be by words, conduct, in writing or by email or any other method. It need not even be made explicitly to the victim, as in *Collister and Warhurst* (1955).

Collister and Warhurst (1955)

Within the defendant's hearing two police officers discussed the chances of them dropping a charge against him in return for payment. They did not make a direct demand. However, their discussion was held to be a demand for the purpose of blackmail.

Making an unwarrented demand with menaces is the *actus reus* of the offence. Once it is made the *actus reus* is complete. The demand does not have to be received by the victim. Where a demand is sent through the post, the demand is considered made at the point the letter is posted. This was decided by the House of Lords in *Treacy DPP* (1971).

Treacy v DPP (1971)

D posted a letter containing a demand with menaces in England to someone in Germany. Even though the letter with the demand in it would not be opened until it arrived in Germany, the House of Lords held that D could be guilty of blackmail in England as this was where D posted the letter.

13.2 Unwarranted demand

Section 21 explains that any demand made with menaces is unwarranted unless two tests set out in s 21(1) are fulfilled. The two tests are that D has to show that he believed:

(a) he had reasonable grounds for making the demand; and

(b) the use of the menaces was a proper means of reinforcing the demand.

These tests focus on D's belief and so give a subjective element to what is an unwarranted demand. If D really thought he had reasonable grounds for making the demand and that the use of menaces was the proper way of reinforcing the demand, then he is not guilty of blackmail. This was shown by *Harvey* (1981).

Harvey (1981)

D and others had paid the victim £20,000 for what was claimed to be cannabis. In fact it was, as D put it, 'a load of rubbish'. The defendants wanted their money back as they felt they had been 'ripped off'. In fact, as the deal was an illegal contract, there is no right in law to recover the money. They kidnapped V, his wife and child and made threats of murder and rape if the money was not returned. They were convicted of blackmail.

The Court of Appeal stated that it was necessary for them to show both that:

(1) they believed they had reasonable grounds for making the demand – on this point the Court of Appeal held that it could be accepted that they did so believe, but it was a matter for the jury to decide; and

(2) they believed the use of the menaces was a proper means of reinforcing the demand – on this point the Court of Appeal upheld the defendants' convictions as they could not have believed that making threats of murder and rape was 'a proper means of reinforcing the demand'.

As *Harvey* shows, the defendant must believe both that he had reasonable grounds for making the demand and that the use of menaces was a proper means of reinforcing the demand.

Genuine claim

The two tests mean that, even though D has a genuine claim, he can still be guilty of blackmail if he does not believe that the use of the menaces was a proper means of reinforcing the demand. For example, if D had lent V money he is entitled to demand its return. He certainly has reasonable grounds for making the demand under the first test in s 21(1). However, if D threatens to beat V up unless V repays the money by the next day and D knows that this is not a proper means of reinforcing his demand, then D can be guilty of blackmail.

13.3 Menaces

The demand must be made with menaces. 'Menaces' has been held to mean a serious threat, but it is wider than just a threat. In *Lawrence and Pomroy* (1971) it was held that menaces was an ordinary English word which any jury can be expected to understand.

Lawrence and Pomroy (1971)

The two defendants had done building repairs on V's house. V was refusing to pay because he claimed the repairs had been poorly done. The defendants went to V's house and D1 said 'Step outside the house and we will sort this out'. D2 said in a threatening way 'Come on mate, come outside'. Later it was found that D1 was carrying a flick knife in his coat. The Court of Appeal upheld the defendants' convictions for blackmail.

In *Clear* (1968) it was said that the menace must be 'of such a nature and extent that the mind of an ordinary person of normal stability and courage might be influenced or made apprehensive by it so as to unwillingly accede to it'. It is not necessary to prove that the victim was actually intimidated. So if the menaces would affect an ordinary person this is sufficient, but if they would not, then blackmail cannot usually be proved. This was shown in *Harry* (1974).

Harry (1974)

D, who was the treasurer of a college rag committee, sent letters to 115 local shopkeepers asking them to buy a poster with the money to go to charity. The poster contained the words: 'These premises are immune from all Rag 73 activities whatever they may be'. The letter sent out indicated that paying for a poster would avoid 'any rag activity which could in any way cause you inconvenience.' Of the 115 shopkeepers who received that letter only about five complained. The trial judge pointed out that as a group the shopkeepers who had received the letter were unconcerned about the supposed 'threat'. He, therefore, ruled that according to the definition given in *Clear*, blackmail was not proved. There had not been any 'threat' which influenced or made them apprehensive so as to unwillingly accede to the demand.

However, in *Garwood* (1987) the Court of Appeal said that where a threat is made which would not affect a normal person, this can still be menaces if the defendant was aware of the likely effect on the victim. So, for example, if D knows that V is extremely attached to an item such as a prize rose or a pet dog, then threats to destroy that item or kill the dog could be menaces for the purpose of blackmail.

The fact that V does not give into the menaces does not prevent D from being guilty. For example V may refuse to pay up and instead go to the police to report D's menaces. D is still guilty of blackmail.

13.4 View to gain or to intent to cause loss

The *mens rea* of blackmail includes that D must be acting with a view to gain for himself or another or with intent to cause loss to another. The interpretation section in the Theft Act 1968, 34(2)(a) defines 'gain' and 'loss'. This states that:

> (2) For the purposes of this Act-
>   (a) 'gain' and 'loss' are to be construed as extending only to gain or loss in money or other property, but as extending to any such gain or loss whether temporary or permanent; and—
>   (i) 'gain' includes a gain by keeping what one has, as well as a gain by getting what one has not; and
>   (ii) 'loss' included a loss by not getting what one might get, as well as a loss by parting with what one has.

So the view to gain for himself or the intent to cause loss to another has to involve money or other property.

Property has the same meaning as for theft. So it covers:

- money
- real property (land and buildings)
- personal property (all moveable items e.g. DVDs, jewellery, cars, clothing)
- things in action (things which give a right – e.g. cheques, logos, tickets)
- other intangible property.

But the gain or loss need not be intended to be permanent, it can be temporary.

Even where D does not succeed in making the gain or causing the loss he intended, he is still guilty of blackmail. The important point is that he made the unwarranted demand with a view to gain or an intent to cause a loss.

An unusual case on view to a gain or intent to cause a loss was *Bevans* (1988).

Bevans (1988)

D, who was suffering from severe osteoarthritis, pointed a gun at his doctor and demanded a morphine injection for pain relief. The doctor gave him the injection. It was held that the morphine was property and, also, that it was both a gain for the defendant and a loss to the doctor from whom it was demanded

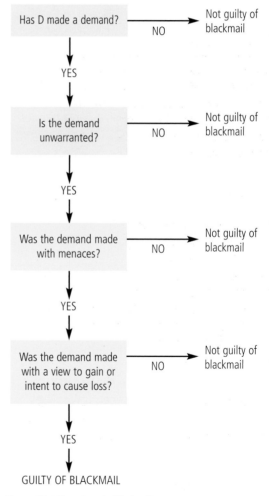

Figure 13.1 Flow chart for blackmail

Key facts

Element	Explanation	Cases
Demand	Can be by any method Can be implicit If the demand is posted, it is effective at the moment of posting	*Collister and Warhurst* (1955) *Treacy v DPP* (1971)
Unwarranted	Not unwarranted under s 21(1) Theft Act 1968 if D believed: (a) he had reasonable grounds for making the demand; and (b) the use of the menaces was a proper means of reinforcing the demand.	*Harvey* (1981)
With menaces	Menaces is an ordinary English word which any jury can be expected to understand Must be 'of such a nature and extent that the mind of an ordinary person of normal stability and courage might be influenced or made apprehensive by it so as to unwillingly accede to it'	*Lawrence and Pomroy* (1971) *Clear* (1968) *Harry* (1974)
With a view to gain or intent to cause loss	Must intend to make a gain or cause a loss of money or other property. The gain or loss need not actually happen	*Bevans* (1988)

Key Facts chart on blackmail

Activity

Explain whether the following situations could be blackmail.

1. Sue sees Tony, a shelf filler in the local supermarket, taking some batteries from a shelf and hiding them in his pocket. She tells Tony she will tell the supermarket supervisor what she has seen unless Tony buys a DVD for her.

2. Romsey tells Vijay that he will destroy Vijay's prize vegetable marrows which Vijay is intending to enter in a local garden competition unless Vijay pays him £500.

3. Two weeks ago Peaches lent Maria £50. She now tells Maria that she will get her brother to beat up Maria unless Maria pays her back the £50 by tomorrow.

Chapter 14

Fraud and making off without payment

14.1 Fraud Act 2006

The previous law on fraud and deception was thought to be in need of a complete reform. As a result the Fraud Act 2006 was enacted. This Act repealed sections 15, 15A, 15B, 16 and 20(2) of the Theft Act 1968 and also sections 1 and 2 of the Theft Act 1978. These previous offences are replaced by an offence of fraud. This can be committed in three different ways. The main way is:

- fraud by false representation (s 2).

The Fraud Act 2006 also creates other offences connected to fraud. One of these is:

- obtaining services dishonestly (s 11).

14.2 Fraud by false representation

Under s 2 of the Fraud Act 2006, the offence of fraud by false representation is committed if D:

'(a) dishonestly makes a false representation, and
(b) intends, by making the representation–

(i) to make a gain for himself or another, or
(ii) to cause loss to another or to expose another to the risk of loss.'

The *actus reus* of the offence is that the defendant must make a representation which is false. The *mens rea* has three parts to it. The defendant must be dishonest, he or she must know or believe the representation to be untrue or misleading and there must be an intention to make a gain or cause a loss.

14.2.1 Representation

The Fraud Act gives some help with what is meant by a representation. Section 2(3) states that:

'"Representation" means any representation as to fact or law, including making a representation as to the state of mind of–
(a) the person making the representation, or
(b) any other person.'

From this, it can be seen that 'representation' covers a wide area. A representation as to fact clearly covers situations where someone uses a false identity or states that they own property when they do not. It also covers situations such as someone stating that a car has only done 22,000 miles when they know it has done double that amount.

A representation as to law covers any situation where the defendant states the law knowing that what they say is not true.

A representation as to state of mind covers such matters as a customer saying they will pay their bill when they have no intention of doing so.

The Act also states that a representation may be express or implied (s 2(4)).

Representations to machines

The representation can be made to a person or to a machine. Section 2(5) specifically covers all devices and systems. It states:

> 'A representation may be regarded as made if it (or anything implying it) is submitted in any form to any system or device designed to receive, convey or respond to communications (with or without human intervention).'

This is designed to cover the many situations in the modern world where it is possible to obtain property via a machine or the internet or other automated system such as cash dispensers or automated telephone services. The provision in the act is wide enough to cover putting a false coin into a machine to obtain sweets or other goods or submitting a claim on the internet.

Express representations

The explanatory notes to the Fraud Act make it clear that there is no limit on the way in which the representation must be expressed. The notes point out that it could, for example, be written or spoken or posted on a website.

A written statement includes where D shows a false identity card or where D provides a false reference.

It also is likely to include giving an excessive quotation for work to be done, especially where it is represented that more work is needed than is actually required. This was decided in the case of *Silverman* (1987). This case was under the old law prior to the Fraud Act 2006 where it was necessary to show that there had been an untrue representation. Although the old cases are no longer binding precedent, it is likely that the courts will look back to these cases for guidance.

Silverman (1987)

D gave an excessive quotation to two elderly sisters for work to be done on their flat. He had done work for them previously and had built up a situation of 'mutual trust'. By giving an exorbitant quotation he was deceiving them as to the true cost of the repairs and the amount of profit he was making. The Court of Appeal accepted that this could be a deception, although they quashed his conviction because of an inadequate summing up to the jury.

NB This situation would now be more likely to be charged as the offence of fraud by abuse of position under s 4 of the Fraud Act 2006.

The explanatory notes to the Act also point out that the offence can be committed by 'phishing' on the internet. That is where a person sends out an email to a large number of people falsely representing that the email has been sent by a legitimate bank. The email asks the receiver to provide information such as credit card and bank numbers so that the 'phisher' can gain access to others' assets.

Implied representations

There are many ways in which it is possible to make an implied representation through one's conduct. This was shown by the old case of *Barnard* (1837).

Barnard (1837)

D went into a shop in Oxford wearing the cap and gown of a fellow commoner of the university. He also said he was a fellow commoner and as a result the shopkeeper agreed to sell him goods on credit. The court said, *obiter*, that he would have been guilty even if he had said nothing. The wearing of the cap and gown was itself a false pretence.

In fact the case of *Barnard* demonstrates both an implied representation and an express representation. The wearing of the cap and gown was an implied representation while the statement that he was a fellow commoner was an express representation.

A more modern example of an implied representation would be standing on a street corner with a collecting box labelled 'Guide Dogs for the Blind'. This is implying that D is collecting on behalf of the charity. If D intends to pocket the money then he is guilty under s 2 of the Fraud Act 2006.

Although there is no definition of what is meant by implied false representation by conduct in the Fraud Act, the explanatory notes to the Act state that:

 'An example of a representation by conduct is where a person dishonestly misuses a credit card to pay for items. By tendering the card, he is falsely representing that he has the authority to use it.'

This example is the same situation as occurred in the case of *Lambie* (1981) under the old law on deception.

Lambie (1981)

D had a credit card (Barclaycard) with a £200 limit. She exceeded this limit and the bank which had issued the card wrote asking her to return

the card. She agreed that she would return the card on 7th December 1977, but she did not do so. On 15th December 1977 she purchased goods worth £10.35 in a Mothercare shop with the card. She was convicted of obtaining a pecuniary advantage by deception contrary to s 16(1) of the Theft Act 1968. The Court of Appeal allowed her appeal but the House of Lords reinstated the conviction.

It is likely that the courts will still look back to decisions under the old law on the point of whether D's acts are an implied representation, though, of course, they do not have to do so.

Under the old law several other situations of implied representation were identified. These included:

- ordering and eating a meal in a restaurant: this is a representation that the meal will be paid for
- paying by cheque: this is a representation that the bank will honour the cheque
- use of a cheque guarantee card: this represents that the user of the card has the bank's authority to use it.

All these situations were considered in cases under the law pre the Fraud Act 2006.

Intention to pay for a meal

DPP v Ray (1973)

D went to a restaurant with three friends. He did not have enough money to pay for a meal but one of his friends agreed to lend him enough to pay for the meal. After eating the meal they all decided not to pay for it. Ten minutes later when the waiter went into the kitchen all four ran out of the restaurant without paying. The Court of Appeal had quashed the defendant's conviction for obtaining a pecuniary advantage under s 16(2)(a) of the Theft Act 1968 (this section has now been repealed). The House of Lords reinstated the conviction. The problem was whether the defendant could be guilty when his original representation that he would pay was genuine. Did the change of mind produce a deception? The House of Lords held that it did.

Paying by cheque

Gilmartin (1983)

D, a stationer, paid for supplies with post-dated cheques which he knew would not be met. This was held to be a deception. By drawing the cheques he was representing that there would be funds in the account to meet the cheques on the dates they were due to be presented.

Use of a cheque guarantee card

Metropolitan Police Commander v Charles (1976)

D had a bank account with an overdraft facility of £100. The bank had issued him with a cheque card which guaranteed that any cheques he wrote up to £30 would be honoured by the bank. D wrote out 25 cheques for £30 in order to buy gaming chips and backed each cheque with the cheque card. He knew that the bank would have to pay the gambling club the money so there was no deception in respect of the fact that the cheques would be honoured. However, he knew that he did not have enough money in his account to meet the cheques and also that the amount would exceed his overdraft limit. He had also been told by the bank manager that he should not use the card to cash more than one cheque of £30 a day.

The House of Lords held that there was a false representation that he had the bank's authority to use the card in the way he did and upheld his conviction under s 16 of the Theft Act 1968 of obtaining a pecuniary advantage by deception.

14.2.2 False

For the purposes of the Fraud Act 2006 a representation is false if:

(a) it is untrue or misleading, and
(b) the person making it knows that it is, or might be, untrue or misleading.

So making a false representation means representing what one knows or believes is untrue or what one knows or believes is a misleading statement. It does not matter whether anyone believes that lie. Nor does it matter whether the defendant gains any advantage from the representation.

It is a matter of fact whether something is true or not. The difficult word in the phrase is 'misleading'. It is not defined in the Act, but the Government, in their paper *Fraud Law: Government Response to Consultation* (2004), stated that a representation was misleading if it was:

> 'less than wholly true and capable of interpretation to the detriment of the victim'.

14.2.3 Gain or loss

This offence requires that D intends to make a gain for himself or another, or to cause loss to another, or to expose another to the risk of loss. Both 'gain' and 'loss' mean gain or loss in money or other property.

Property for this purpose is defined in s 5 of the Fraud Act 2006 as:

> 'any property whether real or personal including things in action and other intangible property'.

Note that this is very similar to the definition of property in s 4(1) of the Theft Act 1968.

'Gain' includes a gain by keeping what one has as well as a gain by getting what one does not have. 'Loss' includes a loss by not getting what one might get as well as a loss by parting with what one has.

The gain or loss can be temporary or permanent.

14.2.4 *Mens rea*

As already stated in the opening section of this chapter, the *mens rea* of the offence of fraud by false representation has three parts to it. The defendant must:

- be dishonest
- know or believe the representation to be untrue or misleading
- have an intention to make a gain or cause a loss.

Dishonesty

The explanatory notes issued by the Government with the Act make it clear that the *Ghosh* test for dishonesty used in theft cases (see 11.4.3) applies to this new offence.

Ghosh sets out a two-stage test. The first question is whether a defendant's behaviour would be regarded as dishonest by the ordinary standards of reasonable and honest people. If the answer to that question is 'yes', then the second question is whether the defendant was aware that his conduct was dishonest and would be regarded as dishonest by reasonable and honest people.

Know or believe the representation to be untrue or misleading

To be guilty the defendant must know that the representation he or she is making is, or might be, untrue or misleading. This is a subjective test. The focus is on what the defendant knew.

Intention to make a gain or cause a loss

The wording of the offence means that it is not necessary for the fraud to succeed. It is only necessary for the defendant to intend to make a gain or cause a loss.

Activity

1. Anika, who owns a shop, puts a collecting box on the counter with a label 'Cancer Research' on it. Customers often put coins in it. Anika keeps all the money which customers put in the box.

2. Bennet and Candy go to a local restaurant. Candy believes they are each going to pay for their own meal but, unknown to her, Bennet has decided that he will leave without paying. They both order a meal. When they have eaten, Bennet gets up to leave. Candy asks him about paying and he says 'Come on, there's no one looking, we can just go' and he walks out the door. Candy waits a few minutes and then decides to leave without paying.

3. Donna has discovered that fake coins provided with one of her child's toys fit into a slot machine selling cigarettes. She uses one of the fake coins to obtain a packet of cigarettes from the machine. Later that day she uses two more fake coins to pay for a magazine in a newsagent's shop.

4. Elvis has a credit card. He has not paid his debt on the credit card for three months and the card company have written to him saying that he must make a minimum payment or else they will ask him to return the card. Elvis does not pay anything off the debt but continues using the card. A month later he receives a letter from the card company. He does not open it, but goes out and buys a new pair of trainers using the card. When he gets home he opens the letter and finds out that the card company have withdrawn his right to use the card and asked him to return it.

Key facts

Definition of offence	D dishonestly makes a false representation and intends, by making the representation • to make a gain for himself or another, or • to cause loss to another or to expose another to the risk of loss	s 2(1) Fraud Act 2006
Actus reus	• make a representation	Can be any representation as to fact or law, including making a representation as to state of mind s 2(3) Fraud Act 2006 Representation can be express or implied s 2(4) Fraud Act 2006 It is false if it is untrue or misleading s 2(2) Fraud Act 2006
	• representation must be false	
Mens rea	• dishonestly • knows or believes representation to be untrue or misleading • intends to make a gain or cause a loss	*Ghosh* two-part test is intended to apply Explanatory notes Gain/loss must be of money or property s 5 Fraud Act 2006
Representations made to machines or automated services	A representation is regarded as being made when it is submitted to any form of system or device	s 2(5) Fraud Act 2006

Key Facts chart on fraud by false representation

Under the old law the prosecution had to prove that the deception had caused the obtaining of property. This led to problems in many cases. An example of such a case is *Laverty* (1970).

Laverty (1970)

D changed the registration number plates and the chassis number on a car and sold the car to P. The changing of the numbers was a representation that the car was the original car to which these numbers had been allocated. However, the conviction was quashed as P had merely said in evidence that he thought that D was the owner of the car. There was no evidence that the deception regarding the number plates had influenced P to buy the car, so there was no proof that D had obtained the purchase money from P as a result of the particular deception.

Under the new offence of fraud by false representation it is not necessary to show that P was influenced to buy the car because of its new number plates. D would now be guilty of the new offence. All the prosecution has to prove is that D intended to make a gain from his act.

It does not matter that the victim becomes suspicious, does not hand over any property, but reports the matter to the police. The defendant has still committed the completed offence as he intended to make a gain or cause a loss.

14.3 Obtaining services dishonestly

This offence was created to replace sections 1 and 2 of the Theft Act 1978 and also s 15A of the Theft Act 1968. All of these had caused considerable difficulty in interpretation.

The new offence is under s 11 of the Fraud Act 2006 which states:

 '11(1) A person is guilty of an offence under this section if he obtains services for himself or another –
　　　(a) by a dishonest act, and
　　　(b) in breach of subsection (2).

11(2) A person obtains services in breach of this subsection if–
　　　(a) they are made available on the basis that payment has been or will be made for or in respect of them;
　　　(b) he obtains them without any payment having been made for or in respect of them or without payment having been made in full, and
　　　(c) when he obtains them he knows–
　　　　(i) that they are being made available on the basis described in paragraph (a), or
　　　　(ii) that they might be, but intends that payment will not be made, or will not be made in full.

The *actus reus* of this offence has several parts to it. These are:

- there must be an act; the offence cannot be committed by omission
- obtains
- services
- not paid for or not paid in full.

The *mens rea* consists of three parts:

- dishonesty
- intending that payment will not be made or will not be made in full
- intention not to pay or not to pay in full.

We will now go on to look at the *actus reus* and *mens rea* in more detail.

14.3.1 *Actus reus* of obtaining services dishonestly

Obtains

The offence requires that the services are actually obtained. This is unlike the offence of fraud by false representation which we considered above in 14.2. For that offence it was not necessary for anything to be obtained. The making of the false representation intending to make a gain or cause a loss was sufficient.

Services

These are not defined by the Act, but the explanatory notes to the Act give examples of situations where services are obtained. These include:

- using false credit card details to obtain services on the Internet
- climbing over a wall and watching a football match without paying the entrance fee.

There are many other situations which would be offences under this section. These could include:

- using a false bus pass to get a free or reduced price journey
- claiming falsely to be under 14 in order to have cheaper admission to see a film in a cinema
- using a stolen decoder card to receive satellite television programmes.

The defendant only has to obtain the service dishonestly. It is not necessary to show that he has deceived anyone. This is shown by the example of climbing over a wall to watch a football match without paying for entry. The defendant has not shown any false ticket or deceived anyone, but he is still guilty of the offence of obtaining services dishonestly.

Not paid for

The offence is only committed if the defendant does not pay anything or does not pay in full for the service. Even if the defendant has made a false statement, but pays full price for the service, then he has not committed the offence of obtaining services dishonestly.

14.3.2 *Mens rea* of obtaining services dishonestly

Dishonesty

This is not defined in the act, nor is any mention made of it in the explanatory notes to the Act. This is different to fraud by false representation where the explanatory notes say that it is intended the *Ghosh* two-part test should apply.

This makes it difficult to know whether the *Ghosh* two-part test will be applied by the courts. However, it seems likely that it will. If so the first question will be whether a defendant's behaviour would be regarded as dishonest by the ordinary standards of reasonable and honest people. If the answer to that question is 'yes', then the second question will be whether the defendant was aware that his conduct was dishonest and would be regarded as dishonest by reasonable and honest people.

Intention not to pay

The prosecution must prove that the defendant intended not to pay or not to pay in full for the services. If the defendant thought that someone else had already paid then he would not be guilty of this offence.

14.4 Making off without payment

This offence was created when it became obvious that Theft Act 1968 left gaps in the law where D was not guilty of any offence, even though his conduct would be seen as 'criminal' by most people.

One of the gaps became apparent in *Greenburg* (1972).

Greenburg (1972)

D had filled his car up at a garage and then driven off without paying. He was not guilty of theft because when he drove away the petrol belonged to him. This is because the civil law rules on the transfer of ownership in a sale of goods state that the goods become D's the moment that the petrol is put into the tank of his car. It was also not possible to prove that he was dishonest when he put the petrol in his tank because he claimed he had driven into the garage intending to pay. He only decided not to pay when he had filled up the tank.

Section 3(1) of the Theft Act 1978 was enacted to cover this situation. The section states:

> '3(1) [A] person who, knowing that payment on the spot for any goods supplied or service done is required or expected from him, dishonestly makes off without having paid as required or expected and with intent to avoid payment of the amount due shall be guilty of an offence.'

The goods supplied or service done must be lawful. If the supply of goods is unlawful (eg cigarettes to someone under 16) or the service is not legally enforceable (eg prostitution), then no offence has been committed.

The offence covers a wide range of situations which include running off without paying for a haircut or a taxi ride. It can also apply to customers in restaurants who go without paying for their meal or hotel guests who leave without paying their bill.

14.4.1 *Actus reus* of making off without payment

There are several points which have to proved. These are that:

- D makes off
- goods have been supplied or a service done
- payment is required on the spot
- D has not paid as required.

Makes off

A key ingredient of the offence is that D 'makes off'. In other words, he leaves the scene where payment was expected. This is a question of fact, as shown in *McDavitt* (1981).

McDavitt (1981)

D had an argument with the manager of a restaurant and refused to pay his bill for a meal. He got up and started to walk out but was advised not to leave as the police had been called. He then went into the toilet and stayed there until the police came. The judge directed the jury to acquit D at the end of the prosecution case as he had not 'made off'.

Goods have been supplied or a service done

If the service is not completed then there is no offence. This was shown in the case of *Troughton v Metropolitan Police* (1987).

Troughton v Metropolitan Police (1987)

D, who was drunk, hired a taxi to take him home but did not give the driver his address. The driver stopped to get directions from D and there was an argument in which D accused the driver of taking an unnecessary diversion. As the taxi driver was unable to get the exact address from D, he drove to the nearest police station to see if someone could help. When the taxi stopped D ran off.

The magistrates convicted D but, on appeal to the Queen's Bench Divisional Court, the conviction was quashed. This was because the journey had not been completed. That meant there was a breach of contract by the taxi driver and so D was not bound to pay the fare.

Payment required on the spot

It has to be proved that payment on the spot was required or expected. If it is not then the offence is not committed. This was seen in *Vincent* (2001).

Vincent (2001)

D had stayed at two hotels and not paid his bills. He said that he had arranged with the proprietors of each hotel to pay when he could. This meant that payment on the spot was not required or expected. At his trial the judge directed the jury that the defendant could not rely on a dishonestly obtained agreement to avoid payment. His conviction was quashed as s 3 merely states that payment on the spot must be required or expected. If there had been an agreement not to expect payment on the spot, it was irrelevant for the purposes of s 3 that that agreement had been dishonestly obtained.

D has not paid

This is a matter of fact. The payment must be of the amount due.

14.4.2 *Mens rea* of making off without payment

The *mens rea* of the offence involves:

- dishonesty
- knowledge that payment on the spot is required
- an intention to avoid payment.

Dishonesty

The test for dishonesty is the same as for theft. This means that the *Ghosh* two-part test applies.

Knowledge that payment on the spot is required

If the defendant does not know that payment is required on the spot, then he is not guilty of this offence.

Intention to avoid payment

The Act only states 'with intent to avoid payment of the amount due' but in *Allen* (1985) the House of Lords held that there must be an intent *permanently* to avoid payment.

Allen (1985)

D owed £1,286 for his stay at a hotel. He left without paying, but his defence was that he genuinely intended to pay in the near future as he was expecting to receive sufficient money to cover the bill. His conviction was quashed because it had not been proved that he intended to evade payment altogether.

It has been argued that this decision in *Allen* allows defendants to put forward fictitious defences of what they hoped to be able to do about payment in the future. But there have been no further cases on this point, so presumably the law is working satisfactorily.

Activity

Discuss the criminal liability, if any, in each of the following situations.

1. Julie, aged 57, goes to her local DIY store on the day when they have a special 10% discount for people over 60. Julie buys goods worth £70 and at the checkout she falsely claims to be over 60 and is given a discount of £7.
2. Kavita fills her car up at a petrol station. She knows she has not got enough money on her to pay so she uses her credit card even though she knows she has exceeded her limit and the credit card company have asked her to return the card. In the shop she uses a fake coin to obtain some chocolate from a machine.
3. Lennox takes a ride in a taxi to the railway station. When the taxi arrives there, Lennox jumps out and runs off without paying the fare.
4. Marcia stays at a health spa for two nights. While there she uses the leisure facilities and has a beauty treatment. She also has meals in the restaurant. When she checks out at the end of her stay she uses a stolen credit card to pay for everything.

Chapter 15

Criminal damage

The law on criminal damage is contained in the Criminal Damage Act 1971. This Act creates four offences which are:

- the basic offence of criminal damage
- aggravated criminal damage
- arson
- aggravated arson.

15.1 The basic offence

The basic offence is set out in s 1(1) Criminal Damage Act 1971 which states that:

> 'A person who without lawful excuse destroys or damages any property belonging to another intending to destroy or damage any such property or being reckless as to whether any such property would be destroyed or damaged shall be guilty of an offence.'

The *actus reus* of the basic offence is made up of three elements. These are that the defendant must:

- destroy or damage
- property
- belonging to another.

15.1.1 Destroy or damage

This phrase is not defined in the Act. However, the same phrase was used in the law prior to the 1971 Act, and old cases ruled that even slight damage was sufficient to prove damage; for example in *Gayford v Chouler* (1898) trampling down grass was held to be damage. The cases prior to the Criminal Damage Act 1971 are, of course, no longer binding but they may still be used as persuasive precedent.

'Destroy' is a much stronger word than 'damage' and it includes where the property has been made useless even though it is not completely destroyed.

Damage covers a wide range of situations as shown by the following cases.

Roe v Kingerlee (1986)

The Divisional Court said that whether property has been damaged was a 'matter of fact and degree'. In that case the defendant had smeared mud on the walls of a police cell, which cost £7 to be cleaned off. It was held that this could be damage even though it was not permanent.

Other cases have also held that non-permanent damage can come within the definition of 'damage'. The courts' approach seems to be based on whether it will cost money, time and/or effort to remove the damage. If so then an offence has been committed, but if not then there is no offence. This is illustrated in the following cases.

Hardman v Chief Constable of Avon and Somerset Constabulary (1986)

CND protesters painted silhouettes on the pavement with water soluble paint, to mark the fortieth anniversary of the dropping of the atomic bomb on Hiroshima. The local council removed the paintings with water jets. The defendants argued that the damage was only temporary, the paintings would have quickly been erased by the weather and by people walking on them, and there was no need for the local council to go to the expense of having the paintings removed by high-pressure water jets. The court held that this was damage.

Blake v DPP (1993)

The defendant wrote a biblical quotation on a concrete pillar. This needed to be cleaned off and so it was held to be criminal damage.

The 'temporary impairment of value or usefulness' was the key factor in *Fiak* (2005).

Fiak (2005)

D was arrested on suspicion of being in charge of a vehicle when he was over the limit for alcohol and for assault on a police officer. He was taken to a police station and placed in a cell. He put a blanket in the toilet in the cell and flushed the toilet several times. This caused water to overflow and flood the cell and two adjoining cells. The blanket was not visibly soiled but it had to be cleaned and dried before it could be used again. The cells had to be cleaned. This was held to be criminal damage.

If there are no costs or effort in clearing up, and the property can continue to be used, then there is no offence. This is shown by *A (a juvenile) v R* (1978).

A (a juvenile) v R (1978)

The defendant spat at a policeman and spit landed on the policeman's uniform. It was held that this was not damage as it could be wiped off with a wet cloth with very little effort. It is possible that a different decision would have been reached if the spit had landed on a light

Activity

Explain whether or not there is damage within the meaning of the Criminal Damage Act 1971 in each of the following situations:

1. Aisha throws a bucket of clean water over Beth. The water thoroughly wets Beth's jacket and skirt. Would it make any difference to your answer if the water was muddy?

2. Conrad writes with white chalk on the brick wall of the local town hall.
3. Dan is working on a construction site. He throws a spanner down. It hits a wall which is being constructed and causes a small piece of brick to chip off. The spanner also hits a scaffolding post and causes a small dent in it. The spanner itself is slightly bent as a result.

coloured T-shirt and left a stain, so that the T-shirt needed washing or dry cleaning. As cost would be incurred in those circumstances, it could be considered as damage.

The type and purpose of the property may be relevant, as in *Morphitis v Salmon* (1990) where it was held that a scratch on a scaffolding pole was not damage. Scaffolding poles are likely to get quite scratched in the ordinary course of use and it does not affect their usefulness or integrity. However, a scratch on a car would almost certainly be considered damage.

15.1.2 Property

Property is defined in s 10(1) Criminal Damage Act 1971. This section says that 'property' means property of a tangible nature, whether real or personal, including money. It includes wild creatures which have been tamed or are ordinarily kept in captivity. It also includes other wild creatures or their carcasses if they are in someone's possession.

Personal property covers all items which can be owned by people. The term is very wide and includes clothing, furniture, electronic equipment, tools, cars, boats etc. The list is almost endless. Real property means land and buildings or other structures attached to the land.

However, property for the purposes of criminal damage does not including mushrooms growing wild on any land or flowers, fruit or foliage of a plant growing wild on any land.

The wording in the 1971 Act is similar to the Theft Act 1968 but there are two main differences. First, land is property which can be damaged although it can only be stolen in certain circumstances and secondly, intangible rights cannot be damaged, though they may be stolen.

15.1.3 Belonging to another

The definition of 'belonging to another' is set out in s 10(2) and is similar to the definition which is used for the purposes of theft. Property is treated

as belonging to any person:

1. having the custody or control of it; or
2. having in it any proprietary right or interest; or
3. having a charge on it.

This gives the same wide definition of 'belonging to' as in theft. It is not restricted to the owner. In fact a co-owner can be guilty of criminal damage as the other co-owner has a proprietary right in the property.

Smith (1974)

The defendant removed some electrical wiring, which he had earlier fitted in the flat which he rented. In doing this he damaged some of the fixtures he had put in. In civil law these fixtures belong to the landlord and this was property 'belonging to another'. However, the defendant was found not guilty because he lacked the necessary *mens rea* (see 15.1.4).

It is important to note that for the purposes of the basic offence, the property affected must belong to another. A person cannot be guilty of the basic offence if the property he destroys or damages is his own. However, for the aggravated offence a person can be guilty even though it is his own property (see 15.2).

15.1.4 *Mens rea* of the basic offence

The defendant must do the damage or destruction either intentionally or recklessly. For the meanings of intention and recklessness the Law Commission, who recommended the reform of the law which led to the passing of the Criminal Damage Act 1971, meant for the previous principles of *mens rea* used in criminal damage cases to continue to apply.

Before the passing of the Criminal Damage Act 1971, the law on criminal damage was contained in the Malicious Damage Act 1861. This Act used the phrase 'unlawfully and maliciously'. Maliciously was taken to have the meaning of either intending the damage or knowing there was a risk of damage and taking that risk. This type of risk-taking is known as subjective recklessness.

When the Law Commission recommended reform of the law, they identified the essential mental element in the malicious damage offences as 'intent to do the forbidden act or recklessness in relation to its foreseen consequences'. They suggested replacing the old-fashioned word of 'maliciously' with the phrase 'intending or being reckless'. This was meant to have the same meaning as the courts had given to the word 'maliciously'.

Intention

The defendant must intend to destroy or damage property belonging to another. Proving the act is not enough; there must be intention to do the damage as was seen in the old case of *Pembliton* (1874).

Pembliton (1874)

The defendant threw a stone at some men with whom he had been fighting. The stone missed them but hit and broke a window. The defendant was not guilty of causing damage to the window as he had no intention to damage the window (or any other property) even though he intended to throw the stone.

The second point is the need to intend to damage property 'belonging to another'. This was illustrated in *Smith* (1974). Smith mistakenly believed that the property he was damaging was his own. His conviction was quashed by the Court of Appeal who said:

> 'Honest belief, whether justifiable or not, that the property is the defendant's own negatives the element of *mens rea.*'

Reckless

Initially the courts used the meaning of subjective recklessness. In *Stephenson* (1979) the defendant was a tramp who sheltered in a hollow in a haystack and, because he was cold, lit a fire there. The haystack caught fire and was destroyed. The Court of Appeal quashed the defendant's conviction on the grounds that, although an ordinary person would realise the risk of the haystack catching fire, he did not realise this as he suffered from schizophrenia and this point should have been left to the jury to decide. The Court of Appeal was using the subjective test for reckless.

However, in *Caldwell* (1981) the House of Lords changed the law. They ruled that a person was reckless if he did an act which in fact created an obvious risk that property would be destroyed and, when he did the act he either:

- had not given any thought to the possibility of there being any risk (objective); or
- had recognised that there was some risk involved, and has nonetheless gone on to take it (subjective).

This was known as *Caldwell* recklessness and, as can be seen, it included both subjective and objective recklessness. The objective test considered whether the risk was obvious to an ordinary prudent person. If so, then the fact that the defendant did not give any thought to the possibility of there being any risk was enough to make the defendant guilty.

This objective test was harsh in its application, particularly where the defendant was young or had learning difficulties. This was seen in *Elliott v C* (1983) where the defendant was incapable of appreciating the risk but was still guilty under this test.

Elliott v C (1983)

The defendant was a 14-year-old girl with severe learning difficulties who had been out all night without food or sleep. She got into a garden shed and, in an effort to get warm, poured white spirit on to the carpet and set light to it. The magistrates found that she had given no thought to the possibility that the shed might be destroyed. They also found that in the circumstances the risk would not have been obvious to her and they acquitted her. The prosecution appealed by way of case stated to the Queen's Bench Divisional Court which ruled that as the risk would have been obvious to a reasonably prudent man, the magistrates had to convict the girl.

This objective test was used up to 2003. Then in *Gemmell and Richards* (2003) the House of Lords overruled *Caldwell* (1981) and reinstated the subjective test for recklessness.

Gemmell and Richards (2003) also known as *G and R* (2003)

The defendants were two boys aged 11 and 12 years. During a night out camping, they went into the yard of a shop and set fire to some bundles of newspapers which they threw under a large wheelie bin. They then left the yard. They expected that as there was a concrete floor under the wheelie bin the fire would extinguish itself. In fact the bin caught fire and this spread to the shop and other buildings causing about £1 million damage. The boys were convicted under both ss 1 and 3 Criminal Damage Act 1971.

The trial judge directed the jury that whether there was an obvious risk of the shop and other buildings being damaged should be decided by reference to the reasonable man, ie the reasonable adult. He told them that the ordinary reasonable man is an adult and that no allowance could be made by the law for the youth of the two boys.

The House of Lords quashed their convictions and ruled that a defendant could not be guilty

unless he had realised the risk and decided to take it. They overruled the decision in *Caldwell* (1981) holding that in that case the Law Lords had 'adopted an interpretation of section 1 of the 1971 Act which was beyond the range of feasible meanings'.

They emphasised that the Law Commission had intended that there should be no change in the *mens rea* required for the offence. They were only replacing the old expression 'maliciously' by the more familiar expression 'reckless'. Parliament must also have intended this as they accepted the Bill in the form drafted by the Law Commission.

The effect of this decision is that 'reckless' in s 1 Criminal Damage Act 1971 is now clearly subjective in its meaning. The defendant can only be guilty if he realised the risk of the damage.

15.1.5 Without lawful excuse

The Act defines two lawful excuses in s 5. These are available only for the basic offence. They apply where the defendant honestly believes either that:

- the owner (or another person with rights in the property) would have consented to the damage; or
- other property was at risk and in need of immediate protection and what he did was reasonable in all the circumstances.

In these situations the important point is that the defendant must honestly believe one of these. It does not matter whether the belief is justified or not, provided it is honestly held.

Belief in consent

In *Denton* (1982) the defendant, who worked in a cotton mill, thought that his employer had encouraged him to set fire to the mill so that the employer could make an insurance claim. The Court of Appeal quashed his conviction as he had a defence under s 5(2)(a).

Intoxicated mistakes

The combination of s 5(2)(a) and s 5(3) allows a defence of mistake to be used, even where the defendant makes the mistake because they are intoxicated.

Jaggard v Dickinson (1980)

The defendant, who was drunk, went to what she thought was a friend's house. There was no one in and so she broke a window to get in as she believed (accurately) her friend would consent to this. Unfortunately in her drunken state she had mistaken the house and had actually broken into the house of another person.

The Divisional Court quashed her conviction holding that she could rely on her intoxicated belief as Parliament had 'specifically required the court to consider the defendant's actual state of belief, not the state of belief which ought to have existed'. They pointed out that a belief may be honestly held whether it is caused by intoxication, stupidity, forgetfulness or inattention.

Belief that other property was in immediate need of protection

Section 5(2)(b) could give a defence in situations where trees are cut down or a building demolished to prevent the spread of fire. A case in which the defence was successfully pleaded in a jury trial was in April 2000 when Lord Melchett and several other members of Greenpeace damaged genetically modified (GM) crops in order to prevent non-GM crops in neighbouring fields being contaminated with pollen from the GM crops. The judge allowed the defence to go to the jury, but they were unable to agree on a verdict. A retrial was ordered and this time the jury acquitted the defendants.

If the defendant has another purpose in doing the damage, then the court may rule that the defence is not available to him as in *Hunt* (1978).

Hunt (1978)

The defendant helped his wife in her post as deputy warden of a block of old people's flats. He set fire to some bedding in order, as he claimed, to draw attention to the fact that the fire alarm was not in working order. The judge refused to allow a defence under s 5(2)(b) to go to the jury as his act was not done in order to protect property which was in immediate need of protection. The Court of Appeal upheld his conviction, despite the very subjective wording of s 5(2)(b).

In the case of *Blake v DPP* (1993) the defendant put forward defences under both s 5(2)(a) and s 5(2)(b).

Blake v DPP (1993)

The defendant was a vicar who believed that the Government should not use military force in Kuwait and Iraq in the Gulf War. He wrote a biblical quotation with a marker pen on a concrete post outside the Houses of Parliament. He claimed that:

- he was carrying out the instructions of God and this gave him a defence under s 5(2)(a) as God was entitled to consent to the damage of property, and

- the damage he did was in order to protect the property of civilians in Kuwait and Iraq and so he had a defence under s 5(2)(b).

He was convicted and appealed, but both the claims were rejected. The court held that God could not consent to damage and that what he did was not capable of protecting property in the Gulf judged objectively, again despite the apparent subjective wording of both s 5(2)(a) and (b).

In order for the defence to succeed the item that D is trying to protect must be property. D cannot cause criminal damage to something in order to protect something which is not in law considered to be property. This was seen in the case of *Cresswell and Currie* (2006).

Cresswell and Currie (2006)

The defendants were opposed to DEFRA's cull of badgers. DEFRA was carrying out this cull in order to determine if there were links between badgers and TB in cows. The defendants destroyed traps set by DEFRA employees for the purpose of trapping badgers. The badgers would then have been killed in the research.

One of the defences the defendants claimed was that they had a lawful excuse under s 5(2) of the Criminal Damage Act 1971. They were convicted and appealed. The conviction was upheld. The court held that the defence was not available as the badgers were not property at the time the traps were destroyed. This was because they had not been reduced into possession since they had not yet been caught. The court also held that the badgers did not belong to another. They were not in the custody or control of DEFRA or anyone else.

Oddly enough the Act does not provide a defence where the defendant believes he is acting to protect a person from harm. In *Baker and Wilkins* (1997) the two defendants believed that Baker's daughter was being held in a house. They tried to enter the house causing damage to the door. They were convicted. Their conviction was upheld on appeal as s 5(2)(b) only provides a defence where other property is in immediate need of protection.

Key facts

Element	Comment	Cases
Destroy or damage	Destroy includes making an item useless even if it is not completely destroyed Damage includes non-permanent damage if it requires effort to remove it It is not damage if it can be easily wiped off	*Roe v Kingerlee* (1986) *Hardman v Chief Constable of Avon* (1986) *A (a juvenile) v R* (1978)
Property	Must be tangible, includes real and personal property Includes wild animals in captivity or possession of another	
Belonging to another	This is wider than owner Includes custody, control or proprietary right	
Mens rea	Intention or recklessness in doing the damage Only subjective recklessness can make the defendant liable	*Gemmell and Richards* (2003)
Lawful excuse	Believed owner would consent to damage Believed damage needed to protect other property	*Denton* (1982)

Key facts chart on the basic offence of criminal damage

Activity

Read the following extract from *The Kent and Sussex Courier* on 9 January 2004 and answer the questions below.

Clingfilm-wrapped yob wrecks lights

A killjoy wrapped in clingfilm caused £700 worth of damage as he climbed up Tonbridge town centre's Christmas tree and smashed some of the decorative lights.

Police are investigating after the vandal wreaked festive havoc at 3.30 am on December 14.

The man, who was caught on CCTV, groped at the colourful illuminations as he clambered up the branches of the tree. In doing so he managed to break some of the decorations.

Tonbridge and Malling Borough Council has since revealed that it cost hundreds of pounds to repair the lights.

Questions

1. Explain the *actus reus* of the basic offence of criminal damage.

2. Explain whether the *actus reus* of the offence has been committed in the scenario above.

3. Explain the *mens rea* of the basic offence of criminal damage.

4. Discuss whether, if a prosecution was brought in the above situation, the defendant could argue that he did not have the *mens rea* for the offence.

15.2 Endangering life

This is an aggravated offence of criminal damage under s 1(2) Criminal Damage Act 1971 which states:

> 'A person who without lawful excuse destroys or damages any property, whether belonging to himself or another –
> (a) intending to destroy or damage any property or being reckless as to whether any property would be destroyed or damaged; and
> (b) intending by the destruction or damage to endanger the life of another or being reckless as to whether the life of another would be thereby endangered;
> shall be guilty of an offence.'

This offence is regarded as much more serious than the basic offence and it carries a maximum sentence of life imprisonment.

15.2.1 Danger to life

The danger to life must come from the destruction or damage, not from another source in which damage was caused. In *Steer* (1987) the defendant fired three shots at the home of his former business partner, causing damage to the house. The Court of Appeal quashed his conviction as they held the danger came from the shots, not from any damage done to the house through those shots. The prosecution then appealed to the House of Lords on the following point of law:

> 'Whether, upon a true construction of s 1(2)(b) of the Criminal Damage Act 1971, the prosecution are required to prove that the danger to life resulted

from the destruction of or damage to the property, or whether it is sufficient for the prosecution to prove that it resulted from the act of the defendant which caused the destruction or damage.'

The House of Lords ruled that as the Act used the phrase 'by the destruction or damage' it could not be extended to mean 'by the damage *or by the act which caused the damage'*. This meant that the defendant was not guilty.

The Law Lords also pointed out that if it did include the act (as opposed to the damage) then there would be an anomaly which Parliament could not have intended, which they illustrated in the following way:

> 'If A and B both discharge firearms in a public place, being reckless whether life would be endangered, it would be absurd that A, who incidentally causes some trifling damage to the property, should be guilty of an offence punishable with life imprisonment, but that B, who causes no damage, should be guilty of no offence. In the same circumstances, if A is merely reckless but B actually intends to endanger life, it is scarcely less absurd that A should be guilty of the graver offence under s 1(2)(b) of the 1971 Act, B of the lesser offence under s 16 of the Firearms Act 1968.'

In the later cases of *Webster* and *Warwick* (1995) the Court of Appeal tried to distinguish them on the facts from the case of *Steer* (1987). In *Webster* three defendants pushed a large stone from a bridge on to a train underneath. The stone hit the roof of one coach and caused debris to shower the passengers in that coach, although the stone itself did not fall into the carriage. In *Warwick* the defendant rammed a police car and threw bricks at it causing the rear window to smash and shower the officers with broken glass.

The Court of Appeal quashed the conviction in *Webster* because the judge had misdirected the jury that an intention to endanger life by the stone falling was sufficient for guilt, but they substituted a conviction based on recklessness. In *Warwick* they upheld the conviction.

They pointed out that, if a defendant throws a brick at a windscreen of a moving vehicle and causes some damage to the vehicle, whether he is guilty under s 1(2) does not depend on whether the brick hits or misses the windscreen, but whether he intended to hit it and intended that the damage from this should endanger life, or whether he was reckless as to that outcome.

Where a case involved dropping stones from bridges, they said a defendant would be guilty under s 1(2) Criminal Damage Act 1971 if he intended or was reckless that the stone would smash the roof of the train or vehicle so that metal or wood struts from the roof would or obviously might descend upon a passenger, endangering life.

15.2.2 Life not actually endangered

Life does not actually have to be endangered. In *Sangha* (1988) the defendant set fire to a mattress and two chairs in a neighbour's flat. The flat was empty at the time and, because of the design of the building, people in adjoining flats were not at risk. The Court of Appeal, using the now discredited test from *Caldwell* (1981), said that if an ordinary prudent bystander would have perceived an obvious risk that property would be damaged and that life would thereby be endangered, the defendant was guilty. The ordinary prudent bystander would not have expert knowledge relating to the construction of the property, neither would he have the benefit of hindsight.

As *Caldwell* (1981) has been overruled by *Gemmell and Richards* (2003) a subjective test would now be applied. So, the test is whether the defendant realised that life might be endangered. If he did then he would be guilty even if there was no actual risk.

15.2.3 Own property

Section 1(2) applies not only where property belonging to another is damaged or destroyed but also where the property damaged is the defendant's own. This can be justified in most situations, as the aim of the section is to make the defendant guilty where he has intended or been reckless as to whether life is endangered by the damage he does. It does not matter whether the damage is to his property or someone else's. However, the case of *Merrick* (1995) shows how the section can be extended to absurd lengths.

Merrick (1995)

Merrick was employed by the householder to remove some old television cable. While doing this he left the live cable exposed for about six minutes. No one was hurt by this but he was charged with endangering life because of the 'damage' to the wiring. His conviction under s 1(2) of the 1971 Act was upheld by the Court of Appeal. In this case the householder was using Merrick as an agent, but if the householder had done the work personally it seems that he would equally have been guilty, even though it was his own property.

The other anomaly shown by this case is that Merrick was guilty only because he was removing old cable and 'damaging' it by this process. If he had been installing new wiring and left that exposed for six minutes it would have been difficult to argue that there was any damage and so he would have been not guilty. Yet the action and the danger in both situations is the same.

15.2.4 *Mens rea* of aggravated criminal damage

There are two points which the prosecution must prove. These are:

1. intention or recklessness as to destroying or damaging any property; and

2. intention or recklessness as to whether the life is endangered by the destruction or damage.

Intention and recklessness have the same meaning as for the basic offence (see 14.1.4). This means that the *Caldwell* test for recklessness has been overruled and the prosecution must prove that the defendant was aware *both* that there was a risk the property would be destroyed or damaged *and* that life would be endangered.

The decision in *R (Stephen Malcolm)* (1984), where the Court of Appeal followed the decision in *Elliott v C* (1983), even though they were reluctant to do so, is presumably overruled after *Gemmell and Richards* (2003). In *R (Stephen Malcolm)* (1984) the defendant was a 15-year-old boy who, with two friends, had thrown milk bottles filled with petrol at the outside wall of a neighbour's ground-floor flat. These had caused sheets of flame which flashed across the window of the flat, endangering the lives of the occupants. The defendant argued that he had not realised the risk, but the Court of Appeal held that the test was whether an ordinary prudent man would have appreciated the risk that life might be endangered. The test following *Gemmell and Richards* (2003) would be whether the defendant had realised the risk. This was confirmed in *Cooper* (2004).

Cooper (2004)

D, who lived in a hostel for people needing support for mental illness, set fire to his mattress and bedding. There was no serious damage. When asked by the police if it had crossed his mind that people might have been hurt, he replied 'I don't think, it did cross my mind a bit but nobody would have got hurt.' He was charged with arson being reckless as to whether life would be endangered. The trial judge directed the jury in accordance with *Caldwell*. D was convicted but the conviction was quashed as the Court of Appeal held that the *Caldwell* test was no longer appropriate. The test for recklessness was subjective.

Key facts

Offence	Law	Comment	Cases
Aggravated criminal damage s 1(2) Criminal Damage Act 1971	Consists of basic offence PLUS intending or being reckless as to whether another's life is endangered	Danger to life must come from damage Recklessness must presumably be subjective Can commit offence by damaging own property	*Steer* (1987) *Gemmell and Richards* (2003) *Merrick* (1995)
Arson s 1(3) Criminal Damage Act 1971	Consists of basic offence committed by fire	Must be property belonging to another	
Aggravated arson	Consists of basic offence committed by fire PLUS intending or being reckless as to whether another's life is endangered	Recklessness must be subjective Can commit offence by damaging own property	*Cooper* (2004)

Key facts chart on aggravated damage and arson

The Court of Appeal made it clear that *Gemmell and Richards* (2003) had affected the law in respect of the level of recklessness required for all criminal damage offences. For all of them a subjective test is now used.

15.3 Arson

Under s 1(3) Criminal Damage Act 1971 where an offence under s 1 Criminal Damage Act 1971 is committed by destroying or damaging property by fire, the offence becomes arson. The maximum penalty is life imprisonment.

The basic offence of criminal damage must be destruction or damage by fire. All the other ingredients of the offence are the same as for the basic offence. Where aggravated arson is charged then it is necessary for the prosecution to prove that the defendant intended or was reckless as to whether life was endangered by the damage or destruction by fire.

In *Miller* (1983) the House of Lords held that arson could be committed by an omission where the defendant accidentally started a fire and failed to do anything to prevent damage from that fire.

Activity

Discuss what offences, if any, have been committed in the following situations.

1. Ali, aged 10, stands at the side of a country road and throws stones across the road. One stone hits the door of a car and causes a slight mark on the door. Another stone hits the side window of the car causing it to smash, showering the driver with glass. The driver swerves but manages to stop the car safely.
   Would your answer be different if Ali was aged 20 and throwing stones on to cars from a bridge across a busy motorway?

2. Charlene has had an argument with her flatmate, Louisa. Charlene decides to teach Louisa a lesson by setting fire to some of her clothes. Charlene hangs an expensive dress out of the window and sets it alight. She then goes out. The flames from the dress set the window curtains alight and the fire spreads to the rest of the flat.

3. Donovan writes abusive words in chalk on the pavement outside a neighbour's house. He also sprays paint on to his neighbour's garden wall. The next day it rains and the chalk is washed away but the paint is still there.

4. Emlyn works one day a week as a gardener for Fiona. Fiona tells him that next time he has a bonfire she would like him to burn some old paperback books which she has put in a box in the garden shed. Emlyn starts a bonfire when Fiona has gone out. He finds two boxes of books in the shed. One box contains old and damaged paperback books. The other box contains some newer hardback books. As both boxes are in the shed, Emlyn believes that Fiona wants both sets of books burnt. He has finished doing this by the time Fiona gets home. She is very angry to find he has burnt the hardback books as well as she did not want these burnt.

5. Gregory lives in a 'squat'. One night when he has taken some drugs he falls asleep while smoking and accidentally drops his cigarette on to his coat which is on the floor alongside his bed. The cigarette causes the coat to burn. Gregory wakes up and realises there is a small fire but he is still very dopey and he goes back to sleep. The fire spreads from the coat to the floorboards and damages these. One of the other people in the squat comes in and puts the fire out before any more damage is caused.

Chapter 16

Defences

16.1 Duress

Duress is a defence based on the fact that the defendant has been effectively forced to commit the crime. The defendant has committed the offence because he has been threatened with death or serious injury. The law therefore allows a defence. The defendant has to choose between being himself killed or seriously injured or committing a crime. In such a situation there is no real choice. The defendant can be considered as so terrified that he ceases 'to be an independent actor'. However, despite this the defendant knowingly does the *actus reus* for the offence and has the required *mens rea*. So, if the law did not allow the defence, he would be liable for the offence.

Duress can be either through a direct threat by another (duress by threats) or through external circumstances (duress of circumstances). Duress of circumstances overlaps with the defence of necessity.

16.1.1 What crimes is duress available for?

Duress can be used as defence to all crimes, except murder, attempted murder and possibly treason. This means that duress, whether by threats or duress of circumstances, is available as a defence to all the offences which are studied in this Unit of AQA A2 Law.

16.1.2 Duress by threats

This is where another person threatens the defendant with serious violence unless the defendant commits an offence. For example, if an armed man pointed a gun at the defendant, gave him a fake credit card, and ordered him to use it in a cashpoint machine to get money. The defendant is stealing the money but he is only doing it because of the threat.

The threat of violence is directed at the defendant by another person who demands that the defendant commit a specific crime or else he will be shot.

Seriousness of the threat

The threat must be of death or serious injury; lesser threats do not provide a defence. For example, a threat to disclose a previous conviction is not sufficient for duress. However, provided there are serious threats, then the cumulative effect of the threats can be considered. This was decided in *Valderrama-Vega* (1985).

Valderrama-Vega (1985)

The defendant illegally imported cocaine. He claimed he had done this because of death threats made by a mafia-type organisation involved in drug smuggling and also because of threats to disclose his homosexuality and because of financial pressures. The trial judge said that the defence was only available to him if the death threats were the sole reason for his committing the offence. The Court of Appeal quashed his conviction as the jury were entitled to look at the cumulative effects of all the threats.

If there had not been a threat of death, then the other threats in this case would not be enough on which to base a defence of duress. But as there had been a threat of death, the jury were entitled to consider the whole of the threats.

Threat to whom?

It used to be thought that the threat had to be to the defendant himself. But in an Australian case in 1967 it was accepted that threats to kill or seriously injure the defendant's common law wife were sufficient.

In recent cases in England it has been accepted that threats to family or even to friends can be a basis for the defence of duress. In *Martin* (1989), in a case of duress of circumstances, the wife of the defendant threatened to commit suicide unless he drove while disqualified (see 16.2). This was held to be sufficient. In *Conway* (1988) the threats were to a passenger in the defendant's car. These were accepted as forming the basis for the defence of duress (see 16.2).

There has been no decision on whether a threat to a complete stranger would be enough to give a defence of duress, but it seems likely that the courts would now allow this. Supposing an armed man seizes hold of someone you do not know and then orders you to go to and firebomb a particular building and cause severe damage to it or else he will kill the stranger. If you do damage the building, can you use the defence of duress? You would be able to if the threat was to a member of your family or, under *Conway* (1988), to a friend. So, it would be reasonable to say that you should have a defence if you choose to commit a crime rather than let an innocent stranger die. In fact the draft Criminal Code proposed that this should be the law.

16.1.3 Subjective and objective tests

In deciding if the defence should succeed, the jury must consider a two-stage test. This involves both subjective and objective tests. These are:

- Was the defendant compelled to act as he did because he reasonably believed he had good cause to fear serious injury or death (a mainly subjective test)?
- If so, would a sober person of reasonable firmness, sharing the characteristics of the accused have responded in the same way? (An objective test.)

These tests were laid down by the Court of Appeal in *Graham* (1982) and approved by the House of Lords in *Howe* (1987).

The first part of the test is based on whether the defendant did the offence because of the threats he believed had been made. This is subjective. However, the belief must be reasonable.

In *Martin (DP)* (2000) the Court of Appeal interpreted this part of the two-stage test as being whether the defendant may have reasonably feared for his safety. So, in considering this test, the jury could take into account any special characteristic of the defendant which may have made him more likely to believe the threats.

Martin (DP) (2000)

The defendant suffered from a condition known as schizoid-affective state, which would lead him to regard things said to him as threatening and to believe that such threats would be carried out. He claimed he had been forced to carry out two robberies by two men who lived on the same estate. The judge ruled that the schizoid-affective disorder was irrelevant to the first part of the test, although it was a characteristic which could be included in the second part of the test.

The defendant appealed saying that the correct test should have been whether, in view of his condition, he may have reasonably feared for his own or his mother's safety. The Court of Appeal allowed the appeal and quashed his conviction. They held that duress and self-defence should be treated in the same way in regard to belief of the circumstances. In self-defence a mistaken belief by the defendant can be a defence, provided it is a genuine mistake. The same applies to duress and so the defendant's mental condition is relevant in deciding whether he reasonably believed that his (or his family's) safety was at risk.

However, in *Hasan* (2005) the House of Lords stated that the belief in the threat must not only be genuine: it must also be reasonable. This statement was *obiter* but it is likely to be followed in future cases.

The second part of the test is based on whether the reasonable man would have responded in the same way. However, the jury are allowed to take certain of the defendant's characteristics into account as the reasonable man is taken as sharing the relevant characteristics of the defendant.

What characteristics can be taken into account was decided in *Bowen* (1996). In this case the defendant had a low IQ of 68 and he obtained goods by deception for two men who had told him they would petrol-bomb him and his family. It was held that his low IQ was irrelevant in deciding whether the defendant found it more difficult to resist any threats. The relevant characteristics must go to the ability to resist pressure and threats. In *Bowen* (1996) it was accepted that the following could be relevant:

- **age**: as very young people and the very old could be more susceptible to threats
- **pregnancy**: there is the additional fear for the safety of the unborn child
- **serious physical disability**: which could make it more difficult for the defendant to protect himself
- **recognised mental illness or psychiatric disorder**: this could include post-traumatic stress disorder or any other disorder which

meant that a person might be more susceptible to threats; this did not include a low IQ
- **sex**: although the Court of Appeal thought that many women might have as much moral courage as men.

16.1.4 No safe avenue of escape

Duress can only be used as a defence if the defendant is placed in a situation where he has no safe avenue of escape. In *Gill* (1963) the defendant claimed that he and his wife had been threatened unless he stole a lorry. However, there was a period of time during which he was left alone and so could have raised the alarm. As he had a 'safe avenue of escape' he could not rely on the defence of duress.

It has also been held that if police protection is possible then the defendant cannot rely on duress. However, in the case of *Hudson and Taylor* (1971) it was accepted that police protection might not always be effective.

Hudson and Taylor (1971)

The defendants were two girls, aged 17 and 19, who were prosecution witnesses in a case against a man called Wright who was charged with wounding another man. When giving evidence in court they lied and said they could not identify Wright as the attacker. They were then charged with perjury (lying in court under oath). In their defence at their trial for perjury they said they lied because a man called Farrell, who had a reputation for violence, had told Hudson that if she gave evidence against the attacker, he would cut her up. They were convicted and appealed. The Court of Appeal quashed their conviction.

At the appeal the prosecution argued that the girls could have sought police protection. On this point the Court of Appeal pointed out that there were cases in which the police could not provide effective protection. They said that in deciding whether going to the police for protection was a realistic course, the jury should consider the age of the defendant, the circumstances of the threats and any risks which might be involved in trying to rely on police protection.

However, in *Hasan* (2005) the House of Lords thought that the Court of Appeal's ruling in *Hudson and Taylor* was too favourable to the defendants. The Lords thought that if the threat was not reasonably expected to be carried out immediately or almost immediately, then there was little room for doubt that the defendant could have taken evasive action by going to the police or in some other way.

The case of *Hudson and Taylor* is also relevant on how immediate the threat has to be and this is considered next.

16.1.5 Imminence of threat

The threat must be effective at the moment the crime is committed. But this does not mean that the threats need to be able to be carried out immediately. In *Hudson and Taylor* (1971) the trial judge in their perjury case ruled that the defence of duress was not available to the two girls. This was because the threat could not be immediately put into effect while the girls were giving evidence, so there was no reason why they could not have given truthful evidence.

On this point the Court of Appeal said that the threat had to be a 'present' threat, but that this was in the sense that it was effective to neutralise the will of the defendant at the time of committing the offence. If the threat is hanging over the defendant at the time he or she commits the offence, then the defence of duress is available.

This was further considered in *Abdul-Hussain* (1999), a case on duress of circumstances.

Abdul-Hussain (1999)

In this case several defendants, who were Shiite Muslims, had fled to Sudan from Iraq because of the risk of punishment and execution because of

their religion. They feared that they would be sent back to Iraq and so they hijacked a plane. The plane eventually landed in the UK. The defendants were charged with hijacking and pleaded duress. The trial judge decided that the danger they were in was not sufficiently 'close and immediate' as to give rise to a 'virtually spontaneous reaction' and he ruled that the defence of duress could not be considered by the jury. The defendants were convicted and appealed.

The Court of Appeal quashed their convictions, holding that the threat need not be immediate but it had to be imminent in the sense that it was hanging over them. They ruled that:

- there must be imminent peril of death or serious injury to the defendant, or to those for whom he has responsibility;

- the peril must operate on the defendant's mind at the time of committing the otherwise criminal act, so as to overbear his will; this is a matter for the jury;

- execution of the threat need not be immediately in prospect.

The Court of Appeal also backed their ruling in *Abdul-Hussain* (1999) by giving a hypothetical example based on the history of Anne Frank whose family hid from the Nazis for a long period of time during the Second World War, because they knew they would be sent to a concentration camp. Anne Frank and all the members of her family were eventually caught and all of them, except her father who survived, died in a concentration camp. The Court of Appeal said:

'If Anne Frank had stolen a car to escape from Amsterdam and been charged with theft, the English law would not, in our judgment, have denied her a defence of duress of circumstances, on the ground that she should have waited for the Gestapo's knock on the door.'

Key facts

Case	Facts	Law
Duress can be by threats or circumstances Duress is not available for murder or attempted murder		
Valderrama-Vega (1985)	Smuggled cocaine because of death threats and threats to disclose homosexuality	Must be a threat of death or serious injury but can consider cumulative effect of threats
Graham (1982)	Helped kill his wife because he was threatened by his homosexual lover	Two-stage test: • was the defendant compelled to act as he did because he reasonably believed he had good cause to fear serious injury or death? • if so, would a sober person of reasonable firmness, sharing the characteristics of the accused have responded in the same way?
Martin (DP) (2000)	Suffered from a schizoid-affective state which would make things seem threatening and believe the threats would be carried out	Correct test should have been whether, in view of his condition, he may have reasonably feared for his own or his mother's safety
Bowen (1996)	Had a low IQ (68) – obtained goods by deception for two men because of petrol-bomb threat	Cannot take low IQ into account Can consider: • age • pregnancy • recognised mental illness • sex
Gill (1963)	Threatened so that he stole a lorry but had time to escape and raise the alarm	Cannot use duress if has a 'safe avenue of escape'
Hudson and Taylor (1971)	Two girls lied on oath because of threats to cut them up	The threat need not be capable of being carried out immediately Also recognised that police protection cannot always be effective Take into account age and sex
Abdul-Hussain (1999)	Hijacked plane to escape from persecution in Iraq	Threat must be 'imminent' and operating on the defendant's mind when he commits the offence

Key facts chart: cases on general principles of duress

16.1.6 Threat to make the defendant commit a specific offence

The defendant can only use the defence if the threats are in order to make him commit a specific offence. In *Cole* (1994) the defendant claimed that he and his girlfriend and child had been threatened (and he had been actually hit with a baseball bat) in order to make him repay money he owed. As he did not have the money he carried out two robberies at building societies to obtain sufficient money to repay the debt. He said he only did this because of the threats of violence to him and his family.

His conviction was upheld because he had not been told to commit the robberies. The threats to him were directed at getting repayment and not directed at making him commit a robbery. This meant there was not a sufficient connection between the threats and the crimes he committed, so the defence of duress was not available to him.

This applies only to duress by threats. In duress of circumstances the defence may be used for any offence which is an appropriate response to the danger posed by the circumstances. As seen in *Abdul-Hussain* (1999) above, the danger was of torture and execution and the offence committed was hijacking which enabled them to reach a safe venue.

16.1.7 Intoxication and duress

If the defendant becomes voluntarily intoxicated and mistakenly believes he is being threatened, he cannot use duress as a defence. A mistake in these circumstances is unreasonable. However, if there is no mistake and the intoxication is irrelevant to the duress, the defendant can use the defence of duress. This could be, for example, where he is threatened by a man with a gun. In this situation there is duress and it is irrelevant whether the defendant is intoxicated or not.

16.1.8 Self-induced duress

This is where the defendant has brought the duress on himself through his own actions; for example where a defendant voluntarily joins a criminal gang and commits some offences, but then is forced to commit other crimes which he did not want to do under duress.

The normal rule is that where the defendant is aware that he may be put under duress to commit offences, he cannot use the defence. This has been held to apply to the following situations:

- where the defendant joins a criminal gang which he knows is likely to use violence
- where the defendant puts himself in a position where he knows that he is likely to be subjected to threats of violence or actual

violence. This could be by being involved in criminal activity although not part of a gang, or by becoming indebted to a drug dealer.

These situations can be illustrated by specific cases.

Sharp (1987)

The defendant joined a gang who carried out robberies. He claimed that he had wanted to withdraw from the robberies before the last one where a sub-postmaster was shot dead. The Court of Appeal ruled that he could not use duress as a defence. He knew when he joined the gang that they were likely to use violence, so he could not claim duress when they threatened him with violence.

A contrasting case to *Sharp* is the case of *Shepherd* (1987).

Shepherd (1987)

The defendant had joined an organised gang of shoplifters. A group of them would enter a shop and while one of them distracted the shopkeeper, the others would steal as much as they could, usually boxes of cigarettes. This activity, although criminal, was non-violent. Shepherd said he wanted to stop taking part but was then threatened with violence unless he continued. The Court of Appeal allowed his appeal and quashed his conviction. If he had no knowledge that the gang was likely to use violence then the defence of duress was available to him.

In *Heath* (2000) the defendant owed money to a drug-dealer. He was then threatened and made to help in the supply of cannabis. He could not use the defence of duress as he knew that by becoming indebted to a drug-dealer he was putting himself at risk of being threatened or having violence used on him.

This situation, where the defendant voluntarily

associates with violent people, was considered by the House of Lords in *Hasan (formerly Z)* (2005). This case now lays down the law on the availability of the defence of duress where a defendant voluntarily associates with others who are engaged in criminal activity.

Hasan (formerly Z) (2005)

D associated with a violent drug dealer. This drug dealer told D to burgle a house in order to steal a large amount of money that was in a safe there. The dealer threatened that if D did not do this then D and his family would be harmed. D, carrying a knife, broke into the house but was unable to open the safe. He was convicted of aggravated burglary. The Court of Appeal quashed the conviction but certified the following question for the consideration of the House of Lords:

'Whether the defence of duress is excluded when as a result of the accused's voluntary association with others:
(i) he foresaw (or possibly should have foreseen) the risk of being then and there subjected to any compulsion by threats of violence; or
(ii) only when he foresaw (or should have foreseen) the risk of being subjected to compulsion to commit criminal offences; and, if the latter
(iii) only if the offences foreseen (or which should have been foreseen) were of the same type (or possibly the same type and gravity) as that ultimately committed.'

The House of Lords reinstated his conviction. They took the view that option (i) in the certified question correctly states the law. The defence of duress is excluded where D voluntarily associates with others who are engaged in criminal activity and he foresaw or ought reasonably to have foreseen the risk of being subjected to any compulsion by threats of violence.

So, if the defendant voluntarily associates with criminals, he will not normally be able to use the defence of duress for any offence he commits due to threats of violence by those criminals. The only time he can use the defence is where he did not foresee that they would try to make him commit an offence through threats AND a reasonable person would not have foreseen this either.

16.2 Duress of circumstances

Although duress by threats has been recognised as a defence for a long time, it is only recently that the courts have recognised that a defendant may be forced to act because of surrounding circumstances. This is known as duress of circumstances. The first case in which this was recognised was *Willer* (1986).

Willer (1986)

Willer and a passenger were driving down a narrow alley when the car was surrounded by a gang of youths who threatened them. Willer realised the only way to get away from the gang was by driving on the pavement. He did this slowly (about 10 mph) and having made his escape he drove to the police station to report the gang. The police charged him with reckless driving for having driven on the pavement and he was convicted.

He appealed and the Court of Appeal said that the jury should have been allowed to consider whether the defendant drove 'under that form of compulsion, that is, under duress'.

Willer shows the difference between duress and duress of circumstances. In *Willer* no-one specifically threatened the defendant telling him to commit the driving offence. He did so because of the threatening circumstances. In duress proper, the defendant would have had to show that someone forced him to commit a driving offence by threatening him with violence unless he did so.

This case was followed by *Conway* (1988) in which a passenger in Conway's car had been shot at by two men a few weeks earlier. The car was stationary when the passenger saw two men running towards the car. He thought they were the two people who were after him (in fact they were plain-clothes policemen) and he yelled at Conway to drive off. Conway did so very fast and was charged with reckless driving. The trial judge refused to leave duress for the jury to consider and Conway was convicted. On appeal the Court of Appeal quashed his conviction and ruled that a defence of duress of circumstances was available if, on an objective standpoint, the defendant was acting in order to avoid a threat of death or serious injury.

There was then a third case involving a driving offence. This was *Martin* (1989) where the defendant's wife became hysterical and threatened suicide unless he drove her son (who was late and at risk of losing his job) to work. The defendant was disqualified from driving but he eventually agreed to do this. He was convicted of driving while disqualified. On appeal it was ruled that duress of circumstances could be available as a defence and the same two-stage test put forward in *Graham* (1982) for duress by threats applied. So the tests were:

- was the defendant compelled to act as he did because he reasonably believed he had good cause to fear serious injury or death?
- If so, would a sober person of reasonable firmness, sharing the characteristics of the accused have responded in the same way?

Although these cases established that there was a defence of duress of circumstances, all the cases involved driving offences. It was not until the decision in *Pommell* (1995) that it became clear that duress of circumstances could be a defence to all crimes except murder, attempted murder and some forms of treason.

Pommell (1995)

The defendant was found by police at 8.00 am lying in bed with a loaded sub-machine gun against his leg. He told the police he had taken it off a 'geezer who was going to do some people some damage with it' at about 1 am. He did not want to risk going round the streets at night with it so he was going to get his brother to hand it in to the police that morning. At his trial for possessing a prohibited weapon the judge ruled that his failure to go to the police straight away prevented him from having any defence.

The Court of Appeal held that the defence of duress of circumstances was available for all offences except murder, attempted murder and some forms of treason. So it was open to the defendant and, as the jury had not been allowed to consider the defence, the Court of Appeal ordered that there should be a re-trial with a new jury.

16.3 Intoxication

The law on intoxication as a defence is set out in Chapter 5, section 5.3. The points made in that section apply when considering intoxication as a defence to offences in this Module. Check that you understand the points made in that section.

Remember that intoxication is only a defence to specific intent offences. It is not available for basic intent offences; that is, offences where the defendant can be guilty if he is reckless.

In this module of the AQA A2 specification the only basic intent offence is criminal damage. The specific intent offences are theft, robbery, burglary, blackmail, fraud by false representation, obtaining services dishonestly and making off without payment. So, for all these offences intoxication is available as a defence.

However, intoxication is a defence only if it means that the defendant did not have the required *mens rea* for the offence. So if the

Activity

Explain whether a defence of duress would be available in the following situations.

1. Clancy is threatened by Neil, a fellow employee, who tells Clancy that he will tell their boss about Clancy's previous convictions for theft. Neil says that Clancy has to help him shoplift from a small corner-shop by distracting the counter-staff while Neil does the stealing. Clancy feels obliged to do this as he does not want to lose his job.

2. Joseph, who is of a timid nature and low intelligence, is told by Katya that she will beat him up unless he obtains goods for her from a shop using a stolen credit card. He does this and obtains a DVD player for her.

3. Natasha's boyfriend, Ross, is a drug-dealer. She also knows that he has convictions for violence. He threatens to beat her 'senseless' unless she agrees to take some drugs to one of his 'customers'. She is caught by the police and charged with possessing drugs with intent to supply.

4. Stewart's wife has previously tried to commit suicide. She is very depressed because they are heavily in debt. She tells Stewart that she will throw herself under a train unless he can get the money to pay off their debts. Stewart obtains the money by robbing a local off-licence.

5. Tamara is due to give evidence against Alexia's boyfriend who is facing a trial for attempted murder. A week before the trial is due to take place, Alexia sends Tamara a text message saying that Tamara will be killed if she gives evidence. Tamara attends the court but lies in evidence saying, untruthfully, that the man she saw was much shorter than Alexia's boyfriend.

defendant takes an item from a shop without paying for it when he is in an intoxicated state, his intoxication will only be a defence if he does not know what he is doing and so is not dishonest.

If the defendant knows he is being dishonest and intends to deprive the other person of the property, then even though he is drunk, he has the required *mens rea* for theft and will be guilty.

16.4 Self-defence/prevention of crime

This defence is also set out in section 5.4. The points made in that section also apply when considering whether self-defence or prevention of crime is a defence to any of the offences in this Module. So again look back to Chapter 5 and check that you understand the law on self-defence and prevention of crime.

A defendant who pushed his attacker away and caused the attacker to fall against a window and smash it, could use the defence of self-defence provided the push was reasonable force in the circumstances as he believed them to be. Self-defence could provide a defence to a charge of criminal damage in these circumstances.

Examination-style questions

Question 1

Rakinder and Nick went into a local clothes shop. Rakinder had previously been suspected of shoplifting and was banned from entering this shop. Once in the shop Rakinder took a blouse from one of the rails and put in her bag. While she was doing this Nick went into the changing rooms to try a pair of jeans on. He put his own baggy combat-style trousers on over the top so that the jeans could not be seen.

He then chose another pair of jeans and took them to the assistant at the till. He paid for them with his credit card. However, he had not paid the debt on the card for several months and that morning he had received a letter saying that the credit company were withdrawing his right to use the card and telling him to return the card to them.

While he was paying for the jeans, Rakinder took a purse from an unattended bag. She was about to walk out of the shop when someone shouted to stop her as she had taken the purse. A woman shopper caught hold of her arm but Rakinder kicked her on the shins and then ran off.

1. Discuss Rakinder's criminal liability for both the incident with the blouse and the incident with the purse. (25 marks)
2. Discuss Nick's criminal liability for the incidents with both pairs of jeans. (25 marks)

Question 2

Steven and Carly decide to enjoy a weekend break at The Great View Hotel. They drive there and, on the way, they stop for petrol. Steven puts the petrol into the car at the pump and then goes into the garage shop to pay. While he is waiting in the queue he picks up a bar of chocolate. When he gets to the till he uses his firm's credit card to pay for the petrol although he is only supposed to use this when driving for business. He has put the bar of chocolate in his pocket and does not pay for it as he has forgotten about it.

That evening at the hotel they drink two bottles of wine with their meal and then have some more drinks afterwards. Carly decides to go to their room to use the bathroom. She goes to the floor where their room is and sees a room with the door open. She thinks it is their room and goes into it. She tries to open a suitcase in the room thinking that it is hers. She cannot open it and damages the lock. She then writes 'Carly loves you' in lipstick on a shirt hanging in the wardrobe thinking the shirt is one of Steven's. She takes a ten pound note which is on the dressing table and goes back to join Steven in the bar.

1. Discuss the criminal liability of Steven for the incidents at the petrol station. (25 marks)
2. Discuss the criminal liability of Carly for the incidents in the hotel room. (25 marks)

Question 3

Nathan decides to go to see his favourite football team play at their home ground. His flatmate, Vincent, is away but Nathan knows that Vincent has a season ticket for all home games. He finds this season ticket and takes it with him. He uses Vincent's motorbike to go to the football ground. At the ground he shows Vincent's season ticket to enter the ground.

At the end of the match he sees a wallet lying on the ground behind the stands. He picks it up and looks inside. It contains £30 but does not have a name inside it. Nathan decides to keep it. He tries to start up the motorbike to get home but finds it will not start.

He leaves the bike and takes the train home. He does not buy a ticket and when the ticket inspector comes round he tells him that he has had his pocket picked and only has a small amount of change, which is not enough for the ticket. He says he will send the money. The inspector asks him for his name and address. Nathan gives a false name and address and the inspector lets him go. When he gets home he puts Vincent's season ticket back.

1. Discuss the criminal liability of Nathan in respect of the motorbike and the wallet.

    (25 marks)
2. Discuss the criminal liability of Nathan in respect of his use of the season ticket and his failure to pay for his train ticket.

    (25 marks)

UNIT 4

Section B: Law of Tort

Table of Cases

Chapter 17

Negligence

17.1 General principles of negligence

17.1.1 *Donoghue v Stevenson* (1932) and the duty of care

The modern tort of negligence begins with Lord Atkin's groundbreaking judgment in *Donoghue v Stevenson* (1932). A new approach was necessary because no other action was available.

The judgment is important for identifying five critical elements:

1. Lack of privity of contract did not prevent the claimant from claiming.
2. Negligence was accepted as a separate tort in its own right.
3. Liability for negligence depends on proving:

   (a) existence of a duty of care owed to the claimant by the defendant
   (b) breach of that duty by falling below the appropriate standard of care
   (c) damage caused by the defendant's breach that was not too remote a consequence of the breach.

4. The means of determining the existence of a duty of care, Lord Atkin's 'neighbour principle':

> 'You must take reasonable care to avoid acts or omissions which you can reasonably foresee would be likely to injure your neighbour. Who then in law is my neighbour? … persons who are so closely and directly affected by my act that I ought reasonably to have them in my contemplation as being affected so when I am directing my mind to the acts or omissions in question'.

5. A manufacturer owes a duty of care towards consumers or users of his products not to cause them harm.

Negligence then developed incrementally, case by case, with a duty of care being established in numerous relationships.

Much later in *Anns v Merton LBC* (1978) (see 17.2.2), Lord Wilberforce developed a two-stage test imposing liability where there was sufficient legal proximity between the parties unless there were policy reasons for not doing so.

However this two-part test was criticised and so the case and the test was overruled in *Murphy v Brentwood D C* (1990) (see 17.2.3). This case approved a three-part test from *Caparo v Dickman* (1990):

1. Were the consequences reasonably foreseeable?
2. Was there a sufficient relationship of proximity between the parties?
3. Is it fair, just and reasonable in all the circumstances to impose a duty of care?

Policy has always been a key consideration in determining liability. As Winfield puts it

❝ '... the court must decide not simply whether there is or is not a duty, but whether there should or should not be one ...' ❞

Many policy factors may influence judges in deciding whether or not to impose a duty.

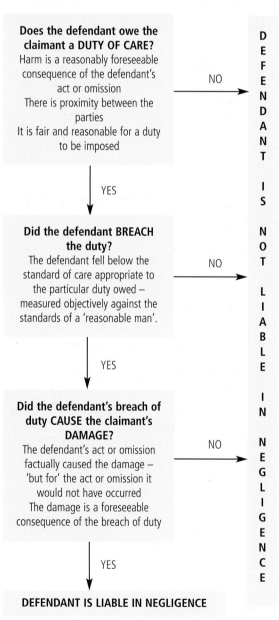

Figure 17.1 The essential elements for proof of negligence

- Loss allocation – judges are more likely to impose a duty on a party who is able to stand the loss, and insurance is also a major determining factor.
- Practical considerations – courts may be willing to impose vicarious liability on companies who can then plan effective policies to avoid future liability.
- Moral considerations – the public may be more prepared to accept a 'good Samaritan' law than judges would.
- Protection of professionals – Lord Denning particularly expressed concern that professionals should not be stopped from working by restrictive rulings.
- Constitutional considerations – judges are not keen to be seen as law-makers as this is Parliament's role.
- The 'floodgates' argument – judges are reluctant to impose liability where it may encourage large numbers of claims; this appears not to be morally justifiable and has affected the development of liability for nervous shock.
- Deterrent value – in *Smolden v Whitworth and Nolan* (1997), the court imposed a duty on a rugby referee who failed to control a scrum properly.

17.1.2 Breach of duty

The 'reasonable man' test

Breach refers to a falling below the standard of care appropriate to the duty in question.

The standard is measured against that of the 'reasonable man'. In *Blyth v Proprietors of the Birmingham Waterworks* (1856), Alderson B explained:

❝ 'Negligence is the omission to do something which a reasonable man, guided upon those considerations which ordinarily regulate human affairs, would do, or doing something which a prudent and reasonable man would not do.' ❞

The 'reasonable man' is an objective standard and has been described in *Hall v Brooklands Auto-Racing Club* (1933) by Greer LJ as '"the man on the street", or the "man on the Clapham Omnibus"'. In *Glasgow Corporation v Muir* (1943) MacMillan LJ concluded that the reasonable man is 'presumed to be free from both over-apprehension and from over-confidence.'

In fact the breach of duty is just another way of saying that the defendant is at fault.

Factors relevant to breach

Through the cases, judges have developed a number of rules concerning what should be taken into account in determining the standard appropriate to the duty.

- Foreseeability of harm – there is no obligation on the defendant to guard against risks other than those that are within his reasonable contemplation: *Roe v Minister of Health* (1954).
- The magnitude of risk – the more likely the risk, the more the defendant should guard against it: *Bolton v Stone* (1951).
- The extent of the possible harm (the 'thin skull' rule) – the defendant will be liable for the full extent of harm caused: *Paris v Stepney BC* (1951).
- The social utility of the activity causing harm – a defendant may be excused where the risk was taken to avoid a worse harm: *Watt v Herts CC* (1954).
- Practicability of precautions – we need only do what is reasonable to avoid risks of harm: *Latimer v AEC* (1953).
- Common practice – this may be strong but not absolute evidence that there is no negligence: *Brown v Rolls Royce Ltd* (1960).
- Experience – the standard is not lowered because of inexperience: *Nettleship v Weston* (1971).

Experts and professionals

Professionals do not conform to the usual rules on the breach of duty in negligence and are more appropriately considered as a special category on their own.

The standard of care appropriate to professionals is not judged according to the reasonable man test. On the contrary a person exercising specialist skills is to be judged by comparison with other people exercising the same skill; *Bolam v Friern Hospital Management Committee* (1957).

The standard is not reduced because the defendant lacks experience. So a junior doctor must exercise the same care and skill as an experienced doctor; *Wilsher v Essex Area Health Authority* (1988).

Most recently the House of Lords has suggested that the court in each individual case should determine what is the standard of care appropriate to the professional against whom the negligence is alleged, rather than for professional opinion; *Bolitho v City and Hackney Health Authority* (1997).

17.1.3 Causation in fact and the 'but for' test

The 'but for' test

The simple starting point in establishing causation is the 'but for' test. As Lord Denning explained in *Cork v Kirby MacLean Ltd* (1952):

> '... if the damage would not have happened but for a particular fault, then that fault is the cause of the damage; if it would have happened just the same, fault or no fault, the fault is not the cause of the damage.'

Often the facts allow the test to operate straightforwardly: *Barnett v Chelsea & Kensington Hospital Management Committee* (1969).

However, sometimes judges will simply ignore the problems associated with applying the 'but for' test in order to give a just result: *Chester v Afshar* (2004).

Problems in proving causation

Sometimes problems occur where the level of knowledge available to the court makes it impossible to pinpoint a precise cause.

If the damage is caused by multiple causes that are acting concurrently, then the 'but for' test appears to be incapable of providing an absolute test of causation. The court may decide that the negligence has '… materially increased the risk…' and that the defendant should therefore be liable for damages: *McGhee v National Coal Board* (1973).

In contrast, where there are a number of possible concurrent causes of the damage and it is impossible to identify the specific one causing the damage, then it is unlikely that the court will hold one cause ultimately responsible: *Wilsher v Essex Area Health Authority* (1988).

The courts will not allow recovery of damages for 'loss of a chance' because of the problem of proving causation: *Hotson v East Berkshire AHA* (1987) and *Gregg v Scott* (2005).

The House of Lords has recently accepted that in certain circumstances where a number of defendants all contribute to the same basic injury, then liability can result if they have materially increased the risk of harm: *Fairchild v Glenhaven Funeral Services Ltd and others* (2002).

However, the House of Lords has recently modified the principle so that damages are apportioned: *Barker v Corus; Murray v British Shipbuilders (Hydromatics) Ltd; Patterson v Smiths Dock Ltd and Others* (2006). The Compensation Act 2006 reversed this position in respect of mesothelioma claims.

Where causes of damage occur one after the other, then liability usually remains with the first event: *Performance Cars Ltd v Abraham* (1962).

Novus actus interveniens

Even though the defendant can be seen as negligent, the chain of causation may be broken by a subsequent, intervening act. If the court accepts that this intervening act is the true cause of the damage, then the defendant may not be liable despite the breach of duty.

This plea is known as *novus actus interveniens*, meaning 'a new act intervenes', and it is an effective defence. The case law seems to fall into three categories.

An intervening act of the claimant

This is closely connected with contributory negligence. However, the plea here is that the claimant is actually responsible for his own damage and therefore the chain of causation is broken and the defendant has no liability at all: *McKew v Holland & Hannen & Cubitts (Scotland) Ltd* (1969).

An intervening act of nature

The defendant may be relieved of liability in those situations where he can show that the act of nature he argues is breaking the chain of causation, is unforeseeable and independent of his own negligence: *Carslogie Steamship Co v Royal Norwegian Government* (1952).

An intervening act of a third party

In order to succeed with a plea in these circumstances, the defendant must show that the act of the third party was of such magnitude that it does in fact break the chain of causation: *Knightley v Johns* (1982).

17.1.4 Causation in law and remoteness of damage

The tests of remoteness

Even though a causal link can be proved factually, according to the 'but for' test the claimant may still be prevented from winning the case if the damage suffered is too remote a consequence of the defendant's breach of duty. The test is a matter of law rather than fact.

The original test was that the claimant could recover in respect of a loss that was a direct consequence of the defendant's breach regardless of how foreseeable: *Re Polemis and Furness, Withy & Co* (1921).

The test was criticised for failing to distinguish between degrees of negligence. As a result, the test was later changed to one of liability for damage that was a reasonably foreseeable consequence of the breach: *Overseas Tankship (UK) Ltd v Morts Dock & Engineering Co (1961) (The Wagon Mound (No 1))*.

The critical part of the test is foreseeability of the general rather than the specific type of damage. It is not therefore necessary for the full extent of the damage to be foreseen: *Bradford v Robinson Rentals (1967)*.

It is not necessary for the precise circumstances to be foreseen if damage is a foreseeable consequence (*Hughes v The Lord Advocate (1963)*); neither will it matter that the damage is more extensive than might have been foreseeable provided that the kind of damage itself is foreseeable (*Vacwell Engineering Co Ltd v BDH Chemicals Ltd (1971)*).

The 'thin skull' rule will also apply so that the defendant will be liable for the full extent of the damage if the type of damage is foreseeable: *Smith v Leech Brain & Co Ltd (1962)*.

17.2 Pure economic loss

17.2.1 The traditional view

The *Hedley Byrne* (1964) case (see 17.3.1) introduced the concept that a claimant could recover for economic loss arising from negligently made statements. However, the courts have always distinguished such an action from 'pure economic loss' arising out of negligent acts. The position here was traditionally very clear; there was no liability for a 'pure economic loss'.

In the past this was based on policy and the idea that 'economic loss' (for instance, a loss of profit) was a concept applicable to contract law rather than tort. The principle has been quite clearly stated and illustrated in past cases.

Spartan Steel v Martin & Co (Contractors) Ltd (1973)

An electric power cable was negligently cut by the defendants, resulting in a loss of power to the claimants who manufactured steel alloys. A 'melt' in the claimant's furnace at the time of the power cuts had to be destroyed to stop it from solidifying and wrecking the furnace. The claimants were able to claim for physical damage and the loss of profit on the 'melt' in the furnace. The court refused to allow their claim for lost profits for four further 'melts', and argued that they could have completed while the power was still off. The loss was foreseeable. Nevertheless, Lord Denning held that a line must be drawn as a matter of policy, and that the loss was better borne by the insurers than by the defendants alone.

There appears to be an artificial distinction here created for policy reasons purely for the purpose of restricting any extension of liability. The distinction has the obvious potential to create unfair anomalies in the law. For instance, it might mean that an architect giving negligent advice leading to the construction of a defective building could be liable, whereas the builder whose negligence leads to a defect in a building may not be.

Nevertheless, other cases have confirmed the principle that a pure economic loss arising from a negligent act is unrecoverable.

Weller & Co v Foot and Mouth Disease Research Institute (1966)

Auctioneers' regular income from sale of cattle was disrupted as the result of a ban on the movement of livestock following an escape of a virus from the defendant's premises. No liability could be accepted for their loss of profit.

However, there have also been situations where an economic loss was recovered, although in less clear-cut situations where the difference between a negligent statement and a negligent act was less obvious.

Dutton v Bognor Regis Urban District Council (1972)

A local authority was responsible for a negligently carried out building inspection that resulted in defective foundations having to be repaired at great financial cost to the owner of the building. The Court of Appeal held that, since a local authority were under no duty to carry out an inspection, they could not be held liable for a negligent inspection. Nevertheless they were prepared to impose liability on the basis of physical damage, that the defective foundations were a risk to the health and safety of the occupants. The claimant as a result was awarded damages to restore the building to a state where it was no longer a danger.

Clearly it is difficult to distinguish between a negligent inspection (an act) and a satisfactory report based on the inspection (a statement). The case did not fit easily under either *Hedley Byrne* (1964) or *Donoghue v Stevenson* (1932), which perhaps explains the court's reasoning.

17.2.2 Pure economic loss under *Anns*

Further erosion of the basic principle that pure economic loss is unrecoverable came as a result of Lord Wilberforce's two-part test.

Anns v Merton London Borough Council (1978)

Here the negligent building inspection had failed to reveal that the foundations were too shallow. On the basis of the two-part test and that there were no policy grounds to avoid imposing a duty, the tenant was able to recover the cost of making the flat safe; economic loss, in other words.

Because of the availability of the *Anns* two-part test, the so-called 'high water mark' was then reached in respect of recovery for a pure economic loss.

Junior Books Ltd v Veitchi Co Ltd (1983)

The claimants' architects nominated the defendants to lay the floor in the claimants' new print works. As a result, they sub-contracted to the main builders to complete the work. In the event the defendants laid a thoroughly unusable floor which then had to be re-laid. The claimants could not sue the builders who had hired the floor layers at the claimant's request, and they had no contractual relationship with the floor layers. Nevertheless they succeeded in winning damages not just for the cost of re-laying the floor, but also for their loss of profit during the delay. There were said to be three key issues:

1. The claimant's architects had nominated the defendants and so they relied on the defendants' skill and judgment.

2. The defendants were aware of this reliance at all material times.

3. The damage caused was a direct and foreseeable consequence of the defendants' negligence.

Lord Brandon dissented and criticised the other judges for creating obligations in a non-contractual relationship only appropriate as between contracting parties.

17.2.3 Pure economic loss after *Anns*

Almost immediately, judges considered that the relaxation of the principle concerning recovery for economic loss had now gone too far. A long line of cases followed in which they tried to limit the scope of the above cases.

Governors of the Peabody Donation Fund v Sir Lindsay Parkinson & Co Ltd (1985)

The court would not accept that there was liability owed for a negligent council inspection that resulted in a drain having to be re-laid because it did not conform to regulations. The council's duty in inspecting was to protect the health and safety of the public.

The cases had often arisen because an action in contract was not available and so the reliance test from *Junior Books* (1983) was argued.

Muirhead v Industrial Tank Specialists Ltd (1985)

Fish merchandisers bought lobsters while they were cheap to sell on when their price increased. They bought storage tanks in which to hold the lobsters and lost money when the French-built pumps in the tanks were defective and the lobsters could not be stored. They originally succeeded against the supplier of the tanks in contract but, when they went into liquidation, bought an action in tort against the manufacturers of the pumps. Their claim that the test of proximity and reliance in *Junior Books* (1983) applied failed. The court held that reliance had only been possible in that case because the claimants nominated the defendants. The case was therefore distinguished.

The argument that costs of repairing defects in property that could lead to a danger to health or safety, approved in *Anns* (1978), was also gradually rejected.

D & F Estates v Church Commissioners (1989)

Liability against builders was rejected when plaster cracked, fell off walls, and had to be replaced as the result of the negligence of sub-contractors. The builders had satisfied their duty by hiring competent tradesmen and, in the absence of injury or an actual risk to health, any loss was purely economic and not recoverable.

These represent only a few of the cases where *Anns* (1978) was argued to allow economic loss and rejected or the case distinguished. The general unease that was felt at Lord Wilberforce's test in *Anns* and at the extension of liability for economic loss led eventually to the overruling of *Anns,* and thus back to a more restrictive attitude towards economic loss.

Murphy v Brentwood District Council (1990)

The House of Lords would not impose liability on a council that had approved plans for a concrete raft on which properties were built and which then moved, causing cracks in the walls. The claimant was forced to sell the house for £35,000 under what its value would have been if it had not been defective but in the absence of any injury, loss was purely economic. So the ratio in *Anns* (1978) was overruled and the principle of law now is that a local authority will not be liable for the cost of repairing dangerous defects (in the case, gas pipes had broken during the settlement of the property) until physical injury is actually caused. *Junior Books v Veitchi* (1983) was not overruled but was allowed to stand on its own facts. It is unlikely, however, to have much impact on future cases.

The principles in *Murphy* (1990) have subsequently been followed.

Department of the Environment v Thomas Bates & Sons Ltd (1990)

The claimant failed to recover the cost of repairing a building built of concrete which was of insufficient strength to support its intended load, although it was not dangerous to carry its existing load. Such cost was purely economic and thus unrecoverable.

So the present policy of the courts in relation to economic loss appears to be that recovery for such loss should be through the normal insurance of the injured party, rather than through the courts using negligence.

Marc Rich & Co v Bishop Rock Marine Co Ltd (1995)

A vessel was negligently classed as seaworthy and then sank. The classification society did not owe a duty of care to the owners of a cargo that sank with the ship. This was economic loss. The House of Lords applied the three-part test from *Caparo v Dickman* (1990) and determined that it was not just and reasonable in the circumstances of the case to impose a duty.

17.3 Negligent misstatement

17.3.1 The origins of liability

The law of torts is concerned mainly with compensating for physical damage or personal injury, not for loss that is only economic. The obvious justification for this stance is that economic loss, or for instance loss of a profit or bargain, is more traditionally associated with contract law, and the judges have always been eager to separate out the two.

Activity

1. What exactly is a 'pure economic loss'?
2. Why are the courts more willing to accept an economic loss caused by a negligently made statement than one resulting from a negligent act or omission?
3. Why were judges in later cases nervous about the judgment in *Junior Books* (1990)?

4. What is the difference between physical damage to property and the cost of repairing defects in property?
5. How would the courts now prefer a claimant to recover compensation for an economic loss?
6. Why did the judges in *Murphy* (1990) decide not to overrule *Junior Books* (1983)?

Key facts

- The courts have always been reluctant to allow liability for 'pure economic loss' because it is felt that it is more to do with contract – *Spartan Steel v Martin* (1973).
- Claims have been successful where there has been a risk to health – *Dutton v Bognor Regis UDC* (1972).
- The position on economic loss was drastically relaxed as the result of Lord Wilberforce's two-part test in *Anns*

(1978) – *Junior Books v Veitchi* (1983) – though this was because of a 'near contractual' relationship between the two parties.
- Judges were never really happy with *Anns* or the two-part test, and these were eventually overruled in *Murphy v Brentwood DC* (1990).

An action for an economic loss caused by a statement was traditionally available in tort, but in the tort of deceit and only in the case of fraudulently made statements.

Derry v Peek (1889)

A representation in a share prospectus that a tram company could use motive power led to loss when the Board of Trade refused the company a licence to use motorised trams. The company had fully expected to be granted the licence so their misstatement was not considered to be fraudulent.

That action for economic loss caused by reliance on a negligently made statement should be available was reaffirmed even more recently, although not without some fundamental disagreement being expressed.

Candler v Crane Christmas & Co (1951)

Accountants negligently prepared a company's accounts and investors then lost money. In the absence of a contractual relationship or fraud, the court was not prepared to declare the existence of a duty of care. Lord Denning, dissenting, felt that there should be a duty of care to the investor and to:

'... any third party to whom they themselves show the accounts, or to whom they know their employer is going to show the accounts so as to induce them to invest money ...'

The House of Lords eventually accepted this dissenting judgment a long time afterwards, and initially only in *obiter*.

Hedley Byrne v Heller & Partners Ltd (1964)

An advertising company was approached with a view to preparing a campaign for a small company, Easipower, with whom they had not previously dealt. The advertisers then did the most sensible thing in the circumstances and approached Easipower's bank for a credit reference. The bank gave a satisfactory reference without checking on their current financial standing, and the advertisers produced the campaign. They then lost money when Easipower went into liquidation. They sued the bank for their negligently prepared advice. They failed because the bank had included a disclaimer of liability in the credit reference. Nevertheless, the House of Lords, approving Lord Denning's dissenting judgment in the last case, held that such an action should be possible, and this has subsequently been accepted as law.

The interesting point of the court's approval of the principle in the case is that they were holding that such a duty could apply despite there being no contractual relationship, and despite the fact that, in effect, they were accepting that they could impose liability for an economic loss.

As a result, the House of Lords in the case laid down strict guidelines for when the principle could apply.

1. There must be a special relationship between the two parties – based on the skill and judgment of the defendant and the reliance placed upon it.
2. The person giving the advice must be possessed of special skill relating to the type of advice given – so the defendant ought to have realised that the claimant would rely on that skill.
3. The party receiving the advice has acted in reliance on it – and in the circumstances, it was reasonable for the claimant to rely on the advice.

The subsequent case law has in general followed these requirements.

17.3.2 The elements of liability

A special relationship

The precise meaning of 'special relationship' was never really examined in *Hedley Byrne* (1964) and so it has become an area for judicial policy-making. The original leaning was towards a narrow interpretation that would then only include a relationship where the party giving the advice was in the business of giving advice of the sort in question.

However, it has since been suggested that a business or professional relationship might in general give rise to the duty if the claimant is genuinely seeking professional advice.

Howard Marine & Dredging Co Ltd v Ogden & Sons Ltd (1978)

Dredging took much longer because the hirers of the barges had misstated the payload weight to the party hiring them. It was accepted that the relationship, while a standard business one, could give rise to a special relationship for the purposes of imposing a duty.

A purely social relationship should not normally give rise to a duty of care, but has done when it has been established that carefully considered advice was being sought from a party with some expertise.

Chaudhry v Prabhaker (1988)

A woman asked her friend, who, while not a mechanic, had some experience of cars, to find her a good second-hand car that had not been in an accident. When it was later discovered that the car advised on had been in an accident and was not completely roadworthy, the friend advising on its purchase was successfully sued.

Common relationships where a duty will be identified though are those where valuers or accountants are providing the advice.

Yianni v Edwin Evans & Sons (1982)

A building society surveyor was held to owe a duty to purchasers of a property valued at £12,000 where it was later discovered that repairs worth £18,000 were required. The duty was imposed because it was shown that at the time, less than 15 per cent of purchasers would have their own independent survey carried out, and therefore it was foreseeable that they would rely on the standard building society survey.

The mere fact that the claimant pays for the advice is insufficient for liability unless there is proximity between the parties.

West Bromwich Albion Football Club Ltd v El-Safty (2005)

The club sent a player with a knee injury to a consultant on the advice of their physiotherapist. The consultant negligently advised reconstructive surgery which failed and the player had to retire when other treatment would have been more appropriate. The club sued for the economic loss arising from the player's premature retirement, claiming a special relationship existed because it had paid for the treatment. The court held that the person really taking the advice was the player and there was insufficient proximity between the club and the doctor to impose a duty.

The possession of special skill or expertise

Ordinarily then, a claim is only possible if the party giving the advice is a specialist in the field which the advice concerns.

Mutual Life and Citizens Assurance Co Ltd v Evatt (1971)

A representative of an insurance company gave advice about the products of another company. The court held that there could only be a duty in such circumstances if the party giving the advice had held himself out as being in the business of giving the advice in question.

So advice given in a purely social context could not usually give rise to liability. The defendant in *Chaudhry v Prabhaker* (1988) was unfortunate in this way, though the result was justified since he should have applied the same caution in advising that he would have had if he had been buying it himself.

Reasonable reliance on the advice

It is only fair and logical that if there has been no reliance placed on the advice given, then there should be no liability on the defendant for giving it.

JEB Fasteners Ltd v Marks Bloom & Co (1983)

A negligent statement of the value of a company's stock did not give rise to a duty. This was because the party buying the company was doing so only to secure the services of two directors, and so placed no reliance on the stock.

The real test is whether there is sufficient proximity between the parties for there to be reasonable reliance on the advice. In *Raja v Gray* (2002) the Court of Appeal held that there was insufficient proximity between valuers appointed by receivers and parties with an interest in mortgaged property generally.

It will not be foreseeable reliance if the claimant belongs to a group of potential claimants that is too large.

Goodwill v British Pregnancy Advisory Service (1996)

Here a man had not been properly advised of the possibility that his vasectomy could automatically reverse itself. It was held that there could be no duty of care owed to a future girlfriend of the man.

But whenever there is foreseeable reliance on advice given, then there will be a duty of care owed.

Smith v Eric S Bush (1990)

A building society valuation had identified that chimney breasts had been removed, but the valuer had failed to check whether the brickwork above was properly secured. It was not and after the purchase it collapsed. There was a duty of care because, as in *Yianni v Edwin Evans* (1982), even though the contract was between building society and valuer, it was reasonably foreseeable that the purchaser would rely on it.

Foreseeable reliance by the party seeking the advice might also prevent an exclusion of liability clause in a contract from operating successfully.

Harris v Wyre Forest District Council (1989)

In the sale of a council house, a negligent survey had been carried out for the local authority. Even though the purchaser did not see the valuation, he could rely on it and a disclaimer of liability inserted in the valuation was ineffective because it was not reasonable within the terms of the Unfair Contract Terms Act 1977.

Where a duty to act is imposed by statute, a civil action is only usually available to a party when the type of harm suffered was that anticipated by the statute. This was one of the reasons why the action failed in *Caparo v Dickman* (1990). However, a duty may apply where the public would generally benefit.

Law Society v KPMG Peat Marwick (2000)

The Law Society was owed a duty of care by a firm of accountants hired to prepare annual accounts for the Law Society because it would be possible for clients of firms to be compensated by the Law Society if the accounts were unreliable.

17.3.3 Recent developments in the law

In *Caparo v Dickman* (1990) the House of Lords had the opportunity to consider the principles involved in liability under *Hedley Byrne* (1964). The financial booms and rapid development in property markets had not only led to a greater increase in home ownership and share ownership; it had also led to a great number of claims for negligent misstatement, particularly against property surveyors and accountants.

The House of Lords preferred an incremental approach to establishing the duty of care, as we have already seen. They also made a number of observations regarding the circumstances in which the *Hedley Byrne* type duty will be owed.

- The advice must be required for a purpose described at the time to the defendant at least in general terms.
- This purpose must be made known actually or by inference to the party giving the advice at the time it is given.
- If the advice will subsequently be communicated to the party relying on it, this fact must be known by the advisor.
- The advisor must be aware that the advice will be acted upon without benefit of any further independent advice.

- The person alleging to have relied on the advice must show actual reliance and consequent detriment suffered.

So the significant feature of this development of the duty is the express or implied knowledge of the purpose for which the claimant acted in reliance of the statement.

Guidance on the factors to be taken into account in deciding whether a duty of care in fact exists have subsequently been provided by the Court of Appeal.

James McNaughten Paper Group Ltd v Hicks Anderson & Co (1991)

Accountants who drew up accounts at very short notice for the chairman of a company had no duty of care to the person who acquired the company in a takeover bid, having inspected the accounts. The Court of Appeal identified the factors that should be taken into account in establishing a duty of care as follows:

1. The purpose for which the statement was made.
2. The purpose for which the statement was communicated.
3. The relationship between the person giving the advice, the person receiving the advice, and any relevant third party.
4. The size of any class that the person receiving the advice belonged to.
5. The degree of knowledge of the person giving the advice.

As a result of this final point, *Caparo* (1990) has been distinguished in some later cases.

This is a very narrow approach to the duty, and some subsequent cases have taken a more relaxed view. Policy considerations are important in identifying reasonable reliance and a special relationship. This was clear in *Caparo* (1990). As a result, the range of possible claimants is limited. The courts will not extend the range where it is not fair, just and reasonable as required in *Caparo*.

Newell v Ministry of Defence (2002)

An army officer claimed negligence when he applied for early release and had no reply for an unreasonable time. While waiting to hear, he had turned down a civilian job and claimed to have lost financially as a result. The court did not accept that the employer had owed the claimant any duty. It would not be fair to impose a duty where the employer was not involved in the officer's applications for civilian employment.

There is a greater chance of proving reliance in arrangements that are contractual. In *Commissioner of Police for the Metropolis v Lennon* (2004), acting on advice the claimant took time off before moving to a new force and as a result lost his housing allowance. The police were held liable under *Hedley Byrne*.

Some cases certainly seem to be at odds with the general principle and liability has been imposed apparently to prevent a party being without any remedy.

White v Jones (1995)

Solicitors who negligently failed to draw up a will before the testator's death were held to owe a duty to the intended beneficiaries who consequently lost their inheritance. Any contractual relationship was with the testator, and since a will can be changed, a beneficiary is not necessarily ensured the inheritance. Nevertheless, the House of Lords were prepared to identify both a special relationship in the circumstances and reliance.

Although in some instances this is because the court is uncertain whether the principle in *Hedley Byrne* (1964) or that in *Donoghue v Stevenson* (1932) is the appropriate one to apply. The latter is certainly less restrictive.

Spring v Guardian Assurance plc (1995)

An employee of an insurance company was dismissed and then prevented from gaining a position with another company because of a negligently prepared and highly unfavourable reference provided by the first company. The House of Lords held that the first employers were liable because of the reference, but the House was split on whether *Hedley Byrne* should apply.

The approach to dealing with negligently prepared references has since been developed by the Court of Appeal. In *Bartholomew v London Borough of Hackney* (1999), the court increased the duty to ensuring that information provided is accurate and that the reference does not create any unfair impression.

This test has now been developed further.

Cox v Sun Alliance Life Ltd (2001)

The claimant was a branch manager who was suspended for reasons not related to dishonesty. An allegation of dishonesty was made during negotiations for a termination agreement. However, the investigation that followed was abandoned and Sun Life agreed that in any references they would make no mention of the allegation. However, they did so in one reference which cost the claimant a job and he sued successfully for negligence. Lord Justice Mummery stated that before divulging information that is unfavourable to an ex-employee in a reference, the employer must believe in the truth of the information, have reasonable grounds for that belief, and make a reasonably thorough investigation before making the statement.

Activity

1. Why did the House of Lords in *Hedley Byrne* (1964) alter the previous rule in *Candler v Crane Christmas & Co* (1951)?
2. What exactly is a special relationship?
3. How can the decision in *Chaudhry v Prabhaker* (1988) be justified?
4. What level of specialist expertise is required for liability?
5. Against what standards is reasonable reliance measured?
6. How can the *Goodwill v BPAS* (1996) case be distinguished from other cases on reasonable reliance?
7. Why was the decision in *Yianni v Edwin Evans* (1982) greeted with such shock by building society surveyors?
8. To what extent does the case of *Caparo v Dickman* (1990) limit liability under *Hedley Byrne*?
9. How do cases like *White v Jones* (1995) and *Spring v Guardian Assurance* (1995) fit in with the normal rule?

Key facts

- Originally there was only an action available for misrepresentations if they were made fraudulently – *Derry v Peek* (1889).
- An action for negligence was originally specifically rejected in *Candler v Crane Christmas & Co* (1951).
- The House of Lords eventually accepted *in obiter* that such an action was possible in *Hedley Byrne v Heller & Partners* (1964).
- But only subject to certain requirements:
  (a) the existence of a special relationship – *Yianni v Edwin Evans* (1982)
  (b) where the party giving the advice has specialist skill and knowledge of the type sought – *Mutual Life & Citizens Assurance v Evatt* (1971)
  (c) the other party acts in reliance of the advice which is known to the other party – *Smith v Eric S Bush* (1990).
- Limitations on these requirements have since been made – *Caparo v Dickman* (1990).
- A list of important factors to be considered has been identified in *James McNaughten Paper Group v Hicks Anderson* (1991) including:
  (a) the purpose for which the statement was made and communicated
  (b) the relationship between all relevant parties
  (c) the degree of knowledge of the defendant.
- But there are also cases that do not fit the principle neatly – *White v Jones* (1995) and *Spring v Guardian Assurance* (1995).

17.4 Psychiatric harm (nervous shock)

This is another area of negligence that has been the subject of uncertain development. The extent to which liability has been imposed has expanded or contracted according to:

- The state of medical knowledge, ie psychiatric medicine and the recognition of psychiatric disorders, has developed dramatically over the past 100 years; the great concern expressed in recent years over soldiers who were executed in the First World War is an interesting example.
- Policy considerations on the part of judges, particularly the 'floodgates' argument, that to impose liability in a particular situation may lead to a rush of claims, and so should be avoided whatever the justice of the case.

Actions failed in the last century for three reasons:

- Because of the state of medical knowledge, psychiatric illness or injury was not properly recognised so there could be no duty if the type of damage concerned was not recognised.

- Another problem of course was the fear that a person making such a claim could actually be faking the symptoms.
- Finally there was the 'floodgates' argument, that once one claim was accepted it would lead to a multitude of claims.

Victoria Railway Commissioners v Coultas (1888)

Nervous shock resulting from involvement in a train crash did not give rise to liability, not least because of the 'floodgates' argument.

Even from the start there were two aspects to determining whether liability should be imposed.

- Firstly, the injury alleged must conform to judicial attitudes of what constitutes nervous shock, a recognised psychiatric disorder.
- Secondly, the person claiming to have suffered nervous shock must fall into a category accepted by the courts as being entitled to claim.

17.4.1 The nature of psychiatric injury

The claim must then involve an actual, recognised psychiatric condition capable of resulting from the shock of the incident, and recognised as having long-term effects.

Reilly v Merseyside Regional Health Authority (1994)

No liability was found when a couple became trapped in a lift as the result of negligence, and suffered insomnia and claustrophobia after they were rescued.

In the modern day, conditions such as post-traumatic stress disorder and acute anxiety syndrome would be recognised where the courts would be reluctant to allow a claim purely for a temporary upset, such as grief, distress or fright from which we all at times suffer.

Tredget v Bexley Health Authority (1994)

Unusually, parents of a child born with serious injuries following medical negligence and then dying two days later succeeded in their claim. They were held to be suffering from psychiatric injuries despite the argument that their condition was no more than profound grief.

The courts in recent times have been prepared to accept a claim that is partly caused by grief and partly by the severe shock of the event.

Vernon v Bosely (No 1) (1997)

A father had witnessed his children being drowned in a car negligently driven by their nanny. He recovered damages for nervous shock that was held to be partly the result of pathological grief and bereavement, but partly also the consequence of the trauma of witnessing the events.

17.4.2 Primary victims, secondary victims and the development of liability

Originally, claims were first allowed purely on the basis of foreseeability of real and immediate fear of personal danger (the so-called 'Kennedy' test from *Dulieu v White* (1901)) so that the class of possible claimants was at first very limited.

Dulieu v White & Sons (1901)

The court accepted a claim when a woman suffered nervous shock after a horse and van that had been negligently driven burst through the window of a pub where she was washing glasses. She was able to recover damages because she had been put in fear for her own safety.

This limitation was later extended to include a claim for nervous shock suffered as the result of witnessing traumatic events involving close family.

Hambrook v Stokes Bros (1925)

A woman recovered damages for nervous shock when she saw a runaway lorry going downhill towards where she had left her three children, and then heard that there had indeed been an accident involving a child. The court disapproved the 'Kennedy' test and considered that it would be unfair not to compensate a mother who had feared for the safety of her children when she could have claimed if she only feared for her own safety.

This principle was even extended at one point to include shock suffered on witnessing events involving close but not related people.

Dooley v Cammell Laird & Co (1951)

A crane driver claimed successfully for nervous shock when he saw a load fall and thought that workmates underneath would have been injured.

Indeed, claims have even been allowed where harm to the person with whom the close tie exists would be impossible.

Owens v Liverpool Corporation (1933)

Relatives recovered for nervous shock when the coffin fell out of the hearse that they were following.

One restriction on this development was to prevent a party from recovering who was not within the 'area of impact' of the event.

King v Phillips (1953)

A mother suffered nervous shock when from 70 yards away she saw a taxi reverse into her small child's bicycle and presumed him to be injured. Her claim failed because the court said she was too far away from the incident and outside of the range of foresight of the defendant.

In contrast, the same principle of reasonable foresight has allowed recovery for nervous shock where the damage was to property.

Attia v British Gas (1987)

A woman who witnessed her house burning down when she arrived home was able to claim successfully for nervous shock. She was within the area of impact. The claim was said to be within the reasonable foresight of the contractors who negligently installed her central heating, causing the fire.

An alternative measure to the area of impact test is whether the claimant falls within the area of shock.

Bourhill v Young (1943)

A pregnant Edinburgh fishwife claimed to have suffered nervous shock after getting off a tram, hearing the impact of a crash involving a motorcyclist, and later seeing blood on the road, after which she gave birth to a stillborn child. The House of Lords held that, as a stranger to the motorcyclist, she was not in the area of foreseeable shock.

It has also been well established in the case law that a rescuer will be able to recover when suffering nervous shock.

Chadwick v British Railways Board (1967)

When two trains crashed in a tunnel, a man who lived nearby was asked because of his small size to crawl into the wreckage to give injections to trapped passengers. He was able to claim successfully for the anxiety neurosis he suffered as a result. This was largely explained on the basis that he was a primary victim, at risk himself in the circumstances.

Usually only professional rescuers will be able to claim, or those present at the scene or the immediate aftermath.

Hale v London Underground (1992)

A fireman claimed successfully for post-traumatic stress disorder he suffered following the Kings Cross station fire.

However, claims for shock suffered at the scene of disasters will not be successful in the case of those people considered only to be bystanders.

McFarlane v E E Caledonia (1994)

A person who was helping to receive casualties from the Piper Alpha oil rig failed in his claim because he was classed as a mere bystander rather than a rescuer.

As we have seen, the tests developed above involve the proximity of the claimant in time and space to the negligent incident, or the closeness of the relationship with the party who is present. The widest point of expansion of liability came under the two-part test from *Anns* (1978), and allowed for recovery when the claimant was not present at the scene but was at the 'immediate aftermath'. Inevitably, 'the meaning of immediate aftermath' was open to an interpretation based on policy.

McLoughlin v O'Brian (1981)

A woman was called to a hospital about an hour after her children and husband were involved in a car crash. One child was dead, two were badly injured, all were in shock and they had not yet been cleaned up. The House of Lords held that since the relationship was sufficiently close and the woman was present at the 'immediate aftermath', she could claim. Lord Wilberforce identified a three-part test for secondary victims that was approved later in *Alcock* (1992) – see below.

17.4.3 *McLoughlin, Alcock* and *White* and the limits on claiming

The House of Lords has subsequently had the opportunity to review all aspects of the duty and to identify fairly restricted circumstances in which a claim can succeed.

Alcock v Chief Constable of South Yorkshire (1992)

At the start of a football match, police allowed a large crowd of supporters into a caged pen, as the result of which 95 people in the stand suffered crush injuries and were killed. Since the match was being televised, much of the disaster was shown on live television. A number of claims for nervous shock were made. These varied between those present or not present at the scene, those with close family ties to the dead and those who were merely friends. The House of Lords refused all of the claims and identified the factors important to consider in determining whether a party might recover. These were:

- The proximity in time and space to the negligent incident – there could be a claim in respect of an incident or the immediate aftermath that was witnessed or experienced directly, there could be none where the incident was merely reported.

- The proximity of the relationship with a party who was a victim of the incident – a successful claim would depend on the existence of a close tie of love and affection with the victim, or presence at the scene as a rescuer.

- The cause of the nervous shock – the court accepted that this must be the result of witnessing or hearing the horrifying event or immediate aftermath.

The case then identifies for the future the classes of claimants who will be successful and those who will not:

- Primary victims – those present at the scene and themselves injured.

Page v Smith (1996)

Here Page was involved in a car accident caused by the defendant's negligence. Although Page actually suffered no physical injury, he suffered a recurrence of 'chronic fatigue syndrome' which he had suffered some years before. The House of Lords held that the defendant was liable for the psychiatric injury caused to the claimant.

So in the case of primary victims the 'thin skull' applies even though the psychiatric injury may appear to be unforeseeable.

Simmons v British Steel (2004)

The claimant was injured through his employer's negligence and then suffered a worsening of his psoriasis, a stress-related skin disease, and of a depressive illness, also leading to a personality change. This resulted from his anger at his

employer's lack of apology and lack of support, rather than from the injury itself. However, the court still imposed liability as the claimant was a primary victim.

- Primary victims – an alternative is those who were present at the scene and their own safety was threatened, as in *Dulieu v White* (1901) where the woman could have been hurt by the horse coming through the glass window, and did in fact suffer a miscarriage.
- Secondary victims – these are people who are not primary victims of the incident but who are able to show a close enough tie of love and affection to a victim of the incident, and witnessed the incident or its 'immediate aftermath' at close hand. The probable limit of this is in *McLoughlin v O'Brian* (1982). In *Alcock* (1992) the judges were reluctant to allow claims there in respect of both proximity in time and space to the incidents at Hillsborough, and turned down claims from people who had identified bodies in the morgue some time after the events of the match. Indeed the courts have engaged in some fairly fine distinctions as to what can acceptably be called 'the immediate aftermath' in later cases.

Taylor v Somerset HA (1993)

The claimant's husband suffered a fatal heart attack while at work. She was told only that he had been taken to hospital, and when she arrived at the hospital she was told that he was dead. She was so shocked that she would not believe he was dead until she identified his body in the mortuary. She later suffered a psychiatric illness and claimed against the hospital. Even though she was at the hospital within an hour, her action failed. The court held that the actual purpose for her visit was to identify the body so that it was not to do with the cause of his death.

- Rescuers – these may well of course be primary victims and at risk in the circumstances of the incident causing the nervous shock; *Hale v London Underground* (1992). However, the question of who qualifies as a rescuer seems uncertain.

Duncan v British Coal (1990)

There was surprisingly no liability where a miner saw a colleague crushed in a roof fall (the fault of the employers), and tried to resuscitate him.

- The House of Lords certainly seem to be hostile towards claims by the emergency services for psychiatric injury suffered while dealing with the aftermath of a disaster in the course of their duties. A rescuer will only be able to claim where he is a genuine 'primary victim'.

White v Chief Constable of South Yorkshire (1998)

Police officers who claimed to have suffered post-traumatic stress disorder following their part in the rescue operation at Hillsborough were denied a remedy by the House of Lords. The reasoning seems to be that they did not actually put themselves at risk, and that public policy prevented them from recovering when the relatives of the deceased in the disaster could not.

The reasoning in *White* has subsequently been followed in *French v Chief Constable of Sussex Police* (2006) in respect of police officers who claimed to suffer nervous shock after being investigated for the shooting of an innocent man.

More recently the courts have been willing to accept that a rescuer can also claim as a secondary victim, but only where the rescuer conforms to all of the requirements for secondary victims in *Alcock* (1992).

Greatorex v Greatorex (2000)

A fire officer attended the scene of an accident caused by the negligence of his son. When he was required to attend to his son he claimed to suffer nervous shock. The court would not accept the claim because of the conflict that it would cause between family members, but had the son not been the cause of the accident, a claim may have been possible in the circumstances.

- Secondary victims watching the events on live television in contravention of broadcasting standards may claim from the broadcasting authority.

Those who cannot claim

Bystanders

The law has always made a distinction between rescuers or people who are at risk in the incident and those who are merely bystanders and have no claim. This point goes back as far as *Bourhill v Young* (1943).

McFarlane v EE Caledonia Ltd (1994)

A person on shore receiving survivors from the Piper Alpha oil rig disaster was not classed as a rescuer and therefore had no valid claim.

Those with no close tie of love and affection to the primary victim

Workmates who witness accidents involving their colleagues will not be able to claim because any ties are not close enough to involve foreseeable harm.

Robertson and Rough v Forth Road Bridge Joint Board (1995)

Three workmates had been repairing the Forth Bridge during a gale. One of them was sitting on a piece of metal on a truck when a gust of wind blew him off the bridge and he was killed. His colleagues who witnessed this were unable to claim. They were held not to be primary victims and had insufficient ties with the dead worker for injury to be foreseeable.

Those suffering gradual rather than sudden shock

If the psychiatric injury is the result of a gradual appreciation of events rather than a sudden shock, then there will be no liability.

Sion v Hampstead Health Authority (1994)

A father claimed to have suffered psychiatric injury as the result of watching his son, over the space of 14 days, gradually deteriorate and then die, when there was the possibility of the death resulting from medical negligence. There could be no claim because there was no sudden appreciation of a horrifying event.

However the Court of Appeal has since accepted that the shocking event itself can last for a long period of time.

North Glamorgan NHS Trust v Walters (2002)

Doctors negligently failed to diagnose that a 10-month-old baby suffering from hepatitis required a liver transplant, and told his mother that he should recover. He then suffered a major fit in front of her and both were taken to another hospital for the baby to have a liver transplant. On arrival he was found to have irreversible and severe brain damage. Permission was gained to switch off life support and the baby died minutes later in his mother's arms. The events took 36 hours. The mother suffered pathological grief

(a recognised psychiatric illness) as a result, and sued successfully. The Court of Appeal held that the whole period from when the baby suffered the fit to when it died was 'a single horrifying event' and part of a continuous chain of events, distinguishing it from cases involving gradual realisation of shocking consequences.

The Court of Appeal referred to this case in *Atkins v Seghal* (2003) where a mother was told of her daughter's death by a police officer but did not see the body until two hours later. The court accepted that this still fell within the immediate aftermath.

Even the House of Lords has extended the situations in which a claim is possible.

W v Essex and Another (2000)

The claimants agreed to foster a fifteen-year-old boy, having been assured by the defendant's officers that the child did not have a record as a child abuser or was not suspected of such. In fact the child had been cautioned for indecent assault and was currently under investigation for rape. He then committed serious sexual assaults on the children of the family and when the parents found out, the marriage eventually broke down and the parents suffered depression as a result of discovering the abuse. The House of Lords rejected the defendant's argument that the injury was not the result of witnessing a shocking event and would not strike out the claim.

Where there is no causal link between the incident and the damage

If the psychiatric injury can be attributed to an event other than the horrifying incident in question, then there is no causal link and no possible claim.

Calascione v Dixon (1994)

The defendant was responsible for the death of a 20-year-old in a motorcycle accident. He was not liable however for the psychiatric injuries suffered by the mother of the young man. It was shown that the psychiatric illness was more the result of the stress of the inquest and a private prosecution rather than the incident itself.

Comment

Clearly the area of recovery for psychiatric injury (nervous shock) has been subject to an erratic development. There is no doubt that secondary victims have been treated harshly by comparison to primary victims, despite the fact that they are just as likely to suffer psychiatric harm as primary victims. Even in the case of bystanders, it seems that it is policy reasons rather than the foreseeability of harm that has led to a denial of liability.

The need for reform in the area has been identified by the Law Commission in a Report (Law Com No 249) in 1998. Their chief recommendations are:

- to retain the requirement of a close tie of love and affection to the primary victim in the case of secondary victims
- to remove the requirements for such claimants to show proximity in time and space, and that the event has been witnessed by the claimant's own unaided senses
- that the injury should be accepted even where not caused by a sudden trauma.

The proposals seem to be much fairer. However, it is not clear whether or not there is any likelihood of them becoming law.

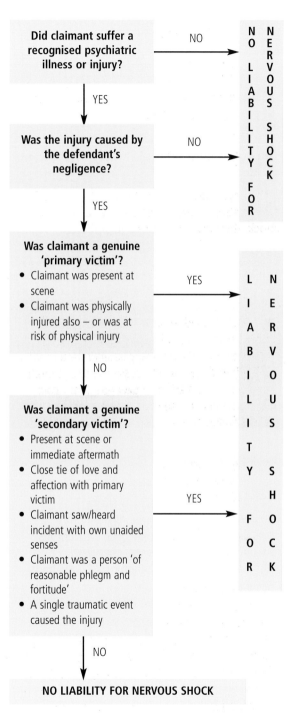

Figure 17.2 The means of determining liability for nervous shock

Key facts

- Originally courts were unwilling to allow actions for nervous shock – *Victoria Railway Commissioners v Coultas* (1888).
- This was because of the primitive state of psychiatric medicine.
- The key requirement is always that the illness amounts to a recognised psychiatric disorder – *Vernon v Bosely* (1997).
- An action was first accepted only because the claimant was also in physical danger – *Dulieu v White* (1901).
- But this was then extended to include a person who was in the area of shock, ie witnessed the accident and had some close tie with the victim – *Hambrook v Stokes* (1925).
- The widest extent of the duty was to include witnessing the immediate aftermath of the accident – *McLoughlin v O'Brian* (1981).
- Strangely a claim has been allowed for nervous shock on witnessing property damage – *Attia v British Gas* (1987).
- Now basic rules identify a restricted range of people who can claim – *Alcock v Chief Constable of South Yorkshire* (1992) – which include:
  - (a) primary victims – present and either injured or at risk
  - (b) secondary victims – close tie of love and affection to the victim, and a witness of the incident or its immediate aftermath

- (c) rescuers – where the rescuer is either a genuine primary victim (*White v Chief Constable of South Yorkshire* (1998)) or a genuine secondary victim (*Greatorex v Greatorex* (2000)) – but there is now no general category of liability to a rescuer
- (d) those witnessing it on live television in contravention of broadcasting requirements.
- There are a number of classes of people who could not claim:
  - (a) mere bystanders – *McFarlane v E E Caledonia* (1994)
  - (b) secondary victims without close ties to the victim – *Robertson and Rough v Forth Road Bridge Joint Board* (1995)
  - (c) those not suffering a recognised psychiatric disorder – *Reilly v Merseyside Regional Health Authority* (1994)
  - (d) those outside of the area of foreseeable shock of the accident – *Bourhill v Young* (1943).
- The Law Commission has suggested relaxing the rules for claims by secondary victims, so that they should only need to prove the close tie of love and affection with the primary victim.

Activity

1. What exactly is 'nervous shock'?
2. Why were courts originally reluctant to allow a claimant to recover for nervous shock and why has this changed?
3. How broad is the definition of 'psychiatric injury'?
4. Has there been any logical kind of development to nervous shock?
5. What is the 'area of impact' and what is the 'area of shock'?
6. What is the difference between a 'primary victim' and a 'secondary victim'?
7. In which specific ways is a primary victim in a better position to claim than a secondary victim?
8. What are the three essential features of a successful claim by a secondary victim?
9. How have the courts defined the meaning of 'immediate aftermath' in the decisions of cases?
10. To what extent is policy a determining factor?
11. To what extent does *McLoughlin v O'Brien* (1982) fit in with other cases?
12. In what way is *Attia v British Gas* (1987) such a strange case?

Activity

In the following series of situations, suggest which of the statements may raise a successful claim of nervous shock:

1. (a) James is present when his dog is run over by Carl's negligent driving, and suffers nervous shock.
   (b) James hears that his mother has been run over by Carl's negligent driving four days ago, and suffers nervous shock.
   (c) James is a passenger in a car when his friend Andrew, the driver, is killed by Carl's negligent driving. He suffers nervous shock.
   (d) James hears screams when Carl crashes his car, and suffers nervous shock.

2. (a) Sally hears that a friend has died in a car crash caused by negligence, and suffers from profound grief.
   (b) Sally sees her friend killed in an accident at work caused by the employer's negligence, and cannot sleep.
   (c) Sally is called to the hospital to identify her mother's body after a car driver has negligently run her over and it makes Sally very angry.
   (d) Sally is with her father when he drowns as a result of negligence when a ferry sinks. She suffers post-traumatic stress disorder.

Chapter 18

Occupiers' liability

18.1 Occupiers and premises

Occupiers' liability concerns the liability of an 'occupier' of land for the claimant's injury or loss or damage to property suffered while on the occupier's 'premises'. Therefore it must be distinguished from damage caused by the defendant's use of his or her land, which the claimant suffers on his or her own land. This would lead to an action in nuisance or possibly the tort of *Rylands v Fletcher* (1868) (see Chapter 20).

The tort is found in two statutes, the Occupiers' Liability Act (OLA) 1957 (concerned with the duty of care owed to lawful visitors) and the Occupiers' Liability Act (OLA) 1984 (the duty owed to trespassers).

While in statutory form, the tort has developed out of negligence, and so much of the terminology and many of the principles are the same. Indeed, though the Acts do contain extensive definition, where definitions are not supplied in the Acts these are to be found in the common law.

Inevitably there is overlap with negligence. The basic liability arises from the loss or injury caused by the 'state of the premises'. Loss or damage arising other than because of the state of the premises should be claimed for under negligence if it is possible.

Ogwo v Taylor (1987)

There was no liability under the Act when a fireman was injured in a fire on the defendant's premises. The fire did not result from the state of the premises, so liability was in negligence.

It can be argued that the Act should apply to damage caused other than by the state of the premises since s 1(1) states that the Act should apply:

> '. . . in respect of dangers due to the state of the premises or to things done or omitted to be done on them.'

Definition of occupiers

Potential defendants are the same under either Act, occupiers of premises.

There is in fact no statutory definition of 'occupier'. Section 1(2) of the 1957 Act merely states that the rules apply:

> '. . . in consequence of a person's occupation or control of premises . . .'.

The established test for determining occupation then is found in common law.

Wheat v E Lacon & Co Ltd (1966)

A manager of a public house was given the right to rent out rooms in his private quarters even though he had no proprietary interest in the premises. When a paying guest fell on an unlit staircase, the House of Lords held that both the manager and his employers could be occupiers under the Act. In the event neither had breached their duty since it was a stranger who had removed the light bulb.

So dual or multiple occupation of premises is possible, and the identity of the defendant, which party was in control of the premises, may depend on the circumstances in which the damage or injury was suffered.

Collier v Anglian Water Authority (1983)

Here a promenade formed part of the sea defences for which the water authority was responsible. The local authority owned the land, and was responsible for cleaning the promenade. When the claimant was injured because of disrepair, the water authority rather than the local authority was liable, though both were occupiers.

Occupation does not require either proprietary interest or possession, so the position is quite different to trespass. All that is required for liability is that the defendant has sufficient control of the premises at the time that the damage was caused.

Harris v Birkenhead Corporation (1976)

Here a four-year-old child had been injured in an empty house, which was not boarded up or secured in any way. Even though the council had

not yet taken possession of the house, they were liable since they had served a compulsory purchase notice and were effectively in control of the premises.

In the final analysis, the identity of the defendant will be influenced by the ability to meet a successful claim whether through insurance or other means.

Definition of premises

The Acts are again relatively silent on the meaning of premises. Some limited reference is given in s 1(3)(a) which refers to a person having occupation or control of any:

> '. . . fixed or moveable structure, including any vessel, vehicle and aircraft . . .'

So the common law again applies, and besides the obvious such as houses, buildings and the land itself, premises has also been held to include:

- ships in dry dock – *London Graving Dock v Horton* (1951)
- vehicles – *Hartwell v Grayson* (1947)
- lifts – *Haseldine v Daw & Son Ltd* (1941)
- even a ladder – *Wheeler v Copas* (1981).

18.2 Liability in respect of lawful visitors and the Occupiers' Liability Act 1957

18.2.1 The scope of the duty

The extent of the duty of care is set out in s 2(1).

> 'An occupier owes the same duty, the common duty of care, to all his visitors except insofar as he is free to do and does extend, restrict, modify or exclude his duty to any visitors by agreement or otherwise'.

The nature of the duty is in s 2(2) to:

> '... take such care as in all the circumstances ... is reasonable to see that the visitor will be reasonably safe for the purpose for which he is invited ... to be there ...'

Three key points need to be made:

1. Firstly, the standard of care is that generally applied in negligence, the standard of the 'reasonable man'. As a result, the occupier is merely obliged to guard against the foreseeable.
2. The duty in the 1957 Act only applies if the visitor is carrying out activities that are authorised within the terms of the visit. So if the visitor strays, he may lose protection under the 1957 Act, although the 1984 Act might still apply.
3. The duty is to keep the visitor safe, not necessarily to maintain safe premises. If the latter were the case it would make industry unworkable. But because of the scope and potential limitations of the duty, the Act sensibly makes some different rules for different classes of visitor.

The duty, however, does not extend to liability for pure accidents and a duty in respect of a specific risk cannot last indefinitely where there could be other causes of the damage hours after he had gone off duty.

Cole v Davis-Gilbert & The Royal British Legion (2007)

The claimant was injured when she put her foot onto a hole in a village green where it was common for a maypole to be erected. She argued that the owner of the village green had a duty to ensure that visitors were safe and that the British Legion had failed to properly fill the hole after a village fete. Her claim failed. The court held that since her claim was nearly two years after the fete the duty on the British Legion could not last that long. Inevitably the hole had been opened again by a stranger and the incident was a pure accident.

18.2.2 Lawful visitors and special classes of visitor

Potential claimants under the 1957 Act

The 1957 Act was passed to simplify a fairly complex common law, whereby the duty owed to a person entering premises varied with the capacity in which the person entered. The Act introduced a common duty to be applied to all lawful visitors.

By s 1(2), the class of people to whom the occupier owes a duty is the same as under common law. These are called visitors under the Act, and as a result of s 1(2) include:

- all invitees – these can be friends making a social call, but they could also include people invited onto land for a purpose, eg to give a quote for work.
- licensees – or people whose entry is to the material interest of the occupier, eg customers. They can include anyone with permission to be on the premises for any purpose (licensees were treated somewhat harshly by the common law, being entitled to no more than warnings of danger) – visitors with an implied licence must prove that the conduct of the occupier created a grant of a licence.

Lowery v Walker (1911)

Certain members of the public used a short cut across the defendant's land for many years. While he objected, he took no legal steps to stop it. When he loosed a wild horse on the land, which savaged the claimant, he was liable. The claimant by the defendant's conduct had a licence.

- those entering under a contractual agreement – in which case the terms of the contract might determine the extent of the duty.
- those not requiring permission to enter because of a legal right to enter, eg meter readers, police officers etc.

No duty is owed under the 1957 Act to trespassers. A more limited duty is owed to trespassers under the Occupiers' Liability Act 1984. Certain other categories of entrants are also not covered by the 1957 Act. These include:

- those using a private right of way
- those entering under an access agreement under the National Parks and Access to the Countryside Act 1949 (both of the above classes are also dealt with under the 1984 Act)
- those using a public right of way – these are excluded by both Acts and fall under common law with the tortfeasor liable for misfeasance but not nonfeasance.

McGeown v Northern Ireland Housing Executive (1994)

The claimant lived in a cul-de-sac owned by the defendants. She was injured on a footpath which had become a public right of way. The injury was due to a failure to maintain the footpath, and her action failed.

Occupiers' liability to children

Under s 2(3) the occupier '. . . must be prepared for children to be less careful than adults . . .' and as a result '. . . the premises must be reasonably safe for a child of that age . . .', so for children the standard of care is measured subjectively.

The reasoning is perfectly logical; what may pose no threat to an adult may nevertheless be very dangerous to a child.

Activity

Consider which of the following potential claimants would be able to class themselves as visitors for the purposes of the OLA 1957, and why.

1. Trevor is a milkman delivering milk to Archie's door.
2. Kurt is a milkman who picks flowers in Archie's garden after delivering milk.
3. Gordon, a football fan with a season ticket for the Wanderers, arrives at the ground on Wednesday night for the match with United.
4. Hannah regularly crosses Farmer Giles' field, using a well-known public path.
5. Greg is at Mavis's house on Monday morning as agreed, to paint the outside.
6. Ali is a police officer who has called at Brian's house for routine enquiries.
7. Tom regularly climbs over his neighbour's back fence and comes through his back garden on his way home, knowing that his neighbour works later so will be out.
8. Parminder calls at her friend Baljinder's house as arranged, to enjoy a meal together.
9. Baljinder is at her friend Parminder's house for a meal, enters Parminder's bedroom and takes a valuable ring.
10. Yuri is an employee of British Gas and has called at Ojukwu's house to read the gas meter.

Moloney v Lambeth LBC (1966)

Here a four-year-old child fell through a gap in railings guarding a stairwell and was injured. An adult could not have fallen through the gap so such an injury would have been impossible. The occupier was liable.

Similarly, children are unlikely to appreciate risks that adults would and might even be attracted to the danger. Thus occupiers should guard against any kind of 'allurement' which places a child visitor at risk of harm.

Glasgow Corporation v Taylor (1922)

Here a seven-year-old child ate poisonous berries in a botanical gardens and died. The shrub on which the berries grew was not fenced off in any way; the occupier should have expected that a young child might be attracted to the berries and was liable.

Nevertheless, the existence of an allurement on its own is not sufficient ground for liability.

Liddle v Yorkshire (North Riding) CC (1944)

A child was injured jumping off a soil bank while showing off to his friends. The defendant was not liable since the child had been warned away from the bank on numerous previous occasions.

In fact, even though an allurement exists, there will be no liability on the occupier if the damage or injury suffered is not foreseeable.

Jolley v London Borough of Sutton (1998) CA and (2000) HL

The council failed to move an abandoned boat for two years. Children regularly played in the boat and it was clearly a potential danger. When two young boys of 14 years jacked the boat up to repair it, the boat fell on one, injuring him. In the Court of Appeal the action for compensation failed, since it was held that, while the boat was an obvious allurement, the course of action taken by the boys and therefore the specific type of damage were not foreseeable. The House of Lords reversed this. As Lord Hoffman said:

> '... the [trial] judge's broad description of the risk as being that children would 'meddle with the boat at the risk of some physical injury' was the correct one to adopt ...'

In any case, the courts will sometimes take the view that very young children should be under the supervision of a parent or other adult. In this case the occupier might find that he is relieved of liability.

Phipps v Rochester Corporation (1955)

A five-year-old child was injured, having fallen down a trench dug by the defendant where the child frequently played. The defendant was not liable because the court concluded that the parents should have had the child under proper control.

Liability to people carrying out a trade or calling

Sensibly, the Act also has a more particular attitude to professional visitors, taking the view that, by s 2(3)(b) in relation to activities carried on within their trade, they should:

> *'. . . appreciate and guard against any special risks ordinarily incident to it . . .'.*

So an occupier will not be liable where tradesmen fail to guard against risks which they should know about.

Roles v Nathan (1963)

No liability was found on the occupiers when chimney sweeps died after inhaling carbon monoxide fumes while cleaning flues. The sweeps should have taken the occupier's advice to complete the work with the boilers off.

Tradesmen might still have an action against their employer if the latter has agreed to an unsafe system of work.

General Cleaning Contractors v Christmas (1953)

Occupiers were not liable for an injury sustained when a window cleaner fell after a window closed on him; his employers were liable.

However, the existence of a skill is not proof *per se* that the occupier is not liable. It depends whether normal safeguards in the trade could have averted the loss or injury.

Salmon v Seafarers Restaurants Ltd (1983)

Owners of a chip shop were liable for the injuries caused to a fireman, which were unavoidable due to the fire's character.

Liability for the torts of independent contractors

Generally the occupier will be able to avoid liability for loss or injuries suffered by his visitors when the cause of damage is the negligence of an independent contractor hired by the occupier. This is under s 2(4).

A reputable contractor will in any case be covered by his own insurance, and so the claimant can still recover compensation.

However, three requirements will apply:

1. It must be reasonable for the occupier to have entrusted the work to the independent contractor.

Haseldine v Daw & Son Ltd (1941)

The occupier was not liable for negligent repair of a lift, a highly specialist activity.

2. The contractor hired must be competent to carry out the task.

Ferguson v Welsh (1987)

Demolition contractors hired by the local authority employed the claimant. When he was injured due to their unsafe working systems, the local authority was liable.

The contractor must be able to demonstrate obvious expertise. The fact that the contractor fails to carry insurance for the activity should be a fair indication to the occupier that the contractor is not competent.

Bottomley v Todmorden Cricket Club (2003)

The club hired a stunt team to carry out a 'firework display'. The team chose to use ordinary gunpowder, petrol and propane gas rather than the more traditional fireworks, and also then enlisted the help of the claimant, an unpaid amateur with no experience of pyrotechnics, for the stunt. The claimant was burnt and broke an arm when the stunt went wrong. The stunt team had no insurance and the court held that this was sufficient to impose liability on the cricket club.

3. If possible, the occupier must check the work (obviously the more complex and technical the work and the less expert the occupier, the less reasonable it is to impose this obligation).

Woodward v The Mayor of Hastings (1945)

Occupiers were liable when a child was injured on school steps that were negligently left icy after cleaning off snow. The danger should have been obvious to the occupiers.

The occupiers' duty is also to inspect that the independent contractor is insured so that he can stand the loss if found liable. This is also part of the duty to ensure that a competent contractor is chosen.

Gwillam v West Hertfordshire NHS Trust (2002)

A hospital trust organised a fund raising fair on its premises and hired a 'splat-wall' from Club Entertainments which also operated it. (A 'splat wall' is a wall that a person wearing a Velcro suit will stick to after bouncing from a trampoline.) The claimant was injured because the wall had been negligently assembled. Club Entertainment was meant to insure, but this had expired four days before the fair, and the claimant sought damages from the trust. The Court of Appeal held that there was a duty to ensure that the contractor had insurance cover, but that the trust had not breached this duty.

The obligation may not apply if there are other accepted means of assessing that the independent contractor is competent.

Naylor (t/a Mainstream) v Payling (2004)

A door attendant, supplied by an independent contractor, threw the claimant out of a nightclub and negligently injured him. The claimant argued that the club had failed to check whether the independent contractor had insurance. The Court of Appeal held that there was no obligation to check on the independent contractor's insurance because the nightclub used a local scheme supported by the local authority and the police for establishing whether door attendants were suitably qualified.

18.2.3 Avoiding the duty and defences

By s 2(1) the occupier may extend, restrict, modify or exclude his duty. The occupier may achieve this in one of three ways:

Warnings

By s 2(4)(a) a warning is ineffective unless:

> '. . . in all the circumstances it was enough to enable the visitor to be reasonably safe.'

What is sufficient warning is a question of fact in each case.

Sometimes a mere warning is insufficient to safeguard the visitor and the occupier may need to set up barriers instead.

Rae v Mars (UK) Ltd (1990)

A warning was ineffective in respect of a deep pit inside the entrance of a dark shed, so the occupier was liable.

But a choice of words, which are nothing more than an attempt to avoid liability, will not be accepted as a warning.

Some risks are possibly so obvious that no additional warning is needed.

Staples v West Dorset DC (1995)

Danger of wet algae on a high wall at Lyme Regis should have been obvious.

This is particularly true where the occupier takes reasonable steps to avoid harm.

Beaton v Devon County Council (2002)

The claimant was injured riding his bicycle through a tunnel. The tunnel was well lit and in good condition. Two gullies that ran through it were well known. The court held that the occupier had done everything practical to keep the visitor safe.

Exclusion clauses

These are allowed by s 2(1) so they can be a term in a contractual licence.

Ashdown v Samuel Williams & Sons Ltd (1957)

The claimant could not recover for injuries sustained in a shunting yard because notices excluding liability were sufficiently bought to her attention, and she was only a contractual licensee when she entered.

Use of exclusion clauses will, however, be subject to various restrictions:

- They will be unavailable in the case of persons entering under a legal right.
- They do not apply in the case of strangers, eg a tenant's visitors, because they will have been unable to agree the exclusion.

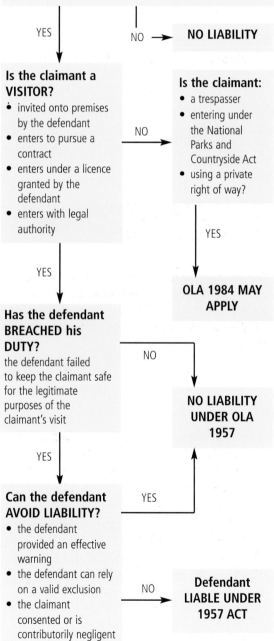

Figure 18.1 The assessment of liability under the Occupiers' Liability Act 1957

- They will probably fail against children, who may be unable to read or to understand their implications fully.
- They are not allowed for death or injury caused by the occupier's negligence because this will be prevented by s 2(1) Unfair Contract Terms Act 1977.
- There is an argument that, since OLA 1984 imposes a minimum standard of care to trespassers, then this should be beyond exclusion, or trespassers have better rights than lawful visitors.

General defences

There are two possibilities:

1. The claimant's contributory negligence. Under the Law Reform (Contributory Negligence) Act 1945, this has the effect of reducing awards of damages.
2. *Volenti non fit injuria* – consent. Section 2(5) allows that the occupier '. . . has no liability to a visitor in respect of risks willingly accepted as his by the visitor . . .'

  - The risk must, however, be fully understood by the visitor.

Simms v Leigh RFC (1969)

There was no liability to a Rugby Football player when the injury was sustained within the normal rules of the game.

- Mere knowledge of the risk is also insufficient; it must be accepted.

White v Blackmore (1972)

General knowledge that 'jalopy racing' was dangerous did not mean that the claimant had accepted inadequate safety arrangements.

- If the claimant has no choice, then consent cannot be used as a defence.

Burnett v British Waterways Board (1973)

A claimant entering the defendant's dry dock on a barge had no choice but to be there, so consent was unavailable as a defence.

- Express warnings that the claimant enters at his own risk may be caught by Unfair Contract Terms Act 1977.

Activity

1. Who exactly is a visitor?
2. What sorts of people are non-visitors?
3. Who is an occupier?
4. Why is the duty called 'the common duty of care'?
5. What exactly is the duty owed?
6. Why are children owed a different duty?
7. What exactly is 'allurement'?
8. What protection does the case of *Phipps v Rochester* (1955) give to an occupier?
9. When will a tradesman be able to successfully sue an occupier?
10. When is an occupier liable for negligent acts or omissions of people who have carried out work on his premises?
11. How can an occupier avoid being liable to a lawful visitor?
12. When will a warning sign protect an occupier from liability?
13. When is an exclusion clause likely to be used and when will one not succeed?

Key facts

Occupiers' liability	Case
Occupiers' liability is covered by two Acts: the Occupiers' Liability Act 1957 for lawful 'visitors' and the Occupiers' Liability Act 1984 for trespassers An 'occupier' is anybody in actual control of the land Premises are widely defined and have included even a ladder	*Wheat v Lacon* (1966) *Wheeler v Copas* (1981)

The duty and the standard of care in the 1957 Act	Case
A 'common duty of care' is owed to all lawful visitors The duty is to ensure that the visitor is safe for the purposes of the visit An occupier must take extra care for children, who are less careful than adults, and not put extra danger or 'allurements' in their path This applies to any foreseeable danger to the child regardless of what injury is actually caused Although it is assumed that parents should keep control of young children A person carrying out a trade or calling on the occupier's premises must prepare for the risks associated with the trade The occupier will not be liable for damage which is the result of work done by independent contractors if: (a) it is reasonable to entrust the work (b) a reputable contractor is chosen (c) the occupier is not obliged to inspect the work.	s 2(1) s 2(2) s 2(3) *Glasgow Corporation v Taylor* (1922) *Jolley v London Borough of Sutton* (1998) *Phipps v Rochester Corporation* (1955) *Roles v Nathan* (1963) *Haseldine v Daw* (1941) *Woodward v Mayor of Hastings* (1945)

Avoiding the duty	Case
It is possible to avoid liability where: (a) adequate warnings are given (b) exclusion clauses can be relied on – subject to the Unfair Contract Terms Act 1977 (c) defences of consent or contributory negligence apply	*Rae v Mars* (1990)

Key facts chart on occupiers' liability

18.3 Liability in respect of trespassers and the Occupiers' Liability Act 1984

18.3.1 The background of the duty

The 1984 Act was introduced to provide a limited duty of care mainly towards trespassers. The Act came about because traditionally at common law, an occupier owed such entrants no duty at all, other than possibly to refrain from deliberately or recklessly inflicting damage or injury.

Bird v Holbreck (1828)

This case finally outlawed mantraps.

An occupier was however still entitled to act reasonably in his own protection.

Clayton v Deane (1817)

This case accepted that an occupier was entitled to use reasonable deterrents to keep trespassers out, eg broken glass on top of a wall, as long as it was reasonably visible.

The common law could be particularly harsh when applied to child trespassers.

Addie v Dumbreck (1929)

Children frequently played on colliery premises and near to dangerous machinery. When one was injured, there was no liability since he was a trespasser.

Because of the growth of more dangerous premises and taking into account the difficulties of making children appreciate danger, the law was changed.

B R Board v Herrington (1972)

A six-year-old child was badly burned when straying onto an electrified railway line through vandalised fencing. The House of Lords, using the practice statement, established the 'common duty of humanity', a limited duty owed when the occupier knew of the danger, and of the likelihood of the trespass.

Because of some of the impracticalities of the rule, the 1984 Act was passed.

18.3.2 The scope of the duty

By s 1(1)(a) a duty applies in respect of people other than visitors (who are covered by the 1957 Act) for:

> '. . . injury on the premises by reason of any danger due to the state of the premises or things done or omitted to be done on them.'

Thus the 1984 Act provides compensation for injuries only. Damage to property is not covered, reflecting an understandable view that trespassers are deserving of less protection than are lawful visitors.

The occupier will only owe a duty under s 1(3) if he:

> (a)   . . . is aware of the danger or has reasonable grounds to believe it exists;
> (b)   . . . knows or . . . believes the other is in the vicinity of the danger; and
> (c)   the risk is one against which . . . he may be expected to offer . . . some protection.

In deciding whether s 1(3) applies, the court must take into account all of the circumstances when the injury occurred.

Donoghue v Folkestone Properties (2003)

The claimant was injured when he was trespassing on a slipway in a harbour and dived into the sea. The injury happened in the middle of winter, at around midnight. The court held that the occupier did not owe a duty of care. A reasonable occupier would not expect that a trespasser might be present or engage in such a foolhardy escapade.

So the occupier is not liable if he had no reason to suspect the presence of a trespasser.

Higgs v Foster (2004)

A police officer investigating a crime entered the occupier's premises for surveillance and fell into an uncovered inspection pit behind coaches suffering severe injuries, causing him to retire from the police force. The police officer was a trespasser and the occupier could not have anticipated his presence so there was no liability.

The occupier is also not liable if he was not aware of the danger or had no reason to suspect the danger existed.

Rhind v Astbury Water Park (2004)

The claimant ignored a notice stating 'Private Property. Strictly no Swimming' and jumped into a lake and was injured by objects below the surface of the water. The occupier had no reason to know of the dangerous objects so there was no liability.

The character of the duty owed is, by s 1(4) to '. . . take such care as is reasonable in all the circumstances . . .' to prevent injury to the non-visitor.

So the standard of care is an objective negligence standard. What is required of the occupier depends on the circumstances of each case. The greater the degree of risk, the more precautions the occupier will have to take. Factors to be taken into account include the nature of the premises, the degree of danger, the practicality of taking precautions, and the age of the trespasser.

Tomlinson v Congleton Borough Council (2003)

The local authority owned a park including a lake. Warning signs were posted prohibiting swimming and diving because the water was dangerous, but the council knew that these were generally ignored. The council decided to make the lake inaccessible to the public but delayed start on this work because of lack of funds. The claimant, aged 18, dived into the lake, struck his head and suffered paralysis as a result of a severe spinal injury. His claim under the 1984 Act succeeded.

Here all three aspects of s 1(3) were satisfied. The Court of Appeal felt that the gravity of the risk of injury, the frequency with which people were exposed to the risk, and the fact that the lake acted as an allurement all meant that the scheme to make the lake inaccessible should have been completed with greater urgency. The trial judge had reduced damages by two-thirds because of the contributory negligence of the claimant. The House of Lords, however, accepted the council's appeal for three reasons. Firstly the danger was not due to the state of the premises. Secondly it was not the sort of risk that a defendant should have to guard against but one that the trespasser chose to run. Thirdly, the council would not have breached its duty even with a lawful visitor as the practicality and cost of avoiding the danger was not reasonable to expect of the occupier.

This can also be seen in *Keown v Coventry Healthcare NHS Trust* (2006).

Keown v Coventry Healthcare NHS Trust (2006)

A child had climbed a fire escape to show off to his friends and fell. The Court of Appeal held that, since the child appreciated the danger, it was not the state of the premises (the existence of the fire escape) but what the child was doing on them which was the cause of harm so there was no liability.

The same principle, that the damage must be caused by the state of the premises and not by a careless act of the claimant, was also evident in *Siddorn v Patel* (2007). Here a tenant danced on a Perspex roof of an adjoining building also owned by her landlord, but failed in her claim.

The mere fact that the occupier has taken precautions or fenced the premises is not proof that the occupier knew or ought to have known of the existence of a danger.

White v St Albans City Council (1990)

The claimant had taken an unauthorised short cut over the council's land. He fell from a narrow bridge that had been fenced. The court did not feel that this was sufficient to make the council liable.

18.3.3 Avoiding the duty and defences

Again, as with the 1957 Act, it is possible for the occupier to avoid liability.

Under s 1(5) the occupier could do so by taking:

 '. . . such steps as are reasonable in all the circumstances . . .'.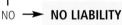

This might, in the case of adult trespassers, be achieved by use of effective warnings.

Westwood v The Post Office (1973)

A notice that 'Only the authorised attendant is permitted to enter' placed on the door of a motor room was held a sufficient warning for an intelligent adult.

Again it is unlikely that such warnings will succeed in the case of children.

Section 1(6) also preserves the defence of *volenti*; the claimant must appreciate the nature and degree of the risk, not merely be aware of its existence.

Ratcliffe v McConnell (1999)

A warning notice at the shallow end of a swimming pool read: 'Deep end shallow dive'. The pool was always kept locked after hours and the claimant knew that entry was prohibited

then. He was a trespasser and when he was injured diving into the shallow end his claim failed. The court held that he was aware of the risk and had accepted it.

Is the defendant an OCCUPIER of PREMISES?
- the defendant has sole control of premises at time harm caused to the claimant
- the defendant is one of many people with interest in premises but was in control at material times

YES / NO → **NO LIABILITY**

Is the claimant a VISITOR?
- invited onto premises by the defendant
- enters to pursue a contract
- enters under a licence granted by the defendant
- enters with legal authority

NO →

Is the claimant:
- a trespasser
- entering under the National Parks and Countryside Act
- using a private right of way?

YES ↓

Is the defendant AWARE of DANGER and:
- knows or believes the claimant is in danger; or
- risk is one against which the defendant should guard

YES ↓

OLA 1984 MAY APPLY
If the defendant is not taking care to avoid risk of injury

YES ↓

OLA 1957 MAY APPLY

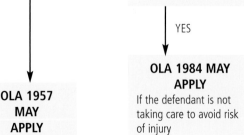

Figure 18.2 The assessment of liability under the Occupiers' Liability Act 1984

There is no reference to exclusions in the Act. It is argued that exclusions should be impossible since the Act creates a minimum standard of care which would then be thwarted. However, this then creates the unhappy situation where a trespasser might be entitled to more care than a lawful visitor.

Activity

Consider the following problem on Occupiers' Liability.

Alsopp Towers is a large pleasure theme park. At the entrance gate there is a sign which reads 'All of the rides are dangerous and customers enter entirely at their own risk'.

Consider any liability that Alsopp Towers may incur for the following customers:

1. Jasbir catches her heel in a gap between the boards while getting off 'The Screw', falls several feet, and injures herself badly.
2. Sean, who is a delivery driver, leaves his lorry to pick flowers from one of the ornamental borders. He tears his shoe and sock, and cuts his foot quite badly on broken glass.
3. Pedro, an electrical contractor who is repairing one of the rides, is electrocuted and badly burnt when Daisy, who operates the ride, carelessly plugs it in.
4. Tom and Jerry, two 10-year-old boys, have sneaked in by climbing over a fence. They are both injured when they walk across the rails on one of the rides and are hit by one of the cars.

Activity

1. What protections, if any, did the law traditionally offer to trespassers?
2. Is it possible for an occupier to legitimately protect against intruders?
3. What type of damage is compensated under the 1984 Act?
4. Does the 'duty of common humanity' and the duty owed to trespassers under the 1984 Act differ at all?
5. Which factors must be present in order to impose a duty on the occupier under the 1984 Act?
6. What difficulties are created by the minimum standard of care in the 1984 Act?

Key facts

The common law	Case/statute
The law was originally merely not to deliberately cause harm	*Bird v Holbreck* (1828)
Because of the harshness of the rule as it applied to children, a common duty of humanity to trespassers was introduced	*BR Board v Herrington* (1972)

The scope of the duty under the 1984 Act	Case/statute
This was given statutory force in the 1984 Act The occupier only owes a duty if he: (a) is aware of the danger or has reasonable grounds to believe it exists; (b) knows or believes the other is in the vicinity of the danger; and (c) the risk is one against which he may be expected to offer some protection. Compensation is only available in respect of personal injury or death not personal property	s 1(3)
The greater the risk the more precautions must be taken	*Tomlinson v Congleton Borough Council* (2003)

Avoiding the duty	Case/statute
The occupier can defend if he has taken reasonable steps to avoid harm so warnings may succeed, but not against children	s 1(5) *Westwood v The Post Office* (1973)
volenti is also possible if the trespasser is fully aware of the risk	s 1(6) *Ratcliffe v McConnell* (1999)

Chapter 19

Nuisance and escape of dangerous things

19.1 Private nuisance

Nuisance is sometimes seen as a quite complex tort. There are a number of reasons for this.

- There are two distinct types – private nuisance and public nuisance which are very different. Besides this, many aspects of nuisance are now found in statutory form, so strictly speaking there is a third type also.
- The tort covers a more diverse range of situations than do most other torts.
- The tort has itself been developed in specific circumstances to create the separate tort of *Rylands v Fletcher* from the 1868 case.
- Finally many of the situations involved can appear to be indistinguishable from ones which might now be covered by negligence. In fact it is probably simpler and more convenient to bring an action under negligence.

Definition and purpose

The usual definition of private nuisance is that in Winfield (*Winfield and Jolowicz on Tort*, Sweet & Maxwell):

> '. . . an unlawful interference with a person's use or enjoyment of land or some right over, or in connection with it.'

To this must be added the word 'indirect', because any direct interference would be actionable under trespass.

Nuisance concerns neighbourhood. It will almost always involve the competing claims of neighbours to do as they wish on their own land. Usually, but not always, it will involve adjoining properties. A number of points stand out in this respect.

- Neighbourhood is a continuous state of affairs, so a problem created by one neighbour may affect another neighbour over a period of time.
- It is not unreasonable to expect to be able to do what you like on your own land. Problems only arise when this affects your neighbour's ability to enjoy his land.
- Disputes between neighbours can be as trivial as disputes within families. It would be an intolerable waste of court time to have to deal with all complaints no matter how trivial they were.

For these reasons nuisance is very often called the 'law of give and take'. It involves balancing the competing interests of individuals, and as Rogers says (*Tort*, Sweet & Maxwell):

> '. . . each of us must put up with a moderate amount of inconvenience caused by others as the price of being able to inflict some inconvenience upon others in the conduct of our own activities.'

So not every intentional interference with the enjoyment of land will be classed as a nuisance, only those also classed as unreasonable. What is reasonable in this respect depends not so much on the conduct of the defendant, but on whether the interference caused by that conduct is sufficient to give rise to a legal action.

19.1.1 The parties to an action

Claimants

Since nuisance involves the competing rights of neighbours to use their land how they wish, the basic rule is that anyone who has the use or enjoyment of the land and is affected by the interference may claim. This will obviously include an owner and an occupier, but also can be any holder of a legal or equitable title.

It could then include an owner not in possession who is suing over permanent damage done to the land by the interference.

A tenant can also sue, though there are some gaps in the law here regarding landlords' responsibilities to their tenants for the condition of the property.

Habiteng Housing Association v Jones (1994)

A tenant was unable to claim compensation for damage caused by a cockroach infestation when there was no vermin control responsibility in the tenancy agreement, and the tenant was unable to prove that the infestation began in the landlord's flat.

The Law Commission in its Report No 238 in 1966 recommended that the implied covenant of fitness for human habitation in the Landlord and Tenant Act 1985 should be updated to cover such eventualities.

Traditionally it was felt that, while the tenant would be able to bring an action, his or her family could not.

Malone v Laskey (1907)

The wife of the householder was unable to sue in respect of personal injury sustained when vibrations from machinery caused the cistern to fall on her in the lavatory.

A recent innovation modified this principle somewhat.

Khorasandjian v Bush (1993)

The right to sue was granted to an occupier's family where they had suffered harassing telephone calls.

However, the House of Lords overturned this principle in *Hunter and Another v Canary Wharf* (1997) preferring the principle that the right to sue in nuisance is linked to a proprietary right in the land.

Defendants

Clearly the creator of the nuisance can be a defendant, and this might be the case whether or not the creator of the nuisance is also occupier of the land.

Southport Corporation v Esso Petroleum Co Ltd (1953)

Here the defendant's oil tanker beached in the estuary and leaked oil that subsequently drifted to local beaches. The court held that there was no reason why a defendant who is not the occupier of neighbouring land but misuses it so as to cause a nuisance should not be liable.

Even though an occupier has not created the nuisance he might nevertheless be liable in law for authorising it.

Tetley v Chitty (1986)

Here a landlord was liable in nuisance by permitting go-kart racing on his premises.

However, the authorisation must apply to the nuisance, not just to the use of land by the creator of the nuisance.

Smith v Scott (1973)

A local authority was not liable for letting a flat to a 'problem family'. The lease specifically prohibited the creation of nuisances by tenants.

In other circumstances where the occupier is not responsible for creating the nuisance, he might still be liable as a result of 'adopting' the nuisance, ie of failing to deal with the nuisance.

This principle can apply where a stranger has created the nuisance.

Sedleigh Denfield v O'Callaghan (1940)

Strangers blocked a culvert pipe on the defendant's land. He knew about it but failed to deal with it and was liable when it led to flooding on the claimant's land.

It can also apply even where the nuisance is the result of natural causes.

Leakey v National Trust (1980)

Following heavy rain, a large natural mound on a hillside slipped and damaged the claimant's cottage. The defendants were liable as they knew that it might happen and did not prevent it.

The occupier is liable because he knew of the nuisance but did nothing about it.

Anthony and others v The Coal Authority (2005)

The defendant was responsible for former bodies that had tipped waste from mining onto a tip on its land. This was later partly landscaped and passed into private hands. Later a fire was started through spontaneous combustion of the coal which lasted for three years. The claimant sued for the interference caused by the fumes and smoke. The defendant was held liable because it was aware of the problem while the tip was still in its control but failed to prevent the nuisance.

This principle of a landlord being liable for adopting the nuisance by actually failing to deal with it quite commonly applies to local authorities acting as landlords.

Page Motors Ltd v Epsom & Ewell Borough Council (1982)

The council was liable in nuisance for failing to deal with gypsies who camped out on council land and then interfered with the claimant's business.

This would apply whenever the council failed to prevent gypsies or other groups from congregating on council land and using it as a base from which to carry out any illegal activities – see *Lippiatt v South Gloucestershire County Council (1999)*.

There are also more complex provisions on repair under landlord and tenant law.

19.1.2 The elements of private nuisance

There are three key elements in proving the existence of a nuisance:

1. An unreasonable use of land
2. leading to an indirect interference
3. with the claimant's use or enjoyment of land.

The unreasonable use of land

Mere interference on its own is insufficient for an action. The claimant must prove that the defendant's activity amounts to an unlawful use of land. Unlawful is not used here in the usual sense of illegal, but rather means that the court accepts that the defendant's use of land is unreasonable in the way that it affects the claimant.

The proper question for the court is – in all of the circumstances, is it reasonable for the claimant to have to suffer the particular interference? In assessing the defendant's conduct, the courts are really analysing fault but with a more flexible approach than might be the case with negligence.

Solloway v Hampshire County Council (1981)

The council was not liable for trees on the highway that damaged the claimant's property, because they lacked the resources to do anything about it.

The opposite answer has been given in *Hurst & Another v Hampshire County Council (1997)* for consistency with other cases.

Because the tort is all about balancing competing interests, a number of factors will have to be considered by the court in deciding whether the use of land by the defendant is unreasonable.

Locality

Nuisance has to do with use of land, and land can be used in very different ways according to the area concerned. Thus, as Thesiger LJ stated it in *Sturges v Bridgman* (1879):

> '… what would be a nuisance in Belgrave Square would not necessarily be so in Bermondsey.'

*   The nuisance might be simply an acceptable activity carried out in the wrong area.

Laws v Florinplace Ltd (1981)

The claimant succeeded in gaining an injunction where a shop in a residential area was converted into a sex shop.

*   The customary use of the area is important in determining liability.

Murdoch v Glacier Metal Co Ltd (1998)

The claimant failed to prove that his use and enjoyment of land was interfered with when he lived close to a busy bypass.

*   Usually the result may be different in an industrial area where claimants might naturally expect noise and pollution. This will not however prevent success in a nuisance action where damage is caused rather than mere interference with comfort.

St Helens Smelting Co Tipping (1865)

Copper smelting, even in an industrial area, could be classed as a nuisance when it resulted in smuts from the process damaging the claimant's shrubs.

- Often in any case the court may reach a compromise between the competing interests of the two parties.

Dunton v Dover District Council (1977)

The opening hours of a local authority playground were reduced following a successful complaint by a neighbouring old people's home.

The duration of the interference

To be actionable, the interference should be continuous. In this way, a noisy one-off party to celebrate A Level results may not be a nuisance, where the continuous vibration of machinery may.

- Usually it will be necessary for both the interference and its cause to be continuous for there to be liability.

Bolton v Stone (1951)

There was no liability when a cricket ball hit Miss Stone. The pitch was 78 yards from the road, she was 100 yards away, and the fence 17 feet above the pitch. Also, it was shown that only six balls had been hit out of the ground in 28 years.

- Isolated instances have been accepted as nuisances when arising from a continuing state of affairs.

Spicer v Smee (1946)

Fire that began as the result of faulty wiring spread to a neighbour's house. This was accepted as nuisance, the faulty wiring being a continuous state of affairs.

- The fact that the interference is only temporary is not on its own sufficient to avoid a claim, if the interference is of a kind and at times when it is an unacceptable interference.

De Keyser's Royal Hotel Ltd v Spicer Bros Ltd (1914)

Building work including the use of pile drivers was carried out at night and interfered with the claimant's sleep. Despite the fact that it was only a temporary state of affairs, the court granted an injunction to prevent the building work taking place at night.

- These principles have more recently been extended to cover events lasting only 15 or 20 minutes.

Crown River Cruises Ltd v Kimbolton Fireworks Ltd (1996)

A barge was set alight by flammable debris, resulting from a firework display lasting only 20 minutes.

- Indeed *Rylands v Fletcher* (1868) has been described as a specific form of nuisance covering isolated escapes.

Cambridge Water Co v Eastern Counties Leather plc (1994)

Chemicals from the tanning process eventually filtered through the ground and polluted the claimant's bore hole.

The seriousness of the interference

The law makes a distinction between mere inconvenience and physical damage.

- In the case of mere discomfort or inconvenience, then the test is all about balancing the competing interests and about what is reasonable. The appropriate test is whether the interference is:

> '… an inconvenience materially interfering with the ordinary comfort physically of human existence, not merely according to elegant or dainty modes and habits of living, but according to plain and sober and simple notions among the English people.' Knight Bruce VC in *Walter v Selfe* (1851)

- Generally where the interference causes damage to the claimant, it will be sufficient to class the use of land as unreasonable.

Halsey v Esso Petroleum Co Ltd (1961)

The claimant successfully claimed for noise coming from the defendant's depot, but also in relation to the damage which smuts caused to the washing.

- Damage may be insufficient cause to claim if the activity is for the public benefit.

Miller v Jackson (1977)

The majority of the Court of Appeal held that cricket balls coming onto Miller's land from the local Cricket Club were a nuisance. Nevertheless, they were not prepared to grant an injunction since it was not in the public interest.

- The use of land in any case might not be considered unreasonable where such use is an absolute right.

Stephens v Anglian Water Authority (1987)

Because the right to appropriate water is an absolute right, it could not be classed as unreasonable even though it caused subsidence in the claimant's property.

The sensitivity of the claimant

- The claimant cannot engage in a use of land that in itself is hypersensitive and then complain of damage caused by normal activities.

Robinson v Kilvert (1889)

No liability was found when the heat required in the manufacture of the defendant's boxes downstairs in a building damaged the brown paper made by the claimant upstairs, as it would not damage any other paper.

- In any case the law has moved away from the idea of 'abnormal sensitivity' to a general test of foreseeability.

Network Rail Infrastructure v Morris (2004)

Morris ran a recording studio near to a railway line. The railway company installed new track circuits which interfered with the claimant's amplification system, causing him to lose business. The Court of Appeal ignored the issue of abnormal sensitivity but held that the interference was not foreseeable.

Malice shown by either party

- Deliberately harmful acts will ordinarily be nuisances.

Hollywood Silver Fox Farm v Emmet (1936)

The defendant objected to the claimant's use of his land as a mink farm fired shotguns near to the property. Normally this would not be unreasonable use of land. However, mink eat their young when frightened. The act was meant to cause harm and was unreasonable.

- Acts of revenge taken in response to unreasonable behaviour can be classed as unreasonable themselves and therefore a nuisance, and any action that might have been brought may in turn be defeated.

Christie v Davey (1893)

The defendant became annoyed by the noise from music lessons next-door, and responded by banging on the walls, beating trays and shouting. An injunction was granted against him.

The state of the defendant's land

- The defendant may not simply ignore nuisances that arise on his or her land, however they are created.

Leakey v The National Trust (1980)

The defendants were liable when a large mound, the Burrow Mump, on their land, subsided and damaged the claimant's cottages.

- So defendants owe a duty to prevent the spread of those things on their land which might create a nuisance.

Bradburn v Lindsay (1983)

The owner of a semi-detached property was held to be liable to his neighbour for the spread of dry rot which he should have prevented.

- Though they will not be liable merely because a natural event is occurring that might create a nuisance, unless they are also aware of the actual danger created by the natural event.

Holbeck Hall Ltd v Scarborough Borough Council (2000)

The claimant's hotel was situated close to the sea, near to a cliff. The local council owned the land between the hotel and the cliff top. After a long period of steady erosion, there was a major landslip that undermined the foundations of the hotel, meaning it had to be demolished. The defendant council were not liable. The Court of Appeal held that the council was not liable. They were unaware of the danger of the major landslip, nor could this be presumed from the previous erosion. They had neither adopted the nuisance, nor had they created it.

The actual cause of the nuisance

- Where an activity is obviously an interference but the cause of the harm is another factor, then there is no actionable nuisance.

Southwark LBC v Mills and others; Baxter v Camden LBC (1999)

In joined appeals, tenants in blocks of council flats complained about normal daily noises coming from the neighbouring flat. The reason that the noises could be heard at all was the poor soundproofing of the flats. It was held that the noise was not unreasonable in this context and could not be a nuisance.

The impact on the claimant's human rights

- Since incorporation of the European Convention of Human Rights, it may be possible for a claimant to argue that the nuisance also affects his human rights. In both *Dennis v Ministry of Defence* (2003) and in *Hatton v UK* (2003), claimants sought remedies for the disturbances caused by aircraft noise. They also argued unsuccessfully that the regulations on aircraft noise were an effective breach of their human rights under Article 8 of the European Convention.

An indirect interference

If the interference involves a direct physical intrusion, then the action should be fought in trespass. Nuisance will only be available if interference is indirect.

In this way a variety of things have been held to be actionable as nuisances:

- Fumes drifting over neighbouring land – *Bliss v Hall* (1838)
- Vibrations from industrial machinery – *Sturges v Bridgman* (1879)
- Loud noises including gunfire – *Hollywood Silver Fox Farm v Emmet* (1936)
- Hot air rising into other premises – *Robinson v Kilvert* (1889)
- Smuts from factory chimneys – *Halsey v Esso Petroleum* (1961)
- Fire – *Spicer v Smee* (1946)
- Continuous interference from cricket balls – *Miller v Jackson* (1977)
- Pollution of rivers – *Pride of Derby & Derbyshire Angling Association v British Celanese* (1953).

The use and enjoyment of land

We have already seen how courts will draw a distinction between interference with the mere enjoyment of the land and actual physical damage.

In this way there has been some judicial control of the extent to which enjoyment of land is protected. This is where the courts are called on most to balance competing interests. It means that certain activities will be beyond protection.

Generally the courts have refrained from protecting purely aesthetic interests.

Bridlington Relay Ltd v Yorkshire Electricity Board (1965)

No nuisance was found when overhead power cables ruined television reception.

This is because, as Lord Hoffman has stated, the inconvenience involved in such cases should be in relation to the land itself, rather than only the landowner.

Hunter v Canary Wharf Ltd (1997)

Families of tenants were denied an action in private nuisance where they complained of dust and poor television reception caused by the erection of a tall building nearby because they lacked *locus standi*. The House of Lords overruled the Court of Appeal, stating that such interference could not be classed as a nuisance.

It is logical to assume, therefore, that there could be no action for lowering the tone of a neighbourhood, and yet that seems to be the substance of the case in *Laws v Florinplace* (1981).

In a recent verdict, interference with a functional use of land supporting a purely entertainment or leisure purpose has been identified as an interest capable of protection; *Crown River Cruises Ltd v Kimbolton Fireworks Ltd* (1996).

Activity

Consider whether there is a possible claim for nuisance in the following situations:

1. Raj and Jas recently received successful A Level results and held a very noisy party that lasted till 3.00 am in the morning. Ada and Florence who live next door were kept awake and were quite annoyed.
2. Tara lives next door to Albert, an amateur shortwave radio enthusiast. When he is using his equipment, it causes interference to both sound and vision on Tara's television.
3. Ricky, a music promoter, proposes to hold an open-air pop concert lasting one week, in parkland at the head of a residential cul-de-sac.
4. Norris is annoyed because Rita's cat regularly comes into his garden and messes on his flowers, some which have died.
5. Residents in a private home for the elderly object to the noise from junior football matches played on local authority playing fields near to the home.

19.1.3 Defences and remedies

Defences

Many defences are particularly appropriate to allegations of private nuisance.

Statutory authority

Since many of the activities that are likely to be the cause of a nuisance are now regulated or licensed by environmental or other laws, then statutory authority is likely to be one of the most effective defences.

Hammersmith Railway v Brand (1869)

Vibrations from trains were an inevitable consequence of the existence of the railway. As Lord Cairns said, it would be a *reductio ad absurdam* to grant injunctive relief since this would prevent the railway from operating.

However, the defence may not be available where discretion to act is exercised improperly.

Metropolitan Asylum District Hospital v Hill (1881)

There was a general power to build a smallpox hospital. The defence was unavailable when it was sited in a place that would cause a nuisance.

The defence will not be available either where there is negligence.

Dorset Yacht Co Ltd v Home Office (1970)

In this case the Home Office could not avoid liability for the damage done by Borstal boys who had been taken to Poole by their warders.

Where statute provides the only possible remedy, an action in nuisance may not in any case be possible and does not necessarily infringe human rights law.

Marcic v Thames Water plc (2003)

Through the failures of the defendants, the claimant's home became flooded with sewage on many occasions. The Water Industry Act 1991 provided the appropriate remedies and excluded an action in nuisance. The Court of Appeal nevertheless held that the interference amounted to an actionable nuisance, and that there was also a breach of Article 8 – the right to respect for private and family life, home and correspondence. The House of Lords, however, held that there could be no nuisance action and that the remedies under the Act were compatible with the Human Rights Act 1998 and Article 8.

Local authority planning permission

This can in some circumstances act as lawful justification for a nuisance.

Gillingham Borough Council v Medway (Chatham) Dock Co (1993)

Planning permission was granted to use part of a dockyard as a commercial port. Neighbours then suffered disturbance from heavy vehicles using the access for 24 hours a day. It was held not to be an actionable nuisance because of the planning permission.

However, local authorities have no power to authorise nuisances, so that planning permission will only be granted where the nuisance is the inevitable result of a change in the character of a neighbourhood that Parliament itself has expressly authorised.

Wheeler v Saunders (1996)

A pig farmer was granted planning permission to expand by building two more pig houses, each containing 400 pigs. One pig house was only 11 metres from the cottage of a neighbour who then took action in nuisance. The defendant's appeal on having planning permission failed because the defence was said to operate only for those nuisances that Parliament had authorised.

Prescription

This is a defence that is unique to nuisance. If the nuisance has continued for 20 years without complaint, then the right to complain will lapse.

Sturges v Bridgman (1879)

The vibrations from the defendant's machinery disturbed the claimant who had bought land next door and was using it as a doctor's consulting room. The defence of prescription failed since the court held that the nuisance only began when the consulting room was built.

Act of a stranger

In other words, the act of a trespasser may be a defence. This will not apply, however, where the defendant adopts the nuisance; *Sedleigh Denfield v O'Callaghan* (1940).

Volenti non fit injuria

A claimant may always consent to the nuisance.

Kiddle v City Business Properties Ltd (1942)

A tenant will generally be said to consent to the risk of nuisances arising from the condition of the premises that are not the result of the landlord's negligence. In this case, the tenant failed in his action when gutters had become blocked and flooded over onto the tenant's stock.

Public policy

The tort, as we have said, is about competing interests. The courts will not then grant a nuisance action where it is not in the public interest.

Miller v Jackson (1977)

Here the court refused to grant an injunction to the neighbour of a cricket ground that had been in existence for more than 70 years, despite the damage the claimant had suffered, rather than lose a recreational facility.

However, the mere fact that something is of public benefit does not mean that it will automatically escape liability for nuisance.

Adams v Ursell (1913)

A fish and chip shop in a residential area was still a nuisance, despite the fact that it was patronised by local people.

The claimant coming fresh to the nuisance is not a defence

Bliss v Hall (1838)

The claimant bought a house close to the defendant's candle works. This had been there for three years but was still held to be a nuisance.

Remedies

Damages are available where the claimant has suffered some loss. The test of remoteness is that in *The Wagon Mound (No 2)* (1967), based on reasonable foreseeability. The claimant may recover for any physical loss, for depreciation in value and for a business loss.

The common remedy for nuisance will be an injunction. This will be prohibitory, ordering the defendant to refrain from the nuisance. The injunction may be coupled with damages where a loss has occurred.

One further remedy available to a claimant is 'abatement'. This may well involve entering the defendant's premises in order to prevent further nuisance. In this way a claimant might enter a defendant's land in order to chop down overhanging branches, although these would need to be returned to the defendant.

Activity

Consider whether any defence to a claim for nuisance is possible in the following situations:

1. The noise from a busy railway line distresses homeowners living in houses next to the railway line.
2. Burglars break into Ravinder's home while he is spending six months in India and leave his radio, TV, and hi-fi all playing on maximum volume.
3. Anna lives in a block of flats in the flat beneath Roger. Anna is very distressed because she has to get up at 6.00 am to go to work, and when Roger returns from his work at around 1.00 am she can hear his footsteps walking around for hours after.
4. Residents of a small estate want to have a nearby local authority playground shut down because of the noise from children playing.
5. For more than 15 years, Archie has kept pigs in his back yard. His neighbour Reggie eventually objects to the smell.

One possible difficulty with this remedy is that it could lead to a counter injunction, as in *Stanton v Jones* (1995) which involved a dispute over a high hedge.

The remedy in any case may not always be possible.

Burton v Winters (1993)

In a dispute over a boundary, a wall was found to be a few inches over the boundary. When the injured party was awarded damages instead and then damaged the other party's garage, she was prosecuted for criminal damage.

Alternatives to an action in nuisance

Civil actions of course are costly to bring, and despite the Woolf reforms may still be slower than other forms of action.

Disputes between neighbours can lead to very strained relations, and indeed television shows have been devoted to the subject of disputes that have become out of hand. The courts in recent times have encouraged the use of Alternative Dispute Resolution (ADR) in general, in civil disputes. Mediation is one way of neighbours approaching the problem from a more productive standpoint than resorting to court actions.

The criminal law has also introduced measures for the protection of people who are the victims of bad behaviour by neighbours as well as by others. These include anti-social behaviour orders, from the Crime and Disorder Act 1998, and criminal offences under ss 2 and 4, and the possibility of a civil claim under s 3 Protection from Harassment Act 1997.

Since Article 8 of the European Convention of Human Rights concerns the right to privacy and the respect for family life, human rights law may now also be used, particularly since the incorporation of the Convention in the Human Rights Act 1998. Indeed, such a course of action has already proved successful.

Marcic v Thames Water plc (2001)

The claimant's land was repeatedly flooded with sewage as a result of the defendant's failure to control it. The Court of Appeal, while acknowledging the claim as an actionable nuisance, also accepted that it amounted to a breach of Article 8. The House of Lords held that it was not.

Activity

1. Why is the law of nuisance sometimes referred to as 'the law of give and take'?
2. When will an action in nuisance be unavailable to a person who has suffered from the nuisance?
3. In which ways will locality affect an action for nuisance?
4. In what circumstances is it possible for an act that is not continuous to be an actionable nuisance?
5. What is the effect of malice in the tort of nuisance? How does this compare with other torts?
6. In what ways is *Hunter v Canary Wharf* (1997) a disappointing judgment?
7. Why should a person's excessive sensitivity prevent them from claiming?
8. In which circumstances is a person liable in nuisance for a nuisance actually caused by someone else?
9. What is generally the most effective defence in nuisance, and why?
10. Which factors will determine a claimant's choice of remedy in nuisance?
11. Why would a claimant bring an action in nuisance rather than negligence?

19.2 Public nuisance

19.2.1 Definition and character

Public nuisance is very different to private nuisance. For one thing it extends beyond neighbours. It has been defined by Romer LJ in *A–G v PYA Quarries Ltd* (1957) as:

> 66 '… something which affects a reasonable class of Her Majesty's citizens materially or in the reasonable comfort and convenience of life.' 99

Public nuisance does not have to be an interference with the use and enjoyment of land, so it is not based on proprietary rights. For this reason, it has also developed as a crime, in which respect it will commonly be prosecuted by the Attorney General.

19.2.2 Requirements for proving public nuisance

It is essential for an action to be successful in public nuisance for there to be a substantial class of people affected by the nuisance.

Attorney-General v PYA Quarries Ltd (1957)

The nuisance complained of was the noise and vibrations from quarrying. The defendant's argument that too few people were affected failed. It was sufficient that a representative class was affected.

To succeed, a claimant must be able to show special damage suffered over and above that which other members of the class have suffered.

Tate & Lyle Industries Ltd v Greater London Council (1983)

The House of Lords characterised an interference with navigation rights in the River Thames as physical damage, making it actionable public nuisance.

- Special damage might include personal injury.

Castle v St Augustine Links (1922)

A taxi driver was hit in the eye by a sliced golf ball. The golf club was liable. In comparison to *Bolton v Stone* (1951), the links straddled the highway so the risk of harm was much greater.

This has been confirmed in *Corby Group Litigation v Corby BC* (2008). The Court of Appeal rejected the defendant's argument that the principle from *Hunter v Canary Wharf Ltd* in private nuisance should apply.

- It can also include damage to goods, as with the washing in *Halsey v Esso Petroleum Co Ltd* (1961).
- It can also include financial loss.

Rose v Miles (1815)

The defendant's barge blocked a navigable river. As a result, the claimant was forced to empty his barge and pay for alternative transport. The defendant was liable for the cost.

This has been confirmed in *Corby Group Litigation v Corby BC* (2008). The Court of Appeal rejected the defendant's argument that the principle from *Hunter v Canary Wharf Ltd* in private nuisance should apply.

- One further example of special damage might be a loss of trade connection, as when shops lose trade during a long-term blockage of the highway such as road repairs; *Wilkes v Hungerford Market Co* (1835).

Most commonly, the tort involves use and abuse of the highway. Interference can be in a number of ways.

- It might involve obstructions to the highway. This might occur as the result of queues for which the defendant is responsible, as at a football match or concert or theatre performance; *Lyons v Gulliver* (1914). It may apply to a picket line; *Thomas v National Union of Mineworkers (South Wales Area)* (1985).
- It can apply to projections over the highway, which cause damage. These could be clocks, hoardings, signs and other artificial structures. In this case, an occupier is liable to ensure that structures do not fall into disrepair. In the case of natural things, the position may be less clear.

Noble v Harrison (1926)

A branch from a tree on the defendant's land fell onto a bus. The defendant was not liable because the defect in the tree was latent and probably beyond his control.

- It will also apply to the condition of the highway, particularly since a local authority will usually have a duty to maintain the highway.

Griffiths v Liverpool Corporation (1974)

It was a nuisance when a person tripped on a flagstone that was standing up by half an inch.

Activity

1. What are the significant differences between private and public nuisance?
2. Who exactly are 'a reasonable class of Her Majesty's citizens'?
3. What exactly is special damage in public nuisance?
4. In what way is the 'highway' so important to public nuisance?

Key facts

- It is possible to have private nuisance, public nuisance, and now statutory nuisance also.
- A private nuisance is defined as an unlawful indirect interference with a person's use or enjoyment of his land.
- Unlawful means unreasonable, and what is unreasonable can depend on:

  (a) Locality – what is a nuisance in Belgravia need not be a nuisance in Bermondsey; *St Helens Smelting v Tipping* (1865).
  (b) Duration of the nuisance – whether the nuisance is continuous or only short-lived; *Bolton v Stone* (1951).
  (c) Sensitivity of the claimant; *Robinson v Kilvert* (1889).
  (d) The seriousness of the nuisance – whether or not damage is caused or merely inconvenience; *Halsey v Esso Petroleum* (1961).

  (e) Malice can also play an important role; *Christie v Davey* (1893).

- The interference must be indirect; direct interference would be a trespass.
- It is insufficient that the interference is with a purely recreational use of land – *Hunter v Canary Wharf* (1997).
- Defences include: statutory authority, prescription, act of a stranger, consent and public policy.
- Public nuisance is defined as an interference with the material comfort of a class of Her Majesty's subjects.
- It must involve damage to the defendant over and above that caused to the public generally – *Tate and Lyle v GLC* (1983).
- It involves the highway: ie damage caused by obstructions to the highway, projections over the highway, and the condition of the highway.

19.3 *Rylands v Fletcher*

The tort of strict liability actually comes from the case of *Rylands v Fletcher* (1868) (see 19.3.1 for details). The rule was defined in the case in the Court of Exchequer Chamber by Blackburn J. He said:

> 66 'We think that the true rule of law is, that the person who, for purposes of his own, brings on his land and keeps there anything likely to do mischief if it escapes, must keep it in at his peril, and, if he does not do so, he is prima facie answerable for all the damage which is the natural consequence of its escape.' 99

This basic definition contains the major ingredients of the tort. Lord Cairns then added to these in the appeal to the House of Lords the further requirement that for the claimant to succeed, the thing brought onto the land must then amount to a 'non-natural' use of land.

The tort is identified as a form of strict liability to deal with dangerous activities and dangerous substances. However, it is arguable how much it can actually be seen as a tort of strict liability, or how much it is rather a particular type of nuisance dealing with isolated but hazardous escapes rather than with continuous interference.

Whichever it is, the tort is not straightforward and it is not simple to bring an action. In fact there are so many defences available to a claim that it is hard to see that it is strict liability at all.

Traditionally it could be said that the liability was strict because there was no particular requirement to show fault, and the defendant could be made liable even if he or she had taken care to avoid the escape. The tort was also originally distinguished from nuisance because of the requirement in nuisance that harm of the type caused by the nuisance should be foreseeable but no such requirement is apparent in *Rylands v Fletcher* (1868).

This is not now the case since the House of Lords has identified the tort as a type of nuisance, and subject therefore to the same test of foreseeability.

Cambridge Water Co v Eastern Counties Leather plc (1994)

The claimants were a water company that used a borehole from which to extract water for domestic consumption and use. The defendants owned a nearby tannery where they used a solvent for degreasing the animal skins. Sometimes this solvent would spill onto the concrete floor. Unbeknown to the defendants, over a period of time the spilt solvent seeped into the ground and eventually filtered through into the borehole contaminating the water. Since the contamination was not foreseeable at the time of the spillages, the House of Lords held that there could be no liability.

There are other factors which make the tort difficult to prove. Lord Cairns added the requirement that there be a non-natural use of land. So the simplest way to defeat a claim is to show that the use of land in question is a natural use.

Moreover, the judges have shown hostility to the general principle of strict liability in the tort and have restricted the application of the rule still further.

- Firstly, according to *Read v Lyons* (1947), there can only be liability if the thing brought onto the defendant's land escapes from that land.
- Secondly, according to *Rickards v Lothian* (1913), there must be a '… special use of land bringing with it increased danger to others.'
- Thirdly, the recent return to foreseeability of type of damage, as in *Cambridge Water Co v Eastern Counties Leather plc* (1994).

Despite this, the tort can still not be seen only as an extension of nuisance. Claimants have recovered damages despite not being occupiers of land as in *Hale v Jennings Bros* (1938). Similarly the tort has been applied to accidental and intentional releases of the thing causing mischief; *Crown River Cruises Ltd v Kimbolton Fireworks Ltd* (1996).

19.3.1 Essential elements of the tort

There are essentially four elements that must be proved in order for there to be a successful claim under the tort of *Rylands v Fletcher* (1868):

- A bringing onto the land and accumulating
- of a thing likely to cause mischief if it escapes
- which amounts to a non-natural use of the land
- and which does escape and causes damage.

In the case itself, all elements were present and the defendants were liable.

Rylands v Fletcher (1868)

The defendant, a mill owner, hired contractors to create a reservoir on his land to act as a water supply to the mill. The contractors carelessly failed to block off disused mineshafts that they came across during their excavations. Unknown to the contractors, these shafts were connected to other mineworks on adjoining land. When the reservoir was filled, water then flooded the neighbouring mines.

All elements of the modern tort were present. The large volumes of water were not naturally present in that form but were brought onto the land. Such a large volume of water could quite obviously do damage if it escaped. Lord Cairns identified that storage of water in these quantities did amount to a non-natural use of land. Finally, in the event, the water did escape through the mineshafts, causing considerable damage to the claimant.

Each of the four elements requires proof and so should be considered individually.

The bringing onto the land

Clearly the starting point is that if the thing in question is already naturally present on the land, then there can be no liability.

Pontardawe RDC v Moore-Gwyn (1929)

There was no liability for the damage caused by the escape of rocks in an avalanche.

There could not be liability if the thing in question was already growing on the land. There must be a bringing onto land.

Giles v Walker (1890)

There was no liability for weeds spreading onto neighbouring land.

There cannot be liability for a thing that naturally accumulates on the land.

Ellison v The Ministry of Defence (1997)

Rainwater that accumulated naturally on an airfield at Greenham Common did not lead to liability when it escaped and caused flooding on neighbouring land.

It is still possible for there to be an action in nuisance where the defendant is aware of the thing causing the nuisance and has in effect 'adopted it' by failing to do anything about it.

Leakey v The National Trust (1980)

Here a mound of loose earth on a hill was particularly subject to cracking and slipping in bad weather. When the mound did in fact slip and cause damage to neighbouring land, the defendants were liable because they knew of this possibility and yet failed to do anything to prevent it.

Besides this, the person who brings the thing onto the land does not have to be the owner or occupier of the land. So a mere licensee falls within the scope of the rule.

Charing Cross Electric Supply Co v Hydraulic Power Co (1914) (The Charing Cross Co Case)

The defendants had a statutory power to lay water mains, which were then situated above electric cables. They were liable, however, when the water main burst and flooded the electric cable, causing a blackout in large parts of London.

The thing brought onto the land must be brought on for the defendants' purposes.

Dunne v North Western Gas Board (1964)

The Gas Board was bound by statute to supply gas to its consumers. It was held, however, not to have collected the gas onto land for its own purposes, so there was no liability.

But the fact that the thing is brought onto the land for the purposes of the defendant does not mean it has to be accumulated there for the defendant's benefit.

Smeaton v Ilford Corporation (1954)

A local authority collected sewage under a statutory authority. It was held that it did so for its own purposes, even though it was accepted that it derived no benefit from collecting the sewage.

One final and quite significant point here is that the thing that is brought onto the land does not necessarily have to be the thing that escapes and causes mischief.

Miles v Forest Rock Granite Co (Leicestershire) Ltd (1918)

The claimant brought the action in respect of injuries suffered when rocks flew onto the highway from the defendants' land where they were blasting. It was the explosives that had been brought onto land that actually caused the rock to escape, but there was still liability.

The thing likely to do mischief if it escapes

It is not the escape itself that must be likely, only that mischief is likely, if the thing brought onto land does escape.

Musgrove v Pandelis (1919)

The rule was applied when a garaged car with petrol in its tank caught fire and the fire spread to the next door neighbour's house. The fire was unlikely, but would certainly cause mischief if it escaped.

Neither must the thing that escapes be dangerous in any intrinsic sense. It is sufficient that it becomes dangerous by the manner of the escape.

Shiffman v Order of the Hospital of St John of Jerusalem (1936)

The thing that 'escaped' and caused the damage was a flagpole.

However, the thing must be a source of foreseeable harm if it does escape.

Hale v Jennings Bros (1938)

A 'chair-o-plane' car on a fairground ride became detached from the main assembly while in motion and injured a stallholder as it crashed to the ground. The owner of the ride was liable. Risk of injury was foreseeable if the car came loose.

Strangely enough, even people who 'escape' have been held to be dangerous and a potential mischief under the rule.

Attorney General v Corke (1933)

A landowner allowed gypsies to camp on his land. When they then committed nuisances and trespass against his neighbours, the landowner was liable. The gypsies were held to be 'likely to do mischief if they escaped'. One potential problem here is whether the landowner would have been in a position to restrict the gypsies' free movement lawfully.

A non-natural use of land

Lord Cairns in the House of Lords in *Rylands v Fletcher* (1868) itself indicated the requirement of a non-natural use of land. He said:

> '... if the defendants, not stopping at the natural use of their close, had desired to use it for any purpose which I may term a non-natural use ... and in consequence of doing so ... the water came to escape ... then it appears to me that which the defendants were doing they were doing at their own peril.'

This concept of non-natural use was developed and explained by Lord Moulton in *Rickards v Lothian* (1913):

> '... it is not every use of land which brings into play this principle. It must be some special use bringing with it increased danger to others, and not merely by the ordinary use of land or such a use as is proper for the general benefit of the community.'

Non-natural use of land is clearly a complex concept, and one which inevitably changes to take into account technological change and changes in lifestyle. It is inconceivable for instance that leaving a car garaged with petrol in the tank could be seen as a non-natural use of land today, though it was seen as such in 1919 at the time of *Musgrove v Pandelis* (1919).

The case law suggests that we must consider that non-natural is something more than artificial and refers to some extraordinary use of land.

In general, as a result things associated with a domestic use of land will not normally be classified as non-natural even though they may be potentially hazardous.

- Fire in a domestic context has been held a natural use

Sochaki v Sas (1947)

There was no liability for a fire that started from a spark from a domestic grate and spread to the claimant's premises.

- as has electric wiring

Collingwood v Home & Colonial Stores (1936)

Defective wiring caused a fire to start that then spread to the claimant's premises. It was impossible to show negligence and the defendants escaped liability.

- and a domestic water supply has also been held to be a natural use of land.

Rickards v Lothian (1913)

The defendant was not liable when an unknown person turned on water taps and blocked plugholes on his premises, so that damage was caused in the flat below.

Even owners of commercial premises may be exempt from the rule because the activity leading to the escape is held to be natural rather than non-natural use of land.

Peters v The Prince of Wales Theatre (Birmingham) Ltd (1943)

The claimant occupied part of a theatre. A sprinkler system in the theatre caused flooding and damaged the claimant's stock. There was no liability since the use of land was not non-natural.

Where such facilities are in question, it will often be the volume, size or quantity involved that will lead to the thing being classed as a non-natural use of land. In the *Charing Cross case* (1914) for instance, it was the volume of water in the main and the pressure at which it was held that made the use of land non-natural, rather than the storage of water itself. This, as we have already seen, is capable of being viewed as a natural use.

It is also at times the context in which the thing is brought onto land and accumulated, that leads to the court holding that it is a non-natural use of land.

Mason v Levy Auto Parts of England (1967)

Large quantities of scrap tyres were stored on the defendant's land. These then were ignited, and a fire spread causing damage to the claimant's premises. The storage of such large quantities of a combustible material, the casual way in which they were stored and the character of the neighbourhood were all then considered by the judge in determining that there was a non-natural use of the land.

On the other hand, the fact that the public may derive a benefit from the particular use of land in question may mean that the court holds it to be a natural use of land.

British Celanese v A H Hunt (Capacitors) Ltd (1969)

The defendants stored strips of metal foil, which were used in the process of manufacturing electrical components. Some of these strips of foil blew off the defendant's land and onto an electricity substation, causing power failures. The court held that the use of land was natural. This was partly because of the benefit derived from the manufacture by the public, and there was no liability under the rule as a result.

The fact that an activity is associated with war does not mean that it constitutes a non-natural use of land merely because it occurs in peacetime.

Ellison v Ministry of Defence (1997)

Bulk fuel installations on a military airfield were held not to be a non-natural use of land, when rainwater that naturally gathered on the airfield ran off flooding neighbouring land.

However, courts have been prepared to accept that certain activities may always lead to a potential level of danger, so that amounts to a non-natural use of land whatever the benefit to the public derived from the activity that has led to the danger.

Cambridge Water Co v Eastern Counties Leather plc (1994)

The storage of particular chemicals on an industrial site was held to be a classic example of a non-natural use of land. The House of Lords, therefore, rejected the defendant's plea that just because the activity was an important source of local employment, this made it a natural use of land.

The thing must actually escape

Blackburn's original rule in the case of *Rylands v Fletcher* (1868) does not appear to contain any specific application of the word 'escape'. It is unlikely, therefore, that it was intended at that point that the requirement should be for the thing to escape onto land in which the claimant held a proprietary interest. If this were the case, then it would support the general idea of a strict liability tort for the control of dangerous activities.

However, the rule was seen as a development of the law of nuisance, in which there is a clear requirement for the claimant to have an interest in land. This explains the opinion expressed by Lord MacMillan that there must be such an escape since the rule derives:

> '... from a conception of mutual duties of adjoining or neighbouring landowners.'

Read v J Lyons & Co Ltd (1947)

A munitions inspector was inspecting a munitions factory and was injured, along with a number of employees, one man dying, when certain shells exploded. The House of Lords held that the rule did not apply because there was '... no escape at all of the relevant kind.'

Viscount Simon explained that an escape in *Rylands v Fletcher* (1868) means

> '... an escape from a place where the defendant has occupation or control over land to a place which is outside his occupation or control.'

This is obviously a very restrictive limitation on the operation of the rule. However, this interpretation of the meaning of escape for the purposes of the rule has not always been accepted as an absolute requirement. In *British Celanese v A H Hunt (Capacitors) Ltd* (1969) Lawton J felt that the escape in question should be:

> '... from a set of circumstances over which the defendant has control to a set of circumstances where he does not.' The test here is far less restrictive and far more appropriate to a tort of strict liability.

Certainly there are cases that appear to operate according to this reasoning rather than that in *Read v Lyons* (1947).

Hale v Jennings (1938)

Both stalls operated on the same piece of land. Neither stallholder owned the land.

A similar principle has been seen where both parties are operating on the same stretch of river.

Crown River Cruises Ltd v Kimbolton Fireworks Ltd (1996)

Inflammable material from a firework display fell onto barges used as a jetty for pleasure cruisers, causing fire damage.

19.3.2 Parties to an action in *Rylands v Fletcher*

Potential defendants

The question of the identity of potential defendants depends very much on the test of an escape that is used in the case.

According to Viscount Simon's test in *Read v Lyons* (1974) a defendant to an action in *Rylands v Fletcher* (1868) will be either the owner or occupier of land who satisfies the four ingredients of the tort, which must all be present for liability.

On the other hand, according to the test as described by Lawton J in the *British Celanese case* (1969), a potential defendant is one who satisfies the four ingredients of the rule, where the escape is from a set of circumstances over which he has control, to a set of circumstances over which he does not.

The natural development of the less restrictive rule is to include a claim where the defendant is merely in control of the highway and not the occupier of land.

Rigby v Chief Constable of Northamptonshire (1985)

The defendant was liable for the damage caused by the negligent release of CS gas canisters on the highway.

Potential claimants

The question of who can sue is not necessarily quite so clear-cut. In the original case, Blackburn J made no suggestion of any requirement for a claimant to have a proprietary interest in land. Nevertheless, Lord MacMillan in *Read v Lyons* (1947) suggested that there is such a requirement.

Lawton J in the *British Celanese case* (1969) felt that Lord MacMillan's requirement was too restrictive, and his test would necessarily include a wider class of potential claimants. Indeed, in the case it was a third party who had suffered damage as a result of the loss of power when the foil landed on the power station.

The logical development of a less restrictive test here is to allow a claim for accumulations that escape, causing damage to the claimant, regardless of where the damage occurs.

Crown River Cruises Ltd v Kimbolton Fireworks Ltd (1996)

The claimant was able to recover in nuisance and negligence despite the fact that the damage caused was to barges moored on the river. However, the opportunity to extend the rule here to cover the escape was rejected.

19.3.3 Defences and remedies

Types of recoverable loss and remoteness of damage

If MacMillan's test is accepted as correct, then this has the effect of limiting claims to recovery only for damage to the land owned or occupied by the claimant and to damage to property found on that land. MacMillan also expressed doubts as to whether a claim for personal injuries was possible under the rule.

On the other hand, if Lawton's test is preferred, then damages that can be recovered for are much wider, and indeed wide enough to include personal injury claims. Certainly there were cases before *Read v Lyons* (1947) including both *Shiffman* (1936) and *Hale v Jennings* (1938) in which the court found no problem in granting damages for personal injury.

Nevertheless, since the modern view following *Cambridge Water* (1994) is to accept *Rylands v Fletcher* (1868) as a form of nuisance, and since in *Hunter v Canary Wharf Ltd* (1997) it was doubted whether personal injury was recoverable in nuisance, then this issue might also be settled in *Rylands v Fletcher*.

It is certainly unlikely that a claim for economic loss will be successful.

Weller v Foot and Mouth Disease Research Unit (1966)

Auctioneers sued for their loss of usual income when there was a ban on the movement of livestock, following the escape of a virus from the defendant's premises. In the case there was in fact held to be no liability, because the claimants had no proprietary interest in land. It is unlikely that they would have succeeded in any case in respect of the type of damages claimed.

The tort is not actionable *per se,* and this means that any claimant must show damage in order to succeed. There can be no liability for the mere interference with the enjoyment of land.

Eastern & South African Telegraph Co Ltd v Cape Town Tramways Co Ltd (1902)

Electric emissions interfered with the transmission of telegraphic messages sent down underground cables. The claimant's action failed because of their 'hypersensitive' use of land. It was also suggested *in obiter* that the damage could not be classified as damage to property.

The rule on remoteness of damage was only recently settled. Blackburn J's original remarks refer to 'the natural consequence of the escape' suggesting that the *Re Polemis* (1921) direct consequence test applies.

However, the House of Lords in *Cambridge Water* (1994) have now stated that reasonable foreseeability of damage is a prerequisite of liability. In other words, the defendant must have known or ought reasonably to have foreseen that damage of the relevant type might be a consequence of the escape of the thing likely to cause mischief.

Possible defences

Despite the tort being described as strict liability, many defences are possible in the event of a claim. Blackburn J identified some of these at the time of the original case; others have developed since.

Volenti non fit injuria (consent)

There will be no liability where the claimant has consented to the thing that is accumulated by the defendant.

Consent is a commonly available defence in the case of multiple occupation of buildings, particularly tall buildings. The claimant will be said to consent when the thing accumulated is for the common benefit of the occupants.

Peters v Prince of Wales Theatre (Birmingham) Ltd (1943)

The claimant's stock was damaged by water from the defendant's sprinkler system. The water supply was nevertheless for the benefit of both and so there was no liability for the escape.

Common benefit

There will in any case be no liability on a defendant when the source of the potential danger is something that is maintained for the benefit of both claimant and defendant.

Dunne v North Western Gas Board (1964)

Gas mains exploded without any negligence by the Gas Board. The court felt that the Board accumulated the gas not for its own benefit but for the benefit of the consumers, and there was no liability.

Act of a stranger

If a stranger over whom the defendant has no control has been the cause of the escape causing the damage, then the defendant may not be liable.

Perry v Kendricks Transport Ltd (1956)

The defendants parked their bus on their parking space, having drained the tank of petrol. When an unknown person removed the petrol cap, a child was then injured when another child threw in a match which ignited the fumes in the tank. The Court of Appeal considered that the burden of proof here was on the claimant to show that such an eventuality was foreseeable. There was a valid defence and no liability.

Nevertheless, in other jurisdictions the strict liability of the rule can mean that there is liability, regardless of who causes the escape or whether it was foreseeable; *Mehta v Union of India* (1987).

Act of God

This defence may succeed where there are extreme weather conditions that '… no human foresight can provide against.' The nature of the defence is that it is only possible in the case of unforeseeable weather conditions.

Nichols v Marsland (1876)

The defendant here made three artificial ornamental lakes by damming a natural stream on his land. Freak thunderstorms accompanied by torrential rain broke the banks of the artificial lakes, that then caused the destruction of bridges on the claimant's land. There was no liability because the weather conditions were so extreme.

Statutory authority

A statute on construction may provide a defence if the escape is a direct result of the carrying out of the duty contained in the statute.

Green v Chelsea Waterworks Co (1894)

The defendants were obliged by statute to provide a water supply. The court held that occasionally burst pipes were an inevitable consequence of this duty, and so there could be no liability without negligence.

In the absence of a duty, there may still be liability when the thing escapes. There was liability in the *Charing Cross* case (1914) because there was only a power rather than a duty to provide the water supply.

Fault of the claimant

A defendant will not be liable when a claimant is in fact responsible for the damage that he suffers.

Eastern & South African Telegraph Co Ltd v Cape Town Tramways Co Ltd (1902)

The defendants were not liable because the interference with the telegraphic transmissions was said to be the fault of their excessive sensitivity.

Contributory negligence

Where the claimant is partly responsible, then the Law Reform (Contributory Negligence) Act 1945 applies and damages may be reduced according to the amount of the claimant's fault.

Points for discussion

The rule in *Rylands v Fletcher* (1868) has a number of problems associated with it. The modern perception of the rule seems to be that it is a more particular development of the law of nuisance, and therefore it not only has all the shortcomings of that tort but also would seem to be far from being strict liability in any straightforward sense. It is certainly unlikely that there is a future possibility of the tort being used as a general means of controlling dangerous activities or things by the use of strict liability. This is a pity, since the introduction of the tort shortly after the major period of the industrial revolution gave the common law the opportunity to have an all-embracing tort of strict liability for the control of hazardous activities, substances and other things. This could, in turn, have been used to make industry more responsible, and one element of tort could have had real deterrent value. The opportunity was wasted, and *Rylands v Fletcher* is merely a tort based on property rights.

In other jurisdictions such as India the tort has been expanded, but that has not been the case in England. On the contrary, the rule has been constantly limited in its scope by the decisions in the cases.

- Lord Cairns limited it immediately in the actual case in the House of Lords, by imposing the requirement of a non-natural use of land for liability.
- The tort was further restricted in its development by the requirement of proprietary interest in land established by Lord MacMillan in *Read v Lyons* (1947). This limits the circumstances in which a claimant can recover for damage caused by dangerous things accumulated on land.
- The *Cambridge Water* case (1994) even seems to be taking the tort towards a negligence style fault liability with the requirement of foreseeability.

The court in *Crown River Cruises Ltd v Kimbolton Fireworks Ltd* (1996) expressly rejected suggestions that the tort could or should be developed. The very breadth of the defences that have been made available in the tort seem in any case to be at odds with the principle of strict liability.

The tort then seems to be of questionable significance in the modern day. Judges are reluctant to allow claims under the tort to succeed. Most claims that could be brought under the tort could probably just as easily be brought under negligence instead, and indeed the requirement of foreseeability means that a claimant has similar concerns in some aspects.

The tort is rarely used and almost never successfully. Indeed shortly after the *Cambridge Water* case (1994), the Australian High Court in effect abolished the rule, claiming that the rule had been absorbed by the general rules of negligence.

Nevertheless, the House of Lords have recently had the opportunity to review the tort in total. In doing so, the House expressly rejected the idea of abandoning the tort or that it should be treated as having been absorbed within the general law of negligence.

Transco plc v Stockport MBC (2003)

The council was responsible for a high pressure water pipe supplying multi-storey flats. This had leaked over a period of time and caused an embankment to collapse, exposing the claimant's gas pipeline and leaving it in a dangerous condition. The claimant sought the cost of repairs from the council. The House of Lords held that there was no accumulation of a thing likely to cause mischief if it escaped, and that also the use of land was a normal use. Lord Bingham felt that the tort involved a defendant doing something that he ought to realise would give rise to a high risk of danger if it escaped, however unlikely the escape. He also considered that a test of 'ordinary' use was preferable to one of 'natural' or 'non-natural' use. So the tort only applies when the defendant's use of land is extraordinary or unusual in the particular circumstances and at the particular point in time.

Most areas of activity that could be affected or controlled by the rule are probably dealt with now by statutory controls. Certainly there are few hazardous activities that are not controlled by some form of statutory regulation.

The Nuclear Installations Act 1965 was used in respect of contamination caused to land by radioactive materials, even though the actual damage involved was economic.

Clearly, one area where the rule could have great potential is in controlling pollution and protecting the environment. The first block on this possibility is the fact that the tort is exclusively concerned with property rights, so a general interest in the environment is not within the scope of the tort. While the House of Lords in the *Cambridge Water* case (1994) recognised the potential for use of the tort in this area, they also dismissed it as unnecessary in the light of available legislation. Certainly under pressure of European directives, much legislation has been introduced; the Environmental Protection Act 1990 and the Environment Act 1995 are examples. Besides these there is a mass of health and safety legislation regulating the use of hazardous activities and substances. So even though the tort could be used to great effect in the area, it is unlikely, given the attitude of the judges, that it will.

Activity

1. What are the key ingredients of the rule in *Rylands v Fletcher* (1868)?
2. To what extent is liability under the rule really 'strict liability'?
3. What exactly is a 'non-natural' use of land?
4. Which things situated on land that are dangerous will lead to liability if they escape?
5. What must escape for the tort to operate?
6. Does the rule help the victims of damage caused by dangerous activities in general?
7. Who will be liable under the rule?
8. What are the different consequences of the tests in *Read v Lyons* (1947) and in the *British Celanese* case (1969)?
9. How limiting are the defences to a successful claim under the rule?
10. How are personal injuries covered under *Rylands v Fletcher*?

Key facts

- The basic rule according to Blackburn J is that a person is liable for the damage caused by things brought onto and accumulated on the land which then escape.
- The tort is seen as strict liability.
- There are four essential ingredients to the tort:

  (a) Bringing onto the land – the thing must not normally be there – *Pontardawe RDC v Moore-Gwyn* (1929).
  (b) Of a thing likely to cause mischief if it escapes – *Hale v Jennings* (1938).
  (c) Which must involve a 'non-natural' use of land – Lord Cairns in *Rylands v Fletcher* (1868).
  (d) The thing must actually escape – *Read v Lyons* (1947).

- Who is a defendant and who can claim, depends on whether the escape has to be from one person's land to another's or from the defendant's control to a situation outside of his control – *British Celanese v Hunt* (1969).
- The tort is now generally seen as a type of nuisance requiring foreseeability of damage – *Cambridge Water v Eastern Counties Leather* (1994).
- There is a wide range of possible defences including: act of God, act of a stranger, consent, common benefit and statutory authority.

Chapter 20

Vicarious liability

20.1 The nature and purpose of vicarious liability

Vicarious liability is not an individual tort such as negligence or nuisance. It is a means of imposing liability for a tort onto a party other than the tortfeaser, the party causing the tort.

It was originally based on the 'fiction' that an employer has control over his or her employees, and thus should be liable for torts committed by the employee. This was possibly less of a fiction when the 'master and servant' laws still reflected the true imbalance in the employment relationship.

In a less sophisticated society with less diverse types of work, control was possible. In domestic service, for instance, a master could dictate exactly the method of the work done by the servant. Modern forms of employment make control less evident. The actual work done by a surgeon can hardly be said to be under the control of a hospital administrator with no medical expertise.

Nevertheless, the origins of the liability are important because it is rare that vicarious liability will exist outside of the employment relationship.

The rule has been criticised for being 'rough justice' since an apparently innocent party is being fixed with liability for something which he has not done. On this level, imposing liability by this method is a direct contradiction of the principle requiring fault to be proved to establish liability.

There are a number of justifications for the practice, many of which have to do with ensuring that the victim of a wrong has the means of gaining compensation for the damage or injury suffered.

- Traditionally, an employer may have had a greater degree of control over the activities of employees. Indeed it may well be that an employee has carried out the tort on the employer's behalf, so it is only fair that the employer should bear the cost.
- Employers, in any case, are responsible for hiring, firing and disciplining staff. An employer may have been careless in selecting staff, and, if employees are either careless or prone to causing harm and the employer is aware of this, then he has the means to do something about it. The internal disciplinary systems allow the employer to ensure that lapses are not repeated, ultimately by dismissing staff. The employer is also responsible for ensuring that all employees are effectively trained so that work is done safely.
- The major concern of an injured party is where compensation is likely to come from. In this respect the employer will usually be better able to stand the loss than the employee will. In any case the employer is obliged to take out public liability insurance and can also pass on loss in prices.
- This is itself a justification for vicarious liability since it is also a means of deterring tortious activities.
- In certain instances, imposing vicarious liability makes the conduct of the case easier for the injured party in terms of identifying specific negligence, particularly in medical negligence.

Proving vicarious liability first depends on satisfying a number of other basic tests:

- Was the person alleged to have committed the tort an employee? There is only very limited liability for the torts of independent contractors.
- Did that party commit the alleged tort 'during the course of his or her employment'? An employer is generally not liable for torts that occur away from work or while the employee is 'on a frolic on his own'.
- Was the act or omission a tort? Again, an employer will not generally incur liability for other wrongs such as crimes carried out by the employee.

20.2 Testing employment status

It is not always possible to determine at first sight whether in fact a person is employed under a contract of service or not. It is often in the interest of an 'employer' to deny that the relationship is one of employment. Definitions such as the one in the Employment Rights Act 1996 that the employer is a person employed under a contract of employment, are no real help in determining employment status. It has been suggested in *WHPT Housing Association Ltd v Secretary of State for Social Services* (1981) that the distinction lies in the fact that the employee provides himself to serve, while the self-employed person only offers his services. This is no greater help in determining whether or not a person is employed.

There is in any case inconsistency in the methods of testing employee status, according to who it is that is doing the testing. For instance, the only concern of the tax authorities in testing employee status is to determine liability for payment of tax, not for any other purpose. So the fact that a person is paying Schedule D tax is not necessarily definitive of self-employed status. Again, industrial safety inspectors may have less concern with the status of an injured party and more with the regulations that have been breached.

Besides this, a number of different types of working relationship defy easy definition. 'Lump' labour was common in the past. Casual and temporary employment is even more prevalent in recent times.

Over the years the courts have devised many methods of testing employee status. They all have shortcomings. Some are less useful in modern society than others.

The control test

The oldest of these is the 'control test'. This test did derive from the days of the 'master and servant' laws, as we have already seen. In *Yewens v Noakes* (1880) the test was whether the master had the right to control what was done and the way in which it was done. According to McArdie J in *Performing Rights Society v Mitchell and Booker* (1924), the test concerns '… the nature and degree of detailed control.'

Lord Thankerton in *Short v J W Henderson Ltd* (1946) identified many key features which would show that the master had control over the servant. These included the power to select the servant, the right to control the method of working, the right to suspend and dismiss, and the payment of wages.

Such a test is virtually impossible to apply accurately in modern circumstances. Nevertheless, there are circumstances in which a test of control is still useful, in the case of borrowed workers.

Mersey Docks & Harbour Board v Coggins and Griffiths (Liverpool) Ltd (1947)

The test was applied when a crane driver negligently damaged goods in the course of his work. The Harbour Board hired him out to stevedores to act as their servant. The Harbour Board was still liable for his negligence, however, as he would not accept control from the stevedores.

An interesting development of the control issue concerns the activities of bouncers.

Hawley v Luminar Leisure Ltd (2006)

A bouncer who was supplied to clubs by a firm of specialists assaulted a customer outside the club. The issue was whether the firm supplying the bouncer or the club were vicariously liable for his actions. The Court of Appeal held that the club exercised so much control over the manner in which the bouncer carried out his work that effectively they employed him.

The integration or organisation test

Lord Denning in *Stevenson Jordan and Harrison Ltd v McDonald and Evans* (1969) established this test. The basis of the test is that someone will be an employee whose work is fully integrated into the business, whereas if a person's work is only accessory to the business, that person is not an employee.

According to this test, the master of a ship, a chauffeur and a reporter on the staff of a newspaper are all employees, whereas the pilot bringing a ship into port, a taxi driver and a freelance writer are not.

The test can work well in some circumstances but there are still defects. Part-time examiners may be classed as employed for the purposes of deducting tax, but it is unlikely that the exam board would be happy to pay redundancy when their services were no longer needed.

The economic reality or multiple test

The courts in recent times have at last recognised that a single test of employment is not satisfactory and may produce confusing results. The answer under this test is to consider whatever factors may be indicative of employment or self-employment. In particular, three conditions should be met before an employment relationship is identified:

1. The employee agrees to provide work or skill in return for a wage.
2. The employee expressly or impliedly accepts that the work will be subject to the control of the employer.
3. All other considerations in the contract are consistent with there being a contract of employment rather than any other relationship.

Ready Mixed Concrete (South East) Ltd v Minister of Pensions and National Insurance (1968)

The case involved who was liable for National Insurance contributions, the company or one of its drivers. Drivers drove vehicles in the company colours and logo that they bought on hire-purchase agreements from the company. They were also obliged to maintain the vehicles according to set standards in the contract. They were only allowed to use the lorries on company business. Their hours, however, were flexible and their pay was subject to an annual minimum rate according to the concrete hauled. They were also allowed to hire drivers in their place. McKenna J developed the test in determining a lack of employment status.

The test has subsequently been modified so that all factors in the relationship should be considered and weighed according to their significance. Such factors might include:

- The ownership of tools, plant or equipment – clearly an employee is less likely to own the plant and equipment with which he works.
- The method of payment – again a self-employed person is likely to take a price for a whole job where an employee will usually receive regular payments for a defined pay period.
- Tax and National Insurance contributions – an employee usually has tax deducted out of wages under the PAYE scheme in schedule E, and Class 1 NI contributions also deducted by

the employer. A self-employed person usually pays tax annually under schedule D and will make National Insurance contributions under Class 2.

- Self-description – a person may describe himself as one or the other and this will usually, but not always, be an accurate description.
- Level of independence – probably one of the acid tests of self-employed status is the level of independence in being able to take work from whatever source, and also to turn work down.

All of these are useful in identifying the status of the worker, but none are an absolute test or are definitive on their own.

Irregular situations

Certain types of work have proved more likely to cause problems in the past than have others. Not every working relationship is clear cut, and judges have been called on to make decisions, sometimes based on the factors we have already considered. Often their answer will depend on the purpose of the case, so that the court might seek to bring a person within industrial safety law although they appear to be self-employed.

Casual workers

Such workers have traditionally been viewed as independent contractors rather than as employed. This may be of particular significance since modern employment practices tend towards less secure, less permanent work.

O'Kelly v Trust House Forte plc (1983)

Wine butlers who were employed casually at the Grosvenor House Hotel needed to show that they were employees to claim for dismissal. They had no other source of income and there were many factors consistent with employment. However, the tribunal held that, since the employer had no obligation to provide work and since they could, if they wished, work elsewhere, there was no mutuality of obligations. They were not employed.

The House of Lords have also confirmed this lack of mutual obligation test of employment status more recently.

Carmichael v National Power plc (1998)

The case involved a tour guide at Sellafield. She was given work as required and paid for the work done; tax and NI were also deducted. But the House of Lords decided that there was no obligation to provide work and no obligation on her part to accept any that was offered, although the Court of Appeal had reached an entirely different result.

Agency staff

Many large companies now hire staff through employment agencies. On past cases, they have not always been seen as employees of the agency.

Wickens v Champion Employment (1984)

Agency workers were not employees since the agency was under no obligation to find them work, and there was no continuity and care in the contractual relationship consistent with employment.

Workers' cooperatives

Again it is uncertain whether such workers would be employees or not. Usually we would expect them to be so. However, there are instances where such workers have been classed as self-employed.

Addison v London Philharmonic Orchestra Ltd (1981)

The orchestra operated as a cooperative. The musicians could do other work on their own account. It was held that they were subjecting themselves to discipline rather than control as employees.

Outworkers

People who work from home, usually women with young children, are a very disadvantaged sector of the workforce. They tend to work for little pay and have few rights. There is obviously little control over the hours that they work. Nevertheless, working in areas such as the garment industry, they normally fall into a general framework of organisation. They were in the past always considered to be independent contractors. Some recent cases have suggested otherwise.

Nethermere (St Neots) Ltd v Taverna & Gardiner (1984)

Workers in the garment industry were held to be employees because it was felt that they were doing the same work as employees in the factory, only at home.

Trainees

Apprenticeships were traditionally subject to their own rules, but there are few of these now. In the case of trainees, the major purpose in their relationship with the 'employer' is to learn the trade rather than to actually provide work. Therefore they are not usually classed as employees.

Wiltshire Police Authority v Wynn (1980)

A female cadet tried to claim unfair dismissal, but needed to prove that she was an employee. While she had been placed on various attachments, was paid a wage, could do no other work, and had set hours, she was only undergoing training with a view to becoming a police officer and was not yet employed.

Labour only sub-contractors (the lump)

Such workers are common in the construction industry where they do work for a lump sum. There are advantages to both sides in not making tax and National Insurance contributions. These workers are classed as self-employed.

Activity

Consider whether the following would be classed as employees using the tests above:

1. Sandra, a machinist, works from home stitching shirts from pieces of cloth pre-cut and delivered by her employer, Tej, who also deducts National Insurance payments from her pay, but leaves her to settle her own tax. Tej owns the sewing machine that Sandra uses.
2. Eric, a plasterer, travels round building sites and works for cash payments. Neither he nor builders that he works for pay tax or NI for him. He uses his own tools.
3. Coco, a circus clown, also sells tickets before performances and helps to pack up the big top when the circus goes on to the next town. He also drives one of the lorries that transports the circus. The circus owner says that Coco is self-employed.
4. Alistair is a consultant orthopaedic specialist. He is paid a full-time salary by an NHS Trust but spends three days per week seeing private patients.

Hospital workers

Obviously vicarious liability for the work of people in health care can be critical. Nevertheless, the traditional view in *Hillyer v Governor of St Bartholomews Hospital* (1909) was that a hospital should not be vicariously liable for the work of doctors. This was justified on the grounds that hospitals generally lacked adequate finance before the creation of the National Health Service. In *Cassidy v Ministry of Heal* (1951) the modern view is that hospitals and health services should be responsible for the work done in them.

20.3 Torts in or out of the course of employment

We have already discussed whether or not it is fair to impose liability on an employee for torts committed by his employee. Since it is a potentially unjust situation, it is strictly limited and the employer is only liable for those torts committed 'in the course of the employment'.

What is in the course of employment or not is a question of fact for the court to determine in each case. It is often difficult to see any consistency in the judgments. It seems inevitable that judges will decide cases on policy grounds, and this may explain the apparent inconsistency.

Regardless of the reasoning applied in them, there are two lines of cases:

1. Those where there is vicarious liability because the employee is acting in the course of the employment;
2. Those where there is no vicarious liability because the employee is said not to be in the course of employment.

Torts committed in the course of employment

It is very hard to find a general test for what is in the course of employment. However, courts have appeared to favour a test suggested by Salmond

that the employer will be liable in two instances:

1. For a wrongful act that has been authorised by the employer
2. For an act that, while authorised, was carried out in an unauthorised way.

Authorised acts

An employer then will inevitably be liable for acts that he has expressly authorised, and, since an employee is only obliged to obey all reasonable and lawful acts, he could refuse to carry out tortious acts that the employer instructed him to.

The more difficult aspect of this rule is whether the employer can be said to have authorised a tortious act by implication and should therefore be liable. At least one case has suggested that this is possible.

Poland v Parr (1927)

The employee assaulted a boy who was stealing from his employer's lorry. The employer was held to be vicariously liable since the employee was only protecting the employer's property.

Authorised acts carried out in an unauthorised manner

An employer can be liable for such acts in a variety of ways.

- Where something has been expressly prohibited by the employer

Limpus v London General Omnibus Company (1862)

Bus drivers had been specifically instructed not to race. When they did and the claimant was injured, the employer was vicariously liable. The drivers were authorised to drive the buses but not in the manner in which they did.

- Where the employee is doing the work negligently

Century Insurance Co. Ltd v Northern Ireland Transport Board (1942)

A driver of a petrol tanker was delivering to a petrol station. He carelessly threw down a lighted match, causing an explosion. The employer was still liable since the driver was in the course of employment, and merely doing his work negligently.

- Where employees gives unauthorised lifts contrary to instructions

Rose v Plenty (1976)

A milkman continued to use a child helper despite express instructions not to allow people to ride on the milk floats. When the boy was injured partly through the milkman's negligence, his employers were liable. The milkman was carrying out his work in an unauthorised manner. Lord Denning suggested that the employers were liable because they were benefiting from the work undertaken by the boy.

- Where the employee exceeds the proper boundaries of the job.

Bayley v Manchester, Sheffield and Lincolnshire Railway Co (1873)

Part of a porter's work was to ensure that passengers boarded the correct train. Here the porter pulled the claimant from the train in order to do so. The employers were vicariously liable for the assault.

Following *Lister v Hesley Hall* (2001) the principle can also now apply in the case of sport where there is a close connection between the tortious act and the employment.

Gravil v Carroll and Redruth Rugby Football Club (2008)

In a semi-professional rugby match the first defendant, a player in the game, punched the claimant, a player from the opposing team, in the eye causing him a fracture to the right orbit which then required reconstructive surgery. The court held that the rugby club was vicariously liable for the claimant's injuries. There was a close connection between the punch and the employment and the club had the means through disciplinary measures to avoid their players engaging in such behaviour. It was fair, just and reasonable to impose liability.

However, the mere fact that a police officer uses his uniform to gain the trust of a victim will not necessarily give rise to vicarious liability.

N v Chief Constable of Merseyside Police (2006)

Two hours after he had gone off duty, the defendant was parked outside a club still in uniform. The defendant offered to take to the police station a young woman about whom a first aider from the club was worried because the woman was very drunk and had taken the drug ecstasy. The defendant in fact took the woman to his house where he committed various sexual assaults including rape. The court held that there was no close connection between the employment and the assaults. The defendant had merely made use of his uniform to gain trust and abuse it.

Torts not in the course of employment

The area is confusing because many cases where the employer has been found not to be liable, appear to cover the same areas as those falling within the course of employment. Usually there is some extra element, but it is still confusing. In general though, an employer will not be liable when the employee's tortious act fell outside of the course of employment or where the employee was 'on a frolic on his own'.

- Expressly prohibited acts

Beard v London General Omnibus Co (1900)

A bus conductor drove the bus despite express orders to the contrary, and injured the claimant. The employers were not vicariously liable. The conductor was not carrying out his own work but something outside of his own employment.

- Where the employee is 'on a frolic of his own'. An employer will not be responsible for acts which occur outside of the normal working day, such as travelling into work. The same applies where the employee does something outside of the scope of the work

Hilton v Thomas Burton (Rhodes) Ltd (1961)

Workmen took an unauthorised break and left their place of work. On returning, one employee who was driving the works van, crashed the van and killed somebody. The employer was not liable since the workmen were 'on a frolic'.

- Giving unauthorised lifts

Twine v Beans Express (1946)

A hitchhiker was injured through the negligence of a driver who had been forbidden to give lifts. The employers were not liable. This contrasts with the same situation in *Rose v Plenty* (1976) because here the employer was gaining no benefit from the prohibited lift.

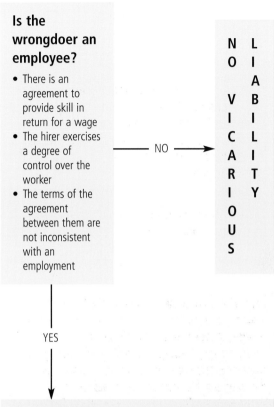

Is the wrongdoer an employee?

- There is an agreement to provide skill in return for a wage
- The hirer exercises a degree of control over the worker
- The terms of the agreement between them are not inconsistent with an employment

NO → NO VICARIOUS LIABILITY

YES ↓

Is the wrong committed in the course of employment?

- Employee is carrying out an authorised wrongful act
- Employee is carrying out an authorised act in an unauthorised manner
- Employee is not 'on a frolic on his own'
- Employee is not travelling to or from work in own time

YES ↓

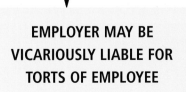

EMPLOYER MAY BE VICARIOUSLY LIABLE FOR TORTS OF EMPLOYEE

Figure 20.1 The process of testing vicarious liability

Activity

Consider whether the employer would be liable in the following circumstances:

1. Roger is employed by 'Eazi-build', a DIY warehouse. While driving to work one morning, his negligence causes a car crash in which Parminder is injured and her car is damaged beyond repair.
2. Simon is a travelling salesman for 'Eazi-build' who works from home. While driving to his first call, he negligently collides with a car driven by Oona, injuring her and damaging her car.
3. Taru is a delivery driver for 'Eazi-build'. One day on completing his last morning delivery, instead of returning to work as he should, he goes to a pub for a few beers. On driving back to work he negligently runs over a pedestrian, Nellie, killing her.

● Acts exceeding the proper boundaries of the work.

Makanjuola v Metropolitan Police Commissioner (1992)

The claimant was persuaded to allow a police officer to have sex with her in return for not reporting her to immigration authorities. There was no liability on the employer. The officer was not doing anything that could be described as falling within his work.

Some situations still defy easy analysis. An employer is generally not responsible for the employee who is travelling to and from work. In some situations, however, this may not be the case. This, for instance, might include where the employee works from home and travelling is part of the work.

Smith v Stages (1989)

The employer was liable here because the employees were paid both travelling expenses and travelling time.

20.4 Other areas of vicarious liability

Liability for the crimes of employees

An employer will not usually be liable for the crimes of an employee that also amount to torts, so that there can be no civil liability.

Warren v Henleys (1948)

A petrol pump attendant assaulted a customer whom he believed was intending not to pay. The court was not prepared to hold that the assault took place in the course of employment.

The courts are more prepared to consider that the dishonesty of an employee falls within the course of employment, and therefore to impose liability on the employer. This might apply in the case of fraud.

Lloyd v Grace Smith & Co (1912)

Solicitors were liable when their conveyancing clerk fraudulently induced a client to convey the property to him.

However, the courts will generally not make an employer liable for an employee's fraudulent activities where they occurred partly in and partly outside the course of the employment.

Credit Lyonnais Bank Nederland NV v Export Credits Guarantee Department (1999)

Two parties were involved in a fraud on the bank, but some of the activities fell outside their employment.

Vicarious liability can also apply in the case of thefts by the employee.

Morris v Martin & Sons (1966)

The employer was liable when the employee working in his dry-cleaning business stole a customer's fur coat.

One area that has caused difficulty for the courts in recent years is where public bodies are accused of being responsible for abuses carried out by their employees.

On the basis of implied duties owed by employers to their employees, employers have been held liable in cases of sexual harassment by other of their employees – *Bracebridge Engineering v Darby* (1990) – and also in the case of racial harassment – *Jones v Tower Boot Co Ltd* (1997).

However, the difficulty of identifying abuse as an 'unauthorised mode of carrying out an authorised act' has led the Court of Appeal to reject claims of vicarious liability for sexual abuse.

Trotman v North Yorkshire County Council (1999)

Here the claimant was a pupil at a special school. He alleged vicarious liability against the local authority after being sexually abused by his deputy headmaster while on a trip with the school. The teacher was sharing the boy's bedroom for nocturnal supervision because of the boy's fits. Butler Sloss LJ found it difficult to reconcile the case with either the harassment cases based on an employer's implied duties to the employee, or with the cases based on fraud. The general feeling of the court was that the more extreme the act of the employee, the less likely that the employer would be held vicariously liable for it.

More recently, the House of Lords have developed a newer test based on inherent risk to cover such situations and enable liability to be imposed more easily.

Lister v Hesley Hall Ltd (2001)

The case is a major development in vicarious liability. Three claimants were sexually abused over a period of time by the warden of a school for children with emotional difficulties, where they were all resident. The warden was then convicted of criminal charges. The claim against the school was on the basis that it had actual or constructive knowledge of the abuse and had failed to prevent it. The trial judge, despite being bound by *Trotman* (1999), allowed the claim on the basis of breach of a duty to the claimants. The Court of Appeal reversed this on the ground that the wrongful behaviour could not be considered to be 'in the course of employment' according to established definitions. In the House of Lords the judges rejected the test in *Trotman* and held that the key test was whether there was sufficient connection between the employment and the torts carried out by the employee. Here the employee's torts were carried out on the school's premises and at times when the employee should have been caring for the claimants. The House of Lords was satisfied that there was an inherent risk of abuse that the employer should have guarded against, and that vicarious liability was appropriate, despite appreciating the applicability of the 'floodgates' argument to the case.

The reasoning in *Lister* has subsequently been approved and applied.

Mattis v Pollock (2003)

A bouncer employed by a nightclub got involved in a fight with customers and the claimant intervened. The bouncer then left the club, went home, returned with a knife and intent on revenge stabbed the claimant outside the club. The Court of Appeal held that what the bouncer did was so closely connected to what his employer expected of him that the employer should be held vicariously liable. The bouncer was supposed to manhandle and intimidate customers.

Liability for the acts of independent contractors

An employer will not usually be liable for the tortious acts of independent contractors whom he has hired. The reason is the lack of control that the employer is able to exercise.

Nevertheless there are some very limited circumstances in which an employer has been shown to be liable for the acts of independent contractors.

These include:

● A situation in which the contractor has been hired for the purpose of carrying out the tort. The employer may be liable, as he would be for his employees

Ellis v Sheffield Gas Consumers Co (1853)

The defendants without authority hired contractors to dig a hole. When the contractors failed to fill the hole and the claimant was injured, the defendants were vicariously liable.

● Where the employers are under a non-delegable duty of care imposed by statute. This

might, for instance, apply where there is an obligation not only to provide but also to ensure that industrial safety equipment is used

● Where a similar non-delegable duty of care is owed in common law.

Honeywill & Stein v Larkin Bros Ltd (1934)

Employers were liable for a breach of the implied duty to provide competent staff and a safe system of work when a freelance photographer set fire to a cinema when using magnesium flares for lighting.

The employers' indemnity

Where the employer is vicariously liable, then both he and the employee are joint tortfeasors. The consequence of this is that the claimant could actually sue either. One further consequence is that the employer who is sued may then sue the employee for an indemnity.

Lister v Romford Ice & Cold Storage Ltd (1957)

A lorry driver knocked over his father who at the time was his driver's mate. The father then claimed compensation from the employers. The employer's insurers on paying out then exercised their rights of subrogation under the insurance contract and sued the driver. The House of Lords accepted that this was possible.

The case is strongly criticised, not least for destroying the reason for imposing vicarious liability. As a result, insurers do not generally exercise their rights under the principle.

Vicarious liability for loaned cars

Another area which creates problems apart from travelling to and from work, is the practice of lending vehicles. The case law again seems confusing. The defining difference appears to be whether or not the vehicle is being used for a purpose in which the owner has an interest.

Britt v Galmoye (1928)

There was no liability on an employer when the car was lent to the employee for the employee's own personal use.

The result will be different where the owner has requested that the other party should borrow the car to carry out the purposes of the owner.

Ormrod v Crosville Motor Services Ltd (1953)

The owner asked the other party to take the car to Monte Carlo where the owner would later join him; the owner was liable.

In some instances, it appears that the logic of the decision is merely that the judges wished there to be liability.

Morgans v Launchbury (1973)

A wife allowed her husband to use her car to go out drinking on the promise that he would not drive while drunk. In the event he allowed another drunk and uninsured driver to drive him home. When there was an accident, vicarious liability was imposed on the wife in order that a claim could be made against her insurance.

Recent developments

There have been two important recent developments in vicarious liability.

Firstly in *Viasystems (Tyneside) Ltd v Thermal Transfer (Northern) Ltd, S & P Darwell Ltd and CAT Metalwork Services* (2005) the Court of Appeal

Activity

1. What justifications are there for making an employer liable for the torts of his employee?
2. In which ways can vicarious liability be said to be unfair?
3. What will a claimant need to show, in order to establish liability on the part of the employer?
4. To what extent is it easy to demonstrate that a person is an employee?
5. Why is the 'control test' an ineffective test on its own?
6. How does the 'economic reality' test operate?
7. What factors are useful indicators of whether a person is employed or self-employed?
8. Is an employer liable for acts done in protection of his property?

9. Explain what is meant by an authorised act done in an unauthorised manner.
10. Why exactly was the dairy liable in *Rose v Plenty* (1976)?
11. What exactly is a 'frolic on his own'?
12. Why were *Limpus* (1862) and *Beard* (1900) decided differently?
13. In what circumstances is an employer liable for the crimes of his employee?
14. Why is *Lister v Hesley Hall* (2001) such an important case?
15. Why is the principle in *Lister v Romford* (1957) criticised and why is it not followed?
16. What consistency, if any, is there between *Morgans v Launchbury* (1973) and other cases on vicarious liability?

declared that there could be dual vicarious liability by two defendants in the same claim.

Secondly the House of Lords has declared that there can be vicarious liability for the acts of employees under s 3 Protection from Harassment Act 1997.

Majrowski v Guy's and St Thomas' NHS Trust (2006)

The claimant was bullied and harassed by his departmental manager because of his homosexuality, which, after investigation, was accepted by the Trust. The claimant succeeded in an action against the Trust under s 3.

Key facts

The nature of vicarious liability	Case
Vicarious liability is where one person is held liable for the torts of another. This is usually where an employer is liable for the tortious acts of an employee. For the employer to be liable: (a) the tortfeasor must be an employee (b) the tort must take place during the course of employment.	

The tests of employment status	Case
Various tests have been developed to determine whether or not someone is an employee rather than an independent contractor (self-employed) – these include the 'control' test and the 'organisation' (or integration) test. The most modern test is the 'economic reality' test – all factors should be considered and their importance weighed.	*Ready Mixed Concrete v Minister of Pensions and National Insurance* (1968)

Torts in the course of employment	Case
Course of employment can include: (a) authorised acts (b) acts done in an unauthorised manner (c) negligently carried out work (d) exceeding the proper bounds of the work.	*Poland v Parr* (1927) *Limpus v General London Omnibus Co* (1862) *Century Insurance v Northern Ireland Transport* (1942) *Bayley v Manchester, Sheffield & Lincolnshire Railway* (1873)

Torts outside of the course of employment	Case
There is no liability for: (a) being on a 'frolic on his own' (b) things outside of the scope of employment.	*Hilton v Thomas Burton* (1961) *Twine v Beans Express* (1946)

Liability for the crimes of an employee	Case
An employer is not usually liable for an employee's crimes: (a) this will apply to fraud (b) and also to crimes generally (c) but now a distinction is made where the criminal act of the employee is an inherent risk that the employer should guard against.	*Lloyd v Grace Smith* (1912) *Warren v Henleys* (1948) *Lister v Hesley Hall* (2001)
There is usually no liability for torts of independent contractors. It is rare but possible to recover the loss from the employee. In some cases it is possible for owners to be liable for torts committed in cars that they have lent to the tortfeasor.	*Ellis v Sheffield Gas Consumers* (1853) *Lister v Romford Ice* (1957) *Morgans v Launchbury* (1973)

Chapter 21

Defences

Specific defences need to be considered when determining whether or not the claimant has either accepted a risk of harm and voluntarily taken it, or indeed has otherwise contributed to his or her own damage by taking insufficient care for his or her own safety.

In this way, a claimant who takes part in sporting activities, particularly in the case of a contact sport, may have voluntarily assumed the risk of injury by taking part and being aware of the nature of the sport.

Similarly, in the case of road traffic accidents there may be contributory negligence, for instance where the claimant has failed to wear a seat-belt, or in the case of an accident involving a motorbike where the claimant failed to wear a crash helmet.

If, on the other hand, the claimant has contributed so much to the damage suffered as to be entirely responsible, then this will probably result in a successful plea of *novus actus interveniens*.

21.1 Contributory negligence

Contributory negligence was originally a complete defence so that no damages at all were payable if the defence succeeded.

Butterfield v Forester (1809)

The defendant obstructed a road by placing a pole across it. The claimant was injured when his horse collided with the pole while he was violently riding the horse. It was held that the claimant had contributed to his own harm. Taking proper care would have avoided the accident and he was unable to claim any damages.

In the nineteenth century this ruling was particularly harsh on people sustaining injuries while at work.

The Law Reform (Contributory Negligence) Act 1945 changed the nature of the rule so that damages could be reduced according to the extent to which the claimant had contributed to his or her own harm. Damages will then be reduced proportionately, according to the degree that the claimant contributed to his own harm.

It should be remembered that the defence can only be applied and damages only apportioned where both the defendant and the claimant are each partly to blame for the damage suffered by the claimant.

Sayers v Harlow Urban District Council (1958)

A lady became trapped in a public lavatory when the door lock became jammed through negligent maintenance. She then stood on the toilet roll holder in an effort to climb out of the cubicle. She had to catch a bus so it was reasonable for her to try to get out in the circumstances, and so her act did not break the chain of causation. The council was liable but the damages were reduced by 25% because of the careless manner in which she tried to escape.

On this basis, 100% reduction in damages has even been held to be possible, although this possibility has also caused some controversy.

Jayes v I M I (Kynoch) Ltd (1985)

The claimant lost a finger at work while cleaning a machine with the guard off. The employers were liable under statutory provisions for a failure to ensure that the guard was in place. However, 100% contributory negligence was held on the part of the claimant, who admitted his fault in taking the guard off.

A successful claim of contributory negligence depends on the defendant showing that the claimant has been negligent himself, and is therefore partly to blame. This will mean that use of the defence, just as in negligence, depends on showing that the behaviour of the claimant meant that harm was foreseeable.

Jones v Livox Quarries Ltd (1952)

The claimant was employed in a quarry and, in defiance of his employer's express instructions, rode on the rear towbar of a 'traxcavator'. The driver was unaware of the claimant and, when another vehicle collided with it, the claimant was injured. His damages were reduced by 5%. Lord Denning stated that:

'A person is guilty of contributory negligence if he ought reasonably to have foreseen that, if he did not act as a reasonable, prudent man, he might be hurt himself; and in his reckonings he must take into account the possibility of others being careless.'

The defence has become a common aspect of claims for injuries or damage sustained in road traffic accidents. Damages can be reduced where a motorcycle passenger fails to take the precaution of wearing a crash helmet.

O'Connell v Jackson (1972)

It was acknowledged that the passenger received much greater injuries because of not wearing a crash helmet. Damages were reduced accordingly.

The defence is also commonly applied to passengers of motorcars who fail to wear seat belts as required by law.

Froom v Butcher (1976)

The passenger suffered greater injuries than would have been the case if wearing a seat belt. Damages were reduced as a result.

Indeed the defence is now commonplace in many everyday situations.

Stinton v Stinton (1993)

Damages reduced by one third for accepting a lift from a drunk driver.

The defence does not require that the claimant owed a duty of care, merely that he failed to take the appropriate care in the circumstances. It is of course always necessary to show causation, ie that the claimant's acts or omissions helped to cause the loss or injuries that he sustained, despite the defendant's liability.

Woods v Davidson (1930)

The defendant negligently ran over the claimant who was drunk at the time. The claim of contributory negligence failed since it was shown that the fact that the claimant was drunk was irrelevant in the circumstances, and the claimant would have been run over even if sober.

Activity

1. What is the effect of a successful plea of contributory negligence?
2. Why exactly did the claimant fail in *Livox* (1952)?
3. Why is the defence of contributory negligence so commonplace in road traffic accidents?
4. In which ways is contributory negligence not a full defence?
5. What was unfair about the defence of contributory negligence before the 1945 Act was passed?
6. What exactly must be shown about the claimant when the defence is used?
7. When will a 100% reduction in damages for contributory negligence be possible?

Key facts

- Following the Law Reform (Contributory Negligence) Act 1945, damages may be reduced where the claimant has helped cause his own damage – *Sayers v Harlow UDC* (1958).
- Damages can be reduced by 100% – *Jayes v IMI (Kynoch)* (1985).

- It must be shown that the claimant failed to take proper care of himself which caused extra harm – *Woods v Davidson* (1930).
- – and that this failure caused the injury or damage – *Sayers v Harlow UDC* (1958).

Smoking is an obvious situation in which the claimant may contribute to his own harm.

Badger v Ministry of Defence (2005)

The claimant died of lung cancer at age 63. The defendant admitted a breach of statutory duty by exposing the claimant to asbestos dust, but argued that damages should be reduced because if the claimant had not smoked cigarettes he would also have been unlikely to die of lung cancer at such a young age. Because the claimant was aware of the risk from cigarettes from 1971, the court reduced damages by 20%.

21.2 *Volenti non fit injuria*

Volenti as a defence concerns a voluntary assumption of the risk of harm by the claimant. Simply translated, it means that no injury is done to one who consents to the risk. It is a complete defence and means that, if successfully used, the claimant will receive no damages. This contrasts with contributory negligence which only reduces damages.

Some judges hold the view that the defence succeeds because there is an express or implied agreement between the defendant and the claimant. However, other judges believe that the defence can still succeed where the claimant has come upon a danger that the defendant has already created.

To succeed, the defendant would have to show three things:

1. Knowledge of the precise risk involved
2. Exercise of free choice by the claimant
3. A voluntary acceptance of the risk.

The rule will not apply merely because the claimant has knowledge of the existence of the risk. On the contrary, the claimant must have a full understanding of the nature of the actual risk for the defence to succeed.

Stermer v Lawson (1977)

Consent was argued when the claimant had borrowed the defendant's motorbike. The defence failed because the claimant had not been properly shown how to use the motorbike, and did not therefore appreciate the risks.

Neither will the defence succeed where the claimant has no choice but than to accept the risk. An assumption of risk must be freely taken and the claimant must actually voluntarily undertake the risk of harm.

Smith v Baker (1891)

A worker was injured when a crane moved rocks over his head and some fell on him. The defence of consent failed. The workman had already done all that he could in complaining about the risks involved in the work taking place above his head. He had no choice but to continue work and did not give his consent to the danger.

Clearly, consent is a defence that can naturally arise in certain types of employment because of the character of the work. However, the more obvious the risk in the industry, the less likely it is that the defence will succeed.

Gledhill v Liverpool Abattoir (1957)

A worker in an abattoir was injured when a pig fell on him. This was accepted as a well-known risk of the work.

Where a person has a duty to act and is then injured because of the defendant's negligence, *volenti* will not be available as a defence. The duty means that the claimant had no choice but act. This would be particularly appropriate in rescue cases.

Haynes v Harwood (1935)

When the defendant failed to adequately tether his horse, the policeman who was injured trying to restrain the animal was not acting voluntarily. He was acting under a duty to protect the public.

Volenti as a defence is appropriate in cases involving negligence, but consent to physical injury is also particularly appropriate in the tort of trespass to the person.

In this context, consent is also a defence that is commonly applied in a sporting context, particularly in the case of contact sports. It will succeed where the injuries sustained fall within the normal activities of the sport.

Simms v Leigh RFC (1969)

A rugby player was injured when he was tackled and thrown against a wall. Because the tackle was within the rules of the sport, there was consent.

But consent cannot be used as a defence where the injuries are a result of conduct that falls outside of what can be legitimately expected in the sport.

Condon v Basi (1985)

A footballer in an amateur match was held liable for breaking another player's leg in a foul tackle. The injured player had not consented to foul play.

We have already seen also that the defence of consent is of critical importance to medical treatment where it can apply to a claim of battery or medical negligence.

Sidaway v Governors of the Bethlem Royal and Maudsley Hospitals (1985)

The doctor in question was required to seek the claimant's consent to an operation. However, the House of Lords was not prepared to accept the existence of a doctrine of 'informed consent' in English law. As a result, there was no liability when the doctor had warned of the likelihood of the risk but not the possible consequences.

An interesting question is whether a person who is a known suicide risk in the care of authorities that are aware of this, has behaved voluntarily when actually committing suicide. In *Reeves v Commissioner of the Metropolitan Police* (1999) *volenti* was said not to apply because of the duty owed by the police to protect the claimant from himself.

If the claimant's behaviour is such that he need not have been in any danger, then *volenti* is clearly a possibility.

ICI Ltd v Shatwell (1965)

The claimant and his brother were quarry workers. The claimant, following his brother's instructions, ignored his employer's instructions on the handling of detonators, and was injured when one exploded. His claims of vicarious liability by the quarry failed. By ignoring his employers and listening to his brother's unauthorised comments, he had assumed the risk of injury voluntarily.

Before the defence can be applied successfully, it must be shown of course that the defendant did in fact commit a tort.

Wooldridge v Sumner (1963)

The claimant attended a horse show as a professional photographer. A rider who was riding too fast lost control of the horse, which then injured the claimant. The Court of Appeal recognised that the rider owed spectators a duty of care. Nevertheless they considered that he had been guilty of an error of judgment in his riding of the horse but not negligence. He had not breached his duty, so *volenti* was not an issue.

The test of *volenti* is subjective rather than objective. It will not help the defendant to argue that the claimant ought to have been aware of the risk. The defence only applies where the claimant does actually know of the risk.

Nevertheless, where a defence of *volenti* may fail for just such a reason, the defendant may still successfully claim contributory negligence and at least reduce the amount of damages that are payable.

Activity

1. What specifically must the injured party have consented to for the defence of *volenti non fit injuria* to apply?
2. Is the test objective or subjective?
3. What are the most common contexts in which the defence of consent operates?
4. When is a person who plays sport said to have consented to the risk of harm?
5. What level of information must be given to a patient by a doctor in order for consent to treatment to be real?
6. What effect does a dangerous type of employment have on the application of the defence?
7. Why could the defence not apply in *Haynes v Harwood* (1935)?
8. What would a defendant have to prove about a claimant for a defence of *volenti* to succeed?
9. Why was the case of *ICI Ltd v Shatwell* (1965) decided in the way it was?
10. What are the basic differences between the defences of *volenti* and contributory negligence?

Activity

Suggest what defence may be argued in each of the following situations, and explain whether or not it is likely to succeed.

1. Jed is being sued for breaking Raj's collarbone during a kick-boxing contest.
2. Manjit accepts a lift from Steven, who already has a car full of passengers. Manjit sits in the open boot of the car, and is injured when another car fails to stop when the traffic lights change and hits Steven's car from behind.
3. Mohammed was injured when he went for a flight in a light aeroplane with Pierre, who he knows does not have a pilot's licence.
4. Helga fell off a horse and was badly injured during a show-jumping contest when the horse pulled up at a large fence.

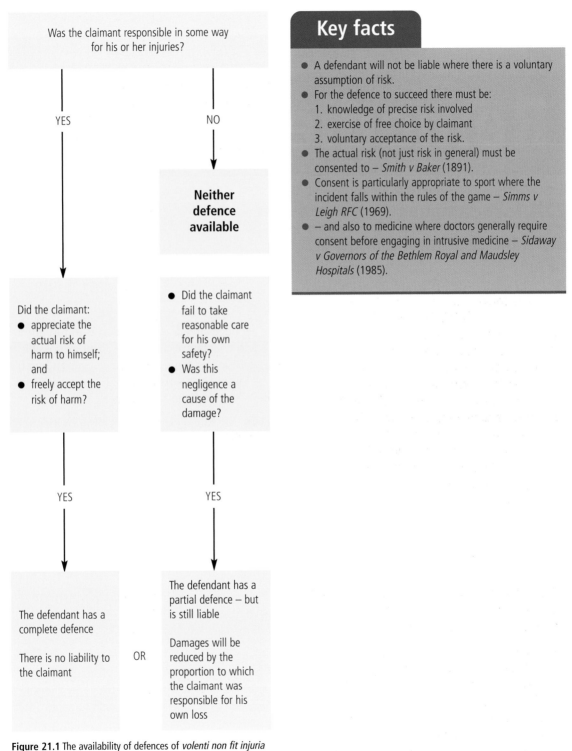

Was the claimant responsible in some way for his or her injuries?

YES

NO

Neither defence available

Did the claimant:
- appreciate the actual risk of harm to himself; and
- freely accept the risk of harm?

- Did the claimant fail to take reasonable care for his own safety?
- Was this negligence a cause of the damage?

YES

YES

The defendant has a complete defence

There is no liability to the claimant

OR

The defendant has a partial defence – but is still liable

Damages will be reduced by the proportion to which the claimant was responsible for his own loss

Key facts

- A defendant will not be liable where there is a voluntary assumption of risk.
- For the defence to succeed there must be:
  1. knowledge of precise risk involved
  2. exercise of free choice by claimant
  3. voluntary acceptance of the risk.
- The actual risk (not just risk in general) must be consented to – *Smith v Baker* (1891).
- Consent is particularly appropriate to sport where the incident falls within the rules of the game – *Simms v Leigh RFC* (1969).
- – and also to medicine where doctors generally require consent before engaging in intrusive medicine – *Sidaway v Governors of the Bethlem Royal and Maudsley Hospitals* (1985).

Figure 21.1 The availability of defences of *volenti non fit injuria* and contributory negligence and their contrasting effects

Chapter 22

Remedies in tort

22.1 Tort damages

22.1.1 The character of damages in tort

Damages is a sum of money paid by the defendant to the claimant once liability is established in compensation for the harm suffered by the claimant. The purpose of awarding damages in tort, however, is altogether different since in the case of damage to property or personal injury or indeed damage to reputation, a sum of compensation is an entirely artificial remedy.

The purpose of damages in tort then is, as far as is possible to do so, to put the claimant in the position (s)he would have been in had the tort never occurred. Inevitably there is a large measure of speculation involved in awarding damages in tort since it involves predicting what would have happened if the tort had not occurred. It is a false remedy because a sum of money will not always repair the harm done to the claimant, and there is always the danger of overcompensating or undercompensating the victim of the tort.

22.1.2 The effect of speculation in tort damages

In tort damages are to put the claimant in the position (s)he would have been in had the tort not occurred. On this basis in tort damages are frequently of a speculative nature, in other words an attempt to assess what the claimant's position would have been if (s)he had not been wronged by the defendant. This is known as general damages

and a major feature of tort claims, for instance in personal injury, is in calculating future losses.

22.1.3 Special damages and general damages in tort – calculating future loss

As we have already seen, damages in tort are to place the victim of the wrong as far as possible in the position as (s)he would have been in had that person not been wronged. In this way there are generally two types of damages:

(a) special damages, which account for losses already incurred up to the date of the claim
(b) future damages or general damages which concern how the claimant's future would have been but for the tort.

In the case of economic losses and property damage these can easily be compensated for as special damages and quantified before trial of the action. There is usually little problem in calculating such loss.

Damages in respect of property damage or loss are calculated according to:

- loss of the property and its value at the time of the tort
- any costs of transporting replacements
- loss of reasonably foreseeable consequential losses associated with or caused by the damage to property
- loss of use until the property is replaced
- reduction in value if the property is to be retained and any costs of repair.

22.1.4 Non-compensatory damages

In some cases in tort, damages are awarded even though there is no quantifiable loss.

These could be in the form of nominal damages where the tort has been proved but there is no actual loss. An obvious example is in a trespass to land action.

Although rare in England and Wales, exemplary damages are also possible. Certainly large awards of damages by juries in defamation actions would be seen as a punishment rather than representing any loss. Exemplary damages are common in other jurisdictions such as the USA.

In England and Wales the leading case on the issue is *Rookes v Barnard* (1964), which involved a dismissal for a refusal to be a member of a Trade Union in a 'closed shop' situation. Such damages are only awarded where:

- government employees have acted in an oppressive, unconstitutional or arbitrary manner, as in *Thompson v Commissioner of Police for the Metropolis* (1998) where the court identified that in cases involving misconduct by police amounting to oppressive or arbitrary behaviour, punitive damages could be awarded; or
- the defendant's conduct was calculated to profit from the tort, as in some defamation actions; or
- where statute expressly allows for such a provision, as in the Copyright Act 1965.

22.1.5 Damages in personal injury claims

Here damages are divided into two types.

Special damages

These account for any quantifiable loss up to the date of trial. Such loss might include damage to any property, cost of medical care, any special equipment or similar requirements, eg modifying an existing residence to allow for effective wheelchair use, laundry, loss of earnings and all other pre-trial losses.

The principle of mitigation of course still applies and thus the court will only allow recovery for losses that it considers are reasonable in the circumstances. On this basis it is possible that private medical care may not be allowed.

General or future damages

These obviously include pecuniary or purely financial losses such as loss of future earnings and of course future medical costs or the cost of special care or other facilities.

They also include non-pecuniary losses that will be assessed as pain, suffering and loss of amenities. Such damages are clearly very difficult to quantify, but judges are guided by set sums for each type of injury. Clearly such calculations are entirely arbitrary. They can also show up various anomalies. For instance, a claimant who has been in a coma will get no award for pain or suffering though a claim for loss of amenities is still possible.

Future earnings are calculated by multiplying what is known as a 'multiplicand' (what the court decides is the claimant's actual net loss after taking account of factors such as payment of benefits) by a 'multiplier' (a number of years based on the claimant's age – but since judgment comes as a lump sum which can be invested and accrue interest the maximum multiplier is actually set quite low in real terms).

The disadvantages to the claimant of being given damages as a lump sum were explored in *Wells v Wells* (1998). Here it was accepted that a claimant might use the money unwisely and lose the benefits. Also, a single sum takes no account of a possible deterioration in the claimant's condition.

Deductions from the multiplicand are possible to take account of, eg private insurance payments, disability pensions and other payments made to the claimant. Deductions can also be made from the multiplier, eg where a known illness would have in any case caused early retirement.

In cases where it is hard to assess the full extent of the injury caused it is possible to seek a split trial with an award of interim damage.

Alternatively, where the claimant's condition is likely to deteriorate over time it is possible to seek provisional damages, allowing the claimant to establish liability but to return to court as the need for a greater level of damages arises with the deteriorating condition.

As is the case with all damages, interest is payable.

22.1.6 The effect of death in tort claims

A distinct possibility in a tort claim is that the claimant will have died as a result of the defendant's wrongful act or omission. Traditionally a person's tort action died with him, which was clearly very unfair. Now it is the case that a person's action against the defendant survives his/her death.

On death there are two possible actions:

(a) Firstly an action is possible under the Law Reform (Miscellaneous Provisions) Act 1934. This is an action brought by the personal representatives of the deceased in the deceased's name. So any damages awarded will go into the estate of the deceased to be distributed to any beneficiaries along with his/her other assets. The action shares many of the characteristics with the action for personal injury from which it has developed.
(b) The second action is on behalf of the dependants of the deceased under the Fatal Accidents Act 1976. It is available to only a very small class of close relatives. As well as losses that have followed death it also includes an arbitrarily set fixed sum for bereavement.

22.2 Equitable remedies in tort

22.2.1 The character of equitable remedies in tort

Equitable remedies are available in tort, although much less so than in contract law with which equity is much more closely associated. The whole purpose of equitable remedies is that they should operate where an award of damages is an inadequate remedy and justice is not served.

On that basis the most common equitable remedy in tort is the injunction. Equitable remedies are at the discretion of the court, unlike an award of damages which is an automatic consequence of liability being established. Because the remedies are discretionary they are awarded subject to compliance with the various 'maxims of equity' such as 'he who comes to equity must come with clean hands' (meaning that the person asking for the injunction must have behaved properly himself).

22.2.2 Injunctions in tort

Probably the most common remedy in tort after damages is an injunction. An injunction will clearly be sought in order to try to put a stop to the tort.

In this way it may be an appropriate remedy in torts such as private nuisance where a householder wants to end the indirect interference, or in the economic torts, where for instance an employer is seeking to end disruption in an industrial dispute. Interestingly, in the nuisance case *Miller v Jackson* the claimant lost the case and had no remedy because Lord Denning considered that, in seeking an injunction, he had gone for the wrong remedy. To allow it would have been in effect to close the cricket ground down.

Injunctions can be classified according to what they try to achieve:

- The most common form of injunction granted is a **prohibitory injunction**, where the defendant is ordered to cease doing whatever amounts to the tortious action. This would clearly be useful in relation to trespass and nuisance, and also in the case of torts protecting reputation such as defamation.
- **Mandatory injunctions**, those ordering the defendant to carry out a particular act, are granted less frequently because it is hard for courts to oversee them.

- On occasions a court may grant a *quia timet injunction*. This has the effect of restraining conduct that is likely to cause severe damage to the party who is seeking the injunction, but before any damage has actually occurred. In this way, in torts that are not actionable *per se* such an injunction would be available in effect before any cause of action has arisen so that the likelihood of substantial damage without the injunction being granted must be demonstrated to the court's satisfaction.

Injunctions can also be classified according to the point at which relief is to be achieved – so they can be:

- **Perpetual** (formerly known as final) – These injunctions contain all of the relief required in the order itself.
- **Interim** (formerly known as interlocutory prior to the Woolf reforms) – These injunctions are an interim measure sought in advance of the actual trial of the issue. So they could be used to prevent continued publication of an alleged libel pending a trial for damages.

Examination-style questions

Question 1

Last year, Alan bought a house in a residential suburban area. During the past ten months, he has been renovating the property. As a result he has had many bonfires that have not only upset his neighbours Sue and Mary, but soot from the fires has dirtied their washing. Piles of rubbish that he has collected in the garden have also caused their fence to collapse. When Sue and Mary complained, Alan answered that he had local authority planning permission and in any case it was none of their business. Since then he has also disturbed them with constant drilling and banging till the early hours of the morning.

Recently Alan invited Roger to his house to see the progress of the work. Contractors that Alan had hired to fit a new central heating system failed to properly secure the floorboards that they had taken up, and Roger fell through one as he stepped on it, breaking his leg.

1. Consider what rights Sue and Mary may have against Alan and the possible remedies if they are successful in their action.   (25 marks)
2. Consider what rights Roger may have against Alan or the contractors.   (25 marks)
3. Discuss the suggestion that in nervous shock claims, the law has dealt unfairly with secondary victims.   (25 marks)

Question 2

Darren is a delivery driver for Pegasus Courier Services. While under his contract he is obliged to pay his own tax and national insurance, he drives a van provided by Pegasus, wears a uniform provided by Pegasus and is prevented from taking other driving jobs. He is forbidden from smoking while at work but one day while making a delivery to Bloggs & Co he carelessly drops his cigarette end on the client's floor, burning an expensive carpet. On his way back to Pegasus he goes off his route to return home and walk his dog. Because he is driving too fast he loses control, mounts the pavement, hits Sandra, a pedestrian and sends her through a plate glass window.

Sandra's injuries are so horrific that the ambulance driver, Frank, who attends her now suffers from post-traumatic stress disorder. Sandra's husband, Aiden, was informed of her accident immediately, and was at the hospital within an hour of her arrival to find that she had been pronounced dead on arrival. Aiden is now grief stricken.

1. Consider what rights and remedies Bloggs & Co and Sandra may have against Pegasus. (25 marks)
2. Consider what rights Frank and Aiden may have against Pegasus or Darren for their injuries.   (25 marks)

3. Discuss the suggestion that the law on psychiatric injury is unfair to secondary victims.
(25 marks)

Question 3

Ron was recently driving home from a party with his girlfriend Freda. They had both drunk several glasses of gin and tonic. Ron was going well over the speed limit, showing off to Freda. He took a bend too fast and was forced onto the wrong side of the road. As he came round the bend, he hit a car which was driven by Sally, head on, writing off her car and causing her to break her collar bone and crack several ribs.

After the accident Ron left his own damaged car on his front drive. The petrol tank was damaged in the crash and petrol seeped out over the drive and soaked several bags of rubbish that he had also left there for some time. Two young boys are walking past one day smoking. One carelessly throws his cigarette end down on Ron's drive. The petrol catches light and sets fire to the rubbish. In the ensuing fire the flames spread to the house of Ron's neighbour, Tej, causing several thousand pounds worth of damage.

1. Consider what rights and remedies Freda and Sally may have against Ron.
(25 marks)
2. Consider what rights Tej may have against Ron.
(25 marks)
3. Discuss whether it is in fact accurate to call *Rylands v Fletcher* a tort of strict liability.
(25 marks)

UNIT 4

Section C: Concepts of Law

Table of Cases

Chapter 23

Law and morals

23.1 The distinction between law and morals

23.1.1 The character of a rule

Rules exist in many contexts, not just in the case of legal rules or even moral rules. The term 'rule' has been defined by academic writers Twining and Miers as 'a general norm mandating or guiding conduct'. In other words, a rule is something that determines the way in which we behave, whether because we submit ourselves to it voluntarily, as would be the case with moral rules, or because it is enforceable in some general way, as would be the case with laws.

Many rules are neither morally binding, nor do they ultimately have the force of law attached to them. Nevertheless, they are necessary and generally adhered to because of the context in which they operate. A classic example of this is the rules that operate in sport. These rules originated to define the sport, and have evolved over time to ensure that each contest conforms to the spirit of that definition. In many instances the rule has developed for the protection of the players.

Rules might also come about through custom or practice, and involve the disapproval of the community rather than any legal sanction if such a rule is broken. All law students learn that the early common law developed out of custom that was commonly accepted. Eventually such rules 'harden into rights' and indeed very often are so widely accepted that they become the law. The Bills of Exchange Act 1882 in effect did little more than to put into statutory form the practices which merchants had willingly followed over many centuries.

Another academic writer, Hart, however, insists that rules should be distinguished from mere habit or practice. He suggests that the defining characteristic of a rule is its enforceability. Rules are generally obeyed for one of three reasons:

1. Because they carry with them a sense of moral obligation – this can be seen in relation to **crime** where most offences, particularly those committed against the person, are seen as morally unacceptable and in fact reflect many religious codes. The basic justification for the House of Lords decision in *Shaw v DPP* (1962) was that the judges are the ultimate guardians of our morals and have a duty to act against immoral behaviour. In contract law, most people would see it as morally outrageous that a man should go back on his word. In a **contractual** situation, this is enforceable because he is bound to carry out his obligations under the terms of the contract. The very nature of the word **tort** (meaning wrong) indicates that there is a good deal of morality attached to it, and that people should be free from invasions with their person or their property.
2. Because the rule is reasonable and relevant – Parliament is said to be legislatively supreme but even parliamentary law may have to be abandoned if it is seen as too irrelevant or too unfair. The classic example of this was the introduction of the so-called 'Poll Tax' in the 1980s.

3. Because a penalty may be imposed if the rule is broken. This explains why people obey rules that they disagree with, such as when compulsory seat-belt wearing was introduced.

23.1.2 The basic nature of morals

The moral values of communities lay down a framework for how people should behave. Concepts of morality differ from culture to culture, although nearly all outlaw extreme behaviour such as murder.

Morality is generally to do with beliefs, so may be affected by religion. We all have a moral code of some kind which defines what we think is and is not acceptable behaviour. Morality can differ from culture to culture and from individual to individual, although some behaviour is universally unacceptable. Inevitably morality has an impact on law, particularly the criminal law. Very often it concerns behaviour of a sexual nature and leads to controversy.

Often morality finds its roots in religion. The Bible provides a moral code for Christian communities both in the very basic and strict rules of the Ten Commandments, and in the more advanced socially aware teachings of Christ. The Koran provides a very extensive moral code for Muslims.

The law of a country will generally reflect the moral values accepted by the majority of the people, but the law is unlikely to be exactly the same as the common religious moral code. A good example of this is adultery. This is against the moral code for both Christians and Muslims, but is not considered a crime in Christian countries. In fact, in England it is merely evidence of an irretrievable breakdown of a marriage sufficient to permit one party to the marriage a divorce. However, in some Muslim countries, though not all, it is against the criminal law and attaches criminal penalties.

In England and Wales there has been a move away from religious beliefs and the way that the law has developed reflects this. Abortion was first legalised in 1967, yet it would be fair to say that

many people still believe it is morally wrong. Indeed the case of *Gillick v West Norfolk and Wisbech AHA* (1986) demonstrates that there are individuals who forcefully reject the idea of giving contraceptive advice and support to underage girls, despite the evidence of the scale of the need demonstrated in the figures of teenage pregnancies.

While English law clings to the idea that euthanasia is unacceptable, there is a clear call for its legalisation in recent cases such as *R (on the application of Pretty) v DPP* (2001) and *Re B* (2000).

R (on the application of Pretty) v DPP (2001)

Mrs Pretty was suffering from motor neurone disease. As a result she was becoming more and more incapable of movement. She knew that eventually she would suffocate to death. She wanted her husband to be able to assist her to take her own life when she felt that her life had become intolerable.

She applied to the courts for a judicial declaration that, if her husband assisted her to commit suicide, he would not be prosecuted. The House of Lords refused the declaration on the basis that any assistance of the husband would be a criminal act.

Re B (2000)

B was paralysed, unable to breathe independently, and on a life support machine. She was mentally fully aware of her situation and she asked for the life-support machine to be switched off. The doctors refused to do this, so she sought a declaration from the courts that she had the right to decide whether on not the machine should be switched off. The courts held that as she was mentally competent she did have this right, even though she knew she would die when the machine was switched off.

Doctors have even shown a moral acceptance of the need for euthanasia in instances of terminally ill patients suffering dreadful pain and indignity as in *R v Cox* (1992) and *R v Arthur* (1981).

A more limited and passive form of euthanasia has been accepted as legal with the ruling in *Airedale NHS Trust* v *Bland* (1993), where it was ruled that medical staff could withdraw life support systems from a patient, who could breathe unaided, but was in a persistent vegetative state. This ruling meant that they could withdraw the feeding tubes of the patient, despite the fact that this would inevitably cause him to die. Again, many groups believe that this is immoral as it denies the sanctity of human life.

23.1.3 The diversity of moral views

One of the key problems with morality is that, while many moral views coincide, there are also many that differ wildly. A French sociologist, Durkheim, suggested that it is almost impossible to find a single set of moral values that would be acceptable to all the members of a modern society.

The views of different societies and even within a society can vary significantly on difficult ethical issues such as euthanasia, pornography, prostitution, the use of soft drugs, vivisection; even subjects as diverse as foxhunting, sex before marriage and body-piercing cause great controversy.

There do appear to be certain core morals which are generally accepted, and these are usually associated with life and death issues. However, even then there is also disagreement. While most people see any form of killing as wrong, there are vastly opposing views on whether abortion is the taking of a human life or merely a woman exercising rights over her own body. In England, the laws on abortion act as a defence to a medical practitioner carrying out the operation where certain conditions are satisfied; ie that the pregnancy is more damaging to the woman or members of her family than termination would be, or that there is a foetal abnormality justifying termination. In the USA on the other hand, following the case of *Roe v Wade* (1973), abortion is a constitutional right of all women, declared in the Supreme Court.

Where lesser considerations such as the concept of dishonesty are concerned, there are as many interpretations as there are individuals. This can clearly be seen in the lack of a positive definition of dishonesty in s 2 Theft Act 1968, and in the criticisms, such as those of Professor Griew, of the test of dishonesty produced in *Ghosh* (1982).

Morals also clearly change and develop. Views on homosexuality have altered dramatically since the trial of Oscar Wilde, and now the argument is more over whether or not gay couples should be able to legally parent children, than whether or not their sexual activities are acceptable or legal.

23.1.4 The differences between law and morality

Despite the fact that law develops from a shared morality, there are nevertheless some very significant differences between the two:

- Morality develops over a long period of time, while it is possible for law to be introduced instantly. Morality cannot be deliberately changed; it evolves slowly and changes according to the will of the people. In the late nineteenth century, the author Oscar Wilde was ruined and imprisoned over his homosexuality. Now gay couples have equal rights to a sexual relationship as heterosexual couples. Law can be altered deliberately by legislation; this means that behaviour which was against the law, can be 'de-criminalised' overnight. Equally, behaviour which was lawful can be declared unlawful.
- Morality inevitably depends on voluntary codes of conduct whereas law is enforceable. Many morals may in any case be difficult to enforce if not unfair, eg *Gillick* (1986). Breaches of moral codes in general carry no official sanction (though some religions may 'excommunicate', which in a deeply religious society may be a powerful persuader to moral behaviour).

Key facts

Law	Morality
A rule is 'a general norm mandating or guiding conduct': Twining and Miers	Moral values generally are to do with beliefs and may be affected by religion
A law is binding and enforceable	Only morally binding
Law can be introduced instantly Law can be altered by legislation and can change overnight	Develops over a long period of time Cannot be deliberately changed Changes slowly according to the will of the people
Mandatory code of conduct Obeyed because: ● of a sense of moral obligation ● they are reasonable and relevant ● a penalty may be imposed if the rule is broken	Voluntary code of conduct Obeyed through a sense of shame and guilt Generally no 'official' sanction for breaches

Both law and morality can dictate the way in which people are expected to behave
The laws of a country are likely to reflect the moral values of the majority of the people
There is an overlap between law and morals, e.g. murder is a crime and is also morally wrong

Figure 23.1 Comparison of law and morals

Morality then relies for its effectiveness on the individual's sense of shame or guilt. Law, on the other hand, makes certain behaviour obligatory with legal sanctions to enforce it.

● Breaches of moral rules are not usually subject to any formal adjudication, while breaches of law will be ruled on by a formal legal system, usually in the courts.

23.2 The relationship between law and morals

23.2.1 Law and morality

Both law and morality are said to be normative. This means that they both dictate the way in which people are expected to behave. Moral viewpoints can clearly have an enormous influence on the making of laws, and some people would argue that the criminal law represents a common moral position.

The moral standards of a community are recognised as having a significant influence on the development of law, but in complex societies, morality and law are never likely to be coextensive. Major breaches of a moral code, such as murder and robbery, will also be against the law, but in other matters, there may not be any meaningful consensus.

The law may appear to be based on moral positions but ones not accepted by everyone. The obvious example to return to is the legalisation of abortion under the Abortion Act 1967. The Act served a vital need in ensuring the safety of women so that they should have abortions in proper clinical conditions.

At the time of the Act, which started as David Steel's private members bill, there was much publicity regarding horrific injuries and even death caused by back-street abortions. Nevertheless, groups such as LIFE and the Association of Lawyers for the Defence of the Unborn Child fiercely contest the morality of abortion. In contrast, many in the women's movement see that the law should be changed and extended so that it reflects a woman's right to choose what to do with her own body.

Arguments can occur even amongst those with scientific knowledge as to the point at which life actually begins. In this way, much of the argument surrounding the amendments to abortion law in the Human Fertilisation and Embryology Act 1990 were over the timescale during the pregnancy during which abortion would be permitted. The Catholic Church of course would argue that abortion is wrongful *per se*, since life in its view begins at conception.

Moral contradictions can also appear in the law so that while abortion can be carried out legitimately, the courts have refused actions for 'wrongful life' in *McKay v Essex AHA* (1982) because it is contrary to the principle of the sanctity of life. Similarly, doctors have been prosecuted for openly practising euthanasia as in *R v Cox* (1992) but withdrawing feeding so that a patient in a permanent vegetative state would die was accepted in *Airedale NHS Trust v Bland* (1993).

Other contradictions involve sexual morality. Many would argue that sex of any kind outside of marriage is morally unacceptable. However this simple viewpoint does not necessarily reflect the law. Adultery and incest could both be classed as morally unacceptable, although probably to different degrees. In English law, the latter is subject to criminal sanctions while the former is not. Lap-dancing and the use of topless waitresses may offend many people's moral sensibilities but they are not against the law. The flippant use of nudity in daily newspapers is also a constant source of controversy.

23.2.2 Natural law and positivism

A major debate is whether law and morality should reflect each other exactly. The idea of natural law is that the two should coincide and that there is a divine source for the law. Taken to the extreme, the supporters of natural law would say that legal rules which did not conform with moral laws should be ignored. In other words, if the legal rules of a country are in contrast to the

moral laws, the legal rules should be disobeyed. Positivists, on the other hand, hold that if legal rules have been enacted by the correct procedures, then those legal rules must be obeyed, even if they are not liked and are in conflict with morality.

23.2.3 The *Hart Devlin* debate

In 1957 the Wolfenden Committee was asked to examine and consider a range of moral issues. The committee recommended the legalisation of both prostitution and homosexuality, and as a result gave rise to much debate on the issues.

Professor Hart approved the findings of the Report and argued strongly that there should be a clear separation of law and morality. He felt that morality was a matter of purely private judgment and that the state had no right to intervene in private morality, and that it was also wrong to punish people who may have done no harm to others. On the other hand, he felt that a legal system should be based on logical ideas producing 'correct' decisions from rules. Nevertheless, he also did concede that society could not exist without a form of morality which mirrors and supplements the legal rules.

Lord Devlin felt that society required the observance of certain moral principles and, even if public opinion was changing, the law should still support those moral principles. He also felt that the judges have a residual right to protect and preserve some sort of common morality. An obvious example of judges exercising this right was in *Shaw v DPP* (1962).

Shaw v DPP (1962)

D published a 'ladies directory'. This was a list of prostitutes with photos of some of the prostitutes and information on the type of sexual behaviour in which they were prepared to participate. D was convicted of conspiring to corrupt public morals.

In this case the House of Lords effectively invented the crime of conspiracy to corrupt public morality to cover the situation.

English law continues to take this line in some cases. A strong example was the case of *R v Brown* (1993).

R v Brown (1993)

A group of men took part in sado-masochistic acts against each other. This was done in private and all the men involved were adults and had consented to the acts. There were some injuries caused but the court accepted that these were transient and minor. Despite all these facts, the House of Lords ruled that their behaviour was a breach of the criminal law of assault and they could not claim the defence of consent to excuse their acts.

In this case the House of Lords were imposing a certain standard of what was considered as acceptable behaviour. However, the judges in the House of Lords were not unanimous as two of the five judges disagreed with the decision.

Even then the contradictions in the law can be shown when the case is compared with *R v Wilson* (1997). Here the Court of Appeal accepted that a man branding his wife's buttocks with his initials could not lead to a criminal conviction because it was consensual on the wife's part and was an entirely private matter in which the law should not intervene.

23.3 The legal enforcement of morals

There are many instances of connections between law and morals in the sections above that can be usefully employed in answers to questions on the subject.

Inevitably, many of them involve the criminal law and the question of morality is particularly appropriate in that area of the law. Inevitably too morality is less of an issue in both contract law

and tort. There are of course included above examples from areas other than these three areas of law, family and matrimonial law being an obvious example.

Criminal law

In criminal law, morals figure very largely in the whole area of sexual offences, and there have been many major recent developments including of course current statutory developments.

The case of *B v DPP* (2000), while answering many existing contradictions in the existing law on strict liability and the defence of mistake, has its focus on sexual behaviour and as such has its roots in morality.

We have already seen how the courts have become involved in controversy surrounding sexual behaviour. The House of Lords in *R v Brown* (1993) held that a group of homosexual sado-masochists could not consent to harming each others' genitalia. The very moral justification given was that it was not in the public interest to allow such behaviour, for the possible corrupting effect on other people.

However, the Court of Appeal in *R v Wilson* (1996) held that a wife could consent to her husband branding his initials in her buttocks with a hot knife. Again morals formed part of the reasoning; it was not the role of the court to interfere in the private pastimes of husbands and wives in a domestic context.

The homicide offences and the non-fatal offences also have their roots in the moral view that it is wrong to kill or physically harm another person with no justification. Even within these offences, the use of partial defences in voluntary manslaughter can be seen as having a base in morality. Hence the notion that it would be wrong to convict a person of murder whose reasoning was impaired by an abnormality of the mind, as with diminished responsibility under s 2 Homicide Act 1957.

The defences also in many ways reflect morality. In insanity for instance, the defendant has a defence because he does not know what he is doing, or if so, he does not know that it was wrong. The rules on voluntary intoxication demonstrate society's natural repugnance for acts done while under the influence of alcohol or drugs. Even in the case of involuntary intoxication, the case of *R v Kingston* (1994) was in many ways a moral judgment.

Contract law

Contract law is not an area that is overly concerned with morals. Nevertheless, there are occasions where morality of varying sorts is an issue.

In the area of vitiation, certain contracts can be declared void in essence because of their association with immorality. In *Pearce v Brooks* (1866) a cab owner failed to enforce a contract with a prostitute who used his cabs for trade because the courts were not prepared to allow contracts for immoral purposes.

Similarly in *Parkinson v The College of Ambulance* (1925) the contract was void because its whole purpose was corruption in public life. The courts have been similarly unprepared to enforce contracts to commit a tort or a crime as in *Dann v Curzon* (1910). Neither will the courts allow parties to take advantage of contracts that set out to defraud, such as one aimed at defrauding the revenue in *Napier v National Business Agency* (1951).

Judges in contract law cases are not prepared to allow violence to be used to secure a contract, hence the development of a law on duress.

The area of fraudulent misrepresentation developed in *Derry v Peek* (1889), while based on the tort of deceit, still reflects the view in contract law that it would be improper to allow a contract to be secured by fraud.

Tort

In tort deceit has already been mentioned as one example of the law adopting a moral standpoint.

We have already seen how the law of tort can become involved in moral difficulties. Cases such as *R (on the application of Pretty) v DPP* (2001) and *Re B* (2000) are on one hand concerned with

criminal liability of those who assist in euthanasia of whatever kind. On the other hand, they may also involve the duty of doctors towards their patients. The starting point for doctors is a moral obligation to treat patients, found in the Hippocratic oath. It is also backed up with legal duties found in a variety of judgments on for instance the duty to examine (*Barnett v Chelsea and Kensington Hospital Management Committee* (1969)), or duties in relation to treatment (*Wilsher v Essex Health Authority* (1988)) etc.

There is also a basic moral contradiction, since all intrusive medical treatment in the absence of consent is a battery in law. This is best illustrated in the judgment of Cardozo J in the American case *Schloendorff v Society of New York Hospital* (1914). It has also been restated in English law in the cases of *Re T (adult: refusal of medical treatment)* (1992) and also in *Re C (adult: refusal of medical treatment)* (1994). Nevertheless, doctors have been able to justify withdrawing feeding and hydration leading to death in the case of a patient in a persistent vegetative state and therefore incapacitated in *Airedale NHS Trust v Bland* (1993). They have also justified sterilisation of a mentally incapacitated patient in *Re F (mental patient: sterilisation)* (1990). They have also even been able to give treatment that is unwanted in *Re S (adult: refusal of medical treatment)* (1992). Clearly these are cases that involve very complex and troubling moral issues.

23.4 Exam questions on law and morality

Section C of Unit 4 is a synoptic section and therefore requires you to make links between the various elements of your course and see the law in a broader context.

In this way, questions on morality will require that you have a firm understanding of the ways that legal rules and moral rules may differ and also when they may coincide. Questions will also require that you also illustrate your understanding of the nature of morality and its relationship and various contradictions with legal rules by reference to the substantive areas of law that you have studied in Unit 3 and sections A and B of Unit 4. Obviously, the way that you are able to illustrate will depend on the two units that you have studied, which may involve only one law if crime is chosen in both units, but otherwise would give you material from two areas. Almost inevitably with this subject, you will have more sources of illustration within the criminal law than with either contract or tort.

In the sections of this chapter above you have many illustrations and useful cases that you can use in your answers.

Sample essay question

Discuss the extent to which morals have had a serious impact on the development of law. Use examples from criminal law or civil law or both in illustrating your answer.

Chapter 24

Law and justice

24.1 The meaning of justice

Generally we would all assume that law and justice are in effect the same thing, or at least that the whole purpose of law is to promote justice. Nevertheless, this is not always the case and it is probably easier to assume that there are many occasions where law and justice quite naturally coincide but that there also occasions when they do not. We have all seen many instances in newspapers of so-called 'miscarriages of justice': the 'Birmingham Six', the 'Guildford Four' and Stefan Kizco are popular examples. These instances are focused on wrongful convictions in the criminal law. The existence of the Criminal Cases Review Commission is an acknowledgement that mistakes are made and that sometimes the law deals wrongly with people and treats people unjustly.

However, such complaints are not restricted to the criminal law, and occur in a civil context also. Many people quite plainly suffer physical problems following medical treatment where tort is the appropriate remedy, but will be unable to gain any compensation because they cannot prove fault. *Wilsher v Essex Area Health Authority* (1988) is a classic example of this. The law is no doubt right on the subject, but it is inevitable that the claimant may walk away feeling that he has been treated less than justly.

The famous case of Tony Martin, in which he was convicted of murder when he shot and killed one burglar and injured another, caused controversy. This was not just because he was convicted within the criminal law, but also because the injured burglar claimed for compensation. We may all feel that we are entitled to take some steps to protect ourselves from burglars, and the case perhaps indicates that the old maxim that 'an Englishman's home is his castle' is not the full truth.

Justice is certainly one goal towards which the law naturally strives, but it is unlikely that law will ever produce 'justice' in every case. The law is concerned with the enforcement of legal rules, and justice is not the primary consideration in every case.

The most immediate problem in any case is defining precisely what 'justice' means. The difficulty of defining justice was once commented on by Lord Wright, who said:

> 'the guiding principle of a judge in deciding cases is to do justice; that is justice according to the law, but still justice. I have not found any satisfactory definition of justice . . . what is just in a particular case is what appears just to the just man, in the same way as what is reasonable appears to be reasonable to the reasonable man.'

In some situations people's concept of what is justice may differ and, depending on what is at stake, it may differ quite widely. Justice can be seen in the idea of conformity, applying the rules in the same way to all people. This is the whole basis of the doctrine of *stare decisis* in common law, treating like cases alike. However, even this can lead to situations which may be seen as injustices.

Indeed it is not surprising that the rigid application of rules may actually produce injustice. Married women before the landmark case of *R v R* (1991), in which the House of Lords used the Practice Statement to alter a 200-year-old rule that a man could not be guilty of raping his wife, may well have thought that they were being treated unjustly by the law. By virtue of their marital status and the identity of their rapist, they were simply being denied the protection that was offered to every other woman. In a similar way it is easy in cases such as *R v Ahluwalia* (1992) to argue that provocation is essentially a male defence, and therefore in effect is discriminating against women.

We have some idea what represents justice. The development of rules of equity were said to be based on justice and fairness. Equity developed because the common law was said to be unfair, because the writ system was closed and so not every litigant had a claim, because many of the rules of common law were too rigid for the claim to be successfully fought, and because the remedies available were often irrelevant to the actual need.

Justice then in its simplest sense is based on fair and equal treatment for all. It is something that we all would naturally demand from any law and would believe should be an integral part of any legal system. However, there are numerous examples from history of societies creating unjust laws.

The majority population in South Africa prior to the new constitution would not have accepted that the apartheid laws were just, and this is why they were resisted by the ANC and other groups over many years until their eventual collapse. Many of the atrocities carried out during Nazi Germany were in fact backed up by the Nuremburg laws passed by the National Socialist party once in power. The view of the international community was reflected in the war trials conducted deliberately at Nuremburg. In modern times we have already seen that there are many examples of miscarriages of justice occurring, even in a legal system that we all consider to be fair.

Aristotle, the Greek philosopher, was one of the earliest people to actually put forward the view that all law should promote justice. However, there are many varied theories on the relationship between law and justice and first it is necessary to consider these.

24.2 Theories of justice

24.2.1 Theories of natural law

Natural law is a strange concept. The basic idea is that all law ultimately derives from a divine source which is superior to man-made law and which is based on moral rules. It therefore promotes the idea that law and morality should therefore absolutely reflect each other.

Different views can be taken on what this natural source is. Aristotle believed that it could be found in nature, while St Thomas Aquinas believed that the natural source of law was God.

The logical extension of the natural law philosophy then is that it is permissible to break the legal rules of a country if they fail to conform to moral laws, and that this is only a representation of justice in action. This was indeed a view that was held by St Thomas Aquinas. His view was that laws that went against the public good had no legitimacy. Nevertheless, he was not prepared to see the law broken if this would lead to social disruption, which he also felt would be against God's will.

Professor L L Fuller is a modern follower of the idea of natural law. His work, *The Morality of Law*, focuses on an 'inner morality' which he argues should be followed. Lord Devlin, as we have seen in the previous chapter, also believed that law is based on morality, but in this case used this as a justification for judges to use the law to interfere in moral issues. The contrary view of course was taken by Professor Hart.

24.2.2 Positivism

Theories of natural law conflict with those of positivist thinkers who essentially believe that, provided that the law is made according to the correct procedures, then it should be followed absolutely, however much it conflicts with morality.

Kelsen was a well known positivist who wrote about his theories in *General Theory of Law and State* in 1911. Kelsen argued that law and morality are entirely separate concepts, and that even though an individual law might be seen as immoral, it should still be followed. He was also of the opinion that justice is too vague a concept to be defined. Since there could be different theories of justice, it was predominantly based on individual perceptions and preferences, and could not be represented in law.

Professor Hart, as we have seen before, also considered that law and morality are separate concepts. He argued that law should be based on logical ideas that will produce correct decisions according to the rules.

Durkheim held the opinion that since society is held together by social structures, the law must operate as an integral means of ensuring that those structures work.

24.2.3 Utilitarianism

Utilitarianism is a philosophy that developed in the nineteenth century predominantly from the writings of Jeremy Bentham and John Stuart Mill. It was also followed to a degree and given some practical application at that time.

As a theory it is essentially different from the basic principles of natural law, although it still in some senses concentrates on the conflict between legal rules and divine law or at least justice. Jeremy Bentham, the originator of this school, argued quite convincingly that the major purpose of law was to achieve the greatest happiness for the greatest number. The most successful law in this sense would be one that in effect achieved the greatest all round good. The idea was clearly a good one that has a lot of merit. However, it also has an obvious defect. The greatest good might not always represent what was in everybody's interest, and indeed it completely ignores the interests of the individual which would be sacrificed for the benefit of the majority.

John Stuart Mill also developed this theme. His opinion was that people should be left to manage their own affairs and that legal intervention should be only minimal. The only justification for interfering with a person's basic freedoms would then be where that person was causing harm to someone else and thus interfering with their freedoms. Bentham was much admired by Chadwick who, to an extent, put the philosophy into practice in his great public health improvements of the late nineteenth century, not always popular for their impact on property rights and for the cost in terms of taxation and the local rate.

24.2.4 Economic views of law and justice

Law inevitably is used to support prevailing political philosophies, Parliament being the supreme law maker. A major focus of politics is property rights and the distribution of wealth. This is in essence what divides the leading parties. Capitalist theories can be contrasted with socialist theories, and governments that tend towards either will introduce laws which protect respectively either viewpoint. A government supporting capitalism will tend to interfere with individual rights in a minimal way and be very protective of property rights. This was evident in the policies of government during the Industrial Revolution following the *laissez-faire* economics of the time. In contrast, a socialist government will tend to be interventionist and the many reforms in labour relations, employment protection, consumer rights, landlord and tenant controls in the late 1960s and late 1970s are an example of this.

Socialism is generally hostile to property rights where they come at the expense of social justice. Karl Marx argued simply that capitalism is an unjust philosophy, because it protects individuals with wealth at the expense of the social needs of the many, and that therefore in any capitalist society all law is essentially unjust since it represents the means by which one class oppresses the class or classes below it. Marxist views of justice, therefore, are based on the redistribution of wealth. A just outcome possibly for the many but tough luck on those from whom the wealth is redistributed.

Robert Nozick, in his 1974 essay 'Anarchy, State and Utopia', on the other hand, was prepared to define a just society. This was one, he said, where the state has the least possible power to interfere with the rights of the individual. Nevertheless, his theory is based not just on the ownership of property but also on the manner in which it has been gained. In this way, Nozick would suggest that if the property has been gained fairly then the state should have no right to interfere. The natural extension of the principle is that redistribution of wealth is unjust because it interferes with basic individual rights.

Clearly all economic views of justice present problems. The clear problem of trying to balance purely economic considerations with notions of justice is that what may be just for society as a whole may be very unjust to a particular individual. The reverse is obviously equally true. A good example of the problem was in the case of *Re B* (1996). The case involved a little girl, Jaime Bowen, who was suffering with leukaemia. She had already received treatment which had not been successful and her father wished for the health authority to try further treatment, and why shouldn't he? Any parent would want every possible step to be taken to prevent their child from dying. The case was much publicised at the time, and the controversy then was over the refusal by the health authority to fund further treatment (although the health authority succeeded on the basis that the refusal to treat was in fact a clinical rather than an economic decision).

Clearly though, very pressing needs, and what we may see as basic rights, can be affected by economic considerations. An example is *R v*

Key facts

Definition of justice	Difficult to define 'What is just in a particular case is what appears just to the just man': Lord Wright	Equity Fair and equal treatment for all	
Theories of justice	Natural law	● Derives from a divine source ● Law and morality should absolutely reflect each other ● An inner morality which should be followed ● Can break legal rules if do not conform to moral laws	Fuller
	Positivism	● Law, if made according to correct procedures, must be followed even if it conflicts with morality	Kelsen, Hart
	Utilitarianism	● Major purpose of law is to achieve the greatest happiness for the greatest numbers ● The interests of the individual are sacrificed to the benefit of the majority	Bentham
Economic theories of justice	Capitalism	● Minimalist interference with individual rights ● Redistribution of wealth is unfair because it interferes with basic individual rights	Nozick
	Socialism	● Interventionist, e.g. employment protection, consumer protection ● Based on redistribution of wealth ● Hostile to property rights	Marx

Key facts chart on law and justice

Gloucestershire County Council ex parte *Barry* (1997). Here the court allowed a local authority to avoid its statutory duty to provide welfare services based on an assessment of their available resources. The difficulty in accommodating an increasing need for welfare provision within a restricted budget is obviously a concern, and one that the court rightly took seriously. Nevertheless, it is easy to argue that the judgment ignores the basic justice of the situation.

24.3 The extent to which legal rules achieve justice

The law does not always provide justice, although it could still be argued that ensuring justice should be an aim of any legal system. Justice, as we have seen, can be difficult to define and may mean very different things to different people. If we take the examples of Marx and Nozick above, the first would see it as unjust that one person should enjoy greater wealth and power than another, the second would see it as unjust to interfere with a person's property rights to achieve a redistribution of wealth. There is a clear conflict and a clear contradiction here.

Clearly the ability of the legal system to achieve justice depends on certain potentially conflicting factors. These are:

- Treating like situations alike
  This of course is the justification for the doctrine of *stare decisis* and judicial precedent in common law. It can be seen also in sentencing policy in criminal law, and indeed in the means of assessing quantum of damages in civil law.
- The need for discretion
  For the law to be just, it may also depend on the presence of discretion to meet the needs of justice in individual situations, rather than being strictly bound by hard and fast rules. The need to give justice, or at least to avoid injustice, is of course one of the principles behind the Practice Statement 1966 giving the House of Lords the power to change law. *B R Board v Herrington*

(1972) and *R v R (Marital Rape)* (1991) are two examples of the practice statement being used for this very purpose. However, *Jones v Secretary of State for Social Services* (1972) is an example that the Lords will not always use the practice statement even if they feel the past law was unjust. Equity is another obvious example of where rules have been developed where the common law rule would lead to injustice.

Of course, the problem with these two factors is that they tend to be mutually exclusive. An example of injustice created by ignoring the individual situation would be the inability of battered women like *Ahluwalia* (1992) to use the law of provocation in defence of murdering their abusive husbands. As convicted murderers they in effect carry the same stigma as the Moors Murderers, Ian Brady and Myra Hindley, or the Yorkshire Ripper, Peter Sutcliffe. The stigma attached to the individuals only varies because of the number of crimes rather than the nature of the crime itself. The sentence in any case is the same, a mandatory life sentence, and there is no discretionary sentencing in the case of murder.

Criminal law

Criminal law has to deal all the time with the concept of justice, or there would be no respect for it and it would prove unworkable.

It does so in two ways:

1. By grading crimes according to their seriousness.
   In this way, crimes are identified according to their seriousness, taking account of factors such as the inherent wickedness of the crime, the extent to which it causes social alarm, the extent to which it interferes with personal or property rights etc. The crime of murder is considered to be one of the worst because of its wickedness; and burglary of a dwelling house is considered to be worse than that of a commercial premises because of the fear it can create in the occupant, particularly if it is carried out when the occupant is there. Even within crimes of the same character a

gradation occurs, so that rape is the most serious sexual offence and while a peeping tom may upset his victim, he is not classed with the same seriousness.

2. By a sentencing policy that reflects both the seriousness of the crime and factors such as whether the crime involves a first offence, or whether or not the convicted person is a recidivist (repeat) offender.
    The sentencing objective of retribution is generally directed at the most serious crimes such as murder, robbery and rape. Denunciation reflects the need to demonstrate society's disapproval of the crime. Reparation reflects the view that the most important resolution is actually to find some way of repaying the victim for the effects of the crime. Rehabilitation on the other hand seeks to reform the criminal where it is felt possible. The process of mitigation also helps to identify other factors that should be taken into account. Sentencing then represents the sensible view taken by the law that if the criminal is to reform and become an upright member of society then he must be dealt with fairly and proportionately according to the nature of the crime he has committed. The development of crime surveys and the use of victim impact statements also demonstrate that there is a need to be fair also to the victim.

We have already seen some examples of the apparent injustices in the criminal law. Another example of apparent injustice is the case of *E v DPP* (2005).

E v DPP (2005)

D was a 15-year-old boy who was charged with unlawful sexual intercourse with a girl under the age of 16 contrary to s 6 of the Sexual Offences Act 1956, which has since been repealed. The girl was also aged 15 and was a willing participant. The defence argued that this was contrary to three articles in the European Convention on Human Rights:

- Article 6 – the right to a fair trial
- Article 8 – the right to respect for D's private life
- Article 14 – the right not to be discriminated against on the ground of sex.

However, the Court of Appeal ruled there was no breach of human rights and upheld the conviction.

By prosecuting the defendant in this case, the state was criminalising his behaviour and treating the girl as the victim, when this was not, in fact, the situation. It appears to be unjust that the boy received a criminal conviction.

Contract law

Contract is essentially about property and its transfer. The law can be seen as both just and unjust in the rule, that it is generally for the parties to determine the terms of the contract themselves. This is demonstrated in consideration where the rule is that it must be sufficient (it must have some value in the eyes of the law) but need not be adequate. This allowed the widow in *Thomas v Thomas* (1842) to enforce an arrangement freely made which otherwise would have run contrary to her dead husband's stated wishes.

Those who see a capitalist economy as unjust would then welcome the inclusion of such measures as the Sale of Goods Act 1979, the Supply of Goods and Services Act 1982, and the Unfair Contract Terms Act 1977 as a just way of protecting consumers from businesses that would take advantage of them. Indeed, the common law through the rules on incorporation of exclusion clauses had also shown concern for justice in cases such as *Olley v Marlborough Court Hotels* (1949) and *Thornton v Shoe Lane Parking* (1971).

The presence of the vitiating factors shows that

the law is concerned with justice and that a party should not be bound by a contract unfairly made. Duress protects a party against unfair pressure, as is evident in the case of *Barton v Armstrong* (1975). The development of a law on undue influence does the same in less extreme circumstances. The case of *Royal Bank of Scotland v Etridge* (2001) demonstrates some of the very complex situations which the courts have had to deal with in developing the law to be just to both wife and lending institution.

The various classes of misrepresentation show that the law will not allow a party to be forced to comply with a contract entered into on the basis of inaccurate information. This applies whether the misrepresentation is fraudulent and deliberately made (although this would be under the *Derry v Peek* (1889) criteria in the tort of deceit) or innocently, where a remedy is available under the Misrepresentation Act 1967. In mistake too, the rules prevent a party from being caught by the mistake unjustly. Here the rules even deal with the justness of retrieving the good from innocent third parties, where the contract with the rogue has been made face to face and more care should have been taken to check his identity, as in *Lewis v Avery* (1972).

Finally, the remedies also are concerned with the justice of the situation. According to the rule in *Hadley v Baxendale* (1854) later developed in *Victoria Laundry v Newman Industries* (1949), damages will only be recoverable for what is a natural consequence of the breach, or a loss that was foreseeable to both parties at the time the contract was formed. Equitable remedies such as injunctions, specific performance and rescission are clearly aimed at representing justice.

Tort

In tort, many people would advocate that the fault system very often produces injustice for a claimant. This is why no-fault schemes have been called for (see Chapter 26).

Justice can be demonstrated clearly in the groundbreaking judgment of Lord Atkin in *Donoghue v Stevenson* (1932). Before that time, the

so-called 'contract fallacy' ruled and there was no general duty of care and little possibility of a remedy. Not only did the case secure a remedy for the claimant against the manufacturer, but the 'neighbour principle' gave the means of identifying other duty of care situations, and is credited with the development of a tort of negligence.

The trespass torts protect individuals from unwanted interference with their person, their land or their personal property.

The tort of nuisance allows for protection against unreasonable use of land.

Defamation protects civil liberties but the defence of justification allows freedom of speech where the slur is in fact the truth. The defence of fair comment protects the freedom of the press, often to reveal things of important public interest; although it does not necessarily always represent justice, as can be seen in the 'McLibel' trial. Privilege as a defence of course may not always represent a just position.

One way in which tort very often is unable to give real justice is in the remedies available. Damages in tort are necessarily an artificial remedy. Even if compensation puts a claimant back in the financial situation that he would have been in but for the tort, that would be scant comfort for instance to the victim of medical negligence paralysed by careless medical treatment, or the widow of a motorist killed by the negligence of a negligent driver.

24.4 Exam questions on justice

Section C of Unit 4 is a synoptic section and therefore requires that you should make links between the various elements of your course, and see the law in a broader context.

Questions on justice will demand that you have a good understanding of the meaning of justice and its relationship with law. You will need to be aware of the various theories of justice and their inherent contradictions.

You will need also to illustrate your

understanding by reference to the substantive areas of law that you have studied in Unit 3 and Sections A and B of Unit 4. There are elements of justice that can be discussed on each area of law, although often in quite different ways. There are in any case many illustrations and examples of all things relating to law and justice given above.

Sample essay question

There are many different theories of justice. Using criminal or civil law or both, consider the extent of the relationship between law and justice.

Chapter 25

Judicial creativity

One view is that Parliament makes UK law through Acts of Parliament and delegated legislation, while the role of the judges is merely to apply the law to the cases before them. However, in reality the judges can and do create law. This can occur through both:

- the operation of the doctrine of judicial precedent; and
- statutory interpretation.

25.1 Precedent and judicial creativity

In precedent there used to be a school of thought that judges did not actually 'make' new law; they merely discovered it. However, it is now recognised that judges do use precedent to create new law and to extend old principles. There are many areas of law which owe their existence to decisions by the judges.

Criminal law

In the criminal law, judges have played a major role in developing the law on intention. For example, the Court of Appeal judges in *Vickers* (1957) created the rule that the intention for murder covers an intention to cause grievous bodily harm as well as an intention to kill. The judges in the House of Lords confirmed this in *Cunningham* (1982).

The relationship of foresight of consequences to intention has also been formulated by judicial

decisions in *Moloney* (1985), *Nedrick* (1986) and *Woollin* (1998) (see 1.3.1); although in this area there was at least a statutory starting point with s 8 Criminal Justice Act 1967 where Parliament provided guidance (see 1.4.2).

Judicial decisions have also effectively created new crimes as in *Shaw v DPP* (1962), which created the offence of conspiracy to corrupt public morals, and in *R v R* (1991) when it was decided that rape within marriage could be a crime.

Contract

Nearly all the main rules which govern the formation of contracts come from cases decided by the judges. Many of the decisions were made in the nineteenth century, but they still affect the law today; for example, *Felthouse v Bindley* (1863) on the rule that silence can be acceptance of an offer; *Hyde v Wrench* (1840) setting out that a counter-offer is not an acceptance; and *Adams v Lindsell* (1818) that where the post is a suitable method of acceptance, the acceptance is made at the point when the letter is posted.

During the second half of the twentieth century, starting with the case of *Solle v Butcher* (1950), the courts developed a doctrine of mistake in equity under which a contract could be voidable in equity for mistake, even though it was not void for mistake under the common law rules. This development in the law was overturned in *Great Peace Shipping Ltd v Tsavliris Salvage (International) Ltd* (2002) when the Court of Appeal declared that the decision in *Solle v Butcher* was wrong and that it was not possible to make a contract voidable for mistake in equity. This example shows how the courts can create law and then change it back again.

Tort

The law of negligence in the law of tort is another major area which has been developed and refined by judicial decisions. An important starting point in this area of law was the case of *Donoghue v Stevenson* (1932) in which the House of Lords, when recognising that a manufacturer owed a duty of care to the 'ultimate consumer', created what is known as the 'neighbour test'. This has been further developed by *Caparo Industries plc v Dickman* (1990) with the three-stage test of first, the consequences being reasonably foreseeable, second, the parties being in a sufficiently

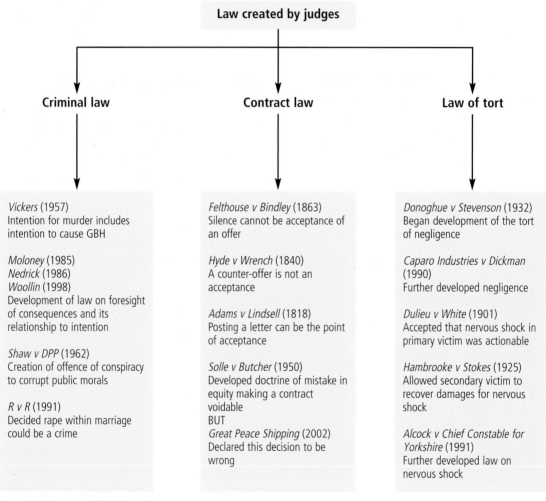

Figure 25.1 Law created by judges

proximity relationship and third, whether it is fair, just and reasonable to impose a duty of care.

There have also been major developments in negligence with case law on liability for nervous shock. The first case in which this was accepted was *Dulieu v White and Sons* (1901) where nervous shock in a primary victim was held to be actionable. This was extended in *Hambrook v Stokes Bros* (1925) when a secondary victim was able to recover damages for nervous shock. There were various further developments leading to the whole of this area of law being reviewed by the House of Lords in *Alcock v Chief Constable of South Yorkshire* (1991). Since then there have been further refinements of the law. However, the important point to note is that there is no statutory law in this area. All the 'rules' have been created by the judges.

25.1.1 The doctrine of precedent

So how can judges create law through the doctrine of judicial precedent? The basic doctrine means that in England and Wales the courts operate a very rigid doctrine of judicial precedent which has the effect that:

- every court is bound to follow any decision made by a court above it in the hierarchy; and
- in general, appellate courts are bound by their own past decisions.

Although this appears very rigid and does not apparently allow the courts to create law, there are ways in which the doctrine of judicial precedent can be avoided, so allowing judges to create law. There are four main ways in which this can occur:

- the House of Lords' use of the Practice Statement
- the exceptions in *Young's* case (1944) for the Court of Appeal
- the extra exception for the Court of Appeal (Criminal Division)
- distinguishing, which can be used by all courts.

Original precedent

In addition to the four ways of avoiding precedent listed above, the courts will on some occasions have to create new law when deciding a case on an area of law for which no law exists. An example of this was the case of *Hunter and others v Canary Wharf Ltd and London Docklands Development Corporation* (1995). Part of the decision in this case involved whether the interference with television reception by a large building was capable of constituting a private nuisance. There was no previous case on this, so a new decision had to be made. It was decided that interference with television reception was similar to interference with a view from a house and so no claim could be made as the law of nuisance had never allowed a claim for interference with a view.

25.1.2 The Practice Statement

Since 1966, this Practice Statement has allowed the House of Lords to change the law if they believe that an earlier case was wrongly decided. They have the flexibility to refuse to follow an earlier case when 'it appears right to do so'. This phrase is, of course, very vague and gives little guidance as to when the House of Lords might overrule a previous decision. This gives the Law Lords considerable scope as to when they decide they should use the Practice Statement and when to leave the law to stand as it is.

Use of the Practice Statement in criminal law

The first use of the Practice Statement in a criminal case was in *Shivpuri* (1986) which overruled the decision in *Anderton v Ryan* (1985) on attempts to do the impossible. An interesting feature of that decision was that the case of *Anderton* had been decided less than a year before.

Since then the Practice Statement has been used several times in criminal cases. For example

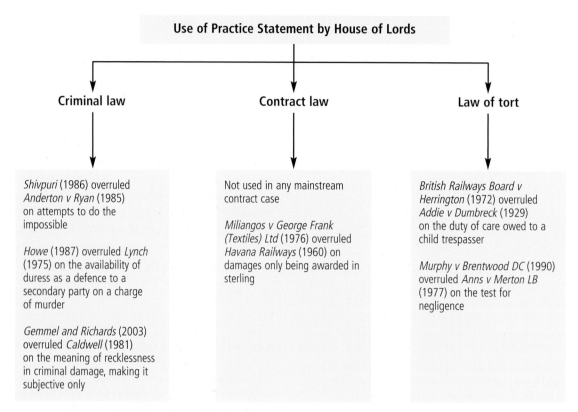

Figure 25.2 Use of Practice Statement by the House of Lords

it was used in *Howe* (1987) which overruled *DPP v Lynch* (1975) on whether the defence of duress was available to a secondary party to murder (ie a defendant who helped but did not actually do the killing).

It was also used in *Gemmell and Richards* (2003) to overrule *Caldwell* (1981) on the meaning of recklessness. This had the effect of abolishing the inclusion of objective recklessness in the *mens rea* for criminal damage. Instead liability for criminal damage can only be based on intention to cause the damage or subjective recklessness; ie realising there is a risk that the damage will be caused and deciding to take that risk.

Although the House of Lords has used the Practice Statement in criminal cases, there are occasions when it has decided that it should not change the law. This has happened even in cases where there has been considerable criticism of the existing law. For example, in *Clegg* (1995) the House of Lords refused to change the law on mistake as to the amount of force required in self-defence.

Use of the Practice Statement in contract law

The Practice Statement shows that the House of Lords is reluctant to overrule decisions in the law of contract. The Statement says:

> ' . . . they will bear in mind the danger of disturbing retrospectively the basis on which contracts, settlement of property and fiscal arrangements have been entered into . . .'

So it is not surprising that there have not been any mainstream contract cases in which the Practice Statement has been used. However, a case which arose from breach of contract where the Practice Statement was used is *Miliangos v*

George Frank (Textiles) Ltd (1976). In this case the Lords overruled the earlier case of *Havana Railways* (1960) on the point that damages could only be awarded in sterling (British pounds) and not in other currencies. In *Miliangos* the Lords recognised that currency exchange rates were no longer as stable as they used to be and that damages could be awarded in the currency used in the contract terms.

Use of the Practice Statement in tort

The first major use of the practice Statement was in *British Railways Board v Herrington* (1972), which involved the law on the duty of care owed to a child trespasser. It overruled an earlier case of *Addie v Dumbreck* (1929) which had decided that an occupier of land would only owe a duty of care for injuries to a child trespasser if those injuries had been caused deliberately or recklessly. In *Herrington* the Lords held that social and physical conditions had changed since 1929, and the law should also change.

Another major use of the Practice Statement occurred in 1990 when, in *Murphy v Brentwood District Council*, the House of Lords overruled the decision in *Anns v Merton London Borough* (1977) regarding the test for negligence in the law of tort.

25.1.3 The Court of Appeal and *Young's* case

The Court of Appeal is normally bound by its own previous decisions. This rule comes from the case of *Young v Bristol Aeroplane Co Ltd* (1944). However, that case does allow for three exceptions where the Court of Appeal need not follow its own past decision. These are where:

1. there are conflicting decisions in past Court of Appeal cases; the court can choose which one it will follow and which it will reject
2. there is a decision of the House of Lords which effectively overrules a Court of Appeal decision; the Court of Appeal must follow the decision of the House of Lords

3. the decision was made *per incuriam*, ie carelessly or by mistake because a relevant Act of Parliament or other regulation has not been considered by the court.

The first two exceptions do not give the Court of Appeal any power to change or create law. It is only the last exception (*per incuriam*) that gives a very small degree of flexibility to correct errors. However, this exception is not often used, but it was used in *Rakhit v Carty* (1990) when the Court of Appeal refused to follow decisions made in 1982 and 1988 because a relevant provision of the Rent Act 1977 had not been considered.

25.1.4 The Court of Appeal (Criminal Division)

The Criminal Division, as well as using the exceptions from *Young's* case (1944), can also refuse to follow a past decision of its own if the law has been 'misapplied or misunderstood'. This exception was recognised in *Gould* (1968). In *Spencer* (1985) it was said that there should not in general be any difference in the way that precedent was followed in the Criminal Division and in the Civil Division of the Court of Appeal. However, it had to be remembered that 'we may be dealing with the liberty of the subject and if a departure from authority is necessary in the interests of justice to an appellant, then this court should not shrink from so acting'.

This exception is not often used but it does exist and it gives the Court of Appeal (Criminal Division) the power to alter law when it is necessary.

25.1.5 Distinguishing

This is a method which can be used by a judge to avoid following a past decision which he would otherwise have to follow. It means that the judge finds that the material facts of the case he is deciding are sufficiently different for him to draw a distinction between the present case and the previous precedent. He is not then bound by the previous case. This way of avoiding precedent can be used by a judge at any level of court.

Criminal cases

Distinguishing has been used in the law on duress. In *Sharp* (1987) (see 16.1.2) it was held that duress was not available as a defence where the defendant joined a criminal gang which carried out robberies. *Shepherd* (1987) (see 16.1.2), in which the defendant joined a gang of shoplifters, was distinguished from *Sharp*. A distinction was drawn between joining a gang known to use violence and a gang which took part in non-violent criminal activity, so *Shepherd* could use the defence of duress when he was threatened into continuing to steal.

Contract cases

The use of distinguishing can be seen in the contract cases of *Balfour v Balfour* (1919) and *Merritt v Merritt* (1971). Both cases involved a wife making a claim against her husband for breach of contract. In *Balfour* it was decided that the claim could not succeed because there was no intention to create legal relations; there was merely a domestic arrangement between a husband and wife and so there was no legally binding contract. The second case was successful because the court held that the facts of the two cases were sufficiently different in that, although the parties were husband and wife, the agreement was made after they had separated. Furthermore, the agreement was made in writing. This distinguished the case from *Balfour* as the agreement in *Merritt* was not just a domestic arrangement but meant as a legally enforceable contract.

Distinguishing was also used in the case of *Ingram v Little* (1960) when the Court of Appeal found that there was a material difference in the facts which allowed them to come to a different decision to that in *Phillips v Brooks Ltd* (1919). In *Ingram v Little* (1960) two sisters who were selling a car initially refused to accept a cheque from the buyer. They only accepted it after they checked that the name given them by the rogue buyer was in the telephone book. This meant according to the Court of Appeal that they only intended to deal with the person of that name and not the man who was present buying the car. This was important as it meant that the ownership of the car had never passed to the buyer and they were able to reclaim the car from a later purchaser who had innocently bought it from the rogue. The fact that they refused to accept the cheque until they had confirmed (as they thought) the buyer's identity distinguished the case from *Phillips v Brooks*.

In a more recent case, *Shogun Finance Ltd v Hudson* (2003), the House of Lords by three judges to two distinguished the facts of the case from *Phillips v Brooks* (1919). In this case the rogue buyer had gone to a car showroom and arranged to buy a car on hire-purchase. He showed a driving licence in the name of a Mr Patel to the salesman in the showroom who faxed a copy of the licence and draft HP agreement, signed by the rogue in Mr Patel's name, through to the finance house (the claimants). The claimants checked the credit rating of Mr Patel and compared the signature on the licence with that on the HP form before they accepted the deal. The House of Lords said that this was not a face-to-face contract as in *Phillips v Brooks* (1919). It was a written contract and Mr Patel was the person with whom they thought they had made the contract. They had not made a contract with the rogue in the car showroom. Again this allowed them to reclaim the car as the ownership in it was always theirs.

Tort cases

Distinguishing is often used in tort cases. An example is when the case of *Read v J Lyons & Co* (1947) was distinguished from *Rylands v Fletcher* (1868) (see 19.3). In *Rylands v Fletcher* the essential point was that there was an escape of a substance from land which caused the damage. In *Read v J Lyons & Co* the explosion occurred inside the factory, causing injury to people in there. There was no escape of anything from the factory. The court distinguished the case on this point and the claim failed.

Another example is *Evans v Triplex Safety Glass Co Ltd* (1938) which was distinguished from

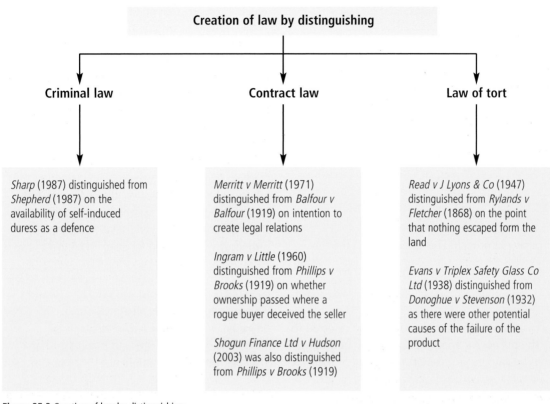

Figure 25.3 Creation of law by distinguishing

Donoghue v Stevenson (1932). This was on the point that manufacturers were not liable in negligence to the ultimate consumer of their goods where there were a number of other potential causes of the fault.

Evans v Triplex Safety Glass Co Ltd (1938)

The claimant bought a car fitted by the makers with a windscreen of 'Triplex Toughened Safety Glass'. While he was driving the car the windscreen shattered, injuring the claimant and his passengers. The defendant manufacturer was held not to be liable for the injuries. The case differed from *Donoghue v Stevenson* and was distinguished from it because:

- the windscreen had been in place for more than a year before it shattered;

- the shattering could have resulted from another cause which occurred during the use of the car rather than a fault in manufacture;

- the windscreen could have been badly fitted.

25.2 Statutory interpretation and judicial creativity

In statutory interpretation the judges are being asked to decide the precise meaning of words in an Act of Parliament. There are conflicting views on the role of judges in this area. Some judges follow the Literal Rule which states that the words should be given their plain, ordinary, grammatical meaning. This can mean using the literal meaning of the words even if the result is not very sensible.

Although this rule was the one most used in the nineteenth century and the first part of the twentieth century, the judges recognised that on some occasions other methods of interpreting the words were needed. The Mischief Rule was first formulated as long ago as 1584. This rule gives a judge more discretion than the Literal Rule. The judge should look to see what the law was before the Act was passed, in order to discover what gap or 'mischief' the Act was intended to cover. Then the court should interpret the Act in such a way that the gap is covered. This is clearly a quite different approach to the Literal Rule. This rule was used in *Smith v Hughes* (1960) to decide that prostitutes who were calling from a house were soliciting in a public place.

More recently judges have applied the purposive approach. This goes beyond the Mischief Rule in that the court is not just looking to see what the gap was in the old law; the judges are deciding what they believe Parliament meant to achieve.

Lord Denning was one judge who preferred to use the purposive approach and explained why, when he said in the case of *Magor and St Mellons v Newport Corporation* (1950):

> 'We sit here to find out the intention of Parliament and carry it out, and we do this better by filling in the gaps and making sense of the enactment than by opening it up to destructive analysis.'

However his attitude was criticised by judges in the House of Lords when they heard the appeal in the same case. Lord Simonds called Lord Denning's approach 'a naked usurpation of the legislative function under the thin disguise of interpretation' and pointed out that 'if a gap is disclosed the remedy lies in an amending Act'.

This highlights the conflict between whether the judges should make law or whether they should only apply it mechanically and leave any reform of the law to Parliament.

25.2.1 Conflicting rules of interpretation

The fact that there are different rules which can be applied means that it is difficult to predict which approach will be taken in a case. The following two examples show how the judges' use of one rule rather than another may lead to different conclusions. In each case the phrase in the relevant Act of Parliament was one which had come to have a special meaning in the law.

Fisher v Bell (1960)

In this case the key phrase for interpretation was 'offers for sale'. This occurred in s 1(1) Restriction of Offensive Weapons Act 1959. The court had to decide whether putting a flick knife marked with a price on display in a shop window was 'offering for sale'. In contract law displaying an article in a shop window is not offering that article for sale but only an invitation to treat. Although the phrase was in an Act which was intended to prevent the sale of flick-knives, the court applied the special meaning in contract law and found the shop-keeper not guilty of an offence.

This is an example of judges refusing to create law but applying the strict literal legal meaning of the phrase. The decision can be criticised because it meant that the Act was partially ineffective and, indeed, another amending Act was passed to ensure that shop-keepers who displayed flick-knives in a shop window would be guilty of an offence.

Jones v Tower Boot Co Ltd (1997)

The opposite happened in *Jones v Tower Boot Co Ltd* (1997) where s 32(1) of the Race Relations Act 1976 states that:

> 'Anything done by a person in the course of employment shall be treated for the purposes of this Act ... as done by his employer as well as by him, whether or not it was done with the employer's knowledge or approval.'

The words 'course of employment' are the critical ones. In the law of tort this phrase has a well-established legal meaning so that an employee is only acting in the 'course of employment' if 'the unauthorised wrongful act is so connected with that which he was employed to do as to be a mode of doing it'.

Clearly in *Jones v Tower Boot* the employees were not employed to carry out the acts they did against Jones. These included burning his arm with a hot screwdriver, whipping him with a piece of welt, throwing metal bolts at his head and calling him unpleasant names. If the Court of Appeal had used the legal meaning of the phrase 'course of employment' the employers of the men would not be responsible for the men's behaviour, nor would they have to try to prevent such incidents happening.

Instead of using the literal approach, the Court of Appeal used the purposive approach. They thought that to do otherwise would allow 'racial harassment on the scale that was suffered by the complainant ... to slip through the net of employer responsibility'; and that it was wrong to apply a common law principle which had been created for another area of the law.

These two cases illustrate how the judges can choose which statutory interpretation rule or approach to use.

Key facts

Method	Specific 'rule'	Comment	Cases
Judicial precedent	Practice Statement	Only available to House of Lords Allows them to overrule a previous decision when 'right to do so'	*BRB v Herrington* (1972) *Murphy v Brentwood DC* (1990) *Shivpuri* (1986) *Howe* (1987)
	Young's case (1944)	Allows Court of Appeal to depart from a previous decision of its own where it was *per incuriam*	*Rakhit v Carty* (1990)
	Liberty in criminal cases	Court of Appeal (Criminal Division) can refuse to follow an earlier decision if the law was 'misapplied or misunderstood'	*Gould* (1968)
	Distinguishing	Applies to all courts Do not have to follow a previous decision if there is a material difference in the case	*Merritt v Merritt* (1971) *Ingram v Little* (1960) *Shogun Finance Ltd v Hudson* (2003)
	Original precedent	If there is no previous decision on the point then the court must create new law	*Hunter v Canary Wharf* (1995)
Statutory interpretation	Literal Rule/approach	Does not allow for law-making	*Fisher v Bell* (1960)
	Mischief Rule	Can fill in the gaps in the law	*Smith v Hughes* (1960)
	Purposive approach	Allows judges to create law by looking for what Parliament intended	*Jones v Tower Boot* (1997)

Key facts chart on judicial law-making

25.3 Balancing the roles of Parliament and the judiciary

As Parliament is the elected law-making body in this country, it would be undemocratic to allow the judges to have too great an influence in law-making. For this reason precedent is subordinate to statute law and delegated legislation. This means that if an Act of Parliament is passed, and that Act contains a provision which contradicts a previously decided case, the case decision will cease to have effect. The Act of Parliament is now the law on that point.

This happened when Parliament passed the Law Reform (Year and a Day Rule) Act in 1996. Up to then judicial decisions meant that a person could only be charged with murder or manslaughter if the victim died within a year and a day of receiving his injuries. The Act enacted that there was no time limit, and a person could be guilty even if the victim died several years later. So, cases after 1996 follow the Act and not the old judicial decisions.

25.3.1 Parliamentary powers of law-making

In theory Parliament has no limit on what law it may enact. The government can choose to change any area of law that they believe is in need of reform. This allows them to make major changes; for example, the law on sexual offences was completely rewritten when Parliament passed the Sexual Offences Act 2003. More recently the law on deception offences has been dramatically altered by the Fraud Act 2006.

There are, however, some limitations on what Parliament can do. The first is a time limit. Parliament also has to debate matters of national and international importance, such as the war in Iraq in 2003. It has to consider financial and social problems of the UK; each year a budget has to be set and taxation changed to ensure that the government has enough money to finance health, education, the armed forces etc. This only leaves limited Parliamentary time for considering new laws on areas such as criminal law.

The second limitation is that the government must do what the people of the country agree to. The government is voted in at a general election, and if they pass unpopular laws they are unlikely to be voted in at the next general election.

25.3.2 Limitations on judicial law-making

Compared to Parliament, judges are very limited in the amount of law which they can create. They can only create or change law when a suitable case is taken to court. Even then they can only change the law on the point of law raised by the case they are hearing. This limits their law-making potential.

This also creates a problem because the law can only be changed by the judges in a piecemeal way. They cannot tackle all the problems that are known to exist in the law. This would not be a problem if Parliament was more active in reforming the substantive law. However, Parliament has been very reluctant to change the law even though there is a great need for the law to be reformed. This is particularly true in the criminal law where a draft Criminal Code was proposed but Parliament has never enacted it. One of the areas creating problems is the wording of the law in the Offences Against the Person Act 1861. The judges have tried to bring some 'sense' to the law, but they can only make minor changes through their interpretation of the Act.

25.4 Human Rights Act 1998

The Human Rights Act 1998 has some effect on both judicial precedent and statutory interpretation where human rights are an issue in a case. For precedent this is because s 2 of the Act requires judges at all levels in the court system to take into account judgments of the European Court of Human Rights. For statutory interpretation, s 3 of the Act requires that legislation be interpreted, so far as is possible, in a way which is compatible with the rights in the European Convention on Human Rights.

Where judges cannot interpret an Act of Parliament in a way which is compatible with the Convention, then under s 4 Human Rights Act 1998 judges can declare that an Act is incompatible with the European Convention on Human Rights. This particular provision preserves the balance between the judges and Parliament. The judges are highlighting the law which they think should be reformed, but they are not themselves changing it.

However, in some cases the courts have interpreted the law very widely so as to give effect to the European Convention on Human Rights. In *Offen* (2001) the Court of Appeal had to consider the meaning of the word 'exceptional' in the Crime (Sentences) Act 1997 where any offender committing a second serious offence had to be given a life sentence unless there were 'exceptional circumstances'. Before the Human Rights Act 1998 came into force, the courts in *Kelly* (2000) had said that 'exceptional' was an ordinary English adjective saying:

> 'To be exceptional a circumstance need not be unique or unprecedented or very rare; but it cannot be one that is regularly or routinely or normally encountered.'

This led to a strict approach where offenders were given life sentences even when the earlier crime had been committed a long time ago and the second offence was not that serious of its type.

In *Offen* (2000) the Court of Appeal said that this restricted approach could lead to the sentence being arbitrary and disproportionate and a breach of Articles 3 and 5 of the European Convention on Human Rights. In order to interpret the Crime (Sentences) Act 1997 in a way which was compatible with the Convention, it was necessary to consider whether the offender was a danger to the public. If he was not then he was an exception to the normal rule in the Act,

and this could be considered exceptional circumstances so that a life sentence need not be given.

This shows how judges can alter the law to take into account human rights.

25.5 Exam questions on judicial creativity

Both precedent and statutory interpretation are topics which had to be studied for AS Law. This section is a synoptic one and gives you the opportunity to show your understanding of the links between these topics which you studied at AS and the substantive areas of law in the options which you have studied for A2.

To answer a question on judicial creativity, it is important to show a good understanding of both judicial precedent and statutory interpretation. Remember that this is A2, and it is at a higher level than AS. You must be able to discuss both how the rules of precedent and statutory interpretation allow judges to develop the law, and also what limitations there are in these methods of law-making. It is also important to be able to illustrate your answers with case examples. You need to have an understanding of the balance between the powers which judges have to make law, and Parliament's powers of law-making.

Finally, remember to focus your answer on the question which is set. An answer which is a general account of precedent and or statutory interpretation will not gain high marks. It is important to use your knowledge to discuss the point required by the question.

Sample essay question

Discuss to what extent judges can develop the law through judicial precedent and statutory interpretation.

Chapter 26

Fault

26.1 The meaning of fault

26.1.1 The concept of fault

Fault as a concept in whichever area of law is really only a simpler way of describing legal blame and responsibility. In this sense it also refers to the mental state of the defendant. The basic principle is that a defendant should be able to contemplate the harm that his actions may cause, and should therefore aim to avoid such actions.

Fault is an essential element of quite diverse elements of law. For instance in family law, certain facts needed to prove an irretrievable breakdown of a marriage in a divorce petition can be described as fault. Examples would be adultery or behaviour.

Fault is also a feature of the options in Units 3 and 4 contained in this book. This is particularly so of criminal law and certain areas of tort, but to a lesser degree in contract law.

In criminal law, the requirement of *mens rea* is used to decide if a defendant has criminal intent when he commits the act and is therefore at fault for the crime. This is so in all crimes except strict liability.

In contract law, a breach can be identified irrespective of the intention of the defendant, but it is still the person who breaches a contract who is liable. Fault is in any case identifiable in the award of damages, where foreseeable loss is an issue under remoteness of damage and also in the behaviour of the defendant in the granting of equitable remedies.

In tort, foreseeable harm is appropriate to all aspects of negligence. This is another way of describing fault. Similarly in the trespass torts intentional and direct harm is required.

26.1.2 Fault contrasted with strict liability

Fault liability requires some intention, or at least a conscious failure to take care by the defendant.

In contrast, strict liability, while recognising certain limited defences, takes no account of the defendant's state of mind.

Criminal law

In criminal law, strict liability is easy to identify as the lack of requirement of *mens rea*, although it is not necessarily so easy to identify and certain rules have developed.

The concept of strict liability appears to contradict the basis of criminal law. Normally criminal law is thought to be based on the culpability of the accused. In strict liability offences, there may be no blameworthiness on the part of the defendant.

Strict liability in criminal law is usually found in regulatory offences. Such offences are often concerned with protecting the public in general, such as regulations on the sale of food, the use of road vehicles and the causing of pollution. For such offences, it is not necessary for the prosecution to prove *mens rea,* as it is considered that protection of society in general is more important than imposing liability on an individual who may not be at fault in any way.

An example is seen in the following case:

Pharmaceutical Society of Great Britain v Storkwain Ltd (1986)

The defendant company was found guilty of supplying prescription-only drugs without a prescription. In fact, the drugs had been supplied because a customer had given in what appeared to be genuine prescriptions, but which were later found to be forged.

There was no finding that the defendants had acted dishonestly, improperly or even negligently. The forgery was sufficient to deceive a pharmacist. Despite this, the House of Lords upheld the defendants' conviction. The defendants were not at fault in any way, but they had supplied the drugs without a genuine prescription and this was enough to make them guilty as it was a strict liability offence.

In this case it is possible to argue that the importance of preventing unauthorised drugs being given out justifies the offence being one of strict liability. However, in other situations, especially where the maximum penalty for the offence is severe, it is less easy to justify strict liability.

The Sexual Offences Act 2003 has created several offences of strict liability in respect of belief in the age of a willing participant in sexual activity. This led to a conviction in the following case under s 5 of the Sexual Offences Act 2003, which carries a maximum penalty of life imprisonment. In addition an offender found guilty under the section will be placed on the sex offenders' register.

G (2006)

D was a boy aged 15 who had had sexual intercourse with a girl aged 12. He was charged under s 5 of the Sexual Offences Act 2003 with rape of a child under 13. The girl was actually 12, but D believed on reasonable grounds that she was 15. She had told him so on an earlier occasion. D was held to be guilty as the offence is one of strict liability and may be committed even if:

- the girl consented to sexual intercourse; and
- D reasonably believed her to be 13 or over.

Contract law

In contract law, strict liability can be identified in statutory terms found in the Sale of Goods Act 1979 (as amended). Here liability is strict in respect of the implied terms requiring that goods should correspond to any description applied to them, s 13; that the goods should be of satisfactory quality, s 14(2); and be fit for the purposes for which they are sold, s 14(3); and, where goods are sold by sample, the bulk should correspond to the sample, s 15. Similar strict liability can be found in the implied terms in the Supply of Goods and Services Act 1982.

Law of tort

In tort, strict liability can also be found. The tort of *Rylands v Fletcher* (1868) was traditionally described as a strict liability for the escape of dangerous things from the defendant's land. However, the additional requirement of non-natural use added by Lord Cairns in the House of Lords and the requirement of foreseeability of harm added in *Cambridge Water Co v Eastern Counties Leather plc* (1994) has meant that this description can no longer be sustained. This has recently been reaffirmed in the lengthy consideration of the entire tort in the 2003 case of *Transco plc v Stockport Metropolitan Borough Council*.

However, there are significant areas of strict liability in statutory torts. The Animals Act 1971 imposes strict liability on the 'keepers' of animals for any non-domestic species.

Possibly more significant is the Consumer Protection Act 1987, which in s 2(1) identifies that:

 '… where any damage is caused wholly or partly by a defect in a product, every person to whom subsection 2 applies shall be liable for the damage …'.

Potential defendants include manufacturers, anyone who 'abstracts' products, anyone carrying out an industrial or other process which adds to the essential characteristic of the product, importers, suppliers and 'own-branders'. In this way, a consumer may sue almost anyone in the chain of production or distribution for defects in a product that renders it unsafe. The Act covers death, personal injury, and loss or damage to property caused by unsafe products. There are some limited defences.

26.2 The importance of fault in criminal law

In the criminal law, fault is an important element. In order to prove a person guilty of an offence, the prosecution has to prove the required *actus reus* and *mens rea* for that offence. The *actus reus* is the physical element of the offence, but without the *mens rea* it does not impose liability except for offences of strict liability. So the *mens rea* can be seen as the main 'fault' element of the offence.

The criminal law imposes liability for different levels of *mens rea*. The law may make the defendant guilty for being negligent, or reckless, or for having specific intention to do or cause something. These are very different levels of fault. Where the defendant is proved to be at fault (and found guilty of an offence) he can be punished. Also, as explained at 26.1.2, it is possible for a defendant to be found guilty even when he is not at fault under the principles of strict liability.

26.2.1 Different levels of fault

The highest level of fault in criminal law is where the defendant has specific intention. The exact

intention varies according to the type of offence. For example, the intention required for murder is an intention to kill or an intention to cause grievous bodily harm. For theft, the intention required is to intend to deprive another of property permanently and to be dishonest.

Recklessness involves fault in the sense that the defendant has realised that there is a risk of the consequence occurring but has decided to take that risk. This level is sufficient to convict a person for an offence under s 47 Offences Against the Person Act 1861. For s 47, the *mens rea* required is either intention or recklessness that the victim might be put in fear of having unlawful force applied to him, or that unlawful force might be applied to the victim. The defendant also has to cause actual bodily harm to the victim – the *actus reus*. Recklessness is also sufficient for an offence of criminal damage.

The test for negligence is based on what the reasonable man would foresee. The defendant must owe a duty of care which is breached by falling below the standard of care appropriate to the specific duty. This standard is judged by the 'reasonable man' test, with the defendant taking care to avoid harm which is foreseeable by the reasonable man. In criminal law, gross negligence can be the basis of fault for involuntary manslaughter. Gross negligence is a higher level of fault than just negligence. The law on gross negligence manslaughter imposes fault where the negligence goes as stated in *Bateman* (1925):

 'beyond a matter of mere compensation between subjects and shows such disregard for the life and safety of others as to amount to a crime against the State and conduct deserving of punishment'.

Criticism of level of fault

There are arguments that the required fault level in murder should not include an intention to cause grievous bodily harm as decided in *Vickers* (1957). Surely an intention to kill is a much higher level of fault than an intention to cause grievous bodily harm. Yet by imposing liability for murder based on an intention to cause grievous bodily harm, the law is treating defendants with different levels of blameworthiness in the same manner. Not only are such defendants found guilty of murder, but there is no difference in their sentence as there is a mandatory sentence of life imprisonment for murder.

26.2.2 Mitigating fault

There are various defences available in the criminal law which can reduce or eliminate fault on the part of the defendant. For example, the defence of mistake if successful will eliminate fault entirely so that the defendant is found not guilty. This occurred in the following case.

Williams (1987)

The defendant mistakenly believed that a youth was being attacked by another man. Williams struggled with the other man, believing that by doing so he was preventing further assaults on the youth. In fact, the man was a police officer trying to arrest the youth. Williams was not guilty of any offence as he thought he was acting in prevention of crime. He was judged according to his honest mistake as to the facts of the situation.

Another defence which completely eliminates fault so that the defendant is not guilty of the offence charged is non-insane automatism (see 5.2). This is a defence because the *actus reus* done by the defendant is not voluntary. In addition, the defendant does not have the required *mens rea* for the offence. The cause of the automatism must be external, such as a blow to the head.

Some defences only reduce liability. The main examples of these are the special defences to murder of diminished responsibility, provocation and suicide pact set out in the Homicide Act 1957. If these defences are successful, the defendant is not guilty of murder but is instead

guilty of the lesser offence of manslaughter. In the situations covered by these defences, the law recognises the need to impose a lower level of liability than would otherwise be the case. Such defendants are seen as less blameworthy. The importance of this is that they can be given any sentence that the judge thinks is suitable, whereas for those guilty of murder, a sentence of life imprisonment has to be imposed.

Sentencing

Another way that the different levels of fault are recognised in the criminal law is through sentencing. In most cases, judges have a complete discretion as to what sentence should be imposed on a defendant who has pleaded guilty to or been found guilty of an offence. The only cases in which they do not are murder and other offences where there is a minimum sentence for repeat offenders of serious offences, drug-dealing or burglary.

Even in murder, the law recognises there are different levels of fault through the tariffs which must be imposed under the Criminal Justice Act 2003. The judge has to state the minimum term a murderer must serve before being able to apply for parole. The Act gives guidelines for these:

- a whole life term where the murder is exceptionally serious, eg abduction and sexual motivation in the murder of a child
- a minimum term of 30 years for serious murders, eg by using a firearm
- a minimum term of 15 years for other cases of murder
- twelve years for offenders under the age of 18.

For other offences where the judge has discretion in sentencing, various factors will be taken into account. These include such matters as whether the offence was premeditated, whether the victim was particularly vulnerable, eg a child or very elderly person, and whether the defendant was the ringleader. All these are considered as making the offence more blameworthy, and the defendant is likely to receive a heavier punishment than otherwise. From this it can be seen that fault plays a central role in sentencing an offender.

26.2.3 Should there be liability without fault?

At 26.1.2 the concept of strict liability was considered. In the criminal law, it can be argued that since a person convicted of an offence is liable to be punished, then there should be a fault element in order for that person to be convicted. However, there are arguments that strict liability should be used even in the criminal law. There are other reasons for imposing liability, not just fault.

In *Wings Ltd v Ellis* (1984) the House of Lords had to consider the Trade Descriptions Act 1968 which creates offences aimed at consumer protection. They pointed out that this Act was 'not a truly criminal statute'. This was because 'its purpose was not the enforcement of the criminal law but the maintenance of trading standards'. In such types of 'offences' the law is not concerned with fault, and finding a person guilty where there is no fault can be justified.

Another justification for strict liability is that allowances for levels of blameworthiness can be made in sentencing. This is an argument put forward by Baroness Wootton. She thinks that where the object of the criminal law is to prevent the occurrence of socially damaging actions, it would be absurd to ignore those which were due to carelessness, negligence or even accident. If the aim is to prevent socially damaging actions, then the question of motivation is irrelevant at the point of deciding guilt. Baroness Wootton believes that the point of sentencing is the time at which the presence or absence of guilty intention is all-important. The courts can deal with the offence according to the level of fault by imposing a sentence which is likely to prevent a recurrence of the forbidden act.

These arguments only apply to offences, which are not truly criminal and which are also socially damaging. For offences which are considered as truly criminal offences, then the requirement of fault should be essential.

26.3 The importance of fault in civil law

26.3.1 Contract

Even though the law of contract basically involves the regulation of agreements made between the parties, fault can still be an issue when a party breaches a contract through the mechanism of remoteness of damage and foreseeable loss. The leading case of *Hadley v Baxendale* (1854) included two tests. Damages could be awarded for loss naturally arising out of the breach, but also for loss within the specific contemplation at the time the contract was formed. The later case of *Victoria Laundry v Newman Industries* (1949) made it clear that this second test had concerned foreseeability.

Fault is also specifically an issue in relation to vitiating factors that might cause a contract to be declared void or voidable.

The defendant's mental state is significant then in areas like misrepresentation. A fraudulent misrepresentation, according to *Derry v Peek* (1889), occurs when the defendant caused the other party to enter a contract on the basis of a false statement that he made 'knowingly or without belief in its truth or recklessly careless whether it be true or false'. In negligent misrepresentation, under the principle from *Hedley Byrne v Heller & Partners* (1964), the defendant is liable because of the reasonable reliance which he knows the other party places on his falsehood. Obviously both areas are sued in tort law rather than contract law, but still apply to contracts based on a misrepresentation.

In unilateral mistake, a contract is vitiated because only one party enters the contract under a mistake, and the other party knew of this mistaken belief and took advantage of it. This applies certainly where the mistake is as to the nature of the contract as in *Hartog v Colin & Shields* (1939), and also where the identity of one party is mistaken as in *Cundy v Lindsay* (1878). It is less likely to vitiate a contract where the mistaken identity occurs in face to face dealings. This was settled in *Lewis v Avery* (1972) and recently reaffirmed in *Shogun Finance Ltd v Hudson* (2003).

While the rules are complex, this element of fault can also be seen in undue influence, both in the case of actual undue influence (prior to *Etridge* (*Royal Bank of Scotland plc v Etridge* (2001)) for a while called Class 1), and in situations where a wife stands as surety to a bank for her husband's debts or loans (prior to *Etridge* called Class 2B).

26.3.2 Law of tort

Fault is a concept that is particularly relevant to the law of torts, and the tort of negligence is based on fault liability. In negligence, a defendant will not be liable unless the claimant can also show fault. This is done by demonstrating that the defendant owed the claimant a duty which he has breached by falling below the standard of care appropriate to the specific duty. It is tested according to the 'reasonable man' test, so the defendant must act so as to avoid foreseeable harm (*Donoghue v Stevenson* (1932)). Professionals, however, are measured according to their own standards (*Bolam v Friern Hospital Management Committee* (1957)). Even in causation, damages will only be awarded where the damage is not too remote a consequence of the breach. This is measured against damage, which is a reasonably foreseeable consequence of the breach according to the test in *The Wagon Mound (No 1)* (1961).

It would certainly also apply in occupiers' liability under the 1957 Act which is basically a specific statutory form of negligence. Here the defendant is liable because he creates foreseeable harm causing the visitor damage or injury, as can be seen in the House of Lords judgment in *Jolley v London Borough of Sutton* (2000).

Fault can also be seen in the trespass torts, to land, to persons, and to goods in the requirement of direct and intentional interference. In assault for instance, the defendant must have intended to cause apprehension of fear. This can be seen in the case of *Smith v Superintendent of Woking Police* (1983) where the defendant peering through a window caused the claimant real alarm even though it was improbable that the claimant could have suffered harm.

While motive is said to have no relevance to the commission of a tort, fault can certainly be recognised where malice is an issue. In private nuisance, malice may be the basis of an action as in *Hollywood Silver Fox Farm v Emmett* (1936). It may also defeat an action for nuisance, where the claimant acts with malice in response to the nuisance, as in *Christie v Davey* (1893).

Fault can even be seen in the tort of defamation because of the requirement that the falsehood is published to a third party. In *Theaker v Richardson* (1962) the defendant was liable when he wrote to another councillor, calling her 'a lying, low down brothel keeping whore and thief' because he would have been aware that her husband, being her agent, might open it believing it to be an election address.

Even in vicarious liability, which is not a tort in itself, an employer is liable and therefore responsible or at fault for the torts of his employees, because he is bound to hire appropriate staff and ensure that they comply with the law during the course of their employment.

Fault liability and the need for reform

Fault liability, particularly in the case of medical negligence as we have seen, seems unfair to claimants because of the problems associated both with amassing evidence and of actually proving fault.

It seems obviously wrong to impose liability on a body such as a health authority, unless that body can be shown to have done wrong. The fact that the defendant satisfies legal tests on fault is nevertheless scant comfort to a person who places his safety in the hands of professional people, and finds himself later to have suffered irreversible and disabling damage.

Fault liability can also be seen as unfair to victims who have suffered harm, because the degree to which a person can easily gather evidence and therefore present a winnable case may depend on the degree of publicity which the case has produced. Inevitably, people involved in an event gaining media attention or involving a number of claimants may be in a better position to find suitable evidence.

In this way, fault liability can also be unfair to society generally in not providing an adequate means of remedying wrongs, since the fault-based system can create classes of victims who can be compensated and classes who cannot. This can be particularly true of the victims of pure accidents and those suffering from genetic disorders.

It can also be seen as unfair to defendants since there are no identified degrees of culpability.

This in turn means that a defendant will not be penalised according to the degree of negligence shown.

The rules concerning the standard of care, as well as the imposing of duties, mean that very often a claimant's ability to recover for the wrong suffered is determined according to the whims of policy, and therefore can be subject to arbitrary and often inconsistent reasoning.

In fairness to the fault-based system, its major justification is that it does punish the wrongdoer and so is said to have some deterrent value.

Key facts

Basic principle	D is only blameworthy if he should be able to contemplate the harm his actions may cause	Intention or conscious failure to take care
Fault in criminal law	The mental element in an offence – *mens rea*	Intention is the highest level
	Sentencing can also reflect the level of fault	Recklessness, in the sense that D has realised the risk of a particular consequence but has taken the risk, is sufficient for some offences
		Gross negligence is required for gross negligence manslaughter: *Bateman* (1925), *Adomako* (1994)
		But there are offences of strict liability in which *mens rea* is not required
Fault in contract law	Breach of contract regardless of intention	Remoteness of damage and foreseeable loss
	BUT fault is identifiable in: • the award of damages	*Hadley v Baxendale* (1854) *Victoria Laundry v Newman* (1949)
	• considering the behaviour of D in the granting of equitable remedies	D must come with clean hands
Fault in the law of tort	Negligence is based on fault liability	Foreseeable harm is required *Donoghue v Stevenson* (1932)
	Type of damage must be foreseeable	*The Wagon Mound* (1961)
	In assault there must be intention to cause fear of violence	*Smith v Superintendent for Woking* (1983)

Key facts chart on fault

However, no-fault systems have been advocated on a number of occasions. The Pearson Committee in 1978 suggested such a system in the case of personal injury claims, though this has never been accepted or implemented. Two no-fault based medical negligence bills have also been introduced unsuccessfully. The principle is not without precedent since such a system has operated in New Zealand.

26.4 Exam questions on fault

Section C of Unit 4 is a synoptic module and therefore requires you to make links between the various elements of your course and see the law in a broader context.

Questions on fault will require that you have a firm understanding of the basics of fault liability, but that you also illustrate your understanding of the concept by reference to the substantive areas of law that you have studied on Unit 3 and sections A and B of Unit 4. Obviously the way that you are able to illustrate will depend on the two units that you have studied which may involve only one law if crime is chosen in both units, but otherwise would give you material from two areas.

The key to answering requires showing a full understanding of what fault liability is, that liability depends on culpability and responsibility in whatever area of law. You may also be able to make obvious criticisms of fault liability, that it denies some deserving people the possibility of a claim. You may also be able to compare fault with 'no-fault' systems such as that in New Zealand, or refer to the ways of mitigating the harshness of fault liability such as *res ipsa loquitur* in tort or strict liability generally.

In the sections of this chapter above you have many illustrations of examples of all these things and of useful cases.

Sample essay question

Discuss whether liability in the law should be based on fault. Use examples from criminal and/or civil law to support your discussion.

Chapter 27

Balancing conflicting interests

27.1 The different interests of parties to a dispute

27.1.1 The nature of rights or interests

Everybody would want to be sure that their interests are protected by the law, and that the law achieves this through various sets of rules. Another way of describing an interest is to call it a right. So in this context it is perhaps simpler to think of law as a set of mutual rights and obligations than merely as a body of rules. In this way, the law protects a person's rights by imposing a corresponding duty on the other party so that they are bound in law not to interfere with those rights. Inevitably, the interests of one individual and the interest of the majority may sometimes fall into conflict. In every area of law, the principle of fault or blame is a concept that is commonly applied in determining whether in fact a person has interfered wrongly with another person's rights or interests.

Nevertheless, interests or rights are not always so easy to define. The law is obviously full of specific rights, for instance rights of ownership. However, while it may appear at first glance to

point to a particular object or even land as being someone's property, it is not as straightforward as it actually looks. Undergraduate students of Land Law and of Trusts would recognise the problem instantly.

Demonstrating a right or interest in property would often involve arguing over an abstract concept of ownership in a court of law, with the court demanding concrete proof or evidence of ownership. In ownership of land, or rights such as debts, actual ownership might be shared and this might not mean half each. In the case of land bought through a mortgage, both the house-owner and the building society in effect own the property at the same time, up to the value of the mortgage. As a result of this, the building society is able to sell the property and take back the loan if the house owner defaults on payment.

The only way that we can often prove a legal right or interest then is by being able to enforce it. An obvious example of this is in a contract where we have an interest in the property to be passed. If the contract is not performed we may sometimes be able to enforce performance, but most often we only have a right to compensation for the loss of the bargain that we made.

27.1.2 Corresponding rights and duties

The way that the law works is that where an individual has an enforceable right, this then imposes on other parties to acknowledge that right, and so there is a duty.

Criminal law

In criminal law for instance, each offence carries with it a right not to be the victim of the offence. The criminal law imposes sanctions on those people who in effect fail in their duty and infringe those rights. The natural right to life means that there is a duty not to kill. The right to personal safety carries with it the corresponding duty not to assault, batter, wound or commit a grievous bodily harm which would be contrary to the offences under the Offences Against the Person Act 1861. It follows easily from this that the various offences under the Theft Acts including theft itself but also robbery, burglary and the deception offences, are based on rights to personal property and a corresponding duty to respect it.

Tort

Some similar rights and duties exist in tort. Again these are rights recognised by the law and duties imposed by law. The right to civil liberties is represented in trespass to the person, and also in defamation and other torts protecting reputation. Negligence is a tort that we all know is based on proving a duty of care, so our rights are interfered with when the defendant fails to prevent his negligent acts or omissions which he should contemplate will lead to foreseeable harm.

Contract law

In contract law, it is quite easy to see the corresponding rights and duties. Generally this is because we set out both in the terms of the contract on formation, although many now are imposed by statute as in the Sale of Goods Act 1979. In simple terms, our rights to receive the goods or services under the contract are based on the duty of the other party to deliver them, and if they fail to, there is an actionable breach of contract.

Other law

Rights and duties of course are not restricted to these three areas of law. Marriage is a voluntary union between a man and a woman. However, the relationship gives rise to rights and duties which are reflected in the five facts that will prove irretrievable breakdown of the marriage justifying the granting of a petition for divorce. So we have a right to faithful behaviour from our partner, and adultery is a breach of the duty that goes with that right. We also have both a right and a duty to live together, so desertion also may justify divorce after a certain period. Neither are we bound to accept unreasonable behaviour from our partners, so domestic violence may be clear evidence of a breach of our duty, although much less than that may be accepted by the courts as behaviour justifying divorce.

Sometimes the right is actually only gained following performance of the duty. Examples of this would include the paying of National Insurance contributions which then entitle us to claim contributory benefits, or the one year's service that in many cases is needed before we can exercise various employment rights (such as the right not to be unfairly dismissed).

Rights often involve both power and choice. People who own property, whether personal property or land, have the right to sell it, but they also have power in that they have the choice whether to sell or not. Of course, people whose rights have been infringed also have the power to sue, but may choose not to do so if an alternative is preferable.

In some cases, what appears to be a right may actually attach no protection. Certain rights have only limited protection because to exercise the right may interfere with another person's interests. A good example of a conflict between rights and freedoms is the right to life of an unborn child. A foetus has no legal protection and so cannot be represented in a legal action. This was firmly stated in *Paton v The UK* (1990) where a father of an unborn child was not allowed to prevent its abortion. The logic, while it may seem unfair to the unborn child, is inescapable; to prevent the abortion would be to interfere with the rights of the mother over her own body.

27.1.3 Balancing competing rights and interests

It can often prove impossible to exercise a right or interest without it infringing another person's right or interest.

In **tort**, an obvious example can be found in the law of nuisance involving neighbouring landowners. Here a landowner may bring an action for an indirect interference with his land. However, the action may fail and the landowner may be unable to enforce his right to quiet enjoyment of the land because the locality is one where the nuisance is allowed as stated *in obiter* in *St Helens Smelting v Tipping* (1865). It may be that it is not in the public interest to allow the claim as in *Miller v Jackson* (1977), where an injunction would have prevented the playing of cricket.

In **contract** law, it is assumed that the parties have the right to enforce the contract, or at least to compensation if it is not carried out. However, a person may be prevented from enforcing his rights under the contract because the contract has been made following an innocent misrepresentation as in *Esso v Marden* (1976), or because the contract was based on the mistaken belief in the existence of the subject matter as in *Couturier v Hastie* (1852), or of the terms of the contract as in *Hartog v Colin & Shields* (1939). Besides this, a party may be prevented from relying on an exclusion clause because he has not done sufficient to draw it to the attention of the other party, as in *Thornton v Shoe Lane Parking* (1971).

In **crime**, a conviction will rarely be achieved in the absence of *mens rea*, even though the victim may feel that his rights have been infringed. The defence of consent is also another bar to a criminal conviction for various assault offences. This can be seen in the case of *R v Wilson* (1996). Even though the wife consented, most of us would probably feel that to be branded on the buttocks was a gross infringement of our rights and would be unlikely to consent to it.

Sometimes an individual's rights or interests are sacrificed for the greater public good. Examples include the defence of statutory authority in tort, strict liability where there is no requirement to prove fault, the defences of absolute privilege and fair comment in defamation actions, the changes to the right to remain silent after caution by a police officer etc.

27.2 Balancing individual rights and public interests

Certain rights are expressed as fundamental human rights. These have been protected under the European Convention of Human Rights, now incorporated into English law by the Human Rights Act 1998.

The Convention is set out as a number of Articles, each of which represents an individual human right. These include:

- Article 2 – the right to life
- Article 3 – freedom from torture or inhuman or degrading treatment
- Article 4 – freedom from slavery
- Article 5 – the right to liberty apart from lawful arrest
- Article 6 – the right to a fair trial
- Article 7 – freedom from any retroactive penal laws
- Article 8 – the right to respect for private and family life, home and correspondence
- Article 9 – freedom of thought, conscience and religion
- Article 10 – freedom of expression
- Article 11 – freedom of peaceful assembly and association
- Article 12 – the right to marry freely
- Article 13 – the right to an effective remedy in a national court
- Article 14 – freedom from discrimination.

However, it would be easy to see how some of these rights could be sacrificed for the general public interest. In the case of Article 10 for instance, freedom of expression may well need to be avoided if it concerns matters of state security. While Article 14 would seem to guarantee freedom from discrimination, there are a number of examples both in the Sex Discrimination Act 1975 and the Race Relations Act 1976 of justifiable exceptions. Similarly, while we all at times might wish to exercise our rights of assembly under Article 11, there are clearly instances when we could equally sympathise with the police in banning demonstrations when rival factions are involved and public order is threatened.

Many basic rights are traditionally classed as basic freedoms. Again, while we might seek to defend the right, there are instances when the right conflicts with a public interest.

Freedom of expression

Freedom of expression is not only guaranteed by Article 10 of the European Convention on Human Rights, but is a traditional right within English law.

Nevertheless, the right is subject to many restrictions:

- In tort, defamation is concerned with preventing publication of false statements that are likely to cause the subject to be lowered in the minds of right thinking people. It also of course has quite a profound impact on freedom of speech, as suggested in the 'McLibel' case. While the defence of fair comment may protect the press, this will only apply to the extent that the statement involves a matter of public interest, that is a genuine opinion rather than a statement of fact, and that is fairly stated.
- There are other restrictions on the freedom in the case of the media. Both broadcasters and the press have Standards Commissions who determine what is acceptable, and a Board of Censors exists to regulate what can be shown

in films and videos. The Obscene Publications Act 1959 adjudicates on pornography. The government too is able to impose restrictions through the use of 'D' Notices.

- Many people in public service are called on to sign the Official Secrets Act 1911. This has the effect of preventing them from speaking out on issues that concern them, as in the 'Spycatcher' case. It may also be used to prevent important information from reaching the public, as led to *R v Ponting* (1985).
- Criminal actions can be used also to restrict freedom of speech in certain contexts. The law of incitement was used to prevent the spread of racial hatred in *R v Jordan & Tindal* (1963), and to prevent an incitement to soldiers to defect as in *R v Arrowsmith* (1975); a charge of blasphemous libel was successful in *R v Lemon* (1979).

Freedom of movement

We all take it for granted that we are free to move anywhere around the country. However, this is not always the case. The right still has restrictions.

- Even though a person is considered to be innocent until proved guilty after a fair trial, it is still possible to be lawfully detained while under arrest, and while on remand pending trial.
- It is possible also lawfully to detain a person against his will by an order under the Mental Health Act 1983.
- Immigration law is used to deport people. People may be denied passports. Even Article 39 of the EC Treaty which ensures the free movement of workers still contains exceptions explained in Directive 64/221 which enables member states to deny entry on grounds of public security, public policy or public health. *Van Duyn v The Home Office* (1984) is an obvious example.
- A practice which was quite controversial at the time was the preventing of pickets travelling to picket lines elsewhere, to prevent breaches of the peace during the miners strike in 1984–5.

- People have been prevented from entering clubs if they are not public places, as in *Dockers Labour Club v Race Relations Board* (1976).
- The tort of trespass may also prevent people from straying onto other people's land without permission.

Freedom of association and freedom of assembly

Article 11 of the European Convention guarantees both rights. Freedom of association is the right to meet with like-minded people, and to form organisations in pursuit of common goals. Obvious examples are trade unions and pressure groups.

Everyone is generally free to join such groups, but there are still restrictions:

- The most important restrictions are in the Public Order Act 1986. Section 14 gives the police wide powers to restrain assemblies (of over 20 people), to move them on, or by s 12 to apply to stop marches or postpone them. The Act contains the offences of riot (12 or more people using or threatening violence); violent disorder (three or more people); and affray (one person).
- The Prevention of Terrorism Act 1989 outlaws membership of terrorist groups. The Public Order Act 1936 ss 1 and 2 also outlawed membership of a paramilitary group or one wearing uniforms in response to the marches of fascist sympathisers at the time.
- Workers at GCHQ were banned from being members of unions by the government, as confirmed in *CCSU v Civil Service* (1984).
- Conspiracy law is another means of restriction that was freely used against trade unionists in the nineteenth century.
- The Criminal Justice and Public Order Act 1994 also gave police the power to deal with 'criminal trespasses', but was mainly aimed at 'new age travellers', 'raves', and 'hunt saboteurs'.

Freedom from discrimination

This freedom used to be limited because, although it applied to areas like race, sex and disability, traditionally it did not include areas such as religion and age. However, EU directives have meant that rights of religion and age are now also covered by law.

The balance at times swings the other way, and the rights of individuals can take precedence over the state. This occurs frequently in administrative law where the *ultra vires* doctrine and the rules of natural justice allow individuals to challenge the decisions of public officials acting in a judicial, quasi-judicial or administrative capacity. The first is where the public body has gone beyond its powers, the second where it has acted unreasonably.

27.3 Exam questions on balancing conflicting interests

Section C of Unit 4 is a synoptic unit which requires you to make links between the various elements of your course so that you see can show that you see the law in a broader context.

Questions on this area will require that you have a firm understanding of the relationship between rights and duties and why different interests may come into conflict. Questions will also require illustration from substantive areas of law, including those that you have studied in Unit 3 and sections A and B of Unit 4.

It is not so easy to restrict examples of competing interests purely to crime, contract or tort. However, in the sections of the chapter you have many illustrations and useful cases that you can use in your answers.

Sample essay question

It is possible to argue that one man's right involves another man's duty, but because of the competing nature of rights it is possible also that not every right is enforceable.

Using examples from criminal law or civil law or both, consider whether or not the above statement is true.

Index

Page numbers in *italics* refer to charts and diagrams.